Contents

COUNCIL OF PUBLICATION.

W. LINDSAY ALEXANDER, D.D.,

Professor of Theology, Congregational Union, Edinburgh.

JAMES BEGG, D.D., Minister of Newington Free Church, Edinburgh. THOMAS J. CRAWFORD, D.D., S.T.P., Professor of Divinity, University, Edinburgh.

D. T. K. DRUMMOND, M.A., Minister of St Thomas's Episcopal Church, Edinburgh.

WILLIAM H. GOOLD, D.D., Professor of Biblical Literature and Church History, Reformed Presbyterian Church, Edinburgh.

ANDREW THOMSON, D.D., Minister of Broughton Place United Presbyterian Church, Edinburgh.

General Editor. REV. THOMAS SMITH, D.D., EDINBURGH.

LONDON:

JAMES NISBET & CO., 21 BERNERS STREET.

1873.

PRINTED BY BALLANTYNE AND COMPANY EDINBURGH AND LONDON

No Condemnation

Sermons on Romans 8

Thomas Manton

Contents

THE EPISTLE DEDICATORY.

To the Eight Honourable PHILIP and ANN, the LORD and LADY WHARTON.

THE inserting your honours' names in this publication so little needs an apology, that it had much more needed one not to have done it. Your deeply inward affection to the excellent author; your most singular and just value for his person, ministry, converse, and memory, as they were too great to be fully expressed, so they are to be wholly concealed and buried in silence. Those acts of your beneficence towards him, wherein love is wont, the sincerer it is, always the more to affect privacy, it would be a rude violence to offer at disclosing. But its paths in that so long-continued friendly commerce with him, unto which your honours were pleased to condescend, could not be hid. Any eye might observe the frequency of your kind visits, the familiar freedom you gladly allowed him at your house, as at his own home; and that when the season invited you to your pleasant country recess, it was also the more pleasant to you if his affairs could allow him there to divert and repose himself with you. In the very common and piercing affliction of his death, which entered into the souls of many, none that were not of his nearer relatives had a greater share than your honours, or in the bitter sorrows caused by it. Your part may be hoped to be as peculiarly great in the advantages and consolations which he that bringeth light out of darkness is pleased to attend and follow it. The decease of any such person (besides that it is otherwise also instructive) is a further enforcing repetition and inculcation of a common but very apt and powerful argument, both for the increase of our faith concerning another world, and the diminution of our love to this. To the former purpose, the argument from this topic cannot but be very convictive unto such whom the forelaid serious apprehension of a Deity hath prepared and made capable of it. Unto others, to whose grosser minds that most important and so easily demonstrable thing is doubtful, one may despair anything should be certain that they see not with their eyes. But who that believes this world hath a wise, holy, righteous, merciful ruler, that disposes all things in it, can take notice that the best of men die from age to age as others do, and allow himself to think no differ ence shall be made hereafter? And that God should order the collecting of so great a treasure in one man; not to say of general learning and knowledge, but of true goodness, grace, sanctity, love to himself, and to men for his sake (his very image, and the lively resemblances of his own holy and gracious nature) to be forever buried in the dust? Or who would not rather conclude (as that blessed apostle) that when the world is passing away and the lusts of it, he that doth the will of God (being thus transformed into it) abideth forever? 1 John ii. 17.

And for that other purpose, Who that beholds what was of so great value, forsaking our world and caught up into heaven, would not less love an earthly station, and covet to be consorted with the holy assembly above? Every such assumption ought to diminish with us the retentive power of this world, and sensibly add to the magnetism and attractiveness of heaven. Doth not God expressly teach and prompt us to despise a world, out of which he plucks such excellent ones, plainly judging it not worthy of them? The general argument to both these purposes, though it hath not more strength in itself from the death of this or that particular person (when we foreknew that such must die) yet hath more emphasis and efficacy upon us, as the instances are repeated; especially when we have a present occasion to consider the death of some one of great value thoroughly known to us, as this worthy person was to your honours. For it is not then a cold, faint idea we have of such a one's worth (as that is which is begot by remote and more general report) but have a lively remembrance of it as it appeared in numerous vivid instances; and thence do, with the more spirit and assurance, conclude such excellences too great to be forever lost, or be an eternal prey -to death and the grave; but therefore that he is certainly ascended and gone into a world more suitable to him: whence also the manifold endearments (which were the effects of former very intimate conversation) recur afresh with us, and carry up our hearts after him thither, making us wish and long to be there too.

But the wisdom and mercy of providence seem especially to have taken care the church of God on earth should be some way recompensed for the loss of so considerable a person out of it, by those so generally acceptable and useful works of his that survive him. Your honours' judicious and very complacent gust and relish of anything that was Reverend Dr Manton's make you the more capable of the larger share and fuller satisfaction in that recompence. And were it known how great a part of them hath had a second birth or resurrection by the diligence of one depending on you, that rescued them from the obscurity of a private closet as from a grave, and who, though deservedly favoured by you upon other accounts, is undoubtedly much the more upon this also, you would be esteemed to have the more special title to them, as well as capacity of advantage by them.

There is, however, enough to make it decent and just, that wheresoever these writings shall be read, your kindness to the author should be told for a memorial of you; and whatsoever your interest was, or is, in him and his labours, it cannot be a lean wish unto you to desire your benefit may be proportional, which is most earnestly desired for you, with the addition of all other valuable blessings, by your honours' greatly obliged, and very humble servants in Christ our Lord,

WILLIAM BATES.

JOHN HOWE.

SERMON I

There is therefore now no condemnation to them which are in Christ Jesus, who walk not after the flesh, but after the spirit.

Romans viii. 1.

IN the former chapter, the apostle in his own person represents a believer groaning under the relics of sin, or bewailing the imperfections of his sanctification. Now, because this conscience of indwelling sin may breed in us fears of condemnation, he showeth here what remedy and relief is provided for us by Jesus Christ 'There is therefore,' &c. So that the words are an inference from the complaint and gratulation expressed in the last verse of the preceding chapter: though in the godly there remain some sin, yet no condemnation shall be to them, observe here

1. A privilege: 'there is no condemnation.'

2. A description of the persons who have interest in it: they are described, first, by their internal estate, 'To them which are in Christ Jesus;' secondly, by their external course of life 'Who walk not after the flesh, but after the spirit.'

[1.] There is a denial of the prevailing influence of the corrupt principle 'They walk not after the flesh.'

[2.] Their obedience to the better principle is asserted and affirmed 'But after the spirit.'

Three points I shall touch upon,

1. That it is a great felicity not to be obnoxious to condemnation.

2. That this is the portion of the true Christian, or such as are in Christ.

3. Those who are in Christ obey not the inclinations of corrupt nature, but the motions of the spirit.

Doctrine 1. It is a great privilege not to be obnoxious to condemnation: there is no condemnation to them that are in Christ.

To understand this, you must consider

First, What condemnation importeth.

Secondly, How we came by this exemption.

First, What condemnation importeth? The terror of it is unspeakable when it is sufficiently understood; and therefore, by consequence, our exemption and deliverance from it is the greater mercy.

In the general, condemnation is a sentence dooming us to punishment. Now, particularly for this condemnation

1. Consider, Whose sentence this is. There is *sententia legis* and *sententia judicis* the sentence of the law and the sentence of the judge. The sentence of the law is the sentence of the word of God, and that is either the law of works or the law of grace. The damnatory sentence of the law concludeth all under the curse, for 'all are under sin:' Gal. iii. 10, 'For as

many as are under the works of the law are under the curse; for it is written, Cursed is he that continueth not in all things that are written in the book of the law to do them'. So all the world is guilty before God, Rom. iii. 10. But the gospel, or the law of grace, denounceth damnation to those that believe not in Christ, and obstinately refuse his mercy: Mark xvi. 16, 'He that believeth not shall be damned'; and also against them that love not Christ and obey him: 1 Cor. xvi. 22, 'If any man love not the Lord Jesus Christ, let him be accursed.' This is the sentence of the law. But then there is *sententia judicis*, the sentence which the judge passeth upon a sinner, and is either—

[A.] The ratifying of that sentence which the word denounceth, be it either law or gospel; for what 'is bound in earth is bound in heaven;' and God condemneth those whom his word condemneth; so that for the present wicked men have a sentence against them; they are all cast in law, 'condemned already' as it is John iii. 18. If men were sensible of their danger, they would be more earnest to get the sentence reversed and repealed before it were executed upon them; they are not sure of a day's respite; it is a stupid dullness not to be affected with this woeful condition; there is but a step between them and death, and they mind it not.

[B.] As pronounced and declared. So it shall be at the last day by the judge of all the earth: Acts xvii. 30, 'Because he hath appointed a day in which he will judge the world in righteousness;' and 2 Thes. i. 8, 'He shall come in flaming fire, taking vengeance on all them that know not God, and obey not the gospel' Then the sentence is full and solemn, pronounced by the judge upon the throne, in the audience of all the world. Then it is final and peremptory, and puts men into their everlasting estate. And then it is presently executed; they go away to that estate to which they are doomed. Of this the scripture speaketh: John v. 39, 'They that have done evil shall arise to the resurrection of damnation' It is miserable to be involved in a sentence of condemnation by the word; now that shuts up a sinner as in a prison, where the door is bolted and barred upon him till it be opened by grace. But doleful will their condition be who are condemned by the final sentence of the judge, from which there is no appeal nor escape nor deliverance.

2. Consider, The punishment to which men are condemned. And that is twofold, either the *poena damni*, the loss of a heavenly kingdom; they are shut out from that: 'But the children of the kingdom shall be cast out into utter darkness: there shall be weeping and gnashing of teeth' Mat. viii. 12; or *poena sensus*, the torments and pains they shall endure, called the 'damnation of hell' Mat. xxiii. 33. Both together are spoken of: Mat. xxv. 41, 'Depart from me, ye cursed, into everlasting fire, prepared for the devil and his angels' Words that should cut a sinner to the heart, if he had any feeling of his condition. Now, to be exempted from condemnation to this punishment is the greater mercy. It is enough to heighten in our thoughts the greatest sense of the love of God, that we are freed from the curse, that Jesus hath 'delivered us from wrath to come,' 1 Thes. i. 10; that we are as brands plucked out of the burning; but much more when we consider that we shall be admitted into God's blessed presence, and see him as he is, and be like him, 1 John iii. 2; and for the present that, 'being justified by faith, we should be made heirs according to the hope of eternal life,' Tit. iii. 7.

The apostle expresseth both parts of the deliverance in one place: 1 Thes. v. 9, 'For God hath not appointed us to wrath, but to obtain salvation by our Lord Jesus Christ.' Mark the antithesis, 'Not to wrath, but to obtain salvation,' which should increase our sense of the privilege, that, when others lie under the wrath of God, we shall see him and love him and praise him in heaven to all eternity.

3. How justly it is deserved by us, by reason of original and actual sins, both before and after conversion. Original sin, for the scripture telleth us, Rom. v. 16, 'The judgment was by one to condemnation;' and again in ver. 18, 'By the offence of one, judgment came upon all to condemnation.' All Adam's children are become guilty before God, and liable to death, or brought into such an estate wherein they are condemnable before God. So by many actual sins it is deserved by us. As we are 'by nature children of wrath' Eph. ii. 3; so for a long time we have 'treasured up wrath against the day of wrath,' Rom. ii. 5. We have even forfeited the reprieve which God's patience allowed to us, and have more and more involved ourselves in condemnation. Till we comprehend our great need of pardon and exemption from condemnation we cannot understand the worth of it. Nay, we have deserved this condemnation since conversion.

He doth not say here, 'There is no sin in us,' but, 'There is no condemnation.' Sin in itself is always damnable, and our redemption doth not put less evil into sin; but in strict justice we deserve the greater punishment: this is another consideration that should endear this privilege to us.

4. How conscience standeth in dread of this condemnation. For if 'our own hearts condemn us,' 1 John iii. 20, they are a transcript of God's law, both precept and sanction; and therefore do not only check us for sin, and urge us to duty, but also fill us with many hidden fears, which sometimes are very stinging. When we are serious, the more tender the heart is, the more it smiteth for sin: Rom i. 32, 'Who knowing the judgment of God, that they that commit such things are worthy of death.' In your consciences you will find an inward conviction that God is your judge, and will call you to an account for the breach of his law. We feel this, living and dying: Heb. ii. 15, 'Who were all their lifetime subject to bondage through fear of death'; and 1 Cor. xv. 56, 'The sting of death is sin' only it is more piercing and sharp when we die.

Secondly, Let us inquire how, or upon what reasons we come to have this exemption from condemnation.

This is—

1. Upon the account of Christ's satisfaction to God's justice. We all in our natural estate lie under the curse and wrath of God; but Christ was 'made a curse for us' to 'redeem us from the curse of the law,' Gal. iii. 13. And the apostle telleth us, 2 Cor. v. 21, that 'he was made sin for us, that we might be made the righteousness of God in him.' Christ became a sacrifice for sin to appease God towards us; he was made a public instance of God's penal justice, that we might be made an instance of God's merciful justice, or that God might deal with us in a way of grace, upon the account of the righteousness of Christ.

2. Upon the account of the new covenant grant: John v. 24, 'Verily verily, I say unto you, He that heareth my word, and believeth on him that sent me, hath everlasting life, and shall not come into condemnation.' Christ would have us mark this as a certain and important truth, for escaping eternal death and obtaining eternal life are not trifles; and God's faithful word is interposed that such an one shall not come into condemnation, verily, verily. Well then, the gospel, or new covenant, offereth pardon and exemption from condemnation to that death which the law hath made our due, to all those who will come under the bond of it.

3. The certainty is considerable, which resulteth or ariseth from these two grounds. It is just with God to pardon them, and to exempt them from condemnation who take sanctuary at his grace, and devote themselves to him: 1 John i. 9, 'If we confess and forsake our sins, he is just and faithful to forgive them.' 2 Tim. iv. 8, we read of a 'crown of righteousness, which the righteous judge shall give at that day.' *Justum est quod fieri potest.* God may do it or not do it, he is not unjust if he doth it; and *justum est quod fieri debet.* This latter is understood here, because of the fulness of the merits and satisfaction of Christ, and his truth in his promises; he must judge men according to the law of grace, and give them that which his promise hath made their due.

4. There must be an appeal to the gospel, where this grace is humbly sued out by the penitent believers; for God is sovereign, and must be sought unto. Appeals from court to court, and from one tribunal to another, are often set down in scripture, as Ps. cxxx. 3, 4, 'If thou, Lord, shouldest mark iniquities, Lord, who shall stand? But there is forgiveness with thee, that thou mayest be feared.' No man could escape condemnation and the curse if the Lord should deal with us in strict justice; but from the tribunal of his strict justice we appeal to the throne of grace, where favour and pardon is allowed to us upon certain equitable and gracious terms. According to the old terms, who is able to appear in. the judgment before God? A sinner must either despair, or die, or run for refuge to this new and blessed hope: so Ps. cxliii. 2, 'Enter not into judgment with thy servant, Lord, for in thy sight shall no man living be justified.' An innocent creature must beg his mercy, and devote himself to his fear.

I proceed to the second proposition

Doctrine 2. That this privilege is the portion of those that are in Christ.

1. I shall here show you what it is to be in Christ.

2. How we come to be in Christ.

First, what it is to be in Christ. The phrase noteth union with him. There is certainly a real, but spiritual, union between Christ and his members, which I have often described to you. But late cavils make it necessary to speak a little more to that argument. All that I will say now is this

1. That it is more than a relation to Christ as a political head.

2. That the union of every believer with Christ is immediate.

1. That it is more than a relation to Christ as a political head. I prove it, because it is represented by similitudes taken from union real as well as relative; not only from marriage, where man and wife are relatively united, but from head and members, who make one

body; not a political, but a natural body: 1 Cor. xii. 12, 'For as the body is one, and hath many members, and all the members of that one body, being many, are one body, so also is Christ'; also by the similitude of root and branches, John xv. 1-3. Yea, it is compared with the mystery of the trinity and the unity that is between the divine persons: John xvii. 21-23, 'That they all may be one; as thou, Father, art in me, and I in thee, that they also may be one in us: and the glory which thou gavest me I have given them, that they may be one, as we av8 one. I in them, and thou in me, that they may be made perfect in one.' Which, though it must not be understood in the utmost strict ness, yet at least there is more than a relation; as also by reason it is not only a notion of scripture, but a thing effected and wrought by the Spirit on God's part: 1 Cor. xii. 13, 'We are by one Spirit baptized into one body,' and by confederation one with another: Cant. ii. 16, 'I am my beloved's, and my beloved is mine.' Christ is ours, and we are his; and he is also in us, and we in him. It is such a real conjunction with Christ as giveth us a new being, that Christ becometh to us the principle and fountain of a spiritual life: 1 John v. 12, 'He that hath the Son hath life.' Christ is the stock, we the graft; he is the vine, we the branches; therefore we are said to be 'planted together in him,' Rom. vi. 5; so that we may grow and live in him. We are united to him as the body is to the soul; all the members of the body are quickened by the soul; the second Adam becometh to all his members a quickening spirit, 1 Cor. xv. 45, as giving them life, not only by his merit and promise, but the influence of his Spirit, which life is begun here, and perfected in heaven. It is begun in the soul, Phil. iii. 20, and Rom. viii. 10, but it is perfected both in body and soul in heaven, for the Spirit is life to the body 'because of righteousness;' and if 'the Spirit of him that raised Christ from the dead dwell in you, he that raised up Christ from the dead shall also quicken your mortal bodies by his Spirit that dwelleth in you.' So that a vivifical[1] influence is the fruit of this union, which showeth that our union with Christ is not only a union with him as a political head (as the king is head and governor of all his subjects), but such a conjunction as maketh way for the lively influence of the Spirit of grace, as well as obligeth us to subjection to him, and obedience to his laws.

2. That the union of every particular believer with Christ is immediate, person with person. The thing is plain; for the scripture saith often that Christ is in us, and we are in Christ; and therefore it is not said truly that we are united with the church first, and by the church with Christ. Christ, who is the head of the church, is the head of every particular member of the church; and he that doth not hold the head and abide in him presently withereth, and can bring forth no fruit. The only place produced with any pretence for that fond conceit is 1 John i. 3, 'That which we have seen and heard declare we unto you, that ye also may have fellowship with us, and truly our fellowship is with the Father, and with his son Jesus Christ.' From whence they conclude that our union and communion is first with the apostles and then with Christ, not immediately, but mediately: we have communion with the church, and we have communion with them, and their communion is with the Father and the Son; but

---

[1] Life-giving

the quite contrary is true, that by faith we have first union and communion with Christ, and then with his church, because of the common relation to Christ. Well, but the apostle saith that ye may have communion with us, and truly our communion is with the Father and the Son. Communion and fellowship with us is not meant of communion between the apostles and them, but that you may have like fellowship with God and Christ as we have; that ye also, that you may have Communion as we have; as if he had said, The communion of which I speak is communion with the Father and his Son Jesus Christ; that is, we have communion with God and Christ, and we desire that you may have also the same communion. Though the thing be evident in itself, yet I shall add reasons, not my own, but another's that is, Episcopius, a man from whom all the modern divinity is derived, as is evident by their homilies and printed discourses. Though they are severe and tragical upon the memory of that blessed servant of God, John Calvin, yet methinks they should not differ from their great master in divinity; now, saith he, upon the place, " This opinion that we are united first to the apostles and then to God is with all diligence to be refuted. First, because it is absurd in itself; and secondly, because of the absurd consequences which are deduced from it."

[A.] "It is absurd in itself", because our communion followeth our union. But our union is not with the apostles themselves, but with Christ; for the apostles are not united to Christ as apostles with a saving union, but as believers; they are united to Christ in the same manner that we are; and so we are all brethren. Now, a brother is not united to the father by his brother, but immediately; for there is no subordination in a family, but a collateral respect to their common parent; as they are apostles, they are instruments whom God employeth to work that in us by which we may be united, not to them, but to God, and Christ immediately, and so have communion with him; so the apostle saith, 1 Cor. xi. 2, 'I have espoused you to one husband, that I may present you as a chaste virgin to Christ.' I will add, and not only the whole church, but particular believers, are said to be married to the Lord, Rom. vii. 4, The union and conjunction is with him immediate, and in this office all ministers or pastors are equal with the apostles, only that they first and immediately were sent by God for this work.

[B.] For the absurd consequences that may be drawn from thence namely, that our union is necessary with some men or company of men that is, some church, before we can have union and communion with God and Christ. Which by degrees, saith he, introduce the papacy; for if such an union be with any men first necessary, certainly with those that first delivered Christian doctrine; but because they abide not forever, others were to be substituted in their place that immediately depended on them, and so onward; and before we have union and communion with God and Christ we must have communion with their successors, how much soever they have degenerated from pure Christianity in doctrine, worship, and government; but, saith he, there is no such necessity. Every single believer, the lowest and least among them, have an equal immediate union and communion with Christ; for the apostles and all other pastors do only preach the gospel to no other end but to bring souls to God, and have authority over us to no other end; therefore what can be more absurd than that our union with any church or head of the church should be necessary before our union with Christ should be obtained? "

I proceed to the second thing which I proposed viz., to open to you,

Secondly: How we come to be in Christ. This is by regeneration, or the converting work of his Spirit. Conversion consists of three parts:

1. There is in it a turning from the creature to God.

2. From self to Christ.

3. From sin to holiness.

1. From the creature to God; that is, from the false happiness to the true from all false ways of felicity here below, to God, as enjoyed in heaven. Certainly our conversion may be understood by our aversion or falling off from God Now we fell from God to the creature: Jer. ii. 13, 'My people have forsaken me.' We sought our happiness, apart from God, in the enjoyment of some sublunary contentment; therefore till God be our end, there is no use of means. *Intentio est finis ultimi, electio est mediorum*, there is no choice of means without intention of the end. And Christ as mediator is to be considered as a means to come to God: John xiv. 6, whose favour we have forfeited, and not only forfeited, but despised; for whilst we are satisfied with our worldly enjoyments, we care not whether God be a friend or an enemy. Worldliness is carnal complacency or well-pleasedness of mind in worldly things, in the midst of soul dangers: Luke xii. 19, 'I will say to my soul, thou hast much goods laid up for many years; take thine ease, eat, drink, and be merry.' And the very first faith is a recovery out of this infatuation, or a settling our minds on eternal life: 1 Tim. i. 16, 'For a pattern to them that should afterwards believe on him to life everlasting'; and so in many other places. Whole Christianity is a coming to God by Christ: Heb. vii. 25; and that is the reason why faith cannot be in the heart of one that is yet entangled in the false happiness: John v. 44, 'How can ye believe, which receive honour one from another, and seek not the honour that cometh from God only? 'Which is to be understood not only *meritorie*, but *effective*, because while they are entangled in the false happiness, Christ is of no use to them; neither will they mind any serious return to God as their felicity and portion.

2. From self to Christ. For we are to flee from wrath to come, or the condemnation deserved by our apostasy and defection from God: Mat. iii. 8, 'generation of vipers, who hath warned you to flee from wrath to come?' Heb. vi. 18, 'Who have fled for refuge to lay hold of the hope set before us.' Therefore none are in Christ but those that thankfully receive him, and give up themselves to him: John i. 12, 'To as many as received him': 2 Cor. viii. 5, 'They first gave themselves unto the Lord'; that is, venturing on his promises, gave up themselves to the conduct of his word and Spirit, and trust themselves- entirely in Christ's hands, while they go on with their duty and pursuit of their true and proper happiness.

3. From sin to holiness, both in heart and life. For we 'are called to be holy,' and must flee not only from wrath but sin, which is the great make-bate between us and God; and therefore we need not only reconciling but renewing grace, which is accompanied in us by the 'Spirit of sanctification': 2 Thes. ii. 13, 'Who hath chosen you to salvation through

sanctification of the Spirit and belief of the truth' The Spirit beginneth it, as the fruit of God's elective love; and by faith and the use of all holy means doth accomplish it more and more, for he acts in us as the Spirit of Christ, and as we are members of his body, for framing us and fitting us more and more for his use and service. The third proposition observed in the text was,

Doctrine 3. Those who are in Christ obey not the inclinations of corrupt nature, but the motions of the spirit. This is brought in here as a fruit and evidence of their union with Christ, and interest in non-condemnation; for being united to Christ, they are made partakers of his Spirit; and they that have the Spirit of Christ will live an holy and sanctified life. The spirit first uniteth us to Christ, and sanctifieth and separateth the soul for his dwelling in us; and the effects of it are life and likeness. We live by virtue of his life: Gal. ii. 20, and walk as he walked: 1 John ii. 6, or else our union is but pretended.

But let us more particularly consider this evidence and qualification. They walk not after the flesh, but after the spirit; where we will enquire:

1. What is meant by flesh and spirit. By flesh is meant corrupt nature; by the spirit the new nature, according to that noted place: John iii. 6, 'That which is born of flesh is flesh, and that which is born of the Spirit is spirit.'

2. Both serve to those that are influenced by them as a guiding and inciting principle. The flesh to those that are 'after the flesh,' and the spirit to those that are 'after the spirit:' Rom. viii. 5. The flesh guideth and prompteth us to those things which are good for the animal life, for things of sense are known easily, and known by all. Carnal nature needeth no instructor, no spur; it doth pollute and corrupt us in all sensual and earthly things; but spiritual and heavenly things are out of its reach: 2 Pet. i. 9, and it inclines as well as guideth; for the things that we see, and feel, and taste, easily stir our affections, 'Demas hath forsaken us, having loved the present world.' Yea, 'tis hard to restrain them, and it is not done without some violence: Gal. v. 24, 'They that are in Christ have crucified the flesh with the affections and lusts thereof'; that the spirit or new nature doth both guide and incline^ is clear by those expressions: Heb. viii. 10, 'I will put my laws into their minds, and write them in their hearts, and I will be to them a God, and they shall be to me a people'

3. That those who are under the prevalency of the one principle cannot wholly obey and follow the other is clear; for those two are contrary: Gal. v. 17, 'The flesh lusteth against the spirit, and the spirit against the flesh;' and contraries cannot subsist together in an intense degree. They are contrary in their nature, contrary in their tendency and aim, contrary in their rule: Gal. vi. 16. The one carrieth us to God and heaven, the other to something pleasing to present sense; the one is fed with the world, the other with heaven. They are contrary in their assisting powers, Satan and the Spirit of God; the good part is for God; and the flesh, which is the rebelling principle, is on the devil's side: 1 John iv. 4. Satan by the lusts of the flesh taketh men 'captive at his will and pleasure': 2 Tim. ii. 26, 'That they may recover themselves out of the snare of the devil,, who are taken captive by him at his will and pleasure;' but the Spirit of God is assisted by the author of it, the Holy Ghost: Eph. iii. 16, 'Strengthened by the Spirit with might in the inner man. 'They are irritated by the spirit

or the flesh, presenting different objects, of sense and faith. The flesh hath this advantage, that its objects are near at hand, ready to be enjoyed; but the objects of faith are to come lie in an unseen world, only they are greater in themselves, and faith helpeth to look upon them as sure enough: Heb. xi. 1.

4. That every Christian hath these two principles in himself; the one by nature, is called flesh; the other by grace, is called spirit. God's best children have flesh in them. Paul distinguisheth in the former chapter betwixt 'flesh' and 'spirit' 'the law of the members' and 'the law of the mind': Rom. vii. 18, 23, as two opposite principles inclining several ways.

5. Though both be in the children of God, yet the spirit is in pre-dominancy; for the acts of the flesh are disowned: 'not I, but sin that dwelleth in me' and a man's estate is determined By the reign of sin, and grace in a man converted to God. The spirit, or renewed part, is superior, and governeth the will, or whole man, and the flesh is inferior, and by striving seeketh to become superior, and draws the will to itself; so that the heart of a renewed man is like a kingdom divided. Grace is in the throne, but the flesh is the rebel which disturbeth and much weakeneth its sovereignty and empire. It must needs be so, otherwise there would be no distinction between nature and grace. A man is denominated from what is predominant in him, and hath the chiefest power over his heart: if it be the flesh, he is carnal; if the spirit, he is regenerate, or a new creature; if his heart be set to seek, serve, please and glorify God, and doth prefer Christ before all the world: Phil, iii. 8. Then he hath not only a spirit contrary to the flesh and the world, but a spirit prevailing above the flesh and the world: 1 Cor. ii. 12, for 'We have not received the spirit of the world, but the Spirit of God.' Then the government of the soul is in the hands of grace.

6. The prevalency of the principle is known, not only by the bent and habit of our wills, but our settled course of life. By our walk, for it is said in the text, 'They that walk not after the flesh, but after the spirit.' A man is not known by an act or two, but by the tenor of his life. Those that make corrupt inclination their ordinary guide and rule, and the satisfaction thereof their common trade, they are carnal and in the flesh, and so cannot please God: Rom. viii. 5; but those whose business it is to serve, please and glorify God, and their end to enjoy him, and by whom this is diligently and uniformly pursued, they 'walk after the spirit;' because they 'live in the spirit, they walk in the spirit': Gal. v. 25.

I come to apply this discourse.

Use 1. Is information.

1. That condemnation yet remaineth upon all those that are out of Christ; for that promise, 'there is no condemnation' hath an exception, limiting it to those that are in Christ. Carnal men think God will not deal so severely as to condemn them; but there is no comfort hence to them. The scripture propoundeth privileges with their necessary limitations and restrictions; where sin remaineth in its power and strength, the law condemneth men, conscience convinceth them, and God will condemn them also. So the brutes are more happy than they, who follow their pleasure without remorse, and offend not the law of their creation as they do; and when they die, death puts an end to their pains and pleasures at

once; but those that walk after their lusts, are but Christians in name, certainly they are not made partakers of the spirit of Christ; for if they did live in the spirit, they would walk in the spirit, and none but such can escape condemnation. They that walk after the flesh are without God, and without Christ; but everyone will shift this off from himself, but the works of the flesh are manifest: Gal. v. 19. Many men visibly declare that they walk not after the spirit, by their drunkenness, adultery, wrath, strife, malice, and envy; others more closely live only to satisfy a fleshly mind; now whether openly or closely, if they cannot make out their living after the spirit, they walk after the flesh.

2. It informeth us, that we can never have solid peace, till justification and sanctification be joined together. Justification: Horn. v. 1, 'Being justified by faith, we have peace with God': Mat. ix. 2, 'Son, be of good cheer, thy sins be forgiven thee.' So for sanctification: 2 Cor. i. 12, 'This is our rejoicing, the testimony of our conscience, that in simplicity and godly sincerity we have had our conversation in the world.' Still there are fears of damnation, while sin is in us; but when it is our honest purpose to please God, and we strive against sin, and do in a good measure overcome it, our consciences may be the better, and the sooner settled.

Use 2. For exhortation.

To quicken us to seek after this privilege. Do you fear damnation, or do you not? If not, what grounds of comfort have you? What course have you taken to escape it? If you do fear it, why do you not 'flee from wrath to come?' Mat. iii. 7. Why do you not 'run for refuge'? Heb. vi. 18. You cannot be speedy and earnest enough in a matter of such concernment.

Again, this calls to those that are in Christ to be sensible of their privilege, so that they may bless God for it. Gratitude is the life and soul of our religion, and it is a cold and dull thanksgiving, only to give thanks for temporal mercies; it cometh more heartily from us when we bless God for spiritual mercies: Ps. ciii. 1, 2, 3, 'Bless the Lord, my soul, and all that is within me, bless his holy name. Bless the Lord, O my soul, and forget not all his benefits, who forgiveth all thine iniquities, who healeth all thy diseases' It also calls to all such, to be tender of their peace. Every sin doth not put you into a state of condemnation again, but every known, willful sin, puts us to get a new extract of our pardon: 1 John ii. 1, 2, 'My little children, these things write I unto you, that ye sin not: and if any man sin, we have an advocate with the Father, Jesus Christ the righteous, who is the propitiation for our sins.' By sin your title is made questionable, and your claim made doubtful; repenting and forsaking sin is necessary when we have been foiled by sin, that we may have a new grant of a pardon.

SERMON II

For the law of the spirit of life in Christ Jesus hath made me free from the law of sin and death.

Romans viii. 2.

That these words are brought as a proof of the former assertion, is clear from the causal particle, *For*; but whether they are a proof of the privilege or qualification, is usually disputed. I think of both; as when they are explained will appear. Therefore I shall first open the words, and then suit the proof to the foregoing assertion.

First, In opening the words observe,

1. Here is law opposed to law.

2. By the one we are freed from the other.

1. There is a perfect opposition of 'the law of the spirit of life in Christ Jesus, to the law of sin and death.' Here is law against law, and the spirit against sin, and life against death. Now, what are these two laws? I think they may be explained by that of the apostle: Rom. iii. 27, 'Where is boasting then? It is excluded; by what law? Of works? Nay, but by the law of faith.' What is there called the law of works, and the law of faith, is here called the law of the spirit of life, and the law of sin and death; in short, by these two laws is meant the covenant of works, and the covenant of grace.

(1.) The covenant of grace is called the 'law of the spirit of life in Christ Jesus.' A law it is, for it hath all the requisites of a law, a precept, and a sanction. They err certainly, that tell us the gospel is no law; for if there were no law, there would be no governor, and no government, no duty, no sin, no judgment, no punishment, nor reward. But of that more by and by.

(2.) A law of the spirit it is. Not only because of its spiritual nature, as it cometh nearer and closer to the soul than the law of outward and beggarly rudiments; and therefore Christ called the ordinances of the gospel, 'spirit 'and: truth': John iv. 24, spirit, in opposition to the duties, or the legal administrations, which are called 'carnal ordinances:' Heb. ix. 10; and truth, in opposition to them again, as they are called 'shadows of good things to come' Heb. x. 1. In this sense the gospel or new covenant, might well be called the law of the spirit; but riot for this reason only, but because of the power of the spirit that accompan ieth it; as 'tis said: 2 Cor. iii. 6, 'Who hath made us able ministers of the New Testament, not of the letter but of the spirit: for the letter killeth, but the spirit giveth life.' *Lex jubet, gratia juvat*; and the grace of the gospel is the gift of the spirit.

(3.) Tis called the spirit of life, because through the preaching of the gospel we are renewed by the Holy Ghost, and have the new life begun in us, which is perfected in heaven; and we are said: Gal. ii. 19, To be 'dead to the law, that we may live unto God'; that is, that by virtue of the Spirit of Christ dwelling in us, we may live righteously and holily to the glory of God.

(4.) It is the spirit of life in Christ Jesus, partly because he is the author and foundation of this new covenant; and partly, also because from him we receive the spirit, as from our head. We have the 'unction from the holy one': 1 John ii. 10; and the renewing of the Holy Ghost is shed upon us abundantly through Christ Jesus our Lord: Titus iii. 6.

Thus I have plainly opened the first law mentioned. Let us address ourselves to the second.

1. The law of sin and death. Thereby is meant the covenant of works, which inferreth condemnation to the fallen creature, because of sin; and in part the legal covenant, not as intended by God, but used by them; it proved to them a law of sin and death, for the apostle calleth it 'the ministration of death': 2 Cor. iii. 7, and verse 9, 'a ministration of condemnation' Now, because it seemeth hard to call a law given by God himself, a law of sin and death, I must tell you it is only called so, because it convinceth of sin, and bindeth over to death; and that I may not involve you in a tedious debate, I shall expedite myself by informing you, that the law of works hath a twofold operation, the one is about sin, the other about wrath, or the death threatened by the law.

[A.] About sin, its operation is double.

(1.) It convinceth of sin, as it is said: Horn. iii. 20, 'By the deeds of the law shall no flesh be justified in his sight: for by the law is the knowledge of sin.' That is, the use of it is to bring us to an acknow ledgment of sin and guilt; for when the law gets before a man what God commandeth and forbiddeth, and a man's conscience convinceth him that he hath offended against it by thoughts, lusts, words, deeds, he findeth himself a sinner, and his heart reproacheth him as one that is become culpable and guilty before God; so that all are concluded under sin by the services of that covenant. Neither will the legal covenant help him, for that is rather an acknowledgment of the debt than a token of our discharge a bond rather than an acquittance'; an hand writing of ordinances against us': Col. ii. 14; which did every year revive again the conscience and remembrance of sins: Heb. x. 3.

(2.) The other operation of the law about sin is, that it irritateth sin, and doth provoke and stir up our carnal desires and affections, rather than mortify them. For the more carnal men are urged to obedience by the rigid exactions of the law, the more doth carnal nature rebel; as a bullock is the more unruly for the yoking, and a river, stopped by a dam, swells the higher. The law requireth duty at our hands, but confers not on corrupt man power to perform it, and denounceth a curse against those that obey not, but giveth no strength to obey. That it is so is plain by that of the apostle: Rom. vii. 5, 'When we were in the flesh, the motions of sins which were by the law did work in our members to bring forth fruit unto death.' While we were under the dominion of corrupt nature, sins that were discovered by the law were also irritated by the law, as ill vapours are discovered and raised by the sun, which where hidden in the earth before; and so sin brought forth those ill fruits, the end whereof is death. But this is not to be charged on the law of God, but the perverseness of man; for the proper use of the law is to discover and restrain sin, and weaken it; not to provoke and stir it up. See how the apostle vindicateth God's law: Rom. vii. 7, 8, 'What shall we say then? is the law sin? God forbid: nay, I had not known sin but by the law: for I had not known lust unless the law had said, Thou shalt not covet: but sin, taking occasion by the commandment, wrought in me all manner of concupiscence.' Thus he answereth the objection, If sin grow more powerful in us by the law, then is the law sin? No, far be it from our thoughts; the law is not the cause, but the occasion only, as sin showeth its power upon the restraint. Well, then, the ceremonies of the legal covenant do riot mend the matter, for these are but a weak fence about our duty, and bridling more of our liberty, stubborn man spurneth the more against the law of God, and will not be subject to it.

[B.] The other operation of the law is about death, or the judgment denounced against sin; and so it is said, 'the law worketh wrath': Rom. iv. 15, as it bringeth punishment into the world, and revealeth God's wrath against the transgressions of men, and raiseth the fears of it in our consciences; and it is called the law of death, because unavoid ably it leaveth man under a sentence of death, or in a cursed and lost estate by reason of sin. These are the two laws.

2. By one law we are freed from the other. The apostle saith me, but he personateth every believer; they are all freed by the covenant of grace, from the bond and influence of the covenant of works; so it is a common privilege; what belongeth to one belongeth to all.

Secondly, My second part is to suit the words as an argument to confirm the former proposition.

1. They confirm the privilege, 'There is no condemnation to those that are in Christ.' They are free from the law of sin and death. He that is freed from the law is acquitted from condemnation; it can have no power over him.

2. The description is double: first, from their internal estate; they are in Christ; therefore they have the privileges and advantages of his new law of the law of the spirit of life, which is in Christ Jesus: secondly, their external course, 'They walk not after the flesh but after the spirit.' They have a spirit, and a quickening sanctifying spirit, grace given them in some measure to do what the law enjoineth. Being under Christ's holy government, saith Diodate, they are freed from the deadly tyranny of sin by the spirit of life, freed from the yoke and dominion of sin, which bringeth death, and so 'walk not after the flesh but after the spirit.' This I think to be the true meaning of the words.

Now I come to the doctrines.

Doctrine 1. That the new covenant is the law of the spirit of life in Christ Jesus.

Doctrine 2. That the new covenant giveth liberty (to all that are really under it) from the slavery of sin, and the condemning power of the law.

For the first point, that the new covenant is the law of the spirit of life in Christ Jesus. I shall divide it and prove,

1. That the new covenant is a law.

2. That it is the law of the spirit of life in Christ Jesus.

First. That it is a law. That the gospel hath the force of a law, I shall evidence by these considerations,

1. That man, being God's creature, is his subject, and standeth related to him, as his rightful governor, and therefore is to receive what laws he is pleased to impose upon him: Is. xxxiii. 22, 'The Lord is our judge, the Lord is our law-giver, the Lord is our king, and he will save us;'

and James iv. 21, 'There is one law-giver, who is able to save and to destroy' Our subjection to God, as our sovereign, is built on our total and absolute dependence upon him, both for our creation and preservation; for we could neither make ourselves, nor preserve ourselves; and therefore we are subject to the will of another, whose we are, and whom we should serve.

2. Man as a reasonable and free agent is bound voluntarily to yield up himself in subjection to his proper lord. All the creatures are under the government of God, and so in a sense are under a law; for there is a certain course, within the bounds of which their natures and motions are limited and fixed: Ps. cxix. 91, 'They continue to this day, according to thine ordinances: for they are all thy servants;' and, Ps. cxlviii. 6, 'He hath established them forever, and made a decree beyond which they shall not pass': so Prov. viii. 29, 'He gave to the sea his decree, that the waters should not pass his commandments. 'All creatures are balanced in a due proportion, and guided in their tract and course by an unerring hand, which is a kind of law to them. So man, as a creature, is subject to the direction of God's providence, as other creatures are; but as a reasonable creature he is capable of moral government, and of a law, properly so called; for so he hath a choice of his own, a power of refusing evil, and choosing good. Other creatures are ruled by a rod of iron, God's power and sovereignty; but man, whose obedience depends upon choice, is governed by laws which may direct and oblige him to good, and warn him and drive him from evil. Man is apt to be wrought upon by hopes and fears, which are the great instruments of government; by hopes of reward, and fears of punishment; and therefore he, not only out of his own interest, but duty to his creator, is bound to give up himself to do the will of God. This is called for; 2 Chron. xxx. 8, 'Yield yourselves to the Lord;' and 2 Cor. viii. 5, 'They first gave themselves to the Lord'; and Rom. vi. 13, 'Yield yourselves to the Lord'; and in many other places.

3. Man, being bound to obey the will of God, needeth a law from God to constitute his duty, and direct him in it; for without his laws, the subject cannot know what is clue to his sovereign, nor can man understand what his duty is to his creator. In innocency he gave him a law written upon his heart, for God made him 'holy and righteous' Eccles. vii. 29, and he was to perform such actions as became an holy and righteous creature; his nature bound him and fitted him to love God, and his neighbour and himself in a regular and due subordination, to God. This law was sufficient to guide him while he stood in his integrity, and to enable him to please God in all things; for this law written upon his heart was both his rule and his principle. But consider men in their fallen estate; surely they needed a law, and that God should show them what was good and evil. The Gentiles had some relics of the law of nature: Rom. ii. 14, 15, and so much sense of their duty left, as leaveth them not only culpable for their neglect of it, Rom. i. 20, 'But they are all become guilty before God,' Rom. iii. 19. With his people he dealt more favourably and graciously: Ps. cxlvii. 19, 20, 'He showed his word unto Jacob, and his statutes unto Israel: he hath not dealt so with any nation: as for his judgments they have not known them.' Alas! in the weakness to which we were reduced after the fall, how miserable should we be, and grope in the dark, if God had

not given us a law, and showed us what is good! Were it not for the relics of nature in the Gentiles, the world would be but a den of thieves, and a stage of wickedness; and every one would do what is right in his own eyes; and though the interests of men causeth them to make laws for their own safety, but yet there is no sure and sufficient direction to guide them in their obedience to God, without his word. The laws of men have no other end than the good of human society, and reacheth no further than the government of the outward conversation; there is little or nothing in them to guide us in our obeying or enjoying God. This God hath done in his word, to the Jews of old, and to us Christians more fully; for 'We are built upon the foundation of the prophets and apostles;' Eph. ii. 20; namely, as they have showed us to live in obedience to God, as our proper and rightful Lord, and to enjoy him as our proper happiness. But to leave this general view of these things.

4. The gospel, which is both our rule and charter, is the law which in Christ's name is given to the world. That appeareth,

[1.] By the titles or terms wherein it is expressed; as, Is. ii. 3, 'Out of Zion shall go forth the law, and the word of God from Jerusalem.' So Isa. lxii. 4, 'The isles shall wait for his law;' and Is. li. 4, 'A law shall proceed from me, and I will make my judgment to rest for a light to the people.' And in the New Testament it is called 'The law of faith' Rom. iii. 27, and the 'Law of Christ,' Gal. v. 2, so that the doctrine of salvation by Christ is that law which we should abide by.

[2.] The reason of the thing showeth it. For here is,

(1.) A governor or ruler, the Lord Christ, who hath acquired a new dominion and empire over the world, to save and to rule men upon his own terms: Rom. xiv. 9, 'For to this end Christ both died, and rose, and revived, that he might be lord both of dead and living'; and, Acts ii. 36, 'Therefore let all the house of Israel know assuredly, that God hath made the same Jesus whom ye have crucified, both Lord and Christ;' and Ps. ii. 7-11, so that he is lord of the new creation; and man doth owe obedience not only to God as creator, but to Christ as redeemer and ruler.

(2.) Christ being possessed of this lordship und dominion, hath made a new law of grace, which is propounded as a remedy for the relieving and restoring the lapsed world of mankind to the grace and favour of God; granting pardon and life to all that sincerely repent and believe in him, and live in new obedience; and peremptorily con cluding and damning those to everlasting death that shall refuse these terms.

(3.) This new constitution and gospel covenant hath all the formalities of a law. And here I shall show you, first, wherein it agreeth; and, secondly, wherein it differeth from the laws of men.

First, Wherein it agreeth. First in the promulgation of it with full authority; it is not only enacted *pleno jure*, by an absolute and uncontrollable right; but proclaimed by authorised messengers sent by the Lord Christ, who in his name were to require the obedience of the world to his new law: Mat. xxviii. 19, 20, 'All power is given to me in heaven and earth: go ye forth therefore and teach all nations, baptizing them in the name of the Father, Son, and

Holy Ghost; teaching them to observe all things whatsoever I have commanded you' He sendeth abroad his heralds, summoning the world to obedience: Acts v. 31, 'Him hath God exalted with his right hand to be a prince and a saviour, to give repentance and remission of sins': and Acts xvii. 30, 'The times of this ignorance God winked at, but now commandeth all men everywhere to repent'; he commandeth all men to repent, because he 'will judge the world in righteousness by the man whom he hath ordained,' Acts xvii. 31; and Acts x. 36, 'We preach peace by Jesus Christ, who is lord of all.' In these places Christ's right and authority is asserted; and the gospel is preached in his name, and the world invited and commanded to obey.

2. In the obligation and force. There is not only direction given to us to obey the gospel, but a charge and obligation is laid upon us. The gospel is sometimes called 'The counsel of God': Luke vii. 30. 'They rejected the counsel of God against themselves.' Sometimes the law of God is called his counsel, as it is the result of his wisdom; and his law, as it is the effect of his legislative will. He would not only direct and instruct the creature by his counsel, but oblige him by his authority; *decretum necessitatem facit, exhortatio liberam voluniatem excitat*, saith the canonist, Exhortation or advice serveth to direct or excite one that is free, but a decree and law implieth a necessity to obey. So Jerome, *Ubi consilium datur, offerentis arbitrium est: ubi praeceptum, necessitas servitutis*. Counsel and precept differ. Precept saith, not only we shall do well to do so, but we must do so. Counsel respects friends, a precept subjects. There is a coactive power in laws; God hath not left the creatures to comply with his directions if they please; no, there is a strict charge laid upon them; they must do it at their peril. Laws have a binding force, from the authority of their law giver. God giveth us counsel as a friend, but commandeth us as a sovereign. Therefore we read much of the 'Obedience of faith:' Rom. xvi. 26, 'The gospel was manifested to all nations, for the obedience of faith,' and Rom. i. 5. "We have received apostleship for the obedience of faith' among all nations: so Acts vi. 7, 'And a great company of priests were obedient to the faith;' and 2 Cor. x. 5, 'Bringing every thought into captivity to the obedience of Christ'; and 1 Pet. i. 22. 'Having purified your hearts in obeying the truth through the spirit'; and Acts v. 32, 'The Holy Ghost which is given to them that obey' All this is said to show it is not arbitrary or indifferent, but we are bound by the authority of this new law.

3. This law hath a sanction, otherwise it were but an arbitrary direction, though delivered in a preceptive form. The sanction is by promises of reward, or by threatenings of punishment; the precept establisheth man's duty, and is the rale of our obedience, which if it be neglected, infers *culpam*, fault or blame. The sanction is the rule of God's proceeding, and so it inferreth *paenam*, punishment: Mark xvi. 16. The law of grace threateneth us with the highest penalties: John iii. 19, 'This is the condemnation, that light is come into the world, and men love darkness rather than light'; and Heb. x. 2, 9, 'Of how much sorer punishment suppose ye shall be thought worthy,' &c.; though in the loss all are equal, yet conscience in hell hath a kind of accusation, or self-tormenting, in reflecting upon the refusal of the remedy, or losing the special advantages we had by the gospel. As the breach of the law is vindicated on the Jew first, Rom. ii. 9, so the gospel when known to be the only way of

peace and life, it is the worse for us in the judgment, if we neglect it. Secondly, the promises are given to sweeten the precepts to us, that we may obey in love, not as slaves, for fear of punishment only. Forced motives change not the heart endure not long; therefore in Christ's law there are promises of pardon of sin, adoption into God's family, and finally eternal life. We make the precept to be the way to the promise; and God maketh the promises to be the motive to the precept. We keep the precept to obtain the promise; but God propoundeth the promise that we may keep the precept more comfortably. We aim at happiness, but God aimeth at obedience, and maketh that the end of all his promises; so that we must obey the command, that we may obtain the blessing of the promise, and be assured of it; and we believe the promise, that we may obey the precept.

4. This sanction supposeth an exercise of government according to law; and so that there is a just governor and administrator, who will take account how this new law of grace is kept or broken. So there is here now in part, both in the way of internal or external government. First, internal government, as 'The kingdom of God is within us': Luke xvii. 20. Soul-government is carried on according to this rule of commerce, between us and God. As there is a sense of our duty written upon our hearts, a remaining inward principle, inclining us to it, Heb. viii. 10; so there is a fear of our judge, who will call us to an account for the violation of his law; an inward sentence of life or death upon us, as we do good or evil; the bitter afflictive sense of God's dis pleasure in case of evil; and the rewards of love and obedience, as tests of God's acceptance, given us by his Spirit upon our fidelity to Christ, a real lively joy, and peace of conscience: 2 Cor. i. 12, 'This is our rejoicing, the testimony of our conscience' Rom. v. 1. 'Being justified by faith, we have peace with God;' Rom. xiv. 17, 'For the kingdom of God is not meat and drink, but righteousness, and peace, and joy in the Holy Ghost.' Secondly, God's external government is according to the law of the gospel. God interposeth now and then, punishing the contempt of the gospel with remarkable judgments: Heb. ii. 1, 2, 3, 'Therefore we ought to give the more earnest heed to the things which we have heard, lest at any time we should let them slip; for if the word spoken by angels was steadfast, and every transgression and disobedience received a just recompense of reward how: shall we escape if we neglect so great salvation, which at first began to be spoken by the Lord himself, and was confirmed by them that heard VOL. xi. 2 o it?' And eminently dispensing his blessing where the gospel is favoured and obeyed, and prospereth, as he blessed the 'house of Obed-edom for the ark's sake'; but more fully at the day of judgment the wicked have their full punishment: 2 Thes. i. 8'; Coining in flaming fire, rendering vengeance to all those that know not God, and obey not the gospel.'

Secondly, I shall show you wherein the gospel, as a law, differeth form ordinary laws among men. (1.) Men in their laws do not debate matters, but barely injoin them, and interpose their authority; but God condescendeth to the infirmity of man; and seemeth to come down from the throne of his sovereignity, and reasoneth, and persuadeth, and beseecheth men that they will not forsake their own mercies: Isa. xlvi. 8, 'Remember this, show yourselves men, bring this to mind again, ye transgressors': and Isa. i. 18, 'Come, let us, reason together.' God is pleased to stoop to sorry creatures, and to plead, and argue with them: so

2 Cor. v. 20, 'We as ambassadors in God's stead, do beseech you to be reconciled.' Men count it a lessening to their authority to proceed to entreaties; but the clemency of the Redeemer's government is otherwise.

(2.) The law of God bindeth the conscience and the immortal souls of men; condemneth not only acts, but thoughts and lusts: Mat. v. 28, 'The law is spiritual, 'Rom. vii. 14. With man, thoughts and desires are free till they break out into act. (3.) Man's laws do more incline to punishment than reward. For robbers and murderers, death is appointed; but the innocent subject hath only this reward, that he doth his duty, and escapeth those punishments. In very few cases doth man's law promise reward. The inflicting of punishment is the proper work of man's law, and the great engine of government, because its use is to restrain evil; but God's law propoundeth rewards equal to the punishment. Eternal life on one hand, as well as eternal death on the other: Deut. xxx. 15, 'See, I have set before you life and good, death and evil;' because the use of God's law is to guide men to their happiness. It is *legis candor*, the equity and favour of man's law to speak of a reward; it commands many things, and forbids many things, but still under a penalty; its natural work is punishment, and it doth not invite men to a duty by a reward: *ex malis moribus humanae leges*, to restrain evil is their work. (4.) Human laws threaten temporal punishment; but God's law threateneth eternal punishments and rewards: Mark ix. 44, 'Where the worm dieth not, and the fire is not quenched.' He is a living God: Heb. x. 31, into whose hands we fall when we die.

Use 1. Is to humble us that we bear so little respect to the precepts of the gospel, and do so boldly break them, and so coldly perform the duties thereof. We fear temporal power more than eternal, a prison more than hell; and therefore can dispense with God's law to comply with our own lusts. A little profit or a little danger will draw men into the snare, when eternal death will not keep them from it. Oh rouse up yourselves. Are you not Christ's subjects? Is not he a more powerful sovereign than all the potentates in the world? Doth he not in his gospel give judgment upon the everlasting state of men? Will this judgment be in vain? Hath he not appointed a day when all matters shall be taken into consideration? Will not sin, when it comes to be reviewed, have another countenance? Awaken then your sleepy and sluggish souls. If you can deny these truths, go on in the neglect of Christ, and breach of his laws, and spare not; but if conscience be sensible of his authority, break off your sins by repentance, sue out your pardon in his name; devote yourselves to God, walk more cautiously for time to come. God will not wink always at your disloyalty.

Use 2. is direction to us. If you would not be flighty in the duties of the gospel, look upon it as a law, and let me commend these rules to you.

1. Never set Christ's mercy against his government. He is a saviour, but he is also our lord, and must be obeyed; and faith implieth a consent of subjection, as well as dependence.

2. Cry not up his merits against his Spirit. His merit is your ransom, but his Spirit is your sanctifier; and this law is the law of his Spirit, the one implieth the other; his Spirit implieth the merit of Christ, by bringing you under the law of grace.

3. Set not the ends of Christ's death one against the other. He that died that he might reconcile you to God, died also to bring you into obedience; it is a mercy to be redeemed from wrath; but it is as great if not a greater mercy to be redeemed from sin. Titus ii. 14.

4. Do not so put all upon Christ as to exempt yourselves from the jurisdiction of God; no, Christ 'redeemed us to God,' Rev. i. 9. To him we were first lost; to him we must be recovered, that he may not lose the glory of his creation in Christ. We are not without law: 1 Cor. ix. 21, not without the law to God, but under the law to Christ; we are not to be irregular, but to rule all our actions by the law of Christ. To carry ourselves as without law, if we challenge it *de jure*, is to affect to be gods; *de facto*, it is to be as devils, the greatest rebels in nature.

I come now to the second doctrine observed.

Secondly. That the gospel is the law of the spirit of life in Christ Jesus. Here I shall inquire,

1. What is the spirit.

2. From whom we receive it.

3. By what law.

1. What is the spirit here spoken of? I answer, both the person of the Holy Ghost, and the new nature.

[A.] The person of the Holy Ghost cannot be excluded; partly, because he is Christ's witness and agent in the world, who is powerfully able to apply whatever he hath procured for us, and to give us the effect of all his offices: John xv. 26, 'But when the comforter is come, whom I will send to you from the Father, even the Spirit of truth that proceedeth from the Father, he shall testify of me': and John xvi. 14, " He shall take of mine, and glorify me.' He revealeth the tenor of Christ's doctrine, and attests the truth of it by his gifts and graces bestowed upon the church, and to every one of us in particular, by his powerful effects in our hearts. Therefore it is said, 'We are witnesses of these things, and so is the Holy Ghost, which he hath given to them that obey' Acts v. 32. Christ that taught us the Christian religion, doth work it in us by his Spirit, and so doth confirm it to us. ^ And partly, because by this means all the divine persons have their distinct work and share in our recovery to God: 1 Pet. i. 2, 'Elect according to the fore-knowledge of God the Father, through the sanctification of the Spirit, unto obedience and sprinkling of the blood of Christ.' The Father concurs by electing, the Son as purchasing, the Spirit as sanctifying and inclining us to God. As the Father must not be without the glory of his free grace, nor the Son of his infinite merit; so neither the Holy Ghost of his powerful and effectual application. And partly also, because this is agreeable to the economy or dispensation that is observed among the divine persons. The Spirit is the effective power of God; therefore he it is that causeth our life, or by regeneration infuseth a new life into us: Ezek. xxxvi. 27, 'I will put my Spirit into you, and cause you to walk in my ways.' I prove it by three arguments. The first is taken from the nature of the thing itself. Certainly we cannot live independently without the influence of God; for all life is originally in him, and from him conveyed to us, and that by his Spirit. In life natural, it is clear, all that God did in creation was done by his Spirit: Job xxvi. 13, 'By his

Spirit he hath garnished the heavens, his hands hath formed the crooked serpent.' The Spirit is the immediate worker in the creation of the world; by his concurrent operation with the Father and the Son, all things were produced; he speaketh there of the heavenly bodies and constellations. And again in Ps. civ. 30, 'Thou sendest forth thy Spirit, and they were created.' And when the creation of man is spoken of: Mai. ii. 15, 'Did he not make one? Yet had he the residue of the Spirit.' It is true also of spiritual life, which is called a new birth; and no man can 'enter into the kingdom of God but he that is born of water and the Spirit,' John iii. 5; and it is called a new creature; all creation is of God: 2 Cor. v. 17, 18, 'A resurrection to life'; or a quickening dead souls, Eph. ii. 1,5,' And you hath he quickened who were dead in trespasses and sins. Even when we were dead in sins, hath he quickened us together with Christ.' And therefore the spirit of life is from God. Now if God effecteth all these things by his Spirit, to whom but him alone is our salvation to be ascribed? as the scripture doth frequently mention. My second argument is taken from our incapacity to help ourselves, and recover ourselves from the devil, the world, and the flesh, to God. So blind are our minds, so depraved are our hearts, so strong are our lusts, and so many are our temptations, and so inveterate are our evil customs, that nothing will serve the turn but the Spirit of God, who doth 'open the eyes of our mind:' Eph. i. 18, change our hearts: Titus iii. 5, reconcile our alienated and estranged affections to God, that we may return to his love, and live in obedience to him, and finally, be presented before him, as fit to live forever in his presence: Col. i. 21, 22, 'and you that were sometimes alienated, and enemies in your minds by wicked works, yet now hath he reconciled in the body of his flesh through death, to present you holy and unblamable, and unreprovable in his sight.' All this doth the powerful and all-conquering Spirit of God, by virtue of the meritorious purchase of Christ. In short, he findeth in us such addictedness to sin, such a love to the present world, such indulgence to the flesh, as beareth down both reason and the authority of God, that no less agent can do the work. My third reason is taken from the subsequent effects. If this life be strengthened by the Spirit, it is much more wrought and infused by the Spirit at first, when all is against it. Now the scripture is copious in asserting the supply of the Spirit of Christ, as necessary to do and suffer the will of God: Eph. iii. 16, 'Strengthened with all might in the inner man, from the Spirit:' 1 Pet. iv. 14, 'The Spirit of God and of glory resteth upon you' Surely he that must help us when we are living must quicken us when we are dead; and he that is necessary to break the force of our carnal affections still after they have received their death wound, was absolutely necessary to overcome them at first, when in full strength. The necessity of strengthening grace doth much more show the necessity of renewing grace; for there needs much more power to overcome the corruptions of nature, than to heal or prevent the infirmities of the saints.

[B.] The new nature is the product of the Holy Ghost: John iii. 6, 'That which is born of the Spirit is spirit.' Men become spiritual in their dispositions, inclinations, actions and aims, from the effects of the spirit of regeneration, which may be considered with respect to God or to man.

(1.) How the converted person or new creature standeth affected to God, seemeth to be set forth by the apostle in that place: 2 Tim. i. 7, 'For we have not received the spirit of fear, but of love and power, and a sound mind.' I shall explain it. Observe in the negative de scription, but one part only of mortification is mentioned deadness to the fears of the world. But that defect may be supplied from another scripture': The spirit lusteth against the flesh': Gal. v. 17, he deadeneth us to the delights and hopes of the world, as well as the fears and sorrows; but the one is understood in the other; for this spirit causeth us to prepare for sufferings in the world, and to look for no great matters here, but to expect crosses, losses, wants, persecutions, injuries, painful sicknesses, and death; and doth fortify us against all bodily distresses, that we are not greatly moved by them, considering our relation to God and interest in blessedness to come, which doth weigh down all so it is not a spirit of fear. But then you must enlarge it by considering the main work of the Spirit, which is to subdue the lusts of the flesh, that the government of God may be set up in our hearts; for the flesh is the great rebel against God and sanctified reason. Therefore we must obey the Spirit, and take part with it in these strivings; yea, we must strive against the flesh, and overcome it, so as to prevent all willful reigning sin; for they that have the Spirit live in no sin, but only smaller human frailties. Surely where the spirit prevaileth it crucifieth the flesh, and causeth men to live above all the glory, riches, and pleasures of the world, and mortifieth our sensuality more and more, and doth conquer and cast down our strongest, sweetest, dearest lusts, that they may not hinder our love and obedience to God in Jesus Christ. But then for the positive part of the description. It is a spirit of love, power, and a sound mind; that is, the three effects of it are life, light, and love. There is a new vital power, called there the spirit of power; and then he possesseth our hearts with predominant love to God, called there the spirit of a sound mind; so that by these three effects, doth the Spirit, renewing and sanctifying the souls of men, discover itself; in enlightening their minds, and opening their hearts, and fortifying their resolutions for God and the world to come; and these three effects do answer the nature of God, whom we apprehend under the notions of wisdom, goodness and power. To his wisdom there answereth the spirit of a sound mind; to his goodness, the spirit of love; and the spirit of power, to the power of God; so that by these graces we are made 'partakers of the divine nature': 2 Pet. i. 4, and do in some sort resemble God. And these suit with the word of God, which is sometimes represented as light, because the wisdom of God shineth forth there, and is represented in the mysteries of the gospel, where the way of salvation is sufficiently taught': We speak wisdom among those that are perfect': 2 Cor. ii. 6, 'The holy scriptures are able to make us wise to salvation': 2 Tim. iii. 15. Sometimes the gospel is called the power of God: Tit. ii. 11, and Jude 4. Or the goodness of God, because it representeth the wonders of God's love in our redemption by Christ, and the rich preparations of grace he hath made for us. And these three effects of the spirit suit with the three fundamental graces, faith, love, and hope The spirit of a sound mind is elsewhere called the 'spirit of faith:; 2 Cor. iv. 13, which is the eye of the new creature; and the spirit of love is with a little variation called 'Love in the spirit:' Col. i. 8, and is the heart of the new creature; and the spirit of power is hope, called elsewhere 'Abounding in hope through the power of the Holy Ghost': Rom. xv. 13, which is the strength of the new creature, whereby we overcome sins and temptations. And in all these effects doth the life and power of true godliness consist; for surely, he is sufficiently furnished for the kingdom of heaven, and all the duties thereof, whose mind is enlightened to know God in Christ Jesus, and inclined to love God, and live to him, and who hath chosen the blessedness of the next world for his portion, and liveth in the joyful hopes and foresight of it; this man hath the true spirit of the gospel, and his conversation will be answerable, for there are three words by which a good conversation is usually expressed holiness, heavenliness, and godliness. Holiness is sometimes spoken of as distinct from godliness: 2 Pet. iii. 11; and so holiness noteth purity and hatred of sin, and abhorrence of sin: this is the fruit of the sound mind, or the love and knowledge of God in Christ; for he that sinneth hath not seen God: 3 John 11, that is, hath no true apprehension of him; for if we rightly beheld 'the glory of the Lord 'in a glass of the gospel, 'We are changed into his likeness, '2 Cor. iii. 18. And faith, which is but the knowledge of the gospel with assent, doth purify the heart: Acts xv. 9. The next property is godliness, or an inclination and addictedness to God, and is the fruit of love which subjecteth all to God, and raiseth the heart, and resigneth it to him, and maketh it fit to serve, please, glorify and enjoy him: 2 Cor. v. 14, 15, 'For the love of Christ constraineth us, because we thus judge, that if one died for all then were all dead: and that he died for all, that they which live should not henceforth live to themselves, but unto him which died for them:' 1 Pet. iv. 6, 'For this cause was the gospel also preached unto them that are dead, that they might be judged according to men in the flesh, but live according to God in the Spirit:' 1 Cor. vi. 20, for 'ye are bought with a price, therefore glorify God in your spirits, which are God's.' Love is most seen in a thorough resignation and obedience unto God, and a desire of communion with him here: Eph. ii. 8, and the full fruition of him hereafter: 2 Cor. v. 1. The last property is heavenliness: Phil. iii. 20, but 'Our conversations are in heaven, from whence we look for a Saviour.' This the Spirit worketh in us by hope, which fortifieth us against all the terrors and delights of sense: 1 John iv. 4-6, 'Greater is he that is in you, than he that is in the world; they are of the world, therefore speak they of the world, and the world heareth them. We are of God; he that knoweth God, heareth us; he that is not of God, heareth not us: hereby know we the spirit of truth, and the spirit of error.' The apostle is speaking there of the trial of spirits, and he puts the difference upon the issue the Spirit of God, and the spirit of the world, and showeth the one must needs be more powerful than the other; so in that other text: 1 Cor. ii. 12, 'For we have not received the spirit of the world, but the spirit which is of God.' A spirit raised to God, and seeking the happiness to come, weaneth us and draweth us off the world, and so giveth us power to overcome not the world only, but the flesh and the devil also.

(2.) Consider this spirit, as it fitteth us and frameth us for our duty to man. That the apostle showeth: Eph. v. 9. 'For the fruit of the Spirit is in all goodness, righteousness, and truth'; that is, the spirit that God hath sent among us by the preaching of the gospel doth bring forth and produce in us all kindness, justice and fidelity. There is not a more benign, affable thing than the gospel spirit, nor anything that doth more fit us to live peaceably and usefully in human society. The first property is all goodness, for God is good to all, and his spirit is called a good spirit: Ps. cxliii. 10. It causeth us to love all mankind with a love of benevolence; and those that are holy and partakers with us in the same grace, with a special love of complacency. This not only keepeth us from doing those things which would hinder their good, but also inclineth us to seek their good, by all means possible, especially the best good for them, and if others do injuries to us, to forgive them, as 'God, for Christ's sake hath forgiven us.' The second operation which the Holy Ghost produceth in us is righteousness, or justice in all our dealings, giving everyone his due, honour to whom honour, tribute to tribute, and praise to whom praise belongeth, not bor rowing without a mind or ability to pay, which is but a specious robbery; and it is a shame so many Christians are guilty of it; I am sure 'tis contrary to the Spirit of God, for when God hath done so much to manifest his justice to the world, all that have the Spirit of God should be very righteous, far from oppression, fraud, or detention of what is another man's. The third thing is truth, or fidelity; whereby we carry ourselves sincerely, and free from hypocrisy and dissimulation, or lying, cozenage and deceit. God is a God of truth, and the holiness _he worketh in us is true holiness; the apostle groundeth his exhortation upon that, 'Wherefore put away lying': Eph. iv. 24, 25, 'and speak truth every man to his neighbour'. Tis a sin inconsistent with sincerity more than any other. Well, then, this is the gospel spirit; now the Holy Ghost doth not only plant these graces in us at first, but doth continually increase them, and assist us in the exercise of them. He doth plant them in us at first. Faith is his gift, and it is he doth change our hearts, and kindle an holy love in us to God, and raiseth the heart to the hope of salvation: 1 Pet. i. 9, 'Begotten to a lively hope.' This is his first work, for men must be good before their actions can be good; then he doth increase grace, making all outward means effectual to this end and purpose; this is called 'the supply of the Spirit of Christ Jesus': Phil. i. 19, meaning thereby a further addition of grace wrought in us by the Spirit, whereby we grow and advance in the way to heaven. These impressions are weak in us at first, but they are increased by the same author or agent in the use of the same means. Lastly, he doth assist us in the exercise of the same grace, still working in us what is pleasing in the sight of God: Heb. xiii. 21. He concurreth to every action, and we do not only 'live in the spirit, but walk in the spirit': Gal. v. 25. All along we are quickened by his influence.

2, Let us in the next place consider from whom we receive it. It is said here the spirit of life 'which is in Christ Jesus' it belongeth to Christ to give the spirit.

[A.] He is the head of the renewed state. Christ was filled with the Spirit to this end, to be the head, or quickening spirit to his mystical body: 1 Cor. xv. 45, 'The first Adam was made a living soul, the second a quickening spirit;' not only as he giveth us the life of glory, but the life of grace also: so Eph. i. 22, 23, 'He is head over all things to the church, which is his body, the fullness of him that filleth all in all.' He is an head, not only to govern and defend the church, but to give them spiritual life and motion, as the head doth to the members; for he filleth all with grace. All believers are supplied from this fountain, and continually supplied, 'Till they be filled with all the fullness of God': Eph. iii. 17, 18, 19, that is, with all the grace he meaneth to impart to us. Well, then, the spirit is given by Christ: John iv. 14, 'Whoso drinketh of the water that I shall give, shall never thirst, but the water that I shall give him,

shall be in him a well of water, springing up to everlasting life.' It is a living conduit: John vii.
38, 39.

[B.] It is his law that is written upon our hearts by the Spirit. The new covenant is made with
sinners in Christ: Heb. viii. 8-10, 'Be hold the days come (saith the Lord) I will make a new
covenant with the house of Israel, not according to the covenant I made with their fathers in
the day when I took them by the hand to lead them out of the land of Egypt, because they
continued not in my covenant; for this is the covenant I will make with the house of Israel, I
will put my laws into their minds, and write them in their hearts.' Now he that taught us the
Christian faith and religion, doth impress it upon us by his Spirit; we find a power, more than
can be from the words alone, in the effects on ourselves. This cometh from Christ, whose
law it is, but it is immediately wrought by the Spirit.

[C.] Christ promised it, therefore Christ giveth it: John xv. 26, 'The comforter shall come,
whom I will send you from the Father.' By virtue of his merit and intercession, Christ, from
the Father, sendeth forth the all-conquering Spirit to subdue the world to himself. He
promised beforehand to send down this sanctifying Spirit into men's souls, to do this work
upon them.

[D.] He giveth it on his own conditions, that is to say, of faith: John vii. 37, 38, 'If any man
thirst, let him come to me, and drink; he that believeth in me, out of his belly shall flow
rivers of living water: but this he spake of the Spirit, which they that believe in him should
receive.' And repentance: Acts ii. 38. 'Then Peter said unto them, Repent and be baptized
every one of you in the name of Jesus Christ, for the re mission of sins, and you shall receive
the gift of the Holy Ghost.' Now these are the conditions of the new covenant, which Christ
brought out of the bosom of God.

3. By what law? By the gospel. This is 'the law of the Spirit of Christ.' There is some little of
the spirit given by the light of nature, to help men to read the book of the creatures: Rom. i.
19. God showed it them; they might see somewhat of God in the creatures, his wisdom,
power, and goodness; and God excited their minds to behold it, and did dart in some light
into their consciences. There was more of the spirit given by the legal covenant; they might
see much more of the power, wisdom and goodness of God in his statutes and laws than
heathens could in the book of nature; but generally it wrought unto bondage. The free spirit
was but sparingly dispensed, and to some few choice servants of God; but these were but as
a few drops of grace; the great flood of grace was poured out by the gospel. The apostle
puts the Galatians to the question, by what doctrine they received the Spirit: Gal. iii. 2, 'This
only would I learn of you, received you the Spirit by the works of the law, or by the hearing
of faith? 'He appealeth to their conscience and experience, what kind of doctrine conveyed
the Spirit to them, the preaching of the law, or the preaching of the gospel; and this is
meant not only of the Spirit that wrought miracles, but the sanctifying Spirit. He speaketh of
both, ver. 5, 'He therefore that ministereth to you the Spirit, and worketh miracles among
you.' Where the ministration of the Spirit is made a distinct branch from working miracles';
doth he it by the works of the law, or by the hearing of faith? 'So that the Spirit of

regeneration, sanctification and adoption, cometh by the doctrine of the gospel. I will prove this by some reasons.

[A.] From the institution of God. God delighteth to bless his own means; and the great institution of God for the benefit of mankind is the gospel, which being a supernatural doctrine, needed to be attested from heaven, that the truth of it might be known by the mighty power that doth accompany it. Therefore this new covenant is the law of the spirit; the powerful influence of the Spirit of God on all those that submit to it, is the seal and confirmation of it. No other doctrine can so change the soul, and convert it to God: John xvii. 17, 'Sanctify them through the truth, thy word is truth.' John viii. 31, 32, 'And ye shall know the truth, and the truth shall make you free.' That is to say, then we know it to be the truth, a doctrine of God, sanctifying us, and making us conquerors over sin and Satan.

[B.] From the nature of the gospel. For God will work agreeably by suitable means, not only agreeable to the subject upon which he worketh, the souls of men, but agreeably to the object by which he worketh.

(1.) In the general. It is a spiritual doctrine. By a spiritual doctrine he will pour out more of the Spirit, which was but sparingly dispensed when the ordinances which he instituted were carnal and bodily; more fully, when he had given a law that suited more with his own spiritual nature, and came closer to the soul of man, than the law of a carnal commandment. This law was the law of the spirit; when he would break the obstinacy of the Jews he tried them by many positive laws and external observances; but when he would reduce the world into a state of liberty, his laws were spiritual and rational, and with them he poureth out a mighty spirit; therefore the apostle intimateth that they served God 'in the oldness of the letter, but we serve him in the newness of the spirit': Rom. vii. 6, that is, in that true holiness whereunto we are renewed by the Holy Ghost, through the preaching of the gospel, which is called the 'ministry of the spirit': 2 Cor. iii. 8. There was more letter then, but more spirit now: Phil, iii. 3. A believer hath 'no confidence in the flesh'; doth not place his hope in the observances of 'carnal ordinances,', but 'rejoiceth in Christ Jesus' serving God in the spirit.

(2.) More particularly, the gospel is suited to the operation of the Spirit; it being a doctrine of profound wisdom, great power and rich goodness, in comparison of which all other knowledge is but cold and dry. The spirit we are possessed withal is but a transcript of the word: Heb. viii. 10: 2 Cor. iii. 3, 'Ye are manifestly declared to be the epistle of Christ, written not with ink, but with the Spirit of the living God.' There is the prescript, there the transcript; as suppose a man would stamp his coat of arms upon wax, there needeth wax, a seal graven with it, and a hand to apply it; this is the case here. God would stamp his image upon our souls, but first the characters of it are upon the word. By this word of wisdom, he will give us the spirit of a sound mind, that we may know God and ourselves, and the difference between good and evil; by this word of grace, or account of his love to us in Christ, he gives us the spirit of love; by this word of power, wherein there are such rich and great promises, he will raise a noble spirit in us to carry us above the world. The stamp is prepared only to make an impression; there is required a strong hand to apply it to the heart of man; for though the gospel doth powerfully excite our dead and drowsy hearts to spiritual and heavenly things, yet it is not enough that the doctrine be opened, but it must be applied to the soul by the Spirit, or else it is not healed and changed. The word is the means, but the Spirit renewethus as the principal cause; for the word doth not work upon all, nor upon all those alike on whom it worketh. The gospel is a fit instrument for it. Everything communicateth its own nature; fire turneth all about it into fire; an holy and heavenly doctrine is fit to beget an holy and heavenly spirit.

(3.) For the honour of our Redeemer; in his lordship or kingly office; who as he requireth new duties of man fallen and disabled, so he giveth strength proportionably. The difficulty of our recovery lay not only in our reconciliation with God, but in the renovation of our nature, and subduing our obstinacy, or changing our hearts. Of his prophetical office; that we might have the effect and comfort of it, external doctrine is not only necessary, but the illumination of the Spirit; who 'leadeth us into all truth.' His priestly office; that his merit may be known to be full, his intercession powerful, it is needful that such a gift should be given to his people as the visible pouring out of the Spirit: Acts ii. 30.

Use 1 is, to convince the rabble of carnal Christians, how little they have gained by that Christianity they have. Alas! In what a case are those poor souls who have not the Spirit of Christ: Rom. viii. 9, 'If any man hath not the Spirit of Christ, he is none of his.' They do not belong to Christ, have no interest in the fruits of his redemption; and then how will ye stand before God in the judgment, and make answer to all that may be alleged against you the accusations of the law, or Satan, or your own consciences? Certainly the guilt of sin remaineth, where the power of it is not broken. There are Christians in name, and Christians in power; in profession, and in deed and in truth; Christians in the letter, and Christians in spirit: these are such as are sanctified by the Spirit unto obedience; and none but such have interest in the comfortable promises of mercy of the new covenant: Gal. vi. 16, 'As many as walk according to this rule, peace and mercy be upon them.' And none other shall be saved at last: Heb. v. 9, 'He is the author of salvation to them that obey him': Heb. xii. 14, 'Without holiness no man shall see the Lord.'

Use 2 is to humble the better sort of Christians, that they have gotten so little of the Spirit, that the effects of it in their souls are so imperfect, clouded with a mixture of remaining infirmities. All that are godly have this spirit, are guided by it, walk after it; but all have it not in a like measure. Some are weak; it doth not subdue their lusts and fears, nor breed such mortification and courage as should be found in the disciples of Christ; these want comfort, if possibly they should be sincere; for their evidences are not clear by which they should be tried. Mortification: Gal. v. 24, 'They that are Christ's, have crucified the flesh, with the affections and lusts thereof.' Courage: 1 Pet. iv. 14, 'If ye be reproached for the name of Christ, happy are ye'

Use 3 is of directions to all sorts of Christians.

1. Do all your duties, as those that are under the law of the spirit of life. Not in the oldness of the letter, but the newness of the spirit; not customarily, formally, but seriously, with a life and a power. Be lieve in the spirit: 1 Cor. ii. 5, 'That your faith should not stand in the

wisdom of men, but in the power of God.' Love in the spirit: Col. i. 8, 'Who also declared to us your love in the spirit' Hope in the spirit: Gal. v. 5, 'For we through the spirit wait for the hope of righteousness of faith.' Hear in the spirit, pray in the spirit, and obey in the spirit: 1 Pet. i. 22, 'Seeing you have purified your souls in, obeying the truth through the spirit.' Let there be a spirit and life in all that you do.

2. Beg of your Redeemer to pour out a fuller measure of his Spirit in your souls; he hath promised it: Zech. xii. 10, 'I will pour upon the house of David, and upon the inhabitants of Jerusalem, the Spirit of grace and supplication': Isa, xliv. 3, 'For I will pour water upon him that is thirsty, and floods upon the dry ground; and I will pour my Spirit upon thy seed, and my blessing upon thine offspring' The saints have begged it earnestly: Ps. cxliii. 10, 'Teach me to do thy will, for thou art my God, thy Spirit is good: lead me into the land of uprightness': and Luke xi. 13, They that ask, shall have. None lack this grace, but those that forfeit it by neglect and contempt, and resistance of the motions of his Holy Spirit.

3. Use ordinances to this end. All these are helps and means to obtain it. The gospel worketh morally and powerfully. It is the 'divine power giveth us all things to life and godliness,' therefore in the use of means you must wait for it: 2 Pet. i. 3 'According to his divine power he hath given us all things.'

4. Let us examine often, and see if we are partakers of his spirit. Two evidences there be of it, and they are both in the text, life and liberty. First, life, for this spirit is called 'the spirit of life in Christ Jesus'; by it we are enabled to live the life of faith and holiness: Gal. ii. 20, 'I live by the faith of the Son of God.' Doth it rule the main course of your lives? Denying the pleasures and profits and honours of the world, we must live in Christ and to Christ; we must not only seek truth in the gospel, but life in the gospel. Secondly, liberty: 2 Cor. iii. 17, 'Where the Spirit of the Lord is, there is liberty.' There is more alacrity, readiness and cheerfulness in obedience: Ps. cxix. 32, 1 1 will run the ways of thy commandments, when thou shalt enlarge my heart.' It is a liberty not to do what we list, but what we ought, and that upon gracious and free motives, with a large heart that can deny God nothing, but is sweetly and strongly inclined to him.

SERMON III

Hath made me free from the law of sin and death.

Romans viii. 2.

We now come to the second point.

Doctrine 2 That the new covenant giveth liberty to all that are under it, from the slavery of sin, and the condemning power of the law. Let me explain this point: and here I shall show you,

1. That liberty supposeth precedent bondage.

2. That our liberty must answer the bondage.

3. I shall show you the manner of getting our liberty.

First, Liberty supposeth preceding bondage; for when Christ spake of liberty, or making them free, the Jews quarrelled at it: John viii. 33, 'We were never in bondage to any man: how sayest thou then that ye shall be made free? 'So much we gather from their cavil, that it is the first thought, or the ready sentiment and opinion of mankind, that to be made free, implieth a foregoing bondage. Now, our bondage consisteth in a slavery to sin and Satan, and being under the condemn ing power of the law, or obligation to the curse, and eternal damnation.

1. That man is under the slavery of sin, which the law convinceth him of; that it is so with us, the scripture showeth: Titus iii. 3, 'We were sometimes foolish and disobedient, serving divers lusts and pleasures.' (1.) There is the condition of natural men; they serve. (2.) The baseness of the master, lusts, and divers lusts. (3.) The bait or motive by which they are drawn into this service, intimated in the word pleasures; for a little brutish satisfaction a man selleth his liberty, his soul, his religion, his God, and all. This word is most proper to our purpose; for that noteth his slavery. Carnal affections so govern us, that we know not how to escape and come out of this thraldom[2]; we suffer the beast to ride the man. It were monstrous in the body, for the feet to be where the head should be, or to have the limbs distorted, to have the arms hang backward; yet such a deordination there is in the soul, when reason and conscience is put in vassalage to sense and appetite. The natural order is this: reason and conscience directs the will, the will moveth the affections, the affections move the bodily spirits, and they the senses and members of the body; but natural corruption inverts all: pleasures affect the senses, the senses corrupt the phantasy, the phantasy moveth the bodily spirits; the affections, by their violence and inclination, enslave the will and blind the mind; and so man is carried headlong to his own destruction. This slavery implieth three things:

---

[2] enthralled

[A.] A willing subjection: Rom. vi. 16, 'Know ye not that to whom ye yield yourselves servants to obey, his servants ye are to whom you obey, whether of sin unto death, or of obedience unto righteousness? 'Servants were made so, either by consent or conquest. The apostle speaketh there not of servants by conquest, but of servants by consent and covenant. When a man yieldeth up himself to be at the disposal of another, he is a servant to him; so in moral matters, by whatever a man is employed, and to which he giveth up his time and strength, life and love, to that he is a servant, be it to the flesh or to the spirit, as we make it our business to accomplish or gratify the desires of the one, or the other. A godly man hath sin in him, but he doth not serve it, yield up himself to obey it; he doth not walk after his lusts.

[B.] Customary practice and observance: John viii. 34'; Whosoever committeth sin is the servant of sin.' The word signifieth he that liveth in an habit and course of sin; he is brought under the power of it, enslaved by such pleasures as he affects.

[C.] Inability to come out of this condition. 'The law is spiritual, but I am carnal, sold under sin': Rom. vii. 14. By the law of nations, service was brought in by conquest, and those that were taken in war were *venditi sub hasta* sold under a spear, merely at the disposal of him that took them: 2 Pet. ii. 19, 'They are servants of corruption: for of whom a man is overcome, of the same is he brought into bondage.' This our service under sin is in part represented by a captive, in regard we cannot rid ourselves of it; in part by an hired servant, because we willingly, and by our own default, run into it. This impotency is most sensible in them that are convinced of better, but do that which is worse; they see their duty, but are not able to perform it, being overcome by their lusts; they have some kind of remorse and trouble, but cannot help themselves.

But how came this servitude upon us? Partly by the natural inclination of our own corrupt hearts. There are *servi natura*, fools and brutish men; so in a spiritual sense are all men: Gen. viii. 21, 'The imaginations of man's heart are evil from his youth.' (2.) It is increased by custom in sinning; these lusts are not only born with us, but bred up with us, and so plead prescription because religion cometh afterwards: Jer. xiii. 23, 'Can the Ethiopian change his skin or the leopard his spots? then may ye also do good that are accustomed to do evil.' It is hard to shake off inveterate customs. Strict education, though it changeth not the heart, hindereth the growth of sin. (3.) Example doth strengthen and increase it: Eph. ii. 3, 'Among whom we also had our conversations in times past in the lust of our flesh, fulfilling the desires of the flesh and the mind, and were by nature children of wrath even as others': and Isa. vi. 5, 'I am a man of unclean lips, and I dwell in the midst of a people of unclean lips.' (4.) By the devil's craft, who observeth our tempers and inclinations, who suiteth every distemper with a diet proper: 2 Tim. ii. 26, 'That they may recover themselves out of the snare of the devil, who are taken captive by him at his will.' Now, this is our bondage till we change masters, and devote and give up ourselves to God.

2. By nature men are under the power of sin, and so by consequence under the sentence of death, for sin and death go hand in hand; These two cannot be put asunder, being joined together by the ordination of God's righteous law. If sin rule in us, it will certainly damn us;

for none are freed from the damning power of sin, but those that are freed from the dominion of it. The same law that convinceth of sin, doth also bind over to death; sin and death suit together like work and wages: Hom. vi. 23, 'The wages of sin is death' To affect you while we are explaining this matter, consider three things:

1. The suitableness of death to sin.

2. The certainty of it.

3. The terribleness of this death.

[A.] The suitableness or correspondence that is between sin and death. This suitableness will appear, if we consider the wisdom, justice and holiness of God.

(1.) The wisdom of God, which doth all things according to weight, measure and order, cannot permit the disjunction of these two things, so closely united together as sin and punishment; but there will be an appearance of deformity and incongruity, if there be such things as good and evil, *bonum et malum morale*, as he is unworthy of the name, not only of a Christian, but a man, that denieth it. Again if there be such a thing as pleasure and pain, joy and sorrow, as the sense telleth us, or that which we call *bonum et malum naturale*, natural good, and natural evil, then it is very agreeable to the wisdom of God, that these things should be rightly placed and sorted, that a moral evil, which is sin, should be punished with a natural evil, which is pain and misery; and moral good, which is virtue, should end in joy and pleasure; or in short, that there should be rewards and punishments. God is naturally inclined, as the creator of mankind, to make his creatures good and happy, if nothing hinder him from it, if there be no impediment in the way. From hence we may see how incongruous it is to the wisdom of God, who permitteth no dissonancy or disproportion in any of his dispensations, to admit a separation of these natural relatives. If there were no other testimony of this, yet the dispositions of our own hearts would evince it, for there we have some obscure shadows of the proper ties which are in God. We compassionate a miserable man, who is made so by the iniquity of the times, and we esteem him not deserving his misery: and we are moved with indignation against one, who by evil arts is fortunate and successful, but altogether unworthy of the happiness which falleth to his share; which is an apparent proof that men are sensible of an excellent harmony, and natural order which is between these two things, virtue and felicity, sin and misery, and to see them so suited, doth exceedingly please us. Now this showeth how fitly these two couples are joined, sin and death, grace and life.

(2.) Let us consider the justice of God, as the judge of the world, and so must and will do right: Gen. xviii. 25, 'Shall not the judge of all the earth do right? 'It belongeth to his general justice, that it be well with them that do well, and ill with them that do evil. God is readily inclined to provide happiness for man, who is his creature, if there were no sin to stop the course of his bounty; and if sin had not entered into the world, there had been nothing but happiness in the world; but when 'sin entered into the world,' death presently trod upon the heels of it: Hom. v. 12, 'As by one man sin entered into the world, and death by sin; so death passed upon all, even for that all have sinned.' Now men are of different sorts; some recover out of the common apostasy, and their cursed estate by sin, and live holy; others wallow in their filthiness still. Therefore it is agreeable to God's general justice to execute vengeance on the one, and to reward the other; at least, the punishment is just: Rom. ii. 9, 10, 'Tribulation and anguish upon every soul of man that doth evil, but glory, honour and peace to every one that worketh good.' So that the justice of God maketh an inseparable connexion between sin and death.

(3.) Let us consider the purity and holiness of God, which inclineth him to hate evil and love that which is good. The first we are most concerned to prove: Ps. v. 5, 'The foolish shall not stand in thy sight, thou hatest all the workers of iniquity.' But the other is true also, 'The upright are his delight': Prov. xi. 20. Well, then, if God loveth good and hateth evil, he will one way or other express his love and hatred. This he doth by promising life to the good, and threatening death to the evil. Out of all this discourse about the wisdom, justice and holiness of God, we conclude the suitableness of death to sin; that the difference between good and evil is not more naturally known, than it is also evidently known that the one is rewarded and the other punished. Other cannot be looked for if we consider the wisdom of God, which suiteth all things according to their natural order; therefore sin, which is a moral evil, is punished with suffering somewhat that is a natural evil, that is the feeling something that is painful and afflictive to nature; or if we consider the justice of God, which dealeth differently with men that differ in themselves; and the holiness of God, who will express his love to the good in making them happy, and his detestation of the wicked in the misery of their punishment.

[B.] The certainty of this connection of sin and death was the second thing proposed.

(1.) Reason showeth in part, that there is a state of torment and bliss after this life, or eternal life and death. All men are persuaded there is a God, and very few have doubted whether he be a punisher of the wicked and a rewarder of them that diligently seek after him. Now neither the one nor the other is fully accomplished in this world, even in the judgment of those who have no great knowledge of the nature and malignity of sin, or what punishment is competent there unto. Therefore there must be some time after that of sojourning in the body, when men shall receive their full punishment and reward, since here we see so little of what might be expected at the hand of God. Surely if man be God's subject, when his work is ended he must look to receive his wages accordingly as he performed his duty, or failed in it. Now our work is not over till this life be ended, then God dealeth with us by way of recompense, giving us eternal life, or the wages of sin, which is death.

(2.) Conscience hath a sense of it. Conscience is nothing else but serious and applicative reason. Now the consciences of sinners stand in dread of eternal death: Rom. i. 32, 'Who knowing the judgment of God, that they which commit such things are worthy of death.' This thought haunts men living and dying: living: Heb. ii. 15, 'And deliver them who through fear of death were all their lifetime subject to bondage;' but chiefly dying: 1 Cor. xv. 56, 'The sting of death is sin.' For then men are most serious, and apprehend themselves nearest to danger. Stings of conscience are most quick and 'sensible then, and a terrible tempest ariseth in sinners' souls when they are to die.

(3.) Scripture, if we take God's word for it, is express. The first threatening: Gen. ii. 17, 'In the day thou eatest thereof thou shalt surely die:' and Horn. vi. 23, 'The wages of sin is death;' and ver. 21, 'What fruit have you in those things whereof ye are now ashamed? For the end of those things is death.' Will you believe this, or venture and put it upon the trial? Oh! take heed of sin. 'The dead are there, and her guests are in the depths of hell': Prov. ix. 18. Men are destroyed by their heedlessness and incredulity. In what a woeful case are you, if it prove true? and prove true it will, as sure as God is true.

[C.] Consider the terribleness of this death. The life to come, and the wrath to come are both eternal. Punishment in one scale holdeth conformity with the reward in the other: as those that escape have an eternal and far more exceeding weight of glory; so they that still remain under the sentence of death for sin, are condemned to an eternal abode both in body and soul under torments: Mat. xxv. 46, 'These shall go away into everlasting punishment; but the righteous into life eternal. 'Oh how woeful is their condition whose bodies and souls meet again at the resurrection, after a long separation; but a sad meeting it will be when both must presently be cast into everlasting fire. If we did only deal with you upon slight and cheap motives, you might refuse to hearken; they are but slight matters that can be hoped or feared from man, whose power of doing good or evil is limited to this life; but, 'It is a dreadful thing to fall into the hands of the living God': Heb. x. 31. The afflictions and sorrows of this life are a part of this death; our miseries here are the fruit of sin, and after them followeth that death which consists in the separation of the soul from the body, called, in the book of Job, the king of terrors; but after that, there is a second death, which is far more terrible, which consists in an eternal separation from the blessed and glorious presence of the Lord. In all creatures that have sense, death is accompanied with some pain; but this is a perpetual living to deadly pain and torment, from which there is no release; there is no change of estate in the other world after our trial is over, and things of faith become mere matter of sense; the gulf is then fixed, there is no passage from torments to joys; Luke xvi. 26. Things to come would not considerably counterbalance things present, if there were not eternity in the case; therefore this death is the more terrible, that men might abhor the pleasures of sin. Well, then, this is the condition of all men once, to be under sin, and under the sentence of this death, which is a woeful bondage.

Secondly. Our liberty must answer the bondage. To be redeemed from wrath is a great mercy; so it is also to be redeemed from sin. These are the branches, Christ delivered us 'from wrath to come': 2 Thes. i. 10'; He hath redeemed us also from all iniquity': Tit. ii. 14. The first part, of freedom from the power of sin, is spoken of, Rom. vi. 18, 'Being then made free from sin, ye became the servants of righteousness.' Man in his natural estate is free from righteousness, ver. 10, that is, righteousness or grace had no hand and power over him; but in his renewed estate he is free from sin. To be under the dominion of sin is the greatest slavery; and to be under the dominion of grace is the greatest liberty and enlargement. They that are free from righteousness, have no inclinations or impressions of heart to that which is good, no fear to offend, no care to please God; are not brought under the awe and power of religion. On the other side, then are we free from sin, when we resist our lusts so as to overcome them, and have a strong inclination and bent of heart to please God in all things, and accordingly make it our business, trade and course of life: Luke i. 75, 'That, being delivered from the hands of our enemies, we might serve him without fear, in holiness and righteousness before him all the days of our life.' The other part of the liberty is when we are freed from the sentence of death passed upon us by the law, and acquitted and discharged from the guilt of sin, and being 'justified by faith,' are made 'heirs according to the hope of eternal life': Tit iii. 7. That I will not speak of now, because before in the first verse.

I now proceed to open unto you the last thing at first propounded; which was,

Thirdly. The manner of getting our liberty. There are three words in the text, Law, Spirit, and Christ Jesus. Let us begin with the last. Christ procureth this liberty for us by the merit of his death and inter cession. The law or gospel offereth this liberty to us, and the Spirit first applieth it and sealeth it to the conscience.

1. Christ procureth and purchaseth this liberty for us, both from the damning power of the law, and the slavery of corruption. We were captives, shut up under sin and death, and he paid our ransom, and so obtained for us remission of sins, and the sanctification of the Spirit. Remission of sins: Eph. i. 7, 'In whom we have redemption by his blood, the remission of sins.' That is one part of our recovery, highly necessary for guilty creatures; how else can we stand before the tribunal of God, or look him in the face with any confidence? But his redemption did not only reach this, but the sanctification of the Spirit also. Therefore it is said: 1 Pet. i. 18, 'Ye are not redeemed with corruptible things, but by the precious blood of Jesus Christ' Thus Christ doth what belongeth to him, and none can share with him in this honour; it is his merit that is at the bottom of the covenant, and procured for us both the favour and image of God, that we might love him, and be beloved by him.

2. There is a law or new covenant, which offereth this grace to us. The law of nature concludeth men under sin, and pronounceth death upon them. Christ hath set up a new remedial law of grace, by which we are called to submit to Christ, and thankfully to accept of his merciful preparations, even the great benefits of pardon and life. The gospel or new covenant doth its part.

[A.] There is grace published or offered to us: Luke iv. 18, 'The Spirit of the Lord is upon me, for he hath anointed me to preach deliverance to the captives' 'It is not enough that our ransom be paid, but the offer must be made; or else how shall it be laid hold upon by faith, and received with thankfulness, and with a due sense of the benefit? Now the gospel showeth, liberty may be had upon sweet and commodious and easy terms.

[B.] The terms are stated in the covenant; that we give up ourselves to the Lord by Christ, and be governed and ruled by the conduct of his word and Spirit: Gal. iii. 2. 'Received ye the Spirit by the works of the law, or the hearing of faith?' and 2 Tim. ii. 25, 26, 'In meekness instructing those that oppose themselves, if peradventure God will give them repentance to the acknowledging of the truth: and that they may recover themselves out of the snare of the devil, who are taken captive by him at his will.' The covenant is not left to our humours and fancies, to model and bring it down to our liking; no, nor are only the benefits offered, but terms stated: Isa. lvi. 4. 'That choose the things that please me, and take hold of my covenant.' When he hath stated his terms, it is too late for man to interpose his vote, or to imagine to bring down Christianity to a lower rate; for we must not new model it, but take hold of it as God hath left it. Be in Christ, and walk after his Spirit.

3. This liberty is assured and established by the covenant. The conscience of sin, and the fears of condemnation, are not easily done away; and we are so wedded to our lusts, that the power of reigning sin is not easily broken; therefore we had need of a sure firm covenant to ratify these privileges to us, because our fears are justified by a former law, made by God himself. Therefore God would not deal with us by naked promise, but put his grace into a covenant-form, that we may have as good to show for our salvation, as we had for our condemnation; yea, and more; and God hath added his oath, 'That the con solation of the heirs of promise might be more strong,' Heb. vi. 18. And it being a latter grant, former transactions cannot disannul it; so that the covenant doth its part also to free believers from the power of sin, and the fears of condemnation.

4. The Spirit applieth this grace, both as to the effects and the sense; [1.] As to the effects, he applieth it in effectual calling; as this quickening Spirit doth regenerate us, and convert us to God, and break the power and tyranny of sin, the wages whereof is death. The gospel is the means, but the blessing is from the Spirit: John viii. 32, 'Ye shall know the truth, and the truth shall make you free'; that is, ye shall know it savingly, so as to feel the power and efficacy of it. To be set free to know, love, serve, and delight in God, is that liberty that we have by the free Spirit: Ps. li. 12, 'Restore unto me the joy of thy salvation, and uphold me with thy free Spirit.'

[B.] The Spirit sealeth it as to the sense, when we come to discern our freedom by the effects of it in our own souls: Eph. i. 13, 'After ye believed, ye were sealed with that holy spirit of promise'; ' and in the fruit of Christ's purchase, Gal. iv. 4, 5, 6, 'But when the fullness of time was come, God sent forth his Son, made of a woman, made under the law, to redeem them that were under the law, that we might receive the adoption of sons. And because ye are sons, God hath sent forth the Spirit of his Son^ into your hearts, crying Abba, Father.' The Spirit's seal is God's impress upon our souls; left there, not to make us known to God (for he knoweth who are his, from all eternity), but for the increase of our joy and comfort; not by guess, but some kind of certainty: 1 John iv. 13, 'Hereby we know that we dwell in God, and God dwelleth in us, by his Spirit that he hath given us.' By the Spirit dwelling and working in us, we know our interest; this is not so absolutely necessary as the former to our safety, but very comfortable. There is a spirit that attendeth the law, reviving fears in men, and a sense of God's wrath; and there is a spirit attending the gospel, inclining us to come to God as a father: Rom. viii. 15. The one is called the spirit of bondage, the other the spirit of adoption. Now, because the law is so natural to us, we the more need this liberty.

Use 1. Since there is a liberty by Christ, and that wrought in us by the Spirit, but dispensed by the gospel; let us seek it in this way.

Therefore consider:

1. Your need, since every man is under the power of sin naturally, and so under a sentence of condemnation to death. If you be not sensible of the evil and burden of sin, yet surely you should flee from wrath to come. Is that a slight matter to you? Our first and quickest sense is of wrath; when our hearts are made more tender, we feel the burden of sin; fear worketh before shame and sorrow; therefore surely he that considereth his deep necessity, should cry out, 'wretched man that I am, who shall deliver me from this body of death? 'Rom. vii. 24.

2. Consider the possibility of your delivery from this bondage by the law of the spirit of life in Christ Jesus. Surely the blood of Jesus can 'purge your consciences from dead works, that you may serve the living God': Heb. ix. 14. There is a covenant, all the promises of which in Christ are, 'Yea, and Amen': 2 Cor. i. 20. The covenant of night and day may sooner be dissolved, than this covenant broken or repealed. There is the Spirit also, who can subdue your strongest lusts, and is ready to help you to mortify the deeds of the body, and to reclaim you from your vain pleasures.

3. How comfortable it will be for you when once this work is in progress, and you begin to pass from death to life; every step will be sweet to you; and as you grow in grace, you do apace advance to heaven: Prov. iii. 17, 'All her ways are pleasantness, and all her paths are peace.'

Use 2. Let us examine whether we have received this regenerating grace, to free us from the reign of sin. Some are free in show, but others are 'free indeed': John viii. 36. Some have the outward badges of liberty, are Christians in name, receive sacraments, and enjoy the ordinances, but not the grace in and by the ordinances. You may know the state of your service by the course of your life. Are you as ready to do anything for God, as before for sin? Rom. vi. 18.

Use 3. If we be free, let us not return to our old slavery again: Gal. v. 1, 'Stand fast in the liberty wherein Christ hath made you free, and be not entangled again in the yoke of bondage.' Especially that chief part of freedom from the dominion of sin: Rom. vi. 12, 'Let not sin reign in your mortal bodies, that ye should obey it in the lusts thereof'; and the 14th verse, 'For sin shall not have dominion over you, for ye are not under the law, but under grace'

SERMON IV

For what the law could not do, in that it was weak through the fleshy God sending his own Son, in the likeness of sinful flesh, and for sin, condemned sin in the flesh.

Romans viii. 3.

HERE the apostle explaineth himself, and showeth how 'the law of the spirit of life in Christ Jesus, doth make us free from the law of sin and death.'

In the words observe three things,

1. The deep necessity of mankind'; for what the law could not do, in that it was weak through the flesh.'

2. The means of our deliverance; or God's merciful provision for our relief. The means are two (1.) Christ's incarnation, in these words; and God sending his own Son in the likeness of sinful flesh. (2.) His passion, and for sin, or by a sacrifice for sin.

3. The end or benefit accruing to us thereby, condemned sin in the flesh.

Doctrine From the whole, that when man could by no means be freed from sin and death, God sent his Son to be a sacrifice for sin, that our liberty might be fully accomplished. The apostle's method is best; I shall therefore follow that.

First. The deep necessity of mankind is argued and made out by this reason, that it was impossible for the law to do away sin, and justify man before God; so he saith, For what the law could not do, in that it was weak through the flesh, that is, through the corruption of our natures, we being sinners, and unable to perform the duty of the law. To understand the force of this reason, take these considerations:

1. That it was necessary, in respect of God's purpose and decree, that we should be freed from sin and death. For God would not have mankind utterly to perish, having chosen some to salvation and repentance, and so leaving others without excuse; therefore the strict judgment of the law is debated upon this argument: Ps. cxliii. 2, 'Enter not into judgment with thy servant, Lord, for in thy sight shall no man living be justified, 'and again: Ps. cxxx. 3, 'If thou, Lord, shouldst mark iniquity, Lord who shall stand? 'According to the first covenant, none can escape condemnation. Now, this consisted not with the purposes of the Lord's grace, who would not lose the whole creation of mankind. God hath showed himself placable and merciful to all men, and hath forbidden despair, and continued many forfeited mercies; and did not presently upon sinning, put us in our everlasting estate, as he did the fallen angels, but rather is upon a treaty with us.

2. God resolving to restore and recover some of mankind, it must be by the old way of the law, or by some other course. The old way of the law claimeth the first respect and precedence of consideration; for, take away Christ and the gospel, nothing more divine and perfect was given to man than the law. This was first intended by God for that end, as the scriptures everywhere witness; and God will not depart from his own institutions, without evident necessity; for he doth nothing in vain, or without necessary cause and reason: Gal. iii. 21, 'If there had been a law given which could have given life, verily righteousness had

been by the law.' God would have gone no further than his first transaction with man. Again, it is said: Gal. ii. 21, 'If righteousness had been by the law, then Christ is dead in vain.' If there had been any other way possible, in heaven or in earth, than the death of Christ, by which the salvation of lost sinners could have been brought about, Christ would not have died; no, our disease was desperate as to any other way of cure, before this great physician took our case in hand. Christ is of no use till our wound be found incurable, and all other help in vain.

3. The law coming first into consideration, as our remedy, its impossibility to justify and give life, needs to be sufficiently demonstrated; for till we are dead to the law, we shall but carelessly seek after the grace of God in Jesus Christ; therefore doth the scripture travail so much in this point, and showeth us, we must not only be dead to sin and dead to the world, but dead to the law, before we can live unto God: Gal. ii. 19, 'I through the law am dead to the law, that I may live unto God'; and again: Rom. vii. 4, 'Ye are become dead to the law, by the body of Christ, that ye may be married to another, even to him that was raised from the dead, that ye may bring forth fruit to God. 'These two places show the means how we become dead to the law, partly through the law requiring a righteousness so exact and full, in order to live, as the corrupt estate of man cannot afford; partly, by the body of Christ introducing a better hope, that is, his crucified body, which is the foundation of the new covenant. Besides Paul argueth this, that the law doth only discover sin, but cannot abolish it, but doth increase it rather; it bindeth over to death, and therefore cannot free from death; and so to fallen man, 'it is a law of sin and death'; and then answereth the objections that might be brought against this'; Is therefore the law sin? God forbid': Rom. vii. 7; and verse 10, 'The commandment which was ordained to life, I found to be unto death'; and so was a law of death, and working wrath, and all not because of any defect in God's institution, but the weakness of our flesh, that is, the corruption of our nature. Nature being depraved, cannot fulfil it, or yield perfect obedience to it. Once more it is said: Acts xiii. 39, 'By him all that believe are justified from all things, from which ye could not be justified by the law of Moses.' The law of Moses was either the ceremonial law. All the oblations and sacrifices, the washings and the offerings then required, could not take away sin, for they were but shadows and figures of what was to come: Heb. ix. 9, 'They were figures which could not make him that did the service perfect, as appertaining to the conscience;' and again, Heb. x. 1, 4, they were 'shadows of good things to come, and it was not possible that the blood of bulls and goats should take away sins.' They might obtain some temporal blessings, or remove some temporal judgments, as they obeyed God in them; but did little as to the ease of the soul, as it was conscious of sin, or under fears of the eternal punishment. They that looked beyond them, to the Messiah to come, with an humble and penitent heart, might have their consciences cleansed from dead works. Every effect must have a cause sufficient to produce it. The blood of bulls and goats was no such cause, had no such virtue; the effect was far above it; there was a more precious blood signified, and shadowed out thereby, that could do it indeed. Or secondly, the moral law given by Moses; partly, because we cannot keep it of ourselves, and the best works that the regenerate

perform, are so imperfect, and mixed with so many infirmities and defects, that they stand in need of pardon: Jam. iii. 2, 'In many things we offend all of us'; our righteousnesses are as filthy rags': Isa. lxiv. 6; and partly, because they cannot satisfy for the least sin, whereby the infinite Majesty of God is provoked. This is only spoken to show why the scriptures do so often speak of the weakness of the law, and how impossible it is the law should give us life, that we may wholly be driven to Christ.

4. The utter impotence of the law to produce this effect, may be known by these two things, which are necessary to salvation, justification and sanctification. The law can give neither of these.

[A.] It cannot give us justification unto life; the law promiseth no good to sinners, but only to those that keep and observe it; he that doth them, shall live in them. Do and live, Sin and die, this is the voice of the law, that was a way whereby an innocent person might be saved, but not how a sinner might be saved. The law considered us as innocent, and required us to continue so'; Cursed is every one that continueth not in all the words of the law to do them:' Gal. iii. 20. But alas, all we have broken with God: Rom. iii. 23, 'We have all sinned, and are come short of the glory of God.' The gospel consider- eth us in this sinful estate, and therefore it promiseth remission, and requireth repentance; both the privilege and the duty concern our recovery to God. Secondly, if the law could be fulfilled for the future, past sins would take away all hope of reward by the law; for the paying of new debts would not quit old scores; what satisfaction shall be given for those transgressions? Let me express it thus, the paying of what we owe, will not make amends for what we have stolen. We have robbed God of his glory and honour; though for the future we should be obedient to him, yet who shall restore that we have taken away, or satisfy for the wrong done to God's justice? Thirdly, the law had no power of taking away of sin, but only of punishing of sin, as it threatened death to the sinner; but how we should escape this death, it told us not. Being all shut up under sin, we are shut up under wrath, and there is no escape but by Jesus Christ.

[B.] It cannot give us sanctification. It calleth for duty, and puts in mind of it, but giveth no strength to perform it; for, being corrupted within, we are little wrought upon by a law without, to which our hearts stand in such enmity and contrariety. But let me prove it by two arguments.

(1.) They that did not keep themselves in innocency, cannot recover their integrity, now it is lost. It is easier to preserve life, than to restore it when once dead. Any fool may open the flood-gates, but when once the waters are broken in, who can recall them? Job. xiv. 4. 'Who can bring a clean thing out of an unclean? not one;' that is, who can purify his heart when it is once defiled with sin? This is an evil not to be remedied by instruction, but inclination.

(2.) Suppose they could recover themselves, they would soon lose it again. As Adam gave out at the first assault, so we would be every moment breaking with God; the sure estate, and the everlasting covenant is provided for us by Christ, and our condition by grace is more stable. God by Christ hath engaged his faithfulness, to give us necessary and effectual grace to preserve the new life: 1 Cor. i. 9, 'God is faithful, by whom ye were called.' Austin compareth the state of Job and Adam: Job was more happy in his misery than Adam in innocency; he was victorious on the dunghill, when the other was defeated on the throne; he received no evil counsel from his wife, when the first woman seduced Adam; he by grace despised the assaults of Satan, when the other suffered himself to be worsted at the first temptation; he preserved his righteousness in the midst of his sorrows, when the other lost his innocency in paradise. So much better is it to stand by the grace of Christ, than our own free will; the broken vessel being cemented again, is strongest in the crack.

Well then, you see that our misery is such, that God only can help us by some new treaty of relief, and therefore let us see what God hath done for us:

Secondly, the means of our deliverance; they are two, his incarnation and passion.

First, His incarnation,

'He sent his Son in the likeness of sinful flesh.' Let me, first, open the words; secondly, show what benefit we have thereby.

[A.] Christ's coming in the likeness of sinful flesh, implieth that it was the nature of sinful men; that he had a true human nature as other men have, but not a sinful nature. In some places it is said he was made in the likeness of men: Phil. ii. 7, and Heb. ii 17, 'Wherefore in all things it behoved him to be made like unto his brethren'; in other places sin is expected'; tempted in all points like us, except sin': Heb. iv. 15: and Heb. vii. 26. He assumed the true and real nature of man, with all the same essential properties, which other men have, only sin is excepted; that infection was stopped by his supernatural conception through the power of the Holy Ghost. In short, he came not in sinful flesh, but in the likeness of sinful flesh; he took not our nature as in innocency, but when our blood was tainted, and we were rebels to God.

[B.] He took not the human nature as it shall be in glory, fully without sin. There will a time come, when the human nature shall be perfectly glorified; but Christ took our nature as it was clothed with all natural, sinless infirmities, even such as are in us. The punishment of sin as he assumed a mortal body; and death to us is the fruit of sin: Rom. vi. 23, and v. 12; he was hungry, weary, pained, as we are.

[C.] He was counted a sinner, condemned as a sinner, exposed to many afflictions, such as sinners endure; yea, bore the punishment of our sin. The Jews accused him of sedition and blasphemy, two of the highest crimes against either table; the standers-by looked on him as one 'stricken and smitten of God': Isa. liii. 4, yea, God made him to be sin: 2 Cor. v. 21. 'He was made sin for us, that we might be made the righteousness of God in him': and Heb. ix. 28, 'So Christ was once offered to bear the sins of many.' Let us next consider,

2. What benefit have we thereby. Because Christ's flesh is meat indeed, to feed hungry souls. I shall a little insist upon that; it being so useful to us when we are sacramentally to eat the flesh and drink the blood of the Son of God.

[A.] He came in our flesh, that thereby he might be under the law. This was given to the whole race of mankind: Gal. iv. 4. 'Made of a woman, made under the law.' His human nature was a creature, and bound to be in subjection to the creator; but then you will say, if Christ obeyed the law for himself, what merit could there be in his obedience? Much every way, because he voluntarily put himself into this condition; as a man that was free before, if he remove his dwelling into another country and dominion, merely for his friends' sake, is bound to the laws of that country, how hard soever they be; and the merit of his love is no way lessened, because he did it voluntarily and for friendship's sake. Well then, there is much in this, that Christ who was a sovereign would become a subject, and obey the same laws that we are bound to keep, not only to be a pattern and example to us, but by his obedience to recover what by our disobedience was lost, and be a fountain of grace and holiness in our nature.

[B.] That in the same nature he might suffer the penalty and curse- of the law, as well as fulfil the duty of it: and so make satisfaction for our sins, which, as God, he could not do. We read 'He was made a curse for us': Gal. iii. 13; and Phil. iii. 8, he was 'obedient to the death, even the death of the cross.' Death was threatened, and a curse denounced against those that obeyed not the law; and we being guilty of sin, could by no means avoid this death; therefore Christ came in the sinner's room to suffer death, and 'bear the curse 'for us, to free us 'from the law of sin and death,' and by this means the justice of God is eminently demonstrated, the lawgiver vindicated, and the breach that was made in the frame of government repaired, and God manifested to- be holy, and a hater of sin, and yet the sinner saved from destruction.

[C.] That he might cross and counterwork Satan's design; which was double: First, To dishonour God by a false representation, as if he were envious of man's happiness: Gen. iii. 5. 'God doth know, that in the day ye eat thereof your eyes shall be open, and ye shall be as gods, knowing good or evil'; that is, sufficient to themselves without his direction. Satan's aim was to weaken the esteem of God's goodness in our hearts. Now when Christ will take flesh, and dwell among us, do whatsoever is necessary for our restoration and recovery, his goodness is wonderfully magnified, and he is represented as amiable to man, not envying our knowledge and happiness, but promoting it at the dearest rates. That God should be made man, and die for sinners, is the highest demonstration of his goodness that can be given us: 1 John iv. 9, 'In this was the love of God manifested towards us, that God sent his only begotten Son into the world, that we might live by him.' What greater proof can we have that God is not envious, but loving, yea, love itself? Secondly, Satan's other design was to depress the nature of man, who in innocency stood so near unto God, that falling off from our duty we might fall also from that firmament of glory wherein God at our creation had placed us, and upon the breach there might be a great distance between us and God. Now, that human nature so depressed and abased by the malicious suggestion of the devil, should be so elevated and advanced, and set far above the angelical nature, and admitted to dwell with God in a personal union, Oh! How is the design of the devil defeated. The great intent of this mystery, 'God manifested in the flesh' was to make way for a nearness between God and us. Christ condescended to be nigh to us by taking human nature into the unity of his person, that we might be nigh unto God; not only draw nigh unto him now in the evangelical estate, but be everlastingly nigh unto him in heavenly glory. When we first enter into the gospel-state, we that were afar off, are said to be 'made nigh in Christ,' Eph. ii. 13;

but this is but a preparation for a closer communion, con junction, and nearness to God, when we shall be ever with the Lord, 1 Thes. iv. 17.

[D.] To give us a pledge of the tenderness of his love and compassion towards us. For he that is our kinsman, bone of our bone, and flesh of our flesh, will he be strange to his own flesh? Especially, since he is not so by necessity of nature, but by voluntary choice and assumption. We could not have such confident and familiar discourse with one who is of another and different nature from us; nor put our suits into his hands with such trust and assurance: it is a motive to man, 'Thou shalt not hide thyself from thine own flesh,' Isa. lviii. 7. A beggar is our own flesh; men in pride and disdain will not own it, and shut up their bowels against them; but Christ had our nature in perfection. This made Laban, though otherwise a churlish man, kind to Jacob: Gen. xxix. 14, 'Surely thou art bone of my bone, and flesh of my flesh.' But this is not all; Christ assumed human nature, that he might experiment infirmities in his own person; and his heart be more endeared towards us: Heb. ii. 17, 18, 'In all things it behoved him to be a merciful and faithful high priest in things pertaining to God, in making reconciliation for the sins of the people; for in that he himself hath suffered, being tempted, he is able to succour them that are tempted.' We have more assurance that he will pity us who is not a stranger to our blood, and hath had trial of our nature, and our miseries and temptations. He knoweth the heart of an afflicted, tempted man, and will mind our business as his own.

[E.] Christ by taking our flesh is become a pattern to us of what shall be done both in us and by us.

(1.) His own holy nature is a pledge of the work of grace, and the sanctification of the Spirit whereby we are fitted and prepared for God. For the same Holy Spirit that could sanctify the substance that was taken from the virgin, so that that holy thing that was born of her might be called the Son of God can also sanctify and cleanse our corrupt hearts. The pollution of our natures is so ingrained, that we are troubled to think how it can be wrought off, and these foul hearts of ours made clean; but the same Spirit that separateth our nature in the person of Christ from all the pollution of his ancestors, can purify our persons and heal our natures, how polluted soever they be: 1 Cor. vi. 11, 'Such were some of you, but ye are washed, but ye are sanctified, but ye are justified in the name of the Lord Jesus, and by the Spirit of God.' So many generations as there are reckoned up in the story of Christ's nativity: Mat. i., 'Abraham begat Isaac, and Isaac begat Jacob,' etc.; so many intimations there are of the deriving of sinful pollution from one ancestor to another, and though it still run in the blood, yet when Christ was born of the virgin, he sanctified the substance taken from her, there the infection was stopped, he was born a holy thing: Luke i. 35: and Heb. vii. 20, 'Who is holy, harmless, undefiled, separate from sinners.'

(2.) His life was a pattern of our obedience; for 'he gave us an example, that we should follow his steps, and walk as he walked': He submitted to all manner of duties both to God and men; Luke ii. 49, 'Wist ye not that I should be about my Father's business?' There was his duty to his heavenly Father; and for his natural and reputed parents: Luke ii. 51, 'He went down and was subject to them'; and still he 'went about doing good,' Acts x. 38. This was the business of his life. Obedience Christ would commend to us, for he never intended to rob God of a creature, and a subject, when he made man a Christian; therefore, he in our nature having the same interest of flesh and blood, the same passions and affections, would teach us to obey God at the dearest rates.

(3.) In the same nature that was foiled, he would teach us also to conquer Satan. He conquered him, hand to hand, in personal conflict, repelling his temptations by scripture, as we should do: Mat. iv. 10. So he conquered him as a tempter. There is another conquest of him as a tormentor, as one that hath the power of death. So he conquered him by his death on the cross, and so his human nature was necessary to that also: Heb. ii. 14, 'Forasmuch as the children are partakers of flesh and blood, he also took part of the same, that he might destroy him that had the power of death, that is, the devil' Christ would stoop to the greatest indignities to free us from this enemy, and to put mankind again into a condition of safety and happiness.

(4.) That he might take possession of heaven for us in our nature: John xiv. 2, 3, 'I go to prepare a place for you, I will come again, and receive you to myself.' The devil's design was to depress our nature, but Christ came to exalt it; Satan endeavoured to make us lose paradise, but Christ came to give us heaven; and to assure us of the reality of the gift, he did himself in our nature rise from the dead, and entered into that glory he spake of, to give us, who are strangely haunted with doubts about the other world, a visible demonstration that the glory of the world to come is no fancy. He is entered into it, and hath carried our nature thither, that, in time, if we regard his offers and his promises, ourselves may be translated thither also.

(5.) After he had been a sacrifice for sin, and conquered death by his resurrection, he hath triumphed over the devil, and led captivity captive, and gave gifts unto men, in the very act of his ascension into heaven: Eph. iv. 8. To teach us, that if we in the same nature continue the conflict, and be faithful unto the death, we shall triumph also, and 'the God of peace shall tread Satan under our feet shortly' Rom. xvi. 20. These things occur to me for the present as the fruits and benefits of Christ's incarnation; but the chief reason why it is brought here, is 'that God might condemn sin in the flesh,' show the great example of his wrath against it, by the sorrows and sufferings of Christ. Secondly, by his passion. This is intimated in the terms, for sin, or by a sin-offering, as we have it in the margin; and is confirmed in other scriptures: as Heb. x. 6, 'In burnt-offerings and sacrifices of sin thou hadst no pleasure.' Therefore in the translation we put the word sacrifices in another sort of letter, as being supplied. So Isa. liii. 10, 'When he shall make his soul sin,' that is, as we will render it, an offering for sin; so 2 Cor. v. 21, 'Christ was made sin for us,' that is, a sacrifice for sin; so here by sin he 'condemned sin in the flesh,' that is, by a propitiatory sacrifice. All things that were in the sin-offering, agree to Christ's death; for instance:

1. Sin was the meritorious cause why the beast was slain. The beasts obeyed the law of their creation, but man had sinned against God: Lev. v. 6. 'He shall bring his trespass offering unto the Lord, for his sin which he hath sinned, and the priest shall make atonement for him concerning his sin.' Here was no other reason the beast an innocent creature should die; so

Christ died for our offences: Rom. iv. 25; not his own, he had no sins of his own to expiate; therefore, while the sacrifice was yet alive, the man was to lay his hand on the head of the sacrifice, confessing his sins, Lev. xvi. 21, and putting them on the sacrifice.

2. The sacrifices were substituted into the place of the offender, and the beasts died for him; so did Christ die, not only in *bonum nostrum* for our good; but *loco et vice omnium nostri* in our stead and room: Isa. liii. 4, 'Surely he hath borne our griefs, and carried our sorrows; he was wounded for our transgressions'

3. The offerings offered to God in our stead were consumed and destroyed; if things of life, they were killed or slain; other things were either burnt, as frankincense; or spilled and poured out, as wine. There was a destruction of the thing offered to God for sin in man's stead. So Christ was to die, or to shed his blood, to put away sin, by the sacrifice of himself: Heb. ix. 26, 'He appeared to put away sin by the sacrifice of himself' All the offerings typified Christ, but more strictly the sacrifices which were of living beasts; some whereof were killed, flayed, burnt, some roasted and fried on coals; some seethed in pots, all which were shadows of what Christ endured, who is the only true propitiatory sacrifice, wherein provoked justice rests satisfied.

4. The effects of the sacrifices all either respect God, or sin, or the sinner. God was pacified or propitiated, the sin expiated, the sinner reconciled, that is to say justified, sanctified.

[A.] God was pacified, propitiated, or satisfied, the law being obeyed which he had instituted for the doing away of sin; not_ satisfied or propitiated as to the eternal punishment, by the mere sacrifice; but so far as to prevent many temporal judgments, which otherwise would fall upon them, for the neglect of God's ordinances; but the true propitiation is Christ: 1 John ii. 2, 'Who gave himself to be a propitiation for our sins.' Propitiation implieth God's being satisfied, pacified, appeased to us, so as to become merciful to us.

[B.] The sin for which the sacrifice was offered was purged, expiated, as to the legal guilt; there was no more fault to be charged on them as to the remedy which that law prescribed; but the true purgation of the conscience from dead works belongeth only to the Son of God: Heb. ix. 14.

[C.] The effect on the sinner himself was, the sinner, coming with his sin offering, according to God's institution, was pardoned, or justified, so far as to quit him from temporal punishment, both before God and man. The magistrate could not cut him off, he having done what the law required for his sin or trespass; nor would God, he having submitted to his ordinance; yea,' he was sanctified, so far as to be capable of legal worship: Heb. ix. 13, 'For if the blood of bulls and goats, and the ashes of an heifer, sprinkling the unclean, sanctifieth to the purifying of the flesh' etc.; but now as to Christ, the sinner is justified by the free and full remission of all his sins: Mat. xxvi. 28, 'For this is my blood of the New Testament, which is shed for many for the remission of sins,' and sanctified with an eternal and real holiness: Heb. x. 10, 'We are sanctified by the offering of Jesus Christ, once for all'; perfectly justified, and perfectly sanctified. Heb. x. 14, 'By one offering he hath perfected forever them that are sanctified,' that is, with a perfection opposite to the legal institution, not with a perfection opposite to the heavenly estate, that cometh afterwards. The ordinances of the legal covenant did what belonged to them; but as to the removing of the internal guilt, and eternal punishment, they were not perfect without looking to Christ.

Thirdly, I come to the end and benefit. When God sent his own Son, surely he designed some great thing thereby; what was his end and design? 'He condemned sin in the flesh.' Two things must be explained. First, What is meant by condemning of sin; secondly, what is meant by these words, 'in the flesh'?

1. What is meant by condemning of sin. To condemn it is to destroy it, because execution ordinarily followeth the sentence. Therefore the sentence is put for the execution; and the word condemn is used for weighty reasons. The gospel is speaking of justification, or our not being condemned. Christ condemned that which would have condemned us, by bearing the punishment of it in his own person. Sin had conquered the world, or subjected man to condemnation; therefore Christ came to condemn sin, that is, to destroy it. The question then is, whether the apostle doth hereby expound the mystery of sanctification or justification. I answer, both are intended, as they are often in these words which express the great undertaking of the mediator, which is to take away sin. There is a damning power, and a reigning power in sin; now if condemning sin be destroying of sin, or taking away its power by his expiatory sacrifice, then not only the pardon of sin, but the mortification of the flesh is intended.

2. What is the sense of those words, 'in the flesh '? Is it meant of the flesh of Christ, or our flesh? Both make a good sense; I prefer the latter. First, he condemned sin in the flesh, or by the crucified body of Christ, exacting from him the punishment due to sin. Secondly, in our flesh, that is sin, which by our flesh rendereth us uncapable of fulfilling the law of God, or obnoxious to his vengeance. This was destroyed by the death of Christ, 'Our old man was crucified with him' Rom. vi. 6: and in conversion the virtue is applied to us, when sin received its death's wound by virtue of Christ's death or sacrifice.

Use 1 is, Information.

1. To show the heinous nature of sin. God hath put a brand upon it, and showed how odious it is to him. Nothing short of the death of Christ could expiate such a breach between God and his creatures; Christ must die, or no reconciliation. Christ's death doth lessen and greaten sin; it greatens the nature of it, to all serious beholders; it lesseneth the damning effect of it to the penitent believer.

2. If Christ came to destroy sin, accursed are they that cherish it. These seek to put their Redeemer to shame, tie the cords which he came to loose: 1 John iii. 8. Christ 'came to destroy the works of the devil.'

3. Christ did not abrogate the law, but took away the effects and consequents of sin committed against the law. The sinner was obnoxious to the justice of the lawgiver and judge; the law could not help him, but the Son of God came to fit us again for our obedience.

Use 2 is, To exhort us to consider first our misery. How unavoidable our perishing was, had not God found out a remedy for us. In our corrupt estate, we neither could nor would obey the law; the duty became impossible, both as to the tenor of the law, and the temper of our hearts, and then the penalty is intolerable.

2. Our remedy lies in the incarnation and passion of the Son of God, that in so entangled a case he could find out a ransom for us. The goodness of God, that he sent his own Son; the power of God, that by this means the guilt and power of sin, with all the consequents of it, are dissolved.

Use 3 is, Direction in the Lord's Supper.

1. Here is the flesh of Christ, which is food for souls: John vi. 51, 'The bread that I shall give is my flesh, which I shall give for the life of the world.' In it he hath purchased grace and pardon of sin, which are the foundations of immortality.

2. The Lord's Supper is a feast on a sacrifice, a commemoration of Christ's sin-offering, or a standing memorial of his passion; a table spread for us in the sight of our enemies. How must we be conversant about it, as the Jews about the sacrifices? First, there is required an humble, broken, and contrite heart, confessing our sins: Ps. xlvi. 17, 'The sacrifices of God are a broken spirit; a broken and contrite heart, O God, thou wilt not despise.' Secondly, sensible, thankful, and comfortable, owning of God's love in Christ. When they had eaten the Passover, they were to rejoice before the Lord: Deut. xvi. 11. So should we after this feast prepared by God to feed and nourish our souls to eternal life.

SERMON V

That the righteousness of the law might be fulfilled in us, who walk not after the flesh, but after the spirit.

Romans viii. 4.

HERE is the second end of our deliverance by Christ, that we might have grace to keep the law of God. The first was, that sin might be condemned in the flesh. In the words we have:

1. A benefit.

2. The persons that receive it.

First, The benefit. That the righteousness of the law might be fulfilled in us. How is this to be understood? of justification, or sanctification?

They that expound it in the former way, make this the sense, that Christ's active obedience, or fulfilling the law, might be imputed, and reckoned to us, as if done by us; but I cannot like this interpretation. First, because it is contrary to the apostle's scope, who speaketh not of Christ's active obedience, but the fruits of his death, or his being made a sin-offering for us. Secondly, the words will not bear it, for the apostle doth not say that the righteousness of the law might be fulfilled for us, but fulfilled in us. Thirdly, the doctrine itself is not sound, unless rightly interpreted; for though God, upon the account of Christ's passive obedience and satisfaction, doth forgive our sins, and his active obedience, as well as his passive, is the meritorious cause of our justification, as being a part of his humiliation, yet that cannot be said to be fulfilled in us, which was done by Christ; for God cannot be mistaken, and reckon us to fulfil the law, which we have not, and will not lie, and say we did it, when we did it not. It is enough to say, Christ obeyed, and suffered for our sakes, so as we might have the fruit and benefit of it. Fourthly, the consequent is pernicious, to say the law is fulfilled in us, as obeyed by Christ, for then we needed not to fulfil it ourselves; it is done to our hands already, and needeth only to be imputed to us by faith; but Christ, who suffered, that we might not suffer, yet did not obey, that we might not obey; but his obedience being part of his humiliation, is an ingredient into his satisfaction for our sins. Christ fulfilled all righteousness, and suffered, that our imperfection of obedience might not be our ruin.

2. It must be meant then of sanctification, that by the merit of Christ's death we are freed not only from the guilt, but tyranny of sin, that we might obtain grace to obey the law, or live holily; which will appear by the answering of two questions:

[A.] What is meant by the righteousness of the law? , I answer, the duty which the law requireth, or anything which God seeth fit to command his people. The law is holy, just, and good, and certainly was not given in vain, but to be a rule to believers in Christ.

[B.] How is it fulfilled in us? For there is the difficulty that pincheth. Can we fulfil the righteousness of the law? The law may be said to be fulfilled two ways:

(1.) Legally, as a covenant of works.

(2.) Evangelically, as the rule of obedience.

(1.) Legally. No man that was once a sinner, and is still a sinner, can possibly fulfil the law; for he cannot be a sinner and no sinner at the same time, nor fulfil the law to a tittle. He that hath broken with God, cannot continue to be innocent; and he that hath flesh and spirit in him, cannot be absolutely perfect. That was determined before: ver. 3, 'what the law could not do, in that it was weak through the flesh'; and this is directly opposed to that.

(2.) Evangelically. And so the law can, and may be kept, or fulfilled sincerely, though not perfectly. The prevalency of the better part constituteth our sincerity. Justified souls have flesh and spirit, but they walk after the spirit. The mixture of infirmities showeth it is not done perfectly; for the corrupt principle hath some influence; yet not a prevailing influence; and God counteth that as done, which is sin cerely done: Rom. xiii. 8, 'He that loveth another, hath fulfilled the law': and Gal. vi. 2, and so 'fulfilling the law of Christ'; and Gal. v. 14, 'For all the law is fulfilled in one word, thou shalt love thy neighbour as thyself.' So the apostle supposeth the Gentiles might in a gospel manner fulfil the law: Rom. ii. 27, 'And shall not uncircumcision, which is by nature, if it fulfil the law, judge thee, who by the letter, and circumcision, dost transgress the law? 'So that in our measure, we do fulfil the law, by the grace of Christ; not perfectly, for he supposeth them to have flesh, or sin in them, but sincerely, as they obey the inclinations of the better part 'walk not after the "flesh, but after the spirit.'

Doctrine That Christ was made a sin-offering for us, that the righteous ness of the law might be fulfilled in us. I shall prove it by these considerations:

1. That Christ came, not only to redeem us from wrath, but also to renew and heal our natures.

2. That our natures being renewed and healed, we are to walk in newness of life, according to the directions of the law of God.

First. That Christ came not only to redeem us from wrath, but to renew and sanctify us. I prove it

1. From the constant drift and tenor of the scriptures. From his nature and office: Mat. i. 21, 'He shall be called Jesus, for he shall save his people from their sins' *Denominatio est a potioribus* from his chief work, which is to save his people from the guilt and power of sin. Guilt inferreth damnation, which is the evil after sin: but he hath his name from saving us from the evil of sin itself; for the great promise made to Abraham was in that: Gen. xii. 3, 'In thy seed shall all the nations of the earth be blessed'; that is, in Christ; but how blessed? That is expounded: Acts iii. 25, 26, 'Ye are children of the prophets, and of the covenant which God made with our fathers, saying to Abraham, And in thy seed shall all the kindreds of the earth be blessed. Unto you first, God having raised up his Son Jesus Christ, hath sent him to bless you, in turning away every one of you from his iniquities." Observe there, what is the mediator's blessing; to turn away his people from sin. Man fallen was both unholy and guilty, liable to the wrath of God, and dead in trespasses and sins; and Christ came to free us from both. We cannot be sufficiently thankful for our freedom from wrath, but we must first mind our freedom from. sin. So when Christ is promised to the Jews: Rom. xi. 26, 'There

shall come out of Sion the deliverer, and shall tur away ungodliness from Jacob,' there is his principal work. So from the end, why he actually came, and was exhibited to the world: Acts v. 31, 'Him hath God exalted to give repentance and remission of sins.' Repentance is nothing but a serious purpose of returning to God, and to that obedience we owe to God: 1 John iii. 5, 'And we know he was manifested to take away our sins, and in him is no sin'; to conform us to the law of God, by his own blessed pattern and example. Again: Titus ii. 14, 'Who hath redeemed us from all iniquity'; and this was the intent of his death: Eph. v. 26. It were endless to bring all that might be said upon this argument.

2. I prove it by reasons taken from the scripture. It must needs be so

[A.] Because the plaster else would not be as broad as the sore; nor our reparation by Christ be correspondent to our loss by Adam. We lost not only the favour of God, but the image of God: and therefore till the image of God be restored in us we do not return to our first estate, nor are we fully recovered. The evil nature propagated from him is the cause of the misery and disorder of mankind. Guilt is but the consequent of sin. Now is he a good physician that only taketh away the pain and leaveth the great disease uncured? Certainly we cannot recover God's favour till we recover his image. A sinful creature, till he be changed, cannot be acceptable to God, neither live in communion with him for the present, nor enjoy him hereafter. We cannot enjoy communion with him now: 1 John i. 5, 6, 7, 'If we say that we have fellowship with him, and walk in darkness, we lie, and do not the truth. But if we walk in the light, as he is in the light, we have fellowship one with another.' Will the Lord take us into his bosom while we are in our sins? The new nature giveth us some knowledge of the nature of God. Can a new creature delight in the wicked? 2 Peter ii. 8, 'Lot's righteous soul was vexed from day to day.' You cannot imagine so, without a reproach to the divine nature; nor can we be admitted into his blessed presence hereafter: Heb. xii. 14, 'Without holiness no man shall see the Lord.' The ungodly, and the unsanctified, are banished out of his presence. Christ came not to make a change in God; to make him less holy, or represent him as less hating of sin. Otherwise,

[B.] Christ's undertaking would not answer the trouble of a true penitent, nor remove our sorest burthen. A sensible and compunctionate[3] sinner is troubled not only with the guilt of sin, but the power of sin. There is the root and bottom of his trouble; his language is, Hosea xiv. 2, 'Take away all iniquity, and receive us graciously.' Pharaoh could say, Take away this plague; but an awakened, penitent, broken hearted sinner will say, Take away this naughty heart. Therefore the promises are suited to this double distress: 1 John i. 9, 'If we confess our sins, he is faithful and just to forgive us our sins': Micah vii. 18, 19, 'Who is a God like unto thee, that pardoneth iniquity, and passeth by the transgression of the remnant of his heritage? He will return again, and have compassion upon us: he will subdue our iniquities, and thou wilt cast all our sins into the depths of the sea.' They do not only desire pardon

---

[3] Compunction: a feeling of guilt or moral scruple that follows the doing of something bad

and release from punishment, but grace to break the power of sin; as a man that hath his leg broken desireth not only ease of the pain, but to have it well set again. Therefore to them that are pricked at heart there is offered the promise of the Spirit: Acts ii. 37, 38. A malefactor condemned to die, and sick of a mortal disease, needeth and desireth not only the pardon of the judge but the cure of the physician.

[C.] To make way for the work of the Spirit. For the divine persons work into each other's hands; as the election of the Father maketh way for the redemption of Christ, so the redemption of Christ maketli way for the sanctification of the Spirit. All the divine persons are glorified in the reduction of a sinner; and they take their turn. The application of the merit of Christ, and the grace of the Spirit, are inseparable: Titus iii. 5, and 1 Cor. vi. 11. These individual companions, sanctification and justification, must not be disjoined. Under the law the ablutions and oblations still went together; the leaven and the altar, the washings and the sacrifices.

[D.] Christ's undertaking was not only for the benefit of man, but for the glory of God, to redeem us to God: Rev. v. 9; and therefore in the work of redemption, our happiness is not only to be considered, but God's honour and interest. Impunity, and taking away the guilt of sin, doth more directly respect our good; but sanctifying, and fitting us for obedience and subjection to God, doth more immediately respect his glory and honour. That he may be glorified again in mankind, who are fallen from him; it was for that man was made at first, and for that are we restored and made again. I proceed to the second consideration propounded.

Secondly. That our natures being renewed and healed, we are to walk in newness of life, according to the directions of the law of God; for principles are given for operation, and habits for acts, and a new heart for newness of life; and therefore regeneration first maketh us good, that afterwards we may do good. But that which I am to prove, is that this righteousness is to be carried on according to the law; for God having made a law, is very tender of it. I shall prove it by four reasons:

1. Christ came not to dissolve our obligation to God, but to promote it rather. Certainly not to dissolve it to free us from obedience to the law; for that is impossible that a creature should be sui juris, or without law; for that were to make it supreme, and independent, and so to establish our rebellion, rather than to suppress it. No, he came upon no such design, to leave us to our own will, to live as we list, without law and rule. He came to restore us to obedience, to bring us back again in heart and life to God: Luke i. 75, 'He hath delivered us from the hands of our enemies, that we might serve him in holiness and righteousness all the days of our lives.' To this end tended his doctrine: 'I came not to destroy the law, but to fulfil it': Mat. v. 17. His example; He came to do what God had commanded, and to teach us to do the same: Mat. iii. 15, 'For thus it becometh us to fulfil all righteousness': and Heb. v. 8, 9, 'Though he were a Son, yet learned he obedience by the things which he suffered; and being made perfect, he became the author of eternal salvation to them that obey him.'

2. Christ dispenseth by virtue of his merit, regeneration, or the spirit of holiness, that all new creatures might voluntarily keep this law, though not in absolute perfection, yet by sincere

obedience. This grace is dispensed to put us into a capacity of loving, pleasing, and obeying God; this is that he promiseth in the new covenant: Ezek. xxxvi. 27, c And I will put my Spirit within you, and cause you to walk in my statutes, and ye shall keep any judgments, and do them.' So Jer. xxxi. 33, 'I will put my law in their inward parts, and write it in their hearts' He doth not say, I will prepare them another law, as if the old law of God were to be abandoned and abolished, and some other precepts substituted in their room; no, but to make them conformable to it in heart and life, the new man is created after God for this end and purpose: Eph. iv. 24, fitted to obey the law; so that the great blessing of the gospel is grace to keep the law.

3. None enter into the gospel state but those that entirely and readily give up themselves to do the will of God; and therefore none can have benefit b^ the sin-offering and satisfaction of Christ but those that consent to return to the duty of the law and live in obedience to God. Surely God never pardoneth any while they are in rebellion, and live under the full power and dominion of sin; no, they must consent to forsake and return to the allegiance due to their proper Lord. This is evident; for the way of entering into the new covenant is by faith and repentance, is nothing else but a sincere purpose of new obedience, or living according to the will and law of God. It is defined to be a 'breaking off of sin': Dan. iv. 27; and therefore the scripture runs in this strain: Isa. lv. 7, 'Let the wicked forsake his way, and the un righteous man his thoughts: and let him return to me, saith the Lord, and I will abundantly pardon': and Isa. i. 16, 'Wash you, make you clean' and then 'though your sins were as scarlet, they shall be as white as snow' The least that can be gathered from these places, is, that a serious vow and thorough resolution of new obedience, are necessary to begin our interest in the grace of the new covenant.

4. The more we fulfil our covenant, vow, and resolution, by obeying the law, our right is the more clear, and evident, and more confirmed to us; our participation of the blessings of the gospel is more full, and our comfort more strong: Ps. cxix. 165, 'Great peace have they that love thy law, and nothing shall offend them;' and Gal. vi. 16, 'As many as walk according to this rule, peace and mercy be upon them.' God loveth us the more, the more we obey his law. It is holiness maketh us more amiable in his eyes, and the objects of his delight. God loveth us as sanctified rather than pardoned; we love him as pardoning and forgiving so great a debt to us; but he delights in holiness or the impress of his own image upon us: Prov. xi. 20, 'The upright in the way are his delight' When the Spirit hath renewed us according to the image of God, we are made objects of his complacency. Now we know God's love by the effects; and therefore the more we act and draw forth this grace, the more God rewardeth our obedience with the sense of his love, and the comforts of his Spirit. The sum of all religion is to love God, and to be beloved of him; to love him and obey him is our work; and to be beloved of him is our reward and happiness. Now the one followeth the other: John xiv. 22. 23, 'Lord! how is it that thou wilt manifest thyself to us, and not unto the world? Jesus answered and said unto him, If a man love me, he will keep my words, and my Father will love him, and we will come unto him, and make our abode with him.' As we increase in holiness and obedience, we increase in the favour of God.

Use 1 is Information. It informeth us of several important truths:

1. That the law is a law of perfect purity and holiness, for he speaketh here of the righteousness of the law. So David: Ps. cxix. 140, 'Thy law is very pure, therefore thy servant loveth it'; and Ps. xix. 8, 'The commandment of the Lord is pure, enlightening the eyes.' It must needs be so, if we consider the author of it, God himself; and everything that hath passed his hand hath his character and impress upon it; it is a law not only fit for us to receive but for God to give; it is the copy of his holiness. It is all one with the image of God which man had in innocency. Now the image of God consisted in righteousness and true holiness. Adam's principle of obedience was also his law and rule; he had that written upon his heart which was afterwards written upon tables of stone; and therefore if a man would cleanse his heart and way, he must study the word of God: Ps. cxix. 9, 'By what means may a young man cleanse his way? by taking heed thereunto according to thy word.' It is not guide his way, but cleanse his way; for even the youngest are defiled. Man's heart naturally is a sink of sin, and there is no way to make his heart clean, and his way clean, but by taking God's counsel in his word. A young man that is in the heat and strength of his lusts, may learn there how to be purified and cleansed.

2. That this law standeth in force. We are freed from the condemning, but not from the directing power thereof; but it always remaineth as a rule of our new obedience. Surely it is in force now; for there is no liberty given to men to live in sin; God will not spare his people when they transgress it by scandalous or heinous sin: Prov. i. 31, 'Therefore they shall eat of the fruit of their own way, and be filled with their own devices.' Though they be the dearly beloved of his soul, the eternal punishment shall not be inflicted upon them, yet they shall smart for the breaches of his law. On the other side they find much encouragement, comfort, and peace when they set themselves exactly to keep it, they can from experience speak much of the gracious reward of obedience: Ps. cxix. 56, 'This I had because I kept thy precepts.' Yea, in the state of heavenly glory, the law as purely moral is still in force; for we are everlastingly bound to love God and one another.

3. That the righteousness of the law may be fulfilled in us. I prove it by this argument. One of these three things we must say, either (1.) that no obedience is now necessary to salvation, or (2.) that the perfect obedience is still necessary, or (3.) some measure of obedience to the law by the ordinary aids of grace, vouchsafed to us in the new covenant, is possible and sufficient. The first we cannot say; for then there would be no necessity of new obedience or holiness. But the scripture condemneth that everywhere, showing us that we are ^God's workmanship, created in Christ Jesus to good works, 'Eph. ii. 10; and 'purified to be a peculiar people, zealous of good works,' Tit. ii. 14. The second we cannot say that a whole perpetual, perfect, personal obedience to the law is still necessary; for then there would be no hope for them that cannot perfectly fulfil the law, which no man living can do: Ps. cxliii. 2, 'Enter not into judgment with thy servant, for in thy 1 sight shall no man living be justified.' Therefore the third thing we must say, that there is such a measure of obedience necessary, as is sufficient to salvation, and possible by grace, and they that attain to it, the scripture

pronounceth them blessed: Luke xi. 28, 'Blessed are they that hear the word of God and keep it'; and John xiii. 17, 'If ye know these things, happy are you if you do them.'

4. That the righteousness of the law not only can, but must be fulfilled in us, or else we are yet in our sins, and have no portion and interest in Christ: 2 Cor. v. 17, 'Whosoever is in Christ is a new creature.' And a new creature must have a new conversation, for 'all old things are passed away, and all things are become new' They are enabled in some measure to fulfil the law of God. Christ being the lawgiver of the Church, or renewed state of mankind, hath set down the terms of life and death; to his terms we must stand or fall: now, 'He is the author of eternal salvation to them that obey him, 'Heb. v. 9. Therefore every one that would be delivered from wrath to come, must look after holiness, and obey God according to his will declared in his law. Certainly Christ died not to purchase an indulgence for us to live in sin; the law hath not its right, it looketh like a law given in vain, if it be not obeyed.

5. This fulfilling of the righteousness of the law is wrought in us by the Spirit, as the fruit of Christ's purchase; this real, solid righteousness is wrought in our hearts by the operation of the Spirit; for those that have it are described to be, 'those that walk after the Spirit, and not after the flesh' Therefore do not resist his work, nor grieve the Spirit of Christ, nor quench his motions when he cometh to work it in you, but submit to all his healing methods. And this Spirit we have from Christ as the fruit of his sin-offering: Titus iii. 5, 6, 'Not by works of righteousness which we have done, but according to his mercy he saved us, by the washing of regeneration, and renewing of the Holy Ghost, which he shed on us abundantly through Jesus Christ our Saviour' He obtained that grace whereby we may keep the law; having satisfied for us as a Mediator, he becometh an author and fountain of life. Upon him you must depend, and to him must you look for it.

Use 2 is Reproof to two sorts of people:

1. To the carnal world, who think that the children of God are too strict and precise, and make more ado about salvation than needs. Certainly if we consider the tenor of God's law, and the exactness of divine justice, what rule and law we must live by, and to whom we must give an account, the best of God's children do no more than needeth; as the wise virgins could not spare one jot of their oil, Mat. xxv, 9, 'Not so, lest there be not enough for us and you' David admireth the brightness of the sun first, and then the purity of the law; and how doth he close up that meditation? See Ps. xix. 12, 'Who can understand his errors? cleanse thou me from secret sins'

2. Professing Christians are also to be reproved for that lazy and cowardly spirit that is in them; and because they are so impotent, and feeble, and backward to their duty. By their backwardness they wrong the law, for they do not give it its due. Christ hath, indeed, freed us from the curse of the law, but not from the obedience of it. And by this feeble and dastardly spirit they wrong the grace of the Redeemer, and the new covenant. Obedience to the law is most strongly enforced out of the grace of the gospel; for thereby we are enabled to perform it. Christ did not only fulfil the law for us, but doth also fulfil it in us by his Spirit; and shall we after such provision, sit down lazily, and be discouraged with every difficulty,

and have our resolutions broken with every assault of temptation? Men spare their pains, and do not improve the grace offered, and then cry out they are weak and unable. This is like lazy beggars, that personate and act diseases, because they would not work. Set your hearts thoroughly to obey God, and see what he will do for you.

Use 3. If this were the end of Christ's coming, and dying, then let us be exhorted to seek after sanctification by the Spirit of Christ.

1. This is one part of our salvation, as well as remission of sins. We often consider Christ as dying for our pardon; we should as much consider him as dying to renew and heal our natures, that we may be recovered to our obedience to God, to crucify the old man, to give us the spirit of holiness. Surely he is made sanctification to us, as well as righteousness; 1 Cor. i. 30, 'But of him are ye in Christ Jesus, who of God is made unto us wisdom, and righteousness, and sanctification, and redemption.' If Christ should abolish wrath, and let alone sin, it were to take away the lesser evil, that the greater may remain.

2. It is not only part of our deliverance, but the better part. Pardon giveth us an exemption from punishment, but sanctification giveth us freedom from a corrupt heart. Surely sin is worse than pain, a moral evil is worse than a natural evil, vice than misery. Once more. By holiness, we more resemble God; for holiness and goodness is his very nature: 1 Pet. i. 4, 'He hath given us precious promises, whereby we are made partakers of the divine nature'

3. Holiness is a means to the rest: pardon and life are the great blessings of the covenant. Now there is no obtaining pardon till regeneration and conversion; for God doth not pardon while we are in our sins; and life and heaven we cannot have till sin be quite done away, for we are not introduced into the presence of God, till we be complete in holiness: Eph. v. 27, 'That he might present it to himself a glorious church, not having spot or wrinkle, or any such thing; but that it should be holy, and without blemish': Col. i. 22, 'To present you holy, and unblameable, and unreprovable in his sight': Jude 24, 'And to present you faultless before the presence of his glory.' During life, obedience is but imperfectly begun; but when it is completed and finished we' do not stay out of heaven one moment; then are we fully made free from sin.

Use 4 is to put us upon trial and self-reflection. Is the righteousness of the law fulfilled in us?

1. We begin to fulfil it when we set ourselves to obey the will of God, taking his law for our rule and his promises for our encouragement. This resolution is the fruit of regenerating grace if it be sincere; and it argueth a renewed heart and conscience: Heb. xiii. 18, 'Pray for us, for we trust we have a good conscience;' and hath in it perfection of parts, though not of degrees.

2. This must be seconded with answerable endeavours. The Greek noteth a continued act; to have the righteousness of the law fulfilled in us is not the work of one day, but implieth a constant walk and obedience to motions after the Spirit.

3. We must endeavour to be more complete every day: Luke i. 6, 'They were righteous before God, walking in all the commandments and ordinances of the Lord blameless'; and Col. iv. 12, 'Labouring for you, that you may stand complete in all the will of God.' So we

read of some that were 'full of all goodness:' Rom. xv. 14, and 'full of good works': Acts ix. 36, as we find in Dorcas. It is the fault of most Christians, that they beat down the price of religion as low as they can, and so make a hard shift to go to heaven.

4. Our begun-sanctification shall be perfected before Christ hath done with us: Col. i. 28, 'That we may present every man perfect in Christ Jesus.' Here we are very imperfect, but it shall be perfectly fulfilled,

SERMON VI

They that are after the flesh do mind the things of the flesh; and they that are after the spirit, the things of the spirit.

Romans viii. 5.

This scripture containeth a notable character of those that are interested in the privileges of the gospel, and will help you in your assuring work, or making out your claim and title. In the words you have:

1. An intimation of two sorts of persons; they that are after the flesh and they that are after the spirit.

2. Their different disposition and practice are compared and set forth:

[1.] By the act: they both mind their several affairs.

[2.] By the object: things of the flesh from things of the spirit Different persons, different objects, and different affections.

Thus you may in one view arid prospect discern the scope and intent of the place. I shall lay it before you in several propositions, and then apply all together.

1. There are two sorts of men in the world some after the flesh and some after the spirit.

2. That these two sorts of men have two different objects the things of the spirit and the things of the flesh.

3. That men discover' their temper and constitution of soul by their favour or affection to either of these objects.

Doctrine 1. There are two sorts of men in the world some after the flesh and some after the spirit. So it must be. There is a twofold original; which produceth a twofold principle, which is acted by a twofold assisting power; and this bringeth them under a twofold covenant, which maketh way for a twofold final estate, into which all the world issueth itself.

1. There is a twofold original; some are only born, others new born; the renewed, and the unrenewed: John iii. 6, 'That which is born of the flesh, is flesh; and that which is born of the Spirit, is spirit.' Some remain under the power of corrupt nature; others are regenerate and renewed by the Spirit.

2. This twofold original produced a twofold principle; that men are led by flesh and spirit, which are always contrary one to another: Gal' v. 17, 'The flesh lusteth against the spirit, and the spirit lusteth against the flesh; and these two are contrary one to the other.' Men, if they be merely such as nature hath left them, are governed by the flesh, or their own carnal inclinations. Others are led by the spirit, walk after it, as ver. 1. They that are born again, have a new principle set up in their natures, to incline them to God.

3. These two principles are supported and assisted with contrary powers. They that are governed by the flesh, are also acted by Satan; he rules and works in them: Eph. ii. 23, 'Wherein in time past ye walked according to the course of this world, according to the prince of the power of the air, the spirit that now ruleth in the children of disobedience;

among whom also we had our conversation in times past, in the lusts of the flesh, fulfilling the desires of the flesh and of the mind' There are all the enemies of our salvation. They that follow inbred corruption as their guide, fall into the devil's share, who hurrieth them on in a way of sin, more vehemently than otherwise they would do. But now those that are led by grace, or a new principle, or the new nature, as their guide, they are assisted and acted by the Spirit of God: Horn. viii. 14, 'As many as are led by the Spirit of God, they are the sons of God; the Spirit is their guardian and keeper; he exciteth and worketh up the habit of grace into greater power and activity' Now, being under such contrary powers, no wonder that they are so different in their courses, and so contrary one to another. It is said, Prov. xxix. 27, 'The wicked is an abomination to the just: and he that is upright in his way is an abomination to the wicked' Their birth is different, the inward principle by which they are guided is different, nature and grace; and they are under different assisting powers, either under the power of Satan, or under the power and conduct of God's Holy Spirit; and therefore no wonder that their course is different, and that there is enmity between both the seeds. A godly man cannot delight in a wicked man, and a wicked man cannot abide the godly. The ground of friendship is *eadem velle et nolle*[4]. Similitude, and likeness of mind and disposition, only the enmity and contrariety is carried on with some difference. The godly pity the wicked, but the wicked hate the godly, because they are against that course of life that they choose. They think it strange they do not run with them to the same neglect of God, and carelessness of heavenly things; and therefore they speak evil of them, 1 Peter iv. 4; and despitefully use them, 1 John iii. 12, as Cain hated Abel.

4. As they are under different assisting powers, so they are under a distinct covenant. The carnal are under the covenant of works, the duty of which is to them impossible, and the penalty intolerable. They are under the condemning power of the law: Horn. viii. 6, 'To be carnally minded is death'; it maketh them liable to the death threatened in the first covenant. But, on the contrary, they that are under the blessed conduct of God's Holy Spirit, and obey the dictates of the new nature begun in them, are under a covenant of grace, where their sincere obedience shall be accepted, and their failings pardoned: Gal. v. 18, 'If ye be led by the Spirit, ye are not under the law.' They are still under the law, as a rule of obedience, but they are not under the curse and rigour of the law. The law in its rigour pronounceth death on every failing; so they are not under the law; but being in some measure enabled to do what the law requires, they are pardoned in what they fall short.

o. These two covenants issue themselves into two places or eternal states, heaven and hell. To the carnal, the scripture denounceth God's eternal wrath; to the spiritual, God's favour and life eternal. The scripture is plain and positive with us: Rom. viii. 13, 'If ye live after the flesh, ye shall die; but if ye, through the spirit, mortify the deeds of the body, ye shall live': Gal. vi. 8, 'He that soweth to the flesh, shall of the flesh reap corruption; but he that soweth

---

[4] To like and dislike the same things

to the spirit, shall of the spirit reap life everlasting.' All mankind, after they have acted their parts in this world, and God cometh to shift the stage, go into one of these two places. Well then, here is our first step, that the whole world is comprised in one of these two ranks; there is no neutral or middle state; either they are guided by the flesh (as all men are in their unregeneracy) and if they continue so in a constant slavery to their lusts, their end shall be everlasting perdition or else they are guided by the Spirit and obey the motions of grace, and make it their business and main employment to please God, and enjoy communion with God; and their end shall be eternal life. It is a question you should often and seriously put to your souls, Shall I be saved, or shall I be damned? If you have any sense and spark of conscience left you when you are sick and dying, you will then put it with great trembling and anxiousness of heart, Poor soul! whither am I now going? It is better to put it now, when you have opportunity to correct your error, if hitherto you have gone wrong. Every man would know his own destiny, what shall become of him, or what is in the womb of futurity, concerning the state of his affairs; as the King of Babylon stood in the heads of the way, to make divination. Now, no destiny deserves so much to be known as this. If the question were, shall I be rich or poor? happy, or miserable in the world? It were not of such great moment; for these distinctions do not out-live time, but cease at the grave's mouth; but this question is of greater moment than so, whether I shall be eternally miserable, or eternally happy? It is foolish curiosity to inquire into other things; they are not of such importance that we should know them beforehand; but it concerneth us much, to know whether we be in a damnable or saveable condition; if we be in a damnable condition, to know it whilst we have time to remedy it; if we are heirs of salvation, the assurance of our interest will preoccupate our blessedness, and will be a great encouragement to us in the way of holiness for the present. Now, nothing will sooner decide this great question than the business we have in hand, whether we be after the flesh or after the spirit; for between these two, heaven and hell is divided. These two divide both the present world and the world to come. I thought good to premise this, that you may consider the weight of the case in hand.

Doctrine 2. That these two sorts of men have two different objects, the things of the spirit and the things of the flesh; the one suits with the one, and the other with the other.

1. The things of the flesh. Let us first know what is meant by flesh, and then we shall better understand what are the things of the flesh.

By the flesh is not meant the mass and substance of our fleshly bodies, or the outward part in which our soul is seated, and by which it performeth its functions and operations, but the vitiosity[5] and corruption of human nature, inclining and addicting itself to the interests of the bodily life. There are the inclinations of the flesh, and the interests of the flesh. The inclinations of the flesh are the evil lustings of corrupt nature; and the interests of the flesh

---

[5] defectiveness

are the things that feed this corruption, or gratify these evil inclinations. Now these are of two sorts:

[A.] Things apparently evil, as all vices and sins: Gal. v. 19, 20, 'The works of the flesh are manifest, which are these, adultery, fornication, uncleanness, lasciviousness, idolatry, witch craft, hatred, variance, emulation, wrath, strife, seditions, heresies, envyings, murders, drunkenness, revellings, and such like.' Though the inward root from whence these things flow be hidden, yet these effects are apparent rank weeds, that smell strong in nature's nostrils. These are not all, but he concludeth it with a such like; and instanceth in these, as the most known, and most commonly practised; as the commandments forbid the grosser sin in the kind, some serve the flesh in a more cleanly manner. And mark in the things enumerated, some belong to the blind and corrupt will, as idolatry and heresy; some to the depraved will, as witchcraft and hatred; some to the affections both of the irascible faculty, as emulation, wrath, strife; some to the concupiscible, as uncleanness, revellings; some to the sensual appetite as adultery and drunkenness. He instanceth not only in the grosser evils, as adultery, but wantonness, or any unseemly behaviour, that tendeth to excite the lust of filthiness in ourselves or others: not only in witchcraft, but hatred or malice, which is a temptation to it; not only in murder, but wrath and strife; not only in drunkenness, but revelling, riotous feasts, and meetings. There is a difference between sins; but the least is to be avoided, if we would shun the greater.

[B.] Things good in their own nature, but immoderately affected, as all the comforts and appurtenances of the bodily life, which are used as baits of corruption, as worldly profits, honours, and pleasures, some that immediately tend to the pleasing of the flesh, as bodily pleasures; others remotely, as they lay in provision for that end. What are here called the things of the flesh, are elsewhere called earthly things: Phil, iii. 19, 'They mind earthly things;' such things as, if rightly used, would be comforts in our passage, but through our folly prove snares. Meat, drink, marriage, pleasures, profits, preferments, ease, idleness, softness, daintiness these things immoderately sought, not in respect to God, or in subordination, but opposition to heavenly things, become baits of corruption, and fuel wherewith to feed the flesh. While men seek them for themselves, and only to please themselves, they are not *adjumenta*, helps to heaven, but *impedimenta*, lets and snares. Our greatest danger doth not lie in things simply evil, but in lawful things. Carnal men esteem these things as the best, and place their happiness in them; these things they affect, and love, and like, and care for: so that the heart is turned off from God and the pursuit of better things, to entertain itself with these baser objects. This is to seek out baits for the flesh; for the flesh is nothing else but the corruption of nature, which inclineth us to any inferior good, and diverteth us from things truly good and spiritual, as communion with and enjoyment of God. Well, now we have suited those that are after the flesh, with an object proper to them, and agreeable with their inclinations.

2. The next thing is, what are the things of the Spirit? 'They are all things pertaining to spiritual life and godliness. You may conceive of them thus:

[A.] Such things as the Spirit revealeth. Now he revealeth the mysteries of salvation, or the deep things of God in Jesus Christ, which the natural man is not capable of: 1 Cor. ii. 14. The whole doctrine of godliness, or salvation offered by God in Christ, is the element of the renewed man, his life and soul is bound up in it: Ps. cxix. 103, 'How sweet are thy words unto my taste? 'But a natural man savoureth not these things, nor knoweth them, nor loveth them, if he be told of them. They that are in a common way partakers of the Spirit, are said to 'taste the good word' Heb. vi. 4. So far as the Spirit worketh upon them, so far they have a relish for these things.

[B.] Such things as the Spirit worketh: Gal. v. 22, 'The fruits of the Spirit are love, joy, peace, long-suffering, gentleness, goodness, faith, patience, meekness'; all internal excellences. The renewed man ever seeks to excel and advance in these things; not to trim the body, but to deck and adorn the soul: 1 Pet. iii. 3, 4, 'Whose adorning, let it not be the outward adorning of plaiting the hair, and wearing of gold, and putting on of apparel: but let it be the hidden man of the heart, in that which is not corruptible, even the ornament of a meek and quiet spirit, which is in the sight of God of great price.' All his desires are to be 'strengthened with might in the inner man by the Spirit' Eph. iii. 16. He rejoiceth, and faints not under troubles, while the inward man is safe; 2 Cor. iv. 1.6, for 'as the outward man decreaseth, the inward man is renewed day by day.' If they can keep grace alive in their souls, that is their care, their business, their comfort. The natural heart is altogether taken up about the outward man, but the renewed heart about the inward man, and an increase in holiness, or spiritual strength; for that is the great product of the sanctifying Spirit, and that which they should mainly look after.

[C.] Such things as the Spirit urgeth and inclineth unto; and these are communion with God here, and the full enjoyment of God hereafter. The great impression which the Spirit leaveth upon the soul is a tendency towards God; for his office is to bring us to God, into communion with him here. God, as a Judge, by the Spirit of bondage, drives us to Christ as a Mediator; and Christ, as a Mediator, by the Spirit of adoption, bringeth us to God as a Father: Rom. viii. 15, 1 Ye have not received the Spirit of bondage again to fear, but ye have received the Spirit of adoption, whereby we cry, Abba Father.' One of the things which the Spirit urgeth us to look after is the favour of God: Ps. iv. 6, 7, 'Lord, lift up the light of thy countenance upon us,' etc.; and communion with him here: Ps. xvii. 15, 'As for me, I will behold thy face with righteousness; I shall be satisfied when I awake with thy likeness'; and the full enjoyment of God hereafter: Rom. viii. 23, 'We ourselves, who have the first fruits of the Spirit, even we ourselves groan within ourselves, waiting for the adoption, to wit, the redemption of our bodies': 2 Cor. v. 5, 'Now he that hath wrought us for the self-same thing, is God, who also hath given unto us the earnest of the Spirit' always groaning, longing to live with God for ever. So when the unregenerate and regenerate are spoken of as two contrary minds and affections, Phil. iii. 19, 20, the one are said to mind earthly things, the others are said to have their conversation in heaven. The flesh draweth us off from God to things earthly and fleshly; but the Spirit's work is to raise the heart to things eternal and heavenly, that our main business might be there. Well now, the things of the Spirit are all those things that are agreeable to the new and spiritual life, as righteousness, peace, grace, and glory, the image of God, and word of God; these things suit with the new nature.

Doctrine 3. That men discover their temper and constitution of soul by their respect to either of these objects. To evidence this to you

1. I will show you what this minding is,

2. Give you some observations,

3. The reasons of the point.

1. What is this minding or respect? Answer. It may be considered simply, and apart; or comparatively, our respects to these contrary objects being compared together.

[A.] Simply, by itself. Our minding is bewrayed by the three operations of man thoughts, words, and actions. That which he minds he often thinks of, speaks of, and seeks after, be they the things of the flesh, or of the spirit, the life and vigour of our souls are seen in thinking, speaking, and acting.

(1.) Men's thoughts will be where their hearts are, and their hearts are where their treasure is; Mat. vi. 21. Carnal men are brought in thinking of their worldly affairs: Luke xii. 17, 29, and he 'dialogued with himself.' Not that it is simply unlawful to mind our earthly business: I bring it to show the temper of the men; their hearts are always exercised with such kind of thoughts, talking with themselves. And on the other side, godly men are remembering God and heaven, and pleased with this kind of thoughts. 'My soul re membered thee in the night'; and they are described: Mai. iii. 16, 'They that feared the Lord, and thought upon his name'

(2.) The same is true of words also, they declare the life and vigour of our spirits, for there is a quick intercourse between the tongue and the heart: 1 John iv. 5, 'They are of the world, and speak of the world, and the world heareth them'; men's speeches are as their temper- is: Prov. x. 20, 'The tongue of the just is as choice silver, but the heart of the wicked is little worth' When the heart is stored with knowledge, and biassed by spiritual affections, they will enrich others with their holy, savoury, profitable discourse; but a drowsy, unsanctified heart in man, bewrayeth itself by his speeches and communications with others.

(3.) By actions, or what we seek after: if all our business be to gratify the flesh, Luke xii. 21; or sowing to the flesh, Gal. v. 8; it argues a fleshly mind. On the other side, they that have a spiritual mind, make it their business to grow in grace: Phil. iii. 13, 'This one thing I do, forgetting the things that are behind, I press forward towards the mark of the prize of the high calling in Christ Jesus.' They labour for spiritual and heavenly things: John xvii. 27, 'Seek the things that are above': Col. iii. 1, 'They mind the things of the Spirit.'

[B.] Comparatively, so the mark must be interpreted. The simple consideration is not so convictive as the comparative.'

(1.) Partly, because all minding the flesh is not sinful, but an over- minding the flesh. The body hath its necessities, and they must be cared for. Yea, take the flesh for sensitive appetite, to please it with lawful satisfactions is no sin; for it is a faculty put into us by God, and in due subordination to religion may be pleased. To please it by things forbidden is certainly a sin; and to prefer it before the pleasing of God is a great sin indeed, for it is a character of them who are in a state of damnation, that 'they are lovers of pleasures more than lovers of God, '2 Tim. iii. 4. Therefore though we must observe our thoughts, words, and actions, yet it must be thus interpreted not to condemn every act, but that we may know in what proportion the vigour of mind is manifested and carried out to either of these objects, by thoughts, words, or actions. If our thoughts of the world shut out all thoughts of God, Ps. xii. 4, 'God is not in all their thoughts.' If our thinking of spiritual things be too rare, unfrequent, and unpleasing to us, we are after the flesh. So for words, if we are heartless in our talk of heavenly things, and we are in our element when speaking of carnal things, and when a serious word is interposed for God, we frown upon the motion. So for actions, compare men's care for the world with their care for their souls; if they more earnestly and industriously seek to please the flesh than to save their souls, it is a sign the flesh and its interests are predominant in them; all things are done superficially, and by the by in religion, not as becomes those that work from and for life, with any diligence and fervency. There is no proportion between endeavours for the world, and their preparations for eternal life; all is earnest on one side, but either nothing is done, or in a very slight manner on the other side; their thoughts, and love, and life, and strength are wholly occupied and taken up about the things of the flesh.

(2.) Partly, because we must distinguish between the sin of flesh pleasing, and the state of flesh pleasing; for a man is to judge of his spiritual condition, not by single acts, but his state, or the habitual frame of his heart. Who is there among God's own children who doth not mind the flesh, and too much indulge the flesh? But they who make it their business to please the flesh, are over careful about it: Rom. xiii. 14, 'Who make provision for the flesh, to fulfil the lusts thereof'; and so indulge the minding of the flesh, as not to mind the things of the spirit, so that vain pleasures do exceed their delight in God, and kill it yet more and more, and bring a slavery upon themselves, which they cannot help: Tit. iii. 3, 'Serving divers lusts and pleasures' and being captivated by the fleshly part, they have contracted a strangeness and enmity to God and his ways: Rom. viii. 7. They that have no relish for the joys of faith, and the pleasures of holiness, and do habitually prefer the natural good of the body, before the moral, spiritual, and eternal good both of body and soul, these are in a state of carnality.

2. The observations upon the point.

[A.] This minding of the flesh must be interpreted not with respect to our former estate; for alas! All of us in times past pleased the flesh, and 'walked according to the course of this world,' and 'had in time past our conversation in the lusts of the flesh, fulfilling the will of the flesh, and of the mind,' Eph. ii. 3. It was God that loosed our shackles: Tit. iii. 3, 'We ourselves were sometimes foolish, disobedient, deceived, serving divers lusts and pleasures, etc., but after the kindness and love of God appeared towards mankind,' etc. If we yet please the flesh we are not the servants of Christ; but if we break off this servitude, Srod will not judge us according to what we have been but what we are.

[B.] To know what we are we must consider what principle liveth in us, and groweth and increaseth; and on the other side, what decreaseth, the interest of the flesh or the interest of the spirit; for these two are contrary, and the one destroyeth the other. The love of the world, and the flesh, estrangeth us from God: 1 John ii. 15, 'Love not the world, nor the things of the world; if any man love the world, the love of the Father is not in him.' On the other side, minding the things of the spirit deadeneth our affections to the world and the baits of the flesh. The conversation in heaven is opposed to the minding of earthly things: Phil. iii. 19, 20, 'Whose God is their belly, whose glory is in their shame, who mind earthly things; but our conversation is in heaven.' So much of affection as we give to the one, we take from the other: Col. iii. 2, 'Set your affections on things above, and not on things of the earth' Now we are to consider if we grow more brutish, forgetful of God, unapt for spiritual things, the flesh gaineth; but if the spiritual inclination doth more and more discover itself with life and power in our thoughts, words, and actions, the flesh is in the wane, and we shall be reckoned among those that walk not after the flesh, but after the spirit; we have every day a higher estimation of God, and Christ, and grace, and heaven, and thereby we grow more dead to other things.

[C.] Some things more immediately tend to the pleasing of the flesh; others more remotely. Immediately, as bodily pleasures, and therefore our inclinations to them are called fleshly lusts, as distinguished from worldly lusts, Tit. ii. 12; or from the lusts of the eye, and pride of life, 1 John ii. 16; and these are intended, when it is said, 1 Peter ii. 11, 'Abstain from fleshly lusts which war against the soul;' that is, those inclinations which carry us to vain and sordid pleasures. Other things more remotely, as they lay in provision for that end, as the honours and profits of the world; as all religion is pleasing God, so all that is opposite to it is pleasing the flesh. Some please it one way, some another; though a man be not voluptuous, yet he may be guilty of minding the things of the flesh, because the world lieth nearest to his heart, and so he is taken off from care of and delight in better things': envy, emulation, wrath, strife, division make us carnal; 2 Cor. iii. 3. Namely, as we bustle and strive for greatness and esteem in the world, though they are not sordidly given to brutish pleasures, and worldly lusts, are called foolish and hurtful lusts, which drown men in perdition and destruction: 1 Tim. vi. 9. Therefore fleshly minding must be applied to anything that inticeth us to neglect things spiritual and heavenly, for the world and the flesh suit; one is the affection, the other the bait.

[D.] Some please the flesh in a more cleanly, others in a more gross manner; as some men's sins are open and manifest, and stink in the nostrils of God, as whoredom, drunkenness, and the like. Now though we fall not into these sins, but escape the pollutions of the world, yet there is a more secret, carnal minding, wherewith we may be tainted, as when we let loose the heart to such alluring vanities as draw us off from God, and Christ, and heaven; and the savour and relish that we have for outward things obstructeth and quencheth the heavenly life, as much as those baser lusts that are more shameful and hateful in the world. Some are disengaged from gross sins, but yet wholly live to themselves, and the pleasures of their fleshly mind; whereas the spiritual living is a living unto God, and subordinateth all things to our great interest; and till we return to God from whom we have strayed, there is little difference what way of sin we choose; we are all gone astray, but everyone his own way, Isa. liii. 6.

[E.] The prevalency of the carnal or spiritual mind is known by observing what we mind seriously, resolutely, willingly, constantly.

(1.) Seriously, and in good earnest. Some seek after worldly things in good earnest, but spiritual and heavenly things in an overly, careless, and perfunctory manner. Now it is easy to know to what sort they are to be reckoned, for where the strength of the soul is employed there our mind is. The scripture adviseth us to moderate our affections to earthly things, to rejoice here, as if we rejoiced not; to mourn here, as if we mourned not; to use all things as not over-using them; and many mourn for sin, as if they mourned not; and rejoiced in God, as if they rejoiced not; seek after heavenly things superficially and by the by, not with their chief strength and care: Mat. vi. 33.

(2.) Resolutely, so as to carry it on whatsoever difficulties and oppositions we meet with: Neh. iv. 6, 'The wall was built, for the people had a mind to the work.' It was a great charge for a wasted people to undergo, being newly returned from the captivity; and there was a great opposition, for they were fain to use sword and trowel together, they did work with one hand, and held the sword with the other hand to fight; but it went on, for the people had a mind to the work. We make our way to heaven by conflict and contest every step, till we are resolved and cleave to the Lord with full purpose of heart, whatever it costs us: Acts xi. 23, 'He exhorted them, that with purpose of heart they would cleave unto the Lord.' We make no work in religion until we so mind these things that we come to such a resolution as Paul had: Acts xxi. 14, 'I am prepared, I am ready, not only to be bound, but to die at Jerusalem for the sake of the Lord Jesus Christ' Such a resolvedness there is also in minding the things of the flesh. When they put up many sad wound and check of conscience, overlook their conveniences in the world, credit, interest, sacrifice whatsoever should, is dear and precious to them, to follow their lusts.

(3.) Willingly. How constrained are most men's duties? Their thoughts of God, their prayers to him, their attendance on his word; doing all they do as a task, rather than going about it as a willing and pleasing employment, as Saul said, that he 'forced himself': 1 Sam. xiii. 12. He pleadeth it as an excuse of his sin, as committing it out of necessity; but it is a just account of most men's worship, they are held to it by force; the heart liketh it not, seeketh to slide away, and they are glad when they are enlarged, and can divert to other things. On the contrary: Ps. civ. 35, 'I will be glad in the Lord, my meditation of him shall be sweet'; this for thoughts. For words: John iv. 32, 'My meat and drink is to do the will of him that sent me.' They are in their element when discoursing and promoting the interest of God. For actions and endeavours: Ps. xl. 8, 'I delight to do thy will, God': 1 John v. 3, 'His commandments are not grievous'; nothing is more pleasing to them than when they are thus employed.

(4.) Constantly. This is that which is mainly to be observed, the constancy of our operations, as to things of the flesh and of the spirit.

(a.) For thoughts. What thoughts have you of God and Christ and the world to come? You mind the world's days, weeks, months, years, it cannot be denied; but if you can never find leisure for God, Christ, and heaven, not in one of a hundred, or a thousand, yea, or twenty thousand thoughts, can you be said to mind the things of the spirit? Did you ever shut the door of your hearts upon vain objects? Cast them out with indignation, as you divert and shift from the thoughts of God, or regarding your last end and great work; we that should retire for the meditation of God banish him out of our minds: Job xxi. 14, 'We say to the Almighty, Depart from us.' We like not these serious reflections, and cast them out.

(b.) For words. How much, how often, and delightfully do you speak of God and the things of the world to come? Do you show this respect for God, or those useful and necessary things which concern your own salvation and the salvation of others? Speech must be guided by prudence, and you must consider not only what you must do, but others will bear; but as to yourselves, you are to observe the vigour of your own spirits, which way it is most let out. To be pent up in carnal company is a grief to a godly heart. It is a grief to him to hold his peace from good: Ps. xxxix. 2, 3, 'I was dumb with silence, I held my peace even from good, and my sorrow was stirred, my heart was hot within me, while I was musing the fire burned.' But in holy company 'they that fear the Lord speak often one to another': Mai. iii. 16. In the general, men will speak as they are affected: Ps. xxxvii. 30, 'The mouth of the righteous speaketh wisdom, and his tongue taJketh of judgment.' He studieth to glorify God, and edify others, because the law of God is in his heart: ver. 31, that is the reason rendered there; that is, because his mind is upon it.

(c.) For actions. Men are known by their constant exercise, what they pursue and seek after; whether their life be a 'sowing to the flesh 'or a 'sowing to the spirit': Gal. vi. 8.

3. The reasons to prove it. That we may fix the reasons we must again, in a shorter method, consider what minding implieth. It implieth our savour, and our walk; or, to divest it from the metaphor, our affections and endeavours. So the reasons will be two, suitable to these two notions.

[A.] As minding implieth our savour and affections. Men's gust is according to their constitutions, and the bait discovereth the temper: for pleasure is *applicatio convenientis convenienti*; when the object and the faculty suit, things please us, and are minded by us, as they are agreeable to our humour: Luke xvi. 25, 'Son. remember that thou in thy life-time hast received thy good things.' Carnal men have their good things and the children of God their good things. Our relish is agreeable to our nature. A fish hath small pleasure on the dry land, or a beast at sea. A fleshly creature can arise no higher than a fleshly inclination moveth it; therefore men's complacency and displacency showeth of what nature they are. The nature is hidden, but the opera tions and affections discover it.

[B.] As it implieth our walk and endeavour. Men's actions are according to their predominant principle. As the tree is, so is the fruit: Mat. vii. 18, 'Every good tree bringeth forth good fruit, but a corrupt tree bringeth forth corrupt fruit' And as a man is, so his work will be; for the course of his life showeth the constitution of his soul: such as the man is, so will his works be. Can a man be said to be after the spirit that only looketh after those things which please the senses, and scarce admitteth a serious thought of God, or the life to come? Or, on the other side, can he be said to be after the flesh that maketh it his business to tame the flesh, and his work to please and enjoy God?

[C.] From both. Things that suit with the disposition and inclination of our hearts do banish all love of contrary things. As the carnal minding is opposite to the spiritual minding, and quencheth and weakeneth it more and more, so the spiritual minding weakeneth the inclinations, and retrencheth the interest of the flesh: Gal. v. 16, 'Walk in the spirit, and ye shall not fulfil the lusts of the flesh' There is no such care of minding the things of the flesh, as by diversion to nobler objects, and obeying a higher principle. Our affections cannot lie idle: while we are awake to the world, we sleep to God; and while we are dead to the spirit, we are alive to the flesh; and so on the contrary.

SERMON VII

They that are after the flesh do mind the things of the flesh; and they that are after the spirit, the things of the spirit.

Romans viii 5.

I PROCEED now to the application of the former discourse:

Use 1. To put us upon serious self-reflection, of what sort are we? after the flesh, or after the spirit? I pray let us go to a thorough search and trial; and to deal more plainly in it,

1. Consider there are three sorts of persons in the world:

[A.] Some are wholly carried away by the desires of the flesh, and seek their happiness here but neglect things to come. The case is clear, that they are after the flesh, and so for the present in a state of death and damnation. And they had need to look to it betimes; for 'to be carnally minded is death' *meritorie et effective*. They provoke God to deny them life, whom they despise for their lusts' sake, and dispense with their duty to him to satisfy some foolish and inordinate desire: and effective, they have no sound belief, nor desire of the world to come: and do you think God will save them against their wills, and thrust and force these things upon them without their consent, or beside their purpose and inclination? No, it will not be. Surely there is no difficulty in the case, to state their condition, who grossly set more by their lusts than by their obedience to God. The things of the flesh are the chief scope and business of their lives; and they care not whether God be pleased or displeased, obeyed or disobeyed, honoured or dishonoured, a friend or an enemy; so the flesh be pleased, that is all their desire and aim.

[B.] There is another sort of men, who do many things that are good, but the flesh too often gets the upper hand; and though they do many things that appertain to the spirit, yet in other things they show they are influenced by the carnal life, as is evident.

[C.] Some unquestionably show they are after the spirit, by their deep sense of heavenly things, their care about them, their diligence and watchfulness over the desires and inclinations of the flesh, and holding a hard hand over the passions and affections thereof, and their serious endeavours to please God. There is no doubt but these are born of God.

All the difficulty is about the middle sort, to understand their condition. They must be again distinguished:

1. Some are not far off from the kingdom of God.

2. Others are actually admitted, though grace be in some weak degree.

(1.) For the first those that are not far from the kingdom of God. They are such as have the grace of the third ground described: Luke viii. 14, 'And that which fell among thorns, are they who, having heard, go forth, and are choked with cares, and riches, and the pleasures of this life, and bring no fruit to perfection.' They have good sentiments of religion, and retain them longer than the stony ground doth, but they are over-mastered with the cares of this world, and voluptuous living, so as that they attain not to the perfection of that holy and heavenly life that should be in Christians. They do not lay aside the profession, but have not felt the power of Christianity in mortifying their fleshly and worldly lusts, that they may be more at liberty for God, and the duties of their heavenly calling; and so cherish a kind of imperfect Christianity, which little honoureth God in the world, or doth good to their own souls. They are neither wholly on nor off from religion. The bane of it is, that carnal and temporal things lie too near their hearts, so that they cannot fully commence into the divine life, and never took pains to overcome the natural spirit, which lusteth to sensuality, envy, pride, and worldliness. There are some good things found in them; but the carnal minding is not mortified, nor doth the meek, holy, heavenly spirit prevail in them. There are others

(2.) Who are regenerate; but grace is weak in them, and corruptions break out, and shake off the empire of grace for a time, though it habitually prevails, and governs their actions. Now for the former, we must persuade them to get a good and an honest heart; that is, that their intentions be more sincere and fixed, their way more thorough and exact, lest they get a name for religion, to do a mischief to it. For most of the calamities of the church, and the prejudices against religion, and hardening by scandals and blemishes, come from that sort of men, and are to be laid at their doors. And for the second, we are to advise them, and call upon them to distinguish themselves from the carnal state more clearly and explicitly. For though God may accept them, yet whilst they border too near upon the carnal world, it is in vain to find out evidences whereby they may assure their hearts before God; for though God possibly hath given them saving grace, and will accept them at last, yet he will not give them assurance; and we do but perplex cases of conscience, to reconcile the tenor of Christianity with their weak state. Exhortation doth better than trial. If they be sincere, they will come on in the way of godliness, and then that which was doubtful will be more clear and satisfactory, and their sincerity will be more unquestionable.

(3.) Because God's dear children write bitter things against themselves, either out of weakness of judgment, or consciousness of too much prevalency of corrupt affections, and tenderness of God's honour, and trouble for their own imperfections, it will be necessary further to state- the point. There is to the very last, flesh and spirit in the best: Gal. v. 17, 'For the flesh lusteth against the spirit, and the spirit lusteth against the flesh'; yet there is enough to distinguish them from the carnal world; and that is the potency and the predominancy of the spiritual principle. *Denominatio est a potiori*; not from what is perfect, but from what is sincere, and habitually reigneth and beareth the upper hand in the soul. But then the question returneth, How shall we know the prevalency? I answer

[A.] Negatively. Not by a bare sense of duty, or a dictate of con science, that showeth what ought to be done; but many times we do quite otherwise; for many 'hold the truth in unrighteousess': Rom. i. 18. A dictate of conscience is unsufficient to change the heart and sanctify the life. Nor barely by the resolution of the will, for that may be ineffectual, and without a full purpose of heart': I go, sir,' said the first son in the parable, 'but went not': Mat. xxi. 30. Many resolve well, but they have not a heart to verify and make good their resolutions: Deut. v. 29. The Jews said, 'All that the Lord hath spoken we will do.' 'Oh! that there were such a heart in them,' saith God. Nor by a faint desire; for many can wish not only for heaven and happiness, but that it might be otherwise with them in point of holiness, that God would change their natures; but they do not use the means': The soul of the sluggard desireth, and hath nothing, 'Prov. xiii. 4. None goeth to heaven by the sluggard's wishes; not by prevailing in one act, or more; for many, in a pang of zeal, may do much for God: Gal. iv. 18, 'It is good to be zealously affected always in a good matter; Ps. cvi. 3, 'Blessed are they that do. righteousness at all times.' Nor by every kind of dislike, and resistance of sin, that may sometimes arise from other lusts; for they sometimes fight among themselves: James iv. 1, 'Whence come wars and fightings among you? come they not hence, even from your lusts, which war in your selves? 'Or from hypocrisy, to hide and feed some other lusts the more plausibly. Or if from conscience, the resistance is too feeble to break the power of sin, till the heart be renewed, or more thoroughly set towards God and heavenly things.

[B.] Positively.

(a.) By the course of our actions. Habits are known by the uniformity of acts, when the effects of the spirit are more constant than those of the flesh, and the drift and business of our lives is for God and our salvation; our bent and business is the pleasing of God, and the saving of our own souls. Men must be judged, not by a few acts, but their walk, or the tenor of their conversations. They that spend their time in knitting one carnal contentment to 'another, and glut themselves with all manner of vain delights, and God hath from them but what the flesh can spare, a little formal slight service, that they may pacify conscience, and enjoy their pleasures with less remorse; what are they doing but the flesh's business?

(b.) By cherishing the best principle with all care and diligence, and mortifying and suppressing the other. The better principle must be cherished; that is, we must get more degrees of faith, love, and hope, that faith may be more strong, love more fervent, hope more lively: 2 Pet. iii. 18, 'But grow in grace, and in the knowledge of our Lord and Saviour Jesus Christ.' On the other side, the flesh would fain be pleased before God; but you must subdue it more and more: 1 Cor. ix. 22, 'I keep under my body, and bring it into subjection'; give it not what it craveth. Rest not in endeavours without success; for, Gal. v. 24, 'They that are Christ's have crucified the flesh, with the affections and lusts thereof.' A Christian is seen *proposito conatu, eventu*. Some victory there must be over the carnal mind. See that the power of the flesh be diminished in you, both as to the motions of it and your obedience to it.

Use 2 is Exhortation.

First. Negatively: Not to mind the things of the flesh. That is, take heed not only of the grosser out-breakings of the flesh, but of serving it in a more cleanly manner, by too free and full a gust and relish in any outward thing; for by this means it securely gets interest, and gaineth upon you. If you freely let loose the heart to every alluring object, and withhold not yourselves from any joy, lust will grow bold and head-strong, and be hardly kept within bounds.

Motives:

1. Consider your engagement, as you are Christ's: Gal. v. 24, 'They that are Christ's have crucified the flesh with the affections and lusts thereof.' Every man is engaged by his profession and covenant, sealed in baptism, so to do; which should be a very moving argument to press us to do things cross and unpleasing to the flesh.

2. Your comfort dependeth on it. For here is your evidence, either you must mortify the flesh, or gratify the flesh; if you gratify the flesh, you are not under the conduct of the Spirit, and so not under the hope of glory; if you mortify it, then you shall live. The only evidence that will content and satisfy you, as to your gracious state, is such a high estimation of God and Christ and grace, as weaneth you, and draweth off the heart from other things. A dull approbation of that which is good will make no evidence, nor a few good wishes; nothing but such a strong bent as deadeneth your affections to the world: Gal. vi. 14, 'God forbid that I should glory, save in the cross of Jesus Christ, by whom the world is crucified to me, and I unto the world.'

3. This will be your wisdom. There is a false wisdom, and a true wisdom: James iii. 15, 'This wisdom descendeth not from above, but is earthly, sensual, devillish:' ver. 17, 'But the wisdom that is from above, is first pure, then peaceable,' etc. This is the true wisdom, to be wise for the spirit. I do the rather insist upon this because there is a notion of wisdom in the word of the text. Carnal men judge their own way wisest, and the way of the godly to be mere folly: 1 Cor. ii. 14, 'The natural man receiveth not the things of the Spirit of God, for they are foolishness to him: neither can he receive them, because they are spiritually discerned.' The godly employ themselves to get things spiritual, and such as God's honour is mainly concerned in; and are not attended with an income of worldly advantage, but rather of loss and detriment but yet the end shall prove that they that thought themselves the only wise men and gainers, have been mere fools; and the greatest losers (those others whom they looked upon as madmen) are the wisest adventurers and the greatest gainers. The issue will show it: Gal. vi. 8, 'He that soweth to the flesh, shall of the flesh reap corruption; but he that soweth to the Spirit, shall of the Spirit reap life everlasting'; Horn. viii. 6, 'To be carnally minded is death, but to be spiritually minded is life and peace.'

4. The flesh is really our enemy; yea, our greatest enemy. Therefore we should not indulge the flesh, but give up ourselves to be ruled by the Spirit: 1 Peter ii. 10, 11, 'Take heed of fleshly lusts which war against the Spirit.' That it is one of our enemies, is clear by that: Eph. ii. 2, 3, 'Wherein in time past ye walked according to the course of this world, according to the prince of the power of the air, the spirit' that now ruleth in the children of disobedience: among whom also we had our conversation in times past in the lusts of our flesh, fulfilling the desires of the flesh and of the mind; and were by nature the children of wrath, even as others.' There is the course of this world, and the prince of the power of the air, and our own flesh. Corrupt nature within us would make us vile enough, without external incitements and suggestions, though there were never a devil to tempt or evil example to follow. If the devil should stand by, and say nothing, there is enough within us to put us upon all manner of evil, though there were no other irritation than God's law: Rom. vii. 9, 'When the commandment came, sin revived, and I died.' Other enemies could do us no

harm without our own flesh. We are tempted to sin by Satan, encouraged to sin by the example and custom of others, inticed to sin by the baits and allurements of the world; but inclined to sin by our own flesh. It is the flesh that holdeth correspondence with Satan, the flesh that openeth the door to temptations, the flesh that maketh our abode in the world so dangerous, the flesh that choketh the good seed, that hindereth all our heavenly thoughts, and maketh the service of God so burdensome. The flesh is within us and maketh a part of ourselves. There is more imminent danger from a plague in the body, than from an enemy that waiteth in the streets to kill us. If we would but keep ourselves from ourselves we should do well enough. It is the flesh that lulleth us asleep in carnal security, that tainteth all our actions, and is so ready to betray us. The devil dealeth with us as Baalam by the Israelites; all his curses and charms pre vailed nothing, till he found a means to destroy them by themselves, to corrupt them by whoredom, and by whoredom to draw them to idolatry. It is the flesh that is the domestical enemy, that dwelleth with us, and in us, and so maketh us a ready prey to Satan. We carry it about with us wherever we go, and so it is ready to do us mischief upon all occasions. When we are about holy duties, it distracteth us with vain thoughts, and taketh off our edge, and make us drowsy and dead-hearted, and weary of God's service. When we are about our callings, it is the flesh that maketh us lazy and negligent, and diverteth us by the proposals of sensual objects; or else to be so earnest in them, that we have no time nor heart for God and soul-necessities. When we are eating and drinking, it is the flesh that turneth our table into a snare, and tempts us to glut ourselves with carnal delights, and to oppress our bodies when we should refresh them and strengthen them for God's service. In our recreations it is the flesh that maketh us inordinate in them, and to forget our great work and last end; and so we are the more entangled in sin when we should be more fit to glorify God. It is the flesh that, being beaten out at one door, entereth by another, and still assaults us afresh, to our great spiritual prejudice. And will you study how to please the flesh, that is so great an enemy to your souls that flesh that resists all the motions of God's Spirit; that cloggeth you in every duty, and draweth you off from the pursuit of everlasting happiness?

5. Consider how ill Christ will take it, and what just cause you give him to withdraw, when you prize the things of the flesh before him and the comforts of the Spirit. Must not the Lord Jesus take it exceeding unkindly, that after all his love, and the discoveries of his grace, you should study to please his competitor, and your own enemy? Is his grace and glory worth no more than so? and hath he deserved no better at your hands? 'God spared not his own Son, but gave him up to the death for us': Rom. viii. 32. 'Christ pleased not himself': Rom. xv. 3. There is nothing so answerable as some self-denial on our part. The most genuine and natural influence from this grace is, that we should spare nothing, please not ourselves: Titus ii. 11, 'The grace of God that bringeth salvation hath appeared unto all men, teaching us to deny ungodliness and worldly lusts' Teaching us, etc., how? By way of precept? No, by way of argument. It persuadeth us to deny ungodliness and worldly lusts.

6. Consider, the more you indulge the flesh, the more it is an enemy, and the more is your slavery and bondage increased; and still you grow the more brutish, forgetful of God, and

unapt for spiritual use for make it a wanton once, and it groweth stubborn and contumacious, and secureth its interest, and gaineth upon you. If you allow yourselves too free and full a gust and relish in any outward thing, and let loose the heart to every alluring object, and withhold not your hearts from any joy and sense-pleasing object, which Solomon acknowledgeth as his sin: Eccles. ii. 10; vicious and inordinate desires increase upon you; and the more you gratify them the more they crave. The way to abate their rage is to deny them, and hold a hard hand over them, to 'bring the body into subjection': 1 Cor. ix. 27. Liberty allowed in satisfying carnal desires doth marvelously increase and nourish them, and will bring you to carelessness, and hardness of heart, if not some foul scandalous fall. I am sure the heart is corrupted strangely. Solomon saith: Prov. xxiv. 21, 'He that delicately bringeth up a servant, shall have him become a son at length'; he will no more know his condition, but grow bold and troublesome. I am sure the flesh was ordained to be a servant, and not a master. Take it in the mildest sense, it was ordained to be God's servant, and our servant, and must be used as a servant, kept fit for work. We are the worse for licence; our natural desires, unless they feel fetters and restraints, will grow unruly; therefore it is good to bridle the flesh, lest it grow masterly. But when the flesh is that which you mind, which you indulge with too free a leave, you deny yourselves nothing, but cocker every appetite; you bring a snare upon the soul; and carnal distempers are the more rooted, and will prove troublesome if not destructive to you.

7. Consider the consequence and weight of these things. If it were a small matter we speak to you about, you might refuse to give ear; but it is in a case of life and death eternal life, and eternal death. We can tell you of many temporal and present inconveniencies that come by the flesh. The body, the part gratified, suffereth, as well as the soul by it: Prov. viii. 11, 'Thou shalt mourn at last, when thy flesh and thy body are consumed.' It betrayeth you to commit such sins as suck your bones, and devour your strength, and give your years to the cruel. It bringeth infamy, and a blot upon the name, sins and scandals. Pleasing the flesh, and minding the flesh, makes one turn drunkard, another a wanton, another a glutton, or a hard-hearted worldling, or an ambitious, vain-glorious fool, or a senseless voluptuary: these are no small things. But rather consider, it will be the eternal ruin of your precious and immortal souls. The more you give up your selves to please the flesh, the more you add fuel to that fire which shall never be quenched, and provide matter of eternal sorrows and confusion of face to yourselves. There will a day come when God will call you to an account for this: Eccles. xi. 9, 'Rejoice, young man in thy youth, and let thine heart cheer thee, and walk in the way of thine own heart, and in the sight of thine eyes: but know that for all these things God will bring thee to judgment.' Mark, young man! We say, *Dandum est aliquid huic cetati;* some allowance is to be made to this age, before they have learned by experimenting pleasures to condemn them; but the young man is admonished: Do what thou pleasest; let thy wanton and wandering eye inflame the lusts of thine heart, smother thy conscience by all manner of sensual and vain delights, but at length thou wilt learn the folly of this to thy bitter cost. These things that are now so pleasing to the senses will one day gnaw and sting the conscience; when God, whom thou now forgettest, shall, whether thou wilt or no, drag

thee forth to judgment, and thou shalt in vain 'call upon the rocks and mountains to cover thee'

8. Consider how contrary it is to our Christian hopes to mind the flesh, or please the flesh: 1 Peter ii. 11, 'Dearly beloved, I beseech you as strangers and pilgrims abstain from fleshly lusts which war against the soul.' You are, or you should be, travelling into another country, where are 'the spirits of just men made perfect;' and this body of thine is to become a spiritual body; will you please it not in a gross, but in a more cleanly manner? Nothing is more unsuitable. Shall we that are going to Canaan hearken after the flesh pots of Egypt? Nothing is so contrary to our profession, and that breedeth such un readiness to depart out of the world, as these vain delights; and therefore if you be strangers and pilgrims, you should not lust after worldly and fleshly things; stop here, lest you forget and forfeit your great hopes.

9. Consider what a vile unthankfulness, and an abuse it is of that liberty which we have by Christ, and all the blessings of God's providence: Gal. v. 13, 'Ye are called to liberty, only use it not as an -occasion to the flesh.' We have a great liberty to use worldly comforts, in order to God's glory, and as encouragements of God's service, and for the sweetening of our pilgrimage; but now, when you use this liberty to please the flesh, you turn it into a bondage, and offer a great abuse to Jesus Christ. Surely he never died to promote the power of sin, he never gave us these comforts richly to enjoy, to hearten our enemy; he was not a man of sorrows that we might live in pleasures, he did not .suffer in the flesh that we might have liberty to indulge and please the flesh; he bestowed not so large a supply of outward comforts to hinder us from those better and eternal things which he purchased for us 1 Tim. vi. 17, 18 or to turn them into occasions of unrighteous ness, and means whereby to dishonour his name, and destroy our souls.

Now if we would not do so, something must be done:

As to sinful inclinations.

As to sinful motions.

As to sinful actions.

As to sinful and fleshly inclinations, observe them, weaken them.

(1.) Observe them. Satan doth, and we should; he observeth which way the tree leaneth, and what kind of diet our soul distempers crave, and suiteth his temptations accordingly, as the angler suiteth his bait as the fishes will take it, for every month a bait: 1 Cor. vii. 5, 'Lest satan tempt you for your incontinency.' He hath a bait of preferment for Absalom, for he is ambitious; a bait of pleasure for Samson, for he is voluptuous; a bait of money for Judas, for he is covetous; thus will he furnish them with temptations answerable to their inclinations; a man by temper voluptuous may despise profit, as an earth-worm doth pleasure, or honour, reputation, and great places, -or at least doth not so much value these things. It is sad that our enemy should know our temper better than we do ourselves, where we are weakest, and how to make his assaults; and therefore observe your inclinations. Flesh-pleasing is the general term by which it is expressed. Three objects there are about which this sin of flesh-pleas ing is exercised: 1 John ii. 16, 'The lusts of the flesh, the lusts of the eye, and the pride of life' credit or honour, profit or riches, sensual pleasure or carnal delight. Now see which of these things do you favour or mind most what carnal interest suiteth with your hearts, and groweth there.

(2.) Weaken and subdue them. It is your uprightness and faith fulness: Ps. xviii. 23, 'I was also upright before him, and I kept myself from mine iniquities.' Let a Christian observe the increase or decay of his master sin, and other things will succeed the more easily. 'Fight not against small nor great, but the king of Israel.' When we can deny ourselves in our dearest lusts, Satan is more discouraged. Samson's strength lay in his locks; so doth the strength of sin, in one- part more than another. Every man is sensible of his darling sin, more or less; but the next thing to be looked after is what we do with it. Herod raged when John the Baptist touched his Herodias; Felix trembled when Paul touched his bribery and intemperance, but puts it off. The young man went away sad and troubled when Christ told him of selling all that he had, for he had great possessions: Mark x. Many are troubled in conscience, not so much for want of assurance, as loathness to part with some bosom lust; but when we must pluck out right eyes, and cut off right hands, Mat. v. 29, 30, it is hard to them. When you pray and strive against this sin, and grow in the contrary grace, this showeth the truth of a man's self-denial; as Abra ham's love appeared in that he did not spare Isaac.

[B.] As to evil motions. Prevent them, and suppress them.

(1.) Prevent them: 1 Peter i. 11, 'Abstain from fleshly lusts that war against your souls.' Which implies not only an abstinence from the outward act, but that you weaken the power and root of sin, that it do not so easily bud forth; those impetus primo primi are sins, not only infelicities but sins; they would not be so rife with us, if the heart were more under command. We are guilty of many sins whereunto we do consent, because we do not more strongly dissent, and more potently and rulingly command all the subject faculties, as a man is guilty of the murder of his child if he seeth his servant kill him, and (loth not his best to hinder it; but chiefly when some partial consent followeth, when the heart is tickled and delighted with them. So an. unclean glance is adultery: Mat. v. 28, 'If a man look on a woman so as to lust after her, he hath committed adultery with her already in his heart.' The more they are mortified, the heart is the less pestered with them.

(2.) Suppress them speedily. When we cannot keep sin under, let us crush it. When the mind dwelleth on it, lust is conceiving, which bringeth forth sin: James i. 15. The flesh riseth up in arms against every gracious motion; so should the spirit against every sinful motion; if you let it alone, it will break out, to God's dishonour. Dash Babylon's brats against the stones.

[C.] As to sinful actions. Prevent them as much as may be; repeat them not, lest they grow into a habit.

(1.) Prevent tliem as much as may be. It is good to stop at last, to hinder the action. When lust hath gained the consent of the will; let it not break forth into action. The very lust is a grief to the spirit, but the act will bring dishonour to God, and give ill example to men: Micah ii. 1, 'Woe to them that devise iniquity, and work evil upon their bed; when the morning is light, they practise it, because it is in the power of their hands. 'If fire be kindled in thy bosom, it is dangerous to let the sparks fly abroad.

(2.) Repeat not these acts; lest they grow into a habit and settled disposition of soul. Evil customs increase by many acts, and so the mischief is more remediless: Jer. xiii. 27, 'I have seen thy adulteries and thy neighings, the lewdness of thy whoredoms, Jerusalem! Wilt thou not be made clean? When shall it once be? 'It is a very difficult thing for a man to leave his inveterate customs; customary exercise in the use of earthly things begets worldly dispositions not easily cured. Augustine saith of his mother Monica: *Ad illud modicum quotidiana modica addenda in earn consuetudinem delapsa erat, ut plenos jam mero calices inhianter hauriebat*. Vinolency[6] crept upon her by degrees. To be gratifying carnal desires now with one thing, now with another, what doth it do, but bring us under the power of a distemper which we cannot remedy: Heb. iii. 13, 'Exhort one another daily whilst it is called to-day, .lest ye be hardened through the deceit- fulness of sin.' Yield a little to sin, and it prevaileth more, till at last you are brought under the power of it: 1 Cor. vi. 12, 'All things are lawful for me, but all things are not expedient: all things are lawful for me, but I will not be brought under the power of any thing.'

Secondly. Positively, as to the things of the spirit.

1. Mind the things of the spirit more than ever you have done. Many stick there in the very acts that properly belong to the mind, never so much as trouble themselves, or come to any reasoning within themselves, about pardon of their sins, peace with God, the sanctification of the spirit, or hopes of eternal life: Ps. x. 4, 'The wicked^ through the pride of his countenance, will not seek after God; God is not in all his thoughts.' Alas! What have you been doing since you came to the use of reason? How have you spent your time in youth or riper age? If you have never thought of God and his grace, nor regarded the offers of mercy in the gospel, certainly you have lost your time, neglected your duty, and betrayed your souls. What have^ you been doing? Have you been governed by the flesh or by the spirit? If all your care hath been about back and belly, and your thoughts have reached no higher than the riches, and honours, and pleasures, and applause, and esteem of the world, and heaven and heavenly things have been little regarded, alas! For the present you are in the highway to hell and everlasting destruction, if you do not correct your error in time, and more earnestly mind other things.

2. You must not only mind the things of the spirit, but prize and choose them for your work and happiness, for some of them belong to your duty, and some to your felicity: Luke x. 42, 'One thing is necessary, and Mary hath chosen the better part, which shall never be taken from her.' Give your hearty consent to seek after that happiness in that way. Without choice, or a determinate fixed bent of heart, you will never thoroughly engage yourselves to God. Determine not only that you must, but you will walk in the way which God hath set

---

[6] drunkenness

forth for you. All will choose happiness before misery, but they are out in the means; they do not choose the good of holiness before the pleasures of sin, nor the life of faith before the life of sense. If you have more mind to keep sin than to let it go, you are still charmed and enchanted with the delights of the flesh, your will and resolution are not fixed.

3. To this add an industrious pursuit and seeking after these things; for our choice is known by our pursuit, and our bent by our work. These things must be diligently sought after, that we may behave ourselves like men that are desirous to have what they seek: Heb. xi. 6, 'God is a rewarder of them that diligently seek him.' Everlasting joys will not drop into the mouth of the lazy soul; these things are not trifles, they will cost us diligence and seriousness: Phil, ii. 12, 'Work out your salvation with fear and trembling.' It is a weighty work, and it must be followed close; if you miscarry in it, you are undone forever; but if you happily get through it, you are in a blessed state indeed.

4. You must seek after the privileges of the gospel in God's way. You cannot have spiritual life, and adoption, and justification by Christ, till you are united to him by faith: 1 John v. 12, 'He that hath the Son, hath life; and he that hath not the Son, hath not life.' You cannot have heaven and glory, but by patient continuance in well-doing: Horn. ii. 3, 'To them that by patient continuance in well-doing seek for glory, and honour, and immortality, eternal life.' You cannot have the end, but in the use of means, and you do not like the end if you do not like the means. Till you come to God by Christ, you cannot live the life of grace; and till you live the life of grace you are not capable of glory. Therefore you must ask your souls often, What have I to show for my title to salvation more than most of the world have?

5. It is not enough that you seek after them in God's way, but you must seek after them above other things. A feeble desire cannot maintain itself against fleshly lusts and temptations. If you have a mind to these things, and a greater mind to other things, your resolution will be soon shaken, carnal things will intercept the vigour and life of your souls. These things must be sought first, and most; all must be sold for the pearl of price: Mat. xiii. 45, 46.

6. You must beg of God to give you a new mind, and a new heart, both to discern and relish spiritual things; for your old corrupt minds and hearts will never do it: 1 Cor. ii. 14, 'The natural man receiveth not the things of the Spirit of God, for they are foolishness to him; neither can he receive them, because they are spiritually discerned.' He cannot accept, nor savingly understand, these things so as to believe them with a sound belief, and a large affection. Exhortations are in vain, for inclination here doth more than persuasion; all things are of God: 2 Cor. v. 17, 18. God must give both, and therefore ask them of him.

SERMON VIII

For to be carnally minded is death; but to be spiritually minded is life and peace.

Romans viii. 6.

The apostle is giving reasons, why the comforts of justification do only belong to the sanctified. He only takes notice of two. First, the difference between the sanctified and unsanctified as to their disposition; secondly, the difference that is between them as to the event and issue. There is a contrary disposition, and a contrary end and issue: first, how they are affected, or what they rnind; secondly, what will come of it, according to God's ordination and appointment.

1. He reasoneth from the contrary disposition of the unsanctified. They, being after the flesh, do only mind and savour carnal things. They study to please the flesh, value all things by the interest of the flesh; therefore, are justly excluded from the privileges of the spiritual life; for it is not fit men should be happy against their wills, or be possessed of privileges they do not care for. God will not cast pearls before swine that trample on them, nor bestow these precious comforts where they are not valued. This argument you have, ver. 5, 'They that are after the flesh do mind the things of the flesh, and they that are after the spirit the things of the spirit.' Because they mind them not, they have them not.

2. He reasoneth from the consequent issue and event, by the ordination and appointment of God. Thus in the text, 'For to be carnally minded is death.' Death belongeth to the carnally minded, and life and peace to the spiritually minded.

In this Scripture there are two ways and two ends, both opposite and contrary to each other:

1. The two ways; the carnal minding, and the spiritual minding

2. The two ends; death and life and peace.

Doctrine That the carnal mind tendeth and bringeth a man to death, but the spiritual mind is the way to life and peace.

The text and the doctrine being a copulate axiom must be explained by parts.

First. To be carnally minded is death. I must open two things. (1.) The carnal minding; (2.) That death which is the fruit and consequent of it.

Question What is this which here we translate 'to be carnally minded,' in the margin 'the minding of the flesh,' and some translations, 'the wisdom of the flesh'?

I answer, it is the influence of the flesh upon all the faculties, understanding, will, and affections; as also upon our practice and conversation, when the wisdom of the flesh governeth our counsels, choices arid actions. It includeth the acts of the mind; there are two acts of the inind, apprehension and cogitation; in both, the flesh bewrayeth itself.

[A.] As to apprehension, we are acute in discerning the nature, worth, and value of carnal things, but stupid and blockish in things spiritual and heavenly: Luke xvi. 9, 'The children of this world are wiser in their generation than the children of light. The Greek signifies more dexterous in the course of their affairs, skillful in all things of a secular interest in back and belly concernments, but very senseless in things that are without the line of the flesh, and beyond the present world: 2 Pet. i. 9, 'He is blind, and cannot see afar off' He can see nothing of the danger of perishing for ever, or the worth of salvation, or the need of Christ to heal wounded souls, or the necessity of making serious preparation for the world to come. It is strange to consider how acute wits are stupid and senseless in these things, being blinded by the delusions of the flesh. Surely none have such a lively knowledge of spiritual things as spiritual men.

Objection But do not many carnal men understand the mysteries of godliness? Yea, sometimes more distinctly and accurately than the sanctified.

I answer, carnal men know not God, nor Christ, nor the things of the Spirit; it is a sottish people of no understanding: Isa. xxvii. 11, and generally the fear of the Lord giveth a good understanding: Ps. cxi. 10, a blunt iron that is red hot will pierce further into a board than a sharp tool that is cold. Love to God enlivens our notions of God and Christ and the world to come, and perfects them; but then it is true that carnal men may be well stocked with literal knowledge: Rom. ii. 20, 'A form of the knowledge of the law'; but they have not those piercing apprehensions and heart- warming thoughts of danger, duty, and blessedness as the spiritual hath; the lively light of the spirit leaveth a greater power and impression upon the heart than this cold knowledge doth or can do. Some carnal men may have more of the notions, words, forms, methods than the unlearned saints have; but they want the thing these were made for. They may dress the meat as cooks, but the godly feed on it, and digest it, and are most capable savingly to understand the things concerning the spiritual life.

[B.] The next act of the mind is cogitation, and so they are said to mind the things of the flesh, whose hearts are continually haunted and exercised with carnal thoughts, or thoughts about sensual, worldly, and earthly things. To make this evident, let me tell you, there are three sorts of thoughts, expressed by three distinct words in scripture.

(1.) There are discourses and reasonings. (2.) There are musings or imaginations. (3.) There are devices. All these ways doth the flesh or spirit bewray itself.

(1.) Sometimes in our discourses, debates, and reasonings. The spirit is seen in debating with ourselves about our eternal condition: Acts xvi. 14, 'She attended to the things that were spoken,' that is, weighed them in her mind; and Luke ii. 19, 'Mary pondered them in her heart,' compared thought with thought: Rom. viii. 31. What shall we say to these things? Now the fleshly minding is seen partly in jostling out these thoughts, and opposing these discourses of the mind, that we have no profit by them; and partly by filling and stuffing the mind with carnal thoughts and discourses, that there is no room for better things: 2 Pet. ii. 14, 'A heart they have exercised with covetous practices' Their hearts are always busied with low, carnal, and base thoughts; therefore it is said. 'The heart of the wicked is nothing worth:' Prov. x. 20. All the debates and discourses of their minds are of no value, and tend to no serious and profitable use.

(2.) Musings, admiring their excellency and. blessing, and applauding themselves in what they have, and hope for in the world: Dan. iv. 30, 'Is not this great Babel that I have built for the house of the kingdom, by the might of my power, and for the honour of my majesty? 'and Ps. cxliv. 15, 'Happy is the people that is in such a case' This self- blessing is a sign of carnal minding; they never set their minds a work upon spiritual and heavenly things. Surely one that belie veth heaven, and looketh for heaven, and longeth for heaven, will be thinking of it Shall an ambitious man find such a savour in thoughts of preferment? a covetous man in the thoughts of wealth and riches? a vain-glorious man in the echoes and supposition of applause? the voluptuous man in reveling and eating and drinking, so that his heart is always in the house of mirth? the unclean person in personating the pleasure of sin by imaginations Mat. v. 28? an envious man in thoughts of revenge? and shall not a spiritual disposition discover itself in our musings? Faith and hope will send the thoughts, as spies, into the land of promise: Heb. xi. 1. Love will be thinking on the object loved. The treasures will take up the mind and heart: Mat. vi. 21. Can a man love God, and Christ, and never think of them? Our pleasant musings should be regarded. A third sort of thoughts are

(3.) Counsels, and contrivances or devices: Rom. xiii. 14, 'Make no provision for the flesh, to fulfil the lusts thereof.' They wholly bend their minds how to compass their worldly ends, and how to advance themselves in the world, carking and caring for these things, but 'God is not in all their thoughts': Ps. x. 4; care not whether God be pleased or displeased, honoured and glorified or dishonoured, nor how to come to enjoy him and carry on the spiritual life with more success, and assure their interest in eternal happiness. The spiritual life is not a thing of hap-hazard and peradventure, but to be carried on with contrivance and needfulness': ponder the path of thy feet': Prov. iv. 26. Now men employ their time and wit upon other projects than how to mortify sin, or 'perfect holiness in the fear of God.' Thus thoughts being the first issues of the mind discover the temper of it. Those that are after the flesh are thorough and true to their principle, they can freely employ their minds about things which are agreeable to their constitution of soul, and can hardly take them off for any serious and grave purpose; they do most readily and delightfully entertain these thoughts, mind the world's weeks, years, days, but never find leisure or time to mind life to come. They never shut the door against vain thoughts; but thoughts of God, Christ, and heaven and hell, sin and holiness, what strangers are they? and when they rush in upon us are thrust forth as unwelcome guests. Anything relating to the flesh is pleasing and welcome, but how to get our hearts washed and cleansed by the blood or Spirit of Christ, is not regarded by them; how to be more holy, to be at peace with God, to keep that peace unbroken by an uniform course of obedience, this is not thought of, nor discoursed of, in the mind, nor the happiness mused on, nor our care and contrivance employed about it.

2. The word also compriseth the will and affections, desires, purposes, choices. What we now read 'mind' is in other translations 'savour,' the Vulgar reads *sapiunt*; Erasmus reads *curant*; Valla *sentiunt*, have a sense or gust; so in these things, we translate it savour: Mat. xvi. S3, 'Thou savourest not the things that be of God'. We translate it elsewhere: Col. iii. 2, 'Set your affections upon things above, and not on things on earth.' But the word as it standeth in our translation will bear it; for when men say they have a mind to it: Neh. iv. 6, 'We built the wall, for the people had a mind to the work' So here it is true of the carnal minding, and the spiritual minding. The relish and taste, which are in the will and affections, floweth from the apprehension of the mind; we relish and delight in objects suitable to that nature which we have; as the constitution is, so are the gust and taste. Tell a carnal person of the joys of the life to come, the comforts of the spirit, the peace of a good conscience, the sweetness that is in the word and ordinances, they find no more savour in these things than

in the white of an egg, or a dry chip; but banquets, merry meetings, and idle sports, they have a complacency for these things, and soon find a. delight free and stirring at the mention of them': their hearts are in the house of mirth 'Eccles. vii. 4. To be well clad, and well fed, maintained in pomp and state, these are the things which are most sweet and pleasing to them, and which they most desire and seek after, for they mind these things, and so bestow their care and delight upon them, and can spend days and hours without weariness in them. Carnal men relish no sweetness in religion: 1 Cor. ii. 14, 'But the natural man receiveth not the things of the spirit of God, for they are foolishness unto him; neither can he know them, because they are spiritually discerned.' As they do not perceive them, so not receive them: these are not the things which are likely to make an impression upon their souls; but, on the contrary, the spiritual minding is discovered by this, because it is best pleased with spiritual things; spiritual minds find a marvellous sweetness and comfort in the word of God, and the means of grace and salvation: Ps. cxix. 103, 'How sweet are thy words to my taste, yea, sweeter than honey to my mouth'; and Ps. lxiii. 5, 'My soul shall be satisfied, as with marrow and fatness;' and Job xxiii. 12, 'I have esteemed the words of his mouth more than my necessary food.' What gladness doth communion with God put into their hearts! One day with him is better than all those flesh- pleasing vanities, wherewith others are deluded and enticed from God. 3. It reacheth also to practice, and implieth earnest prosecution. And so, to be carnally minded, is to make the things of the flesh our work and scope; to be spiritually minded is to make that our work and trade, to seek after the things of the spirit; therefore the course of men's actions, and the trade of their lives are to be considered. Our business showeth our bent; and what we constantly, frequently, and easily practise, discovereth the overruling principle. Wicked men have their good moods, and godly men have their carnal fits, the con stant practice showeth the prevailing inclination. To mind the things of the flesh or spirit is to seek after them in the first place, when men are seriously, constantly, readily, willingly carried to those things which please the flesh, without any respect to God and eternal life. Effects show their causes. If the drift and bent of our lives be not for God and salvation, and our great business in the world be not the pleasing of God and the saving of our own souls, and this be not chiefly minded and attended more than all the pleasures, honours, and profits of the world, God hath not the precedency, but the flesh walking after the flesh or the spirit, is the great discriminating note in this place; pro pounded, ver. 1. amplified afterwards by minding the things of the flesh, and then living after the flesh, ver. 13; so Gal. vi. 8, 'He that soweth to the flesh, shall of the flesh reap corruption: but he that soweth to the spirit, shall of the spirit reap life everlasting.' We must see whether our lives be a sowing to the flesh or the spirit. The mind leaveth a stamp upon the actions. As a godly man showeth spirit in all things, so a carnal man showeth flesh in all things: Zech. xiv. 21, 'On every pot in Jerusalem, and in Judah, shall be Holiness to the Lord of hosts' As God showeth his divine power in every creature, in a gnat, or pile of grass, as well as the sun; so a Christian showeth grace in all things. On the contrary, carnal men show their mind in all things, not only in eating and drinking and trading, but in preach ing, praying, and conference about holy things. The one goeth about his worldly business with a heavenly mind, casts all into the mould of religion; the other goeth about his heavenly business with a carnal and worldly mind; the flesh doth not only influence his common actions, but his duties, either to feed or hide a lust, to serve his worldly mind and vain glory; or else that he may more plausibly carry it on without blame before men, or check of conscience; and so maketh one duty excuse another. It is the flesh maketh him pray, preach, confer about holy things, give alms, and seemingly forgive enemies, or do that which is outwardly and materially just.

Thus you see what is the carnal minding; only I must tell you, that, because the apostle saith it is death, or the high way to everlasting destruction, we must more accurately state the matter.

1. The minding of the flesh must be interpreted not barely of the acts but the state. Who is there among God's children that doth not mind the flesh? and too much indulge the flesh? But yet he doth not make it his business to please the flesh, but rather mortifieth and subdueth it: Gal. v. 24, 'And they that are Christ's have crucified the flesh' and they are still labouring that they may subdue it more and more: 1 Cor. ix. 27, 'But I keep under my body, and bring it into subjection.'

2. This minding of the flesh or spirit must be understood as to the prevalency of each principle; that is to say, when we mind the flesh so as to exclude the minding of the spirit, and the things that belong to the spirit: 1 John ii. 15,' If any man love the world, and the things of the world, the love of the Father is not in him.' And so on the other side, when we so mind the spirit, as that it deadeneth our affections to the world and baits of the flesh: Gal. vi. 14, the 'conversation in. heaven 'is that which is opposite to 'minding earthly things': Phil, iii. 19, 20. Therefore if the flesh can do more, constantly and ordinarily, to draw us to sin than the spirit to keep us from it, we are under the power of the fleshly mind.

3. This minding of the flesh must be interpreted with respect to continuance, not with respect to our former state; for, alas! All of us in time past pleased the flesh, and walked according to the course of this world in the lusts of the flesh: Tit. iii. 3, 'We were sometimes foolish and dis obedient, serving divers lusts and pleasures'; and 'if we yet please the flesh, we are riot the servants of Christ' But if we break off this servitude, and do at length become servants of righteousness, God will not judge us according to what we have been but what we are. Therefore it is our duty to consider what principle liveth in us, and groweth, and increaseth; whether the interest of the flesh decreaseth or the interest of the spirit. If we grow more brutish, forgetful of God, unapt for spiritual things, the flesh governeth; but if the spiritual life doth more and more discover itself with life and power in our thoughts, words, and actions, the flesh is on the wane, and we shall not be reckoned to have lived after the flesh, but after the spirit; we have every day a higher estimation of God and Christ, and grace weaneth and draweth off the heart from other things, that we may grow more dead to them, and live to God in the spirit, and more entirely pursue our everlasting hopes.

4. Some things more immediately tend to the pleasing of the flesh, as bodily pleasures; and therefore the inclinations to them are called the 'lusts of the flesh': 1 John ii. 16. Other things more remotely, as they lay in provisions for that end, as the honours and profits of the world. Now, though a man be not voluptuous, he may be guilty of the carnal minding,

because he is wholly sunk and lost in the world, and is thereby taken off from a care of and delight in better things. Envyings, emulations, strife, and divisions make us carnal: 1 Cor. iii. 3, 'For ye are yet carnal: whereas there is among you envyings, strife, and divisions, are ye not carnal, and walk as men?' They have little of the spirit in them that bustle for greatness and esteem in the world, though they be not wholly given to brutish pleasures; and those that will be rich are said to 'fall into foolish and hurtful lusts, which drown the soul in perdition and destruction': 1 Tim. vi. 9. These are taken off from God and Christ and the world to come, and therefore the fleshly minding must be applied to anything that will make us less spiritual and heavenly: Luke xii. 21, 'So is he that layeth up treasure for himself, and is not rich towards God.' They seek outward things in good earnest, but spiritual things in an overly, careless, or perfunctory manner.

5. Some please the flesh in a more cleanly manner, others in a more gross: Gal.v. 19, 'The works of the flesh are manifest: adultery, fornication, uncleanness, lasciviousness, idolatry, witchcraft.' These are the grosser out-breakings of the flesh; now, though we fall not into these, yet there is a more secret carnal minding, when we have too free a relish in any outward thing, and set loose the heart to such alluring vanities as draw us off from God and Christ and heaven; and these obstruct the heavenly life, as well as the other; therefore, still all must be subordinated to our great interest; some are disengaged from baser lusts, but are full of self-love and self- seeking. I proceed to the second thing

Secondly. What is that death which is the consequence of it? Death signifieth three things in Scripture death temporal, spiritual, and eternal. The first consisteth in. the separation of the soul from the body; the second in the separation of the soul from God; the third in an eternal separation of both body and soul from God,' in a state of endless misery.

1. Death is a separation of the soul from the body, with all its antecedent preparations; as diseases, pains, miseries, dangers, these are death begun': in deaths often, '2 Cor. xi. 13, that is, in dangers; that he may take from me this death, Exod. x. 7, meaning the plague of the locusts; and death is consummated at our dissolution, 1 Cor. xv. 55. Now all this is the fruit of sin, and they forfeit their lives that only use them for the flesh; they are unserviceable to God, and therefore why should they live in the world?

2. Spiritual death, or an estrangement from God, as the author of the life of grace; so we are said to be 'dead in trespasses and sins', Eph. ii. 1; and so it may hold good here: 1 Tim. v. 6, 'She that liveth in pleasure, is dead while she liveth.' That is, hath no feeling of the life of grace. But

3. Eternal death, which consisteth in an everlasting separation from the presence of the Lord, called the second death: Rev. xx. 6, 'On such the second death hath no power'; and v. 14, 'death and hell were cast into the lake of fire, this is the second death.' This is most horrible and dreadful, and is the portion of all those that are slaves to the flesh. Now this is called death, because, in all creatures that have sense, their dissolution is accompanied with pain. Trees and vegetables die without pain, and so doth not man and beast; and death to men is more bitter, because they are more sensible of the sweetness of life than beasts are, and have some forethought of what may follow after; and because it is a misery from which

there is no release; as from the first death, there is no recovery into the present life. This second death is set forth by two solemn notions': The worm that never dieth, and the fire that shall never be quenched': Mat. ix. 44; by which is meant the sting of conscience, and the wrath of God. Both these make the sinner forever miserable; the sting of conscience, or the fretting remembrance of their past folly, when they reflect upon their madness in following the pleasures of sin, and neglecting the offers of grace; and besides this, there are pains inflicted upon them by the wrath of God. There is no member or faculty of the soul free but feeleth the misery of the second death.

As no part is free from sin, so none shall be from punishment; in the first death, the pain may lie in one place, head or heart, but here all over; the agonies of the first death are soon over, but the agonies and pains of the second death endure forever. The first death, the more it prevaileth, the more we are past feeling; but by this second death there is a greater vivacity than ever, the capacity of every sense is enlarged and made more receptive of pain, while we are in the body. *Veliemens sensibile corrumpit sensum* the more vehemently anything doth strike on the senses the more doth it deaden the sense; as the inhabitants about the fall of Nilus are deaf with the continual noise, and too much light puts out the eyes, and taste is dulled by custom; but here the capacity is improved by feeling the power of God sustaining the sinner whilst his wrath torments him. As the saints are fortified by their blessedness, and can endure that light and glory, the least glimpse of which would overwhelm them here, so the wicked are capacitated to endure the torments. In the first death, our praying is for life, we would not die; there, our wish shall be for destruction, we would not live. Every man would lose a tooth rather than be perpetually tormented with the tooth-ache; these pains never cease; this death is the fruit of the carnal life.

Secondly. To be spiritually minded is life and peace. Here all will be easily and soon despatched.

1. What is it to be spiritually-minded? I answer, when we know the things of the spirit, so as to believe them, and believe them so as to affect and esteem them; and esteem and affect them, so as to seek after them; and so seek after them, as to seek after them in the first place. (1.) We must know them; for the things of the spirit must be understood before they can be chosen and desired: John iv. 10, 'If thou knewest the gift.' The brutish world know not the worth of spiritual and heavenly things, therefore mind them not. (2.) Believe them. None will seek after that which they judge to be a fancy, or of the certainty of which they are not persuaded, especially when they must forego present delights and contentments to obtain it: such is salvation by Christ: 2 Pet. i. 5, 10, 16, 'And besides this, giving all diligence to add to your faith virtue, and to virtue knowledge: wherefore the rather, brethren, give all diligence to make your calling and election sure.' (3.) Affect and esteem them above all other things: Heb. xi. 13, 'Being persuaded of these things, they embraced them; so esteem them, that your desires may not be checked and controlled by other things: Heb. xi. 26, 'By faith, Moses, when he was come to years, refused to be called the son of Pharaoh's daughter.' (4.) To pursue after them with all diligence: Phil. ii. 10, 'Working out yoursalva tion with fear and trembling;' and John vi. 27, 'Labour not for the meat that perisheth, but

that which endureth to everlasting life.' (5.) Seek them in the first place, that you may not only make it your busi ness, but the chiefest business of your lives to obtain these things: Mat. vi. 33, 'First seek the kingdom of God.' This is to set your faces heavenward, when you make it your great business to please God, and save your souls.

2. This is life and peace. By life and peace are meant eternal blessedness. He addeth to the word life the term peace, because in eternal life there is freedom from all evil, and the presence of all good; for there can be no true solid peace where there is the fear of any evil, or a want of any good; but here being neither, the soul is fully at peace and rest; therefore it is said that God 'will give glory, honour, and peace to everyone that doeth good:' Horn. ii. 10. Heaven is the new Jerusalem, the city of peace, where we converse with God, who is a God of peace, and enjoy full peace and rest from all our molestations; but though it be meant of heaven, yet peace of conscience is not excluded, partly because it is the beginning and earnest of it, that peace which we now have in the kingdom of the Messiah by our recon ciliation with God: Rom. v. 1, 'Being justified by faith, we have peace with God and the testimony of a good conscience;' 2 Cor. i. 20, 'This is a continual feast.' Now the fruit of righteousness is peace; peace in heaven, and peace on earth: Luke ii. 14, and Luke xix. 38, 'Blessed be the king that cometh in the name of the Lord'; Peace in heaven, and glory in the highest.' It is begun here, and perfected there. And partly because whatever the spirit worketh tendeth to our peace and blessedness, not only hereafter, but now: Rom. xv. 13, 'Now the God of hope fill you with all joy and peace in believing.' The reasons are in common.

1. With respect to God's justice. God, who is the most righteous governor of the world, will make a just difference between the righteous and the wicked by rewards and punishment. It belongeth to his general justice *ut bonis bene sit, et mals male* that it should be well with them that do well, and ill with them that do ill: Ps. xi. 5, 6, 'Upon the wicked he shall rain snares, fire, and brimstone, and an horrible tempest shall be the portion of their cup: for the righteous God loveth righteousness, his countenance beholdeth the upright. Surely God is not indifferent to good and evil, to them that will please the flesh, and them that obey the spirit. His justice will not permit that the carnal and the regenerate, who are so different in their lives, should meet together in the end. No, surely; the end of the one will be death, and the other life and peace.

2. To suit his motives to the profit of men

[A.] There needeth something frightful to make sin a terror to us; therefore doth he counterbalance with advantage the pleasures of sin, that are but for a season. We are vehemently addicted to carnal delights; therefore to check this inclination, God balanceth the choicest and highest pleasures with eternal pain, that by setting one against the other we may be deterred from pleasing the flesh: Rom. viii. 13, 'If ye live after the flesh, ye shall die.'

[B.] To encourage the godly in their self-denying obedience. The godly quit and forego many pleasures which others enjoy. Now, to restrain and deny the flesh seemeth a pain and trouble; therefore to encourage them to continue in a holy course, though it be distasteful to the flesh, and to renounce worldly pleasures and sensual delights while they may enjoy them, God hath told them of life and peace; they shall have joy enough.

Use 1 is Information, to show us the folly of wicked men, who are self-destroyers, and wrong their own souls, while they despise the ways of wisdom, and prefer carnal satisfactions before the pleasing of God': All that hate me, love death,' Prov. viii. 36. Not formally, but con sequentially; a wicked man sinneth not purposely that he may be damned, but that is the issue.

2. It showeth us the security of the wicked. They sleep most soundly when their danger is nighest, as Jonah in the storm that was raised for his sake; they are upon the brink of hell, yet they go on merrily, lulling their consciences asleep with outward and vain delights; but though they sleep, 'their damnation sleepeth not.' It were better to waken and escape the danger: Prov. xxvii. 12, 'A prudent man foreseeth the evil, and hideth himself; but the simple pass on, and are punished.' A little sober consideration of this truth may be of use to them.

Use 2 is Admonition. Oh! let this stop us from going on in a flesh- pleasing course. Consider whither it will lead you; what followeth upon this:

1. It is death. If it were a small thing, you might bear it; but it is a case of life and death eternal life and death. This will be the eternal ruin of your precious and immortal souls. The more you please the flesh, the more you add fuel to that fire which shall never be quenched; and provide matter for that never-dying worm, or eternal sorrow and confusion of face to your souls. Those things that now please the senses, will one day sting the conscience. We should not affect that which will be death to us. Remember the hook, when the flesh looketh only to the bait.

2. It is death threatened in the word of God, and therefore certain, as well as dreadful: Rom. vi. 23, 'The wages of sin is death'; and Rom. vii. 5, 'The motions of sin did bring forth fruit unto death.' If a man warn you of apparent death in a way wherein you are going, you will be cautious. Surely God deserveth more credit than man. He giveth you warning of the danger of this way; and will you go on, and try what will come of it? Surely men do not believe the carnal life will be so mortal and deadly to them as it will be. The false prophet in every man's bosom deceiveth him, that it may destroy him.

3. Consider how willing God is to reclaim you: Ezek. xxxiii. 11, 'Why will you die, house of Israel? 'Hath God any pleasure in your destruction? He delighteth in your conversion rather, and threateneth death, that he may not inflict it.

Use 3. Let us examine what is our frame and temper the carnal minding or the spiritual minding. This is the great test, or the true and lasting difference between men and men, in life and death. The great difference and division is begun here, and continued forever. Other differences cease at the grave's mouth, but this distinguisheth between heaven and hell.

1. What do you seek after, the gratifying of the flesh, or the perfectives of the soul? that the inner man may be renewed and quickened: 2 Cor. iv. 16'; That it be strengthened: Eph. iii. 16, decked and adorned: 1 Pet. iv. 3, to keep grace alive in your souls that is our care, our business, and our comfort.

2. To what end do you live? That you may please, glorify, and enjoy God, or live after the flesh? You were made by God, and for God, that you might have fellowship and communion with him here and hereafter: Ps. lxxiii. 25, 'Whom have I in heaven but thee? and there is none upon earth I desire in comparison of thee' This God's people long for, and labour after, and wait for.

3. In what mariner do we mind it? Is this our constant care, and earnest desire, and choice delight? A naked approbation of that which is good will make no evidence; nor a few cold wishes, or faint endeavours; but your constant business: 2 Cor. v. 9, 'Wherefore we labour, that whether present or absent, we may be accepted of him.'

SERMON IX

Because the carnal mind is enmity to God; for it is not subject to the law of God, nor indeed can be.

Romans viii. 7.

IN the words a reason is given, why the carnal minding will be deadly to us, because it is enmity to God. God surely will be avenged on all his enemies: those that are enemies to God will shortly be dealt with as enemies.

Therefore to be carnally minded is death, because the carnal mind is enmity to God, &c.

In the words here is

1. A proposition.

2. A reason; First. From the contumacy of the carnal mind; Secondly. From its impotency to overcome it: it is a weak wilfulness, or a wilful weakness.

First. The proposition. And there is to be considered the subject, the carnal mind. The predicate is enmity to God.

1. The subject, or thing spoken of: the carnal mind, or the minding of the flesh, or the wisdom of the flesh. But that hath in a great measure been shown before; therefore

[A.] By the carnal mind is meant the rational powers, corrupted by our sensitive appetite, and disposed to obey it; or a mind deceived by the flesh, and enslaved by it; called elsewhere 'a fleshly mind' Col. ii. 18.

[B.] It is here considered in its prevalency and reign, as it depresseth the mind from rising up to divine and spiritual things, and wholly bindeth it, and causeth it to adhere to things terrene and earthly, such as gratify sense, and conduce to please the flesh. The wisdom of the flesh is described: James iii. 15, 'The wisdom that descendeth not from above is earthly, sensual, devilish': and 1 John ii. 16'; All that is in the world is the lust of the flesh, the lust of the eyes, and the pride of life.'

2. The predicate. It is enmity to God. It is more emphatical; an enemy may be reconciled, but enmity cannot. That which is black may be made white, but blackness cannot. This emphatical expression is to set forth the perfect contrariety that is in our desires, affections, inclinations, and actions, to the will of God. We love what he hateth, and hate what he loveth. It is not only an enemy, but enmity.

Doctrine That the wisdom of the flesh is downright opposition and enmity to God.

To evidence this, take these considerations:

1. It is possible that human nature may be so far forsaken as that among men there should be found haters of God and enemies to him. We bless ourselves from so great an evil; and men scarce believe that there are such profligate and forlorn wretches in the world as to profess themselves to be enemies to God, who is so good and the fountain of all goodness; and, for our own part, are ready to defy those that charge it upon us. But the matter is clear. The Scriptures show expressly, that there are 'haters of God', Rom. i. 30; and Ps. cxxxix. 21,

'Do not I hate them, Lord, that hate thee?' and Ps. xiii. 2, 'They that hate thee, are risen up against us without a cause.' And we need not go among the pagans and infidels to seek or find out them that are haters of God; there is an opposite party to God nearer at hand; and they are all those that walk contrary to him: Col. i. 21, 'Enemies in your minds by evil works'; and Ps. lxviii. 21, 'He will wound the head of his enemies, and the hairy scalp of such as go on still in their trespasses.' Now many such live within the verge of the church, and are not to be sought among Turks and infidels only.

2. That hatred and enmity to God may be determined by three things: (1.) If we love not God at all; (2.) If we love him not as much as we ought to do; (3.) If we rebel against him and disobey his laws.

(1.) If we love not God at all; for not to love, is to hate, in things worthy to be beloved. Surely, in divine matters, there is no medium: lie that is not with God, is against him: Mat. xii. 30; and he that loveth him not, hateth him. To be a neuter, is to be a rebel, because God doth so much deserve our love, and we are so much obliged to him, and depend upon him. So it is said, Prov. viii. 36, 'All that hate me, love death: he that sinneth against me, wrongeth his own soul' They that do not seek after wisdom, hate it; they care not for God, whether he be pleased or displeased. You speak all manner of misery to that man of whom you may say, that he loveth not God. So Christ brandeth his enemies': I know that you have not the love of God in you' John v. 42. Men are in a woeful case, if void of the love of God. Love being the fountain of desiring all communion with him, and the root of all obedience to him; therefore, if men, blinded by the delusions of the flesh, or diverted by the world, love not God, being so deeply engaged to God, and God so deserving their love, they are enemies to him: 1 John ii. 15, 'If any man love the world, the love of the Father is not in him': 1 Cor. xvi. 22, 'If any man love not the Lord Jesus Christ, let him be Anathema Maranatha' It is danger enough not to love him, though we break not out in open opposition against his ways.

(2.) If we love him not so much as we ought to do, or not so much as we love some other thing. For, in the sacred dialect, a lesser love is hatred; as, for instance, in the notion of the law of the hated wife: Deut. xxi. 15, 16, 'If a man have two wives, one beloved and another hated, and they have born him children, both the beloved and the hated,' etc. Not that she was not loved at all, or absolutely hated; but she that was not loved as much as the other, is called the hated wife. So in that proverb, Prov. xiv. 20, 'The poor is even hated of his own neighbour; but the rich hath many friends' There, hatred is taken for slighting, or a lesser degree of love. So in this case between us and God: Mat. x. 37, 'He that loveth father or mother more than me, is not worthy of me' But in Luke xiv. 26, it is, 'If any man hate not father and mother, and brothers and sisters; yea, and his own life, he cannot be my disciple' There, the lower and lesser love is called hatred. For Christ's religion teacheth us, not to be unnatural; but in comparison of Christ, we should hate them, trample upon the comforts and benefits which result from such relations, if they be snares to us: so Mat. vi. 24, 'No man can serve two masters, for either he will hate the one and love the other, or hold to the one and despise the other. Ye cannot serve God and Mammon.' God is of that excellent nature, that to esteem anything above him, or equal with him, is to hate him.

Now, because men love the world, and the things of the world over much, yea, more than God, they hate him are enemies to him. All carnal men are guilty of this, as they are lovers of pleasure more than lovers of God. This over-love of sensual satisfactions, or terrene and earthly things, is the highest contempt and affront that can be put upon God, in comparison of our love to him. All the pleasures and contentments of the world should be hated rather than loved. So far as our hearts are set upon those things, which the flesh savoureth and delighteth in, so far are they estranged from God; and then you will neglect him, or easily part with him for the world's sake. If a father should come to his child, and say, 'If you love such vain and enticing company, I shall take you for mine enemy, you must either hate me or them,' would not an ingenuous child refrain his haunts, rather than forfeit his father's love? This is the case between us and God': Love not the world,' saith he, 'nor the things of the world; if you love the world, you do not love me.' Therefore for us only to savour and relish these things is flat enmity to God.

(3.) We are said to hate God, and be enemies to him, if we rebel against him and disobey his laws. God's love to us is a love of bounty, and our love to him is a love of duty, shown rather by obedience than a fellow-like familiarity. Here in the text, our respects to God are interpreted and judged of by our respects to his law. By this, God measureth our love and hatred to himself. It is enmity to God, 'because it is not subject to the law of God.' So, elsewhere, love is determined by obedience: 1 John v. 3, 'For this is the love of God, that we keep his commandments'; and John xiv. 21, 'He that hath my commandments, and keepeth them, he it is that loveth me.' On the other side, hatred is expressed by disobedience: Deut. v. 9, 'On them that hate me, and keep not my commandments.' All sin is a hatred of God; actual sin is *odium Dei actuale*, and habitual sin is *odium Dei habituale*. It is *finis operis*, if not *operantis*. We think not so, but the Scripture judgeth so; and it appears from reason. We apprehend God standeth in the way of our desires; and because we cannot enjoy our lusts with that freedom and security, as we might otherwise were it not for his law, therefore we hate God. He commandeth that which we cannot, and will not do, being enticed and inveigled by the flesh.

3. There is a twofold hatred: *odium abominationis* and *odium inimicitiae* the hatred of abomination, and dislike, and the hatred of enmity. The one is opposite to the love of good will, the other to the love of complacency: Prov. xxix. 27, 'The wicked are an abomination to the righteous.' Surely a righteous man hateth not his neighbour with the hatred of enmity, to seek his destruction; but with the hatred of offence, so as not to delight in him while he is wicked, in opposition to the love of complacency. We may hate our sinful neighbour, as we must first hate ourselves, and loathe ourselves, because of our sins: but in opposition to the love of benevolence we must neither hate our neighbour, nor our enemy, nor ourselves.

[A.] Apply this distinction to the case between God and us, it will be hard to excuse any carnal man from either hatred; certainly not from the hatred of offence or abomination, there being such an unsuitableness and dissimilitude between God and them in pure nature.

We were created after his image, and then we delighted in him; but when we lost our first nature, we left our first love; for love is grounded upon likeness, or willing and nilling the same things. But, alas! Now we love what he hateth, and hate what he loveth; and therefore, because of this dissimilitude, there is a hatred. How can we delight in a holy God, and a God of pure eyes delight in such sensual polluted creatures? What can carnal men see lovely in God, or God in them? See Zech. xi. 8, 'My soul loatheth them, and their soul abhorreth me' Therefore from this hatred of loathing, offence, and abomination, none can excuse themselves; till they come to hate what God hateth, and to love what God loveth, there is, and will be, the hatred of offence: Prov. viii. 13, 'The fear of the Lord is to hate evil;

[B.] For the other branch. The hatred of enmity, is that which implieth all endeavours of mischief, and seeketh the destruction of the thing hated. We cannot excuse the carnal man from this either; for there is a secret positive enmity in them against the being of God; and this is the effect of slavish fear. We hate God under a double notion, as a lawgiver, thwarting our lusts by his precepts; and as an avenger, punishing our disorders. This latter we are upon. Slavish fear apprehendeth God as an avenger of sin, or as a condemning God. Men hate those whom they fear. The Roman historian observeth it: *proprium est humani ingenii odisse quos laeserit*. Why? Because we fear their revenge. We have wronged God exceedingly, and know that he will call us to an account; and, therefore, being sensible of the righteousness of his vindictive justice, we hate him. All that are afraid of God, with such a fear as hath torment in it, *aut extinctum Deum cupiunt aut exanimatum*, it is a pleasing thought to them if there were no God: Ps. xiv. 1, 'The fool hath said in his heart there is no God.' As the devils tremble at their own thoughts of God so do wicked men. It were welcome news to them to hear there were no God.

4. God's enemies carry on a double war against him, offensive and defensive. The offensive war is when men break his laws; employ all their faculties, mercies, comforts, as weapons of unrighteousness against God: Rom. vi. 13, 'Yield not your members as instruments of unrighteousness to sin; but yield yourselves to God. Our faculties, talents, and interests are employed either as armour of light for God, or as weapons of unrighteousness against God. The defensive war is when we slight his word, despise his grace, resist the motions of his Spirit: Acts vii. 51, 'Ye stiff-necked and uncircumcised in heart and ear, ye do always resist the Holy Ghost' When God bringeth his spiritual artillery to batter down all that which lifteth up itself against the obedience of Christ, 2 Cor. x. 4, 5. When he besiegeth our hearts, and battereth them daily by the rebukes and motions of his Spirit, yet men will not yield the fortress, but stand it out to the last; take delight to go on in the obedience of their natural corruptions; will not have Christ to reign over them; and so they increase their enmity, and double their misery, by a resistance of grace, and are rebels, not only against the law, but the gospel, stand out against their own mercies. They are enemies to an earthly prince, that not only infest his country with continual inroads and incursions, but those also that keep his towns and strongholds against him. And in this sense an impenitent person, and an enemy to God, are equivalent expressions in scripture. Though you do not break out into

open acts of hostility against God, yet if you will not come out of your bondage, and come out of the misery and folly of your carnal estate, you are enemies to him.

5. That herein the enemies of our salvation agree, that they all make us rebels to God. The devil, world and flesh, are equal in this. The devil's servants and subjects are opposite to Christ's kingdom: Eph. vi. 12, 'Rulers of the darkness of this world'; and Col. i. 13, 'Who hath translated us out of the kingdom of darkness, into the kingdom of his dear Son' While we remain in the one kingdom we are enemies to the other: Luke xix. 27, 'But for those, mine enemies, that would not that I should reign over them, bring them hither, and slay them before me. The world: James iv. 4, 'Know ye not that the friendship of the world is enmity with God? whosoever therefore will be a friend to the world, is an enemy to God.' They whose hearts are set upon the pleasures, profits, and honours of the world, they are withdrawn from God, as their proper Lord, and chief hap piness, and will neither be ruled by his will, nor seek his love and favour. First, They will not be ruled by His will; for God and the world command contrary things. The world saith, slack no opportunity of gain; to stand nicely upon conscience is to draw trouble upon ourselves; that to give is wasteful profuseness; and to forgive, folly and weakness. God, on the contrary, biddeth us deny ourselves take up our cross; telleth us, that giving is receiving, and the glory of a man is to pass by an offence, or to forgive the wrongs done to him. So the flesh: as the world tempts us to rebellion against God, so the flesh swalloweth the temptation; it carrieth us to do what we list, and disposeth us to a flat rebellion against God, and a contempt of his authority: 2 Sam. xii. 9, 'Wherefore hast thou sinned, and despised the commandments of God? 'The flesh will have it so: Ps. ii. 3, 'Let us break his bands, and cast away his cords from us.' Affectation of carnal liberty is the very effect of sense-pleasing and flesh-pleasing; so that the carnal mind implieth a downright opposition to the law of God: all our ways are enmity to it, and a direct repugnancy against it. Secondly, Nor do we seek his love and favour as our happiness. The world propoundeth objects that are pleasant to our senses, necessary in part for our uses, in subordination to other things; and so enticeth us from God. But it could not entice us, were it not for the flesh, which greedily swalloweth the bait: 2 Tim. iv. 10, 'Demas hath forsaken us, and embraced the present world'; and 2 Tim. iii. 4, 'Lovers of pleasure more than lovers of God'; and John v. 44, 'How can you believe that receive honour one of another? 'And so we are detained from God by the creature, which should be a step and stair that should lead us up to him. The world is full of allurements to the flesh; and those mercies which would raise the mind to God are made the fuel of sensuality, and the greatest means to keep it from him. None neglect him so much as those that have most of the world: Jer. ii. 31, 'O generation! See ye the word of the Lord; have I been a wilderness to Israel a land of darkness? wherefore say my people we are lords, we will come no more at thee?' So Mark x. 24, 'How hard is it for them that trust in riches to enter into the kingdom of God': they are most apt to live an ungodly sensual life, as having less occasion than others to drive them to God.

6. This enmity arising from the flesh, is the more strengthened and increased the more it gaineth the mind and corrupts the mind; for two reasons:

[A.] Then the leading part of the soul, which should guide and command the rest, is corrupted also. There is in the upper part of the soul a directive and imperial power to fit him to obey God. Now it is blinded as to the directive power, and weakened as to its imperial and commanding power; all must needs fall into disorder, and man will live a rebel to the law of his creation, and so be an enemy to God.

(1.) As to the leading and directing part of the soul, that is the understanding, there is a great blindness come upon us by the lust of the flesh, so that we have neither a due sense of our happiness, nor our duty. Not of our happiness, for till the eyes of our minds are opened by the Spirit, we have no real persuasion of the world to come: Eph. i. 18, 'The eyes of your understanding being enlightened, that ye may know what is the hope of his calling, and the riches of the glory of the inheritance of the saints in light': and 2 Pet. i. 9, 'He that lacketh these things is blind, and cannot see afar off.' Nor of our duty; for though some moralities be evident to corrupt nature: Rom. ii. 14, yet for a full resignation, obedience, and love to God, nature owneth little of it, and depraved reason is blind, or sleepy, so that we may have no clear, deep sense of our duty impressed upon our hearts, so as that conscience (which is applicative reason) should warn us of sin, or mind us of our duty upon all necessary occasions.

(2.) The commanding power is weakened. For our senses are so masterly, inordinate, and eagerly set upon the objects, that we yield ourselves to the conduct of them, how unreasonable soever the acts are: Tit. iii. 3, 'For we ourselves were sometimes foolish and disobedient, serving divers lusts and pleasures, living in malice and envy, hateful, and hating one another.' We give way to that which is evil, and oppose that which is good, even against the urgings of conscience': The law of our members warreth against the law of our minds': Rom. vi. 22; and it is a trouble to the flesh to be restrained from what it desireth, as an headstrong horse is loath to be curbed.

[B.] Because, as the leading part of the soul cannot hinder sin, so it doth promote it. And the more wit and wisdom we have, if it be carnal, the more is our enmity against God, as appeareth by those men in a carnal estate who have most of natural acquisitions; the devil's cause is varnished by them, and they prostitute all their sufficiencies to the interest of the flesh, and to cast off the government of God. How many wit themselves into hell? But it is common to all, as appeareth by the two principal effects of the carnal minding, arguing and contriving, by these two the malignity of the flesh doth most betray itself.

(1.) By the arguings of the flesh. What carnal reasons have men for every sin, and against every duty? Which showeth the corruption of nature hath not only taken hold of the appetite and senses, but hath over-spread the mind and reason. Let any temptation come to inordinate pleasure, they will palliate it and honest it with some excuse, that the bait is soon swallowed; or to unlawful gain, by it they pretend they shall be enabled to do good to the church of God; if to honour and applause, they will say religion shall have the advantage of it; so if the temptation be against duty, they will say that they will recompense it another time.

(2.) By contriving: Rom. xiii. 14, and 'make no more provision for the flesh to fulfill the lusts thereof' Wherein do men usually spend their time, but in studying to please the flesh, or to fulfil their fleshly desires? All their wit is wholly employed to this end.

Use 1 is Caution, not to stroke the carnal minding with a gentle censure, as if it were no great matter; it is enmity to God; and if you indulge it, you live in a state of rebellion against him. It is an evil; first, as a wrong done to God, whose we are, and whom we should serve; because it is an usurping of the government of ourselves against God's right, as if we were at our own disposal, as if we might do with ourselves and faculties as we list, without giving an account to an higher Lord. Now to rob God of his authority over his creature, is no small evil: Ps. xii. 4, 'Who have said, with our tongue we will prevail, our lips are our own, who is Lord over us? 'To challenge anything as our own, is to affect to be as God. Secondly, It is a wrong to ourselves, for so we set up our senses and appetite above our reason, and make the beast ride the man; for the lower faculties rule, when the mind is debauched to serve the flesh, and to cater for it, and contrive about it, when it should govern our senses in order to our true happiness and felicity: Jude 10, 'In what they know naturally, in those things as brute beasts, they corrupt themselves'; that is, against the light of nature they engulph themselves in all manner of sensuality. Thirdly, It is a contempt of that glorious happiness which God hath provided for us, Heb. iii. 2. When soul, and heaven, and God, and all things are despised for our carnal ends, how can we look upon it as a light sin? Is it nothing to cast off God and Christ, and despise our own souls, and all the happiness of the world to come, which God hath encouraged us to expect, as if a little worldly transitory pleasure of sin were much better. Fourthly, It is the worse because it is natural. Your very natures being destitute of original righteousness, incline you to please the flesh before God; so that this opposition against God being natural, it is first, the more lasting, for natural antipathies are not easily broken and cured, as that between the wolf and the lamb, the raven and the dove; and the spirit that dwelleth in us, lusteth to envy: Jam. iv. 5: and, Gen. vi. 5, 'Every imagination of the thought of his heart is only evil continually.' We find it early, we find it to be constant; after grace received, the understanding is not so clear and watchful as it should be, but a dark, imperfect guide to us, our will not so powerful as it ought to be; the wisdom of the flesh is kneaded into our natures that we cannot get rid of it, and there is too great a rebellion in the appetite and senses, and in the best a great averseness to their duty; our reason still too often stoopeth to our sensuality. Fifthly, Accidental evil is matter of compassion; but natural, of indignation; we pity a dog poisoned, but hate a toad that is poisonous. If it were only a slip of our natures, or a frailty, it were another thing; but it is the rooted disposition of our hearts. We can better dispense with a fit of anger, than with cankered malice; a blow and away may be forgiven, but an abiding enmity provoketh us to take revenge. Thus it is necessary to know the evil, that we may seek after and admire the" cure.

Use 2 is to press us to come out of this estate of carnality: will you live in enmity against God?

1. Can you make good your part against him? 1 Cor. x. 22, 'Will you provoke the Lord to jealousy? are you stronger than he? 'Secondly, He hath *potestatem vitae et necis*: Jam. iv.

12, 'There is one lawgiver, who is able to save and to destroy.' Thirdly, God is an enemy to those that are enemies to him: Ps. v. 5, 'He hateth all workers of iniquity'; and Ps. vii. 11, 12, 'He is angry with the wicked every day: if he turn not, he will whet his sword, he will bend his bow, and will make it ready.' God's justice, if it doth for a while spare the wicked, yet it doth not lie idle; he can deal with us, comminus and eminus at a distance, and near at hand. He is whetting his sword, and bending his bow; if he fall upon us, what shall we do? If a spark of his wrath light upon the conscience, how soon is man made a burden to himself? Ps. ii. 12, much more when he stirreth up all his wrath against us. What shall we do? First, Accept of the conditions of peace God hath provided: 2 Cor. v. 19, 20, 'to wit, that God was in 'Christ reconciling the world to himself, not imputing their trespasses to them; and hath committed to us the word of reconciliation. Now then we are ambassadors of Christ, as though God did beseech you by us, we pray you in Christ's stead, be ye reconciled to God.' We read of princes that, Luke xiv. 31, while their enemy is yet a great way off, they send an embassy, and desire conditions of peace. God sendeth the embassy to us, let us accept of the offer; we are no match for God. Secondly, Get corrupt nature healed, and the heart renewed by the Spirit: for there is no peace as long as the old heart remaineth. When renewed, we are reconciled; we receive the atonement, if God sanctifieth; he is a God of peace. Be once after the spirit, and then you will be spiritually minded; and to one that is spiritually minded, there is life and peace.

Secondly. The next thing is our impotency to recover ourselves out of this estate; for it is not subject to the law of God, neither indeed can be. Hence observe:

Doctrine That while we remain carnally minded, there is no breaking off this enmity between God and us. The reasons of this repugnancy, or why the carnal mind standeth in such direct opposition to the law, are

1. 'The law is spiritual, and we are carnal, sold under sin,' Rom. vii. 14. Men in an habitual state of carnality, cannot obey a spiritual law.

2. The law is pure and holy: Ps. cxix. 140, 'Thy law is very pure, therefore thy servant loveth it.' But it is otherwise with fleshly creatures, *impuritas est mixtura vilioris.*

3. The law is directly contrary to the fleshly mind, and therefore the fleshly mind is directly contrary to it. The law of God forbiddeth many things that are pleasing to carnal nature, as all excess of bodily pleasures, inordinate seeking after the profits and honours of the world; commandeth many things tedious to flesh and blood, as the loving God with all our hearts, serving him with all our might and strength, loving enemies, doing good to all, seeking others' welfare as our own. Secondly, Besides its repugnancy, there is an utter incapacity. But may it not be brought to obedience by the law demanding its right and due in the name of God? (1.) Not by a bare prohibition, for that exasperateth the evil: Rom. vii. 5, 'For when we were in the flesh, the motions of sins which were by the law, did work in my members to bring forth fruit unto death' (2.) Not by persuasions or instructions; for spiritual arguments work little with a carnal heart; persuasion alone prevaileth not against inclination: 1 Cor. ii 14, 'For the natural man receiveth not the things of the Spirit of God.' (3.) Nor will resolutions, vows, and covenants, make us subject, for these are but the dictates of

conscience, till the will be renewed. It is our judgment we should, but the bent of our hearts lieth as a weight against it: Rom. ii. 18,- 'Thou approvest the things that are excellent, being instructed out of the law.'

Use is information. Since the unregenerate are altogether flesh, and the regenerate in part flesh, the one can do nothing good, the other nothing perfect.

1. It giveth us a true account of man's natural incapacity to what is good. First, there is a natural propensity or inclination to the body before the soul, and earth before heaven, the creature before God: John iii. 6, 'That which is born of flesh is flesh.'

2. This is increased in us by being accustomed to a sinful life: Jer. xiii. 13, 'Can the Ethiopian change his skin, or the leopard his spots? then may ye also do good that are accustomed to do evil.'

3. This custom is more confirmed and rooted by the general practice of all about us: Is. vi. 5, 'Woe is me, for I am undone, because I am a man of unclean lips, and dwell in the midst of a people of unclean lips.'

4. It is not only practised, but countenanced generally in the world: 1 Pet. iv. 4, 'Wherein they think it strange, that you run not with them into the same excess of riot.'

5. The encouragements of another course, lie wholly in a world to come: Mat. v. 12, 'Rejoice and be exceeding glad, for great is your reward in heaven.'

6. The precepts to renounce this sensuality, are given by an invisible God; who, though he hath given sufficient demonstration of the truth of his being, is little cared for: Ps. x. 4, 'The wicked through the pride of his countenance will not seek after God: God is not in all his thoughts.'

SERMON X

So then they that are in the flesh cannot please God.

Romans viii. 8.

THIS verse is consectary[7] from the whole discourse, especially from the former verse. They who are in the flesh, are professed enemies to God, and therefore they cannot please him. In the words here are two things

1. The persons spoken of.

2. What is said of them.

1. The persons spoken of. They that are in the flesh, that is, who are unregenerate, in the state of corrupt nature. He saith not, if the flesh be in you, ye cannot please God, but if you be in the flesh, that is in a carnal state. As to be in the faith, 2 Cor. xiii. 5, implieth being in a gospel state; and to be in Christ: Rom. viii. 1, noteth a state of true Christianity; so to be in the flesh is to be under the dominion and power of the flesh, so as to serve the lusts and passions thereof; during this carnal and corrupt estate, till men are converted and changed, they cannot please God.

2. What is said of them? They cannot please God. Which may be interpreted two ways, *quoad conatum, vel quoad eventum.* First, With respect to their endeavour, they will not frame their doings, nor make this their business and scope to please the Lord, as it is said of the Jews that rigorously kept up the ritual observances of the law: 1 Thess. ii. 15, 'They please not God, and are contrary to all men.' They were as far from fulfilling the true meaning of the law, as they were from observing the gospel; and all men as long as their lusts are untamed and unbroken, they cannot do those things which are pleasing in his sight. Secondly, With respect to God's acceptance and favour, they are not accepted with him so as to obtain life and peace, and be exempted from condemnation.

Doctrine Carnal men do not, cannot please God.

To prove this I shall lay down some propositions:

1. That it is man's duty and happiness to please God. For this end was he made and sent into the world, not that he might live to himself, but unto God. I prove it by this argument; It is man's happiness to please him upon whom he dependeth; all the world goeth upon this principle, that dependence begetteth observance, or a study to please; and as the dependence is less or greater, so men take themselves bound more or less to please those from whom they receive their supplies, as children their parents, servants their masters; and if any breach and displeasure fall out, their dependence obligeth them to see it made up again. We have an instance in scripture: Acts xii. 24, 'Herod was highly displeased with them of Tyre and Sidon, but they came with one accord to him, and desired peace, because their

---

[7] Consequence; corollary

country was nourished by the king's country.' What their interest taught them to do to man, our interest teacheth us to do to God; we depend upon none so much as God, from whom we have both our being and well-being: 'In his hand is our breath, and all our ways,' Dan. v. 23. Our business lieth more with God, than with all the world besides, and therefore him should we love and study to please.

2. That this being man's duty and happiness, it should be our work and scope to approve ourselves to God; for man is never in his proper posture, till he mindeth his true work and happiness, but is either out in the end or way; his end, if pleasing God and being accepted with him be not his scope; the way, if he doth not those things which God will accept. Therefore God's children are sometimes described by their intention, which is of the end, *intentio est finis ultimi*: sometimes by their choice, which is of the means, *electio est medii*; by their scope and intention: 2 Cor. v. 9, 'Therefore we labour, that whether present or absent, we may be accepted with him'. This is the honour we affect, the end which we propound to ourselves, and which our minds are principally set upon. Some seek to please God, others to please their fleshly mind by the fruition of some inferior good. That is our end which we love most, and are pleased best with, and would do most for; so the people of God are sometimes described by the choice of their ways: Isa. lvi. 4, 'They choose the things that please him, and take hold of his covenant'; that is, resolve to do what is pleasing to God, or to behave themselves in such a manner as they may be accepted with him.

3. That it is no easy matter to make this our scope and work to please God. This I shall prove by two reasons.

[A.] Because of the thing itself.

[B.] Because of the requisites thereunto, which are, that a man be renewed and reconciled, &c.

[A.] The matter of itself. God is a great and holy God, and will not be put off with anything, but expecteth worship and service from us becoming his majesty; and lest we should mistake, hath stated our duty in his holy law; which we are to study and fulfil, we are to study it, and know how God will be pleased: Rom. xii. 2, 'That we may prove what is that good and acceptable and perfect will of God.' It is a good and perfect rule that we must live by, for this is only acceptable or well-pleasing unto God: so Eph. v. 10: Proving what is acceptable unto the Lord. We must not serve God hand over head, but prove and try our way, and every step of it, whether it be well pleasing unto him; and consult often, not what is our interest, but our duty; not what is for our advantage, and will gratify our lusts and please the world, but what will please God; and again, v. 17, 'Be not unwise, but understanding what the will of the Lord is.' We may mistake, and therefore we must search again and again, *crassa negligentia dolus est*. It is a sign men have no mind to practise, when they have no mind to know, or be informed. And we are to fulfil our duty as well as to understand it, and that not in a few things, but all: Col. i. 19, 'That ye walk worthy of the Lord unto all pleasing.' Some men are in with one duty, and out with another; but this is to please ourselves, not to please God. Some will rest in rituals, and neglect morals, though the moral duty hath the attestation not only of the word of God, but of conscience: Rom. xiv. 17,

18, 'For the kingdom of God is not meat and drink, but righteousness and peace, and joy in the Holy Ghost: for he that in these things serveth Christ, is acceptable to God, and approved of men.' Many will rest in ordinances and church- privileges, this will not satisfy God: 2 Cor. x. 5, 'With many of them, God was not well- pleased.' Some rest in moralities, and cast off faith and the love of God; others please .themselves in an overly religion, without moral duties.

Nor must this be minded superficially; no, we must be every day more exact in our walking, that no cause of offence, or breach may arise between us and him: 1 Thess. iv. 1, 'As ye have received of us, how to walk, and how to please God, so you would abound therein more and more.' You never please God so much, but you are to please him better; he expecteth more from you, the more you are acquainted with him; and that we should not always keep to our first weaknesses.

[B.] Consider what is requisite thereunto, viz., that a man be in a reconciled and renewed estate.

(1.) Reconciled to God by Christ. All mankind is fallen under the displeasure of the most high God, by preferring the pleasure of the flesh before the pleasing of God; and there is no atonement found to pacify him, but only Jesus Christ, who is his. beloved Son, in whom he is well pleased: Mat. iii. 17. Upon his account grace may be had, both to justify and sanctify us. Now while men are in rebellion against God, they have no interest in Christ, or the grace purchased for them, but are under death and damnation, and therefore cannot be accepted with God, so far as to obtain the great reward; yea, to do nothing acceptably to him, till we believe and are in Christ Jesus, and have his merits applied to us; therefore it is said: Heb. xi. 6, 'Without faith it is impossible to please God'; for till there be some means, that God be a re warder rather than a punisher to the fallen creature, nothing is done kindly, or taken kindly. Well then, nothing can please God but what is done in faith, or in a reconciled estate; and that both in respect to the person working, or the work itself. With respect to the person working; for he is not within the covenant of grace till he believe, but the wrath of God abideth on him: John iii. 36; he is an enemy to God. 2. With respect to the work itself; for till it be quickened by a true and lively faith, and love to God as the consequence of it, it is but the carcase of a good work, and so not acceptable to God; the life and soul of it are wanting, that obediential confidence which should enliven it. Certainly there is no bringing forth fruit unto God, till married to Christ: Rom. vii. 4. As children are not legitimate who are born before marriage, it is a bastard offspring; so neither are works acceptable till we are married to Christ.

(2.) It is also requisite that the person be renewed by the Spirit of Christ; for otherwise he cannot have his spirit, affections, and ways, such as to please God. Nature can rise no higher than itself; it is grace carrieth the soul to God; there needeth renewing grace: Heb. xii. 28, 'Let us have grace, whereby we may serve him acceptably with reverence and godly fear.' To serve him in an acceptable manner, and with that reverence and seriousness as is necessary, is a work above our natural faculties; till God change them, we cannot please him. So also actual grace: Heb. xiii. 21, 'Working in you that which is pleasing in his sight' The best actions of wicked men please him no more than Cain's sacrifice, or Esau's tears, or the Pharisees prayers, it is but a shadow of what a man reconciled and renewed doth, or an imperfect imitation, as an ape doth imitate a man, or a violent motion doth resemble a natural.

Use 1. Is to show us what to- think of the good actions of carnal men; they do not please God; they are for the matter good, but there are manifold defects in them.

1. There is a defect in their state, they are not renewed and reconciled to God by Christ, and therefore God may justly say: Mai. i. 10, 'I have no pleasure in you, neither will I accept an offering at your hands.' They live in their sins, and therefore he may justly abhor and reject all their services; they live in enmity to him, and in neglect of his grace, and will not sue out their atonement.

2. There is a defect in the root of these actions. They do not come from faith working by love, which is the true principle of all obedience, Gal. v. 6. Without love to God in Christ, we want the soul and life of every duty. Obedience is love breaking out into its perfect act: 1 John ii. 5, 'If we keep his word, herein is love perfected.'

3. There is a defect in the manner. They do not serve God with that sincerity, reverence, seriousness, and willingness, which the work calleth for; they show love to him with their lips, when their hearts are far from him, Mat. xv. 8; there is an habitual aversion, whilst they seem to show love to him. All their duties are but as flowers strewed upon a dunghill.

4. There is a defect in the end. They do not regard God's glory in their most commendable actions; they have either a natural aim, as when they are frightened into a little religiousness of worship in their extremities: Hos. vii. 14, 'They howl upon their beds for corn and wine.' And then they are like ice in thawing weather, soft at top, and hard at bottom. Or a carnal aim, out of bravery and vain glory, Mat. viii. 2. Or a legal aim, when they seem very devout, to quiet conscience, or to satisfy God for their sins, by their external duties: Mic. vi. 6, 7, 8, 'Wherewith shall I come before the Lord, and bow myself before the high God? Shall I come before him with burnt-offerings, and calves of a year old? Will the Lord be pleased with thousands of rams, or with ten thousand rivers of oil? Shall I give my first born for my transgression, the fruit of my body for the sin of my soul? 'But Solomon telleth us, Prov. xxi. 27, 'The sacrifice of the wicked is an abomination to the Lord,' much more when he bringeth it with an evil mind. At best it is an abomination, much more when it is to buy an indulgence in some licentious practice, by performing some duties requiring a sin-offering, not a thank-offering. But this cannot please God, so as to obtain an eternal reward. God temporarily rewardeth moral obedience, to keep up the government of the world; as Pagan Home while it excelled in virtue, God gave it a great empire and large dominion. And Ahab's going softly and mourning, was recompensed with a suspension of temporal judgments: 1 Kings xxi. 29, 'Because he humbleth himself before me, I will not bring the evil in his days.' Again, there is a difference between a wicked man going on in his wickedness, and a natural man returning to God. When wicked men pray to God to prosper them in their wickedness, as Balaam's altars were made; or to beg pardon while they go on in their sins; so 'the sacrifice of the wicked is an abomination to the Lord,' Prov. xv. 8. Namely, as they rest in external performances, and think by their prayers or some other

good duties to put by the great duties of faith, repentance, and new obedience, so these prayers and good things are abominable; but in sinners returning to God, and using the means, and expressing their desires of grace, though but with a natural fervency, and with some common help of the Spirit, though the action doth not deserve acceptance with God, and the person is not in such an estate that God hath made an express promise to him that he will accept him, yet he hath to do with a good God, who doth not refuse the cry of his creatures in their extremities, and it is a thousand to one, but he will speed. The carnal man is to act these abilities, and common grace he hath, that God may give more.

Use 2. Is to exhort us. 1. To come out of the carnal estate into the spiritual life; for whilst you are in the flesh, you cannot please God. Now what is more unhappy than to do much to no good purpose; to be acquainted with the toil of duties, and not to be accepted in them? Men are apt to rest in some superficial good actions, and so neglect the grace of God in Christ. We cannot sufficiently beat men from this false righteousness wherewith they hope to please God. Certainly while you are ruled by the world, the flesh, and the devil, you are unfit to obey God; therefore you must renounce the flesh, the world and the devil, and give up yourselves to God the Father, Son, and Holy Ghost, as Creator, Redeemer and Sanctifier. All after-duties depend on the seriousness of the first: 2 Cor. viii. 5, 'They first gave themselves to the Lord, then unto us, by the will of God'; and Rom. vi. 13, 'Neither yield ye your members as instruments of unrighteousness unto sin, but yield yourselves unto God, as those that are alive from the dead, and your members as instruments of righteousness unto God.' The more heartily you give up yourselves to obey God, and look for his favour upon the account of Christ's righteousness, and wait for the healing grace of his Spirit, in the use of fit means, the more easily, readily, and comfortably will the spiritual life be carried on; and the more hearty and serious you are in this, the more peace you will have, and such graces will be heaped upon you, as will be the evident tokens of God's approbation and acceptance. Till you renounce God's enemies, and consent to be the Lord's, you are in the state of rebels; rebels in heart, though subjects in show; and what you perform, is by constraint, and not by a willing mind. God hath right to our duties, before we consent, and therefore it is a sin in carnal men to omit them, but our consent and self-obligation is necessary to our voluntary obedience and acceptation with God. Besides, when this resignation, willingness and consent, is deep rooted, it becometh as a nature to us, and carrieth the force and authority of a principle in our hearts, and puts the soul upon such sincere obedience as God will take kindly at our hands; it habituateth the mind to an obediential frame, and then the particular acts will not be very difficult.

2. To exhort us to please God. This must be managed,

[A.] Negatively:

(1.) Not to please the flesh; flesh-pleasing is the fortress of sin, for all sin tendeth to flesh-pleasing. Now Christians are to crucify the flesh, not to gratify the flesh; our Lord Jesus Christ pleased not himself, Rom. xv. 3; he sought not to gratify that life he had assumed; not that we should deny the body all delight in the mercies of God; then the soul would soon be clogged, which perfecteth its operations by the body. We are to abstain from fleshly lusts which war against the soul, but not to abstain from worldly comforts, which would produce the same effect, hindering our cheerful service of God. Common mercies must be received as mercies, else there would be no room for humiliation and thanksgiving. Not of humiliation, when God correcteth us for sin by depriving us of those mercies, and so there would be no distinction between mercy and punishment; nor for thankfulness, for we cannot be thankful for what we do not esteem and relish in some subordinate degree. Is it a mercy, or is it not? If it be a mercy, we may use it with thanksgiving; if not, then you cannot bless God for it. But in the use of these things, we must take heed that the soul be not drawn away from God, and the interest of the flesh be not set up against him. It becometh a Christian much more to mortify the deeds of the body, than to fulfil his lusts; and he must be cautious that he do not displease God by pleasing the flesh; that Satan who is ever laying his baits to catch unwary souls, do not draw him to such an use of bodily pleasures, as are immoderate and sinful.

(2.) Not to please men, who have power, or many advantages over us. That we please not them to the wrong of God: the apostle saith; Gal. i. 10, 'If I yet pleased men, I were not the servant of Christ.' There is a twofold man-pleasing, which is sinful; the one respects the matter, the other the scope. First, The matter, when we seek to please them by something that is sinful, or by dispensing with our duty to God. To do this voluntarily and deliberately, is to forsake our vowed duty in the covenant, and to renounce our happiness, and therefore a damnable sin; we forsake our duty, when man must be pleased by some known sin; no, our absolute dependence is on God, and therefore his will must be regarded in the first place: Acts v. 29, 'We ought to obey God, rather than man.' And therefore no man must be pleased by sin, it is a renouncing of our happiness, as if their favour were to be pre ferred before the favour of God: John xii. 42, 'Nevertheless among the chief rulers also, many believed on him: but because of the Phari sees, they did not confess him, lest they should be put out of the synagogue'; and chap. v. 44, 'How can you believe that seek honour one of another? 'No, God is enough to a gracious soul: Ps. lxiii. 3, 'Because thy loving kindness is better than life, my lips shall praise thee.' His approbation should satisfy us; the people of God have felt what it is to have displeased God, and what it is to be reconciled to him by the death and intercession of Christ; that to them it is a small matter whether man be pleased or displeased; if God be pleased, it is no matter who is displeased.

Secondly. As to their scope, when the matter is pleasing both to God and men, but you regard man's eye most: Eph. vi. 6, 'Not with eye- service as men-pleasers; but as the servant of God, doing the will of God from the heart'; and Col. iii. 22, 'Not with eye-service as men-pleasers, but with singleness of heart, fearing God.' As your happiness lieth not in man's approbation, so this is the only constant motive of pure and sincere obedience. .

[B.] Positively. Pleasing God is your great duty and business m the world; this is uprightness, and this will be your safety and happiness; for if you study to please God, then God is ever with you. Christ hath given you an instance of that: John viii. 29, 'And he that sent me is with me, the Father hath not left me alone: for I do always those things that please him.' And then it is no matter who is dis pleased and angry with us: Prov. xvi. 7, 'When a man's ways please the Lord, he maketh his enemies to be at peace with him.' God will hear your prayers: 1 John iii. 22, 'And whatsoever we ask, we receive of him, because we keep his commandments. He will give you ever lasting happiness and glory: Heb. iv. 5, and truly he is not hard to be pleased: Mai. iii. 17. Man- pleasing is a more difficult and unprofitable task; God is pleased with nothing that hurts yourselves or others. 3. Let me exhort you, to beg more of the spirit: for whilst we are in the flesh, we cannot please God; and therefore you must beg more plentiful grace to change your natures, and to fix your intention right that you may please God in all things. Your natures are never changed till your love be altered, nor till God direct your love: 2 Thes. iii. 5, 'And the Lord direct your hearts to the love of God.'

SERMON XI

But ye are not in the flesh, but in the spirit; if so be the Spirit of God dwell in you.

Romans viii. 9.

In these words the Apostle applieth the property of the justified, unto the Romans. In this application you may observe both his charity and his prudence;

1. His charity, but you are not in the flesh, but in the spirit.

2. His prudence, if so be the Spirit of God dwell in you.

1. For that clause which expresseth his charity. The phrases of being 'in the flesh' or 'in the spirit,' are the same with being 'after the flesh,' and 'after the spirit,' ver. 5, or 'walking,' or 'living after the flesh' or 'after the spirit' used in other verses of this chapter.

2. In the other clause which expresseth his prudence. The word is either causal or conditional, and signifieth either for so much, or if so be; our translation preferreth the latter rendering; and the sense is, if it were not so, I would not judge you to belong to Christ. As to the latter, observe two things. (1.) To be in the spirit, or to have the spirit dwelling in us, is the same, for the inhabitation is mutual; we are in the spirit, and the spirit in us. (2.) That the Spirit of God and of Christ are all one, witness the proof here subjoined, for he that hath not the Spirit of Christ, is none of his.

Doct. That they in whom the Spirit of God dwelleth, though they live in the flesh, they do not live after the flesh.

1. The terms must be explained.

2. The connection proved.

1. The terms must be explained. Two terms there are: [A.] What is the indwelling of the spirit; [B.] What it is to live in the flesh.

[A.] What the Spirit dwelling in us meaneth. Three things are implied, intimacy, constancy, sovereignty; intimacy with us, constancy of operation in us, and sovereignty over us.

(1.) Intimacy, or familiar presence. As the inhabitant in his own house, he is more there than elsewhere. God is everywhere essentially; his essence and being is nowhere included, and nowhere excluded: Ps. cxxxix. 7, 'Whither shall I go from the Spirit? or whither shall I flee from thy presence? 'He is said more especially to be there where he most manifests his power and presence, so his dwelling is known by his operation, he is in us *virtute insignis aliciujus effectus*, by some notable and eminent effect which he produceth in us. As to the effects of common providence, it is said: Eph. iv. 6, 'That God is above all, and through all, and in all.' But he dwelleth in believers, not by the effects of common providence, but by the special influence of his grace, as Christ's agent begetting and maintaining a new spiritual life in their souls. So he is in them as he is nowhere else, by his gracious operations performed there: Acts xxvi. 18, 'Opening their hearts': Acts xvi. 14, comforting and guiding them upon all occasions. This is his gracious and familiar presence, which the world is not capable of: John xiv. 17, 'I will send unto you the Spirit of truth, whom the world cannot receive, because it seeth him not, neither knoweth him: but ye know him, for he dwelleth with you, and shall be in you.' The world of natural men are great strangers to the Spirit of Christ; they were never acquainted with his gracious and saving operations; but he intimately discovereth his presence to those that enjoy him in the exercise of grace; they feel and discern his motions, and have that comfort and peace which others are strangers to. This then is the intimate and familiar presence of the Spirit in the hearts of believers. Some have raised questions, whether the person of the Holy Ghost be in believers, or only his gifts and graces. The person questionless. We have not only the fruit but the tree, the stream but the fountain; but he doth not dwell in us personally. The Spirit was in Christ *somatikos*, bodily or personally, for his soul dwelt with God in a personal union; in all creatures he is *pneumatikos*, by the common effects of his power and providence; but in believers *energetikos* spiritually by gracious effects, which is all the conception we can have of it.

(2.) Constancy. Dwelling noteth his residence, or a permanent and constant abode. He doth not act upon them, or affect them by a transient motion only, or come upon them as he came upon Sampson, at times, or as he came upon the prophets or holy men of God, when in some particular services they were specially inspired and carried beyond the line of their ordinary abilities; but he dwelleth in us by working such effects as carry the nature of a permanent habit. On the carnal he worketh *per modum actionis transeuntis*[8], but on the sanctified there are effects wrought, not transient, but permanent, *per modum habitus permanentis*[9], as faith, love, and hope. There is difference between his acting upon us and dwelling in us; the Holy Spirit cometh to us not as a guest but as an inhabitant; not for a visit and away, but to take up his abode in us. Therefore, when the Spirit is promised, Christ saith, 'He will give us a well of water always springing into eternal life': John iv. 14, Not a draught nor a splash of water, nor a pond, but a living spring: so John xiv. 23, 'We will come to him, and make our abode with him. He liveth in the heart, that, by constant and continual influence, he may maintain the life of grace in us, Gal. v. 25; by degrees he deadeneth and mortifieth our dearest and strongest sin, Rom. viii. 13, and continually stirreth us up to the love and obedience of God in Christ: 1 Peter i. 22; exciteth us to prayer, and quickeneth our spiritual desires, Rom. viii. 26; giveth us consolation in crosses, 1 Peter iv. 14, and counsel in all our ways, and Rom. viii. 14; and sets us a longing for heaven, Rom. viii. 23. In short, the Spirit is said to dwell there where his ordinary and constant work is, and where he doth by his constant and continual influence form and frame men's hearts and lives to holiness.

(3.) Sovereignty. This is implied also in the notion of dwelling; take the metaphor either from a common House, or from a temple. From an house: where the spirit dwelleth, he dwelleth there as the owner of an house, not as an underling. The apostle inferreth from the Spirit

---

[8] Mode of transitory actions
[9] Mode of permanent habits

dwelling in us, that we are not our own, 1 Cor. vi. 19. We were possessed by another owner before we were recovered into his hands; our hearts are Satan's shop and workhouse; the evil spirit saith, Mat. xii. 44, 45, 'I will return to mine own house.' But he is dispossessed by the Spirit, and then it becomes his house, where he commandeth and doth dispose and govern our hearts after his own will. But it more clearly floweth from the other notion of a sacred house or temple: 1 Cor. iii. 16, 'Know ye not that ye are the temple of God, and that the Spirit of God dwelleth in you?' and 1 Cor. vi. 19, 'What? Know ye not that your body is the temple of the Holy Ghost which is in you? 'A temple is a sacred house, and must be employed for the honour of the God whose temple it is. The heart of man naturally is a temple full of idols; every dunghill-god is worshipped there, Mam mon, the belly, Satan; but when this temple is cleansed, and becometh a mansion for the Holy Spirit, he must be chief there, and all things must be done to his honour, that he may be obeyed, reverenced and worshipped in his own temple. This much we get from either notion: of a common house, that the Spirit is owner or lord of that house; or from a sacred house or temple, that he is the god of that temple; and so wherever he dwelleth he is chief, and principally beareth sway in the heart; whatever opposeth or controlleth his motions, it is as an intruder in a common house, or as an idol set up in a temple.

[B.] What it is to be, or live in the flesh. It noteth two things, the natural life, or the carnal life.

(1.) The natural life, as Gal. ii. 20, 'The life that I now live in the flesh, I live by the faith of the Son of God;' that is, while I exercise the functions and actions of this natural life: Phil. i. 22, 'But if I live in the flesh, this is the fruit of my labour'; that is, if I still enjoy this natural life: for the apostle was in a strait which to desire, to be in the flesh, or out of the flesh.

(2.) The carnal life, as the 8th verse of this chapter, 'They that are in the flesh cannot please God' Sometimes it is put for some acts belonging to the carnal life; but more usually for the state of carnality': if ye live after the flesh, ye shall die.' Now I say, the children of God having his Spirit dwelling in them, though they live in the flesh, though they live a natural life, and having not divested themselves of the interests and concernments of flesh and blood no more than others, yet they do not 'live after the flesh.' A life carnal, see it notably expressed: 1 Pet. iv. 2, 'That he should no longer live the rest of his time in the flesh, to the lusts of men, but the will of God.' Though the life be in the flesh still, yet it is not ordered by the will of the flesh, but the will of God. It is in the flesh we live, but not after the flesh, mortifying and subduing the inclinations of corrupt nature yet more and more. Thus we see the sense of the words.

(2.) Let me prove the connection, that though they live in the flesh, yet they do not live after the flesh. The very explication doth sufficiently show it.

[A.] For if the dwelling of the Spirit implieth intimacy and familiarity, or such operations in the hearts of believers as are not common to others, but peculiar to them, then certainly God's children, though they live in the flesh as others do, yet they should and do live above the rate of flesh and blood; for they have an higher principle in them, which others have not. It is a charge on Christians, that they walk as men 2 Cor. iii. 3, 'car av0p<07rov. If we do no more than ordinary men do, wherein do we differ? What peculiar excellency do we show forth? Some live as beasts, as if they had forsaken all humanity, and had no reason, but sense; others only as men that have reason, but not the spirit. But our way should be with the wise, above, as having a more excellent spirit dwelling in us.

[B.] If it implieth the constancy of his operations; he doth not sojourn for a season, but dwelleth in us by his continuance and abode in our hearts; for he hath constant work to do there, to quicken and enliven our graces, and check the flesh, and abate the force of it. Surely then the tenor of our lives must not be after the flesh, but after the spirit. There are but few but have their good moods and fits; but a constant habitual influence or principle of life, inferreth more than some good moods now and then, a constant living in obedience to God.

[C.] If it implieth sovereignty, that he dwelleth as lord in his own house, then he must not be controlled, nor grieved by the indulging the desires of the flesh: so that the terms explained do evidence themselves, and make out their own truth to any man's consideration. But yet we shall give you some other reasons.

(1.) The Spirit dwelleth nowhere, but where he hath changed the heart so far as to put a new nature in us. He writeth the word of God upon the heart: Heb. viii. 10, and thereby imprinteth his image upon them: 2 Cor. iii. 18, 'But we all as with open face beholding the glory of the Lord, are changed into the same image'; so fitting us for God, and making us amiable in his sight. Now they that are thus prepared, are in the flesh, but not after the flesh; they keep the affections which belong to the bodily life, but they are mortified and subdued, they are not governed by them: 2 Pet. i. 4, 'To us are given great and precious promises, that by these you might be partakers of the divine nature, having escaped the corruption which is in the world through lust.' In which place is intimated a new principle, and that is the divine nature; a new rule, and that is not the course of the world, but the will of God revealed in his word; new ends and motives, and those not the satisfying of our fleshly lusts, but the vision and fruition of God, intimated in the great and precious promises. Now if the Spirit of God dwelleth nowhere but where he hath thus fitted the heart for his residence by sanctifying it and inclining it to God, and the world to come as our happiness, and the word of God as our sure direction thither, it must needs follow, that where the Spirit of God dwelleth, they do not live after the flesh, though they live in it; for then there is a contrary principle, the new nature, which must needs be a curb upon the flesh if we obey the inclinations of it: Gal. v. 16, 'Walk in the spirit, and you shall not fulfil the lusts of the flesh.' And a contrary rule, which is the will of God: Rom. xii. 2, 'Be not conformed to this world, but be ye transformed by the renewing of your minds, that ye may prove what is that good, and acceptable, and perfect will of God.' For by it they are new formed, and to it they are suited; and there is a contrary end and tendency, which is to love, please, serve, glorify and enjoy God. As the natural soul looketh after the conveniences of the body, and catereth only for the body; so the renewed soul looketh after the pleasing of God: 1 Pet iv. 6, 'We live to God in the spirit.' Their business lieth with God, and their happiness lieth in God; it is his favour they seek, his work they do, and the fruition of him they aim at. Spiritual life carrieth a resemblance with the life of Christ as Mediator. Now Christ, 'in that he liveth, he liveth unto God': Rom. vi. 10; so doth a Christian, his whole life is a living unto God: Gal. ii. 1 9, 'The life that I live in the flesh, I live by the faith of the Son of God.'

(2.) When the heart is thus prepared, the Spirit of God cometh to dwell in them, to take possession of them for God's use: 2 Cor. vi. 10, 'I will dwell in them, and walk in them; for I will be their God, and they shall be my people.' They have given up themselves to God, and God owneth the dedication, and sendeth his Spirit into their hearts, first, to take possession of them, and then to maintain and keep afoot his interest in their souls against all the assaults of the devil': For stronger is he that is in us, than he that is in the world': 1 John iv. 4. The world is governed by the evil spirit, but they that are regenerated and enlightened by the Spirit of God, have the knowledge of his will, which is more mighty to establish the saints in truth and holiness, than the spirit of error and persecution to draw and drive them from it. So against the world: 2 Cor. ii. 12, 'We have not received the spirit of the world, but the Spirit of God, that we might know the things that are freely given us of God.' He showeth us better things, and so causeth us to believe them, and to live above all the glory, riches, and pleasures of the world. For the flesh, as he hath set up a contrary opposite principle against it, so his constant working in the heart is to maintain it in predominancy, bringing us more and more to abhor all licentiousness and sensuality, and warning us of our snares and dangers, that we may not make provision for the flesh, to fulfil the lusts thereof. Indeed this doth not exclude our duty: we are to be led by the Spirit, or else we are not what we do pretend to be. We are not to grieve the Spirit, or else we carry it unthankfully towards him, and resist and forfeit his grace; nor do we fulfil our covenant- vow made with the Holy Ghost, if we disobey his sanctifying motions; but it is a great advantage, that we have not only an opposite principle, but an opposite power, which is an enemy to the flesh, and is still contending against it in our hearts.

Use 1 is information.

1. How much this is for the glory of God, that he can maintain grace in the hearts of his people; that whilst they live in the flesh, they do not live after the flesh. Take living in the flesh in the softest sense, for the natural life, it is a state of great frailty and weakness. The natural life only seeketh what is good for itself. Christians have the same bodies, and the same affections that other men have, yet they live quite after another manner; their natural inclination is overruled; while they are in the flesh, they are humbled with many wants, afflictions, and weaknesses, but God's power is made perfect in our weakness: 2 Cor. xii. 9. The word made perfect is notable; excellent things suffer a kind of imperfection till there be an occasion to discover them. Now our many infirmities give an occasion to show forth the perfection that is in the power of grace, which can maintain us in life and comfort, notwithstanding reproaches, pain, sufferings. Were it not for the animal life, there would be no place for temptations and the exercise of grace; but all that are in the flesh have all these things accomplished in them: 1 Pet. v. 19. During our worldly state, we must expect hardships; there goeth more grace to preserve a man in his duty, than goeth to preserve the

good angels in their estate; they are out of gunshot and harm's way. To glorify God upon earth is the greater difficulty: John xvii. 4, 5, 'I have glorified thee on earth, and now, Father, glorify thou me with thine own self, with the glory I had with thee before the world was.' Christ pleadeth that now for the saints, in the midst of so many afflictions; to maintain their integrity and delight in God is the great glory of grace; for surely we stand not by our own strength. But besides the natural life which exposeth us to these difficulties, the carnal life is not wholly extinguished; there is flesh in us, though we be not in the flesh: Gal. v. 17, 'For the flesh lusteth against the spirit, and the spirit against the flesh, and these are contrary the one to the other' Now not only to maintain the combat, but to obtain conquest and victory, is the great wonder of grace, when there are not only temptations without, but mixed principles within. Surely not only in this frail, but this mixed estate, it is as great a wonder to maintain grace in the soul as to maintain a spark of fire in wet wood. The world hath usually an advantage of us in matter of principle; but we have the advantage of them in matter of motive and assisting power, to whom the glory of the conquest alone is to be ascribed. We have, indeed, a principle which directeth and inclineth us to higher ends than the children of this world look after; but their principles are more entire and unbroken, for they are altogether flesh: Gen. vi. 5, 'And God saw that the wickedness of man was great upon earth, and that every imagination of the thoughts of his heart was only evil continually.' But ours are mixed, flesh and spirit. They pour out their whole heart in their sinful and worldly courses: Jude 11, 'They run greedily after the error of Balaam for reward'; they were poured forth, as water out of an open vessel; and Luke xvi. 8, 'The children of this world are wiser in their generation than the children of light.' The reason is manifest; grace, though it be forcible, it is weak, like a keen sword in the hand of a child. But we have the advantage in matter of motive; the flesh cannot propound such excellent rewards as faith propoundeth, eternal happiness in the vision and fruition of God; but now general motives do little prevail against inclination, and our great motives lie in an unseen world; therefore our best security lieth in the assisting power, which is the mighty Spirit of God dwelling in us, who cherisheth and strengtheneth the new creature not only to keep up the combat, but to get a victory, and to overcome the carnal inclination more and more. Therefore thanks be unto God, who giveth us the victory through Jesus Christ our Lord; not only over external temptations, but our indwelling flesh: Rom. vii. 25, 'I thank God through Jesus Christ our Lord.' By the Spirit of Christ we have strength to overcome the oppositions of the flesh, and have grace to perform what God will accept, and so far accept, that notwithstanding weaknesses we shall be reckoned rather to be in the spirit, than in the flesh, and obtain the privileges of the justified.

2. It showeth us the reason why carnal men think so meanly of the people of God, and the spirit that dwelleth in them. They think Christians are but as other men, and that there is no such great matter to be found in those that profess strictness in religion, no such spirit of God and glory, but what others have. I answer, no wonder that they who are blinded with prejudice and malice, and are loath to see the excellency of others whom they hate, lest it disturb their own carnal quiet, will not see what else would plainly discover itself. But some

reason there is for it. This life is a hidden life: Col. iii. 3. It is hidden, partly under the veil of the natural life. It is a life within a life; they live in the flesh as others do, but they do not live after the flesh; they eat, drink, sleep, trade, marry, and give in marriage, as the rest of the world do, but all these things are governed by grace, and carried on to high and eternal ends. The spirit and life are not seen and felt by others, but only discovered in the effects; as these things are carried on holily and with a sincere respect to God's glory: 1 Cor. x. 31. Besides, the effects are imperfect, and clouded with a mixture of remaining infirmities; the best Christians show forth too much of the flesh, and do not act as those that have the Spirit of God dwelling in them; now this is a great hindrance to the converting of the world, and a means of hardening to prying atheists, who think all strictness is but a pretence: 1 Cor. iii. 3, 'While there is yet strife, envyings, and divisions among you, are ye not carnal, and walk as men? 'Mat. xviii. 7, 'Woe to the world because of offences: for it must needs be that offences come, but wo to the man by whom the offence cometh.' It is dangerous to scandalise the world; but the chief cause is their secret enmity to holiness; they censure and traduce good men by reproaches and base misprisions, and cannot endure that those that take a contrary course should have an excellency owned that might alarm their con sciences to reverence: 1 Pet. iv. 6, 'Judged according to men in the flesh, but live to God in the spirit; as deceivers, and yet true' So reputed in the world as a company of dissemblers; the world's malice will not give them leave to see any good in those whom they dislike.

3. It showeth how much it becometh Christians to give such a demonstration and proof of the Spirit's dwelling in them, that others may be able to say they are not in the flesh but in the Spirit. So did these Romans to Paul; they gave ground for his charity to think them justified; so should all that are sincere do. Now these others may be either the godly or the carnal world. First, For the godly, who are best able to judge, they have cause to think so, when you are companions with them in the faith, holiness, and patience of the gospel; the men in the world are tied to one another, like Samson's foxes by their tails, though their heads look several ways, by their mutual interests and common agreement in mischief and enmity to the godly; but the godly themselves should be joined together in the communion of the spirit, loving one another with a Christ-like- love, and seeking each other's good as their own, and being affected with mutual sympathy towards each other's condition, as if it were their own case, and with one mind and mouth glorifying God, and promoting the interests of his kingdom; and by their personal holiness bringing his honour in request in the world. Surely whoever do so, we are to judge them heirs with us of the same grace of life, and to bless God for them. Secondly, For the carnal world; you must keep up the majesty of your profession, that they may see there is a generation of men whose 'life is not spent in carnal pleasures and delights, who are not as other men, nor as themselves once were, and do things which can be accomplished in them by no other means or agent than the Spirit of God; who in their common business act upon reasons and principles of religion, and turn all duties of the second table into duties of the first, discharging all their respects to men out of the love of God, and fear of God; and are led by con science rather than interest; and begin and end with God in all they do, and cast their whole lives into a holy and heavenly mould,

making straight steps to their feet, and walk with a temper becoming religion, in all the inequality of conditions they pass through in the world, looking for no great matters here, but fetching their main supports and comforts from the world to come.

[A.] Those that do so, will in time overcome malice and prejudice, and convince the world that God is in them of a truth, and they are a heavenly and holy people, and have a spirit and a presence that others have not: Prov. xii. 26, 'The righteous is more excellent than his neighbour.'

[B.] They will reprove the world: Heb. xi. 7. Noah condemned the world by his ready obedience to God's warning.

[C.] They will make the world wonder: 1 Peter iv. 4, 'They think it strange you run not into the same excess of riot with them.' It is no wonder to see men proud, covetous, revengeful, carnal, self-seeking: corrupt nature will sufficiently prove this. As it is no wonder to see the sun move, though it was a wonder in Joshua's time when the sun stood still; so it is no wonder to see men loose and wicked; but it is a wonder to see men holy, heavenly, mortified, self-denying.

[D.] You will justify the ways of God against the cavils of atheists and profane carnal men: Mat. xi. 19, 'Wisdom is justified of her children'; and Israel justified Sodom, Ezek. xvi.

Use 2 is to exhort us to get this Holy Spirit to dwell in our hearts, that he may work in us a divine nature, or that spiritual and divine temper which will teach us to live above and against the inclinations of the flesh.

1. The means of infusing the divine nature into us is the doctrine and example of Christ. First, His doctrine, which discovereth higher things than the flesh inclineth us unto, and is the oply cure of the carnal spirit. This word was indited[10] 'by the Holy Spirit': For holy men spake as they were moved by the Holy Ghost': 2 Pet. ii. 21. He inspired the holy apostles, first to speak, and then to write, the doctrine of Christ; he 'led them into all truth:' John xvi. 13. The same Spirit attested this doctrine by miraculous gifts: Heb. ii. 4; is conveyed by it: Gal. iii. 2, 'Received ye the Spirit by the works of the law, or the hearing of faith?' He prepareth and assisteth the ordinary ministry, that they may be fitted to convey this great gift: Acts xx. 28, 'Take heed therefore unto yourselves, and to all the flock over which the Holy Ghost hath made you overseers'; and 2 Cor. iii. 6, 'Who also hath made us able ministers of the New Testament, not of the letter but of the spirit.' He writeth this doctrine upon the heart: Heb. x. 8, and 2 Cor. iii. 3. Doth so renew and sanctify our souls, that we may live unto God. Secondly, The example of Christ, for he had the days of his flesh: John i. 14; and Heb. v. 7; lived in the world, as men do, but not after the flesh; and God in our nature is the fit pattern for us to imitate, that we may be in the world as he was in the world, and not please the flesh, as he pleased not himself. To this example we are to be

---

[10] written

conformed; but it doth not barely work as an example, but as sanctified and accompanied by the Spirit; for it is said: 2 Cor. iii. 18, 'Beholding the glory of the Lord, as in a glass, we are changed into his image and likeness'; and so we are made partakers of this new and divine nature.

2. When the Spirit cometh to work it in us, we must not neglect and refuse his help, but give place to his motions; as when the waters were stirred, they presently put in for cure. To smother convictions breedeth atheism and hardness of heart. When he reproveth, you must hearken and observe: Prov. i. 23, when he knocketh you must open: Rev. iii. 20; when he draweth, you must run: Cant. i. 4. The smarter the reproof, the louder the knock, the stronger the drawing, the more you are bound to improve it, or else you are left in worse condition than before, by resisting or quenching the Spirit. It will be your advantage to obey him speedily, before the heart cool again: Isa. liv. 6. It is a time of finding which God may not give you again; delaying and shifting is a sign the help offered is rather looked upon as a trouble than a favour; and it is but a deceit of heart to elude the importunity of the present conviction: Mat. xxvii. 24, 25, 'Pilate took water and washed his hands, saying before the multitude, I am innocent of the blood of this man' His conscience boggles, and he makes use of this shift to put off the conviction. Surely God demandeth a present obedience: Heb. iii. 7, 8, 'To day if ye will hear his voice, harden not your hearts'; and all serious people will take the advantage: Gal. i. 16, 'Immediately I consulted not with flesh and blood;' Ps. cxix. 60, 'I made haste, and delayed not to keep thy commandments.'

2. Obey him thoroughly. Many will yield to him in some things, but reserve others. He must be obeyed in all things, even in renouncing our sweetest and dearest lusts: Mat. v. 29, 30. Nothing must be spared; every way of pleasing the flesh must be renounced; a partial obedience is rather a following our own humour and inclination than an obeying the Spirit, for he is contrary to all sin; and one sin let alone and allowed, is Satan's nest-egg in our hearts, that he may come thither again and lay more.

3. Obey him constantly, for he is still your guide and monitor, to put you in remembrance of your snares and duties: Eph. iv. 30, 'Grieve not the Holy Spirit, whereby you are sealed to the day of redemption.' When he hath sealed you, and stamped God's image and impress upon your hearts, he must not be grieved by your folly and disobedience. The children of God, that are first regenerated by the Spirit, are still guided and led by him: Rom. viii. 14, 'For as many as are led by the Spirit, are the sons of God.' You are not only to obey at first, but obey still. Jesus Christ, that was at first conceived by the Holy Ghost, was led by him: Luke i. 4, 14. So Christians are always under his conduct. You interrupt the course of his love when you are deaf to his motions.

Use 3 is to put us upon serious reflections. Are we in the flesh, or in the spirit? We are never Christians indeed, till we are in the spirit; you will have flesh in you, but which principle is the most pre dominant? Surely, that principle is predominant whose object is our chiefest good, or esteemed as our felicity. Objects of the flesh, are contentments of the present world; the objects of the spirit are God and heaven; what do you count your happiness? Ps. cxliv. 15, 'Happy is the people that is in such a case. 'Many judge them happy that have much of the world'; Yea, happy is the people whose God is the Lord.' There is the natural happiness, and the spiritual happiness; which is most valuable, or most prized by you? Secondly, That principle is most predominant, which doth most employ us. What do we most industriously pursue? the pleasure and prosperity of the body, or the happiness of the soul? All the care of some is about the body and the bodily life, but their neglected soul may complain of hard usage; what have you done to get the soul furnished and adorned with grace, or established in the comfort and hope of the gospel? Mat. vi. 33, 'First seek the kingdom of God, and his righteousness, and all these things shall be added'; John vi. 27, 'Labour not for the meat that perisheth, but the meat that endureth to everlasting life.' Thirdly, When, to the hurt of the soul and displeasure of God, you frequently gratify the flesh, this is such a constant disobedience to the Spirit's discipline that you cannot be said to be influenced by him.

SERMON XII

Now if any have not the Spirit of Christ, he is none of his.

Romans VIII. 9.

IN the context, we have an assertion of a general truth, 'There is no condemnation to them who are in Christ Jesus, who walk not after the flesh, but after the spirit' We have this application in the beginning of this verse, lest any should raise up a vain confidence that they were in Christ, and therefore freed from condemnation, without regarding what he had before said, expounding himself: ver. 1, 'Who walk not after the flesh, but after the spirit' He here further adds as an application of the proposition, 'he who hath not the Spirit of Christ, is none of his'; which, because they were Christians in profession, was more accommodate to them. Here observe

Doctrine That all true Christians have the spirit of Christ.

1. I suppose there are Christians, or Christ's disciples in name, and disciples indeed: John viii. 31. As an Israelite indeed: John i. 47; Rom. ii. 29. The apostle distinguished of a Jew in the letter, and a Jew in the spirit. So, by just analogy and proportion, there are Christians in the letter, that have the outside of Christians, but not the life and power. We are only Christians in name and profession till we have the Spirit.

2. I assert, that which discriminateth the one from the other, is the having the Spirit. It is a mark both exclusive and inclusive; some marks are exclusive, but not inclusive: John i. 47, 'He that is of God, heareth God's word: ye, therefore, hear them not, because ye are not of God'; that is exclusive. Acts xiii. 46, 'But seeing ye put away the word of God from you, and judge yourselves unworthy of eternal life;' that is also exclusive. But if we depend upon these marks, we put a false reasoning upon our souls: James i. 22, 'But be ye doers of the word, and not hearers only, deceiving your own souls,' 7rapa\oy^6fievoi,. There are inclusive marks, but not exclusive, as: Rom. ix. 1, 2, 3, 'I say the truth in Christ, I lie not, my conscience also bearing me witness in the Holy Ghost, that I have great heaviness and continual sorrow in my heart; for I could wish that myself were accursed from Christ for my brethren, my kinsmen according to the flesh' They that can prefer a public good, before their own personal eternal interest, have an undoubted evidence of their love to Christ; but we cannot say that none love Christ, but those which arrive at that height and degree: but this is both exclusive and inclusive. The text showeth it to be exclusive; he that hath not the Spirit, is none of his; that is, not grafted as a living member into Christ's mystical body for the present, nor will he be accepted or approved as a true Christian at last, at the day of Christ's appearing; to be none of Christ's, is to be disowned and disclaimed by Christ, 'Depart from me, I know you not.' How grievous is the thought of it to any good Christian! Secondly, It is inclusive: 1 John ii. 13, 'Hereby we know that we dwell in God, and he in us, because he hath given us of his Spirit.' These are magnificent words, and such as we should not have used, if God had not used them before us. It is much nearness to dwell one with another, it is more nearness to dwell one in another; this is mutual and reciprocal between God and a believer; if we have his Spirit we may safely conclude it. To prove this, let us see,

1. What it is to have the Spirit.

2. Why this is the evidence that we are true Christians. First. For the first question take these explanations:

1. By the Spirit of Christ is not meant any created habit and gift For the new nature is sometimes called the spirit: John iii. 6. But the third person in the Trinity, called the Holy Ghost, is here meant; for he is spoken of as a person that dwelleth in believers, in the former part of the verse; and dwelleth in them as in his temple, as one that leadeth, guideth, and sanctifieth them; yea, as one that will at length quicken their mortal bodies, ver. 11, which no created habit and quality can do. Yea, he is called the Spirit of God, and the Spirit of Christ: 'If so be the Spirit of God dwell in you'; and in the words of the text, 'If any man have not the Spirit of Christ.' Because he proceedeth from the Father and the Son: John xv. 26, 'When the comforter is come, whom I will send you from the Father, even the Spirit of truth, which proceedeth from the Father.' This is the Spirit which is spoken of in this place.

2. This Spirit is had, or said to be in us. We have not only the fruit, but the tree. But how have we him? We have a right to his person, he is given to us in the covenant of grace, as our sanctifier; as God is ours by covenant, so is the Spirit ours, as well as the Father and the Son; and he is present in our hearts, as the immediate agent of Christ, and worker of all grace. It is true, in respect of his essence, and some kind of operation, he is present in all creatures: Ps. cxxxix. 7, 'Whither shall I go from thy Spirit? Whither shall I fly from thy presence? 'God filleth all things with his Spirit and presence. And therefore when some are said to have him, and others not to have him, it is understood of his peculiar presence, with respect to those eminent operations and effects which he produceth in the hearts of the faithful, and nowhere else; for he is such an agent nowhere, as he is in their hearts. Therefore, they are called temples of the Holy Ghost 1 Cor. iii. 16 and 1 Cor. vi. 19 because he buildeth them up for a holy use, and also dwelleth and resideth there, maintaining God's interest in their souls.

3. These eminent operations of the Holy Ghost are either in a way of common gifts, or special graces; as to common gifts, reprobates and hypocrites may be said to be partakers of the Holy Ghost, Heb. vi. 4, Balaam had the gift of prophecy, and Judas the gift of miracles, as well as the rest of the apostles: 1 Cor. xii., the apostle discourseth at large of the gifts of the Spirit, and concludeth'; but I shew you a more excellent 'way' verse 31; and then taketh it up again: 1 Cor. xiii. 1, 2, 'Though I speak with the tongue of men and angels, and have not charity, I am become as a sounding brass, or a tinkling cymbal; and, though I have the gift of prophecy, and understand all mysteries and all knowledge; and though I have all faith, so that I could remove mountains, and have no charity, I am nothing.'

There are *dona ministrantia*, gifts for the service of the church; such as profound knowledge, utterance in preaching, or praying, or any other ministerial acts; and *dona sanctificantia*, such as faith, hope, and love; the former may render us useful to the church, but not acceptable to the Lord. The superficial Christianity is rewarded with common gifts, but the real Christianity with special graces; all that profess the faith are visibly adopted by

God into his family, and under a visible administration of the covenant of grace; so far as they are adopted into God's family, so far are they made partakers of the Spirit. Christ giveth to common Christians those common gifts of the Spirit, which he giveth not to the heathen world; as, knowledge of the mysteries of godliness, abilities of utterance and speech about heavenly things; some affection also to spiritual and heavenly things, called a tasting of the good word; the heavenly gift, and the powers of the world to come; these will not prove us true Christians, or really in God's special favour, but only visible, professed Christians.

4. The Spirit, as to sanctifying and saving effects, may be considered as *spiritus assistens aut informans*; either as moving, warning, or exciting, by transient motions; so the wicked may be wrought upon by him, as to be convinced, warned, excited; how else can they be said to resist the Holy Ghost? Acts vii. -51. And the Lord telleth the old world, Gen. vi. 3, that his Spirit should not always strive with them. Surely, besides the counsels and exhortations of the word, the Spirit doth rebuke, warn, and excite them, and moveth, and stirreth, and striveth in the hearts of all carnal creatures, or else these expressions could not be used.

5. There are such effects of his sanctifying grace, as are wrought in us, *per modum habitus permanentis*, to renew and change us, so as a man from carnal, doth become spiritual, the Spirit of God doth so dwell in us as to frame heart and life into holiness; this work is sometimes called the new creature, 2 Cor. v. 17, and sometimes the divine nature, 2 Pet. i. 4. It differeth from gifts, because they are for out ward service; but this conduceth to change the heart: it differeth from actual motions and inspirations, because they may vanish and die away, without any saving impression left upon the heart: it differeth from those slighter dispositions to godliness, which are many times in temporaries; because they are but a light tincture, soon worn off, and have no power and mastery over sensual affections; if they restrain them a little, they do not mortify and subdue them. Good motions are as a dash of rain; and those weak inclinations and good dispositions which are in temporaries, are as a pond, or pool, which may be dried up; hut this saving and sanctifying work is as a spring: John iv. 14. Two things are considerable in it: 1. Its continuance and indication. 2. Its efficacy and predominancy.

[A.] The radication is set forth by the notions of the Spirit's dwelling in us: John xiv. 17, 'He shall be in you, and dwell in you.' Its resting upon us: 1 Pet. iv. 14, 'The Spirit of God and of glory rest upon you' He taketh up his abode with us: John xiv. 23, 'We will come to him, and make our abode with him' It is not a visit and away, or a lodging for a night, but a constant residence; he taketh up his mansion in our hearts. Some have fits and qualms of religion, motions of conviction and joy, but not a settled bent of heart towards God and heaven.

[B.] Its prevalency and predominancy; for where the Spirit dwelleth, there he must rule, and have the command of the house; he dwelleth in the soul; he dwelleth so as to govern, directing and inclining us so as to do things pleasing unto God, weaning us from the world: 1 Cor. ii. 12. This is called the receiving, not the spirit of the world, but that which is of God. Mastering and taming the flesh, both its gust and savour: Rom. viii. 5, 'For they that are after the flesh, do mind the things of the flesh' Its deeds and motions: Rom. viii. 13, 'If ye mortify the deeds of the body, ye shall live' The flesh will rebel, but the Spirit gets the upper hand, for the dominion and sovereignty of the flesh are not consistent with the having of the Spirit; the flesh is subdued more and more; where the Spirit cometh, he cometh to govern, to suit the heart to the will of God, and to give us greater liberty towards him: 2 Cor. iii. 17, 'Where the Spirit of the Lord is, there is liberty' The objects of sense which feed the flesh make less impression upon us; and the love of sin is more arid more conquered. Now take it thus explained, you may know what it is to have the Spirit, namely, the dwelling and working of the Spirit in our souls, mortifying the flesh, and causing us to live unto God.

Secondly. Why is this an evidence that we are true Christians? Here I shall prove two things.

1. That all true Christians have this sanctifying Spirit.

2. That it is the certain evidence and proof of their being Christians, or having an interest in Christ.

1. That all that are true Christians have it. I prove it

[A.] From the promise of God, who hath promised it to them; and surely his love and faithfulness will see it made good: Zech. xii. 10, 4 1 will pour upon them the Spirit of grace and supplications'; and Prov. i. 23, 'Turn unto me, and I will pour out an abundance of Spirit unto you;' and Rev. xxii. 17,' Whosoever will, let him drink of the water of life freely' By the water of life is meant the Spirit; as appeareth, John vii. 38, 39; so in many other places. Now surely God's word will not fall to the ground, but must be accomplished.

[B.] From the merit of Christ. Two things Christ purchased and bestowed upon all his people, his righteousness and his Spirit: 2 Cor. v. 21, 'He was made sin for us, that we might be made the righteous ness of God in him ': Gal. iii. 14, 'That we might receive the promise of the Spirit through faith; the rock was smitten by the rod of Moses twice,' 1 Cor. x. 4. And these two gifts are inseparable; where he giveth the one, he giveth the other; we have both, or none: 1 Cor. vi. 11. 'But ye are justified in the name of our Lord Jesus, and by the Spirit of our God': and Tit. iii. 5, 6, 7, 'But according to his mercy he saved us by the washing of regeneration, and the renewing of the Holy Ghost, which he shed on us abundantly through Jesus Christ our Saviour, that being justified by his grace, we should be made heirs according to the hope of eternal life.' He freeth us at the same time *a malo morali*, which is sin; and *a malo naturali*, which is punishment.

[C.] When we enter into the covenant of grace, we enter into covenant i Father, Son, and Holy Ghost; with God, and with the Redeemer, and with the Sanctifier: Mat. xxviii. 19, 'We are baptized in the name of the Father, Son, and Holy Ghost.' What is our covenant with the Holy Ghost? It implieth both our duty and our benefit; our benefit is that we expect that the Holy Ghost should regenerate us, and renew us to the image of God, and plant us into Christ by faith, and then dwell in us, and maintain God's interest in our souls, and so make us saints and believers: and our duty is to consent to give up ourselves to him as our sanctifier, and to obey his powerful motions, before we are made partakers of the Holy Ghost.

[D.] The necessity of having the Spirit appeareth, in that without him we can do nothing in Christianity from first to last; it is the Spirit uniteth us to Christ, and planteth us into his mystical body: 1 Cor. xii. 13, 'By one Spirit we are baptized into one body'; it is by the Spirit we give up ourselves to God as our God and reconciled Father in Christ, and to Christ as our Redeemer and Saviour and so are planted into his mystical body: 1 Cor. vi. 17, 'But he that is joined to the Lord is one spirit' As a man and a harlot are one flesh, so we are one spirit; the union is spiritual for kind, and the Spirit is the author of it. So for further sanctification, and consolation, and mortification; take it either for the purging out lusts or suppressing the acts of sin; for the purging out of lusts: 1 Pet. i. 22, 'Seeing ye have purified your souls in obeying the truth through the Spirit.' Pride, worldliness, and sensuality, these are purged out more and more by the Spirit. Or suppressing the acts of sin: Rom. viii. 13, 'If ye through the Spirit do mortify the deeds of the body.' So for vivification, he infuseth life, and quickeneth and maintaineth it in our souls: Gal. v. 25, 'If we live in the Spirit, let us also walk in the Spirit.' Strengthening it: Eph. iii. 16, 'That he would grant you according to the riches of his grace to be strengthened with might, by his Spirit.' He maketh it fruitful and exciteth it: Ezek. xxxvi. 27, 'I will put my Spirit into you, and cause you to walk in my ways.' For consolation, to uphold our hearts in the midst of all trials and difficulties; then we may go on cheerfully, and in a course of holiness: Acts ix. 31, 'They walked in the fear of God, and the comforts of the Holy Ghost.' To comfort us with the sense of God's love in all our tribulations: Rom. v. 5, 'Because the love of God is shed abroad in our hearts by the Holy Ghost, which is given unto us.' To wait for eternal life: Gal. v. 5, 'But we through the Spirit do wait for the hope of righteousness by faith,' that is, which is built upon it.

2. This Spirit is the evidence of men being true Christians, the only sure and proper evidence: this will appear,

[A.] By the metaphors and terms by which the Spirit is set forth; he is called a seal, a witness, and an earnest': Who hath sealed us, and given us the earnest of his Spirit in our hearts': 2 Cor. i. 22; and Eph. i. 13, 14, 'After ye believed, ye were sealed with the Holy Spirit of promise.' Men used to set their mark and stamp upon their wares, that they might own them for theirs. God sealeth by his Spirit; his stamp is his image: 2 Cor. iii. 18, 'We are changed into his image from glory to glory.' So he is also set forth under the notion of a witness: Rom. viii. 16, 'The Spirit itself beareth witness' What is the witness of the Spirit? Not an immediate revelation or oracle in your bosoms, to tell you that you are God's children, but the renovation of the soul, and the constant operation of the Holy Spirit, dwelling and working in you; this testifieth to our consciences or spirits, that God hath adopted us into his family; thus the Spirit is a witness to the scriptures. So he is set forth as an earnest: 2 Cor. v. 5, 'Now he that hath wrought us to this self-same thing is God, who hath also given us the earnest of his Spirit.' An earnest is part of the sum; we have somewhat of the life, and peace, and joy of the Spirit now. which enableth us to wait with the more comfort and assurance for our future blessedness.

[B.] From the congruity of this evidence.

(1.) The coming down of the Holy Ghost upon him as the evidence of God's love to Christ, and the visible dempnstration of his affiliation and sonship to the world. The evidence of God's love: John. iii. 34, 1 The Father loved the Son, and gave him the Spirit without measure' Now Christ prayed: John xvii. 26'; That the love wherewith thou hast loved me may be in them'; and v. 23, 'That the world may know that thou hast sent me, and hast loved them as thou hast loved me' None will think in degree, therefore in kind, that God would manifest his love to us, as he did to him, by the gift of the Holy Spirit, or his filiation. John knew Christ to be the Son of God, by the Spirit descending and abiding on him: John. i. 32, 'I saw the Spirit descend from heaven like a dove, and it abode on him'; yea, God himself owned this as a demonstration of his sonship: Mat. iii. 17, 'This is my well-beloved Son, in whom I am well pleased' So do we know ourselves to be the children of God, by the Spirit's inhabitation and sanctifying work upon our souls.

(2.) The pouring out of the Spirit was the visible evidence given to the church of the sufficiency of Christ's satisfaction. When God was reconciled, then he shed forth the Spirit: Acts ii. 33, 'Therefore being at the right hand of God exalted, and having received of the Father the promise of the Holy Ghost, he hath shed forth this which ye now see and hear'; so John vii. 38, 39, 'He that believeth in me, (as the scripture saith) out of his belly shall flow rivers of living water: this he spake of the Spirit, which they that believed on him should receive; for the Holy Ghost was not yet given, because Jesus was not yet glorified' Now this is true of God's love and reconciliation to us in particular; when he is pacified, he giveth the Spirit, because the part followeth the reason of the whole; and the atonement made, and the atonement received, Rom. v. 11, are evidenced the same way, even by this fountain of living water, which is given to all believers.

(3.) This is the witness of the truth of the gospel, and therefore the best pledge of the love of God we can have in our hearts; for the believer's hopes are confirmed in the same way the gospel is confirmed; that which confirmeth Christianity, confirmeth the Christian; the extract and original charter are confirmed by the same stamp and impression; the Spirit confirmeth the love of God to sinners, and therefore the love of God to me: Act. v. 32, 'And we are witnesses of these things, and so is the Holy Ghost, whom God hath given to them that obey him.' The word was confirmed by the great wonders wrought by the Holy Ghost: Heb. iii. 4, 'God bearing them witness, with signs and wonders, and divers gifts of the Holy Ghost.' The sanctifying Spirit: John xvii. 17, 'Sanctify them through the truth, thy word is truth': 1 John v. 10, 'He that believeth on the Son, hath the witness in himself.' The Spirit comforting the conscience by the blood of Christ, and sanctifying the heart, and cleansing it as with pure water, this also is our evidence.

[C.] From the qualities of this evidence, and so it is most apt to satisfy the doubting conscience concerning its interest in Christ and his benefits.

(1.) It is a great benefit, becoming the love of God, to give us his Holy Spirit; it is more than if he had given us all the world. Persons that have been at variance will not believe one another, unless their reconciliation be verified by some remarkable good turn and visible testimony of love. A great offender reconciled to Augustus, yet would not believe it, unless he put some notable mark of his favour upon him; as David to Amasa, making him general of his army. Surely the breach hath been so great between us and God, that we shall have no peace and joy in believing, till we have some gift that may be a perfect demonstration that he is at peace with us: Rom. v. 11, 'We joy in God, as those that have received the atonement'; the pledge of it is in the gift of the Spirit. Most men's patience cometh from their stupidness, their confidence from their security, their quiet from their mindlessness of heavenly things; but the soul that is in good earnest must have a witness of God's love, or a sufficient proof that he is reconciled and taken into God's family, made an heir according to the hope of eternal life, which is the spirit of adoption: Gal. iv. 6, 'And because ye are sons, God hath sent the Spirit of his Son into your hearts, crying, Abba, Father'

(2.) It is most sensible, as being within our own hearts: the death of Christ was a demonstration of God's love, but that was done without us on the cross, and before we were born. Justification is a blessed privilege, but either that is God's act in heaven accepting us in Christ, or else, in the sentence of the law, by which we are constituted just; but this cometh into our hearts; Gal. iv. 6, 'God hath sent the Spirit of his Son into our hearts'; so 2 Cor. i. 22, 'He hath given us the earnest of the Spirit in our hearts'; so 1 John v. 11, 'He that believeth hath the witness in himself'; compare the eighth verse.

(3.) It is a permanent and abiding testimony. By his constant opera tion we are acquainted with him, and know him; what moveth and stirreth in us but now and then we understand not, but the Holy Ghost is familiar with us, resideth and dwelleth in our hearts; we feel his pulse and motions: John xiv. 17, 'I will send you the Spirit of truth, whom the world cannot receive, because it seeth him not, neither knoweth him; but ye know him, for he dwelleth in you, and shall be in you'. They that constantly feel his operations in comforting, quickening, instructing them, they may see how they are beloved of God, and minded by him upon all occasions. The effects of the Spirit are life, holiness, faith, strength, joy, comfort, and peace; he enlighteneth our understanding, confirmeth our faith, and assures us of salvation; exciteth us to prayer, stirreth up holy desires and motions, comforteth us in crosses, awakeneth us in groans after heaven. Now those that have such constant experience of the illuminating, sanctifying, quickening work of the Spirit on their souls, cannot but know what kind of spirit dwelleth and worketh in them.

(4.) The sanctifying Spirit is the surest note of our reconciliation with God, as that which will not deceive us; when he sanctifieth, he is pacified towards us: Heb. xiii. 20, 21, 'Now the God of peace, that brought again from the dead our Lord Jesus, the great shepherd of the sheep, through the blood of the everlasting covenant, make you perfect in every good work to do his will, working in you that which is well pleasing in his sight'; and 1 Thes. v. 23, 'The very God of peace sanctify you wholly in body, soul, and spirit;' 2 Cor. v. 17, 18, 'If any man be in Christ, he is a new creature; old things are passed away, behold all things are become new; and all things are of God, who hath reconciled us to himself by Jesus Christ' A man lieth open to delusions by other evidences, and may be long enough without true and solid comfort.

[D.] From God's constant government. But there is a twofold way of providence by which he governeth the world, or else conducteth souls to glory; there is an external sort of government, by prosperities, and adversities, and afflictions, and worldly blessings. Now these have their use, to invite us to obedience, and to caution us against sin; but these things are not dispensed as sure evidences of God's love and hatred, Eccles. ix. 2. Worldly good things may be given in anger, lest men should be marked out by their outward condition, rather than the disposition of their souls. God would not distinguish the good by the blessings of his common providence, nor brand and mark out the bad by their afflictions. Therefore these mercies that run in the channel of common providence, are dispensed promiscuously. But God hath another way of internal government, carried on within the soul by troubles of conscience for sin, and the comforts of a good conscience as the reward of obedience. Now in this sort of government, the influence of the Spirit is mainly seen; God showeth his anger or his love, his pleasure or displeasure, by giving and withholding the Spirit; when he is pleased, we have the testimony of it in our consciences by the presence and comforts of the Spirit; when displeased, he with- draweth the Spirit; this is reward and punishment, the accesses and recesses of the Spirit, if we have sinned: Ps. li. 10, 'Cast me not away from thy presence, and take not away thy Holy Spirit from me.' The retaining and witholding the Spirit is one of the greatest calamities in the world; ver. 2, 'Renew a right spirit in me'; ver. 12, 'And uphold me by thy free Spirit. On the contrary the reward of obedience is the increase of the Spirit: Rom. xiv. 17, 'For the kingdom of God is not in meats and drinks, but righteousness, and peace, and joy in the Holy Ghost.' Now this being God's constant way of internal government, whereby he manifesteth his pleasure or displeasure by witholding, or withdrawing, or giving out his Spirit; and this is a surer way than the effects of his external providence. I cannot say God hateth me, because he denieth earthly blessings, or blasteth them when bestowed; this may be for other reasons than to manifest his anger or hatred: I cannot say God loveth me because I enjoy outward prosperity; but if I have the Spirit, that is never given in anger.

Use 1 is to persuade us to seek after the presence of the Spirit in our hearts. It is not enough to be baptized, to have the common faith and profession of Christians, no, we must also have the Spirit of Christ; for, while we are carnal, we are Christians only in the letter. Two things I will press you to to receive and retain him; to get him and keep him.

[A.] Get him. See that he be entered into your hearts to recover your souls to God, John iii 5, see that you 'be born again of water, and of the Spirit'; and not only so, but get an increase and supply of the Spirit of Jesus Christ: Phil. i. 17, 'Through your prayers, and the supply of the Spirit of Jesus Christ.' Seek more of the Spirit, and lose him not in part, nor in whole': Quench not the Spirit' Eph. iv. 30. To encourage you, consider,

God is ready to give the Holy Spirit, Luke xi. 13, and Christ hath purchased it, that it might not be shed on us in a sparing manner, Tit. iii. 5. 6. It is applied to us by the word, or gospel-dispensation, 2 Cor. iii. 18. Baptism hath its use, Tit. iii. 5; it doth not signify so much the blood of Christ, as the sanctifying, cleansing Spirit purchased thereby. The promise of the Spirit is sometimes made absolutely: as Zech. xii. 10, 'I will pour out a spirit of grace and supplication.' As implying the first grace, you must take your lot; if you miss of it, it is long of yourselves; you resisted former warnings, motions, and strivings of the Spirit; wait in the use of means. Sometimes, conditionally, to faith: John vii. 39, 'This he spake of the Spirit, which they that believe on him, should receive.' Sometimes to repentance: Acts ii. 38, 'Repent, and thou shalt receive the gift of the Holy Ghost' Prov. i. 38. Now these must be often renewed, if we would get more of the Spirit into our hearts, for the Spirit is continued and increased to us by the same acts by which it is gotten at first, by faith and repentance; faith assenting, or consenting, or denying.

(1.) Assenting with admiration of the infinite goodness and love of God shining forth to us in our redemption by Christ. The assent must be strong, that it may more effectually lead on other parts of faith, and because the actions of the three persons are a great mystery: 1 Pet. i. 2, 'Elect according to the foreknowledge of God the Father, through the sanctification of the Spirit, unto obedience and sprinkling of the blood of Jesus' Here is the eternal love of the Father, the infinite merit of Christ, and the all-powerful operation of the Spirit. An assent with wonder and astonishment, because so much wisdom, love, and grace was discovered in it, Eph. iii. 17-19.

(2.) Consent must be often renewed to that covenant by which the Spirit is dispensed. Often enter into a resolution to take God for your God, for your sovereign lord, your portion and happiness; and Christ for your redeemer and saviour; and the Holy Ghost for your guide, sanctifier and comforter. Every solemn consent renewed doth both confirm you in the benefit of the Spirit, and bind you and excite you to the duties required by God in all these relations. Your constant work is to love and seek after God as your happiness, and Jesus Christ as your saviour, and the Spirit for your guide and direction.

(3.) Dependence upon the love of God, and the merits of Christ, and the power of the Spirit, that you may use Christ's appointed means with the more confidence. That soul that thus sets itself to believe, findeth a wonderful increase of the Spirit in this renewed exercise of faith, assenting, consenting, and depending: Rom. xv. 13, 'The God of hope fill you with all joy and peace in believing, that you may abound in hope through the power of the Holy Ghost'

[B.] Your repentance must be renewed by a hearty grief for sin, and resolutions and endeavours against it. The more sin is made odious, the more the Spirit hath obtained his effect in you; and the more heartily you study to please God in the work of love and obedience, the more you are acquainted with the Spirit and his quickenings, the Spirit and his comforts: Acts ix. 31, 'They walked in the fear of the Lord, and the comforts of the Holy Ghost.' His business is to make you holy; the more you obey his motions and follow his directions, the more he delighteth to dwell in your hearts.

Use 2 is self-reflection. Let me put that question to you: Acts xix. 3, 'Have ye received the Holy Ghost since ye believed?' Is the first great change wrought? are you called from darkness to light? from sin to holiness? turned from Satan to God? Are you made partakers of the divine nature? 2 Pet. i. 4. The change must be perfected more and more by the Spirit: 2 Cor. iii. 18, 'Beholding as in a glass the glory of the Lord, we are changed into his image from glory to glory, by the Spirit of the Lord' Do you obey his sanctifying motions? Rom. viii. 14, 'For as many as are led by the Spirit of God are the sons of God' His motions all tend to quicken us to the heavenly life, inclining our hearts to things above: 2 Thes. ii. 13, 'But we are bound to give thanks always to God for you, brethren, beloved of the Lord, because God hath from the beginning chosen you to salvation through sanctification of the Spirit, and belief of the truth,'

SERMON XIII

And if Christ be in you, the body is dead because of sin, and the Spirit is life because of
righteousness.

Romans VIII. 10.

THE text is manifestly a *prolepsis*, or a preoccupation of a secret objection against our
redemption by Christ. If believers die as well as others, how are they freed from death?
Questionless, Christ was sent into the world to abolish the misery brought in by Adam's sin;
now death was the primary punishment of sin: Gen. ii. 17, 'In the day thou eatest thereof,
thou shalt surely die;' and this remaineth on believers. The apostle answereth in the words
read,

First, By supposition, 'if Christ be in you'; that he might fix the privilege on the persons to
whom it properly belongeth.

Secondly, By concession, 'The body is dead because of sin.'

Thirdly, By correction, 'And the Spirit is life because of righteous ness.'

First, The supposition showeth that the comfort of the privilege is drawn from the spiritual
union which believers have with Christ: 'If Christ be in you.' Secondly, the concession
granteth what must be granted, that death befalleth believers; their bodies return to the
dust as others do. But, thirdly, the correction is, that they are certain to live forever with
Christ both in body and soul; and this upon a twofold ground; first, there is a life begun,
which shall not be quenched, but perfected. 'The Spirit is life'; the ground and procuring
cause is Christ's righteousness. Sin deprived them of the life of grace, and forfeited the life
of glory; but here the righteousness of Christ hath purchased this life for us, and the Spirit
applieth it to us.

Doctrine That Christ in believers, notwithstanding death, is a sure pledge and earnest to
them of eternal life both in body and soul.

This point will be best discussed with respect to the several clauses in the text the
supposition, the concession, the correction, or contrary assertion.

[A.] The supposition 'If Christ be in you.' Here I will prove to you, that a true Christian is one
that doth not only profess Christ, but hath Christ in him: 2 Cor. xiii. 5, 'Know ye not that
Jesus Christ is in you, except ye are reprobates? 'that is senseless, stupid wretches, not
accepted of God: so Col. i. 27, 'Christ in you the hope of glory.' Now Christ is in us two ways,
objectively and effectively: objectively, as the object is in the faculty, or the things we think
of and love are in our hearts and minds; so Christ is in us, as he is apprehended and
embraced by faith and love; so he is said, Eph. iii. 17, 'To dwelt in our hearts by faith'; and
again, 'He that dwelleth in love, dwelleth in God, and God in him' 1 John iv. 18. Which is not
to be under stood of the acts only, but the habitual temper and dispositions of our souls; for
else by the ceasing of the acts, the union at least in our hearts would be broken off.
Secondly, effectively, so Christ is in us by his Spirit and gracious influence. Now, the effects
of his Spirit are first, life, he is become the principle of a new life in us: Gal. ii. 20, 1 Christ

liveth in me; and the life that I live in the flesh, I live by the faith of the Son of God.' Where he is, he maketh us to live; and we have another principle of our lives than ourselves or our own natural or renewed spirit. Secondly, Likeness or renovation of our natures: Gal. iv. 19, 'Until Christ be formed in you.' The image of Christ is impressed on the soul: 2 Cor. v. 17, 'if any man be in Christ, he is a new creature.' It is all to the same effect, our being in Christ, or Christ's being in us, for both imply union, and the effect of it a near conformity to Christ in holiness. Thirdly, Strength by the continued influence of his grace to overcome temptation: 1 John iv. 4, 'Ye are of God, little children, and have overcome him, because greater is he that is in you, than he that is in the world.' The Spirit keepeth afoot God's interest in. the soul against all the assaults of the devil; so for the variety of conditions we pass through: Phil. iv. 12, 'I know both how to be abased and how to abound; everywhere, and in all things I am instructed both to be full, and to be hungry; both to abound, and to suffer need'; so for all duties that we are called unto: 1 Cor. xv. 10: 'By the grace of God I am what I am; and his grace which was bestowed upon me was not in vain, but I laboured more abundantly than they all, and yet not I, but the grace of God which was in me'; and Heb. xiii. 21, 'Working in you that which is pleasing in his sight through Jesus Christ' Now, you see what it is to have Christ in us; none but these are real Christians.

(1.) Because we must first be partakers of Christ before we can be partakers of any saving benefit purchased by him, as members are united to the head before they receive sense and motion from it. Christ giveth nothing of his purchase to any but to whom he giveth himself first, 1 John v. 12. And to whom he giveth himself, to them he giveth all things needful to their salvation.

(2.) Where Christ once entereth, there he taketh up his abode and lodging, not to depart thence; dwelling noteth his constant and familiar presence; he doth not sojourn for a while, but dwelleth as a man in his own house and castle. There is a continued presence and influence, whereby they are supported in their Christianity'; He dwelleth in us, and we in him, and we know that he abideth in us by his Spirit': 1 John iii. 24, and John xiv. 23, 'If a man love me he will keep my words, and my Father will love him, and we will come unto him, and take up our abode with him' Not a visit and away, but a constant residence: John xv. 5, 'He that abideth in me, and I in him, the same bringeth forth much fruit'

(3.) Where Christ is, he ruleth and reigneth; for we receive him as our Lord and Saviour: Col. ii. 6. 'As ye received Christ Jesus the Lord, so walk in him' We received him, that he may perform the office of a mediator in our hearts, and teach us, and rule us, and guide us by his Spirit. All others know him by hearsay, but these know him by experience; the testimony of Christ is confirmed in them. Others talk of Christ, but these feel him; others have him in their ears and tongues, but not in their hearts; or if the heart be warm and heavenly for a fit, it quickly falleth to the earth again. Then here doth our true happiness begin, to find Christ within us; this is that which giveth the seal to Christ without us, and all the mysteries of redemption by him; for you have experienced the power and comfort of it in your own souls; you find his image in your hearts, and his Spirit conforming you to what he commandeth in the word, and have a suitableness to the gospel in your souls; you may look with an holy confidence for help to him in all your necessities, when others look at him with strange and doubtful thoughts, because nearness breedeth familiarity, and the sense of his continual love and presence begets a holy confidence to come to him for mercy and grace to help; in short, when others have but the common offer, you have a propriety and interest in Christ. Christ without us is a perfect Saviour, but not to you; the appropriation is by union; he came down from heaven, took our nature, died for sinners, ascended up into heaven again to make intercession at the right hand of the Father; all this is without us. Do not say only there is a Saviour in heaven; is there one in thy heart? There is an intercessor in heaven, is there one in thy heart? Rom. viii. 26, 'But the Spirit itself maketh intercession for us with groanings which cannot be uttered.' He was born of the virgin, is he formed in thee? Gal. iv. 19. He died, are you planted into the likeness of his death? Rom. vi. 5. He is risen from the dead; do you know the power of his resurrection? Phil. iii. 10. Are you raised with him? Col. iii. 1. He is ascended, are you ascended with him? Eph, ii. 6. Christ without us established the merit, but Christ within us assureth the application.

Secondly, I come now to the concession, 'The body is dead, because of sin.' Here observe the emphasis of the expression, 'the body is dead'; not only shall die, or must die, but is dead. He expresseth himself thus for two reasons, first, because the sentence is passed: Gen. ii. 17, Heb. ix. 27, 'It is appointed for all men once to die.' Therefore, as we say of a condemned man, he is a dead man, by reason of the sentence passed upon him; so by reason of this sentence, our body is a mortal body, liable to death, sentenced, doomed to death, and must one day undergo it. The union between it and the soul after a certain time shall be dissolved, and our bodies corrupted. The execution is begun; mortality hath already seized upon our bodies, by the many infirmities tending to, and ending in, the dissolution of nature. We now bear about the marks of sin in our bodies, the harbingers of death are already come, and have taken up their lodging aforehand. The apostle saith, 'in deaths often.' How many deaths do we suffer, before death cometh to relieve us, by several diseases, as colics, meagrims, catarrhs, gout, stone, and the like? All these prepare for it; and therefore this body, though glorious in its structure, as it is the workmanship of God, is called a vile body, as it is the subject of so many diseases; yea, and itself is continually dying: Heb. xi. 12, 'Therefore sprang there even of one, and him as good as dead.' We express it, a man hath one foot in the grave.

[B.] The reason is assigned, 'Because of sin' Death is the most ordinary thing in the world, but its cause and end are little thought of. This expression will give us occasion to speak of both its meritorious cause, and its use and end; both are implied in the clause, 'Because of sin.'

(1.) It implieth the meritorious cause. Death is not a natural accident, but a punishment; we die not as the beasts die, or as the plants decay; no, the scripture telleth us by what gate it entered into the world, namely, that it is an effect of the justice of God for man's sin: Horn. v. 12, 'By one man sin entered into the world, and death by sin.' And it is also by covenant, therefore called wages, Rom. vi. 23. Sin procured it, and the law ratifies it. Ay, but doth it so come upon the faithful? I answer, though their sins be forgiven, yet God would leave this mark of his displeasure on all mankind, that all Adam's children shall die, for a warning to the world. Well then, sin carries death in its bosom, and to some this death is but a step to hell, or death to come; it is not so to the godly; yet in their instance, God would teach the world the sure connexion between death and sin; whosoever hath been once a sinner, must die.

(2.) Its end and use, 'The body is dead because of sin': that is, the relics of sin are not abolished but by death; there is a twofold end and use of death to them that are in Christ.

First, To finish transgression and make an end of sin. We groan under the burden of it, while we are in our mortal bodies, Rom. vii. 21. But when the believer dieth, death is the destruction of sin, rather than of the penitent sinner; the veil of the sinful flesh is rent, and by the sight of God we are purified all in an instant; and then sin shall gasp its last, and our physician will perfect the cure which he hath begun in us, and we shall be presented faultless before the presence of God.

Secondly, To free us from the natural infirmities which render us incapable of that happy life in heaven which is intended for us. The state of Adam in innocency was blessed, but terrene and earthly, a state that needed meat, drink, and sleep. If Christ would have restored us to this life, it may be death had not been necessary, and the present state of our bodies needed not to be destroyed, but only purified; but our Lord Jesus had a higher aim: Eph. i. 3, 'Who hath blessed us with spiritual blessings in Christ.' Adam enjoyed God among the beasts in paradise; we enjoy God among the angels in heaven; it is a divine and heavenly life that he promiseth, a life like that of the blessed angels, where meat, and drink, and sleep hath no use. Now this nature that we now have, is not fitted for this life; therefore Paul telleth us: 1 Cor. xv. 50. 'That flesh and blood cannot inherit the kingdom of God; that is, that animal life which we derived from Adam cannot inherit the kingdom of God. Therefore we need to bear the image of the heavenly, which cannot be till this terrene and animal life be abolished. To this end God useth death. So that which was in itself a punishment, becometh a means of entrance into glory; the corn is not quickened unless it die: 1 Cor. xv. 36, 37, 38. The believers that are alive at Christ's coming must be changed, ver. 51, 52. Christ himself by death entered into glory; therefore whatever is animal, vile, and earthly, and weak, must be put off, before we are capable of this blessed estate.

(3.) The cause of this mortality is, 'Because of sin.' Had it not been for sin, we had never had cause to fear dissolution; there had been no use for coffins and winding sheets; nor had we been beholden to a grave, to hide our carcase from the sight and smell of the living; there was a *posse mom* in innocency, else death could not be threatened as a penalty; but there was a *posse non mori*, or else immortality could not be propounded as the reward of obedience; therefore man is mortal, *conditione corporis*; but immortal, *beneficio conditori*; God could have supported him. Well then, death must make sin odious; or else sin allowed will make death terrible.

3. We come to the assertion or correction, 'The Spirit is life because of righteousness.' In which observe,

[A.] That believers have a life, notwithstanding death. Though death be appointed by God, and inflicted upon believers as well as others, yet they live, notwithstanding this death: John xi. 25, 'He that belie veth in me, though he were dead, yet shall he live.' The fountain of life can raise him when he will; no bands of death can hinder his quickening virtue. Though the union between body and soul be dissolved, yet not their union with God.

[B.] This life is to be understood of body and soul. It is only indeed here said life, but he explaineth himself in the 2d ver. 'If the Spirit of him that raised up Jesus from the dead dwell in you, he that raised up Christ from the dead, shall also quicken your mortal bodies by his Spirit that dwelleth in you' Man is compounded of a body and soul; death deprives him of his body for a time, only the body shall at last be reunited to partake of the happiness of the soul.

(1) The soul, being the noblest part, is presently, and most happily provided for, being sanctified and purified from all her imperfections, and is brought into the sight and presence of God: Luke xx. 38, 'They all live to God.' And they are gathered to the great council and assembly of souls, Heb. xii. 23. There they serve God day and night, and are under a happy necessity of never wandering from their duty, and no longer busied to maintain a war against sin, but we are always employed in lauding, praising, and blessing God, and delighting in him. Well then, this is the happiness of the faithful , that though they put off the body for a time, yet the soul hath an eternal house, to which it retireth, and remains not only in the hand of God, but enjoy eth the sight and love of God: 2 Cor. v. 1, 'For we know that if our earthly house of this tabernacle were dissolved, we have a building of God, an house not made with hands, eternal in the heavens.'

(2.) For the body. At the resurrection the soul shall assume its body again. We cannot easily believe that part shall be placed in heaven, which we see committed to the grave to rot there; but there is no impediment to God's almighty power: Phil. iii. 21, 'Who shall change our vile body, that it may be fashioned like unto his glorious body, according to the working whereby he is able to subdue all things unto himself.' This place doth prove that God hath provided for the happy estate of the body as well as the soul. The dead are God's subjects, put into the hands of Christ; he must give an account of them: John vi. 40, 'And this is the will of him that sent me, that every one that seeth the Son, and believeth on him, may have ever lasting life, and I will raise him up at the last day.' They are likewise members of Christ, 1 Cor. vi. 15. Now this mystical body will not be maimed; they are temples of the Holy Ghost: 1 Cor. vi. 15 temples wherein we offer up to God reasonable service. Now since the Spirit possesseth both body and soul, he will repair his own dwelling-place which he hath once honoured with his presence, and not let corruption always abide on it. And we have the pattern of Christ; he is the first fruits of them that slept: 1 Cor. xv. 20. The soul hath an inclination to the body still; therefore that our happiness may be complete, a glorified soul shall animate an immortal body.

[C.] The grounds are, first, the Spirit's renewing; secondly, Christ's purchase.

(1.) The Spirit is life. He doth not draw his argument from the immortality of the soul, for that is common to good and bad; the wicked have a soul that will survive the body, but little to their com fort; their immortality is not a happy immortality; but he taketh his argument from the new life wrought in us by the Spirit, which is the beginning, pledge, and earnest of a blessed immortality. The soul is an immortal being, but the new life is an eternal principle of happiness; as soon as Christ beginneth to dwell in us, eternal life is begun in our souls, 1 John iii. 15; the immortal seed, 1 Pet. i. 23.

(2.) The meritorious cause is the righteousness of Christ; or the pardon of our sins, and the justification of our persons by the blood and merits of Jesus Christ. When once forgiven, we are out of the reach of the second death: 1 Cor. xv. 56, 'The sting of death is sin.' We are freed from the damning stroke, not the killing stroke, of death; Christ having freed us from the curse of the law, and merited and purchased for us a blessed resurrection, Heb. ii. 14, 15.

Use. Is to enforce the great things of Christianity.

There are but two things we need to regard, to live holily and die comfortably. These two have a mutual respect one to another; those that live holily take the next course to die comfortably': the end of that man is peace'; and to know how to die well, is the best way to live well; both are enforced by this place.

1. To live holily; there are several arguments from the text.

[A.] The comforts of Christianity are not promiscuously dispensed; they are common to all indifferently, but suspended on this condition, 'if Christ be in you,' by his sanctifying Spirit. If you be deceived in your foundation, all your life, hope, and comfort, are but delusive things; but when quickened by the renewing grace of the Spirit of Christ, and made partakers of the divine nature, you have then the earnest of your inheritance: Eph. i. 4, 2 Cor. v. 5, 'He who hath wrought us to' this same thing is God, who hath given us the earnest of his Spirit' Others die uncertain of comfort, or, it may be, most certain of condemnation.

[B.] From the concession, the body is dead; sentence is passed, and in part executed; this awakeneth us to think of another world, and to make serious preparation; when the walls of the house are shaken and are ready to drop down, is it not time to think of a removal? The body is frail and mortal, and that is enough to check sin: Rom. vi. 12, 1 Let not sin reign therefore in your mortal bodies, that ye should obey it in the lusts thereof.' But it is made more frail by actual sin: Gal. vi. 8, 'If we sow to the flesh, of the flesh we shall reap corruption' Shall we sow to the flesh and pamper the flesh, which must soon be turned into stench and rottenness? Man consulting with present sense carrieth himself as if he were a body only, not a soul; and therefore out of love to sensual pleasures, he maketh no account of anything but sensual pleasures and satisfactions; but shall we bestow all our time and care upon a body that was dust in its composition, and will shortly again be dust in its dissolution? The body is not only dying, but dead; you think not of it now, but this death cometh before it is looked for. Saul trembled when the spirit answered him: 1 Sam. xxviii. 19, 20, 'To-morrow thou and thy sons shall be with me.' Would you sport and riot away your time, if you should receive such a message? Surely the dust, and stench, and rottenness of the grave, if we thought of it, would take down our pride and check our voluptuousness, for we do but pamper worms' meat; it would prevent our worldliness. All a man's labour is for the body, and usually in a body overcared for there dwelleth a neglected soul. The body is not only the instrument, but the incitement of it; the soul is wholly taken up about the body, but doth the dead body deserve so much care? Death doth disgrace all the seducing pleasures of the flesh, and the profits and honours of the world. Who is so mad as wilfully to sin with death in his eye? Alas! All the pleasures and honours of the world will be vanity and vexation of spirit to us when we come to die.

[C.] We come now to the corrective assertion, and there is the life promised for body and soul; this breedeth the true spirit of faith: 2 Cor. iv. 13, 14, 'We having the same spirit of faith, (according as it is written, I believed, therefore have I spoken), we also believe, therefore speak, knowing that he that raised up the Lord Jesus shall raise us up also.' The true diligence and godliness: 1 Cor. xv. 58. 'Be steadfast and unmoveable, always abounding in the work of the Lord, for your labour shall not be in vain in the Lord' And patience: Rom. ii. 7, 'Who by patient continuing in well doing, seek for glory, immortality, eternal life'. Christians! We that have souls to save or lose, and have an offer of happiness, shall we come short of it for want of diligence, and spend our time in eating and drinking, and sporting, or in the service of God?

[D.] It is the effect both of the Spirit's renewing, and the righteousness of Christ. Both call for holiness at our hands, as the effect of the renovation of the Spirit, and our title to the righteousness of Christ; so that this life doth not belong to us unless we are in Christ, and walk not after the flesh, but after the Spirit: Rom. viii. 1. Which begun this discourse the double principle and ground of hope enforceth it.

2. To die comfortably. Christianity affordeth the proper comfort against death, as it is a natural and penal evil; a natural evil it is, as it puts an end to present comforts; it is a penal evil too, as it maketh way for the final judgment, Heb. ix. 27. Heathens could only teach them to submit to it out of necessity, or as a debt they owed to nature, or an end of the present miseries; but Christianity, as the sting of it is gone, 1 Cor. xv. 56. As the property is altered: 1 Cor. iii. 22, 'Death is yours,' and that upon solid grounds; as the life of grace is introduced and sin is forgiven, and the conclusions drawn from thence. First, The life of grace introduced. How bitter is the remembrance of death to the carnal man, much more the enduring of it. A dying body and a startling conscience maketh them afraid of everlasting death; and so much sin as you bring to your death-bed, so much bitterness you will have; so much holiness so far you have eternal life in you; and the more it is acted in the fruits of holiness, the more comfort: Isa. xxxii. 17. A little without is grievous, when all is amiss within. Secondly, Sin is forgiven upon the account of the righteousness of Christ, for we shall then be soiled if found in no other righteousness than our own: Phil. iii. 8, 9, 'That I may be found in him, not having my own righteousness' In short, the worst that can befall believers is, that it is the death but of a part, the worst and basest part, and that but for a season. The bodies of the saints shall not always lie in the grave: nor can it be imagined they shall perish as the beasts; no, but be raised up from the grave, and their vile bodies be changed like unto the glorious body of their Redeemer.

SERMON XIV

If the Spirit of him that raised up Jesus from the dead dwell in you, he that raised up Christ from the dead shall also quicken your mortal bodies by his Spirit that dwelleth in you.

Romans VIII. 11.

The Apostle is answering a doubt, How there is no condemnation to them that are in Christ, since death, which is the fruit of sin, yet remaineth on the godly?

Answer

1. By concession, that sin is indeed the seed and original of mortality': the body is dead because of sin' Not only the carnal undergo it, but the justified; though the guilt of sin be taken away by a pardon, and the dominion and power of it be broken by the Spirit of Christ, yet the being of it is not quite abolished; and as long as sin remaineth in us in the least degree, it maketh us subject to the power of death.

2. By way of correction he opposeth a double comfort against it. Destruction by sin is neither total nor final. First, not total; it is but a half death: ver. 10. 'The Spirit is life because of righteousness' Secondly, nor final; it hath a limit of time set, which when it is expired, the body shall have a happy resurrection, and that by virtue of the same Spirit by which the soul is now quickened. So that mark both parts receive their happiness by the Spirit the soul and the body; the soul though it be immortal, in itself, yet the blessed immortality it hath from the Spirit; the Spirit is life because of righteousness'; and the dead body shall not finally perish, but be sure to be raised again by the same Spirit: 'If the Spirit of him'

In the words we have

1. The condition upon which the resurrection is promised, 'If the Spirit'

2. The certainty of performance set forth. [A.] By the author or efficient cause, 'He that raised up Jesus from the dead' [B.] 'By his Spirit that dwelleth in you,' the way and manner of working.

1. The condition. A resurrection is necessary, but a happy resurrection is limited by a condition: Phil. iii. 11, 'If by any means'

2. The certainty of performance.

[A.] From the author God, described by his eminent and powerful work, 'He that raised up Jesus from the dead.' This is mentioned, partly as an instance of his power, and partly as an assurance of his will. First, An instance of his power: Eph. i. 18, 19, 'According to the working of his mighty power, which he wrought in Christ when he raised him from the dead' Our resurrection is a work of the same omnipotency with that which he first evidenced in raising Christ from the dead; the same power is still employed to bring us to a glorious eternity. Secondly, It is an assurance of his will, for Christ's resurrection is a pattern of ours: 1 Cor. vi. 14, 'God hath both raised the Lord, and will also raise up us by his own power'; 2 Cor. iv. 14, 'Knowing that he hath raised up Jesus, shall also raise us up by Jesus.'

[B.] For the way and manner of bringing it about. 'By his Spirit that dwelleth in us.' Where take notice, first, of the relation of the Holy Spirit to God; secondly, his interest in, and nearness to us.

(1.) His relation to God. He is called his Spirit, and the Spirit of him that raised Jesus from the dead, that is, of God the Father.

The Holy Spirit is sometimes called the Father's Spirit, and sometimes Christ's Spirit, because he proceedeth both from the Father and the Son; the Father's Spirit, John xv. 26, 'When the Comforter is come, whom I will send to you from the Father; even the Spirit of truth.' He is also called, Acts xi. 4, 'The promise of the Father;' and Christ's Spirit, Rom. viii. 9, 'If any man have not the Spirit of Christ, he is none of his'; and Gal. iv. 6, 'God hath sent forth the Spirit of his Son into our hearts.' Now the Spirit being one in essence, and undivided in will and essence with the Father and the Son, surely the Father will by, or because of the Spirit dwelling in us, raise us again; for Father, Son, and Holy Spirit are one and the same God.

(2.) His interest in, and nearness to us'; He dwelleth in us' All dependeth upon that mark; he doth not say he worketh in us *per modum actionis transeuntis*; so he worketh in those that resist his work, and shall perish forever; but *per modum habitus permanentis*, as we are regenerated and sanctified. And the effects of his powerful resurrection remain in those habits which contribute the new nature; so the Spirit is said to dwell in us; and in the former verse, Christ to be in us': If Christ be in you, the body is dead because of sin' verse 10.

Doctrine That the bodies of believers shall be raised at the last day by the Spirit of holiness which now dwelleth in them.

1. I shall a little open this inhabitation of the Spirit.

2. Show you why it is the ground and cause of our happy resurrection. 1. For the first, The inhabitation of the Spirit. Dwelling may relate

to a double metaphor, either to the dwelling of a man in his house, or of God in his temple. Of a man in his house: 1 John iii. 24, 'And he that keepeth his commandments dwelleth in him, and he in him;' so it noteth his constant familiar presence. Or of God in his temple: 1 Cor. vi. 16, 'Know ye not that you are the temple of God, and the Spirit of God dwelleth in you? 'Which noteth a sacred presence, that pre sence as a God to bless and sanctify; the Spirit buildeth us up for so holy a use, and then dwelleth in us as our sanctifier, guide, and comforter. The one maketh way for the other; first a sanctifier, and then a guide; as a ship is first well rigged, and then a pilot; and by both he comforts us. He hath regenerated and guided us in the way of holiness. First, he sanctifieth and reneweth us: Tit. iii. 5, 'But according to his mercy he saved us, by the washing of regeneration, and the renew ing of the Holy Ghost;' and John iii. 6, 'That which is born of the Spirit is spirit' First he buildeth his house or temple, and then cometh and dwelleth in it. Secondly, he guideth and leadeth us in the ways of holiness: Rom. xv. 14, 'And myself also am persuaded of you, my brethren, that you also are full of goodness, filled with all knowledge;' 'If we live in the Spirit, let us also walk in the Spirit: Gal. v. 25. Before, we were influenced by Satan: Eph. ii. 2. 'Wherein in times past ye walked according to the course of this world, according to the prince of the power; of the air, that now worketh in the children of disobedience.' He put us upon anger, malice, envy, unclean lusts, and noisome and filthy ways, and we readily obeyed. 2 Tim. ii. 28. 'And that they may recover themselves out of the snares of the devil, who are taken captive at his will.' But the old inmate is cast out, and now we are guided and influenced by another lord. Thirdly, He comforts us with the sense of God's fatherly love, and our eternal inheritance: Rom. viii. 16. 'The Spirit itself beareth witness with our spirit, that we are the children of God.' 2 Cor. ii. 22, 'Who hath also sealed us, and given us the earnest of the Spirit into our hearts.' By both he leaveth upon the soul a sweet taste and relish of spiritual and heavenly things.

2. Why this inhabitation is the ground of a blessed resurrection.

[A.] To preserve the order of the personal operations. To make this evident, consider

(1.) That rising from the dead is a work of divine power; for to him it belongeth to restore life, who gave life at first: 2 Cor. i. 10. 'Who hath delivered us from so great a death,' etc., and is verified in plain experience.

(2.) That this divine power belongeth in common to Father, Son, and Holy Ghost, who being one and the same God, concurred in the same work; and whatever is done by the Father or Son, is done by the Spirit also; and whatever is done by the Spirit, is done by the Father and Son also. As for instance, apply it to the resurrection of Christ, or our resurrection. To the resurrection of Christ, it is ascribed to the Father, 'and God the Father, who raised him from the dead' To God the Son in other places; Christ is said to rise again by his own virtue and power: Rom. iv. 25, 'He died for our offences, and rose again for our justification;' not raised only, but rose again. So the Spirit is said to raise Christ: Rom. i. 4, 'And declared to be the Son of God with power, according to the spirit of holiness, by the resurrec tion from the dead. So 1 Pet. iii. 18, 'Crucified in the flesh, and quickened in the Spirit.' So our resurrection; we are raised by the Father; for in the text it is said, we are raised by the Spirit of him that raised Jesus from the dead. We are raised by Christ: John v. 21, 'For as the Father raiseth up the dead, and quickeneth them, even so the Sou quickeneth whom he will.' So by the Spirit we are raised, as in the text, 'He shall quicken your mortal bodies by his Spirit that dwelleth in you.'

(3.) They all concur in a way proper to them. In all their personal operations it is ascribed to the Father as the first fountain of working, and spring and well-head of all grace, who doth all things from himself; and by the Son and Holy Ghost, as it refers to Christ's resurrection, and ours also. So Christ's resurrection; it is ascribed to God the Father, who in the mystery of redemption hath the relation of supreme judge: Acts ii. 32, 'This Jesus hath God raised up;' and Acts x. 40, 'Him hath God raised up the third day.' And there is a special reason why it should be ascribed to God, as the Apostles when they stood upon their privilege, 'Let them come and fetch us out' Acts xii. 39; so, 'The God of peace that brought again from the dead the great shepherd,' etc., as referring it to his judicial power: Heb. xiii. 26. Though Christ had power to rise, yet no authority; our surety was fetched out of prison by the judge. And then it is ascribed to Christ himself: John ii. 19, 'Destroy this temple, and in three days I will raise it up: which he spake of the temple of his body.' To prove the divinity of his person, it was necessary that he should thus speak; or to prove himself to be God: John x. 18, 'I have power to lay down my life, and to take it up again' He could put a period to his sufferings when he pleased. So for the Holy Ghost, he raised Christ, because the Spirit sanctified his humanity, and by him the human nature of Christ was made partaker of created holiness, and so qualified to rise again when he had done his work. All the created gifts came from the Spirit, and therefore they are called the anointing of the Holy Ghost, with which he was anointed. So to our resurrection, God raiseth the dead, as it is usually said in scripture; and Christ raiseth the dead, 'Every one that believeth on the Son hath everlasting life, and I will raise him up at the last day' John vi. 40. The Spirit raiseth, and still in a way proper to each person; to understand which, we must observe that there are three ways of subsistence in the divine nature, which carry a great correspondence with the prime attributes in God, which are power, wisdom, and goodness. Power we conceive eminently in God the Father, it being the most obvious by which the Godhead is apprehended, and so proper to him who is the beginning of being and working: Rom. i. 20, 'His eternal power and Godhead are seen by the things which are made.' Wisdom is appropriated to Christ, who is often represented in scripture as the wisdom of the Father: especially, Prov. viii. And goodness to the Spirit, therefore often called the good spirit: Neh. ix. 20; and Ps. cxliii. 10. Not but that all these agree to each person, for the Father is powerful, wise, and good; so the Son, and so the Holy Ghost; and love is sometimes appropriated to the Father; namely, the fountain and original love; but the evangelical, operative, and communicative love of God is more distinctly ascribed to the Spirit, because all benefits come to the creature this way; we have our natural being from him: Job. xxxiii. 4, 'The Spirit of God hath made me, and the breath of the Almighty hath given me life.' 'The first clause relateth to the body, the Spirit of the Lord hath made me'; that is, framed the body; the second to the soul, that spirit of life that God breathed into man when his body was framed and organised to receive it: The Spirit created and formed in man the reasonable soul; so the new being which is communicated to us by the Redeemer through the covenant of, grace: Tit. iii. 5, 6. Our glorious being, which is considered either as to soul or body; as to soul, 'the Spirit is life because of righteousness;' as to body, the words of the text. Well then, the Holy Ghost is the operative love of God, working from the power of the Father, a-nd grace of the Son; and whatever the Father or Son doth, you must still suppose it to be communicated to us by the Spirit.

[B.] Because the Holy Ghost is *vinculum unionis*, the bond of union between us and Christ. We are united to him, because we have the same spirit which Christ had; there is the same spirit in head and members, and therefore he will work like effects in you and him; if the head rise, the members will follow after; for this mystical body was appointed to be conformed to their head, as in obedience and suffering, so in happiness and glory: Rom. viii. 29, 'Predestinated to be conformed to the image of his Son.' Christ was raised, therefore they shall be raised; Christ was raised by the Spirit of holiness, so you are raised by the same power of the Holy Ghost. Christ is as tender of his mystical body as of his natural body, therefore will not lose one member or joint of it: John vi. 39, 'I must lose nothing'; and the Spirit doth his office in you, as in him, for you are to be raised up with him, and as he was raised. We feel the power of our resurrection in our regeneration, and we feel the comfort of it in our being raised to glory; head and members do not rise by a different power. How then, you will say, are the wicked raised by Christ? They are raised *ex afficio judicis*, but not *beneficio mediatoris* by him as a judge, not by him as a Redeemer. There will be a resurrection both of the wicked and the godly, the one by the power of Christ as judge, the other by the power of his Spirit as redeemer; the one are forced to appear, the other go joyfully to meet the bridegroom; the one, by Christ's power as judge, shall have the sentence of condemnation executed upon them; the other, by virtue of Christ's life and resurrection, shall enter into the possession of the blessed; a state of bliss and eternal life, wherein they shall enjoy God and Christ, and the company of saints and angels, and sing hallelujahs forever.

[C.] Because the Spirit of sanctification worketh in us that grace which giveth us a right and title to this glorious estate; for by regeneration we are made children of God, and so children of the resurrection: Luke xx. 35, 36, 'But they which shall be counted worthy to obtain that world, and the resurrection from the dead, neither marry, nor are given in marriage; neither can they die any more, for they are equal to the angels, and are the children of God, being the children of the resurrection' Being admitted into his family here, we may expect to be admitted into his presence hereafter. And then actual holiness, if we live to years of discretion, is necessarily required to a blessed and glorious resurrection: Gal. vi. 8. 'If we sow to the flesh, we shall of our own flesh reap corruption; but if we sow to the Spirit, we shall of the Spirit reap life everlasting.' There is no harvest without sowing; and as the seed is, so will the harvest be; they that lavish out their time, and care, and estates, in feeding their own carnal desires, must expect a crop accordingly, which is death and destruction; but they that obey the Spirit, and sow to righteousness, shall obtain eternal life; for till the cause of death be taken away, which is sin, we may fear a resurrection, but cannot expect a resurrection to our comfort.

[D.] The Spirit doth not only regenerate and convert us, which giveth us a right, but abideth in us as an earnest: Eph. i. 14, 'We were sealed with that Holy Spirit of promise, which is the earnest of our inheritance, until the redemption of the purchased possession.' Where observe three things. First, How the heirs of promise are distinguished from others; Secondly, The use of this mark and distinction; Thirdly, The time how long this abideth with us; and all this will fully prove the point in hand.

(1.) The mark of all those whom God adrnitteth into the gospel state. They are sealed with that Holy Spirit of promise; that is, secured, set apart, as those that have interest in the new covenant, by that Spirit of holiness which is promised to believers; for the Spirit is called the promise of the Father; the renewing and sanctifying work of the Spirit, or the image of Christ impressed upon the soul, is this seal; and the comfort and joy that floweth thence, is an appendage to it. As the work of sanctification is more and more carried on, and is fruitful in holiness of life; so we are more and more distinguished as a people set apart to serve, and please, and enjoy the holy and blessed God. Now you that are exercised with so many doubts and scruples about your interest in the promise, would it not be exceeding comfortable to you, if you had your seal and warrant for a secure claim to the privileges of the gospel, by the saving graces of the Spirit, or the impression of the image of Christ upon your hearts? You may be abundantly satisfied; for where these saving graces and fruits of holiness are found, your right and interest in the promise of eternal life is clear and manifest; for this is the mark of the Holy Spirit, and the seed of life eternal.

(2.) The use for which the Holy Spirit and saving graces bestowed on them serveth, is to be the earnest of the inheritance. An earnest is a pledge, or first part of a payment, which is an assurance or security that the rest of the whole price shall not fail to follow; so the Spirit and his graces is the earnest given by God to confirm and assure the bargain, that at last he will bestow upon us our full portion, or salvation and eternal life itself. The presence and working of the Spirit in our hearts is this earnest; as soon as you give up yourselves to God in covenant, you have a right; but the possession is delayed for a season; therefore he giveth us part in hand, to assure us he will bestow the whole in due time; for we need to be satisfied, not only as to our pre sent right, but our future possession. The Spirit and his work of grace received here is glory begun; a part it is, though but a small part in regard of what is to ensue.

(3.) The time how long the use of this earnest is to continue': until the redemption of the purchased possession' The words are somewhat obscure. What is the purchased possession? It is taken for the persons acquitted and purchased, that is to say, the church and people of God, holy and sincere Christians; for they are Christ's possession whom he hath dearly bought, 1 Cor. vi. 10, and recovered out of the hands of Satan their old possessor and master: Col. i. 13. The redemption of them is till their full and final deliverance: Eph. iv. 30. 'Whereby ye are sealed to the day of redemption.' Their deliverance is but begun now, and their bonds but in part loosed; but they are fully freed from the effects of sin at the last day, when death itself is abolished, and their bodies raised up in glory. The earnest is given; the Holy Spirit with his graces to abide with us till then; at that time there is no further use of an earnest, for there is no place left for doubts and fears. Till this day comes, God's earnest abideth with us, that is, in our souls, till our bodies be reunited to them; and this fully proveth the matter in hand.

[E.] His respect to his old dwelling place; he once dwelt in cm- bodies as well as in our souls: 1 Cor. vi. 19, 'Know ye not that your bodies are temples of the Holy Ghost? 'Our bodies were his temple, and honoured by his presence; he sanctified our bodies as well as our souls: 1 Thes. v. 23. 'I pray God sanctify you wholly, your whole spirit, soul, and body.' He sanctifieth the body, as he maketh it obedient to his motions, and a ready instrument to the soul. Now when the body was given up to the Spirit to be sanctified, it was consecrated to immortality; it is by the Spirit's sanctifying the soul that it was made capable of seeing and loving God; so the body of serving the soul in our duties to God. Now shall a temple of God be utterly demolished? that body that was kept clean for the Holy Ghost to dwell in, and to be presented immaculate at the day of Christ, come to nothing? Indeed for a while it rotteth in the grave, but his interest in it is not made void by death, and his affection ceaseth not; this body was once his house and temple, and he had a property in it; therefore he hath a love to our dust, and a care of our dust, and will raise it up again.

[F.] Because the great work of the Spirit is to retrench our bodily pleasures, and to bring us to resolve by all means to save the soul, whatever becometh of the body in this world, and to use the body for the service of the Lord Jesus Christ. Now the Spirit would not put us upon the labours of the body, and take no care for the happiness of the body; these two always go together: 1 Cor. vi. 13, 'The body is for the Lord, and the Lord for the body'; Christ expecteth service from the body, and gave up himself for the redemption of it, as well as the soul: 1 Cor. vi. 20. The body is his in a way of duty, and his in a way of charge; this reason should the more sink into you, because spirit and flesh are so opposed in scripture. Flesh signifieth our inclinations to the bodily life, as spirit doth the bent and inclination of soul to God and heaven; the great work of the Holy Spirit is to subdue the lusts of the flesh: Rom. viii. 13, 'If ye through the Spirit do mortify the deeds of the body, ye shall live'; if we obey him in his strivings against the flesh: Gal. v. 16, 'Walk in the Spirit, and you shall not fulfil the lusts of the flesh' Christ giveth us his Spirit to draw us off from bodily pleasures, that tasting manna, the diet of Egypt may have no more relish with us. So Gal. v. 24, 'They that are Christ's, have crucified the flesh, with the affections and lusts thereof'; they hold a severe hand over all the appetites and passions of the flesh: Rom. xiii. 14, 'Make no provision for the flesh, to fulfil the lusts thereof.' Do not addict yourselves to pamper and please the body. One great part of practical religion is to bring us to love the pleasures that are proper to the immortal soul, above the sottish and brutish pleasures of the body. Well then, was religion intended only to make a great part of us miserable, which part yet is the workmanship of God's hands, when there is so much hardship put upon the body, such labours and pains, such care and watchfulness? His very self-denial is an argument, that the Spirit in us thus commanding and governing us, is a pledge of glory.

[G.] There is in the soul a desire of the happiness of the body; not only a natural desire to live with it, as its loving mate and companion, which maketh us loath to part with it; and if the will of God were so, the saints would 'not be unclothed, but clothed upon, that mortality might be swallowed up of life': 2 Cor. v. 4. They would desire not to put off these bodies, at least not to part with them finally. But a spiritual desire is kindled in us by the Holy Ghost that now dwelleth in us; for the apostle addeth, ver. 5, 'He that wrought us for the self-same thing is God.' God hath framed us to desire this impassible, eternal, and immutable life in our bodies as well as our souls. More plainly elsewhere: Rom. viii. 23, 'We that have the first fruits of the Spirit, groan within ourselves, waiting for the adoption, the redemption of our bodies' That is, the resurrection of the body; to be redeemed from the hands of the grave. Mark, these groans are stirred up in them by the first fruits of the Spirit; now, would the Holy Ghost stir up these groans and desires, if he never meant to satisfy them? That were to mock us, and vex us. which cannot be imagined of the Holy Spirit. Well then, since these desires are of God's own framing, raised up in us by his Spirit, they will not be disappointed, but will in time be fulfilled.

[H.] From the nature of death. Death is that power which God hath given the devil over men by reason of sin: Heb. ii. 14, 'That he might destroy him that had the power of death, even the Devil'; the power of separating soul and body, and keeping us from eternal life, God inflicteth it as a judge, but the devil as an executioner; he is not *dominus mortis*[11], *sed minister mortis*. The devil enticeth them to sin, by which they deserve death, and the sting of death is sin: 1 Cor. xv. 56. The devil hath the power of death; as carnal men are taken captive in his snares: 2 Tim. ii. 26; and when they die, he may have a hand in their torments. While men live, they are in the house of God, are under the protection of God, and have the offers of grace; but if they harden their hearts, and despise these offers, they are cast forth with the devil and his angels; the judge giveth them over to the jailor, and the jailor casts them into prison, from whence they come not forth, till they have paid the utmost farthing: Luke xii. 58. But Christ came to deliver us from this; and all that embrace his salvation, the Spirit puts them into a state of freedom and liberty of the children of God. And as to them, Satan is put out of office, he cannot keep them from entering into eternal life; the power of death is taken from him, and therefore, though their bodies be kept for a while under the state of death, yet at length the Spirit freeth them from the bondage of corruption, and bringeth them into the glorious liberty of the children of God. They shall at length rejoice and triumph in God'; death, where is thy sting? O grave, where is thy victory?' 1 Cor. xv. 55, 56, 67. They die as well as others, but death is not the power of the devil over them, but one of those saving means by which God worketh their life and happiness; it is the beginning of immortality, and the gate and entrance into life; they are not in the custody and power of the devil, as the spirits in prison and the bodies of the wicked are; but in the hand and custody of the Holy Ghost, 'Thy dead men shall live; with my body shall they arise' Isa. xxvi. 19. The key of the grave is in Christ's hand; he is the guardian of their dust, keepeth their bones. Well then, if the Spirit of Christ hath freed you from the snares of sin, he hath freed you also from the bands of death; or as it is said in the Revelations, if you have part in the first resurrection, the second death <hath no power over you: Rev. x. 6; that is, you shall not be cast into the lake that burneth with fire and brimstone; the good Spirit hath prevailed over the evil spirit, and therefore your resurrection will be joyful.

Use 1 Let us give up ourselves to the Holy Spirit as our sanctifier; set open your hearts, that he may come into them as his habitation; do not receive him guest- wise in a pang, or for a turn, or in some solemn duty; but see that he dwelleth in you as an inhabitant in his house. A man is not said to dwell in an inn, where as a stranger or wayfaring man, he goeth aside to tarry for a night; or in the house of a friend, where he resorteth; no, use all Christ's holy means that he may fix his abode in your hearts; that he may dwell there, as at home in his own house; that he may be reverenced there as a God in his temple.

Motives.

---

[11] Lord of death

1. He richly requiteth[12] us; he keepeth up the house and temple where he dwelleth; the Spirit is our seal and earnest: 'The Spirit of God and of glory resteth upon you' 1 Pet. iv. 14.

2. The heart of man is not a waste; you will have a worse guest there, if not the Holy Spirit; Satan dwelleth and worketh in the children of disobedience: 1 Sam. xvi. 14, 'But the Spirit of the Lord departed from Saul, and an evil spirit from the Lord troubled him'; and Eph. ii. 2, 'The spirit that now worketh in the children of disobedience'; and Eph. iv. 27, 'Neither give place to the devil' That cursed inmate will enter, if we give place to him and hearken to his motions; so that then he will make the body a sink of sin, and a dung hill of corruption; he tempts you to scandalous sins, which do not only waste the body for the present, but are a pledge of eternal damnation.

3. Consider how many deceive themselves with the hopes of a glorious resurrection. Alas! They are strangers to the Spirit; it may be not to his transient motions they resist the Holy Ghost, which will be their greater condemnation but to his constant residence; for where he dwelleth, he maketh them more heavenly, acquainting them with God, Col. i. 6; more holy, that is his office to sanctify, 1 Pet. i. 22; to love God more, for he is the operative love of God, Rom. v. 5; 1 John iv. 8; to hate sin more, that bringeth death; and his business is to come as a pledge of life. Alas! In most, the spirit that dwelleth in them lusteth to envy; they are ruled by an unclean spirit, by the spirit of the world: 1 Cor. ii. 12; have no love to God, no real hatred of sin.

Use 2. Live in obedience to his sanctifying motions: Rom. viii. 14, 'As many as are led by the Spirit are the sons of God' The Spirit of God by which you are guided and led, is that divine and potent Spirit that raised up Christ's dead body out of the grave; and if you be led and governed by him, you shall be raised by the power of the same Spirit that raised Christ's body; his power is the cause, but your right is by his sanctification.

Use 3. Use your bodies well; possess your vessel in sanctification and honour: 1 Thes. iv. 4.

[A.] Offer up yourselves to God. For every temple must be dedicated: Rom. xii. 1, 'I beseech you therefore, brethren, by the mercies of God, that ye present your bodies a living sacrifice, holy, acceptable unto God, which is your reasonable service;' Rom. vi. 13, 'Neither yield ye your members as instruments of unrighteousness unto sin, but yield yourselves unto God, as those that are alive from the dead.'

[B.] When devoted to God, take heed you do not use them to sensuality and filthiness; which wrong the body here and hereafter; the pleasures of the body cannot recompense the pains of your surfeit or intemperance, much less eternal torments; for what will be the issue? 'If you live after the flesh (Rom. viii. 13), you must die'; therefore you should daily keep the flesh in a subordination to the spirit: 1 Pet. ii. 11, 'I beseech you as strangers and

---

[12] make appropriate return for (a favor, service, or wrongdoing)

pilgrims, that ye abstain from fleshly lusts'. To please and gratify the flesh, is to wrong the soul.

[C.] We should deny ourselves even lawful pleasures, when they begin to exercise a dominion over us: 1 Cor. vi. 12, 'All things are lawful for me, but I will not be brought under the power" of any.' It is a miserable servitude to be brought under the power of any pleasure, either in meat, drink, or recreations; enchanted with the witchery of gaming, though it grieve the Spirit, wrong the soul, defraud God of his time, rob the poor of what should feed charity, yet they are enslaved.

SERMON XV

Therefore, brethren, we are debtors, not to the flesh, to live after the flesh.

Romans VIII. 12.

IN the words we have,

1. A note of inference.

2. The truth inferred. In this latter we find,

[1.] A compellation—*Brethren*

[2.] An assertion that *we are debtors*.

[3.] An instance or exemplification, *to whom* we are debtors. The negative is expressed, 'not to the flesh, to live after the flesh;' and the affirmative is implied, and must be supplied out of the context, 'to the Spirit' to live in obedience to the Holy Spirit.

1. The inference, 'therefore' he reasoneth from their privileges; the privilege is asserted ver. 1, 'There is no condemnation to them that are in Christ, who walk not after the flesh, but after the Spirit.' It is applied to the Christian: Rom. v. 9, 'But ye are not in the flesh, but in the Spirit' These reasonings are pertinent and insinuative from the privilege asserted; exhortation must follow doctrine, for then it pierceth deeper, and sticketh longer. On the other side, doctrine becometh more lively, when there is an edge set upon it by exhortation, from the privilege implied; certainly privileges infer duty, and therefore, having comforted them with the remembrance of their condition, he doth also mind them of their obligation, 'Ye are not in the flesh, but in the spirit'; 'therefore we are not debtors to the flesh, to walk after the flesh'; but to walk after the Spirit.

[A.] The truth inferred. Where first, observe the compellation, 'Brethren' a word of love and equality; of love, to sweeten the exhortation; for men are unwilling to displease the flesh; of equality, for he taketh the same obligation upon himself; this debt bindeth all, high and low, learned or unlearned, ministers or people; greatness doth not exempt from this bond, nor meanness exclude it.

[B.] The assertion, that we are debtors. Man would fain be sui juris, at his own disposal; affecteth a supremacy and dominion over his own actions: Ps. xii. 4, 'Our tongues are our own, who is lord over us? 'But this can never be; we were made by another, and for another, therefore we are debtors.

[B.] The exemplification, to whom. (1.) Negatively, not to the flesh; this is expressly denied for two reasons, because the flesh maketh a claim upon us. It hath a double claim, one by usurpation; when God is laid aside, self interposeth as the next heir; and that which we count ourself, is the flesh, which doth all in all with men. The other is in pretence; it seemeth to challenge a right by God's allowance; something is due to the body, and no man ever yet hated his own flesh. But we must distinguish of flesh, as it is taken for the body and natural substance; so we are debtors to the body by necessity of nature, for we owe it food, and physic, and raiment. As it is taken for corrupt nature, which inclineth us to seek the happiness of the body and bodily life without God, and apart from God; so we owe nothing to the flesh, so as to obey its lusts, or frame our lives according to the desires of it; we owe it hatred, but not obedience; the motions of corrupt nature tend to feed the habits of sin, sensuality, pride, worldliness; thence come ignorance, unbelief. (2.) Positively, we are debtors to the Spirit, to be led by the Spirit, ver. 14. The Spirit mindeth us of our duty, externally, by the word; internally, by his sacred motions and inspirations, restraining us from sin: Rom. viii. 13, 'If ye through the Spirit do mortify the deeds of the body, ye shall live'; quickening us to holiness: Gal. v. 25, 'If we live in the Spirit, let us also walk in the Spirit.'

Doctrine That believers are debtors, not to the flesh, but to the Spirit.

I shall prove it by considering them in a double capacity.

1. With respect to the order of nature.

2. Or the condition of their spiritual being. Take them as men or Christians. If you look upon them as men, they are debtors to God for all they have; if you look upon them as Christians that have received the faith of Christ, they are much more debtors not to the flesh, but to the Spirit

1. With respect to the order of nature; man is a debtor, for he is a dependent creature; not an owner or a lord, but a steward. I prove it by two arguments. We depend upon God for being and preserva tion, and therefore we are debtors to God for all that we have. Secondly, depending upon God, we are accountable to him. Or thus: God that is a creator and preserver, is therefore an owner; and being an owner, is therefore a governor and ruler, and, by consequence, a judge; his being a creator goeth before his being an owner; and his being an owner goeth before his being; a ruler, and is the foundation of it; for his absolute propriety in us giveth him a power and dominion over us; and there are two parts of his governing power, legislation and execution, or judgment.

[A.] His being a creator maketh him an owner. We have nothing but what we have from God; nothing that we ourselves can keep one moment without God; and therefore we have nothing but what is for God; for we hold it at his will and pleasure: Ezek. xviii. 4. 'All souls are mine'; and Prov. xvi. 4, 'God hath made all things for himself'; and Rom. xi. 36, 'For of him, and to him, and through him are all things.' Among men, whosoever maketh anything by his own proper art and labour, and that of his own stuff, must needs have a full right to it, and a full power to dispose of it. No man ever made anything but of matter pre-existing, but God made all things out of nothing; and therefore if he that planteth a vineyard hath right to eat of the fruit thereof, certainly he that gave us life and being, and made us after his own image to serve and worship him, hath a full right in man, to dispose of man and all the rest of his creatures, as being the work of his hands. He that gave them their being when they were not, and still supporteth them new they are, hath an un doubted just right to order them according to his own will and pleasure.

[B.] His being an owner qualifieth him for being a ruler. For the dominion of jurisdiction is founded in the dominion of property; we are his own, therefore we are his subjects: Mat. xx.

15, 'Is it not lawful for me to do what I will with my own?' Surely he that possesseth all things, hath full right to govern all things; as parents have an authority over their children, who are a means under God to give them life and education. The most barbarous nations have acknowledged the authority of parents; how much greater then is the authority of God, who hath given us life and breath, being and well-being, and all things? He created us out of nothing; and being created, he preserveth us, and giveth us all the good things which we enjoy, and therefore we are obliged to him to be subject to him, and to obey all his holy laws, and to be accountable to him for the breach thereof. The supereminent excellency of his nature giveth him a sufficiency for the government of mankind; and creation and preservation give him a full right to make what laws he pleaseth, and to call man to an account whether he hath kept them, yea or nay. The right of God is greater than the right of parents; for in natural generation they are but instruments of his providence, acting only by the power which God giveth them; and the parents propagate to the children nothing but the matter of the body, and such things as belong to the body, called therefore the 'fathers of our flesh': Heb, xii. 9. Yea, in framing the body, God hath a greater hand than they, for they cannot tell whether the child will be male or female, beautiful or deformed; know not the number and posture of the bones, and nerves, and arteries and sinews; God formeth these things in the womb: Zech. xii. 1, 'And formed the spirit of man within him.' All that they can do, cometh to nothing without God's blessing; so that God is the governor of all creatures, visible and invisible, from whose empire and jurisdiction they neither can nor ought to exempt themselves.

[C.] There are two parts of government or jurisdiction legislation and judgment as the Lord is called, Isa. xxxiii. 22, 'Our king, our lawgiver, our judge' First, as the lawgiver, he by his precepts showeth what is due from man to God: Micah vi. 8, 'He hath showed thee, man, what is good, and what the Lord thy God requireth of thee.' The way of pleasing God is clearly revealed. Many things the light of natural conscience calleth for (Rom. ii. 14); but the light of the holy scripture much more: Ps. cxlvii. 19, 20, 'He hath showed his word to Jacob, his statutes and judgments to Israel; he hath not dealt so with any nation.' " If we are contentious and obey not the truth, and against the light of scripture and reason gratify our brutish lusts, we disclaim God's authority, and do not carry ourselves as debtors to the Spirit, but the flesh. Secondly, judgment or execution. God's laws are not a vain scare-crow; we are accountable for our obedience or disobedience to them. Two things come into the judgment; the laws, the benefits and advantages given us to keep them. First, the laws: 2 Thes. i. 8, 'In flaming fire, taking vengeance on them that know not God, and obey not the gospel'; and Rom. ii. 12, 'For as many as have sinned without law, shall also perish without law; and as many as have sinned in the law, shall be judged by the law.' Secondly, benefits and abilities given us to keep them: Luke xix. 23, 'Wherefore then gavest not thou my money into the bank, that at my coming I might have required my own with usury? 'Every benefit we receive from God, increaseth the debt; we are accountable for all these gifts of grace we have received from God; they are *bona*, things good in their own nature; they are *dona*, things freely given and delivered to us; and talenta, a trust for which we are to be accountable; not as money is given to a beggar, but as an estate put into the hands of a factor. As *bona*, we must esteem them according to their just value; as *dona*, with thankfulness; as *talenta*, with faithfulness. Well then, since we have received our whole being from God, with all the appendant benefits, and since we have it for his use and service, we have all that we have upon these terms, to use it for his glory; it clearly followeth that we are debtors not to the flesh, which inclineth us to please ourselves, but to the Spirit, which inclineth us to please God.

[D.] I shall add one proposition more, that this debt and obligation cannot be dissolved; for as long as we depend upon God in being and operation, so long we are bound to God. Man hath *principium et finem*, a principle upon which he dependeth, and an end to which he is appointed; a superior to whom he is subject, and to whom he must give an account.

(1.) This power and right cannot be alienated by us, or vacated and made void by our sin; we indeed sold ourselves for nought, but that was to our own loss, not to God's: Isa. lii. 3. He hath a full right to command us to keep the law, whether we be faulty or innocent. A drunken servant is a servant, though disabled to do his master's work; no man's right can be vacated without his consent; for the default of another doth not make void our right, especially if inferiors; as the rebellion of the subject doth not exempt him from the power of his prince.

(2.) God doth not make it away by bestowing his gifts on the creature; for he hath given us only *dispensationem*, the employment of these things; not dominium, the sovereign power over them; man hath nothing that is his own, but as he hath it from God, so for God; as to life, man is not *dominus vitae*[13], but *custos*[14]; this is true not only of life, but of time, wealth, strength, parts, yea, of all that we have and are. There is a higher lord, to whom by the law of our creation we owe the debt of duty, love, and obedience; and to whom we are account able for the mercies of his daily providence; and who hath an absolute and uncontrollable right in all that we have and are; all our owning is but a stewardship: Luke xvi. 2. We have a right to prevent the encroachment of our fellow creatures, but not a right to exclude our accountableness and obligation to God; we have a right by way of charge and trust, as a steward in things committed to him, or a factor in the estate consigned to his hands, or a workman in his tools and instruments, which the master giveth him to do his work withal; but not an absolute independent right; they are not ours to use as we think meet. When God disposed his gifts, he did not dispossess himself; as the husbandman doth not intend to throw away his seed, when he scattereth it in the furrows of the earth, but soweth it to receive it again with increase.

(3.) This right in us is so inherent in God, and proper to him, that God himself cannot communicate it to another; for he hath told us that he will not give his glory to another; to

---

[13] Lord of life
[14] guardian

make the creature independent, is to make it no creature. God is God still, and the creature is the creature still, obnoxious to the law of its creator, or else to his punishment for the breach of it. It implieth a contradiction that he should cut off the creature from dependence upon himself, and therefore from subjection to himself; while God is God, and we are creatures, there will be a debt due from us to him, because we depend upon him for our being and preservation; our petty interests may be alienated, as a lord may make his vassal absolutely free, or a prince his subject; as Saul proclaimed, that whosoever encountered Goliath, he would make his house free in Israel, 1 Sam. xvii. 25; that is, free from taxes, imposts, services in war, but not free from being a subject; but no creature can be exempted from duty to God, or made free from his debt; for dependence upon God, and our subjection to him, are so twisted together, that the one cannot be without the other; we wholly depend upon him for being and all things else, and therefore we must be wholly subject to him. Well then, consider man in the order of creation, and he is a debtor to God, not to his own flesh; bound to refer his service, strength, time, care, life, and love to him from whom he received them; these are sound reasonings not to be reproved.

2. By the condition of their spiritual being, so they are much more debtors to God: and therein consider,

[A.] The foundation on which this new estate is built, and that is our emption by Christ. This doth infer the debt mentioned in the text, whether we respect the state from whence we were redeemed, the price paid for us, or the end why we were redeemed. The state from whence we were redeemed, was a state of woeful captivity; from God's debtors we became Satan's slaves. Now if a captive were ransomed by another man's money, his life, service, and strength did belong to the buyer, 'for he is his money': Exod. xxi. 21. Christ hath bought us from a worse slavery, therefore all that we have belongeth to him; we are debtors. So for the price that was paid for our ransom; as from the worst slavery, so with the greatest price: 1 Pet. i. 18, 'We are not redeemed with corruptible things, such as silver and gold, but with the precious blood of Christ'. Now this maketh us debtors, and destroyeth all right and property in ourselves: 1 Cor. vi. 19, 20, 'Ye are not your own, ye are bought with a price, therefore glorify God with your bodies and souls, which are God's.' Take in the end, and the argument is the more conclusive; he hath redeemed us 'to God': Rev. v. 8; Rom. xiv. 4, 'For to this end Christ both died, and rose again, and revived; that he might be Lord both of dead and living' Well then, we are not to live as we list, but to live unto God; not debtors to the flesh, to live after the flesh, but debtors to the Spirit, to be led by the Spirit of God; *ex ordine justiciae*[15], justice requireth this, we are the Lord's.

[B.] The benefit of this spiritual new being itself, or our regeneration, inferreth it; for we are justified and sanctified, and by both obliged, and also inclined to live unto God. Obliged, for these benefits of Christ's righteousness and Spirit given to us, are such excellent benefits,

---

[15] From the order of justice

that for them we owe our whole selves to God. If Paul could tell Philemon, 'thou owest thyself to me': Phil. i. 9, because he had been an instrument in converting him to God; how much more is our obligation to Christ, who is the principal author and proper efficient cause of this grace! Surely we owe our whole selves, and strength, and time, and service to him, *jure beneficiario*, as God's beneficiaries. We are in debt to him as our benefactor; and not only obliged but inclined by the gift of Christ's righteousness and Spirit; he hath formed us for this very thing, and fitted us to perform the more easily what we owe to God. Everything is fitted for its use, so we are prepared and fitted for the new life, and all the duties that belong thereunto: Eph. ii. 10, 'We are his workmanship in Christ Jesus, created unto good works'. The new creature is put by its proper use, if we live after the flesh; for all this cost and workmanship is bestowed upon us in vain, if it doth not fit us to live unto God.

[C.] Our own vow and covenant sworn and entered into by baptism. Baptism doth infer this debt, for there we renounced the flesh, and gave up ourselves to God as our proper lord. Baptism is a vowed death to sin, and a solemn obligation to live unto God; therefore every Christian must reckon himself dead to sin: Rom. vi. 11, 'Likewise reckon ye also yourselves to be dead unto sin, but alive unto God': and Col. iii. 3, 5, 'Ye are dead, therefore mortify your members'; and Rom. vi. 2, 'How shall ye that are dead unto sin, live any longer therein?' He argueth not *ab impossibili*[16], but *ab incongruo*[17]; for a baptized person, or one that is entered into the oath of God. And being made servants of God, we are bound to live in all new obedience: 1 Pet. iii. 21, 'The like figure whereunto, even baptism doth now save us; not the putting away the filth of the flesh, but the answer of a good conscience towards God' The answer of a good conscience saveth.

[D.] In regard of the benefits we do hereafter expect from Christ; our resurrection and glorious estate in heaven. That is mentioned ver. 2, as binding us to the spiritual life. Certainly where we have received good, and expect more good things, we are the more obliged to obedience. From the flesh we can look for nothing but shame and death; but from the spirit, life and peace. Therefore in prudence we are bound to make the best choice for ourselves, and to live not carnally, but spiritually. Sin never did us any good office; nor can you expect anything from it for the future; it hath never done you good, and will do you eternal hurt; and are you so much in love with sin, as to displease your God, and lose your souls for it, which might otherwise be saved in a way of obedience to the Spirit's sanctifying motions? This argument is again repeated in the 13th. ver, 'If ye live after the flesh, ye shall die,' that we might seriously consider it. Can the flesh give you a sufficient reward to recompense the pains you incur by satisfying it?

The first *Use* is information. It informeth us of divers truths.

---

[16] From impossibility
[17] From disharmony

[A.] If your obedience be a debt, then there can be no merit in it; for what is *debitum*[18] is not *meritorium*: Luke xvii. 10, 'When ye have done all that is commanded you, say, We are unprofitable servants; we have done that which was our duty to do'. We owe ourselves, and all that we have, are, and possibly can do, to God, by whom we live and are; and therefore deserve no further benefit at his hands. Put case we should do all, yet in how many things are we come short? Therefore, surely God is not bound to reward us by any right or justice arising from the merit of the action itself, but only he is inclined so to do by his own goodness and bound so to do by his free promise. The creature oweth itself wholly to God, who made it; and God standeth in such a degree of eminency, so far above us, that we can lay no obligation upon him. Aristotle said well, 'That children could never merit of their parents'; and all their kindness and duty they perform towards them, is but a just recompence to them from whom they received their being. If no merit between children and parents, surely not between God and men.

[B.] When a believer gratifieth the flesh, it is not of right, but tyrannous usurpation. For he is not a debtor to the flesh, he oweth it no obedience. 'Let not sin reign in your mortal bodies': Rom. vi. 11,14. Sin shall not reign; it may play the tyrant. Chrysostom saith, that a child of God may be overtaken through inadvertency, or overborne by the impetuous desires of the flesh, and do something which his heart alloweth not; his sins are sins of passion rather than design; and though the reign of sin be disturbed, yet it is not cast off. Our lives should declare whose servants and debtors we are; for whom do you do most? Your lives must give sentence for you, whether you are debtors to the flesh, or to the spirit. If you spend your time in making provision for the flesh, to fulfil the lusts thereof, Horn. xiii. 14, you are debtors to the flesh. If you check the flesh, and tame it, cut off its provisions, though now and then it will break out, you are not debtors to the flesh, but the Spirit.' The flesh may rebel for a time, but the grace of the Spirit reigneth. Some are wholly governed by their fancies and humours, or the passions, appetites, and desires of the flesh; are carried on headlong by their own carnal and corrupt inclinations to every sense-pleasing object, are not masters of themselves in anything, but serve divers lusts and pleasures, against the dictates of their own reason and conscience. Now, it is easy to pronounce sentence concerning them. Others are led by the Spirit of God to the earnest pursuit of heavenly things. Now these, though so often fomented to self-pleasing and compliance with their lusts and corrupt inclinations, yet the heavenly mind hath the mastery; they complain of this tyranny, are grieved for it, troubled, and do by degrees overcome it.

[C.] It informeth us what answer we should make when we are tempted to please the flesh. Say, 'We are not debtors' When Satan tempteth, or sin enticeth, say, 'I owe thee nothing, I have all from God'; if the flesh tempteth to neglect your callings, to misspend your time, say, 'This time is the Lord's'; as the Apostle: 1 Cor. vi. 15, 'Shall I take the members of Christ, and

---

[18] Paying a debt is not meritorious.

make them the members of an harlot?' Luther speaketh of a virgin that would answer all temptations with this, '*Baptizata sum*, I am baptized.' So the faithful hath but this to answer to every tempter and temptation, I am dedicated to God; or, I am the Lord's. This soul, this body, this time, this strength is his; my business is not to please the flesh, but to please the Lord. Nothing will be such a help in defeating temptations, as to consider his full right and interest in us, and how justly he may expect fidelity from us, from whom we receive and expect all things.

The second *Use* is to exhort us to pay the debt of obedience. Common honesty requireth that every man pay his debts. Now we are debtors unto God.

[A.] Consider how reasonable this debt is, that creatures should serve their creator; that those that cannot live of themselves, should not live to themselves; and not do what they please, but what they ought. If God should put us to preserve ourselves, or keep ourselves but for one day, how soon should we disappear, and return into our original nothing! As God sendeth his people to their idols for deliverance: Judges x. 14, 'Go and cry to the gods which you have chosen, let them deliver you in the time of tribulation'. This would make the case sensible; if you can keep yourselves, please yourselves. As protection draweth allegiance, so doth dependence enforce subjection. Since therefore in him we live, and move, and have our being, let us live to him and for him.

[B.] Consider how unavoidable it is. You are the Lord's whether you will or no. No creature is free from this debt. Not the angels, who have many immunities above us; yet Ps. ciii. 20, 21, 'Bless the Lord, ye his angels that excel in strength, that do his commandments, hearkening to the voice of his word; bless ye the Lord all ye his hosts, ye ministers of his that do his pleasure'. Not the human nature of Christ, Gal. iv. 4. The devil and wicked men are, but it is against their wills; but his people are a voluntary people: Ps. ex. 3. They own God's right in them; his they are, and him they will serve: Acts xxvii. 23.

[C.] How comfortable the debt is made by God's new title of redemption. The former ceased not, but will continue whilst there is a relation between the creature and the creator. But this is a power cumulative, not destructive, but superadded to the former; and it is more comfortable and beneficial to us, that Christ would set us in joint again, and restore the creature to a capacity of serving and pleasing God. What a blessed thing is it to take a law of duty out of the hand of a mediator! A double advantage both to assistance and acceptance; now God will help us, and will accept of it, as we can perform it; from the Mediator we have his Spirit and his righteous ness. First, his Spirit to help us, and give us grace to serve God acceptably, to break the bondage of sin: Rom. viii. 2; to help us against it all along, ver. 13, And by his Spirit of grace we are enabled to love him, and serve him: 'Whom I serve in the Spirit'; and the more we use this grace, the more it is increased upon us; and the more we pay this debt, the more we are enabled to pay: Prov. x. 29, 'The way of the Lord is strength to the upright'. We grow the richer for paying, for we pay God out of his own exchequer: 1 Chron. xxix. 14, 'Of thine own have we given thee.' 1 Cor. xv. 10, 'But by the grace of God I am what I am, and his grace which was bestowed upon me was not in vain; but I laboured more abundantly than they all; yet not I, but the grace of God which was with me. 'The laborious, diligent soul hath more abundance of his Spirit. Secondly, as we have his righteousness. God accepts of our imperfect endeavours: Eph. i. 6, 'He hath made us accepted in the beloved': Mai. iii. 17, 'I will spare them as a man spareth his own son that serveth him.' This double comfort we have by the Mediator.

[D.] The debt is increased by every benefit which we receive from God: Luke xii. 48, 'To whom much is given, of him shall much be required; and to whom men have committed much, of him will they ask more' As our gifts increase, so doth our debt; as our debt, so doth our account; they that have received most, are bound to love him more, and serve him better, because they are more in debt than others.

[E.] How necessary it is for us to be debtors to God. If not debtors to God, we are debtors to the flesh; there is no medium; and if debtors to the flesh, servants to every base lust: Tit. iii. 3, 'Serving divers lusts'; *quam multos habet dominos qui unum habere nevult!* We are slaves to everything, if not debtors to God, and behave ourselves as such. Every fancy and humour captivateth us.

[F.] By paying this debt, we receive more than we pay, in present comfort and peace, but certainly in future glory and blessedness: Rom. vi. 22. 'Ye have your fruit to holiness, and the end everlasting life' The fruit of holiness for the present is peace; no greater comfort than in the discharge of our duty: Gal. vi. 16, 'As many as walk according to this rule, peace and mercy be upon them.

[G.] If we pay not the debt of obedience, we incur the debt of punishment: Mat. vi. 11, 'And forgive us our debts, as we forgive our debtors'; and Rom. vi. 23, 'The wages of sin is death.' A man by pleasing the flesh runneth himself further into debt than all the gain he gets by sin doth amount unto, be it ever so pleasing and profitable; he runneth in debt to God's justice, which at length will take him by the throat, and say, Pay what thou owest; it will cast you into the prison of hell, and you shall not depart thence till you have paid the utmost mite: Luke xii. 59. For the present it bringeth you trembling of conscience, and hereafter eternal vengeance; these things should be minded; because the devil gets into our hearts by the back-door of sensual affections; he doth not bring the temptation to our reason. To consider it as a remedy,

(1.) Own the debt by directing yourselves to God. Everyone should have his own; give unto Caesar the things that are Caesar's, and to God the things that are God's: Mat. xxii. 21. Nothing more reasonable than that God should have his own: 2 Cor. viii. 5, 'They first gave themselves to the Lord'

(2.) Keep a constant reckoning how you lay out yourselves for God: Phil. i. 21. 'To me to live is Christ' Neh. i. 11': The Lord show me favour in the sight of this man, for I have been the king's cupbearer.'

(3.) Pray God to bless you, and ever keep in remembrance the former debt: 1 Cor. vi. 15, 'Know ye not that your bodies are the members of Christ? Shall I then take the members of Christ, and make them the members of an harlot? God forbid.' Here is another reason rendered why Christians should not live after the flesh; before, *a debito*[19]; now *a damno*[20];

or if you will take the whole verse, you have the danger of the carnal life, and the benefit of the spiritual; both propositions are hypothetical or conditional, both include perseverance in either course. The apostle saith not, 'If you have lived after the flesh, ye shall die.' All have lived after the flesh before they lived after the Spirit; and in the other part, if ye go on to mortify in the one branch, the doom is heavy death, not only temporal, but eternal; in the other, the boon or benefit is as much as we can desire, and far more than we can ever deserve or requite; both have their use, for man is apt to be moved by hope or fear; if honesty and duty will not persuade us, yet danger and benefit may have an influence upon us.

Let us now consider the first clause, where death is propounded as the necessary consequent of carnal living; we need not only milk, but salt; as milk to nourish the new creature, so salt to fret out the corruption of the old man. A sore penalty is threatened to them that fulfil the desires and inclinations of the flesh; we buy carnal delights at too dear a rate, when we must die eternally to enjoy them.

Doctrine That God threateneth those that live after the flesh, with eternal death and destruction.

I shall speak to this point.

First. *By way of explication.*

Second. *By way of confirmation.*

In the explication I shall show you. 1. What is meant by flesh. 2. What by living after the flesh. 3. What is the death threatened.

By way of confirmation. 1. That this threatening is every way consistent with the wisdom, and goodness of God. 2. The certainty of its being accomplished and fulfilled.

First. *By way of explication.*

1. What is meant by flesh.

[A.] The flesh is sometimes taken for the natural bodily substance, that corporal mass we carry about us: so it is said, 'No man ever hated his own flesh, but nourisheth it, and cherisheth it': Eph. v. 29. The body is a part of us, and deserveth due care, that it might be an holy temple for the Spirit to dwell in, and sanctify, and make use of it for God.

[B.] For corruption of nature, which inclineth us wholly to things grateful to the body and bodily life, with the neglect of God and our precious immortal souls: John iii. 6, 'That which is born of flesh is flesh.' Now flesh in this latter sense is taken,

---

[19] From debt
[20] From injury

(1.) Largely, For the whole dunghill of corruption, in whatever faculty it is seated, in the understanding, will, or rational appetite: so Gal. v. 17, 'The flesh lusteth against the spirit'; that is, corrupt nature.

(2.) Strictly, or in a limited sense, for the corruption of the sensual appetite: 1 John ii. 16, 'All that is in the world is either the lust of the flesh, the lust of the eye, or pride of life.' Sensuality is expressed by the lust of the flesh; and Eph. ii. 3, 'Fulfilling the wills of the flesh and of the mind.' As it is taken more generally for natural corruption, both in will, mind, and affections; so more particularly for the disorder of the sensual appetite, which carrieth us to meats, drinks, riches, pleasures, honours; therefore there are two branches. Flesh must not be confined to this latter sense, but taken in the latitude of the former; 'The wisdom of the flesh' Rom. viii. 7; and of a 'fleshly mind'. Col. ii. 18. Man is a corrupt, carnal creature in all the faculties of the soul, even those which are more noble, the understanding and will; and when the apostle reckoneth up the works of the flesh (Gal. v. 19), he doth not only reckon up fornication and adultery, unclean- ness, wantonness, which belong to the sensual appetite; but idolatry and heresy, which are the fruits of blind and corrupt reason; and witchcraft, hatred, variance, emulations, wrath, strife, sedition, envyings, murder, which belong to the depraved will; we must take flesh then in the largest sense.

2. What it is to live after the flesh. Living doth not note one single action, but the trade, course, and strain of our conversations; they are said to live after the flesh, where the flesh is their principle, their work, and their scope.

[A.] Where it is the governing principle, or that spring which sets all the wheels a-going. Once it was thus with us all; we were wholly actuated by the inclinations and desires of the flesh, and did nothing but what the flesh moved us unto, and therefore natural men are said to be in the flesh: Rom. viii. 8; and after the flesh, v. 5; and to serve divers lusts and pleasures: Tit. iii. 3. But when our cure is wrought, we are actuated by another principle, the spirit or new nature: Rom. viii. 1.; and Gal. v. 16, Not that the old principle is quite abolished, it is in us still: Gal. v. 17, 'The flesh lusteth against the spirit, and the spirit lusteth against the flesh.' And it is in us not as dead, but as working and operative, and there is a mixture of the respective influence and efficacy of these two principles in every action; yea, in some actions a prevalency of the one above the other. The worse part in a particular conflict may get the upper hand; yet there is a sensible difference between the people of God and others; the better principle is habitual and constant, and in predominancy, and doth not only check and thwart the other, but overcome it; and the interest of the flesh decreaseth, and that of the spirit prevaileth, and keepeth the carnal part in subjection; but when the flesh is the chief principle that beareth rule in our hearts, and we are actuated and guided by it in our course of life, we live after the flesh.

[B.] Their work and trade, or the business of their lives. Men are said to live after the flesh, that wholly mind the things of the flesh: Rom. viii. 5; that take no other care, but to spend their time, wit, and estate upon the service of their own fleshly lusts; their whole life, study, and labour is to please the flesh, and satisfy the flesh. If God gets anything from them, it is but for fashion's sake, and it is only the flesh's leavings: so Gal. v. 8, 'To sow to the flesh';

there is their business, to 'make provision for the flesh': Rom. xiii. 14. Neglecting God, and the eternal welfare of their precious and immortal souls, be it in the way of sensuality, or be it in the way worldliness, all their toiling, and excessive care and pains, are for the worldly life; in short, they follow after earthly things with greatest earnestness, and spiritual things in an overly, formal, and careless manner. A carnal man may do many things in religion, which are good and worthy. Man that hath an appetite, hath also a conscience; though the flesh is importunate to be pleased, and unwilling to be crossed, yet it giveth way to a little superficial duty, that conscience may be pacified, and so itself may be pleased with the less disturbance. Religion is but taken on as a matter by the by, as you give way to a servant to go upon his own errand. Nay, sometimes the flesh doth not only give leave, but it sets them a- work, to hide a lust, or feed a lust; to hide a lust from the world, as in hypocrites; as the Pharisees made their worship serve their rapine: Mat. xxiii. 14; or from their own consciences. Every man must have some religion; therefore the flesh alloweth a few services, that it may the more securely possess the heart; it is not for the interest of the flesh to have too much religion, or none at all; the carnal life must have some devotion to cover it, that men may take courage in sin the more freely. Or feed a lust; pride or vain-glory may put men on preaching or praying before others: Phil. i. 16. 17, 'The one preacheth Christ out of contention.' Or give alms: Mat. vi. 1, 'Take heed that you do not your alms before men, to be seen of men'; and a sacrifice may be brought with an evil mind: Prov. xxi. 27. The devil careth not what means we use, so he may have his ends; that is, to keep men in a carnal condition.

[C.] That make it their scope, end, and happiness. That is our scope and end that solaceth our minds, and sweeteneth our labours; that which they aim at is to be rich and great in the world, or enjoy their pleasure without remorse: Phil. iii. 19, 'Whose end is destruction, whose God is their belly, who mind earthly things.' That is our god which lieth next our hearts, to which we offer our actions, and from which we fetch our inward complacency, be it the pleasing of the flesh, or being accepted with God. All their delight and contentment is to have the flesh pleased in some worldly thing; this giveth them a joy and rest of mind, and quencheth all sentiments of religion and delight in God. They that aim at pardon, grace, and glory, no worldly thing will satisfy them; God and heaven are preferred above all the pleasures, honours, and profits they can enjoy here: Psal. iv. 7, 'Thou hast put gladness into my heart, more than at the time when their corn and wine increased.' But it is otherwise with the carnal; for their hearts run out more pleasingly after some worldly thing; and when they obtain it, it keepeth them quiet under the guilt of willful sin, and all their soul-dangers; and they forget eternity, because they have their heart's desire already: Luke xii. 19, 20, 'And I will say to my soul, thou hast much goods laid up for many years; take thine ease, eat, drink, and be merry; but God said unto him, thou fool, this night thy soul shall be required of thee; then whose Shall these things be thou hast provided? 'And the peace and pleasure which they daily live upon, is fetched more from the world than from God, and Christ, and heaven; the flesh is at ease, and hath nothing to disturb it; and they design the conveniences of the flesh in their whole lives; this is their principle, their chief scope and aim; whatsoever he doth, he still designeth the contentment of the flesh, or some temporal good that shall accrue to him. Thus you see who live after the flesh: where no contrary principle is set up to check it; where it is our daily work to please the flesh, and our great scope and solace to have it pleased.

3. What is this death that is here threatened: 'ye shall die'? Surely the natural death is not intended, for that is common to all, both to those that please the flesh, and those that crucify the flesh: Heb. ix. 27, 'It is appointed for all men once to die.' And besides to the godly it is matter of comfort, a thing which they should rather desire than fear, 1 Cor. iii. 22, death is theirs; therefore death is but a softer word for eternal damnation, yet used with good reason. The apostle saith, 'Ye shall die,' rather than 'ye shall be damned.'

[A.] Because death to the wicked is an inlet to their final and eternal misery; it is dreadful to them, not only as a natural evil, as it puts an end to their worldly comforts, but as a penal evil: Heb. ii. 14, 15, 'Who are all their life -time subject to bondage through fear of death' because of the consequences of it; then their torment beginneth.

[B.] Because it is more liable to sense. We know hell by faith, death by sense; now that notion that is more known, affects us more; all abhor death as a fearful thing. Briefly, then, this death consists not in an extinction and abolition of the creature, but in a deprivation of the favour and presence of the blessed God, who is the fountain of all comfort; and in the everlasting pains and torments which the soul and body being cast out of God's presence feeleth in hell; all that weeping and gnashing of teeth, that bitter remembrance of what is past, that acute sense of what is present, that despair and fearful looking for of the fiery indignation of the Lord; what the scripture speaketh of, it is all included in this word, 'ye shall die.' It is, in short, to be separated from God and Christ, and the saints and angels, and to have eternal fellowship with devils and damned spirits, together with those unknown pains inflicted on us by the wrath of God in the other world.

[C.] It would not be sufficient to restrain men from sin, if God should only threaten temporal death, and not eternal. Every murderer would venture to execute his malice, every adulterer follow his lusts, and voluptuous man his swinish and brutish pleasure, if it were only to endure a short pain at death, and then be free from misery ever after. We see how offenders venture on man's punishment, and how many shorten their days for their vain pleasure; therefore unless the death were everlasting, the world would be little awed by it, unless the bitterness be greater than the present sinful pleasure; therefore eternal torment is that which God threateneth, and will surely execute on the sensual and carnal; so that the sinner hath no hope to escape, except by repentance, and breaking this course of living after the flesh.

Secondly. Now, by way of confirmation, we must show the fit connection between these two things, the carnal living, and this terrible death; and there we must show you, [A.] That this threatening is everyway consistent with the justice, and wisdom, and goodness of God. [B.] Since it is threatened, the certainty of its accomplishment.

[A.] Its consistency with the justice, wisdom, and goodness of God.

(1.) His justice: First, because those that live in the flesh, continue in the defection and apostasy of mankind; and so the old sentence is in force against them, 'in the day thou eatest thereof thou shalt die': Gen. ii. 17. To shew you this, let me tell you, that by the creation man was to be subject to God, and by his own make and constitution was composed of a body and soul, which two parts were to be regarded according to the worth and dignity of each; the body was subordinated to the soul, and both body and soul to God; the flesh was a servant to the spirit, and both flesh and spirit unto the Lord. But sin entering, defaced the beauty, and disturbed the order and harmony of the creation; for man withdrew his subordination and obedience unto God his maker, and set up himself instead of God, and the flesh is preferred before the soul; reason and conscience are enslaved to sense and appetite; and the beast doth ride the man, the flesh becoming our principle, rule, and end. Now it is horrible wickedness, if you consider either of these disorders; our contempt of God, for it is great depreciation, and disesteem of his holy and blessed majesty, which is neglected and slighted for a little carnal satisfaction, and every perishing vanity is preferred before his favour. The heinousness of the sin is to be measured by the greatness of him who is offended by it: 1 Sam. ii. 25. 'If one man sin against another, the judge shall judge him; but if a man sin against the Lord, who shall entreat for him? 'Now for creatures to seek their happiness without God, and apart from God, in such base things, deserveth the greater punishment. The other disorder is, we love the happiness of the body above that of the soul; man carrieth it as if he had not an immortal spirit in him: Ps. xlix. 12, 'is as the beast that perisheth'; and is altogether flesh, his wisdom and spirit is sunk into flesh, and sin hath transformed him into a brutish nature. Well now, if men will continue in this apostasy, what then more just, than that God should stand to his old sentence, and deprive them of that happiness which they despise; that those who dishonour their own souls, should never be acquainted with a blessed immortality; and those that contemn their God, and banish him out their thoughts, and do in effect say to the Almighty, Job. xxi. 14, 'Depart from us, we desire not the knowledge thy ways,' that they may spend their days in mirth that God should banish them out of his presence with a curse never to be reversed? They do in effect bid God be gone, the very thoughts of him are an interruption to that sort of life they have chosen, that he should bid them 'depart ye cursed,' who bid him depart first? In short, that the carnal life, which is but a spiritual death, should be punished with eternal death: 1 Tim. iii. 6, 'She that liveth in pleasure is dead while she liveth,' a kind of carcass, or rather a living creature dead, estranged from the life of God, and then deprived of eternal life?

Secondly. They refuse the remedy. The great business of the Christian religion, is to dispossess us of the brutish nature which is gotten into us. I say, this is the drift and tenure of Christianity, to recover us from the flesh to God; to turn man into man again, that was become a beast; to draw him off from the animal life, to life spiritual and eternal; to drive out the spirit of the world, and intro duce a divine and heavenly Spirit purchased by Jesus Christ, and offered to us in the promises of the gospel. The world is mad and brutish, enslaved to lower things; but this healing institution of Christ is to make us wise and heavenly; to recover the immortal soul, that was enslaved to earthly things, and depressed and tainted by the objects of sense, into its former liberty and perfection, that the spirit might command the flesh, and man might seek his happiness and blessedness in some higher and more transcending good, than the beasts are capable of. In short, as sin was the transforming of a man into a beast; so Christianity is the transforming of beasts into man again; to restore humanity, and elevate it from the state of subjection to the flesh. John iii. 6, 'That which is born of the flesh is flesh, and that which is born of the Spirit is spirit.' 2 Pet. i. 4, 'Whereby are given us great and precious promises, that by these you might be partakers of the divine nature; having escaped the corruption that is in the world through lust' 1 Cor. ii. 12, 'Now we have received, not the spirit of the world, but the Spirit which is of God, that we may know the things that are freely given us of God.' Now, after this is done with such cost and care, if men will love their bondage, despise their remedy, surely they are worthy of the severest punishment: John iii. 19, 'And this is the condemnation, that light is come into the world, and men love darkness rather than light, because their deeds are evil'. If we refuse this Spirit that is offered to change our natures, arid lift us up from earth to heaven, and we will not be changed and healed, but wallow in this filth and puddle still, we are doubly culpable for not doing our duty, and refusing our remedy.

But you will say, the punishment is eternal; how will that stand with the justice of God, to inflict it for temporal offences?

(1.) Answer. Till the carnal life ceaseth, the full punishment doth not begin or take place; as when men have done their work they receive their wages. It is not inflicted till after death, and in the other world there is no change of state; our trial is over, our sentence is passed, the gulf is fixed between hell and heaven, that the inhabitants of the one cannot come into the other place, Luke xvi. 26.

(2.) There was eternal life in the offer. Now if men will part with this for one morsel of meat, this is profaneness indeed: Heb. xii. 15, 16. The things propounded to their choice are eternal happiness and eternal misery; if they refuse the one, they in justice deserve the other.

(3.) If they be Christians, they do not pay their great debt, or fulfil their covenant-vow; and so make the forfeiture. The apostle here inferreth the great danger out of the debt': Ye are debtors'; that if we live after the flesh, we shall die; they are entered into the bond of the holy oath. So elsewhere: Gal. v. 24, 'They that are Christ's, have crucified the flesh, with the affections and lusts thereof.' How are we Christ's? As dedicated to him in baptism, they have renounced the devil, the world, and the flesh; they are Christ's not only dejure[21], they ought to do so; but de facto, they have crucified the flesh. It is hypocrisy and perjury that the carnal and brutish nature should reign in us. Baptism implieth a vow, we are 'baptized into the likeness of his death,' Rom. vi. 3. Christ bound himself to communicate the virtue of his death; and we bind ourselves to die unto sin, and to use all Christ's instituted means to

---

[21] according to rightful entitlement or claim; by right

that end and purpose. Now, if after that we are washed, we still wallow in the mire, and affect that life which we have renounced, and gratify what we should crucify; cherish the flesh, rather than use Christ's healing means to subdue it and purge it out, our very baptism will solicit the more severe vengeance, and be a swift witness against us. It were better scalding oil had been poured upon us, than the water of baptism; and if there be any place in hell hotter than others, it is for hypocrites and perjured persons that have broken the vow of their God which is upon them; this should the more sink into us, because every covenant hath a curse included in it, *implicite*, or *explicite*. A consecration implieth an execration or imprecation of vengeance if we do contrary; the scripture abhorreth not this notion; it is said, Neh. x. 29, they entered into a curse and an oath to walk in God's law. So it is in the new covenant, for all Christians do con sent to the threats and punishments of the gospel in case of failing in their duty; as the Israelites were to give their amen, Deut. xxvii. 15, to the curses of the law; so we profess to submit to the law of grace, and tenor of it: in Mark xvi. 16, 'He that believeth not, shall be damned.' We profess our consent to this law, not to a part only, but to the whole. Now whatever faith and baptism calleth for, that must be done; or if it be wilfully left undone, we approve the penalty as just, and that God may rightly inflict it upon us. Thus for the justice of God.

[B.] Now for the wisdom. The punishment is the greater, to check the greatness of the temptation. Much of the fleshly life is pleasant, like the Eden of God, to the besotted soul; therefore God hath guarded it with a flaming sword, that fear may counterbalance our delight. It is a hard thing to bring a man to strive against his own flesh; it is born and bred with us, and is importunate to be pleased, but the end is death. There must be a separation between the soul and sin, or between the soul and God; milder motives would do us no good against boisterous lusts, and are not powerful enough to wean us from accustomed delights; therefore is the punishment threatened the more dreadful, and the sinful fear is checked by the severity of the intermination; though sense-pleasing and flesh-pleasing be sweet to a carnal heart, it will cost him dear. The wisdom of God is seen in three things,

(1.) In punishing sin, which is a moral evil, with death and misery, which is a natural evil; in appointing that it should be ill with them that do evil. These are fitly sorted: Deut. xxx. 15, 'See, I have set before thee life and good, death and evil.' The evil of sin is against our duty, and the evil of punishment against our interest and happiness; now if men will willingly do what they should not, it is equal they should suffer what they would not, what is against their wills; these two are natural relatives, sin and misery, good and happiness; we find some of this in ourselves, we have compassion of a miserable man, whom we esteem not deserving his misery; we think it is ill placed there; and we are also moved with indignation against one that is fortunate and successful, but unworthy the happiness he enjoys; which showeth man hath an apprehension of a natural harmony and order between these things, sin and misery, goodness and felicity.

(2.) The wisdom of God lieth in this, that the love of pleasure, which is the root of all sin, should end in a sense of pain. Man is a very slave to pleasure: Tit. iii. 3, 'Serving divers lusts and pleasures.' It is engrained in our natures; therefore to check it, the Lord hath threatened the pains of the second death; and this method our Lord approveth as most useful to draw us from our beloved sin: Mat. v. 29, 30, 'Better one member suffer, than the whole body to be cast into hell.' In short, God hath so proportioned the dispensation of joy and sorrow, pleasure and pain, that it is left to our choice, whether we will have it here or hereafter, whether we will have pleasure as the fruit of sin, or as the reward of well-doing; both we cannot have, you must not expect to enjoy the pleasures of earth and heaven too, and think to pass from Delilah's lap into Abraham's bosom: Luke xvi. 25, 'Son, in thy life time thou receivedst thy good things'; and Jam. v. 5, 'Ye have lived in pleasure upon earth'; you have been merry and jocund; but your time of howling and lamenting then cometh, far beyond the degree of your former rejoicing. (3.) By setting eternal pains against momentary pleasures, that ye may the better escape the temptation; *momentaneum est quod delectat, eternum quod cruciat*. 'The pleasures of sin are but for a season' Heb. xi. 25; but the pains of sin are for evermore; if the fearful end of this delightful course were soundly believed or seriously considered, it would not so easily prevail upon us. It is the wisdom of our law giver that things to come should have some advantage in the proposal above things present; that the joy and pain of the other world should be greater than the comfort and pleasure of this world, which is a matter of sense; for things at hand would certainly prevail with us, if things to come were not considerably greater; therefore here the pain is short, and so is the pleasure, but there it is eternal. Those that will have their pleasure here, they shall have it, but to their bitter cost; but those that will work out their salvation with fear and trembling, will by the Spirit mortify the deeds of the body, will pass through the difficulties of religion, shall have pleasure at his right hand for ever more, Ps. xvi. 11.

[C.] It is consistent with his love and goodness. This is necessary to be considered,

(1.) Because we are apt to think hardly of God for his threatenings. It is for our profit to give warning, and to bring us to repentance, and that we may take heed and escape these things; he threateneth that he may not punish; and he punisheth in part, that he may not punish forever. The first awakening is by fear, afterwards shame, sorrow, and indignation; the curse driveth us to the promise; first, we look upon sin as damning, then as defiling; first, as it fits us for hell; then, as it unfits us for heaven.

(2.) It is a benefit to the world. Punishment among men, because of the degeneracy of the world, is a more powerful engine of government than reward; we owe much of our safety to prisons and executions; so in God's government, though love be the mighty gospel motive, yet fear hath its use, at least for those who will not serve God out of love; slavish fear tieth their hands from mischief.

(3.) For the converted, they find all help in this part of the Spirit's discipline, to guard their love. When their minds are in danger of being enchanted by carnal delights, or perverted by the terrors of sense; when the flesh presents the bait, faith shows the hook, Mat. x. 28; or are apt to abuse their power, because none in the world can call them to an account: Job xxxi. 23, 'Destruction from God was a terror to me.' He stood in awe of God, who is a party against the oppressor, and will right the weak against the powerful.

2. Since it is threatened, we may conclude the certainty of its accomplishment. The world will not easily believe that none shall be saved but the regenerate, and those that live not after the flesh but the Spirit, and love God in Christ above all the world, even their own lives; that besides these few, all the rest shall be tormented in hell for ever; flesh and blood cannot easily go down with this doctrine; but God's threatenings are as sure as executions.

[A.] Because of the holiness of his nature: Ps. xi. 6, 7, 'Upon the wicked he will rain snares, fire and brimstone, and horrible tempest; this shall be the portion of their cup, for the righteous Lord loveth righteousness.' But men feign God as they would have him to be, and judge of God's holiness by their own interest: Ps. 1. 21, 'Thou thoughtest that I was altogether such a one as thyself.' As if God were less mindful because he is so holy; and will not be so indulgent to their flesh and sin, as they are themselves, and would have him to be.

[B.] His unalterable truth. 'God cannot lie' Tit. i. 2. Though the threatening in the present judgment doth not always show the event, but merit, yet it follows afterwards; for the scripture must be fulfilled, or else all religion will fall to the ground. He cannot endure any should question it, it is not a vain scare-crow: Deut. xxx. 19, 20, 'I call heaven and earth to record this day against you, that I have set before you life and death, blessing and cursing; therefore choose life, that thou and thy seed may live; that thou mayest love the Lord thy God, that thou mayest obey his voice, and that thou mayest cleave unto him, for he is thy life, and the length of thy days'

[C.] His all-sufficient power: 2 Thes. i. 9, 'Who shall be punished with everlasting destruction from the presence of the Lord and the glory of his power'; and Rom. ix. 22, 'What if God, willing to show his wrath, and to make his power known, endureth with much long-suffering the vessels of wrath fitted to destruction? 'If God will do so, surely he can, there is no let there: Heb. x. 29, 30, 'Vengeance belongeth to me, and I will recompense, saith the Lord; and again, the Lord shall judge his people.' He liveth for ever to see vengeance executed; if it seem to be so terrible to you, God knoweth it is with a resign of love, to awaken those that are carnal. What a case am I in then! And to make the converted more cautious that they do not border on the carnal life. God maketh no great difference here between the righteous and the wicked; hereafter he will.

SERMON XVI

If ye live after the flesh ye shall die.

Romans VIII. 13.

THE first *Use* is information.

1. To show the lawful use of threatenings. 2. The folly of two sorts of people. [A.] Of those that will rather venture this death, than leave their sinful pleasures. [B.] Those that would reconcile God and flesh, God and the world.

1. The lawful use of threatenings.

Threatenings are necessary during the law of grace. Two arguments I shall give for the proof thereof: (1.) If threatenings were needful to Adam in the state of innocency and perfection, much more are they useful now, when there is such a corrupt inclination within, and so many temptations without; in the best there is a double principle and many inordinate lusts, that we need the strongest bridle and curb to suppress them. (2.) If Christ came to verify God's threatenings, surely God hath some use of them now; but so it is, the devil would represent God as a liar in his comminations[22]: Gen. iii. 4, 'Ye shall not surely die.' Christ came to confute the tempter, and would die rather than the devil's reproach of God's threatenings should be found true; surely this is to check thoughts of iniquity.

(2.) The folly of two sorts of people. [1.] Of those that will rather venture this death than leave their sinful pleasures, and live a holy life. Carnal men think no life so happy as theirs, being escaped out ot f of religion and bonds of conscience, in the apostle's expression, 'Free from righteousness,' Rom. vi. 20. Whereas the truth is, none are more miserable; for they carry it so, as if they were in love with their own death- Prov. viii. 36, 'He that sinneth against me, wrongeth his own soul - and they that hate me, l6ve death.' You hazard soul and body, and all that is near and dear to you, for a little carnal satisfaction; for the present you get nothing but the guilt of conscience, hardness of heart, and the displeasure of the eternal God; and for the future, everlasting destruction from the presence of the Lord, when the body and soul shall be cast into hell-fire. Consider this before it be too late; there is no man goeth to hell or heaven, but with violence to conscience or lusts; those that go to hell offer violence to their conscience.

[B.] Those that would reconcile God and flesh, God and the world, and secure their interest in both; that hope to please the flesh, and yet to be happy hereafter for all that; would keep up a profession of godliness, while they live in secret league with their lusts. God will not halve it with the world, nor part stakes with the flesh; you cannot please the flesh, and enjoy God too; for you have but one happiness; if you place it in contenting the flesh, you cannot have it in the fruition of God': Their end is destruction, whose God is their belly, and who

---

[22] Commination: the action of threatening divine vengeance

mind earthly things,' Phil. iii. 19. Worldly pleasures will end in eternal torments; and so much delight, so much more will your torments be, for contraries are punished with contraries: Rev. viii. 7, 'How much she hath glorified herself, and lived deliciously, so much sorrow give her.' Therefore, so much as you gratify the flesh, so much you endanger the soul. Will you, for a little temporal satisfaction, run the hazard of God's eternal wrath?

The second *Use* is to dissuade you from this course. To this end I shall lay down some motives, and some means.

1. Motives are these.

[A.] You think the flesh is your friend, do all that you can to please it; whereas indeed it is your greatest enemy. That it is one of your enemies is clear, by that place where all our enemies appear abreast, Eph. ii. 2, 3. There is 'the course of this world, the prince of the power of the air,' and our own flesh. If there were never a devil to tempt, or example to follow, yet, 'out of the heart proceed (Mat. xv. 19,) murder, adultery, theft, blasphemy.' Among other things he reckoneth up murder, which striketh at the life of man; and blasphemy, which striketh at the being of God. If the devil should stand by and say nothing, there is enough within us to put us upon all manner of evil; other enemies would do us no harm, without our own flesh. Corruption may be irritated by God's law, Rom. vii. 9; we may be tempted to sin by Satan, 1 Cor. vii. 5; encouraged to sin by the exam pie and the evil conversations of others, Isa. ix. 16; enticed to sin by the baits of the world, 2 Pet. i. 4; but only inclined to sin by our own flesh; and at length no man is a sinner but by his own consent: Jam. i. 14, 'He is drawn away by his own lust, and enticed.' In vain do temptations knock at the door, if there were nothing within to make answer and admit them; if we could keep ourselves from ourselves, there were no danger from what is without; as Balaam by all his curses and charms could do nothing against the Israelites till he found out a way to corrupt them by whoredom, and by whoredom to draw them to idolatry; and so found a means to destroy them by themselves. So it is the domestic enemy, the flesh within us, which maketh us a prey to Satan, and doth us mischief upon all occasions; it is the flesh distracts us in holy duties with vain thoughts, and abateth our fervours; that maketh us idle in our callings; that tempts to sensuality and inordinate delight when we are repairing nature; and turneth our table into a snare, so that nature is rather oppressed than refreshed for God's service. It is the flesh maketh us forget our great end, and the eternal interests of our immortal souls.

[B.] The more you indulge the flesh, the more it is your enemy, and the more your slavery and bondage is increased; so that still you grow more brutish, forgetful of God, and unapt for any spiritual use. By using to please the flesh, you do increase its desires, and know not at length how to deny it, and displease it; by being made a wanton, it groweth stubborn and contumacious. The more you gratify the flesh, the more inordinate it groweth, and the more unreasonable things it craveth at your hands; therefore you must hold a hard hand upon it at first. Through too much indulgence the reins are loosened to sin, and the enemy is heartened, and our liberty is every day more and more lost. Solomon was fearfully corrupted when he withheld not his heart from any joy: Eccles. ii. 10. This brought him to a lawless excess, and to fall so foully as he did; if you give corrupt nature its full scope, and use pleasures with too free a license, the heart is insensibly corrupted, and our very diseases and distempers become our necessities. Solomon saith (Prov. xx-ix. 21), 'He that delicately bringeth up a servant, shall have him become a son at length'; he will no more know his condition, but grow bold and troublesome. We are all the worse for license; therefore unless natural desires feel fetters and prudent restraints, they grow unruly; therefore that the flesh may not grow masterly, it is good to bridle it. To deny ourselves nothing, bringeth a greater snare upon the soul, and distempers are more rooted: 1 Cor. vi. 12, 'I will not be brought under the power of any creature.' A man is brought into vassalage and bondage, and cannot help it.

[C.] The engagement that is upon Christians to abhor carnal living. By their solemn baptismal vow, which obligeth us to take this yoke of Christ upon ourselves, even to tame and subdue the flesh: Col. iii. 3, 5, 'Mortify your members which are upon earth.' All are strictly bound to mortify the deeds of the body, under pain of damnation; kings as well as subjects, nobles and base; for God is no accepter of persons; no man of what degree soever can presume of an exemption from the duty, or hope for a dispensation. We are all debtors, and this duty taketh place as soon as we come to the use of reason; we all then begin to feel the corruption and imperfection of nature; and we are bound to look after the cure of it, and to use all Christ's healing means that it may be effected. Then we begin to perceive the enemies against whom we are to fight, and a necessity laid upon us of killing them, or being killed by them. It is our great fault that we made conscience of our solemn vow no sooner; surely we should no longer dispute it now: 1 Pet. iv. 3 'For the time past of our life may suffice us to have wrought the will of the Gentiles, when we lived in lasciviousness, lusts, excess of wine, reveling, banquetings, and abominable idolatries.' But set about the work, and undertake the battle against the devil, the world, and the flesh. Your first enemy is the old man; and it is the last, for it is not extinguished in us till death; therefore as soon as we pass out of infancy into youth, we must look upon ourselves under this obligation, not to live after the flesh, but after the Spirit; to weaken the corruption of nature more and more. There was but one man and no more, who was first good and afterwards bad; and that was the first Adam. Another there is, who was never bad, but always good'; and that was Christ Jesus, the second Adam, our Lord, blessed forever. Of all the rest, none proved good that was not sometimes bad; the apostle saith, 'first that which was natural, and afterwards that which is spiritual.' It is true, here first we put off a corrupt nature before we are renewed; the duty lieth upon us by our baptismal engagement, though Christ supplieth the grace.

[D.] The qualities of a Christian, or his condition in the world, engageth him not to live after the flesh. I shall mention two: as they are strangers and pilgrims, or as they are racers and wrestlers. First, Sometimes it is pressed upon them as they are strangers and pilgrims, who have no continued abode: 1 Pet. ii. 11, 'I beseech you as pilgrims and strangers, abstain from fleshly lusts, which war against the soul.' You are, or should be, travelling into another country, where are the spirits of just men made perfect, and where even this body of ours will become a spiritual body; and for you to please the flesh is contrary to your Christian hopes. Nothing so unsuitable for them that are going to Canaan as to hanker after the flesh-pots of Egypt; nothing is so contrary to our profession, and breedeth such an unreadiness to depart out of the world, as these vain delights; therefore if you be strangers and pilgrims, you should not lust after worldly things, lest you forget or forfeit your great hopes. Secondly, you are racers or wrestlers: 1 Cor. ix. 24, 'Know you not that they which run in a race run all, but one receiveth the prize? So run that you may obtain.' They that exercised in the Isthmian games had a prescribed set diet both for quality and quantity, and had their rule chalked out to them; they knew their work and their reward; so v. 27, 'But I keep under my body, and bring it into subjection, lest that by any means, when I have preached to others, I myself should be a cast-away'; that is, denied himself those liberties which otherwise he might enjoy, having prescribed to others the way of striving and getting the victory. They for an oaken or olive crown dieted themselves, kept themselves from all things which should hurt them, or disable them in the race or combat; and should we cocker every appetite, that have an eternal crown of glory in view and pursuit? Our danger is greater if we should miscarry and miss of it; theirs, the loss of a little vain glory; ours, of eternal glory; therefore we should strive that we be not found unworthy to receive it. There the victory was uncertain; here all that are runners may be sure of the crown.

[E.] Consider the malignant influence of the flesh, and how pernicious it is to the soul. If it were a small thing we spake to you about, you might refuse to give ear; but it is in a case of life and death, and that not temporal but eternal. We can tell you of many present and temporal inconveniences that come by the flesh. The body, the part gratified, is in many oppressed by it: Prov. v. 11, 'Thou shalt mourn .at last, when thy flesh and body is consumed.' It betrayeth you to such sins as suck your bones and devour your strength, and give your years to the cruel; to such enormities and scandalous practices as bring infamy and a blot upon your name. Pleasing the flesh maketh one turn a drunkard, and the very sin carrieth its own punishment with it; a second, a wanton; a third, a glutton; a fourth, a hard-hearted world ling; and all these sins waste the conscience, and debase the body, and spend our wit, time, strength, and estates. But we have a more powerful argument to present to you; it will be the eternal loss and ruin of your souls. There will a day come when you shall be called to an account for all your vain delights and pleasures: Eccles. xi. 9, 'Rejoice, young man, in thy youth, and let thine heart cheer thee in the days of thy youth, and walk in the ways of thine own heart, and in the sight of thine own eyes; but know that for all these things God will bring thee to judgment.' The young man is cited before the tribunal of God, and we think somewhat must be allowed to that age, before men have learned by experience to contemn pleasures, and the young man is spoken to in his own dialect. Let his wanton and wandering eye inflame the lusts of his heart, and smother his conscience by all manner of sensual delight; yet at length he will know the folly of this to his bitter cost. These things which are now so pleasing to the senses shall gnaw and sting his conscience, when God, whom he now forgetteth, shall bring him to the judgment, and he shall have nothing to plead for his brutish folly.

[F.] What vile unthankfulness it is, and a great abuse of that liberty which we have by Christ: Gal. v. 13, 'Ye are called to liberty, only use it not as an occasion to the flesh'. We have a great liberty to use our worldly comforts, with a respect to God's glory, and as encouragements of God's service, and for the sweetening of our pilgrimage; but it is strangely perverted when we use these things to please the flesh; you turn it into a bondage, and offer a great abuse to Jesus Christ. Surely he never died to promote the power of sin, or gave us these comforts to defeat the ends of his death. Was he a man of sorrows that we might live in pleasure? Did he suffer in the flesh to purchase us liberty to please the flesh? Or die for sin, to give sin the mastery? Did the Lord vouchsafe these comforts that we might dishonour his name, or undo our own souls?

2. Means to come out of this estate and course of sin. I shall give you a few directions:

[A.] To those that never pretended to the spiritual and heavenly life, and are as yet to be drawn out of the common apostasy and defection of mankind to God. All that I shall say to them is to observe checks of conscience and motions of the Spirit, and what help is given to weaken the flesh.

(1.) Checks of conscience, however occasioned, either by a lapse into some sin, which is wont to scourge the soul with some remorse: Mat. xxvii. 4, saying 'I have sinned in betraying innocent blood' Conscience, working after the fact or by the conviction of the word: Acts xxiv. 25, 'And as he reasoned of righteousness, and temperance, and judgment to conic, Felix trembled.' Do not smother these checks; this breedeth atheism and hardness of heart. Suppose one, dissolutely bent, yet upon some loathsome concomitants which follow his riot and intemperance, beginneth to be troubled; God's providence is to be- observed as well as his own sin. This is a kind of softening his heart; if he revert to his old frame, the man is the worse. No iron so hard as that which hath been often heated. Water, after it hath been heated by the fire, congealeth the sooner after it is taken off. If he doth not take notice of God's warnings, his soul is more unapt to be wrought to repentance; yea, God injustice may deprive him of those common helps: Hos. iv. 17, 'Let him alone'; or give him up to his own heart's counsels. It is dangerous not to make use of those intervals of reason and sober thoughts which arise in our minds.

(2.) The motions of the Holy Spirit, when he cometh to recover you from the flesh to God; and you are troubled not only with remorse for actual and heinous sins, but about your eternal estate; and are haunted with thoughts of the other world, -and urged to resolve upon the heavenly life. Surely, when the waters are stirred, we should put in for a cure, John v; when he draweth, we should run, Cant. i. 4; when he knocketh, we should open, Rev. iii. 20, and not obstruct the work of godliness, but seriously employ our thoughts about it: Acts xvi. 14, 'Whose heart the Lord opened, that she attended unto the things that were spoken by Paul.' We should not rebel against the motions of the Spirit, lest we grieve our sanctifier, and he forsake us, because we for sook him first, and so our hearts be hardened in a carnal course. Briefly, God doth all in our first conversion; yet these three things lie upon us; first, to observe the touches of God's punishing and chastising hand reclaiming us from our wanderings: Ps. cxix. 59. 'Before I was afflicted I went astray' Secondly, To reflect upon the motions of his Spirit to draw us out of this estate, that we may not resist the Holy Ghost, Acts vii. 51. Thirdly, To examine every day what advantage the Spirit hath gotten against the flesh; how the interests of it are weakened, its lusts checked, its acts restrained, Gal. v. 16. Every one that doth seriously mind the business of his salvation cannot but see these things of great advantage to his spiritual estate; and there is no great difficulty in them to the serious soul that hath a mind to be saved.

[B.] To those that seem to be recovered, and to have a care of the spiritual life, that they may not revert to this bondage, and that the work may be more thoroughly wrought in them.

(1.) Look to the mind; take heed there be not flesh there, for the fleshly mind is a great enemy to godliness: Rom. viii. 7, 'The carnal mind is enmity to God'; and it is a low poor mind, blinded with the love of present things: James iil 15, 'The wisdom that descendeth not from above is earthly, sensual, devilish;' it hindereth us from discerning the reality of our hopes, and from having a true sense of our duty impressed upon our hearts: 1 Cor. ii. 14, 'But the natural man receiveth not the things of the Spirit of God, for they are foolishness to him; neither can he know them, because they are spiritually discerned'; and also from applying our rule to particular cases, either in judging of our estate or in guiding of our actions. It is strange to see how the world, or the delusion of the flesh, do blind very knowing men, and how unacquainted they are with their own hearts, or unable to discern their duty in plain cases, when the performance of it is likely to be displeasing to the flesh. What strange disguises it puts upon temptation, and how they wriggle and distinguish themselves out of their duty, when either God must be disobeyed or the flesh displeased. The flesh is always partial for itself; therefore get a sound mind and this spiritual discerning.

(2.) Look to the heart, that there be no flesh there. Sinful inclinations must be observed and mortified. Satan doth observe them, and shall not we? He seeth which way the tree leaneth, and what kind of diet their soul-distempers crave, and suiteth his temptations accordingly. As the skillful angler suiteth his bait as the fishes will take it, every month: 1 Cor. vii. 5, 'Lest Satan tempt you for your incontinency.' He hath a bait of preferment for Absalom, for he is ambitious; a bait of pleasure for Samson, for he is voluptuous; a bait of money for Judas, for he is covetous. Thus will he furnish them with temptations answerable to their inclinations. A man by temper voluptuous esteems not profit much, nor an earth-worm pleasure, nor an ambitious man much either of them, but honour, and reputation, and great place. Now, it is sad that our enemy should know our temper better than our selves. Your uprightness and faithfulness to God is seen in weakening your particular inclination to sin: Ps. xviii. 23, 'I was also upright before him, and kept myself from mine iniquity.' Observe the decay of your master-sin, and other things will come on the more easily; fight not against small or great, but the king lust, the domineering sin. Satan is the more discouraged when we can deny our domineering lusts. As Samson's strength lay in his locks, so doth the strength of sin in one lust more than another. Every man knoweth his darling commonly; but that which is our great care is to wean our hearts from it. Herod raged when John the Baptist touched his Herodias; Felix trembled when Paul touched his bribery and intemperance; and the young man goeth away sad when Christ discovereth his worldliness, Mark x. 22. We have all our tender parts, which we cannot endure should be touched. But now, when you are willing to part with this sin, pray, strive, and watch against it; grow in the contrary grace; it sheweth your self-denial and sincerity; you will not spare your Isaac. Well then, see that no worldly thing be too near and dear to you, and that God hath a greater interest in your heart than the flesh, or anything that belongeth to it.

(3.) Let not the senses cast off the government of reason, and be the ruling power in your souls. They were not made to govern, but to be governed, and to be subjected to God and reason. Man by the fall is inverted: Tit. iii. 3, 'hateful and hating one another.' Man in his right constitution should be thus governed. The understanding and conscience prescribe to the will, the will according to right reason and conscience moveth the affections, the affections move the bodily spirits and the members of the body. But by corruption all is inverted and changed; pleasure affects the senses, the senses corrupt the fancy, the fancy the bodily spirits; they the affections; and the affections by their violence and impetuous inclination to forbidden things, move the will; and the will yielding, blindeth the mind; and so man is carried headlong to his own destruction; the feet are where the head should be, e contra. Well then, you must guide the senses, as Job made a covenant with his eyes: Job xxxi. 1. and David prayeth: Psal. cxix. 37, 'Turn away mine eyes from beholding vanity.' They let in objects, and objects stir up thoughts, and thoughts affections, Mat. v. 28. Now take heed they do not grow masterly; if they transmit temptations and stir up evil motions crush the scorpion on the wound.

(4.) Keep up a readiness for your work, which is to obey the will of God. It argueth some prevalency of the flesh, when our duty beginneth to grow troublesome and uneasy; therefore the spirit or the better part cannot so readily produce its operation. The soul in the right temper doth willingly and cheerfully obey God: I John v. 3, 'This is the love of God, that we keep his commandments, and his commandments are not grievous.' Psal. xl. 8, 'I delight to do thy will, my God: thy law is in my heart'; and Psal. cxii. 1, 'Blessed is the man that feareth the Lord, that delighteth greatly in his commandments.' Therefore it is time for you to check the flesh, and overcome it, lest further mischief increase upon you.

(5.) Refer all things to your ultimate end; and consider whether what you do doth hinder or further you therein; for all things are to be regarded and valued as they conduce to God's service and your salvation: Eccles. ii. 2, 'What doth it? '1 Cor. x. 31, 'Whether ye cat or drink, or whatsoever ye do, let all be done to the glory of God'. Be true to your scope.

(6.) Take heed of the servitude and bondage which the flesh is wont to bring upon the soul where it reigneth. It maketh men very slaves; the heart groweth weak, and lust strong, Ezek. xvi. 30. They are not under the government of the Spirit, but under the tyranny of their fleshly lusts, doing whatever it commandeth, be it never so base, foolish, and hurtful. If anger provoke them to revenge, they must fight, kill, and slay, and hazard their worldly interest for anger's sake, or at least cannot forgive injuries for God's sake; if filthy lusts send them to the lewd woman, away they go like a fool to the correction of the stocks; and though they dishonour God, ruin their estates, stain their fame, hazard their lives, yet lust will have it so, and they must obey. If covetousness say they must be rich, however they get it; they rise early, go to bed late, eat the bread of sorrow, and pierce through themselves with many cares: yea, make no question of right or wrong, trample conscience under foot, cast the fear of God behind their backs, and all because their imperious mistress, ambition, urgeth them to it. If envy and malice bid Cain kill his brother, he will break all bonds of nature to do it; if ambition bid Absalom rebel against his father, and kill him too, it shall be done, or he shall want his will. If covetousness bid Achan take a wedge of gold, he will do it, though he know it to be a cursed thing; if it bid Judas betray his Lord and Master, though he knew if he should do it, it had been better he had never been born, yet he will do it. Thus they are not at their own command, to do what reason and conscience inclineth them to do. If, sensible of their bondage, they would think of God and the world to come, and the state of their souls, lust will not permit it; if to break off this sensual course, they are not able; they are servants of corruption. Some, God hangeth up in chains of darkness for a warning to the rest of the world of the power of drunkenness, gluttony, avarice and wretched worldliness; yea, of every carnal man it is true: (John viii. 34,) 'Whoso ever committeth sin, is the servant of sin.' Therefore if the slavery and imperious disease begin to grow upon you, the flesh hath prevailed very far, and you need more to look to it, and that betimes.

Third Use. Here is ground of trying your estate before God. It is a question you ought often seriously to put: 'Shall I be saved, shall I be damned?' If you have any spark of conscience left you, when you are sick or dying, you will put it with anxiousness and trembling of heart': Poor soul, whither art thou now a-going? 'It is better put it now, while you have opportunity to correct your error, if hitherto you have gone wrong. We see in worldly things, men would fain know their destiny; the king of Babylon stood upon the head of the ways to make divination; we would fain know what God hath hidden in the womb of futurity. No destiny deserves to be known so much as this; not whether I shall be poor or rich, good success in this enterprise, or bad; it is not of so great moment; these distinctions do not outlive time, but cease at the grave's mouth; but it is a question of greater moment, Whether eternally miserable, or eternally happy? It is foolish curiosity to enquire into other things, when we have a good God to trust to; but it chiefly importeth us to consider whether we are in the way to salvation or damnation. Nothing will sooner determine this great question, than this text, 'If ye live after the flesh, ye shall die; but if ye through the Spirit do mortify the deeds of the body, ye shall live.' The latter branch we shall examine afterwards; now for the first clause.

1. Some live in defiance of the Spirit; cherish the flesh, fulfil the works of the flesh: Gal. v. 19. It is no subtle matter to find them out; they declare their sin as Sodom, while they are drinking, whoring, sporting, quarrelling, scoffing at godliness.

2. Others please the flesh in a more cleanly manner; but have no due regard to that spiritual and eternal happiness, which lieth in the enjoyment of God. Though their carriage be blameless and separated from the gross pollutions of the world, they care not whether God be pleased or displeased, honoured or dishonoured, angry or reconciled. And besides, the works of the flesh are not always interpreted in the gross sense, but according to the scale

of the sanctuary. When he saith, adultery, fornication, murder, are works of the flesh; we must not only think of the gross acts, but the very first seeds of these sins, the secret inclinations and desires of the flesh in this kind, Mat. v. 27, 28. So lasciviousness; not the sinful attempt only, but every motion of tongue, heart, senses, by which the eyes and ears, the soul and consciences of ourselves and others may be polluted to idolatry, anger, inordinate affection of the heart to any creature, Eph. v. 5. So by murder, not only when it proceedeth to blood, but hatred, variance, strife, heresies, Mat. v. 21, 22. So in short, emulation, and affectation of applause, Gal. v. 26.

3. The prevalence of the divine or carnal principle must determine our condition. Now its reign is known:

[A.] By our savour, relish and taste, Rom. viii. 5. For every man's gust is according to his constitution, which breedeth oblectation[23], or pleasure of mind. Now when we savour only the things of the flesh, that if it be pleased, quiets us in the want of other things, contents us in the neglect of God and his service; that we have no appetite after, or savour or relish any sweetness but in fleshly things; this is an ill sign.

[B.] By our course of walking; which is often insisted on in this chapter. There may be some blemishes in God's children, some unevenness of obedience through the relics of the flesh; but their main, constant course, for which they labour and strive, is to approve themselves to God, and to be accepted with God, and to live in obedience to the motions of his sanctifying Spirit. But where there is a carelessness in the heavenly life, the influence of the fleshly life is most discovered in all our actions.

[C.] By our tendency and scope. When the heart is turned to, or alienated from God. The flesh reigneth if the world turn our hearts from him, and the flesh be pleased before him, and we mind our own things; we are lovers of pleasure more than lovers of God.

---

[23] Pleasure; satisfaction; delight.

SERMON XVII

If ye through the Spirit do mortify the deeds of the body, ye shall live.

Romans VIII. 13.

WE come now to the second clause, wherein we have two things: (1.) The condition to be performed. (2.) The blessedness promised. First, In the condition we have,

1. The parties interested.

2. The duty required.

1. The parties interested are justified believers, who are not in the flesh, or after the flesh. Yet two persons are mentioned: the principal author, and the subordinate agent. We are the principal parties in the obligation; but in the operation, the Spirit is the principal. The particle through is usually the note of an instrument, yet the Spirit is not our instrument, but we are his; he first worketh on us as objects then by us as instruments; and therefore though the duty falleth upon us, and we are said to do it by the Spirit; yet it must be thus under stood: we are the principal parties as to obligation of duty; but as to operation and influence of grace, the Spirit is the principal.

2. In the duty there is the act, 'mortify'; the object, 'the deeds of the body'

[A.] The act, 'mortify.' I shall open it more fully by and by; only note for the present,

(1.) Sin is alive in some degree in the justified; otherwise what need it to be mortified? The exhortation were superfluous if sin were wholly dead.

(2.) It noteth a continued act. We must not rest in a mortification already wrought in us. He saith not, 'If ye have mortified' but, 'If ye do mortify'; this must be our daily practice, not done now and then, or by fits; if we always sincerely labour to mortify the deeds of the body, we are in the way of life.

(3.) It showeth that this work must not be attended slightly, or by the by, but carried on to such a degree, that corruption may be weakened, or lie a-dying, or be upon the declining hand. The success and event is considerable, as well as the endeavour. Where the event dependeth upon outward and foreign causes, a man hath comfort in doing his duty whatever the success be, but here where the event falleth within the compass of our duty itself, there it must be regarded. We must so oppose sin, that in some sort we may kill it or extinguish it, and not only scratch the face of it, but seek to root it out; at least that must be our aim.

(4.) Mortifying noteth some pain or trouble. For nothing that hath life, will be put to death without some struggling; and the flesh cannot be subdued without some trouble to ourselves, or violence offered to our carnal affections. Only let me tell you, if it be painful to mortify sin, you make it more painful by dealing negligently in the business, and drawing out your vexation to a greater length; the longer you suffer this Canaanite to live with you, the more will it prove as a thorn or goad in your sides. Here, if ever, it is true our affection procureth our affliction; sin dieth when our love to it dieth; your trouble endeth, your delight in it ceaseth, as you can bring your souls to a resolution to quit these things. *Quam suave mihi subito factum est, carere suavitatibus iniquorum.* No delight so sincere as the contempt of vain delights.

[A.] The object, 'the deeds of the body,' that is, our sins. So called, (1.) Because sin is compared to a body: Rom. vii. 24, 'Who shall deliver me from this body of death?' and Col. ii. 11, 'In putting off the body of the sins of the flesh.' There is besides the natural body, a body of corruption, which doth wholly compass about the soul; there is the head of wicked desires, the hands and feet of wicked executions, the eye of sinful lusts, the tongue of vain and evil words; therefore it is said, (Col. iii. 5), 'Mortify your members which are upon earth'; not of the natural body, but of the mass of corruption; particular sinful lusts are as members of this body. (2.) Sins are called the deeds of the body, because they are executed by the body: Rom. vi. 22, 'Let not sin reign in your mortal bodies, that ye should fulfil the lusts thereof'; and Rom. vi. 19, 'As ye have yielded up your members servants to uncleanness, and to iniquity unto iniquity' All the members of the body are employed as instruments to serve our sin; now affections are manifested in action; therefore by the deeds of the body, he meaneth not outward acts only, but lusts also. Well then, fight we must, but not with our own shadows; sin is gotten within us; by the soul it hath taken possession of the body; the gates of the senses are always open to let in such objects and temptations as take part with the flesh; and the flesh is ready to accomplish whatever the corrupt heart doth suggest arid require.

Secondly, The life that is promised to them that mortify sin—'Ye shall live' a spiritual life of grace here, and an eternal life of glory hereafter. Heaven is worth the having, and therefore the reward should sweeten the duty. From this clause the points are three:

1. That justified persons are bound to mortify sin.

2. That in the mortifying of sin, we and the Spirit concur. The Spirit will not without us, and we cannot without the Spirit.

3. That eternal life is promised to them who seriously improve the assistance of the Holy Ghost for the mortifying of sin.

1. *Doctrine* That justified persons should mortify sin. It is their duty so to do.

First. What is the mortification that lieth upon us?

1. Negatively, What it is not; we must distinguish between the mock mortification, the counterfeit resemblances of this duty, and the duty itself.

[A.] There is a pagan mortification. I call it so, because such a thing was among the heathens, which is nothing else but a suppressing such sins as nature discovereth, upon such reasons and arguments as nature suggesteth: Rom. ii. 14, 'The Gentiles do by nature the things contained in the law': namely, as they abstained from gross sins and performed outward acts of duty. This was a kind of resemblance of mortification, and but a resemblance. We read of this in history; the answer of Socrates to the physiognomist, *oimai paiderasten,* when his scholars enraged at his character *Paiderastes etairoi eimi phusei all epecho.* So of Palaemon, who coming in a drunken fit to scoff at the lecture of Xenocrates, with his head crowned with a garland of rosebuds, was by his grave and moral discourse, reduced from his riot and licentiousness, which was a kind of moral conversion; but this we fault, because it is but a half turn from sins of the second table, or lower hemisphere of duty; and because these sins were suppressed and hidden, rather than mortified and subdued; *Sapientia eorum abscondit vitia, non abscindit. Lact.* As Haman refrained himself, when his heart boiled with rancour and malice, Esther v. 10, their wisdom tended to hide sin, rather than to mortify it. And besides this kind of conversion was not a recovery of the soul from the flesh and the world to God; but only an acquiring a fitness to live more plausibly, and with less scandal among men.

[B.] There is a popish and superstitious mortification; which standeth in a mere neglect of the body, and in some outward abstinences and austerities, and such observances as are prescribed by men without any warrant from God; as in abstaining from marriage, and some sort of meats or apparel, as unlawful; yea, from the necessary functions of human life; the apostle telleth us that these things have 'A show of wisdom' (Col. ii. 23), a specious show, and are highly cried up by the carnal world; but have no real worth to commend us to God, as being not commanded by God, or warranted by the best example of the most holy and mortified men. Suppose abstinence from marriage: 'Enoch (Gen. v. 22.) walked with God, and begat sons and daughters.' And we have more instances of true piety in married folks, than in monkery and cloistral devotions. Jesus Christ sanctified a free life, using all sorts of diet and company, not abstaining from feasts themselves: Mat. xi. 19, 'The Son of man came eating and drinking.' So when the vow of voluntary poverty is recommended by the papists as an estate of perfection. Certainly beggary, which is threatened as a punishment, is not to be wished or desired; much less to be chosen or wilfully incurred; least of all to be made the matter of a vow. Surely it is greater self-denial entirely to devote and faithfully to use our riches for God, than to cast them away and rid our hands of them; as he is a better steward that improveth his master's stock, than he that casts off the employment, and lazily refuseth to meddle with it. So for penance and self-discipline; they look more like the rites of Baal's priests, who gashed and lanced themselves to commend them to their idol, than the practices of Christ's votaries and believing penitents; who hath indeed commanded us to mortify our lusts, but not to mangle our bodies; to retrench the food and fuel of the flesh when need requireth; but not to bind ourselves to a course of rigorous observances, which gratify the flesh in one way, as much as it seems to contradict it in another; namely, as they breed in us pride and presumption of merit above other Christians. In short, these external rigours, though they are greatly admired by the world, which is wholly governed by sensual desires, yet they are not acceptable to God, as having more in them of ridiculous pageantry and theatrical stage-holiness, rather than serious devotion.

[C.] There is the mortification of the hypocrite, which is an outward forbearing evil, though they do not inwardly hate it; which proceedeth from divers causes:

(1.) Because they have no inclination to some sins; or rather, a greater inclination to other sins, which intercept the nourishment by which these sins should be fed. Though we are all gone astray from God, yet every one hath his way: Isa. liii. 6, 'All we like sheep have gone astray; we have turned everyone to his own way' So Eccles. vii. 29, 'God made man upright, but he hath found out many inventions.' As the channel is cut, corrupt nature in us findeth a vent and issue; some are sensual, but not greedy of worldly gain; shall we therefore call them mortified? Some that are greedy of gain, are not proud and aspiring, or given to carnal pleasures; do you think therefore sin is dead in them? No, their corruption breaketh out another way, more suitable to their temper and constitution, or custom and course of life; in some, nature is more sullen and rigid; in others, more facile, and obvious to the grosser temptations.

(2.) Sometimes it is because we make one lust give way to another. For certain weeds destroy one another, as wild beasts also prey upon one another. So when men abstain from pomp and pleasure, because of the cost, their covetousness starveth their riot; so on the contrary, when men check their sensual inclination by their sparing humour. But mostly it is seen in those that run into extremes, and bend the crooked stick too far the other way, as the lunatic in the Gospel fell sometimes into the water, and sometimes into the fire, Mat. xvii. 15. Or as our ancestors to drive out the Picts or wild Britons, called in the Saxons, a worse enemy; or as if there were no better physic for a dead palsy, than a burning fever. Sins take the throne by turns; as the voluptuous in youth prove the most worldly and covetous in age; but this is not to quit sin, but to exchange it.

(3.) Sometimes because men have not strength and opportunity to act sin. They may seem weaned and mortified, when they are but spent and tired out with executing their lusts; and it is not hatred of sin, but indisposition of nature to fulfil it: Job xxxiii. 20, 'His soul abhorreth dainty food.' No thanks to the glutton, but to his disease. Old age is described as 'days that have no pleasure in them' Eccles. xii. 1. It is not the weakness of sin, but nature in them; their lusts leave them, rather than they leave their lusts; sin goeth out rather than is put out, rather dieth to us than we to it.

(4.) It may come to pass through outward respects, of carnal fear and shame. A debauched creature, that walloweth in all filthy lusts, is an abhorring to all that wear the heart of a man; therefore credit may keep some from running into excess of riot, for lewdness is odious and disgraceful; their iniquities are found hateful, as the Psalmist saith. Mere shame and men-pleasing may restrain many within the compass of their duty. Joash was good all the days of Jehoiada, but afterwards hearkened to the lewd princes, 2 Chron. xxiv. 17. In such cases there is no true hatred of sin, no true gracious principle set up against it; this abstinence is but for a while; take away the restraint, and they soon return to their own bent and bias; and besides, this keepeth them but from a few sins.

(5.) Restraining grace. God may restrain and bridle men by the power of his word on their consciences, when yet their hearts are not renewed; or by common instincts of natural modesty and ingenuous ness; or by the power of his providence, as God withheld Abimelech, Gen. xx. 6. Though the sin be not subdued, yet the act and exercise may be suspended. Balaam had a mind to curse Israel, but God suffered him not, though he strove by all means to please Balak.

(6.) Terrors of conscience. A man that is under them, *non proponit peccare*[24]; a renewed man, *proponit non peccare*[25]; the one hath for the tune no actual will or purpose to sin; the other a purpose not to sin; no will to sin, yet have a great deal of sin in the will. Thus negatively I have showed you what is not mortification.

2. Positively, What it is. Here again we must distinguish. Mortification is twofold, passive and active; passive, whereby we are mortified; and active, whereby we mortify ourselves; the one is God's work, the other our own.

[A.] Mortification passive, whereby God mortifieth sin in us; which he doth either, (1.) At conversion, when a principle of grace, contrary to sin and destructive of it, is planted in our hearts: Ezek. xi. 19, 'I will put a new spirit into them, and I will take away the heart of stone, and I will give them an heart of flesh, that they may walk in my statutes.' So Ezek. xxxvi. 26, 'I will put a new spirit into them'. In the work of regeneration God doth give a deadly wound to sin; the reign of it is broken, that it cannot with such strength bring forth the deeds of the body. (2.) By the continual and renewed influence of his grace. He doth more and more weaken the power of sin: Mic. vii. 19, 'He will have compassion on us, and subdue our iniquities.' It is God's work; alas! Without this, if we be left to ourselves, the more we resist sin, the more it is irritated and increased in us. (3.) God doth it by his word, which is the great instrument which he useth to convey the power of his grace, John xvii. 17. There we see the evil of sin, and the danger of it; are stirred up to resolve, cry, and pray against it, and are told of the great remedy, which is Christ's death. (4.) He mortifieth us by his providence, as he taketh away the fuel and provision of our lusts, and awakeneth us to a more earnest conflict with sin. Out of love to our souls he crosseth our humours: John xv. 2, 'Every branch that beareth fruit, he purgeth it, that it may bring forth more fruit' The vine-dresser cutteth and pareth off the luxuriant and superfluous branches: Isa. xxvii. 9, 'By this therefore shall the iniquity of Jacob be purged; and this is all the fruit, to take away his sin.' Now all this is passive mortification, necessary to be observed by us, that we may submit to God's work, and improve the impressions of his word, Spirit, and providence.

[B.] Active mortification is the constant endeavour of a renewed soul to subdue sin dwelling in us, that we may be more at liberty to serve, please, and glorify God. It is a constant endeavour; for in a leaking ship there is a continual use of the pump. Sin is a continual burden and clog to the new nature, and it is every day's business to get rid of it; we groan under it, Rom. vii. 24; and we must strive as well as groan. The spirit or new nature lusteth against the flesh, Gal. v. 17, not only by a disliking thought which may check actual motions of the flesh, but also by a constant use of all holy means, that we may get the mastery of it. They are bound to die unto sin, therefore will not let it reign, Rom. vi. 11, 12; and the end of mortification is vivification, or liberty towards God, which the soul aspireth after, more and

---

[24] No intent to sin
[25] Intends not to sin

more; for we grow dead to sin, that we may be alive to righteousness. In short, this work must be continued till we have gotten some power against our corruption, and it be weakened, though not subdued totally.

There is a general and particular mortification. The general mortification is, 'The putting off the whole body of the sins of the flesh' Col. ii. 11. The particular mortification is, when we subdue or weaken this or that particular lust: Ps. xviii. 23, 'I was also upright before him, and kept myself from mine iniquity' Now the rule is, that the general mortification must go before the particular; otherwise all that we do, is but stopping a hole in a ruinous fabric that is ready to drop down upon our heads; or to make much ado about a cut finger, when we have a mortal disease upon us. Besides, particular mortification dependeth on the general; for till we be renewed by God, how can we mortify sin? Col. iii. 8, 'Put off all these, anger, wrath, malice, blasphemy, filthy communication out of your mouths, seeing ye have put off the old man with his deeds.' Seeing you have put off all corruption, allow yourselves to live in no one sin. Alas, to set against a particular sin, before we set upon the whole body of sin, it is but to put a new patch upon a torn garment, and so make the rent the worse; or to cut off a branch or two, while the root or trunk remaineth in full life and vigour, and so sprouteth the more for cutting. First look after the general work, that sin be stabbed at the heart, and then the particular branches and limbs of it die by degrees.

[C.] There is a double way of mortification, privative, and positive. The one standeth in the cutting off the fuel and provisions of the flesh, or those things by which sinful and corrupt nature is kept alive; the other lieth in resistance and active endeavors against it; as fire is put out, either by withdrawing wood or combustible matter, or pouring on water; or an enemy is destroyed by starving or battle, as Antigonus answered to a captain, that kept a garrison in a city subject to rebellions and mutinyings, that 'he should not only fasten the clog, but starve the dog'; meaning thereby, that he should strengthen the garrison, and weaken the city. Both these ways must Christians go to work in the business of mortification.

The one by shunning the occasions of sin, and cutting off the provisions which feed the distemper in our souls: Rom xiii 14, 'Make no provision for the flesh, to fulfil the lusts thereof.' When men entertain themselves with all sensual delights, as if their business were to hearten the enemy, to keep the flesh alive, after they have undertaken its death in baptism. The other is using the means which tend to the subduing of it; such as prayer: 2 Cor xii 8, 'For this thing I sought the Lord thrice.' Hearing the word: John xv 3, 'Now are ye clean, through the word which I have spoken to you'; and such like. As on the one side we must not provide oil to feed the flame; so on the other, there must be striving, praying, exercising ourselves unto godliness, that grace may be strengthened in war against sin.

[D.] There is a daily and ordinary course of mortification; and a solemn extraordinary setting about this work in special seasons. The daily course is needful, because sin is at continual work in our hearts; and as soon as a Christian neglects his soul, the effects do soon appear. In this sense, a Christian must die daily, that is, to his sins and corruptions; he must still watch, and strive, and get some advantage against them, by every prayer he maketh to God, every act of receiving the Lord's Supper, or hearing the word; it is his constant task; but there are certain seasons when he must solemnly set about this work; as—

(1.) When God maketh sin bitter by afflictions, and we are threshed, that our husk may fly off. Affliction is a special time of dealing against sin, Jer ii 19. We must not hinder the working of God's physic, but further it rather, exercise ourselves under the rod: Heb xii 11, 'It yieldeth the peaceable fruit of righteousness, to them that are exercised thereby.' Use it to God's ends and purposes; the smartness of the rod should make sin more hateful to us.

(2.) When you have some serious stirrings upon hearing the word, or some new powerful consideration is given you to quick your hatred against sin; when a truth is borne in with great light, power, and evidence upon the heart. There is a providence that goeth with sermons; many gracious opportunities are lost by our negligence; certainly when the waters are stirred, it is good getting into the pool: see Jam i. 23, 'If a man be a hearer of the word, and not a doer, he is like unto a man beholding his natural face in a glass.' If so, there is a season lost; there is some duty pressed, some sin discovered, some want laid open; mortification is much promote by observing and improving these seasons: 1 Pet i. 22, 'Seeing ye have purified your souls, in obeying the truth through the Spirit'; and Ps cxix. 104, 'Through thy precepts I get understanding, therefore I hate every false way.' By attending on the word, we get new degrees of light, and hatred against sin; sometimes God weakeneth sin this lust, sometimes that, according as he is pleased to direct it to your consciences.

(3.) After some notable fall, or sin against God. See the core of the distemper pulled out. To get a pardon is not enough, but mortification must be looked after; the longer sin defileth the heart, the deeper it is rooted; therefore speedily recover yourselves at such a time; a green wound is more easily cured, than an old rankled sore; and David complaineth his wounds did stink through his foolishness, Ps xxxviii 5. The longer these wounds be neglected, the worse. If a member is sprained, or out of joint, if you delay to set it, it never growth strong or straight. Peter did not lie in the sin, but went out immediately and wept bitterly, Matt xxvi 75. The longer corruption is spared, it acquireth the more strength, secureth its interest more firmly, and is more deeply rooted in the soul, and bringeth a custom on the body also.

Secondly. Why justified persons must mortify the deeds of the body.

1. With respect to Christ.

2. With respect to sin.

3. With respect to grace received.

1. With respect to Christ. And there — (1.) What he did, and is to us. (2.) Our relation to him.

[A.] What he did, and is to us; for what end he suffered for us, and for what end he is offered to us. (1.) He suffered for us, to take away sin, or to purchase grace whereby sin may be mortified; he paid the price to provoked justice: 1 Pet ii 24, 'He bore our sins in his body upon the tree, that we being dead unto sin, should live to righteousness.'

Naturally we are dead to righteousness, and alive to sin; but Christ's intention in dying for sinners, was to remedy this, that sin might die and grace live; and therefore our old man is said to be crucified with Christ, Rom vi 6. Then the price was paid, and grace purchased. He came not only to free us from punishment, but cut also the power of sin. The guilt of sin is contrary to our happiness; the power of sin, to God's glory. (2.) The end for which he is offered to us. God propoundeth Christ, not only as a foundation of comfort, but as a fountain of grace and holiness: 1 Cor i. 30, 'Who of God is made to us, wisdom, and righteousness, and sanctification, and redemption'; to be our sanctification, as well as our righteousness; where he is the one, he is the other; one principal blessing is to turn us from our sins, Act iii. 36; and that is mortification, or weakening the power and love of sin in our hearts. Now that we may receive him as God offereth him, and not rend and divide him by a broken and imperfect faith; as we look for comfort in Christ in the sense of our justification and pardon; so an experience of his power in mortifying sin, otherwise we have but half of Christ.

[B.] Our relation to him, both by external profession, and real implantation, both bind us to mortify sin.

(1.) External profession obligeth us to die unto sin; it was a part of our baptismal vow, and we quite nullify and frustrate the intent of that ordinance, unless we mortify the deeds of the body. The flesh was renounced in our answer to God's covenant-questions: 1 Pet. iii. 21, Baptism is called 'the answer of a good conscience towards God' It is an answer to the Lord's offers propounded in the gospel when we were first consecrated to this warfare; and that dedication must never be forgotten: 2 Pet. i. 19, 'And hath forgotten that he was purged from his old sins.' To neglect, is to forget; as 'to distribute and communicate, forget not'; that is, neglect not. So here, 'hath forgotten that he was purged from his old sins.' While they please the flesh, they neglect their baptismal vow, and so make that ordinance of none effect to them. We are said (Col. ii. 13), to 'put off the body of the sins of the flesh.' That is, in vow and obligation, being buried with him in baptism. Now if we do not stand to our vow, our solemn admission into Christ's family was in vain.

(2.) By real implantation. Surely they that are united to Christ cannot live in the servitude and slavery of sin; for by this union with him they are assimilated and conformed to him: Gal. ii. 20, 'I am crucified with Christ'; and it was not his privilege alone, but all the justified: Gal. v. 24, 'And they that are Christ's have crucified the flesh, with the affections and lusts thereof.' This conformity is called by the apostle, a being 'planted into the likeness of his death' Horn. vi. 5. Christ was crucified in his human nature, and we in our corrupt nature; we crucified him by our sins, and we are crucified with him by the Spirit; Christ died for sin, and a Christian dies unto sin.

2. With respect to sin, which remaineth in us after we are justified. Here are three considerations demonstrating why we should mortify sin.

[A.] That sin still abideth in us after we are taken into the justified estate. While we dwell in flesh, this woeful and sad companion dwelleth with us; we cannot get rid of this cursed inmate, till the house itself be pulled down; we die struggling with it; and when one of our feet is within the borders of eternity, yet it departeth not. As hair groweth after shaving, as long as the roots remain; so is corruption sprouting; therefore must be always mortifying;

always cleansing: 2 Cor. vii. 1, 'Having these promises, let us cleanse ourselves from all filthiness of flesh and spirit'; always purifying, 1 John iii. 3, 'He that hath this hope in him, purifieth himself as Christ is pure'; always 'laying aside the weight, and the sin that doth so easily beset us' Heb. xii. 1. Since sin is not nullified, it therefore must be mortified; the war must last as long as the enemy liveth, and hath any strength and force.

[B.] It still worketh in us, is very active and restless, not as other things, which as they grow in age, grow more quiet and tame: James iv. 5, 'The spirit that dwelleth in us lusteth to envy.' The flesh is not a sleepy habit, but a working stirring principle: Rom. vii. 8, 'Sin wrought in me all manner of concupiscence'; that is, sinning nature; it is always inclining us to evil, or hindering that which is good. (1.) Inclining us to that which is evil. It doth not only make us flexible and yielding to temptations; but doth urge us, and impel us thereunto: Rom. vii. 23, 'But I set) another law in my members, warring against the law of my mind.' We think and speak too gently of sin, when we think it a tame thing, that worketh not till it be irritated by the suggestions of Satan. No, it is like a living fountain that poureth out its waters, though nobody come to drink of them; it is irritated by the law of God many times, and the motions of the Spirit; these corrupt humours within us, are in a continual fermentation: Gen. vi. 5, 'And God saw that the wickedness of man was great upon earth, and that every imagination of the thoughts of his heart was only evil continually.' Temptations only make them more violent. (2.) Hindering us from that which is good. Either it draweth away the heart from duty, or distracteth the heart in duty. It draweth away the heart from duty: Rom. vii. 21, 'I find then a law, that- when I would do good, evil is present with me.' It abateth the edge of our affections, discourageth us by many unbelieving carnal thoughts, and so the heart is drawn away from God, that sin may the more domineer; or distracting our minds in duty: Ezek. xxxiii. 31, 'Their hearts go after their covetousness'; filling our minds with thoughts of the world, vain pleasures; revenge turneth our duties into sins.

[C.] The sad consequence of letting sin alone. When sin is not mortified, it groweth outrageous, and never ceaseth acting till it hath exposed us to shame before God, men, and angels; or hardeneth us in a carnal, careless course. Lusts let alone end in gross sins, and gross sins in a casting off all religion. Love of pleasures let alone, will end in drunkenness and uncleanness; envy, in murder and violence. Judas allowed his covetousness, and that brought him to betray his master; Gehazi was first blasted with covetousness, then with asking a bribe to God's dishonour, then with leprosy, and so became a shame and burden to himself; Ananias and Sapphira were taken off by a sudden judgment. The devil loveth by lust to draw us into sin; and by sin to shame; and by shame to horror and despair. Sin is no tame thing. But do the people of God run into such notable excesses and disorders? Yes, when they let sin alone, and discontinue the exercise of mortification; witness David, that run into lust and blood; and Peter into curses and execrations; Solomon into sensuality and idolatry. Old sins long laid asleep may awaken again, and hurry us strangely into mischief and inconvenience.

3. In regard of grace received.

[A.] The grace of justification. Reliance upon the righteousness of Christ for justification doth not shut out the work of mortification, but conduceth much towards it; it doth not exclude it, for the justified must be mortified; it pleadeth for it, 'Grace teacheth us to deny ungodliness' Tit. ii. 11. That sin may be mortified and put to death for Christ's sake, Christ was crucified and put to death for our sakes. God doth not require it in point of sovereignty, but pleadeth with us upon terms of grace. Grace hath denied us nothing, it hath given us Christ and all things with him, and shall we stick at our lusts? Grace thought nothing too good for us, not the blood of Christ, nor the favour of God, nor the joys of heaven; and shall we count anything too dear to part with, for grace's sake? Mortification is an unpleasing task; but grace commands and calls for it, and that with such powerful oratory as cannot be withstood.

[B.] In regard of the grace of sanctification: To exercise it, preserve it, and increase it.

(1.) That we may exercise it to that end for which it was given to us. It was given to us to avoid sin: 1 John iii. 9, 'Whosoever is born of God doth not commit sin, for his seed remaineth in him, and he cannot sin, because he is born of God'; and 1 John v. 18, 'We know that whosoever is born of God, sinneth not; but he that is begotten of God, keepeth himself, and the wicked one toucheth him not' There is a seed and principle within us, to curb and restrain sin too, and keep us from falling into the power of the devil, or being brought back into our old bondage. This other principle was set up in us, on purpose to excite us unto what is good, so also to abate the power of sin; as the way to destroy weeds is to plant the ground with good seed; and it is given us as a bridle actually to restrain the exorbitances, and hold it in, when it flieth out. Now this grace of God will be in vain, unless it be used to such purpose; and one of God's most precious gifts would lie idle; therefore we should act it, or walk in the spirit, that we may not fulfil the lusts of the flesh.

(2.) Preserve it in power and vigour. For the life of grace dependeth very much upon the dying of sin; as health and strength in the body cometh on as the disease abateth: 1 Pet. ii. 24, 'That we being dead unto sin, might be alive unto righteousness.' But as the life of sin increaseth, grace languisheth and wither eth, and is ready to die, Kev. iii. 2. The flesh and the spirit are contrary, and always are encroaching upon one another; and there is this advantage on the flesh's side, that it is a native, not a foreigner. Home-bred plants, which the soil yieldeth naturally without any tillage, as nettles, will sooner preserve themselves, and get ground upon better plants, because the earth bringeth them forth of its own accord; or as water heated, the cold is natural to it, and will prevail against the heat, unless it be driven out by a constant fire. Whether the prevalency of sin doth weaken grace effective or *meritorie*, by its malignant influence, or as deserving such a punishment from God, I will not now dispute; but weaken it, it doth; that is clear by experience; for though grace be planted in us by God, it is not settled in such an indivisible point, as that it cannot be more or less; there is a remission of degrees: Mat. xxiv. 12, 'The love of many shall wax cold.' Faith may grow sick and weak; there are soul- distempers as well as bodily; and then a man is altogether unfit for action, and performeth duties in a very heartless and uncomfortable fashion; therefore still we must be mortifying sin.

(3.) That we may increase it. Grace is not only *donum*, a gift to be preserved; but *tolentum*, a talent to be improved and increased upon our hands, that we may be the more fit to glorify God. This appeareth by the many excitations in scripture to growth: 2 Pet. iii. 18, 'But grow in grace, and in the knowledge of our Lord and Saviour Jesus Christ.' It is not enough to maintain that measure of grace which we have already received, but we must get more; always look after the growth of it in ourselves; and indeed the one cannot be done without the other; there is no possibility to keep what we have, unless it be improved; he that roweth against the stream, had need ply the oar; and he that goeth up a sandy hill, must never stand still. And it is our own fault, if it doth not grow; God loveth to multiply and increase his gifts; 'Grace be multiplied' 2 Pet. ii. 2. There is more to be had, and more will be given, unless our sins obstruct the effusion of it; if we get it not, we may blame ourselves, for God doth nothing to hinder the increase; and indeed when grace is in any life and vigor, it will be growing: Prov. iv 18, 'The way of justice is as a shining light, which shineth more and more unto the perfect day.' The morning light increaseth; a wicked man groweth worse and worse; he sinneth away the light of his conscience, rejecteth the light of the word, till he stumbleth into utter darkness. It is like the coming on of the night; the other like the coming on of the day. Now mortification of sin is the great means of growing in grace, *removet quod prohibet*; it maketh room for grace in the soul, as it taketh away that which letteth, that it may diffuse its influence more plentifully. In heaven we are perfect, because there is no sin; opposite principles are wholly gone; so here, the more you weaken sin, the more is grace introduced with power and success: 1 Pet. ii. 1,2,' Wherefore laying aside all malice, and all guile, and hypocrisy, and envy, and evil-speaking, as new-born babes, desire the sincere milk of the world, that ye may grow thereby.' There is no way of growth, till evil frames of spirit be laid aside.

The First use, is to enforce this duty upon all those that are called unto, or look for any hopes by Jesus Christ, to mortify the deeds of the body: Oh! Do not think you are past mortification, because you are in. a state of grace; there is need of it still; yea, it concerneth you more than others.

1. There is still need of it, if you consider the abundance of sin of all kinds that yet remaineth with us, and the marvellous activity of it in our souls, and the cursed influences of it; or the mischief that will accrue to us, if it be let alone. Let me a little press you by all these considerations.

[A.] The abundance of sin of all kinds that remaineth with the regenerate, or those that are called to grace. I shall evidence that by some scriptures: 1 Pet. ii. 1, 'Wherefore laying aside all malice, and all guile, and hypocrisies, and envies, and evil speaking'; to whom is this spoken? The word *wherefore* biddeth us look back; when we look back, we find it was spoken to those that were called, effectually called, and born again; yea, those that had made some progress in mortification, that had purified their hearts to the obedience of the truth, 1 Pet. i. 22. Who would think that the seeds of so much evil should lurk in their hearts? but alas! it is so. They are in part envious, malicious, hypocritical to the last; and unless they shall keep mortifying, these sins will get the mastery of them, and bewray themselves to their loss and prejudice, and God's dishonour. See another place: Col. iii. 5, 'Mortify therefore your members which are upon earth; fornication, uncleanness, inordinate affection, evil concupiscence, and covetousness, which is idolatry.' You would think all this were spoken to loose and ungoverned men, that have not the least tincture and show of religion. No; it is spoken of those whose life was hidden with God in Christ, men acquainted with spiritual things, and brought under the power of the life of Christ. We foolishly imagine that such should only be told of the remainders of unbelief, or spiritual pride, or such like evils as are very remote from public infamy and scandal; but the Spirit of God is wiser than we; and knoweth our hearts, and the secret workings of them, better than we do ourselves; and it is better these sins should be laid open in the warnings of the word, and dis covered to us, rather than in us, by the prevalency of a temptation. An over-spiritual preaching, hath not refined but destroyed religion; God thought it fit it should be said to them that are taken into the communion of the life of Christ, 'mortify 'what? your spiritual pride? no; but fornication, uncleanness, inordinate affection; the root of the foulest sin is in our nature, and if we do not keep a severe hand over them, will sprout out in our practice: so Gal. v. 19, 20, 'Now the works of the flesh are manifest, which are these; adultery, fornication, unclean- ness, lasciviousness, idolatry, witchcraft, hatred, variance, emulation, wrath, strife, sedition, heresy' The apostle thought good to warn pro fessing Christians, who had given up themselves to the leading of the Spirit, of the works of the flesh; he giveth a black catalogue of them, and he concludeth all, 'of which I told you before, as I have also told you in times past, that they that do such things shall not inherit the kingdom of God.' The apostles, that were divinely inspired, and full of the wisdom of God, did not soar aloft in airy speculative strains, or refined spiritual notions; but thought meet to condescend to these particulars, not only when they spake to Gentiles, but churches, and professing Christians, to give warning against fornication, and drunkenness, and other such gross sins; and that not once, but often; for they knew the nature of man, and that nice speculations are too fine to do the work of the gospel; all that have corruption in them had need stand upon their guard to prevent sins of the blackest hue, and foulest note among them. I will give but one instance more, and that is of our Saviour Christ, who thought meet to warn his own disciples, who surely were good men: Luke xxi. 34, 'Take heed lest at any time your hearts be overcharged with surfeiting and drunkenness, and the cares of this life, and so that day come upon you unawares' This is a lesson for Christ's own disciples; a man would think it more proper for haunters of taverns, and boon companions, whose souls are sunk and lost in luxury and excess; but Christ Jesus thought this caution needful for those that were taken into his own company, and bosom friends. Let not all this be interpreted as any excuse to them that swallow the greatest sins without fear, live in them without sense, and commit them without remorse. Cautions should not be turned into excuses; there is some inclination in our nature to these things; but these are not the practices of God's people; it is spoken that they may not at any time be so.

[B.] As there is abundance of sin, so it is active and stirring even after some progress in mortification. It is enticing, vexing the new nature, urging to evil, opposing that which is good; it is warring, working, always present with us, that the best Christians grow weary of themselves: Rom. vii. 24. 'Oh wretched man that I am, who shall deliver me from this body of death? 'Was Paul an underling in grace? Is not sin the same in all hearts? Have not we as much need to keep humble and watchful, and make use of Christ's mercy and power, as he had? Is sin grown more tame and quiet? Or are we more fool-hardy and secure? Surely we need to mortify corruption as much as others; and whatever degree of grace we have attained unto, this must be our daily task and exercise. If sin be stirring, we must be stirring against it; and when the enemy is active and warring against the soul, it is a folly for us to hold our hands. Especially since corruption is ever ready to renew the assault there, to return after it hath been foiled, and by several ways and kinds venteth itself; when one branch of it is cut off, and one way of it stopped up, it breaketh out in another.

One sin hath several ways of manifesting itself. Worldliness, take it off from greedy getting, showeth itself in sparing, or withholding more than is meet; the folly of that sin is seen in its delight and carnal complacency': Soul, take thine ease, thou hast goods laid up for many years.' He had enough, now takes his fill of pleasure. So pride, if kept from vain conceit of ourselves, bewrays itself by detracting from others; so envy, or vain ostentation, as some venomous humour in the body; heal up one sore, and it breaketh out in another place; there is 'all malice, all guile' etc. All sorts of it.

[C.] The pestilent and mischievous influence of sin, if it be let alone. Sins prove mortal, if they be not mortified. Either sin must die, or the sinner. There is an evil in sin, and the evil after sin; the evil in sin is the *anomia*, or the violation of God's righteous law; the evil after sin is the just punishment of it; eternal death and damnation. Now those that are not sensible of the evil in sin, shall feel the evil that cometh after sin; all God's dispensations towards his people are to save the person, and destroy the sin: 1 Cor. xi. 32, 'But when we are judged, we are chastened of the Lord, that we should not be condemned with the world.' God took vengeance on the sin, to spare the sinner; but the unmortified spareth the sin, and his life goeth for it; the sin liveth, and he dieth; as the apostle Paul speaketh of himself, when the power of the word came first upon him: Rom. vii. 9, 'Sin revived, and I died.' Sin exasperated, and he felt nothing but sin and condemnation. Oh! Consider with yourselves, it is better sin should be condemned, than that you should be condemned; sin should die, than that you should die; his life shall go for its life, in the prophet's parable, 1 Kings xx. 39.

Ay, but what is this to the justified person? 'There is no condemnation to them that are in Christ.'

I answer, you must take in all; because they are supposed to live not after the flesh but after the Spirit. But if it can be supposed that ye can live after the flesh, then ye die, as in the text; that is, ye justified persons. *Paena potest dupliciter timeri, ut est in constitutione Dei, vel ut malum nostrum*, as Bernard. Eternal death may be considered as an evil which God hath appointed to be the fruit of sin, or as an evil that will certainly befall us. A justified person, one that is not so putatively[26] only, but really so; not in his own conceit only, but indeed and in truth, may fear it in the first sense. There is such a connection between continuance in sin, and eternal destruction, that he ought to reflect upon it, so as to represent to his soul the danger of yielding tamely to his sins; and to fear it, so as to eschew it. For this is nothing but to make an holy use of threatenings, and to see the merit of our doings; but as to the event, so not to allow perplexing doubts, but to quicken us to break off our sins, and to look up to God in Christ for pardon. Now to direct you,

1. Strike at the root of all sin: 'they that are Christ's, have crucified the flesh, with the affections and lusts thereof,' Gal. v. 24. The prophet, to cure the brackishness of the waters, did cast salt into the spring, 2 Kings ii. 21. We must begin with the heart, and then go on unto the life; if the root of bitterness be not deadened, it will easily sprout forth and trouble us; as inbred corruption is weakened, so actual sins flowing thence are weakened also. The root of corruption is carnal self-love, for it is at the bottom of other sins; because men love themselves, and their flesh as themselves, more than God. Now this is weakened by the prevalency of the opposite principle, the love of God; and the more we strengthen the love of God, the more is original sin weakened, and we get again into a good constitution and state of soul. Carnal men are self-lovers, and self-pleasers; but spiritual men love God, and please God, and seek to honour God. Love is the great principle that draweth us off from self to God; such as a man's love, nature, and inclination is, such will the drift of his life be. Now men will not be frightened from self-love; it must be another more powerful love which draweth them from it, as one nail driveth out another. Now what can be more powerful than the love of God, which is as strong as death, and will never be quenched or bribed? Cant. viii. 7. This overcometh our self-love; and then time, strength, care, and all is devoted to God; yea, life itself: Kev. xii. 11, 'They loved not their lives to the death.' Self-love is deeply rooted in us, especially love of life, so that it must be something very strong and powerful, which must overcome it; for what is nearer and dearer to us than ourselves? Now the great means to overcome it, is Christ's love; when the soul is possessed with this, that nothing deserveth its love so much as Christ, the natural inclination is altered. This is done by sound belief and deep consideration, as the means: 1 John iv. 19, 'We love him because he loved us first'; 2 Cor. v. 14, 15, 'For the love of Christ constraineth us, because we thus judge, that if one died for all, then were all dead; and that he died for all, that they which live should not henceforth live unto themselves, but unto him which died for them, and rose again' By the Spirit as the author of grace: Rom. v. 5, 'Because the love of God is shed abroad in our hearts by the Holy Ghost given unto us' Then the soul knoweth no happiness but to enjoy his love and favour, and so it prevaileth over their natural inclination, they live not to themselves but to God; not according to the wills of the flesh, but the will of, God.

2. Consider the several ways how this root sprouteth forth. Two are mentioned by the apostle in the fore-cited place: Gal. v. 24, 'With the affections and lusts,' *pathemasi*,

---

[26] generally considered or reputed to be

passions; *epithumiais*, affections; the first word noteth vexing passions, the next desirable lusts. There are two dispositions in the soul of man, of aversation and prosecution; by the one we eschew evil, by the other we pursue good. Corruption hath invaded both, and therefore grace is necessary to rectify and govern both: 2 Cor. vi. 7, 'By the armour of righteousness both on the right hand, and on the left.'

[A.] We must crucify our passions, which have to do with evil vexations to the flesh; and we must subdue our lusts or affections, which have to do with those good things which are pleasing to the flesh. There are vexing evils in which the mind suffereth a kind of affliction; but it is a disorder arising from self-love, and therefore it must be mortified; as envy, which corrodeth and fretteth the heart of him that is surprised by it; but yet self-love is the cause of it, for we are troubled that any water should pass by our mill; or that others should enjoy any honour, or esteem, or trade, or profit which we covet for ourselves. So anger at anything done by man, which is displeasing to us, if given way to, is a short fury and madness; and hindereth a clear discovering of what is right and equal, Jam. i. 20. So worldly sorrow at anything done by God displeasing to the flesh: 2 Cor. vii, 'Worldly sorrow works death.' So inordinate fear, which betrayeth the succours which reason and grace offereth to fortify us upon any sudden incursion of evil': The fear of man bringeth a snare' Prov. xxix. 25. So worldly cares, which divert us from God and dependence on his providence , Phil. iv. 6, 7; yea, set up an anti-providence in our own hearts. The like may be said of malice and revenge, all which bring a torture with them; and if allowed or indulged, would soon destroy our love to God or men; as, if God withholdeth from us any good that we desire, or sendeth that which we desire not, but crosseth our humour; as sickness, want, reproach, or disrespect, or whatever the heart is carried to eschew; or if men enjoy anything more than we would have them, or do anything contrary to the convenience of our flesh, we storm and fret, and justify our passions, think we do well to be angry. Though these are a sort of sins which are a punishment to themselves, and do destroy not only our duty, but our peace; and disquiet and torment the soul that harbours them; yea, will soon destroy that love we owe to God or man; therefore they must be mortified.

[B.] Not only our passions, but our affections must be mortified, our more pleasant lusts, to which we are carried by a sweeter inclination of nature; such as are stirred up by carnal baits and pleasures, as to instance, in sins of the more sordid and brutish part of mankind, motions to intemperance, luxury, uncleanness, and brutish satisfactions; or to instance, in the more refined part of the world, to worldly greatness, honour, and vain delights, to be distinguished from others by estate, rank, and outward dignity; as every man is apt to be carried away by some inordinate lust or other. Now whatever the distemper be, it must be purged out of the heart, if we would have Christ have any interest there. And here we must not only restrain the act, but mortify the habits; for otherwise we cannot be safe; for every temptation falleth in with some or other of these sins, and giveth a new life to it; unless the lusts are weakened, the conversation cannot be Christian: 1 Pet. ii. 4, 'Abstain from fleshy lusts; having your conversation honest;' and Jam. iv. 1, 'From whence come wars and fightings?' Come they not hence, even from your lusts that war in your members?' All their strifes and contentions come from their carnal hearts, or sensual inclinations, which first rebelled against the upper part of the soul, or the dictates of grace and reason, and then broke out into outrageous or misbecoming practices. And our Saviour telleth us that murders, thefts, adulteries, come first out of the heart, Mat. xv. 19. From the polluted fountain of the heart, floweth all the pollution of the life; and if the act should be restrained, yet unless the heart be cleansed, all is loathsome to God, Mat. xxiii. 27. Therefore kill the lusts in your heart, and ye shall more easily curb the sins of the outward man, that they may not break out to God's dishonour. Many think to fashion the life, but neglect the heart; and if they keep from scandal, yet they do not advance the authority and power of grace in the heart, but self-love securely beareth rule in the soul. Many die by inward bleeding as well as by outward wounds; therefore unless our irascible or concupiscible faculty be bridled, and made pliable to the conduct of the heavenly mind, we shall do nothing in Christianity to any good effect.

3. As to actual temptations, when they stir indwelling sin, complain of the violence to God: Rom. vii. 24, 'Oh wretched man that I am! Who shall deliver me from this body of death?' Bemoan yourselves to him who alone can help you, and is ready to do so, when you are afraid of doing anything contrary to your duty; and an humble sense of your impotency is not only a good preparative to receive his graces, but also to defy and rebuke the temptation: Mat. iv. 10, 'Get thee behind me, Satan'; and Gen. xxxix. 9, 'How shall I do this great wickedness and sin against God?' These are best smothered in the birth.

4. Take heed of those sins which the people of God are most in danger of. It is hard to say what they are; for all sins when they are near, and importune the flesh, by the easy and profitable practice of them without danger, or discovery, may tempt an unwary heart. Therefore we must have always our eyes in our head, and stand upon our guard; the secure are next to a fall; there is no cessation of arms in this warfare, or treaty and conclusion of peace to be made with our lusts. Sin is a bosom-friend, but yet the sorest enemy; and if we be not resolute and vigilant, our appetites and senses, or our passions may betray us; and if you be not daily deadening worldly inclinations, self- esteem, and conceit, you cannot stand out against the smallest temptation. But they are most in danger of those sins which the temperature of body and constitution do incline them unto; though we must watch against all sins, for all are hateful to God, and contrary to his law, and incident to us; yet we are inclined to one sin more than to another; there is something that is our privy sore, and may be called the plague of our own hearts, 1 Kings viii. 38 Now this must be watched and striven against; and here the victory is never cheap or easy. Many a groan, many a prayer, many a serious thought, many a hearty endeavour it will cost us; these master-lusts (they never go alone, like great diseases that have petty ones attending them), must be chiefly attended by us, and we must not discontinue the work, till we have gotten some power against them, and they be considerably weakened. Be it lust or passion, or sloth and dulness, or worldliness, or pride, we must pray, and pray again, as Paul prayed. thrice; grace must watch over it and keep it under, and abate it by contrary actions, that we may the better govern this inclination, and reduce it to reason.

5. Take heed of an unmortified frame of spirit. There are certain dispositions of heart which argue much unmortifiedness, and do loudly call for this remedy and cure, even the grace of the Spirit whereby we may be healed.

[A.] As impotency of mind, whereby temptations to sin are very catching, and do easily make impression upon us. The heart, like tinder, soon taketh fire from every spark; certainly there is great life in our lusts, when a little occasion awakeneth them. As it is said of the young fool in the Proverbs, 'he goeth after her suddenly' Pro. vii. 22, that is, as soon as enticed. Upon the least provocation, we grow passionate; the temptation findeth some prepared matter to work upon, as straw is more easily kindled than wood. Now this calleth upon us to weaken the inclination.

[B.] When the temptation is small; a little adversity puts us out of all courage and patience: Pro. xxiv. 10, 'If thou faint in the day of adversity, thy strength is small.' If we be so touchy that we cannot bear the common accidents of the world, how shall we bear the most grievous persecutions, which we are to endure for Christ's sake? For the other sort of corruptions, for handfuls of barley, or a piece of bread, will that man transgress. So 'selling the righteous for a pair of shoes' 'selling the birthright for one morsel of meat' She is a common prostitute that will take any hire. A little thing makes a stone run downhill. Certainly the heart must be looked after; the bias and inclination of it to God and heaven, more fixed.

[C.] When lusts are touchy, storm at a reproof. If the word break in upon the heart with any evidence, carnal men cannot endure it: 1 Kings, xxii. 8, 'He doth not prophesy good concerning me, but evil.' It is a bad crisis, and state of soul, when men would be soothed in their lusts, cannot endure close and searching truths; but either affect general discourses, that they may creep away in the crowd without being attacked; or loose garish strains that please the fancy, but do not reach the heart; or must be honeyed and oiled with grace; scarce can endure the doctrine of mortification; none need it so much as they; or love flattery more than reproof; it is a sign sin and they are agreed, and they would sleep securely. Not only did Herod put John in prison, but an Asa put the prophet in the stocks, 2 Chron. xvi. 10.

[D.] In case of great spiritual deadness. The heart hath too freely conversed with sin, and so groweth less apt for God: Ps. cxix. 37, 'Turn away mine eyes from beholding vanity, and quicken me in thy ways;' and Heb. ix. 14, 'How much more shall the blood of Christ purge your consciences from dead works to serve the living God? 'Our vivification is according to the degree of our mortification, and therefore great deadness argueth the prevalency of some carnal dis temper.

6. Live much in doing good. The intermitting of the exercise of our love to God maketh concupiscence, or the carnal love, to gather strength; and when men are not taken up with doing good, they are at leisure for temptations to entice them to evil; our lusts have power indeed to disturb in holy duties, but it is when we are remiss and careless; and usually it is the idle and negligent who are surprised by sin; as David walking on the terrace, 2 Sam. xi. 2. *Diabolus quem non invenit occupatum*[27], etc. I will close all with these two remarks—

1. That it is more sweet and pleasant to mortify your lusts than to gratify them. 'Stolen waters are sweet, and bread eaten in secret is pleasant; but the dead are there:' Prov. ix. 16, 17. So Job. xx. 12, 13, 14, 'Though wickedness be sweet in his mouth, though he hide it under his tongue, though he spare it, and forsake it not, but keep it still within his mouth, yet his meat is turned in his bowels, it is the gall of asps within him.' Sin is but a poisoned morsel; mortification is not pleasant in itself, yet in its fruits and effects it is rewarded with joy. And more occasions of thanksgivings we shall have: Rom. vii. 24, 25, 'Oh wretched man that I am, who shall deliver me from the body of this death? I thank God through Jesus Christ our Lord.'

2. If you enter not into a war with sin, you enter into a war with God. Shall sin be your enemy, or God? The eternal living God? Ezek. xxii. 14, 'Can thine heart endure, or can thine hands be strong, in the days that I shall deal with thee? I the Lord have spoken it, and will do it.'

---

[27] The devil did not find him occupied.

SERMON XVIII

If ye through the Spirit do mortify the deeds of the body.

Romans VIII. 13.

DOCTRINE That in mortifying of sin, we and the Spirit must concur. Here I shall handle,

1. The manner of this co-operation.

2. The necessity of it.

First, To state the manner of this co-operation.

1. We must know what is meant by the Spirit; it is put either for the person of the Holy Ghost, or for his gifts and graces, the new creature, or the divine nature wrought in us. The person of the Holy Ghost: Mat. xxviii. 19, 'Baptize all nations in the name of the Father, Son, and Holy Ghost.' The new nature: John iii. 6, 'That which is born of the Spirit is spirit' The former is here intended, the uncreated Spirit or author of grace, called the 'Spirit of Christ,' ver. 11. Which leadeth and guideth us in all our ways, ver. 14, which witnesseth to us, ver. 16.

2. The Spirit is the author or principal agent in this work; for he doth renew and sanctify us. We are merely passive in the first infusion of grace: Ezek. xxxv. 25, 'I will sprinkle clean water upon you, and you shall be clean from all your filthiness.' Eph. ii. 1, 'You that were dead in trespasses and sins, yet now hath he quickened'; but after wards we cleanse ourselves; 1 Pet. i. 22, 'Seeing ye have purified your souls in obeying the truth through the Spirit' First he worketh upon us as objects; then by us as instruments; so that we concur not as co-ordinate causes, but as subordinate agents; being first purified and sanctified by him, we purge out sin yet more and more.

3. Though the Spirit be the principal author, yet we must charge ourselves with the duty. It is our work; they destroy all human industry and endeavour, that make mortification to be nothing else but an apprehension that sin is already slain by Christ; no, it is charged on us: Col. iii. 5, 'Mortify therefore your members which are upon earth' And it is our act, or else we can have no comfort in it. Gal. v. 24, 'They that are Christ's have crucified the flesh with the affections and lusts thereof'; and 2 Cor. vii. 1, 'Let us cleanse ourselves from all filthiness of flesh and spirit' Under the law, the leper was first to be cleansed by the priest, and afterwards to wash himself in running water, and shave his hair, Levit. xiv. 8. After being sprinkled by the priest, the necessary ceremony, he himself was to wash. The ceremonies which the priest used are considerable, therefore I shall explain them a little. Two sparrows were to be taken, and one of them killed in an earthen vessel over running water; the other after he was dipped in the blood of the sparrow that was killed, let loose in the open field, to fly up in the air as it were in the sight of God. There was a notable mystery couched under this type; for the bird killed over the running water signified the death of Christ, accompanied with the sanctification of the Spirit, typed by the running water, the only means to cleanse us from our leprosy; and the bird that was let go alive, having his wings sprinkled with blood, signifieth the inter cession of Christ, who is gone with blood to the

mercy-seat; and we are told that Christ came not by water only, but by water and blood. No other bath for spiritual leprosy but water and blood, the merit of Christ's sacrifice and intercession; and the Spirit of grace to heal our natures. But after all this, the man was to wash himself; which figured endeavours that God's people should use to cleanse themselves from all filthiness of flesh and spirit.

4. It being our duty, we must use the means which tend to mortification. For to dream of a mortification which shall be wrought in us without our consent or endeavours, as well whilst we are sleeping, as whilst we are waking, is to delude ourselves with a vain fancy. No, we must set a careful watch over our thoughts, affections, and works. The Spirit's operation doth license no man to be idle; we must join with him, and obey him in his strivings against the flesh-; for the Spirit worketh not on a man as a dead thing, which hath no principle of activity in himself. Therefore those that, upon the Spirit's doing all, will lie idle, abuse the Spirit, who both urgeth us to the duty, and quickeneth us to the use of means, or stirreth us up to use our endeavours, that the end may be obtained. Otherwise we neither obey the Spirit, nor desire the benefit. We do not obey the Spirit; for he doth first sanctify us, then quicken us to use the means, and blesseth the means so used; and we do not desire the benefit; it is but a wish, not a desire; a velleity[28], not a volition: as Prov. xiii. 4, 'The soul of the sluggard desireth, and hath nothing, because his hands refuse to labour.' Many a man hath wishes that he could leave his sins, especially when he thinketh of the shame and punishment; as many an incontinent person, adulterer, glutton, or drunkard, hath a wish to part with his sin, but not a will; for he doth not seriously strive against it, his love to it remaineth unconquered and unbroken. Well then, let us see how far we have gained the point in hand: First, every Christian must determine that the flesh must be mortified; secondly, mortified it must be by us, every man must mortify his own flesh; thirdly, that mortified it cannot be by us without the Spirit; the Spirit will not without us, and we cannot without the Spirit, neither when we are first to begin this work, nor can we carry it on without his assistance.

5. The Spirit mortifieth sin in us, as a Spirit of light, life, and love.

[A.] As a Spirit of light, affecting the soul with a sight and sense of sin, so as we groan under the burden of it. Nothing cometh to the heart but by the understanding; conviction maketh way for compunction, and compunction for a detestation and hatred of sin; and detestation and hatred, for the destruction and expulsion of it. Sin is always loathsome, but we have not always eyes to see it. When we look upon it through Satan's spectacles, or the cloud of our own passions and corrupt affections, we make nothing of it; it seemeth lovely, rather than loathsome to us. But when the Spirit anointeth our eyes with his eye-salve, it is the most hateful thing to the soul, that can be imagined. Jer. xxxi 18, 'After I was instructed, I smote upon the thigh, yea, I was ashamed, and confounded.' We see sin to be another manner of

---

[28] a wish or inclination not strong enough to lead to action

thing than ever we thought it before. Ps. cxix. 108, 'Through thy precepts I get understanding, therefore I hate every false way' When the heart is thoroughly possessed of the evil of sin, we dare not dandle and indulge, or pass it over as a thing of nought. Fear of punishment may suspend the act of sin, but the sight of the evil of it doth help to mortify the root.

[B.] As a Spirit of life; for Jesus Christ to all his seed is a quickening Spirit, 1 Cor. xv. 45. We have life natural from Adam, but life spiritual and eternal from Christ, and that by the Spirit; for we are said to be born again of the Spirit, John iii. 5. The Spirit reneweth us, and maketh us partakers of the life and likeness of God, Titus, iii. 5. Now when this life is infused, there is an opposite principle set up in us to subdue the lusts of the flesh, and also to prevent the power of the objects of sense, which serve and feed them; for the flesh doth obstruct the operations of this new life, and cross the tendency of it. The operations of this new life are obstructed by the flesh'; for (Gal. v. 17.) the flesh lusteth against the Spirit;' and life is sensible of what annoyeth it. The operations of it are the serving and pleasing of God: Gal. v. 25, 'If we live in the Spirit, let us also walk in the Spirit.' And we see a weight hanging upon us, and sin doth easily beset us, that we cannot serve God with that liberty, purity, and delight, that we desire. And therefore this is an heavy grievance and burden to the new nature, that we desire to get rid of it by all means, and labour, and strive in it, and that with good effect A new life also hath a tendency; as soon as it is infused it discovereth itself by its tendency to its end and rest, which is God and heaven; so the objects of sense have the less force and power upon us. Well then, the flesh is an enemy to this new life, and this new life an enemy to it, as having contrary operations and tendencies. Now how doth this new life discover its enmity? Partly by complaining of it, as a sore burden and annoyance: Rom. vii. 24, 'wretched man that I am! who shall deliver me from this body of death? 'Paul was whipped, scourged, imprisoned, exercised with many vexations and sorrows; but the relics of the corruption were his greatest burden. Not, *When shall I come out of these afflictions?* but, *Who shall deliver me from this body of death?* Partly, by endeavours and skiving[29] against it. There may be some dislike of sin in a natural heart, for conscience will sometimes take God's part, and quarrel against our lusts; otherwise a wicked man could not be self-condemned, and hold the truth in unrighteousness; but checks of conscience are distinct things from the repugnancies of a renewed heart; a wicked man's conscience telleth him he should do otherwise, when his heart inclineth him to do so still. But a renewed heart hateth sin, and therefore there is a constant earnest endeavour to get it subdued; and doth watch, pray, plead for God; use means; dare not rest in sin, or live in sin. Yea, also prevail against it so far, that the heart is never turned away from God to sin: 1 John iii 9, 'Whosoever is born of God, doth not commit sin; for his seed remaineth in him; and he cannot sin, because he is born of God.' His heart cannot easily be brought to it; he looketh upon it as a monstrous incongruity: Gen. xxxix. 9, 'How can I do this great wickedness, and sin against God? '2 Cor.

---

[29] avoid work or a duty by staying away or leaving early

xiii. 8, 'For we can do nothing against the truth'; and Acts iv. 20, 'For we cannot but speak the things which we have seen and heard' There is a natural *cannot*, and a moral *cannot*; the natural *cannot* is an utter impossibility; the moral *cannot* is a great absurdity; the new life breedeth such an aversion of heart and mind from sin, such constant rebukes and dislikes of the new nature. A child of God is never in a right posture, till he doth look upon sin not only as contrary to his duty, but his nature; they have no satisfaction in themselves till it be utterly destroyed.

[C.] As a Spirit of love. The great work of the Spirit is to reveal the love of God to us, and to recover our love to God; for the Spirit cometh to us as the Spirit of Christ, by virtue of his redemption. Now the infinite goodness and love of God doth shine most brightly to us in the face of our Redeemer; in the great things which he hath done and purchased for us, and offered to us, we have the fullest expression and demonstration of the love of God, which we are capable of, and which is most apt to kindle love in us to God again: Rom. v. 8, 'God commendeth his love to us, in that while we were yet sinners, Christ died for us;' and 1 John ii. 1, 2, 'My little children, these things write I unto you, that ye sin not; and if any man sin, we have an advocate with the Father, Jesus Christ the righteous. And he is the propitiation for our sins, and not for ours only, but also for the sins of the whole world.' And Eph iii. 18, 19, 'That you may be rooted and grounded in love, and comprehend with all saints, what is the breadth, and length, and depth, and height; and may know the love of Christ which passeth all knowledge.' Now the Spirit attending this dispensation, surely his great work and office is to shed abroad the love of God in our hearts, Rom. v. 5; and Gal. iv. 6, 'Because ye are sons, God hath sent forth the Spirit of his Son into your hearts, crying, Abba, Father'; that being persuaded of God's fatherly love, we may love him again, and study to please him. Therefore nothing doth stir us up against sin, so much as the sense of God's love in Christ. Shall sin live, which is so contrary to God? Shall I take delight in that which is a grief to his Holy" Spirit? cherish that which Christ came to destroy? live to myself, who am so many ways obliged to God? Displease my Father to gratify the flesh? Alas! how many read and hear of this, who are no way moved into an indignation against sin! It is not the love of God called to mind by a few cold thoughts of ours, that worketh so, but the love of God shed abroad in our hearts by the Spirit. That melts the heart, maketh us ashamed of our unkindness to God, and stirreth up an hatred against sin.

6. After conversion, and the Spirit's becoming a spirit of light, life, and love to us; after grace is put into our hearts to weaken sin, still we need the help of the Spirit. Partly, because habitual grace is a created thing; and the same grace that made us new creatures, is necessary to continue us so. For no creature can be good independently, without the influence of the prime good; all things depend *in esse, conserves, operari*, on him that made them. 'In him we live, and move, and have our being,' Acts xvii. 28. If God suspend his influence, natural agents cannot work, as the fire cannot burn, as in the case of the three children; much less voluntary. And if there be this dependence in natural things, much more in supernatural, Phil ii. 12, 13. Will and deed are from God; first principles of operation, and final accomplishment. Partly, because in the very heart there is great opposition against it;

there is flesh still, the warring law, Rom. vii. 23, *Gratia non totaliter satiat*; the cure is not total as yet, but partial; therefore they need the Spirit to guide, and quicken, and strengthen them. Partly, as it meeteth with much opposition within, so it is exposed to temptations without. Satan watcheth all advantages against us; and the soul is strangely deluded by the treachery of the senses, and the revolt of the passions, and our corrupt inclinations, when temptations assault us; so that unless we have seasonable relief, how soon are we overtaken or overborne! Adam had habitual grace, but gave out at the first assault. A city besieged, unless it be relieved, compoundeth and yieldeth; so without the supply of the Spirit, we cannot stand out in the hour of trial: Eph. iii. 16, 'That he would grant you according to the riches of his glory, to be strengthened with might by his Spirit in the inner man.'

Secondly. The necessity of this concurrence and co-operation—1. Of the Spirit with us. 2. We by the Spirit.

1. Of the Spirit's work. We cannot, without the Spirit, mortify the deeds of the body.

[A.] From the state of the person who is to be renewed and healed. A Dinner lying in a state of defection from God, one that hath lost original righteousness, averse from God; yea, an enemy to him, prone to all evil, weak, and dead to all spiritual good; how can such an one renew and convert himself? There is no sound part left in us to mend the rest. It is true he hath reason left, and some confused notions and apprehensions of good and evil; but the very apprehensions are maimed and imperfect; and we often call evil good, and put good for evil, Isa. v. 20. However to choose the one and leave the other, that is not in our power. We may have some loose desires of spiritual favours, especially as apprehended under the quality of a felicity or natural good, and as separated from the means: Numb xxiii. 10, 'O that I might die the death of the righteous! and my last end be like his.' They may long for the death of the righteous, though loath to live their life; but these desires are neither truly spiritual, nor serious, nor constant, nor laborious; so that if we consider what man is in his natural estate, blind in his mind, perverse in his will, rebellious in his affections; this work can only be wrought by the Spirit of God. Will a nature that is wholly carnal, ever resist and overcome the flesh? But so we are by nature, John iii. 6. Can flesh destroy itself? Can a man of himself be brought to abhor what he dearly loveth; and he that drinketh in iniquity like water, be brought to loathe sin, and expel, and drive it from him? On the other side, will he be brought to love what he abhorreth? There is enmity to the law of God in a carnal heart, till grace remove it, Rom. viii. 7. Can we that are worldly, and wholly governed by sense, look for all our happiness in an unseen world, till we receive another spirit? The scripture will tell you, No: 1 Cor. ii. 12, 14, 'Now we have received, not the spirit of the world, but the Spirit which is of God, that we may know the things that are freely given us of God; but the natural man receiveth not the things of the Spirit of God, for they are foolishness unto him; neither can he know them, because they are spiritually discerned' And 2 Pet. i. 9, 'He that lacketh these things is blind, and cannot see afar off.' What man of his own accord will deny present things, and lay up his hopes in heaven? Can a stony heart of itself become tender, or a dead heart quicken itself, or a filthy heart cleanse itself, bring a clean thing out of an unclean? It cannot be.

[B.] The honour of our Redeemer requireth that our whole and entire recovery to God should be ascribed to him. Not part only, as our freedom from guilt, while the power of sin is subdued and broken by ourselves. Renewing grace is his gift, as well as reconciling grace; and we can no more convert ourselves to God, than we can reconcile ourselves to him; both go together; both are obtained by the same merit; and both are received from the same hand: Act v. 31, 'Him hath God exalted with his right hand to be a prince and a saviour, for to give repentance to Israel, and remission of sins'; and 1 Cor. vi. 11, 'And such were some of you; but ye are washed, but ye are sanctified, but ye are justified in the name of our Lord Jesus, and by the Spirit of our God' As by the virtue of his blood and sufferings he reconciled us to God; so by the almighty power of his grace, he doth cure and heal our natures, and imprint God's image upon our souls. The work of redemption would have ceased forever if Christ had not paid our ransom for us, Ps. xlix. 8. So the work of renovation: Job. xiv. 4, 1 Who can bring a clean thing out of an unclean? Not one' Surely Christ hath purchased this grace, and purchased it into his own hands, not into another's; and sendeth forth his conquering and prevailing Spirit to bring back the souls of men to God. This work must not be disparaged, or looked upon as a low, natural, common thing; for this is to lessen the benefit of the new creation, which is so much magnified in scripture.

2. The necessity of our co-operation, 'If we by the Spirit.' [A.] We may: [B.] We must.

[A.] We may. God hath given us gifts which are not in vain, the Christ is pure' Love, which looketh backward or forward, 'teacheth us to deny all ungodliness and worldly lusts.' Tit. ii. 11-14. So that we may, or can, if we be not wanting to ourselves, do something to the crucifying of the flesh. Certainly after regeneration, we are or may be active; otherwise there would be no difference between the renewed and the carnal, and some of God's best gifts would be in vain. You are to improve the death of Christ to embitter sin to you by his sufferings; to improve the grace received; to pray for the supply of the Spirit; to retrench the provisions of the flesh; to walk as in the sight of God, and prepare for a better world; to maintain a constant conflict with sin, and watch over all your ways. There are means of grace appointed to weaken sin; as the word, and sacraments, and many providences, which might be of great use to you if you did improve them.

[B.] We must. For two reasons,

(1.) That God may apply himself to us in our way.

(2.) That we may apply ourselves to God, and meet him in his way.

(1.) That God may apply himself to us in our way. God being our creator, doth preserve the liberty of his workmanship; he applieth himself to every creature according to the nature of it, so as to improve it, not destroy it; he offereth no violence to our natural faculties, but super-addeth grace; draweth, that we may run, Cant i. 4; not hoisteth up, as dead things by pulleys and engines. The will is not compelled, but overcome by the sweet efficacy of grace; being actuated by God, we act under God; that is, by our own voluntary motion, and in a way of operation proper to us. I say, God influenceth all things according to their natural inclination; he enlighteneth by and with the sun, burneth by and with the fire; reasoneth with man; acts necessarily with necessary causes, and freely with free causes; draweth us with the cords of a man, Hos. xi. 4. Now we pervert this order, if we lie upon the bed of ease, and cry, 'Christ must do all.' Christ that doth all for you, doth all in you, and by you; he propoundeth reasons which we must consider, and so betake ourselves to a godly course; he showeth us our lost estate, the possibility of salvation by Christ, sweetly inviting us to accept of grace, that he may pardon our sins, sanctify our natures, and lead us in the way of holiness to eternal life.

(2.) That we may meet with God in his way. He hath appointed certain duties to convey and apply this grace; we are to lie at the pool, till the waters be stirred; to continue our attendance upon God with all diligence and seriousness, till he giveth grace. Mar. iv. 24, 'And he said unto them, Take heed what you hear; with what measure ye mete, it shall be measured to you; and unto you that hear, shall more be given.' God will have believers bestir and put forth themselves, and lie will help them in and by their own endeavours. We must not idly think that grace will drop to us out of the clouds; he was an evil and a slothful servant that did not improve his talent. To neglect duty is to resist grace, and to run away from our strength. God hath promised to be with us, while we are doing; therefore we are to wait for this power in the use of all holy means, that our corruption may be subdued and mortified.

The *Use*. Is to exhort, with all diligence, to set about the mortify ing the deeds of the body, by the Spirit.

Two things I shall press you to;

1. Improve the death of Christ.

2. A right carriage towards the Spirit.

1. Improve the death of Christ. For the term, mortify, or crucify, often used in this matter, respects Christ's death; and everywhere the scripture showeth that the death of Christ is of excellent use for the mortifying of sin. I shall single out a few places: Gal. ii. 20, 'I am crucified with Christ' Three propositions included: 1. Christ crucified. 2. Paul crucified. 3. With Christ. It doth not imply any fellowship with him in the acts of his mediation; there Christ was alone; only that the effects of his death were accomplished in him, a participation of the benefits of his mediation. So Rom. vi. 6, 'Knowing this, that our old man is crucified with Christ, that the body of sin may be destroyed, that henceforth we should not serve sin' Then was there a foundation laid for the destruction of sin, when Christ died; then was the merit interposed, or price paid, and the obligation laid upon us to mortify it. Something there was to be done on God's part; the body of sin was to be destroyed, which intimateth the communicating of his Spirit of grace to weaken the power and life of sin; and something done on our part, that henceforth we should not serve sin. There was a time when we served sin; but being converted, we must change masters, and betake ourselves to another service, which will be more comfortable and profitable to us. One place more: 1 Pet. iv. 1,

'For as much as Christ hath suffered for us in the flesh, arm yourselves likewise with the same mind; for he that hath suffered in the flesh, hath ceased from sin' That is, since Christ hath suffered for you, you must follow and imitate him in suffering also, or dying with him, namely, in dying to sin, as he died for sin; or mortifying our lusts and passions. For 'one that hath suffered in the flesh' or is crucified in his carnal nature, it hath not respect to suffering afflictions, but mortifying sins; for it is presently added, 'He hath ceased from sin,' given over that course of life; so 'that he should no longer live the rest of his life in the flesh to the lusts of men, but the will of God' He inferreth the obligation of this correspondence and conformity from Christ's dying. From all these places we collect:

[A.] It is an obligation. This was Christ's end, and we must not put our Redeemer to shame: 1 John iii. 8, 'For this purpose the Son of God was manifested, that he might destroy the works of the devil'; that the interest of the devil might be destroyed in us, and the interest of God set up with glory and triumph. Shall I go about to frustrate his intention, or make void the end of his death? cherish that which Christ came to destroy? tie those cords the faster, which he came to unloose? By professing his name, we bind ourselves to die to sin: Rom. vi. 2, 'How shall we that are dead to sin, live any longer therein?' not *ab impossibili*, but *ab incongruo*.

[B.] That the death of Christ was a lively and effectual pattern of our dying to sin. For the glory of God, and our salvation, Christ died a painful, shameful, accursed death. Now we must crucify sin, Gal. v. 24; be crucified to the world, Gal. vi. 14. That is to say, Christ denied himself for us, and we must deny ourselves for him; he suffered pain for us, that we should willingly digest the trouble of mortification, and suffer in the flesh, in our carnal nature, as he did in the human nature.

(1.) The death of Christ was an act of self-denial; he pleased not himself, Rom. xv. 3; minded not the interest of that nature he had assumed; parted with his life in the flower of his age, when he had most cause to love it. And will you part with nothing, make it your business to please the flesh, and gratify the flesh? He loved you, and gave himself for you, and will not you give up your lusts?

(2.) The death of Christ was an act of pain and sorrow. Of all deaths, crucifixion is the most painful and shameful. Sinful nature is not extinguished in us without trouble; as sin is rooted in self-love, self-denial is a check to it; as this self-love is mainly a love of pleasure, or the delight we take in sin, so the pains of Christ's death check it. Shall we wallow in fleshly delights, when Christ was a man of sorrows? Christ's sufferings are the best glass wherein to view sin. Will you take pleasure in that which cost him so dear? He was mocked, spit upon, buffeted; he bare the shame due to our vain conversation; a malefactor was preferred before him. Therefore when you remember Christ's death, you learn how to deal with sin. The Jews would not hear of Christ's being king: 'Away with him'; 'we have no king but Caesar' Such an holy indignation should there be in a renewed soul: Rom. vi. 12, 'Let not sin reign therefore in your mortal bodies, that ye should obey it in the lusts thereof.' Let it not king it; we have no king but Christ.

(3.) It was a price paid, that we might have grace. Every true Christian is a partaker of the fruits of Christ's death; and one fruit is, that we might die unto sin: 1 Pet. ii. 24, 'Who his own self, bare our sins in his own body on the tree, that we being dead unto sin should live unto righteousness' This is communicated to us by the Spirit; he bought sanctification as well as other privileges: Eph. v. 25, 2, 'As Christ also loved the Church, and gave himself for it, that he might sanctify and cleanse it with the washing of water by the word' And Tit. ii. 14, 'Who gave himself for us, that he might redeem us from all iniquity, and purify unto himself a peculiar people zealous of good works.' 1 Pet. i. 18, 'Redeemed us from our vain conversations' We are ready to say, 'I shall never get rid of this naughty heart, renounce these sensual and worldly affections'; our hearts are so wedded to the interests of the flesh; but, Mat. xix. 26, 'With God all things are possible'

2. Carry it well to the Spirit.

[A.] Believe that the Holy Ghost is your sanctifier, and resign up yourselves to him as such, that he may recover your souls to God. This is but fulfilling our baptismal vow: Mat. xxviii. 19, 'Go baptize all nations, in the name of the Father, Son, and Holy Ghost' To God the Father as your lord and happiness; to Christ as your redeemer and saviour; to the Holy Ghost as your guide, comforter, and sanctifier. We renew this consent in the Lord's Supper, that we may bind ourselves the faster to him, to submit to his spiritual discipline, that our cure may be wrought in us.

[B.] You must obey his sanctifying motions, for otherwise this resignation was in vain; therefore we must faithfully endeavour, by the power and help which he giveth us, to mortify sin. We must strive against sin, and we must strive with them. To strive against him and resist him, argueth great profaneness, Gen. vi. 3; Acts vii. 51; not to strive with him, much neglect and laziness. You must strive with your hearts, when the Spirit is striving with you; and take the season of his special help. It is not at our command, for 'the wind bloweth as it listeth'; take it when you have it. It is an offence to the Spirit, when the flesh is obeyed before him; men are easily entreated by sin, but deaf to his motions.

[C.] Use the appointed means by which the Spirit worketh. There are means of obtaining the Spirit at first, by the word and prayer. The Spirit is conveyed by some doctrine; for God's operative power is applied to man as a reasonable creature, not for necessity. For the word: Gal. iii. 2, 'Received ye the Spirit by the works of the law, or the hearing of faith?' So for prayer: If not for friendship's sake, Luke xi. 8, 13, yet because of his importunity. 'If ye, being evil, know how to give good gifts to your children, how much more shall your heavenly Father give the Holy Spirit to them that ask it? 'Beg it of God, upon the account of Christ, Titus iii. 5, 6. But we speak now of another thing, not the gift of the Spirit at first, but the supply of the Spirit. It is gotten the same way; the Spirit joineth his power and efficacy with the proper instituted means, the word, which is the sword of the Spirit, Eph. vi. 17. This sword was made by the Spirit: 'Holy men spake as moved by the Holy Ghost' Used by the Spirit to vanquish Satan: 1 John ii. 14, 'And the word of God abideth in you, and ye have overcome the wicked one' It is used for the defence of the better part; the sword of the flesh is the excessive love of pleasures, some carnal bait. And by it the power of the Holy

Ghost came upon us: Acts x. 44, 'While Peter yet spake these words, the Holy Ghost fell on all them that heard the word'; a spirit of sobriety, godliness, meekness, and the fear of the Lord. We cannot make use of this sword, without the Spirit: 1 Pet. i. 22, 'Seeing ye have purified your souls, in obeying the truth through the Spirit' So sacraments: 1 Cor. xii. 13, 'And have been all made to drink into one Spirit' Prayer; looking up to God who helpeth us in our conflicts; openeth their ears to discipline; and commandeth that they return from iniquity, Job xxxvi. 10; and breaketh the yokeless disposition and opposition in our hearts.

[D.] To forbear those wilful sins, which grieve the Spirit: Eph. iv. 30, 'Grieve not the Spirit;' 1 Thes. v. 19, 'Quench not the Spirit;' do not provoke him to withdraw his assistance from us; as David was

sensible of his misery: Ps. li. 10, 11, 12, 'Create in me a clean heart, God, and renew a right spirit within me; cast me not away from thy presence, and take not thy Holy Spirit from me; restore unto me the joy of thy salvation, and uphold me by thy free Spirit.'

SERMON XIX

Ye shall live.

Romans VIII. 13.

WE come now to the" promise, 'ye shall live'.

Doctrine That life is promised to those that seriously improve the assistances of the Spirit, for the mortifying of sin.

First. What is the life here promised, the life of grace, or the life of glory? I shall give my answer in three considerations.

1. The more we die unto sin, the more fit we are to live that new life which becometh Christians, or new creatures; for mortification and vivification do mutually help one another. So much sin as remaineth in us, so far is the spiritual life clogged and obstructed; therefore it is called a weight that hangeth upon us, and retardeth and hindereth us in all our heavenly flights and motions, Heb. xii. 1. That weight is there explained to be sin, that doth easily beset us; it is the great impediment to the heavenly life, and maketh our progress therein slow and troublesome. Well then, the more these inordinate inclinations are broken and mortified, the more we are alive unto righteousness, as the scripture everywhere witnesseth; and the more we tame and subdue the flesh, the more doth the spirit or better part thrive and prosper; therefore it may be truly said, 'If ye through the Spirit do mortify the deeds of the body, ye shall live' that is, spiritually.

2. The spiritual life is the pledge and beginning of the life of glory. Here it is begun by the Spirit, and there perfected; the spirit of holiness is the surest pledge of a resurrection to eternal life, as I proved, ver. 10. 11. The reasonable nature inferreth immortality, and the new nature a blessed immortality; everywhere the new birth is made the seed of eternity, called therefore the immortal seed, 1 Pet. i. 23. And he that is born of God is said to have eternal life abiding in him; he hath the pledge, and earnest, and first-fruits of it; the spiritual life consists in the knowledge, love, and contemplation of God, and perfect love and subjection to him; so that if it were meant of the life of grace, the life of glory cannot be excluded.

3. As it cannot be excluded, so it is principally intended; as is evident, partly, because it is put in opposition to death, which is the fruit of the carnal life'; if ye live after the flesh, ye shall die'; such a life is intended as is directly opposite to that death. And partly, because it is propounded by way of motive, and motives are seldom taken from things co-ordinate, such as are vivification and mortification, a dying to sin; but from things of a superior rank and order, as the glorious reward is to duty. And partly, because this suiteth with the apostle's scope, that justified persons shall not tie condemned, but glorified, because of the life of the Spirit in them.

Secondly. To confirm the point;

1. By Scripture. The offer of eternal life is everywhere propounded in scripture, as the great encouragement of all our endeavours, either in subduing sin, or perfecting holiness: as Prov.

xii. 28, 'The way of righteousness is life, and in the path thereof is no death.' There is the hope of life asserted, and the fear of death removed. Death else where is propounded as the reward of sin, and life as the great motive to keep us in the true love and obedience of God: Gal. vi. 8, 'He that BOwetn to the Spirit, shall of the Spirit reap life everlasting'; so Ezek. xviii. 18, 'Because he considereth, and turneth away from all his transgressions which he hath committed, he shall live and not die' The one is removed, the other asserted; the one is the wages of sin, the other the fruit of God's mercy and free gift; death we naturally abhor; and life we naturally love; therefore the one is threatened, the other promised.

2. To prove it by reasons.

[A.] If we partake with Christ in one act, we shall share with him in all; if dead with him, we shall live with him: Rom. vi. 8, 'If we be dead with Christ, we believe that we shall live with him' That is, if we imitate Christ in his death, then we have sure grounds of believing that after his example we shall have a joyful resurrection to eternal life. He had said before, ver. 5, 'If we be planted in the likeness of his death, we shall be also in the likeness of his resurrection'; that is, be first raised from the death of sin to the life of grace; and then the life of grace shall be swallowed up in the life of glory.

[B.] The mortified soul is prepared to enjoy the heavenly life; as being weaned from worldly and sensual delights: Col. i. 12, 'Who hath made us meet to be partakers of the saints in light' There is a double meetness[30]; first, a meetness in point of right; secondly, a meetness in point of congruity and preparation of heart; the one respects God's appointment, those who are qualified according to the covenant; the other, the suitableness of our affections.

(1) They are in respect of God deemed meet and worthy, whom God vouchsaf th to account worthy. Thus he doth the mortified, as we proved before; he then that would live when he is dead, must die when he is alive.

(2.) Preparation of heart. Heaven would be a burden to a carnal heart, that hath no delight in communion with God, or the company of the saints, or an holy life. What would he do with heaven? A Turkish paradise would suit better with such sensual and brutish souls Now those who are dead to the flesh and the world, do the better relish those things which are heavenly; it is not their trouble, but their happiness; they have the consummation of their hopes and aims.

[C.] They desire this life, and groan and wait for it; which desires, groans, and longings, being stirred up in them by God's Spirit, will not be in vain. They cannot be satisfied with the wealth, pleasures, and honours of the world; they must enjoy something beyond all these things, and that is God; and here they enjoy him but imperfectly. The more the flesh is mortified, our desires to love, know, and enjoy God are more kindled in us. Now by this these are marked out as heirs of promise; for God infuseth the desire, that they may be

---

[30] Appropriateness; proper

satisfied; and where they are laborious, they will certainly be satisfied; for otherwise God would entice us to the pursuit of a happiness, which he never meaneth to give.

[D.] God promiseth it to the mortified, the more to sweeten the duty. Those that think it is easy to forsake sin, never tried it. Mortification is of a harsh sound in a carnal ear; to contradict our carnal desires, and displease the flesh, which is so near and dear to us, will not easily down with us. God might exact it out of sovereignty, but he propoundeth rewards; if we must pass through a strait gate and narrow way, it leadeth unto life, Mat. 7. 14. Sin is such a disorderly thing, and doth so invert the course of a rational nature, that we should part with it by any 'means; but especially when the case is so stated, that we must live or die for ever. This motive should work upon us, because of our desires and fears.

(1.) Our desires. Corrupt nature will teach us to love ourselves, and so to desire happiness, which we cannot enjoy, if we live not; for the. dead are neither capable of happiness nor misery. Though we are unwilling to deny the flesh, or renounce the credit, profit, or pleasure of sin, or grow dead to the world, or worldly things, yet we are willing enough for life and happiness; therefore God promiseth that we desire, that we may submit to those things which we are against; as we sweeten bitter pills to children that they may swallow them down the better; they love the sugar, though they loathe the aloes. So God would invite us to our duty by our interest; if mortification be an unpleasing task, it conduceth to our life: Prov. viii. 35, 36, 'He that findeth me, findeth life' saith wisdom, 'and he that sinneth against me, wrongeth his own soul; and he that hateth me, loveth death.' Who would be so unnatural as to wrong his own soul? to murder himself, to court his own death and destruction? It is not only against the dictates of grace, but the desires of nature. There is nothing can be supposed to enfeeble this argument, but these two things, (a.) Men's vehement addictedness to their carnal courses, that they will rather die than part with them. (b.) That this life, which the promises of the gospel offer, is an unknown thing, it being to be enjoyed in the other world. Both are truths, yet the motive is still forcible.

(a.) How addicted soever men are to any outward thing, yet to preserve life, they will deny themselves: Job. ii. 4, 'Skin for skin, and all that a man hath will he give for his life' It was a truth, though it came out of the devil's mouth. Nothing is so dear to a man as his own life; men will spend all that they have upon the physician to recover their health, Luke viii. 43. Yea, they will hazard the members of their own body, cut off a leg or an arm, for preserving life; and shall not we part with a lust to get life? Who would sell his precious life at such a cheap rate, as the pleasing of a vain and wanton humour?

(b.) But this life, which is not a matter of sense, but of faith, is not likely to be much valued.

Answer. There is some inclination in the heart of man to eternal life; nature gropeth and feeleth about for an eternal good, and an eternal good in the enjoyment of God, (Acts. xvii. 27), as blind men do in the dark. Though man by nature lieth in gross ignorance of the true God, as our lord and happiness; yet the sense of an immortality is not altogether a stranger to nature. Such a conceit hath been rooted in the minds of all nations and religions, not only Greeks and Romans, but barbarians, and people least civilized; they have thought so, and been solicitous of a life after this life. Herodotus telleth us that the ancient Goths thought their souls perished not, but went to Zamblaxis, the captain of their colony, or founder of their nation; and Diodorus Siculus, of the Egyptians, that their parents and friends when they died, went to some eternal habitation. Modern heathens, when they are asked about eternal life, and judgment to come, as to judgment to come, they know it not; but this thing they know, that the condition of men and beasts is different; but what their condition after this life is, they cannot tell; whether they live above or below the earth, but that they subsist and have a being, is their firm persuasion; and therefore are wont to assign to the dead part of the goods which they possessed; if they lose anything, they think some of their friends in another world have taken it to supply their wants there. The Chinese are fully persuaded of a state of happiness and torment after this world. Acosta telleth us, in Peru they were wont to kill some of their slaves, to attend the dead in the world to come; and so Mexico, and other places. It is enough for us that it is an inbred notion or tradition, received from hand to hand by their ancestors; such a conception is not a stranger to human nature; and the nearer any lived to the first original of mankind, the more clear and pressing hath been the opinion hereof; lapse of time, which ordinarily decayeth all things, hath not been able to deface it out of the minds of men; who though they have been gradually depraved and degenerated, according to the distance by which they have been removed from their first originals, yet they could never wholly blot out the sense of an immortal condition after this life; nor could any solid and undubitable reasons be brought against it, to convince it of falsity. Well then, this persuasion being spread through the universe, and with extreme forwardness received by all nations, has borne up against all encounters of time, and constantly maintained itself in the midst of so many revolutions of human affairs, even among them with whom other truths are lost, and who in a great degree have for gotten humanity itself. Certainly this motive hath its use, for the reducing of man to God, especially of those who have been bred in the bosom of the church.

(2.) The argument is of great force in regard of our fears. We desire life, but guilt maketh us fear death. Sin impresseth this torment upon the consciences even of those who little know what sin meaneth: Rom. i. 32, 'They know the judgment of God, and that those who commit such things as they do, are worthy of death.' Natural con science looketh upon sin as mortal and baneful, and knows not how to be delivered from this fear. Nature owneth a distinction between good and evil; and for evil, feareth a punishment; because of those natural sentiments which we have of God, as a holy and just God. Therefore now this tender of life is made to them that not only desire happiness, but are in bondage through fear of death, and by the Christian doctrine involved in the curse of the law, and obnoxious to the flames of hell. Therefore for sinners to hear of life, must needs be an inviting motive. Mortify sin, and it shall not hurt you; you shall live. The sting of sin, which so torments you, shall be plucked out: Ezek. xviii. 13, 'Repent, and iniquity shall not be your ruin.' We are all sinners; but how shall we do that sin may not be baneful to us? Deal gently with it, and it stingeth you to the death; deal severely with it, and it shall do you no harm. When we are dead to sin, we shall not die by sin; you have deserved death; but life is offered, if you will use God's healing methods to get rid of so great a mischief.

Thirdly, I will show you the expediency of the promise; and that we may make use of such a motive as is drawn from the consequence, the death which followeth the carnal life, and that eternal life which by the merciful grant of God is the fruit of mortification. For many question whether it be a true mortification which looketh to the reward; they say we must work from life, but not for life.

I answer, 1. To be over-spiritual and nice above the word, which is the true instrument of sanctification, doth not cherish religion, but quench it. We may make use of God's motives, without sin; why doth God plead with us so often upon the terms of life and death, but that we may plead with ourselves? I know no reason to press men to a holiness abstracted from all respect to the reward. I confess it is a base self-seeking, to eye outward advantages in religious endeavours; for then the end is far beneath the work, and the spirit is made to serve the flesh, not the flesh the spirit i and by-ends taint us, but do not refine us.

2. The doubt proceedeth upon a mistake of the reward. What is this life propounded, but the seeing, loving, and enjoyment of God, and the adoring and praising of God? And can it be -a fault to aim at these things? Doth not the tendency of the new nature directly carry us to them, as the perfection of that estate unto which we are called by Christ, as naturally as the seed cast into the earth works through the clods to get up into stalk and flower? Indeed the objection is fit for them that look for a carnal heaven, as the Jews did for a carnal Messiah, a heaven that consists in ease and fleshly delights. However, to deal throughly in this argument: In the life and happiness which we expect, two things may be considered:

[A.] The nature of that life and happiness.

[B.] The personal benefit and comfort that hence results to us.

[A.] The nature of that happiness consisteth in seeing God, and being like him: 1 John iii. 2, 'When he shall appear, we shall be like him, for we shall see him as he is.' To aim at this is a fruit of the new nature, which aimeth at a perfect fruition of God, and conformity to him. Surely this cannot be in any reason questioned or scrupled at, as our great end. For it is a pure motive, and doth engage the soul to the greatest and best tempered strictness that is imaginable: 1 John iii. 3, 'He that hath this hope,' the hope spoken of in the former verse, 'purifieth himself as Christ is pure'; is every day growing up into a nearer conformity to Christ, whom he hopeth to see, and to be more perfectly like him hereafter. He whose heart is set upon the vision of God, and that pure and sinless estate which he shall enjoy in heaven, that man hath not a light tincture of religion, but is deeply dyed into the spirit of it; for such things cannot be seriously and really minded without grace; yea, no act we do is religious, unless it be directed and influenced by this aim and end. It is a rooted thought; or the impression of a powerful habit.

[B.] There is a personal benefit and happiness which resulteth to us from the fruition of God; as we are freed from the pain and sorrows of this life, in which respect it is often called a rest; especially as we are freed from the misery of those that die in their sins, in which respect it is often called salvation; and most especially, as the soul, fully sanctified, dwelleth in a glorified and immortal body, enjoying all the content and happiness belonging to such an estate. Now of this the objection may be supposed to speak; namely, as we are without misery, in an endless state of blessedness both as to our souls and*, bodies. Now this is a matter of faith, and therefore cannot be the fuel of hypocrisy; temporal convenience may be such; as credit, reputation, and respect in the world are; and therefore this we labour for, and aim at.

3. We must distinguish between *ratio formalis*[31] and *ratio motiva*[32]; our first motions and inducements, and the formal and proper reasons of our love to God; we first love God for his benefits, and they are still motives to quicken and increase our love; but afterwards we love and delight in him for his excellences, both essential and moral, the perfection of his being and holiness. That which first draweth our hearts to God, is his benignity and bounty, his offers of pardon and life; and we must look at those, or we shall never begin with God; but after wards we love him upon other reasons; and holiness itself hath our heart and love.

To bring it to the case in hands. That hatred is most pure, which is carried out against sin, as sin; because of the contrariety that is in it against the pure and holy nature and law of God: Ps cxix. 140, 'Thy word is very pure, therefore thy servant loveth it.' And so by consequence to hate sin as it is *anomia* a transgression of this pure and righteous law; but this is not our first, or only motive of obedience and thankfulness to God. Surely what things were necessary to preserve man in his natural frame, are necessary to reduce and bring him back again into it, and to preserve him in it when once reduced; such were penalties and rewards, life and death; yea, much more now the enemy hath invaded us. Therefore besides the inclination of the new nature, which carrieth us to God, and holiness, and heaven, our happiness, well-being, and personal benefit, are good and powerful motives.

4. There is a threefold use of the reward of life in this work of mortification.

[A.] To quicken a backward heart, which hangeth off because we are loath to come under so severe a discipline. Sorrow for sin is trouble some to the flesh, but the reward sweeteneth it. A carnal man thinketh that if he should give up himself to this course, he shall never see a merry day more, but grow mopish and melancholy. Now when the flesh paints out the spiritual life in such a black and dark lineaments, it is good to reflect upon the glorious life that shall ensue. There is some difficulty at first, though not so much as the flesh imagineth; but it will turn to eternal life and peace. Christ keepeth the best at last; Satan may set out his best commodities at first, but the worst come after. Christ may begin with you roughly; but the longer you are acquainted with him the better. When you come to die, you will not repent that you have not pleased the flesh, and satisfied your carnal desires. It is good to consider what things will be at the end, either of the carnal or spiritual life. The devil seeketh to glut men in their best days with the sweetest pleasures and contentments; but at last, the misery, the shame, the horror! Therefore it is good to reflect upon the issue of

---

[31] Formal reason
[32] Reasons of motive

things, that we may not stand off from God. Consider not what they are now, but what they will be hereafter: 2 Cor. vii. 10, 'For godly sorrow worketh repentance to salvation, not to be repented of.' Many have repented of their carnal mirth; never any of their godly sorrow.

[B.] In your conflict, to baffle a temptation. Heaven and hell should always be before the eyes of a watchful Christian, but especially in< actual conflicts, that you may declare your higher esteem of your hopes, than all the baits that are presented to you in the temptation. God hath promised better things. Moses counterbalanced the pleasures of sin, with the recompence of reward, Heb. xi. 25, 26. The devil offer- eth you to your loss; the glory set before you doth outweigh all.

[C.] To put us upon a conformity, and greater suitableness to our hopes: 1 John iii. 3, 'He that hath this hope in him, purifieth himself as Christ himself is pure.' I hope for such a pure estate; shall I allow either stains in my soul, or spots and blemishes in my conversation? 2 Pet. iii. 14, 'Seeing ye look for such things, be diligent that you may be found of him in peace, without spot, and blameless' They do not look for such things, that are not careful to clarify and refine their souls for the present.

Fourthly. I shall show the sufficiency and powerfulness of this motive. 1. Because of the certainty of this life promised. Surely there is a life after this life is ended; nature guesseth at it, but Christ hath brought it to light, 2 Tim. i. 10. The Scripture revealeth it as the great benefit promised by Christ: 1 John ii. 25, 'And this is the promise that he hath promised us, even eternal life'; it argueth for it: 1 Cor. xv. 19, 'If in this life only we have hope in Christ, we are of all men most miserable.' God would not proselyte us to a religion that should be our undoing, and make us more miserable than other men, by a voluntary denying of the pleasures of the flesh, and exposing us to sufferings from others. It giveth us a visible demonstration of it, by Christ's resurrection and ascension; he is gone into that glory which he spake of: 1 Pet i. 2, 'Who by him do believe in God, that raised him up from the dead, and gave him glory.' God's expressions about it are strong and clear, but our persuasions of it are too weak, or else a small contentment would not so often persuade us from our duty. Surely we doubt of the reality of the world to come, or else we would be sooner persuaded to curb the flesh, and restrain its desires, and wean ourselves from a vain world, that we may be prepared for a better.

2. The excellency of this life above all other lives that may be compared with it.

[A.] With life natural; so it is a glorious life, and it is eternal.

First, a glorious life; for we live immediately upon God, who is all in all to us; not only the soul, but the body, is incorruptible and spiritual. The contentments of the present life are base and low; it is called 'the life of our hands'; because with much labour we get the provisions necessary to supply it. It is a life patched up by the creatures; we have our clothing from the sheep, and silk-worm; our food out of the earth, or things nourished by the earth. We are forced to ransack all the store-houses of nature, that we may keep up a ruinous fabric, which is ready to drop down upon all occasions: 1 Cor. vi. 13, 'Meats for the belly, and the belly for meats, but God shall destroy both it and them.' But there the contentments are high and noble, and our faculties are more enlarged. Then, if ever, it is our meat and drink to do our Father's will. Secondly. The life is eternal; we are never weary of it, and never deprived of it. The present life is a kind of death; like a stream it floweth from us as fast as it cometh to us. It is called a vapour (Jam. iv. 14,) that appeareth, and disappeareth; a flying shadow, Job. xiv. 2. We die as fast as we live; it is no permanent thing; but there our years shall have no end; the pain and trouble of duty is short, but the reward is eternal.

[B.] Compare it with life spiritual; this is like it but differeth from it; it is a blessed and perfect life. First, it is a blessed life, free from all miseries; all tears are wiped from our eyes, and sorrow and pain shall be no more; we shall always be before the throne of God, and behold the glory of Christ, and live in the company of saints and angels; but the spiritual life doth not exempt us from miseries, rather it exposeth us to them. To outward troubles it doth: 2 Tim. iii. 12, 'Yea, and all that will live godly in Christ Jesus must suffer persecution.' And as to inward troubles, we are not freed from all doubts of God's love; though the wounds are cured, the scars remain; Absalom when pardoned, was not to see the king's face. Secondly, it is a perfect life. There is a perfect freedom, not only from misery, but from sin. There is no spot or wrinkle on the face of the glorified saints, Eph. v. 27. Here the spiritual life is clogged with so many infirmities and corruptions, that the comfort of it is little perceived; as a child in infancy, for all his reason, knoweth little of the delights of a man.

Here we only get so much grace as will keep us alive, in the midst of defects and failings, and have much ado to mortify and master corruption; but then it is nullified and quite abolished, that we shall never be in danger of sinning again. Oh, think then of this blessed estate! believe it, for God hath revealed it; hope for it, because Christ hath promised it; and if you submit to the discipline of the Spirit, you shall be sure to find it. Christ, when he went to heaven, sent the Spirit to lead us thither where he is; and the great preparation he worketh in us, to make us capable of this blessed estate, is by mortifying the deeds of the body; the sooner that is done, the more meet and ready you are.

Use. Let all this that hath been spoken, quicken you to mortification. Many things are required of us but the blessing of all cometh from the Spirit. The two great means we have already handled; but now some more.

1. The heart must thoroughly be possessed of the evil of sin; we think it no great matter, and so give way to it, and pass it over as a matter of nought. Oh, let it not seem a light thing to you; do not dandle it, or indulge it, or stroke it with a gentle censure; it is the creature's disobedience and rebellion against the absolute and universal sovereign: 1 John iii 4, 'He that committeth sin, transgresseth also the law; for sin is a transgression of the law.' It is a depreciation and contempt of God's authority: 2 Sam. xii. 9, 'Wherefore hast thou despised the commandment of the Lord, to do evil in his sight? 'It is the deformity of the noblest creature upon* earth, Rom. iii. 24. We have sinned, and are come short of the glory of God. A stain so deep, that nothing could wash it away but the blood of Christ, Heb. ix. 14; a flood that drowned a world of sinners, but did not wash away their sin: 2 Pet ii. 5, Bringing in the flood upon the world of the ungodly' Hell itself can never end and purge it out; therefore it

hath no end. God loathed the creature for sin, and nothing else but sin; his own people, Deut. xxxii. 19, 'he abhorred them because of the provoking of his sons, and of his daughters' God doth not make little reckoning of sin; he doth not overlook it; why should we?

2. Watchfulness not only against less acts, but lusts; not only lusts, but tendencies; especially an ill habit of soul, pride, worldliness, or sensuality: Mark. iii. 37, 'What I say unto you, I say unto all, watch'

3. With watching must go prayer: Mat. xxvi. 41, 'Watch and pray, that ye enter not into temptation; the spirit indeed is willing, but the flesh is weak' For God is our preserver; we watch, that we may not be careless; and we pray, that we may not be self-confident.

4. Keep up heart government: Prov. xxv. 28, 'He that ruleth not his spirit is like a city whose wall is broken down,' a thoroughfare for temptations, open to every comer. Unbridled passions and affections will soon betray us to evil, if anger, envy, grief, (ear, be not under restraints. As in a town that is broken down and without walls, the inhabitants may go and come at pleasure, night and day; there is nothing to hinder, no gates, no bars, friend or foe; there is nothing to hinder egress or regress; so it is with an ungoverned soul.

5. Live always as in the sight of God: 1 John iii. 6; Eph. v. 11, 'He that doth evil, hath not seen God' Job xxxi. 4, 'Doth not he see my ways, and count all my steps? 'A serious sight of God is a great check and awe to sin'; Will he force the queen before my face? 'Shall we sin, when God looketh on?

6. Serious covenanting with God, or devoting ourselves to him: 1 Pet. iv. 12, 'Forasmuch then as Christ hath suffered for us in the flesh, arm yourselves likewise with the same mind; for he that hath suffered in the flesh hath ceased from sin; that he should no longer live the rest of his time in the flesh to the lusts of men, but to the will of God'; and Rom. vi. 13, 'Neither yield ye your members as instruments of unrighteousness unto sin; but yield yourselves unto God, as those that are alive from the dead, and your members as instruments of righteousness unto God.

7. Humiliation for sin. This checketh the pleasure we take in it; this is begun in fear, continued in shame, and carried on further by sorrow, and ended in indignation; we fear it as damning; we are ashamed of it as defiling; we sorrow for it, as it is an act of unkind- ness against God; and we have indignation against it, as unsuitable to our glorious hopes, and present interest: Isa. xxx. 22, 'And thou shalt cast them away as a menstruous cloth; thou shalt say unto it, get ye hence' Hos. xiv. 8, 'Ephraim shall say, what have I any more to do with idols? 'This is the soul's expulsive faculty.

8. Thankfulness for the grace received: 1 Sam. xxv. 32, 33, 'Blessed be God, that kept me from shedding of innocent blood'; Gen. xx. 6, 'I withheld thee from sinning against me.' Disappointments of providence, restraints of grace, the power of saving grace: Rom. vii. 25, 'I thank God through Jesus Christ our Lord.'

9. Diligence in God's work. Standing pools are apt to putrify; when men are not taken up for God, they are at leisure for evil: 2 Sam. xi. 2, 'And it came to pass in the evening tide, that

David arose from his bed, and walked upon the roof of the king's house, and from the roof he saw a woman washing herself; and the woman was very beautiful to look upon, and the king sent for her' etc.

10. The remembrance of the other world, whither you are hastening: 1 Pet. ii. 11, 'I beseech you, as strangers and pilgrims, abstain from fleshly lusts, which war against the soul.' "You need not long for the flesh-pots of Egypt, when you are going to a land that floweth with milk and honey.

SERMON XX

For as many as are led by the Spirit of God are the sons of God.

Romans VIII. 14.

THESE words are given as a reason of what went before; that which immediately went before is a promise of eternal life to those who by the Spirit do mortify the deeds of the body. The reason may be supposed to relate to the promise, or the qualification: first, to the reward promised. Thus; they shall live in eternal happiness and glory, for they are the sons of God; if we be children, God will deal with us as children, bestow the inheritance upon us, and therefore we shall live. Secondly, the qualification. They do by the Spirit mortify the deeds of the body; the Spirit of God sustaineth a double relation, as our sanctifier, and our comforter. The former is proper to this place; he is our sanctifier, either with respect to the first infusion of grace, or the continual direction and ordering of grace so infused. Now this must be interpreted with respect to the twofold work of a Christian, the mortifying of sin, or the perfecting of holiness; his restraining or inviting motions. The first belongeth to the one, the second to the other; if we obey the Spirit's motions in the curbing and restraining evil, and subduing our proneness thereunto, then we shall live; 'for as many as are led' etc. He proveth it a *signo notificativo*; this being led and guided by the Holy Ghost is an in fallible proof of our adoption, or being taken into God's family: 'for as many as are led by the Spirit of God' etc. Observe here,

1. A sure note and qualification, 'as many as are led by the Spirit'

2. A blessed privilege, 'are the sons of God.' In the former—

1. The note itself, or the duty which evidences our claim, 'being led'.

2. The universality of it, 'as many' It is to be understood inclusive and exclusive; they, and none but they. There is in the proposition that which they call *simplex conversio*, all that are led are the sons of God; and backward, all that are the sons of God are led by the Spirit of God.

Doctrine That all that are led by the Spirit of God may know and conclude themselves to be children of God.

I shall first explain, (1.) The qualification; (2.) The privilege.

First, the qualification; We are said to be led by the Spirit.

It must be understood actively, with respect to his direction; and passively on our parts, as we submit to that direction. The Spirit is our guide, and we must obey his motions.

1. The Spirit performeth the office of a guide and leader to the godly.

The Spirit giveth us life, motion, and direction these three things are inseparable in nature and grace; life, motion, and conduct. The same causes which make us live, make us act. The creature dependeth upon God in his motion, as well as his being, Acts xvii. 28; and the regulation of our motions belongeth to the same power. It is so in nature, and it is much more so in grace, and they succeed in this order; it is a work that followeth regeneration;

first, we are born of the Spirit, before we are moved and guided by the Spirit. The Spirit first infuseth the gracious habits: Ezek. xxxvi. 26, 'A new heart will I give you, and a new spirit will I put into you' Secondly, He exciteth the soul to act, and assisteth the new creature in acting according to these habits and principles: Phil. ii. 13, 'He worketh in us both to will and to do according to his own pleasure;' Gal. v. 25, 'If we live in the Spirit, let us walk in the Spirit' Thirdly, He directeth our actions by enlightening our understandings, and governing and guiding our inclinations, to do that which is pleasing to God. This is that which I am to speak of; and here I shall show you, that.

[A.] This direction is promised: Isa. xxx. 21, 'And thine ears shall hear a word behind thee, saying, This is the way, walk in it, when ye turn to the right hand, and when ye turn to the left.' God guideth his people in all their ways to heaven and happiness; not only by general directions, but particular motions and excitations: Ps. xxv. 9, 4 The meek will he guide in judgment, and the meek will he teach his way.' This is the privilege of poor, meek, and humble souls, that they shall not want a guide to direct them in the way to heaven; so ver. 12, 'What man is he that feareth God? him will he teach in the way that he shall choose.' An humble believer, that would not displease God for all the world, and counts the least sin a greater evil than the greatest temporal loss, may be encouraged to expect light and direction from God, to order all his actions so as he may best please God: Isa. xlviii. 17, 'Thus saith the Lord, thy Redeemer, the Holy One of Israel, I am the Lord thy God, which teacheth thee to profit, that leadeth thee by the way thou shouldest go.'

[B.] So it is begged by the saints, as a great and necessary blessing: Ps. xxv. 4, 5, 'Show me thy ways, God, teach me thy paths; lead me in thy truth, and teach me; for thou art the God of my salvation; on thee do I wait all the day long.' Mark how earnest he is show me, teach me, lead me; as if he could never enough express his desire and value of this benefit. Mark his argument, 'Thou art the God of my salvation' in covenant with us, and the God of our salvation; so he hath undertaken in the covenant to save us; as God is our God, so he hath undertaken to be our guide, to teach and lead us; and doth not lay aside this relation till our salvation be accomplished. And mark his continual necessity, 'on thee do I wait all the day long'; as if he would not be left for a moment in the hand of his own counsel. So, Ps. cxix. 33, 'Teach me, God, the way of thy statutes, and I shall keep it unto the end.' The way to heaven is a narrow way, hard to be found, hardly to be kept, and easily mistaken, except God teach us daily by his Spirit. There are innumerable by paths from terrors and allurements without, and we of ourselves are weak, and subject to errors within: so Ps. cxliii. 10, 'Teach me to do thy will, for thou art my God; thy Spirit is good, lead me into the land of uprightness' They that would walk circumspectly, and incur no blame from God, and hazard to their souls, need ever to seek direction from God according to his covenant. We need such teaching, as hath with it leading; and such direction, as hath with 'it strengthening unto obedience; such as will not only help us to understand the general rule, but also how to apply it to particular actions, that no part of our duty may be left upon ourselves; and this only can we have from the Spirit of God, who directeth and leadeth us in all our choices and actions. Well then, whosoever would walk in a regular course of life, in an exact obedience to all the commands of God, and do nothing but what is all perfectly good and acceptable in God's sight, must thus beg for the leading of his gracious and sanctifying Spirit, who is the only fountain of all goodness and holiness, to direct him and assist him in every turn and motion of his life.

[C.] The necessity of it; because we are unable to guide ourselves: 'the way of man is not in himself' Jer. x. 23; 'it is not in man that walketh to direct his steps.' The metaphor of leading is taken from the blind or the weak; the blind who cannot see their way, must have one to lead them; and the lame, who though they can see, yet cannot walk of themselves, but must have one to help them. The ignorant traveller needs a guide, and the weak child a nurse to attend upon him. It is true, the children of God are light in the Lord; besides their natural reason, they have some understanding of the way of godliness; but yet to a steady, constant course of obedience, strict and righteous living, we need to be directed by the good Spirit, to make that light which we have both directive and persuasive.

(1.) Directive: Though we have a general understanding of our duty, yet to make use of it in all particular cases needeth new grace from God. The heathens were wise in generals, Rom. i. 20; they became vain *en dialogismois*, in their imaginations, and their practical inferences from these general truths; their foolish heart was darkened, and professing themselves to be wise, they became fools. And though the people of God have greater advantages by that knowledge they have from the scripture, whereby they are made wise unto salvation, and get more by God's putting his laws into their minds in regeneration, whereby they become light in the Lord; yet being not impeccable, and having many mixtures of sin yet remaining in every faculty, in particular cases are apt to err, and turn out of the way, being in part ignorant and heedless, and too often blinded by their own rebellious lusts and passions; therefore they desire that God would not leave them to themselves, but warn them of their snares and dangers, that they may still keep the path of life without defection or turning aside: Ps. cxix. 133, 'Order my steps in thy word; and let not any one iniquity have dominion over me.' They would not only have their path right, but their steps ordered; as not their general course wrong, as those who walk in the way of everlasting perdition, so not a step awry; they would not miss the way to heaven, either in whole or in part. Men that have such a tenderness upon them, see a continual need of God's counsel, which careless and slight spirits do not; they would not be corrupted by their covetousness, or sensuality, or ambition; these things blind them in particular cases, though they see their way, or know their duty in the general. Therefore they need the constant assistance of the Spirit, to rescue them from the power of every known sin, and to keep them in exact obedience. For all our general light, pride or passion, or sensual and worldly inclinations may make us err.

(2.) That our light may be persuasive, and overcome temptations and inclinations to sin. Alas! how weak are our arguings, and how easily are our considerations of our duty overborne, when a temptation set's our lusts to work, and comes on upon us with fresh strength! We see what we should do, but, yet we are carried away by our rebellious affections to do the contrary; or through sloth and negligence omit to do that which conscience calleth for at our hands. Poor truth is taken captive, and held prisoner, detained in unrighteousness, Rom. i. 18; it may talk, like a man in chains, but hath no power, can do nothing to break the force of the temptation. But now the Spirit's leading is lively and effectual; to be led is to be excited, moved, stirred forward, yea, effectually inclined to do those things which please God; he leadeth us not only *monendo*, by warning us of our duty, or enlightening our minds; but *movendo*, by inclining our hearts. The Holy Ghost doth enlighten our minds, and warm our affections, and purge away their impurities; we are moved, that we may move; and we receive the impression of his grace, that we may act, and do the things he inclineth us unto. This powerful leading the saints beg: Ps. cxix. 34, 35, 1 Give me understanding, and I shall keep thy law; yea, I shall observe it with my whole heart. Make me to go in the path of thy com mandments, for therein do I delight.' God's teaching begets obedience; he showeth us the path of life, and he maketh us to go in it. It is such direction that giveth strength, that exciteth the sluggish will, and breaketh the force of corrupt inclinations; it removeth the darkness which corruption and sin have brought upon the mind, and maketh us pliable and ready to obey; yea, it giveth not only the will, but the deed; in short, it engageth us in a watchful, careful, uniform, and constant obedience.

[D.] The nature or manner how the Spirit performeth the office of a guide, or a leader to us. He guide thus, partly by his word; and partly by his inspirations and motions, or the light of internal grace. By his word, that containeth the matter of his guidance and direction: Ps. cxix. 105, 'Thy word is a lamp unto my feet, and a light unto my path.' Mark, there is path, sand, feet; not only direction for our general choice and course, but our particular actions; and mark also the notions by which the word is expressed, lamp, and light. We have the light of the sun by day, and we make use of a lamp or candle by night; whether it be day or night, in all conditions, as well as in all actions, here is a sure direction; therefore the word is called the sword of the Spirit; now this is the light the Spirit maketh use of. Partly, the inward inspirations and motions of his grace, that we may have a spiritual discerning, 1 Cor. ii. 14. Besides the outward letter, there must be an inward light, that the understanding be opened, as well as the Scriptures; as it is said of Christ, Luke xxiv. 45, that he first opened the scriptures, and then opened their understandings. Otherwise our light is only literal and speculative, not operative and efficacious.

[E.] The parts and branches of this leading are two; First, His restraining motions for the mortifying of sin, and his inviting motions for the perfecting of holiness. He teacheth us, as he leadeth us into all truth, what we are to reject, what to believe in religion. Again, what is to be left undone in the practice of our lives; and he backeth both with what we ought to hope and fear after death in the other world.

(1.) His leading consisteth in his restraining motions, for the mortify ing of sin, or the avoiding of sin. When we are running into the snare, he mindeth us of our danger; as when any evil habit, or spiritual disease is growing upon our spirits, or when we are about to do something unseemly and offensive to God, the Spirit in effect saith, 'do not this abominable thing which I hate! but cast out pride, worldliness, and sensuality; do not give way to such and such lusts.' The Holy Ghost is in a singular manner familiar with God's people, taking up a place of abode in their hearts, and furnishing them with sweet and necessary counsel and advice from time to time; therefore he is said to strive with us, when he opposeth himself to our corrupt inclinations: Gen, vi. 3, 'My Spirit shall not always strive with man.' He striveth by inward motions and checks of conscience, by which he seeketh to humble us for sin, and to reclaim us from sin; if we struggle against these, we lose our advantage: Neh. ix. 20-30, 'Thou gavest them also thy good Spirit to instruct them. Thou testifiedst against them by the Spirit to bring them back to thy law' In these and many places, we read of the Spirit's guidance': If ye through the Spirit mortify the deeds of the body.' We must avoid those things he dissuadeth us from.

(2.) There are his inviting and quickening motions, to bring us on in a way of holiness, and to perfect the work of grace in us, and fit us more for God's use and service. He doth not only close us at first with. Christ, but is the agent and worker of the life of Christ within us, to do his work, and maintain his interest, and sanctify us throughout, as we have experience of his restraining motions, that we may be more and more conformed to God's blessed will, and seek our delight and happiness in communion with his blessed self: Ps. xxvii. 8, 'The Lord said, Seek ye my face: and my heart said, thy face, Lord, will I seek.' God speaketh to us by the injection of holy thoughts, and the secret inspirations of his grace, and we speak to God by the inclinations and resolutions of our own souls. This dialogue is carried on in soul language; there need no audible words between God and the soul; so in other places, how often doth he solicit us by his holy motions and inspirations! The Spirit inclineth and presseth us to that which is good.

2. As the office of the Spirit is to guide and lead, so it is our duty to submit to his direction; to be led by him. That maketh the evidence in the passive sense, if we suffer ourselves to be led and guided by him in all things; for otherwise the Spirit worketh on many, but they will not hear; they either neglect or resist his motions. There is a double voice within us, the flesh and the Spirit; and men's spiritual estate is determined by submission and compliance with either: Rom. viii. 1, 'That walk not after the flesh, but after the Spirit. 'The flesh is near and dear to us, and very imperious and importunate to be pleased. Now some men live in. a perfect obedience to the flesh, according to the fancies and appetites of corrupt nature, and deny it nothing which it craveth at their hands; but there is another voice within us, saying, This is the way, walk in it; thus you must do, if you mean to be happy. Now let us not hear and pass by, as if you heard not; no, you must suffer yourselves to be led and governed by this voice, or this blessed Spirit in all; you must improve his assist ance, wait for his approaches, obey his sanctifying motions, direct ali the actions of your lives according to his guidance and counsel; that is your evidence.

[A.] I shall urge it in conformity to Christ. There is a perfect likeness between Christians and Christ; all the privileges which Christ had, are conveyed to us by the Spirit. If Jesus be the natural Son of the Father, the Christian is his adopted son, John xx. 17; if Jesus be the heir of all things, a Christian is a co-heir with Christ, Rom. viii. 17; if Jesus be innocent, the Christian is justified; if Jesus be born of the Spirit, or framed by the Holy Ghost, the Christian is regenerated, born also of water, and the Holy Ghost, John iii. 5; if Jesus be evidenced to be the Son of God by the coming down of the Holy Ghost upon him, the Spirit beareth witness with our spirits, that we are the sons of God. Jesus was led by the Spirit continually, so we; if he retire into the desert, if he come back again into Galilee, he is still led by the Spirit: Mat. iv., 'Jesus was led up of the Spirit into the wilderness' the Holy Ghost aiding him in that conflict; when it was ended, Luke iv. 14, 'Jesus returned in the power of the Spirit into Galilee,' that is, to preach, or to execute his prophetical office; if he cast out devils, Mat. xii. 14, 'I cast out devils by the Spirit of God.' Thus it was with Christ; certainly therefore whatever design we conceive, whatever resolution we take, whatever enterprise we would bring to pass, we are always bound to depend upon the Holy Ghost; the Spirit must still lead us and move us in all our operations.

[B.] The great mischief which will ensue, if we obey not his sanctifying motions and inspirations. You will resist the Spirit and vex him: Isa. lxiii. 10, 'They rebelled, and vexed his holy Spirit; and therefore he turned to be their enemy.' The other expression, Eph. iv. 30, 'Grieve not the holy Spirit.' He is grieved when the flesh is obeyed before him; the Spirit sustaineth a double relation, our sanctifier, and our comforter; let us not resist our sanctifier, nor grieve our comforter. Surely we should not be ungrateful to this Holy Spirit; if we be holy, he sanctifieth us; if free, it is he who sets us at liberty; if wise, he enlighteneth us. If gratitude cannot prevail, yet our interest should; he is our comforter, and we blot our evidence, darken his seal, and so deprive ourselves of that joy and peace which we might have in our souls, if he were obeyed. There is one great mischief above this, which God sets up as a dreadful warning for our caution, despiting the Spirit of grace, Heb. x. 29. To resist the Spirit is dangerous. To resist the Father speaking in the law; to resist the Son speaking in the gospel, offering our remedy; but to resist the Holy Ghost, who would help us to accept this remedy, there is no other relief for us, no other divine person to give it us. The mission of the Holy Ghost is the last offer for the recovery of mankind; there is nothing more to be expected; if we submit not to his inspirations, and wilfully refuse to give ear to his counsel, our salvation is hopeless.

Secondly, let me now open the privilege—*they are the sons of God*. This privilege may be considered,

1. As to the real grant on God's part.

2. As to their own sense of their adoption on the believers' part.

1. As to the real, grant on God's part. It was intended to the elect from all eternity: Eph. i. 5, 'Being predestinated to the adoption of children'; in time it is brought about by Christ's death, or the work of redemption, Gal. iv. 4, 5; But actually instated upon us, when we are regenerated, and do believe: John i. 12, 13, 'To as many as received him, to them gave he power to become the sons of God, even to them that believe in his name; which were born, not of blood, nor of the will of the flesh, nor of the will of man, but of God.' They are born of God, and so made the sons of God. Being called out of nature to grace, in their effectual calling, they are made sons and daughters to the Most High God; first he doth renew their natures, and make them holy, then reconciled to God as their Father in Christ; this is the first grant.

2. As to their own sense of their adoption, that is spoken of here; they show themselves to be God's children, and so may know themselves to be God's children.

[A.] Because they have the certain evidence that they are received for children by God, through faith in Christ; and that is holiness. If our carriage be suitable to our estate and privileges, why should we doubt? Eph. i. 4, 5, 'Elected to be holy, without blame before him in love, having predestinated us to the adoption of children.' They have the true pledge of God's love, and that is the Spirit; and they show the true fruit of their love to God, and that is obedience to his sanctifying motions; they are led by the Spirit, and so without blame before him in love; as they have a greater measure of the fruits, so it is every day more clear to them.

[B.] The same Spirit that leadeth them, doth assure and ascertain them; for our sanctifier is our comforter. And the more a sanctifier, the more a comforter; first in a darker way, leaving a child-like impression upon them, inclining them to go to God as a father; though their adoption be not so explicit and clear: ver. 15, 'Ye have not received the spirit of bondage again to fear, but the spirit of adoption, whereby we cry, Abba, Father'; and Gal. iv. 6, 'And because ye are sons, God hath sent forth the Spirit of his Son into your hearts, crying Abba, Father.' The children of God deal with God as a father, cry to him as a father, cannot keep away from him, when they dare not so expressly entitle themselves his children. Secondly, in a clearer way, when he manifests his presence by a supernatural and powerful change wrought in the heart, and discovered; whereby they conclude their own gracious estate: ver. 1 6, 'The Spirit itself beareth witness with our spirits that we are the children of God' The Spirit helps to discern his own work, or the image of Christ stamped upon them, in a fair and bright character.

[C.] This is a great privilege; that will appear if we consider our present relation to God, or our future inheritance.

(1.) Our present relation to God: 1 John iii. 1, 'Behold what love 1he Father hath showed us, that we should be called the children of God.' We are his children; and God is, as our father, pleased to own us as his children; we are not born sons, but made so by grace; by nature we are children of wrath, Eph. ii. 3; the very term adoption implieth it. A child by adoption is opposed to a child by nature; for men are not said to adopt their own children, but strangers; now that strangers and enemies should not only be reconciled, but also be called the sons of God, O what unspeakable mercy is it! To have the blessed God, whom we had so often offended, to become our reconciled father in Christ! It is not an empty title that he assumeth; but hath more abundant love and tenderness to our welfare than any title can make us understand.

(2.) Our future inheritance. Our right floweth from our sonship: Rom. viii. 17, 'And if children, then heirs; heirs of God, and joint heirs with Christ'; Titus iii. 5, 6, 7, 'Not by works of righteousness which we have done, but according to his mercy he saved us, by the washing of regeneration, and the renewing of the Holy Ghost, which he hath shed on us abundantly through Jesus Christ our Saviour; That being justified by his grace, we should be made heirs according to the hope of eternal life.' 1 Pet. i. 3, 4, 'Blessed be the God and

Father of our Lord Jesus Christ, which, according to his abundant mercy, hath begotten us again to a lively hope, by the resurrection of Jesus Christ from the dead, to an inheritance incorruptible, and undefiled, that fadeth not away, reserved in heaven for you.' Luke xii. 32, 'Fear not, little flock, it is your Father's good pleasure to give you a kingdom.' What may we 'not expect from the bounty of such a father? Surely he that would pardon his enemies, will bless his children, and that for evermore. Use 1. Is to inform us,

1. Of the nature of the Spirit's conduct. It is sweet, but powerful: it accomplished its effect without offering violence to the liberty of man; we are not drawn, taken, or driven as beasts, but led, guided to happiness; not forced thither against our wills, or without our consent. The inclinations of man are free; there is not a violent impulsion, but a sweet guidance and direction; yet he is subject to the leading, government, and drawing of the Spirit.

2. It informeth us of the great condescension of God to new creatures. [1.] In his care over them. They are led by the Spirit during their pilgrimage; well-guided, and well-guarded: Heb. i. 14, 'Are they not all ministering spirits, sent forth to minister for them who shall be heirs of salvation?' They have the Spirit for direction, and the angels for defence; their charge is not *cura animarum*, but *custodia corporis*.

[B.] In the great honour he puts upon them, and reserveth for them. Now these are the children of God; hereafter they shall have the inheritance; then is adoption complete: Rom. viii. 23, 'Even we ourselves groan within ourselves, waiting for the adoption, the redemption of our bodies.' If annihilated after death, or their life drawn out to all eternity upon earth, allowing them so tolerable contentment, there had been a favour, comparing their estate with damned reprobates; but he hath done better for them; having after a short time of trial and service here, appointed endless joys and pleasures for them at his right hand for evermore. Now he taketh them into his family, then into his bosom.

Use 2. Is to press us to put ourselves under the conduct and government of the Holy Spirit. It is implied in our baptism: Mat. xxviii. 19, 'Go therefore, teach and baptise all nations in the name of the Father, Son, and Holy Ghost' By our express consent, we take God for our lord and portion, and Christ for our redeemer and saviour; and the Spirit for our guide, sanctifier, and comforter. There is all the reason to press us to it: First, From his excellency. He cannot deceive us, because he is the Spirit of truth; he cannot engage us in evil, because he is the Spirit of holiness. From his readiness to do good: Ps. xxv. 9, 'Good and upright is the Lord, therefore he will teach sinners in the way,' the poor sinner that is weary of his wandering, that is truly humble for his failings and wanderings, and comes to him for pardon and grace. Secondly, From our necessity. Our heedless headlong spirit will soon transport us to some inconvenience: Prov. iii. 5, 6, 'Trust in the Lord with all thine heart, and lean not on thine own understanding; in all thy ways acknowledge him, and he shall direct thy path' It is the greatest judgment to be given up to our own hearts' counsels. Thirdly, From the effects, the peace and comfort which followeth his guidance: Jer. vi. 16, 'Stand ye on the ways and see, and ask for the good old paths, where is the good way, and walk therein, and you shall find rest to your souls'; and Ps. cxliii., 10, 'Teach me to do thy will, for thou art my God; thy Spirit is good, lead me into the land of uprightness.'

Question But what must we do?

Answer

1. Continually desire his assistance and powerful conduct: Luke xi. 13, 'If ye then, being evil, know how to give good gifts to your children, how much more shall your Heavenly Father give the Holy Spirit to them that ask him? 'It is pleasing to God: 1 Kings iii. 9, 10, 'Give therefore thy servant an understanding heart, to judge thy people, that I may discern between good and bad; and the speech pleased the Lord.'

2. Let us co-operate with his motions, mortifying the wisdom and the desires of the flesh; avoiding all those things he dissuadeth us from. You grieve him, when you disturb his comforting work, or disobey his sanctifying motions: Eph. iv. 30, 'And grieve not the Holy Spirit, whereby ye are sealed to the day of redemption.' Do not break through when he would restrain you, or refuse or draw back when he would impel and invite ydu to good. The Spirit of God will not forsake you, unless you forsake him first; he is grieved when the wisdom of the flesh is obeyed before his counsel, and his holy inclinations smothered, and we yield easily to the requests of sin, but are deaf to his motions.

3. Let us humble ourselves when we sin through frailty, and leave the directions of the Holy Ghost; let us ever be more wary afterwards: Ps. li. 6, 'In the inward parts shalt thou make me to know wisdom.' We catch many a fall when we leave our guide; as the child when without his nurse he will take to his own feet.

Use 3. Is trial; for it is propounded as a mark of the children of God. Now by whose counsel are you guided? Some follow their own spirit, not the Spirit of God; are guided by the wisdom of the flesh, and their own. carnal affections; led away from God by the lusts of their own heart, and the temptations of the devil; taken captive by him at his will and pleasure, 2 Tim. ii. 26. Our conversations will declare that which is prevalent. *Principiata respondent suis principiis*, the constant effects declare the prevailing principle.

1. The effects of the Spirit's leading are an heavenly life: 1 Cor. ii. 12, 'Now we have received, not the spirit of the world, but the Spirit of God, that we might know the things that are freely given us of God'; and Eph. i. 17, 18, 'That the God of our Lord Jesus Christ, the Father of glory, may give unto you the Spirit of wisdom and revelation in the knowledge of him; the eyes of your understandings being enlightened, that ye may know what is the hope of his calling, and what the riches of the glory of his inheritance in the saints' The Spirit leadeth us to those tilings that are above; the flesh leadeth us to those things here below; to flesh-pleasing vanities, vain perishing delights, grateful only to sense.

2. The Spirit leadeth to an holy life, and obedience to God: Eph. iv. 24, 'And that ye put on the new man, which after God is created in righteousness and true holiness'

3. To spiritual things: Rom. viii. 5, c They that are after the flesh, do mind the things of the flesh; but they that are after the Spirit, the things of the Spirit'; and Gal. vi. 8, 'He that soweth to the flesh, shall of the flesh reap corruption; but he that soweth to the Spirit, shall of the Spirit reap life everlasting,' to excel in these things, though with the loss of carnal pleasures.

4. To all duties to our neighbour: Eph. v. 9, 'For the fruit of the Spirit is in all goodness, and righteousness, and truth'; Gal. v. 22, 23, 'But the fruit of the Spirit is love, joy, peace, long-suffering, gentleness, goodness, faith, meekness, temperance; against such there is no law.'

SERMON XXI

For ye have not received the spirit of bondage again to fear; but ye have received the spirit of adoption, whereby we cry, Abba, Father.

Romans VIII. 15.

THE words contain a reason why those who are led by the Spirit are the children of God. The reason is, because they have received the covenant of grace; and the spirit which accompanieth the new covenant is not the spirit of bondage, but adoption. It is propounded—1. Negatively; 2. Affirmatively.

1. Negatively. They were freed from the servile fear of condemnation, which the legal covenant wrought in them.

2. Affirmatively. They were endowed with the spirit of adoption, or a persuasion of their Father's love, or of God's admitting them into his family, and the right of inheritance; and so were drawn to obedience by noble motives, suitable to the covenant they were under.

For the first clause in the text, ye have not received the spirit of bondage again to fear.

In which words observe,

1. The state of men under the law-covenant it is a state of bondage.

2. The operation of the Spirit during that dispensation, it made men sensible of their bondage: 'Ye have not received the spirit of bondage' There is the Spirit mentioned, and, *palin*, again, implying that during that dispensation they had it.

3. The impression left upon the heart of man, *eis phobon*, unto fear. There is a twofold fear, filial and servile, child-like and slavish. The one is a lawful and necessary fear, which doth quicken us to our duty: Phil. ii. 12, 'Work out your salvation with fear and trembling;' and is either the fear of reverence, or the fear of caution. The fear of reverence is nothing but that awe which we, as creatures, are to have of the divine majesty, or an humble sense of the condition, place, and duty of a creature towards its creator. The fear of caution is a due sense of the importance and weight of the business we are engaged in, in order to our salvation. Certainly none can consider the danger we are to escape, and the blessedness we aim at, but will see a need to be serious; and therefore this fear is good and holy. Secondly, There is besides this, a slavish fear, which doth not further, but extremely hinder out work; for though we are to fear God, yet we are not to be afraid of God. This servile fear may be interpreted either with respect to the precept or the sanction of the law. First, with respect to the precept; and so it showeth us how men stand naturally affected to the duty of the law; whatever they do is merely for fear of being punished. Secondly, to the sanction, penalty, and curse. The fear of evil is more powerful upon us than the hope of good; the greater the evil, the greater the fear, and the more tormenting.

Doctrine That men under the law-covenant are under a spirit of bondage.

Here I shall enquire,

1. What is the spirit of bondage?

2. How is it the fruit of the law-covenant?

3. Whether it is good or bad?

1. What is the Spirit of Bondage? To open it, we must explain three things, (1.) The nature of the object; (2.) The work of the Spirit; (3.) The disposition of man.

[A.] The nature of the object, the law requiring duty of the fallen creature, and threatening punishment in case of disobedience. For the law hath a twofold office; to convince of sin, Rom. iii. 20, 'Now by the law only cometh the knowledge of sin'; and to bind over to punishment; therefore it is said, 'The law worketh wrath' Rom. iv, 15. In both respects the old covenant is called the law of sin and death, Rom. viii. 2. The law as a covenant of works is called a law of sin, because it only showeth our sin; and a law of death, because it bindeth us over to death.

[B.] The work of the Spirit. Every truth is quickened by the Spirit, and made more powerful upon our hearts. The comfort which we have from the truth of the gospel is by the Spirit, and therefore it is called joy in the Holy Ghost. So law-truths are applied to the conscience by the Spirit: Jer. xxxi. 19, 'After I was instructed, I smote upon the thigh'; and 'when the commandment came' that is, in the light and power of the Spirit, 'sin revived, and I died' Rom. vii. 9, that is, was made sensible of his sinful and lost condition. And indeed the usual work wherewith the Spirit beginneth with men, is to show them their sin and misery, their alienation from God, arid enmity to him, and insufficiency to help themselves.

[C.] The disposition of man, which is corrupted, under the workings of the spirit of bondage. And so this spirit of bondage, or servile fear, worketh several ways, according to the temper of men.

(1.) In the profane it giveth occasion of further sinning, as conscience being awakened by the Spirit, urgeth either the precept or the curse. The precept, as a bullock at first yoking groweth more unruly, or a river swelleth when it meeteth with a dam and restraint: Rom. vii. 5, 'For when we were in the flesh, the motions of sin, which were by the law, did work in our members, to bring forth fruit unto death.' Sinful practices were more irritated by the prohibition; and so our obligation to death increased. Or else by urging the curse, which produceth the sottish despair: Jer. xviii. 12, 'And they said, there is no hope; we will walk after our devices' There is a double despair of pleasing, or being accepted; there is a lazy, sottish despair, as well as a raging and tormenting despair, by which men cast off all care of the soul's welfare: 'There is no hope' (2.) In a middle sort of men, that have a legal conscience, it puts them upon some duty and course of service to God; but it is not done comfortably, or upon any noble motives. That which is defective in it is this: First, it is constrained service. This bondage, which is a fruit of the law, doth force and compel men to some unpleasing task. A Christian serveth God out of love, but one under the spirit of bond age serveth God out of fear; a love to God and true holiness prevaileth with the one, more than the fear of wrath and punishment; for the spirit of adoption disposeth and inclineth him to God as a father; but one under the spirit of bondage is forced to submit to some kind of religiousness, for fear of being damned. Indeed both are constrained, the one by love, the other by fear, 2 Cor. v. 14; only the constraint of love is durable, and kindly, and sweet; the other, his task is grievous and wearisome, Mai. i. 11, and holdeth most in a fit; when danger is nigh, they are frighted into some devotion, Ps. lxxviii. 34-38. Secondly, That service which they are forced and compelled to yield to God, is outward service and obedience, Isa. lviii. 7; hanging the head for a day, like a bulrush; and as they do, Mic. vi. 7, offer thousands of rams and ten thousands of rivers of oil, or the firstborn of their body, for the sin of their souls. It is a sin-offering rather than a thank-offering; more to appease conscience, than to please God; con sists in rituals rather than substantiate; and those invented by men, rather than commanded by God. Whereas the true Christian is otherwise described: Phil. iii. 3, 'For we are the circumcision, which worship God in the spirit, and rejoice in Christ Jesus, and have no confidence in the flesh.' But the false Christian is one (Mat. xv. 8) that draweth nigh to God with the mouth, but their heart is far from him; their heart is averse from God, though they must have an outward religion to rest in; and so they serve God not as children do a father, but as slaves serve a hard and cruel master.

(3.) In some the Lord may make use of it to bring on conversion; for according to our sense of sin and misery, so is a saviour and redeemer welcome to us, and prized by us. There must be a sensible awakening knowledge of our great necessity, before we will make use of Christ for our cure and remedy. None but the sick will care for the physician, Mat. ix. 12; the burdened for ease, Mat. xi. 28, 29; the pursued for a sanctuary and refuge, Heb. vi. 18; none but the condemned, to be justified and acquitted, Rom. viii. 33, 34; the lost and miserable to be saved, Luke xix. 10.

2. How is it the fruit of the law-covenant? The law-covenant is double: either the covenant of nature, which concerned both Jevy and Gentile; or the first administration of the covenant of grace, made with the Jews only.

[A.] The covenant of nature, which we are all under naturally, breedeth bondage and shyness of God; we are sensible that we are his creatures, and so owe him duty and subjection; that we have failed in our duty to him, and therefore lie obnoxious to his wrath and punishment. Heathens, that had but some obscure notions of God, felt somewhat of this bondage, Rom. i. 32; they 'knew the judgment of God, and that they which commit such things are worthy of death.' They stood in dread of angry justice; and not only they, but all mankind are under it, Rom. ii. 15. According to that natural sense which men have of religion, so is their bondage more or less; still under fear of death, and the consequence thereof. This sense or conscience of sin and wrath, which the breach of God's law hath made our due, is so engrained in the nature of man that he cannot dispossess himself of it. The apostle compareth it to the bond of marriage, which is indissoluble till one of the parties die, Rom. vii. 1-3. The conscience of man is either married to the law as its husband, or Christ as its husband; not to the latter, till it be dead to the former: ver. 4, 'Ye are become dead to the law by the body of Christ, that ye might be married to another, even to him that was raised from the dead'. Well then, this bondage is the effect of the law, or covenant of nature, impressed upon the heart of man, and ariseth from a consciousness of guilt, and obnoxiousness to God's wrath and displeasure, because of God's broken covenant.

[B.] The first administration of the covenant of grace. That bred a spirit of bondage; witness that allegory, Gal. iv. 22-26. Abraham's two wives did represent the two covenants; the first and second administration of the covenant of grace. The first gendered to bondage, men of a servile spirit, doing what they did, not out of love, but slavish fear: 2 Cor. iii. 9, 'But if the ministration of death, written and engraven in stones, was glorious, so that the children of Israel could not steadfastly behold the face of Moses, for the glory of his countenance, which glory was to be done away'; 'for if the ministration of condemnation be glory, much more doth the ministration of righteousness excel in glory.' Their gospel was dark, and had little efficacy to change the heart of man; it did little allay and vanquish this shyness of God; rather increased it, as it conduced to revive the knowledge of God in their minds, and held forth the ransom and way of appeasing God's angry justice obscurely and darkly; rather showed our distance from God. Israel was God's first-born, and so his heir, but an heir in non-age, Gal. iv. 1, 2; their ordinances were a bond, ours an acquittance; but what is this to us? *Answer.* Much every way:

(1.) That we may bless God for the greater advantages that we have to breed a child-like spirit in us by the new covenant; where the Lord who is offended by sin, is propitiated by the death of Christ, and willing to admit man into his presence; and bless him, that God as a judge driveth us by the spirit of bondage to Christ as mediator; that Christ as mediator by the spirit of adoption may bring us back again to God as a father; and then having God for our father, we may have Christ for our advocate, and the Spirit for our comforter and sanctifier, to enable us to observe the gospel precepts of repentance towards God, and faith in our Lord Jesus Christ; and so be made capable of the promises of pardon and life. One covenant maketh us sensible of the grace of the other; Christ dealeth with us as children of the family, requiring duty from us upon reasonable and comfortable terms.

(2.) Because those that live under the gospel dispensation, and have not received the power of it, may be yet under a spirit of bondage, and cherish a legal way of religion. In every one that entertaineth thoughts of religion, law and gospel are at conflict in his heart, as well as flesh and corruption; this is clear by Gal. v. 17, 18'; For the flesh lusteth against the spirit, and the spirit against the flesh, and these are contrary the one to the other, so that ye cannot do the things that ye would; but if ye be led by the Spirit, ye are not under the law.' As spirit and flesh do lust against, and constantly oppose one another, and labour to suppress and diminish each other, so do law and grace. Those that are slaves to their sinful lusts, and are not enabled by the spirit of the new testament to do in some measure what the rule enjoin eth, have their comforts obstructed; and while sin reigneth, the law reigneth: Rom. vi. 14, 'For sin shall not have dominion over you, for ye are not under the law, but grace.' Partly, by its irritating power; and partly, by its condemning power; leaving them under a fear of condemnation, and urging them to do what they cannot do.

(3.) The children of God by regeneration and adoption, while sin remaineth, may have somewhat of bondage remaining in them. Look: as under the old testament, when the ingenuous and noble motives of the gospel were in a great measure unknown, there was somewhat of a free spirit in the eminent saints, Ps. li. 12, though but sparingly dispensed; so under the gospel dispensation, there are many sad and drooping Christians who do not improve the comforts provided for them, and when they are called upon to rejoice in the Lord always, Phil, iv, 4, rather go mourning all the day long; but it is their fault. The people under the law -dispensation were either the godly, or the wicked, or the middle sort; the eminently godly then had a free spirit; the wicked were either terrified, or stupified; the middle sort, who were touching the righteousness of the law blameless, Phil. iii. 6, had a zeal for outward observances, but not according to knowledge, Rom. x. 2; were merely actuated by a legal spirit. So under the gospel there are the eminently godly, who evermore rejoice, 1 Thes. v. 16, or at least are swayed more with love, than fear; the weak godly, who have much of their ancient fears, and the love of God in them is yet too weak to produce its effects; though this love to God do prevail over sin, yet not ordinarily over fear of punishment; but much of that influences their duties, more than their love to God. There is too great averseness in their hearts from God and holiness, and they seek to break it by the terrors of the Lord. Not sin, but fear is predominant.

3. Is this spirit of bondage good, or bad? I answer,

[A.] We must distinguish of the three agents in it. This bondage cometh partly from a good cause,' the Spirit of God breeding in us a knowledge of our duty, and a belief of the threatenings of God, from whence ariseth a sense of our sinful and miserable condition; so far it is good and useful. Partly from an ill cause, the devil, who delighteth to vex us with unreasonable terrors: 1 Sam. xvi. 14, 'The Spirit of the Lord departed from Saul, and an evil spirit from the Lord vexed him'; the devil both tempteth and troubleth; as the huntsman hideth himself till the poor beast be gotten into the toils, then he appeareth with shouts and cries. Partly from the corruption of man's heart, which either turneth this work to an utter aversation from God, or some perfunctory and unwilling way of serving him. Some know the right use of the covenant, others not; and therefore we must consider not only how it is wrought by the Spirit, but how it is entertained by man through our corruption; our conviction of sin and misery by the Spirit turneth into bondage and servitude.

[B.] The spirit of bondage is better than a profane spirit. Some cast off all thoughts of God and the world to come, and are not so serious and mindful of religion as to be much troubled with any fears about their eternal condition; it were happy for them if they were come so far as a spirit of bondage; they that are under it have a con science of their duty, but such as perplexeth them, and lasheth, and stingeth them with the dread and horror of that God whom they serve. Now this is better than the profane spirit that wholly forgets God: Ps. x. 4, 'God is not in all their thoughts'; whether he be pleased or dis pleased, honoured or dishonoured. This may tend to good; the *gradus ad rem, gradus in re*; yea, it may in some degree be consistent with sincerity; for though to have no love to God is inconsistent with a state of grace, or to have less love to God than sin; yet to have more fear than love is consistent with some weak degree of grace, especially if the case be so, that in act, love is less felt than fear; and therefore, though men are conscious to much backwardness, yet keep up a serious ness; though to their feeling it is more fear than love which moveth them, yet we dare not pronounce them graceless; for there may be a love to

God, and a complacency in his ways, though it be oppressed by fear, that the spirit of adoption is not so much discovered for the time.

[C.] That it is an ill frame of spirit to be cherished or rested in. For while men are under the sole and predominant influence of it, they are never converted to God; fear doth begin the work of conversion, but love maketh it sincere. The Spirit by fear doth awaken men to make them see their condition, terrifying them by the belief of God's threatening, and the sense of his indignation, that they may flee from wrath to come, Mat. iii. 7; or cry out, 'What shall I do to be saved? 'Acts ii. 37. But yet, though they have a sensible work, they have not a saving work. Some by these fears are but troubled and restrained a little, and so settle again in their sensual course, but to their great loss; for God may never give them like advantages again. Others betake themselves to a kind of religiousness, and forsake the practice of those grosser sins which breed their fears; and so resting here, continue in a state of hypocrisy and self-deceiving religiousness.

Use 1. Is information and instruction, to teach us how to carry it as to the spirit of bondage.

[A.] It is not to be slighted; partly, from the matter which breedeth the fear and bondage, which is the law of God, the supreme rule and reason of our duty, by which all debates of conscience are to be decided; partly, from the author; this sense of sin and misery is stirred up in us, and made more active by the operation of the Spirit of God; partly, from the faculty wherein it is seated, the conscience of a reasonable creature, the most lively and sensible power of man's soul, which cannot be pacified, but upon solid grounds and reasons; partly, from the effect, the fear of eternal death, the greatest misery that can befall us; for surely 'it is a dreadful thing to fall into the hands of the living God' Heb. x. 31. To smother and stifle checks of conscience doth increase our misery, not remove it; and produceth hardness of heart, and contempt of God; therefore when our souls are at this pass, that we see we are in bondage to sin, and know not how to help it; in bondage to wrath, and know not how to quench these fears which are awakened in us by the Spirit; surely we should look after solid satisfaction and peace of soul, settled on us upon gospel terms; run to the blood of sprinkling, Heb. x. 22.

[B.] Yet it is not a thing to be chosen, prayed for, or rested in. Partly, because it is a judiciary impression, a spark of hell kindled in the conscience. A tender conscience we may and must pray for, but not a stormy conscience; when we ask legal terrors, we know not what we ask; a belief of the threatenings belongs to our duty, as well as a belief of the promises; but we must not so reflect upon terrors, as to exclude the comfort and hope of the gospel. When under a spirit of bondage, we are in a most servile condition, far from all solid comfort, courage, and boldness. But is it not an help to conversion? Answer, Let God take his own way; we are not to look after the deepness of the wound, but the soundness of the cure; not terrible representations of sin and wrath, but such an anxiousness as will make us serious and solicitous. Partly, because the law-covenant is an antiquated dispensation, the law of nature bindeth not as a covenant; for the promise of life ceased upon the incapacity of the subjects, when under a natural impossibility of keeping it; the threatening and penalty lieth upon us indeed, till we flee to another court and covenant. The Jewish covenant was abolished when Christ repealed the law of Moses; that covenant dealt with us as servants, the gospel dealeth with us as sons, in a more ingenuous way, and inviting us to God upon nobler motives. And partly, from the nature of that fear that doth accompany it; it driveth us from God, not to God, Gen. iii. 8. Adam hid himself among the bushes; and he gives us this reason, because he was afraid; and still we all fly from a condemning God; but to a pardoning God we are encouraged to come nigh: Ps. cxxx. 4,' There is forgiveness with thee, that thou mayest be feared.' In the wicked, the fear of God's wrath once begun, it increaseth daily, till it come to the desperate fear of the damned; and the fault is not in the law, or in the Spirit, but in man, who runneth from his own happiness, and maketh an ill use of God's warnings.

Use 2. Is to put us upon trial, and self-reflection. All that attend upon ordinances, receive some spirit or other a spirit of bondage, or a spirit of adoption; now what kind of spirit are we actuated withal? God's children, who are adopted into his family, may have some degree of the spirit of bondage, great mixtures of fears and discouragements; for only 'perfect love casteth out fear' 1 John iv. 18; but these fears are overbalanced by the spirit of adoption; they have some filial bold ness, a better spirit than a slave; do not wholly sin away the love of a father, though the delight and comfort be much obstructed. It was n sad word for a child of God to speak: Ps. lxxvii. 3, 'I thought of God, and I was troubled.' The remembrance of God may augment their grief, when conscience representeth his abused favours as the cause of his present wrath and displeasure with them; but this is not their constant temper, but only in great desertions. For a constancy, while sin remaineth, somewhat of bondage remaineth; but there is a partial and a predominant legality. The partial maybe found in the regenerate, who do by degrees overcome the servile fear of condemnation, and grow up more and more into a gospel spirit; certainly where that prevaileth, there will be liberty: 2 Cor. iii. 17. Though for a while the heir differeth nothing, or nothing to speak of, from a servant, yet in time he behaveth himself as a son, and is treated as a son; and they get more comfort and joy in the service of God. But the predominant legality is in the carnal; it may be known by the governing principle, fear or love; the inseparable companion of the spirit of bondage is fear; and love and sonship, the spirit of adoption, go together. Where slavish fear prevaileth and influenceth our religion, it may be known by these two things:

[A.] By their unwillingness and reluctancy to what they do for God. The good they do, they would not; and the evil they do not, they would do; that is, they would fain live in a sinful life if they durst, and be excused from religious duties, except that little outward part which their custom and credit engages them to perform; like birds that in a sunshine day sing in the cage, though they had rather be in the woods. They live not an holy life, though some of the duties which belong to it they observe, out of a fear to be damned; if they had their freest choice, they had rather live in the love of the creature than in the love of God; and the pleasures of the flesh than the heavenly life. But now they that have the spirit of adoption, and are inclined to the love of God and holiness, have hearts suited to their work: Ps. xl. 8, 'Thy law is in my heart'; and Heb. viii. 10, 'I will put my law into their minds, and write them upon their hearts.' They obey, not from the urgings of the law from without, but from the poise and inclination of the new nature; not barely as enjoined, but as inclined. They do not say, that this were no duty, or this sinful course lawful! but, how I love thy law! Ps. cxix. 97. 'that my ways were directed!' Ps. cxix. 5. They do not groan and complain of the strictness of the law, but of the remainders of corruption, Rom. vii. 24. Not, who will free me from the law? but who will free me from this body of death? Their will is to serve God more and better, not to be excused from the duties of holiness, or serving him at all.

[B.] By the cause of their trouble about what they have done, or left undone. They are not troubled for the offence done to God, but their own danger; not for sin, but merely the punishment; as Esau sought the blessing with tears, when he had lost it, Heb. xii. 17. He was troubled, but why? *Non quia vendiderat, sed quia perdiderat.* Not because he sold it, which was his sin; but lost the privileges of the birthright, which was his misery. So many carnal men, whose hearts are in a secret love and league with their lusts, yet are troubled about their condition, not because they are afraid to sin, but afraid to be damned; it is not God's displeasure they care for, but their own safety. The young man went away sad and grieved, Mark x. 22, because he had great possessions; because he could not reconcile his covetous mind with Christ's counsel and direction. Felix trembled, being convinced of sins, which he was loath to discontinue and break off. Slavish fear, though it doth not divorce the heart from its lusts, yet it raiseth trouble about them.

Use 3. Is to press you to get rid of this spirit of bondage, and to prevail upon it more and more. For motives,

[A.] It is dishonourable to God, and supposeth strange prejudices and misrepresentations of God; as if his government were a kind of tyranny, grievous and hurtful to man; and we think him a hard master whom it is impossible to please; as the evil and slothful servant, Mat. xxv. 24, 25, '1 knew that thou were an hard man, reaping where thou hast not sowed, and gathering where thou hast not strawed; and I was afraid, and went and hid thy talent in the earth.' His fear was the cause of his negligence and unfathfulness; which fear is begotten in us by a false opinion of God, which rendereth him dreadful, rigorous, and terrible to the soul. While we look upon God through the glass of our guilty fears, we draw a strange picture of him in our minds, as if he were a rigid lawgiver, and a severe avenger, harsh, and hard to be pleased, and we are therefore unwilling to submit to him.

[B.] It is prejudicial to us, in many regards.

(1.) It hindereth our free and delightful converse with God. The legal spirit hath no boldness in his presence, but is filled with tormenting fear and horror at the thoughts of him; the spirit of adoption giveth us confidence and boldness in prayer, Heb. iv 16; and Eph. iii. 1 2; but on the contrary, the spirit of bondage maketh us hang off from God. As Adam was afraid, and ran to the bushes, Gen. iii. 8; and David had a dark and uncomfortable spirit, and grew shy of God after his sin, Ps. xxxii. 3, 4, fain to issue forth an injunction or practical decree in the soul to bring his backward heart into his presence, ver. 5. 'And Cain went out from the presence of the Lord of Hosts' Gen. iv. 16, as unable to abide there, where the frequent ordinances of God might put him in remembrance of him. And Jam. ii. 19, 'The devils believe, and tremble'; they abhor their own thoughts of God, as reviving terror in them. The Papists think it boldness to go to God without the mediation and intercession of the saints; the original of that practice was slavish fear, when God had opened a door of access to himself.

[B.] It breaketh our courage in owning the ways of God, and truths of God. The apostle when he presseth Timothy not to be ashamed of the testimony of the Lord, nor his servants, and to be partakers of the afflictions of the gospel, urgeth this argument, 2 Tim. i. 7, 8, 'For we have not received the spirit of fear, but the spirit of love, and power, and of a sound mind: *pneuma doulias* is *pneuma deilias*, a poor, cowardly, dastardly spirit, mated or overcome with every difficulty; but now a spirit confirmed in the love of God, and the faith and hope of the gospel, is a spirit of power and fortitude. 'The righteous is as bold as a lion' Pro. xxviii. 1. Dan. iii. 17, 18, 'If it be so, our God whom we serve is able to deliver us from the burning fiery furnace, and he will deliver us out of thine hand, king! but if not, be it known unto thee, king, that we will not serve thy gods, nor worship the golden image which thou hast set up.' And Rom. viii. 37, 38, 'I am persuaded, that neither life, nor death, nor angels, nor principalities, nor powers, nor things present, nor things to come, nor height, nor depth, shall be able to separate us from the love of God which is in Christ Jesus our Lord.'

[C.] It hindereth the readiness and cheerfulness of our service, and crippleth our endeavours. The slothful servant was afraid, Luke xix. 21, 22. When we do not know whether we shall please or be accepted or no, it is a very discouraging thing; and we drive on heavily, when nothing appears to us but fear; but love maketh a willing people: 1 John v. 3, 'For this is the love of God, that we keep his command ments; and his commandments are not grievous.

[4.] It resisteth sin unwillingly; we had rather let it alone than go about it; the mortifying of lust is like the cuting off of an arm with a rusty saw; rather let go anything than sin; but grace furnisheth us with the most powerful arguments.

For means,

1. Cherish good thoughts of God. The spirit of bondage is increased upon us by unreasonable fears and jealousies of God'; The Lord is good, and doth good' Ps. cxix. 68. His commands are not grievous: Mat. xi. 30, 'My yoke is easy and my burden is light.' The trials sent us by him are not above measure, nor beyond strength: 1 Cor. x. 13, 'Who will not suffer you to be tempted above what you are able'; nor his punishments above deserving: Neh. ix. 13, 'Thou hast punished us less than we deserved.' He is not hard to be pleased, nor inexorable upon our infirmities: Mai. iii. 17, 'And I will spare them as a man spareth his own son that serveth him.' 'He is a rewarder of them that diligently seek him' Heb. xi. 6.

2. Study the nature and constitution of the gospel, which maketh rich preparation of grace, help, and comfort for you. This is God's act of oblivion, which easeth you of your troubles; for here God promiseth to blot out your transgressions, and remember your sins no more; this is a sanctuary and refuge for your distressed souls to fly unto, when pursued by the law's curse; the charter of your hopes, or the word of salvation which secureth you against the law's curse, or the fears of the damnation of hell. The law is good, as a rule of duty, but

the gospel is glorious, 1 Tim. i. 8, 11. In short, your souls will never sit easily within you, till you resolve not to seek for that in the law which is only to be found in the gospel, peace of conscience, and reconciliation with God; the law can save only the innocent; but the gospel pardoneth the penitent sinner. Look not for that in self, which is only to be found in Christ, a perfect righteousness and merit to appease God's justice, and propitiate him to us; this is only by the blood and obedience of Christ; never look for that on earth which is only to be had in heaven, which is exact and unspotted holiness, Jude 21. 'Then we are presented faultless in his presence.'

3. A hearty and sincere love to God: 1 John iv. 18, 'There is no fear in love, for perfect love casteth out fear, because fear hath torment, and he that feareth is not made perfect in love' He speaketh not of a child-like reverence of the divine majesty, or a carefulness not to displease him; but of slavish fear of condemnation, which is the life and soul of many men's religion; but they are never soundly converted till God hath their hearts, that is, their love. Now this strong and fervent love, arising from faith in Christ, driveth and forceth this tormenting fear out of the heart. Men will never be afraid of him whom they love; and on the other side, will not love him whom they look upon as ready to condemn them, and cast them into hell. Surely God will never damn the soul that loveth him; therefore if we would get rid of the fear of wrath or hell, let us love God with our highest and best affections. We have reason to love him, if we consider the wonder of his love and good will to sinners, manifested to us in and by Jesus Christ.

4. Live holily, and obey the motions of the sanctifying Spirit. We deprive ourselves of comfort by falling into sin; the more the Spirit is a sanctifier, the more a comforter. Holiness breedeth a generous confidence: 1 John iii. 2, 'Behold, now we are the sons of God' Gal. v. 18, 'But if ye be led by the Spirit, ye are not under the law' If we are not watchful against sin, our bondage returneth; therefore David saith, Ps. li. 12, 'Restore unto me the joy of thy salvation, and uphold me by thy free Spirit' The Holy Spirit withdraweth and suspendeth his comforts, when we walk vainly and loosely; then we cannot serve God with any delight and readiness of mind; it is not a free spirit, but a servile, that then governeth us, and influenceth our actions.

SERMON XXII

But ye have received the Spirit of adoption, whereby we cry, Abba, Father.

Romans VIII. 15.

IN the words we have,

First, A privilege, 'Ye have received the spirit of adoption'

Second. One special fruit and effect of it, 'Whereby we cry, Abba, Father'

In setting down the effect, the change is emphatical; ye received; we cry; he includeth himself, and puts in his own name together with theirs, to show that it is a privilege common to all that receive the new testament; the meanest and least of God's children have an affectionate and child-like way of praying unto God.

Doctrine That the spirit which we receive under the new covenant dispensation, is a spirit of adoption.

I shall explain these five things:

1. The state of adoption which we obtain under the new testament.

2. The spirit of adoption consequent thereupon.

3. Whether all that live under the new testament dispensation have the spirit of adoption.

4. Whether all that have it, know it.

5. The reasons why this is the fruit of the new covenant. dispensation. 1. What is the state of adoption? Our admission into God's family,

that he will be a father to us, and we shall be his children: 2 Cor. vi. 18, 'I will be a father unto you., and ye shall be my sons and daughters, saith the Lord Almighty' Which is a great privilege, if we consider three things, (1.) His relation to mankind in the general; (2.) His relation to the ancient church under the legal covenant; (3.) The estate wherein his grace found us, when he was pleased to take us into his family.

[A.] His relation to mankind in general. So he is the father of all the world, as he created them; and Adam is called the son of God, Luke iii. 38. He is a father to any, who giveth them being, and hath a right to govern them; so is God to us; he made us, and is the sole cause of our being and not being, and so hath a right in us to dispose of us at his own pleasure. But the relation that we have to God by adoption is distinct from the natural being; this is our new being, which we have from him as his redeemed ones; our natural being flowed from his benignity and common bounty, but our spiritual being from his special grace and love to us in Christ. By creation we are his children, as he formed us in the womb, and created the soul within us; called therefore the Father of spirits, Heb. xii. 9, in opposition to the fathers of our flesh; but he is our father by adoption, as we are regenerated by the Holy Ghost: John i. 12, 13, 'To as many as received him, to them gave he power to become the sons of God; being born not of blood, nor of the will of the flesh, nor of the will of man, but of God.' Our new birth and spiritual being in Christ, is the next ground of our adoption, and so we come into a nearer relation to him, that we may be capable of receiving the fruits of his special love; it is the benefit of our redemption applied by his sanctifying Spirit to all them that shall be heirs of life. By the common relation, God hath a title to our dearest love, but we have no title to his highest benefits; and therefore he is our father in a more comfortable sense, as we are his workman ship in Christ.

[B.] His relation to the ancient church through the legal covenant. So God was a father to them, and they were his children; for Israel was called his first-born, Exod. iv. 22, in opposition to other nations, who were left to perish in their own ways; and their descendants are called 'the children of the kingdom' Mat. viii. 12, because they had the ordinances and means of grace. But the gospel-church is properly 'the church of the first-born' Heb. xii. 23, as they have a clearer knowledge of the privileges belonging to God's children, and a larger participation, and more comfortable use of them; and so are freed from that rigour and servitude which belonged to the first administration of the covenant of grace. They have that which answereth the privilege of primo geniture, *jus sacerdotis*[33], *et jus haereditatis*. The right of priesthood, as they are 'a royal priesthood' 1 Pet. ii. 9'; made kings and priests unto God' Rev. i. 5, because they 'offer up spiritual sacrifices accept able to God by Jesus Christ' 1 Pet. ii. 5. They are separated by the election of God from the rest of the world, and have an unction from his Holy Spirit, 1 John ii. 20; and so are qualified to offer up themselves, Rom. xii. 1, and prayers and praises, and alms unto God, Heb. xiii. 15, 16. The other privilege of the birthright is, *jus haereditatis*; the first-born had a double portion, not only of possessions, but of dignity and honour, above their brethren. All God's children are heirs, and heirs of the heavenly inheritance; the multitude of co-heirs doth not lessen the inheritance, nor make the privilege less glorious; they are 'heirs of salvation' Heb. i. 14.

[C.] The estate wherein his grace found us, when he was pleased to take us into his family. We were by nature children of wrath, wretched children, Eph. ii. 3, that had deprived ourselves of the inheritance, wasted our patrimony, forfeited our right to the promises; but our inheritance is redeemed, and the forfeiture taken off by Christ; we are brought back again into the family, dignified with the privileges of the first-born, made priests unto God; and above all his other creatures, do become his special portion: Jam. i. 18, 'Of his own will begat he us, to be a kind of first fruits of his creatures'; and made heirs of the kingdom, James ii. 5. Now for us to have the blessed God, whom we had so often offended, to become our reconciled father in Christ, what wonderful love is this! That we should be admitted into the church of the first-born, have free liberty to worship God, and have a right to such a blessed and glorious inheritance!

2. What is the spirit of adoption? First, We are made sons, and then we have the Spirit of his Son, Gal. iv. 6; being adopted into God's family, we have a spirit suitable. They that use to adopt children give them some kind of token to express their love; so here is a gift

---

[33] Right of holy price (?)

answerable to the dignity of our estate, and the love of a father, and that is the gift of the Spirit; the dignity is inward and spiritual; and the gift answereth it: 'He hath sent the Spirit of his Son into your hearts.' God would not distinguish the good from the bad, the heirs of promise from the children of wrath, by the blessings of his common providence; but with what suiteth better with that intimate communion that we have with him as a father: 1 John iii. 24, 'Hereby we know that we dwell in God, and God dwelleth in us, by his Spirit that he hath given us.' Spiritual things are best manifested and discovered to us in a spiritual manner, and by the effects proper to them. Secondly, it is the highest demonstration of God's love to us. In giving us worldly things, he giveth something without himself; but in giving us the Spirit he giveth us himself; for the Godhead is undivided, and God hath no greater thing to give us than himself; as the apostle saith, Heb. vi. 13, that when God had no greater thing to swear by, he swore by himself, so we may say here, it was the evidence of God's love to Christ as mediator: John iii. 34, 'He loved him, and gave him. the Spirit without measure'; so those that are Christ's, because God loveth them, he giveth them the Spirit. Other things may be given in anger, but not the Spirit: Prov. iii. 32, 'The f reward is an abomination to the Lord, but his secret is with the righteous'; implying, that those that are an abomination to the Lord may have other things, and perish forever; but if his secret be with us, his illuminating, sanctifying, comforting Spirit, we have a sure pledge of his love. The context showeth wicked men may have worldly felicity, even to envy, but they have not his secret, which the righteous have. Though their condition be very mean and base in the world, he dealeth with them as with friends, yea, as children; the one hath the visible blessings, the other hath his secret, the inward comforts and operations of his Spirit.

But yet the business is not dispatched. The text speaketh not only of the gift of the Spirit, but of the spirit of adoption. What is that? Answer. We must distinguish between the spirit of regeneration, and the spirit of adoption; they are two acts of the same Spirit, and the one maketh way for the other; yet the consideration of them is different. The Holy Ghost, as a Spirit of regeneration, doth close us first with Christ; and afterwards, as a Spirit of adoption, maketh his abode in our hearts. As a Spirit of regeneration, he worketh in us the first grace, and causeth us to believe unto justification and adoption r and having made his entry into our souls after believing, he is given to us in a more eminent manner than before, and doth possess us in the name of Christ, as his agent, and keepeth a-foot his interest in our souls. The spirit of regeneration is tied to no condition, but is dispensed according to the good pleasure of God; only we are to use the means; to attend upon the word and pray, and our heavenly Father will give the Holy Spirit to them that ask him, Luke xi. 13. If any miss the gift, it is of themselves; if they have it, it is the mere grace of God. But the Spirit of adoption is tied to conditions, and is promised to those that with true faith and repentance do seek after the grace of God in Jesus Christ: Eph. i. 13, 'After ye believed, ye received the Holy Spirit of promise'; and Gal. iii. 14, 'Receive the promise of the Spirit by faith'; and Acts ii. 38, 'Repent, and be baptized for the remission of sins, and you shall receive the gift of the Holy Ghost'; and Prov. i. 23, 'Turn you at my reproof, and I will pour out my Spirit upon you;' Acts xix. 2, 'Have ye received the Holy Ghost since ye believed? 'John vii. 39, 'This he spake of the

Spirit, which they that believe on him should receive'; Acts v. 32, 'The Holy Ghost, which he hath given to them that obey him.' In these and many more places, the Spirit of adoption and further sanctification is spoken of. As a Spirit of regeneration, he buildeth an house for himself; and then, as a Spirit of adoption, he dwelleth in the house so built and furnished; as bees first make their cells, and then dwell in them. By repentance and faith there is a fit mansion prepared for him, and then he taketh up- his residence and abode in us. The first grace is given that we may believe; the second upon believing; the first is the Spirit's renewing; the second is the Spirit's inhabiting.

But yet the business is not finished. The Spirit is called the Spirit of adoption, from his use and effect; and implieth that work of the Holy Spirit whereby the souls of believers are framed to a son-like disposition. One effect is mentioned in the text, his inclining us to have recourse to God as a Father': The spirit of adoption, whereby we cry, Abba, Father'; but other things are intended. They may be reduced to these three heads: 1. Child-like love. 2. Child-like obedience. And 3. Child-like hope and dependence.

[A.] A child-like love to God. The design of the gospel is the revelation of God's love to us, and the recovery of our love to God; therefore the work of the Spirit is to reveal the love and mercy of God to sinners or the way of reconciliation to God by Christ; not God's love to us in particular at first. For we do not as yet see our own particular interest, but come afterward, when we are reconciled to God, and live in obedience to him. Then he becometh a witness to us, verse 16; but at first he openeth a door of hope to us, by revealing God's love to sinners on gracious terms; it is revealed in the gospel; but it is 'shed abroad in our hearts through the Holy Ghost' Rom. v. 5. That love spoken of there respects the offer of pardon and life founded on the death of Christ; therefore a spirit of love bred in us by the wonderful grace discovered in the gospel, is the first effect of the spirit of adoption. It is great love that God will so freely pass by our many offences, and adopt and take us into his family; that we do no longer fly from him as a condemning God, but have recourse to him as a pardoning God. This love is manifested by our desires after him, delight in him, and frequent recourse to him in prayer, representing all our grievances and wants to him. This crying to him as a father mentioned in the text, through the hope we have by Christ, is the instinct of the spirit of adoption.

[B.] A child-like obedience. The great duty of children is to love, please, and honour their father; and God standing in this relation to us, expecteth it from us: Mai. i. 6, 'If I be a father, where is mine honour? If I be a master, where is my fear? 'He will do all that can be expected from a father, a-nd therefore we must do all that belongeth to children: So 1 Pet. i. 14, 'As dear children, not fashioning yourselves to the former lusts of your ignorance'; and verse 17, 'If ye call on the Father' etc. 'Be ye followers of God, as dear children,' Eph. v. 1. Now the Spirit enableth and inclineth us to an affectionate and child-like way of serving God; partly, as he reneweth and healeth our natures, and sanctifieth us unto God: 'I will put my Spirit into them, and they shall walk in my ways' Ezek. xxxvi. 27; and partly, by gratitude and filial love he possesseth us with a desire and care to please him. For as the benefits we have from God's fatherly love are the best, and greatest, and surest; so it calleth for the best returns of our thankfulness and obedience; the privileges of our adoption being the sweetest and strongest bonds and obligations to duty that can be laid upon us; therefore it must be done in. a free and child-like way.

[C.] A child-like hope and dependence, not only for what we want in this world, but chiefly for the happiness of another and better world. What may we not expect from a father, and from an almighty father? If God be your father, you can want no good thing, either for soul or body. Our Lord dissuaded anxiety and carefulness of mind upon this ground, because we have a father, and a father that careth for us, Mat. vi. 25, 32. But chiefly, he doth incline us to the blessed inheritance; being made children, we begin to look after a child's portion. He revealeth the truth and worth of it, Eph. i. 17, 18; and farther confirmeth us of the certainty of it, as a pledge and earnest, by working and dwelling in our hearts: 2 Cor. i. 22, 'Who hath sealed us, and given us the earnest of the Spirit'; prepareth us, fits us for it: 2 Cor. v. 5, 'He that hath wrought us to this selfsame thing, is God'; raised our hearts to long after it, and comforts our hearts with the hopes of it: Rom. viii. 23, 'And not only they, but ourselves also, which have the first fruits of the Spirit, even we ourselves groan within ourselves, waiting for the adoption, to wit, the redemption of our bodies;' and so begetteth that free, noble, and princely spirit which upholdeth us with courage in the midst of all trials and difficulties, and maketh us go on cheerfully in the work of holiness, waiting for the end of our faith, the salvation of our souls. This in short, is the spirit of adoption, a spirit of love, holiness, and heavenly-minded- ness. Love inclineth us to God; holiness suiteth us to our work, that we may have a complacency in it; heavenliness giveth us a confidence, and a princely noble spirit, that is gotten above the hopes and fears of the world.

3. Whether all that live under the New Testament dispensation, have the spirit of adoption?

Answer. No; But take these considerations:

[A.] This showeth what the doctrine of the gospel can do, and should do: But it doth not always do it, because many come under the profession of the gospel, but not under the power of it. But this is the Spirit that came down to accompany the gospel, and the ministry of it; and if it be not received and entertained by men, they may blame themselves. The gospel is serviceable to this end and purpose, to produce such a spirit. If men carry it as if they knew not whether there be a Spirit of adoption, yea or no, there is no fault or defect in the gospel, but they are wanting to themselves, strangers to the grace of the covenant under which they live, by their own negligence and folly. If manna fall about the tents of Israel, and the people will not go to gather it to fill their omer, they may starve, though the bread of heaven be dispensed by such a liberal provision. The Spirit is ready, but they are lazy; the Spirit, by accident, is a cause of servile fear; but these motions are his proper effects.

[B.] A superficial Christianity is rewarded with common gifts, but the real Christianity with special graces. All that profess the faith, and are baptized into Christ, Gal. iii. 26, 27, are visibly adopted by God into his family, and are under a visible administration of the covenant of grace. So far as they are adopted into God's family, so far they are made partakers of the Spirit. Christ giveth to common Christians those common gifts which he giveth not to the heathen world; knowledge of the mysteries of godliness; abilities of utterance and speech about spiritual and heavenly things; some affection also to them, called 'tasting of the good word, the heavenly gift, and the powers of the world to come' Heb. vi. These will not prove us true Christians, or really in God's special favour, but only visible professed Christians.

[C.] Among the sincere, some have not the spirit of adoption at so full a rate as others have; neither so pure and fervent a love to God; nor such a respectful obedience and submission to him; nor such an holy confidence and boldness, becoming that great happiness which they are called unto, who have the right and hope of the blessed inheritance; and so not so much of that son-like disposition, which the Spirit worketh by revealing the love and mercy of God, contained in the gospel, in the hearts of his people. Some do more improve their privileges than others do; now they cannot rationally expect the best and richest fruits of this gift, and to be enabled and enlarged by the Spirit, who do not give such ready entertainment and obedience to his motions, as the more serious and fruitful Christian doth.

4. But do all that have it, know that they have it? I answer,

[A.] The spirit of adoption is in some weak, and therefore not so perceptible as it is in others; for small and weak things are hardly discerned. All God's children have the spirit of adoption in the effects, though not in the sense and feeling of it. They have the spirit of comfort, though not the comfort of it; for 'if any have not the Spirit of Christ, they are none of his' Rom. viii. 9. The witness of his Spirit is spoken of, as distinct from receiving the Spirit, ver. 16; there is a child-like inclination and impression left upon them, though they know it not, own it not. There is a difference between the thing itself, and the degree; we cannot say we have not the spirit of adoption, because we have not so much of this spirit, calming our hearts, rebuking our fears, and filling us with joy and peace in believing. The Spirit was given to Christ without measure, but to Christians in a different measure and proportion, as they yield up themselves more or less to the conduct of his grace, and overcome the enemies of their peace, the devil, the world, and the flesh. The impression is left upon some in a smaller, upon some in a larger character; all are not of a growth and size; some are more real Christians, others only *en onomati*[34]: eminent grace will more discover itself, than a little grace under a heap of imperfections; a fervent love will be felt, and a lively hope of heaven demonstrate itself, and an exact obedience less liable to dispute, as we increase in love, and heavenly mindedness; so the Spirit discovereth his presence in us.

[2.] Where the Spirit of adoption acteth at the lowest rate, there is something to difference it from the spirit of bondage.

(1.) They are carried on to wait upon God upon gospel grounds, though they cannot apply the comforts, and enter themselves heirs to the privileges thereof; some know they are of the truth, and can make out their title with clearness and satisfaction: 1 John iii. 14, 'And

---

[34] Greek: "in the name"

hereby we know that we are of the truth, and shall assure our hearts before him'; others depend on God's general offer, while their claim and sincerity is as yet questionable. God offereth to be a father in Christ to all penitent believers, and so we are encouraged to come to him by Christ; the apostle telleth us, Heb. vii. 19, that the gospel brought in a better hope, by virtue of which we draw nigh to God. There is a child-like inclination, when there is not a child-like familiarity and boldness; the soul cannot keep away from God, but will come to him that he may pardon our sins, and heal our souls, and save our persons. Now this is the spirit of adoption in the lower, or more obscure way of addressing ourselves to God as a father.

(2.) There are child-like groans, as well as child-like comforts; com pare Rom. viii. 26, 'The Spirit itself maketh intercession for us, with sighs and groans, which cannot be uttered'; with 1 Pet. i. 8, 'In whom, though now you see him not, yet believing, ye rejoice with joy unspeakable, and full of glory.' In some the Spirit only discovereth himself by hungering and thirsting after righteousness; in others he worketh peace which passeth all understanding, and joy unspeakable and full of .glory.

(3.) There is a child-like reverence, when there is not a child-like confidence. They are afraid to offend their heavenly Father, though they cannot challenge all the fruits and effects of his fatherly love as belonging to them; when they cannot own him as a father with delightful confidence, yet they dare not offend him; for all God's children have a child-like love to him, when they have not a full sense and assurance of his paternal love to them; for he hath a title to our dearest love, before we can make out a title to his benefits. Now they that love God, hate evil, Ps. xcvii. 10; are tender of omitting any duty, or committing any offence. Where there is this holy awe, there is a spirit of adoption; it is an owning of God as a father: 1 Pet. i. 17, 'If ye call on the Father,' &c., and therefore this reverence we call filial fear.

(4.) The heart is carried out to heavenly things, though we cannot call them ours; all that are children do look after a child's portion. There is a twofold hope, First, a hope which is the effect of regeneration, 1 Pet. i. 3; and a hope which is the effect of experience, Rom. v. 4. Now this puts a difference between the spirit of bondage, and the servile mercenary spirit, when the current of thine affections is carried out after the eternal inheritance; servants and mercenaries must have pay in hand; they covenant with you from day to day, or from quarter to quarter, or from year to year; a child in the family tarrieth for a child's portion: Mat. vi. 4, 'When thou dost thine alms, do not sound a trumpet before thee, as the hypocrites do in the synagogue, and in the street; they have their reward'. Present wages they look for, discharge God from other things; if he will give them the honour and pleasure of the world, they are satisfied, and look for no more.

5. Why this is the fruit of the new covenant dispensation? There are three things which must not be severed, [A.] The object. [B.] A powerful agent. [C.] The disposition of the subject thence resulting.

[A.] There is an object, and that is the gospel, offering pardon and life, reconciliation with God, and the everlasting fruition of him in glory. In the gospel or new covenant, we have the highest discovery of God's fatherly goodness, that he might be more amiable and lovely to us, and be loved by us. The great end of reconciling and saving lost man by Christ, his wonderful condescension in his incarnation, life, sufferings and death, was to commend his love to us: Rom. v. 8, 'Herein God commended his love to us, in that when we were yet sinners, Christ died for us'. To this end also tend his merciful covenant and promises, that we might not look upon God as a condemning judge, but as a gracious and reconciled father, offering to be so to all that will accept Christ, and submit to him. God would not immediately beget this persuasion in our minds by his own secret power, but use this objective means, work upon our love by love, because he will work on man agreeably to the nature of man; his covenant shall speak him a father, that we may apprehend him as a father.

[B.] There is an internal powerful agent, and that is the Spirit. Besides the external objective means, there must be an internal effective cause; for though God's fatherly love doth shine resplendently without us, in the person of the mediator, and the riches of the gospel; yet the dead and dark heart of man is not affected with it: John i. 5, 'And the light shineth in darkness, and the darkness comprehendeth it not' till God shine into our hearts: 2 Cor. iv. 6, 'For God, who commanded the light to shine out of darkness, hath shined in our hearts, to give the light of the knowledge of the glory of God in the face of Jesus Christ'; unless this doctrine of God's fatherly love and grace be accompanied with his illuminating, sanctifying, comforting Spirit, who sheds abroad this love in our hearts which is revealed in the gospel.

[C.] The disposition thence resulting from the application of this object to us by the Spirit. Such as the object is, such are the affections stirred up in us; as by law-truths the Spirit worketh conviction, terrors of conscience, legal contrition, Acts ii. 37, and thence, bondage ariseth; so by the gospel, where God is represented as the Father of mercies, and the God and Father of our Lord Jesus Christ, and in him our God and Father, the impression must be suitable. This Spirit that worketh by the gospel, must needs be the spirit of adoption, or such a spirit as worketh a child-like disposition in us, for the impression must always be according to the stamp.

Use 1. To persuade us to look after the spirit of adoption. We never do seriously and closely Christianize, till we get it; but either have a literal Christianity, a form of knowledge in the gospel, without the life and power; or a legal, old-testament spirit. To quicken you, consider these motives or privileges which you will have by it,

[A.] Peace of conscience, a rest from those troubled and unquiet thoughts which otherwise would perplex us: Rom. xiv. 17, 'For the kingdom of God is not meat and drink, but righteousness, and peace, and joy in the Holy Ghost'; and Rom. xv. 13, 'Now the God of hope fill you with all joy and peace in believing.' This calm of mind differeth from the deadness and benumbedness of a stupid conscience; that is a thing we never laboured for, groweth upon us we know not how; it is maintained by idleness, rather than by watchfulness and diligence; and is inconsistent with serious thoughts of God and our eternal condition; but this is the fruit of our reconciliation with God, and those blessed privileges we enjoy in his family; it stirreth up admiration and thankfulness.

[B.] Liberty in prayer. For the great help we have in prayer is from the spirit of adoption: Zech. xii. 10, 'I will pour out upon you the spirit of grace and supplication.' That Spirit which cometh from the grace and free favour of God, stirring up child-like addresses to God, Rom. viii. 26; Jude. 21, 'Building up yourselves on your most holy faith, praying in the Holy Ghost.' Without this, our prayers are but a vain babbling.

[C.] Readiness in duty: 2 Cor. iii. 17, 'Where the Spirit of the Lord is, there is liberty.' They serve God with a free spirit; the holy life is carried on with more sweetness and success; riot by compulsion, but with ready mind: Ps. li. 12, 'Uphold me with thy free Spirit'; John viii. 32, 'If the truth shall make you free, then are you free indeed' Men are under shackles and bondage if they have not the spirit of adoption; they drive on heavily, have not largeness of heart, and love to God, heaven, and holiness: Ps. cxix. 32, 'I will run the ways of thy commandments, when thou shalt enlarge my heart.' When the heart is suited to the work, there needs no other urgings; but if we force a course of religion upon ourselves, contrary to our own inclination, all is harsh, and ingrate, and cannot hold long.

[D.] Comfort in afflictions. Their true consolation and support in afflictions is the spirit of adoption: Heb. xii. 5, 'Have you forgotten the exhortation which speaketh unto you as unto children?' and therefore he pursueth it all along. They that enjoy the privileges of the family, must submit to the discipline of the family; God will take his own course in bringing up his children; 'he scourgeth every son whom he receiveth,' Heb. xii. 6, 7, 8. While we have flesh in us, there is use for the rod; if God should suffer us to go on in our sins, we were not legitimate, but degenerate children; children take it patiently if beaten by their parents for their faults. Parents may err through want of wisdom; their chastisement is arbitrary and irregular; there is more of compassion than passion in God. God's rod is regulated with perfect wisdom, ordered by the highest love, and tends to the greatest end, our holiness here, and happiness forever; and we have Christ's example, John xviii. 11, 'The cup which my Father hath- given me, shall I not drink it?' The bitterest potions come not from God as a judge, but as a father; are tempered by a father's hand.

[E.] Hope of the benefits of the new covenant, pardon and life. First, Pardon. We often forget the duty of children, but God doth not forget the bowels of a father; our adoption giveth us hope that he- will not deal severely with us, Mai. iii. 17; Ps. ciii. 13. The relation of a child is more durable, not so easily broken off, as that of a servant; a child is a child still, and therefore allowed to remain in the family, when a servant must be gone. Secondly, For life everlasting and glory: Rom. viii. 17, 'And if children, then heirs, heirs of God, and joint heirs with Christ; if so be that we suffer with him, that we may also be glorified with him.' 1 John iii. 1, 2, The spirit of adoption doth both encourage, and incline us to wait for it, Rom. viii. 25. But what shall we do to get this spirit of adoption?

(1.) It is certain that the gift of the Spirit is the fruit of our reconciliation with God. The general reconciliation with mankind, was evidenced by pouring out the Spirit; personal and particular reconciliation with God, is the ground of giving the spirit of adoption to us: Rom. v. 11, 'We joy in God, through our Lord Jesus Christ, by whom we have received the atonement.' Therefore do what God requireth in order to reconciliation; enter into conditions of peace; enter into covenant with God; abhor your former disobedience; cast away the weapons of defiance; and love God, and delight in him.

(2.) Steep your minds in frequent thoughts of God's fatherly goodness: 1 John iii. 1, 'Behold what manner of love is this, that we should be called the sons of God!' Consider it, and admire it!

Use 2. Reflection. Have we the spirit of adoption? It is known,

[A.] By a kind of naturalness to come to God, and open our hearts to him; in all our wants to go and cry, Abba, Father. The spirit of adoption much worketh and discovereth itself in prayer; to cry to our Father is an act becoming the sons of God; the manner is fervent, affectionate; this cry is not by the tongue, but by the heart; the Lord needeth no interpreter between him and the hearts of his children; he that heareth without ears can interpret our desires, though not uttered by the tongue; desires are strong cries: Ps. x. 17, 'Thou hast heard the desires of the humble; Ps. xxxviii. 9, 'Lord! All my desire is before thee, and my groaning is not hid from thee.' This crying is opposite to that careless formality and deadness, which is in other men's prayers; this crying to God, as one that is able and ready to help us, is a great fruit of the spirit of adoption; it is a childlike boldness.

[B.] A childlike ingenuousness in the course of obedience to him; both in our abstaining from sin, as the Rechabites are an emblem: Jer. xxxv. 6, 'We dare not break the commands of our father' and in a ready diligence in our obedience: 2 Cor. v. 14, 'The love of God constraineth us; for we thus judge, if one died for all, then were all dead' &c. The will of our Father is instead of all reasons; Christ ever urged this, 'This is the will of my Father' John vi. 26, 38. So to Christians, 1 Thes. v. 18, 'This is the will of God in Christ concerning you': 1 Thes. iv. 3, 'This is the will of God, even your sanctification.' That is enough, beyond all enforcements.

[C.] As to the inheritance, they are very chary of it, and will not hazard the hope and comfort of it upon easy terms: Heb. xii. 16, 'Let there not be found a profane person, as Esau, who sold his birth-right for a mess of pottage'; 1 Kings xxi. 3, 'And Naboth said to Ahab, the Lord forbid it me, that I should give the inheritance of my father to thee.'

Use 3. Is direction to us in the Lord's supper. This is the seal of the new covenant; the table which God keepeth for the entertainment of his family; the feast for souls; God's children are sure of welcome; it is children's bread we eat; we come hither both to remember the grounds of our adoption, and to receive the comfort of it; we come to meditate on the fatherly love of God, and to get a new taste and experience of it in our own souls. Here we have special communion with him as children with a father; we come for a further participation of the Spirit, 'for we all drink into one Spirit' 1 Cor. xii. 13. Here we look up unto God, and in our hearts cry, Abba, Father. We bind ourselves also to perform the duty of children; with new resolution to submit to his fatherly government, both in his laws and providences, to his commanding and disposing will; and we lift up our hope for the eternal inheritance.

SERMON XXIII

The Spirit itself witnesseth to our spirits, that we are the children.

Romans. VIII 16.

IN the words we have, 1. The privilege assured: *That we are the children of God*. 2. The double testimony by which it is confirmed, *The Spirit itself beareth witness to our spirits*; or if you will, here are *testes, et testimonium*; the thing witnessed, that we are the children of God; and the witnesses, they are two, the Spirit itself, and our spirits; and in the mouth of two or three witnesses everything is established. The Spirit itself is the Holy Ghost, and our spirits are our renewed consciences.

Doctrine That our adoption into God's family is evidenced by the testimony of the Spirit to our spirits.

First, I shall show you the worth and value of the privilege; Secondly, Speak something of this double testimony by which it is assured to us.

First, It is certainly a great privilege, for we are excited to consider it with wonder and reverence: 1 John iii. 1, 'Behold what manner of love the Father hath bestowed upon us, that we should be called the sons of God!' It is a blessed privilege, questionless, to have God for our father, and Christ for our elder brother, and heaven for our portion; what can we desire more? And this will appear to you, if you consider,

1. The person adopting: the great and glorious God, who is so far above us, so happy within himself, and needeth not us, nor our choicest love and service; who had a Son of his own, Jesus Christ the only begotten of the Father, who thought it no robbery to be equal with him in power and glory, Phil. ii. 6; a son that was 'the express image of his person,' Heb. i. 3'; the son of his love,' Col. i. 13; in whom his soul found full complacency: Prov. viii. 30, 'I was daily his delight, rejoicing always before him'. If men adopt, it is *in orbitatis solatium*[35], a remedy found out for the comfort of them that have no children. Seldom was it heard that a father who had a son should adopt a son; therefore it heightens the privilege, that God should vouchsafe to poor creatures such a dear and honourable relation to himself.

2. The persons who were adopted; miserable sinners, who were once strangers and enemies, Col. i. 21'; children of wrath, even as others' Eph. ii. 3; who had cast away the mercies of their creation, and involved themselves in the curse. Now that strangers should be taken into the family, and put in the place of children, and dealt with as children; that enemies should riot only be reconciled, but have liberty to own the blessed God as their father in Christ; that children of wrath should be called to inherit a blessing; that those who had so often offended God, and were become slaves to Satan, should be called into the

---

[35] Loss of comfort

liberty of the children of God; this is that which we may wonder at, and say, Behold what manner of love is this!

3. The dignity itself; compared,

[A.] With the honours of the world. David saith, 1 Sam. xviii. 23, 'Seemeth it a light thing to you to be a king's son-in-law?' We may with better reason say, Is it nothing to be taken into God's family, and to become sons and daughters of the Most High God? All relations may blush and hide their faces in comparison of this; all the splendid titles which are so ambitiously affected by the world, are but empty shows and gilded vanities, and do much come short of this privilege, both in honour and profit. Therefore it is a greater instance of the love of God, than if he had made us monarchs of the world; or if a man could deduce his pedigree from an uninterrupted line of nobles and princes. Alas! How much better is it to be born of the Spirit, than of the froth of the blood? and to have a title that will be our honour and interest to all eternity, than to be distinguished from others by a title that will cease at the grave's mouth?

[B.] Compared with God's relation to other creatures. There is a relation between God and all his creatures; as he gave being to all, so he hath an interest and propriety in all. Sun, and moon, and stars are called his servants, Ps. cxix. 91; all creatures are subject to the law of his over-ruling providence; but man is under his proper government. Adam, by the covenant of works, was rather God's subject, and hired servant, than his son. The people of Israel were his children; but as children in their non-age; for 'an heir as long as he is a child (Gal. iv. 1), differeth little from a servant, though he be lord of all'. A servile spirit was upmost in that dispensation. With respect to the covenant of grace, we are most strictly said to be children of God; Gal. iii. 26, 'For ye are all children of God by faith in Christ Jesus'. Some live only under the visible administration of the new covenant, but not under the efficacy and power; and by the ordinances of the gospel have the badges of liberty, but they are not free indeed, sons indeed. There are among them others whom God hath begotten by his Spirit, and adopted and taken into his family; he hath a paternal affection towards them, and they a filial disposition towards him; he hath a paternal care and providence over them, and they have a filial confidence and dependence on him; he expects the honour of a father, and they may expect the privileges of children. His special relation is distinct from his common relation to other men, for it proceedeth not from his common goodness, but his special and peculiar love. The whole commerce and communion that is between us and him, is on God's part, fatherly; on our part, child-like; he giveth us his choicest benefits, and we perform to him the best service we can.

4. The manner how it is brought about.

[A.] The first foundation of it was laid in the election of God. He is the bottom-stone in this building: Eph. i. 5, 'Predestinated to the adoption of children, according to the good pleasure of his will'. Now what are we, that the thoughts of God should be taken up about us, so long ago?

[B.] Before God's eternal purposes could be executed, and conveniently made known to the world, redemption by Christ was necessary. Therefore it is said, Gal. iv. 4, 5, that he was 'made of a woman, made under the law, that we might receive the adoption of children.' Sin needed to be expiated by the Son of God in our nature, before God would bestow his honour upon us; Christ was to be our brother, before God could be our father; to take a mother upon earth, that we might have a father in heaven; and to endure the law's curse, before we could be instated in the blessing.

[C.] It is necessary that we should be regenerated and born of God, before it can be applied to us. For this new relation dependeth upon the new birth; and none are adopted but those that are regenerated, and renewed to the image arid likeness of God. Nominal Christians are bastards, and not sons; not illegitimate, but degenerate children. The relative change goeth before the real: John i. 12, 13, 'To as many as received him, to them gave he power to become the sons of God; which are born not of blood, nor of the will of the flesh, nor of the will of man, but of God.' And the next foundation of this relation is not our being, which we have from God as a creator, but our new being, which we have from him as our father in Christ. As we are men, God is a governor to us, and we are his subjects; as we are new men, God is a father to us, and we are his children.

[D.] The immediate issue of 'regeneration is faith: John i. 12, 'To as many as received him, to them gave he power to become the sons of God, even to as many as believe in his name.' Receiving Christ is an hearty consent to take Christ to the ends for which God offereth him: namely, that he may be our lord and saviour, that we depending upon the merit of his obedience and sacrifice, and assurance of his covenant and promises, may obey his laws, and wait for our final reward.

5. The benefits occurring to us thereby. I shall instance in three:

[A.] The gift of the Spirit, to be our sanctifier, guide, and comforter. This is a gift which he giveth to none but his children, and which he giveth to all his children; a gift which suiteth with the greatness and love of our Father; and is absolutely necessary for us as children. God as a creator giveth us our natural endowments; but as a father in Christ he giveth us his Spirit: Gal. iv. 6, 'And because ye are sons, God hath sent forth the Spirit of his Son into your hearts' If we have this high privilege of adoption, we have also the Spirit of adoption, to reside and dwell in our hearts as our sanctifier, guide, and comforter. As a sanctifier he doth first change our hearts, and transform us into the image of God in Christ: 2 Cor. iii. 18, 'But we all with open face, beholding as in a glass the glory of the Lord, are changed into his image from glory to glory'; And Titus iii. 5, 6, 'Not by works of righteousness which we have done, but according to his mercy he saved us, by the washing of regeneration, and the renewing of the Holy Ghost, which he hath shed on us abundantly through Jesus Christ our Saviour'; and so he maketh us children. But as bees first frame their cells, and then dwell in them; so he doth dwell in us, that he may further sanctify us, restraining us from sin: Rom. viii. 13, 'If ye live after the flesh, ye shall die; but if ye through the Spirit do mortify the deeds of the body, ye shall live.' And quickening us to holiness: Gal. v. 25, 'If we live in the Spirit, let us also walk in the Spirit.' As a guide, leading us into all truth: John xvi. 13, 'When the Spirit of truth is come, he shall guide us into all truth.' And regulating all the motions of the spiritual life: Rom. viii. 14, 'As many as are led by the Spirit'; especially our prayers: Jude 20, 'Praying in the Holy Ghost'; Rom. viii. 26,' 'We know not what we should pray for as we ought, but the Spirit maketh intercession for us' As a comforter, confirming our present interest and future hopes: 2 Cor. v. 5, 'Now he that hath wrought us for the self-same thing is God, who also hath given us the earnest of his Spirit' Indeed, the Spirit is not so necessarily a comforter as a sanctifier; yet a comforter he is; and if not so explicitly and manifestly, we may blame ourselves. This is God's allowance, and we deprive ourselves of the benefit of it by our own folly.

[B.] Such an allowance of temporal mercies as is convenient for us: Mat, vi. 32, 'For your heavenly Father knoweth that ye have need of all these things' A Christian hath two things to relieve him against all his distrustful fears and cares, adoption, and particular providence. He hath a father in heaven, and his father is not ignorant of his condition, nor mindless of it; and therefore though he hath little or nothing in hand, it is enough that his father keepeth the purse for him, whose care extendeth to all things, and all persons, and hath the hearts of men in his own hands, and performeth all things according to his own will. He knoweth their persons, necessities, and temptations; and if we trust him for our heavenly inheritance, we may trust him for our daily maintenance, which he vouchsafeth to the fowls of the air, and beasts of the field; yea, to his enemies, while they are sinning against him, dishonouring his name, oppressing his servants, opposing his interest in the world. He that feedeth a kite, will he not feed a child? He that supplieth his enemies, will he not take care of his friends? Those of his own family? Indeed, he chooseth rather to profit us, than please us, in his dispensations; but it is your duty to refer all to his wisdom and love.

[C.] Eternal blessedness is also the fruit of this adoption: Rom. viii. 17, 'If sons, then heirs, co-heirs with Christ' As soon as we are taken into God's family, we have a right to the blessed inheritance; and the right and hope that we have now, is -enough to counterbalance all temptations. Alas, what are all the carnal pleasures and delights of sin, which tempt us to disobey our Father, to those blessed things which he hath provided for us in heaven! It was Esau's profaneness to sell his birth-right: Heb. xii. 16. So all the fears and sorrows of the present life: Luke xii 32, 'Fear not, little flock, it is your Father's good pleasure to give you a kingdom'; if we have the kingdom at the last, it is no great matter what we suffer by the way; but hereafter we shall fully receive the fruits of our obedience: Rom. viii. 23, 'We ourselves groan within ourselves, waiting for the adoption, to wit, the redemption of our bodies'. In heaven we have the fullest and largest demonstration of God's love and favour. It is love now, and grace now, that he will take us into his family, and employ us in his service; but then it is another manner of love, when taken not only into his family, but presence and palace; where we have not only a right, but possession; not only some remote service and ministration, but ever lastingly enjoying, delighting, and praising God.

Secondly. We now come to the proof and testimony of our interest in this privilege, 'The Spirit beareth witness with our spirit.' Here let us,

1. Open the double testimony.

2. What the one super-addeth above the other.

3. The necessity of their conjunction to our full comfort. [A.] The nature of this double testimony; and there,

[A.] Let us begin with that which is more known to us, and under stood by us, and that is the testimony of a renewed conscience. Let us consider it, as conscience, and as renewed.

(1.) As conscience. There is a secret spy within us, that observeth all that we think, or speak, or do, Rom. ii. 15, 'Their conscience bearing them witness, and their thoughts in the meantime accusing or excusing'. Now this conscience must not be slighted. Partly, in respect of ourselves, because it is so intimate to us; it is a spy in our bosoms, and can give a better judgment of us and our actions, than anything else can. The judgment of the world by way of applause or censure, is foreign, and grounded upon appearance; therefore not so much to be valued: 1 Cor. ii. 11, 'The spirit of a man which is in him, knoweth the things of a man' Who knoweth more of us than we do ourselves? And this witness cannot be suspected of partiality and ill will; for what is dearer to 'ourselves than ourselves? Therefore if our hearts condemn us, what shall be said for us? 1 John iii. 20, 21, 'For if our hearts condemn us, God is greater than our hearts, and knoweth all things. Beloved, if our hearts condemn us not, then have we confidence towards God.' And partly, because of its relation to God; it is called 'the candle of the Lord' Prov. xx. 27; it is God's deputy judge, and in the place of God to us; and therefore if it doth accuse or excuse, it is to be regarded, for it is before God's tribunal that it doth condemn or acquit us. It is his sentence that we are to stand in fear and dread of; to whom doth it accuse us, but to God? Whose wrath doth it fear, but God's, even then when there is no outward cause of dread and fear? Conscience is the vicegerent of the supreme judge; partly, because of the rule it goeth by, which is the will of God, by which good and evil are distinguished; which is either revealed by the light of nature, or the light of Scripture. The light of nature; Rom. ii. 14, 15, 'For when the Gentiles, who have not the law, do by nature the things contained in the law; these having not the law, are a law to themselves, which show the work of the law upon their hearts; their consciences also bearing witness, and their thoughts the meanwhile accusing, or else excusing one another.' The apostle proveth the heathen had a law, because they had a conscience; for conscience ever inferreth some rule and law by which good and evil are distinguished. The light of Scripture comprehendeth either the covenant of works, or the covenant of grace. Works, and so conscience condemneth all the world as 'guilty before God' Rom. iii. 19; and there is no escape from this sentence, but a regular appeal, and passage from court to court: Ps. cxxx. 3, 4, 'If thou shouldest mark iniquities, Lord, who shall stand? But there is forgiveness with thee, that thou mayest be feared;' Ps. cxliii. 2, 'Enter not into judgment with thy servant, for in thy sight shall no man living be justified' where poor condemned sinners may take sanctuary of the Lord's grace, and humbly claim the benefit of the new covenant. Grace wherein the penitent believer, and those that sincerely obey the gospel, are accepted. The legal conscience condemneth all the world; but the evangelical conscience acquitteth is if we sincerely and thankfully accept the new covenant; that is, if we take the privileges offered for our happiness; and the duties required for our work. Therefore it is said, 1 Pet.

iii. 21, 'Baptism saveth, not the putting away of the filthiness of the flesh, but the answer of a good conscience toward God;' not the bare ordinance, but the covenant which is sealed by it. And what doth the covenant require? Accepting the Lord's offers, and resolving to obey his commands.

(2.) As renewed. By nature conscience is blind, partial, stupid; but by grace it is made pure, tender, pliant, and more able to do its office. The Spirit is not said here to witness to our heart, but to our spirit; that is, to conscience as renewed and sanctified. Now such a conscience implieth these things, *First*, Some knowledge of and consent to the new covenant; for without knowledge the heart is not good, Prov. xix. 2. It erreth in point of law and rule, and therefore cannot well witness in the case. And, *secondly*, consent there must be; for we cannot claim privileges by a charter which we never accepted. Therefore, Isa. lvi. 4, 'And choose the things that please me, and take hold of my covenant.' They thankfully accept the offered benefits, and resolve by the strength of the Lord's grace to perform the required duties. *Thirdly*, That our hearts be set to fulfil our covenant vow; for otherwise we double, and deal insincerely with God: Heb. xiii. 18, 'We trust we have a good conscience, willing in all things to live honestly.' The habit and bent of the heart is for God, and obedience to him. *Fourthly*, that there be some answerable endeavours, and pursuance of this resolution and care to please God in all things: Acts xxiv. 16, 'And herein do I exercise myself, to have always a conscience void of offence towards God and towards men.' *Fifthly*, That these endeavours be uniformly carried on, that our sincerity maybe evidenced to conscience. For then it is matter of rejoicing and assurance to us: 2 Cor. i. 12, 'This is our rejoicing, the testimony of our conscience, that in simplicity and godly sincerity we have had our conversation in the world'; 1 John iii. 19, 'And hereby we know we are of the truth, and shall assure our hearts before him.' Grace, constantly and self-denyingly exercised, hath an evidence in the conscience, and conduceth also to give liberty and boldness before God.

[B.] The witness of the Spirit. Because this is often mistaken, I shall the more distinctly lay it before you.

(1.) The Spirit layeth down marks in scripture which may decide this question, whether ye are the children of God, yea or no. As for instance: 1 John iii. 10, 'In this the children, of God are manifested, and the children of the devil; whosoever doth not righteousness is not of God; neither he that loveth not his brother' And again, Rom. viii. 14, 'As many as are led by the Spirit, are the sons of God.' So everywhere in the Scripture God expressly telleth us who shall go to heaven, and who shall go to hell; and that there is no neutral and middle estate between the holy and carnal; all are of one sort or other. Now if we should go no further, the text would bear a good sense. The Spirit beareth witness with our spirit, when our conscience can witness our sincerity in a course of obedience unto God. The Spirit's witness in Scripture, that this is a sound, so a true evidence; and the testimony of conscience confirmed by Scripture; for whatever is spoken in scripture, is supposed to be the very voice and testimony of the Spirit: as Acts xxviii. 25, 'Well spake the Holy Ghost by Isaiah the prophet unto our fathers'; so Heb. iii. 7, 'Wherefore as the Holy Ghost saith, today if ye will hear his voice.' So the Spirit speaketh or witnesseth to our spirits, namely, in the word;

supposing what is to be supposed, this must not be slighted. Yet this is not all; for the context speaketh not of a witness without, but motion within, whereby we are restrained from sin, and inclined to cry, Abba, Father.

(2.) He worketh such graces in us, as are peculiar to God's children, and evidences of our interest in the favour of God; as when he doth renew and sanctify the soul. And so many of the choicest divines take the word witness for evidence, or the objective testimony; namely, that the presence, and dwelling, and working of the sanctifying Spirit in us is the argument and matter of the proof, upon which the whole cause or traverse dependeth. That it is so to be taken, is clear in that exclusive mark: Rom. viii. 9, 'But ye are not in the flesh, but in the Spirit, if so be the Spirit of God dwell in you. Now if any man have not the Spirit of Christ, he is none of his.' And in that positive mark: 1 John iii. 24, 'And he that keepeth his commandments dwelleth in him, and he in him; and hereby we know that he abideth in us, by the Spirit which he hath given us'; and again, 1 John iv. 13, 'Hereby know we that we dwell in him, and he in us, because he hath given us his Spirit.' That holy and charitable spirit; the gracious operations of his presence, are the argument whence we conclude.

(3.) He helpeth us to discern this work in our souls more clearly. Conscience doth its part to discover it; and the Spirit of God doth his part; namely, as he helpeth us to know and see that grace which he giveth and actuateth in us; for he revealeth 'the things given us of God' 1 Cor. ii. 12, not only in the gospel, though chiefly; but also in our hearts. The workman that made a thing can best warrant it to the buyer. First he sanctifieth, and then he certifieth; sometimes we overlook our evidences, through the darkness and confusion that is in our hearts. Hagar saw not the fountain that was near her, till God opened her eyes, Gen. xxi. 19. There is a misgiving in the conscience; we cannot see grace in the midst of weakness and imperfections. Mary wept for the absence of Christ, when yet he stood by her, John xx. 14, 15. The Spirit dwelleth and worketh in their hearts, but they know it not.

(4.) He helpeth us not only to see grace, but to judge of the sincerity of grace. It is more easy to prove that we believe, than to know that our faith is saving; to love Christ, than to know that we love him in sincerity; because of the deceitfulness of the heart, and the mixtures of unbelief, self-love, and other sins; and some degrees may be in hypocrites, as temporary faith, tastes, imperfect love, partial obedience. And besides, grace where it is weak, is hardly perceived; the air will show itself in a windy season; the fire when it is blown up into a flame, it is no more hidden. Grace strengthened, increased, acted, is more evident to conscience; habits are discerned by acts and exercise, and God is wont to reward the faithful soul with his assuring seal of light and comfort: 1 John iii. 18, 'Love not in word, or in tongue only, but indeed and in truth.' The less we are Christians in show, and the more in sincerity, the more joy and peace.

(5.) He helpeth us with boldness to conclude from these evidences. Many times when the premises are clear, the conclusion is suspended. We find in case of condemnation, it is suspended out of self-love; many know that they that live after the flesh shall die, yet they will not judge themselves; and the same may be done in case of self-approbation, out of legal fear or jealousy; for persons of great fancy, and large affections, are always full of scruples, or loathness to apply the comforts due to them. The Spirit concludeth for them, that they are the children of God: 1 John iii. 14, 'We know that we have passed from death to life'; 1 John ii. 3, 'And hereby we know that we know him.'

(6.) He causeth us to feel the comfort of this conclusion: Rom. xv. 13, 'Now the God of hope fill you with all joy and peace in believing'; it is an impression of the comforting Spirit; and Acts ix. 31, 'They walked in the comfort of the Holy Ghost.' The Spirit is necessary to this actual joy; for it is possible a man may be persuaded of his sincerity, or have no doubting of it, and have too much deadness and dulness of soul; not so comforted. Well then, it is not an oracle, as to Christ. Mat. iii. 17; nor an internal suggestion, Thou art a child of God; we have no warrant for that from scripture. It is not only to, but with conscience. Now conscience goeth upon rational evidence; and we reason and argue from what we feel, or find in ourselves; and it is according to the covenant, where privileges are assigned the believer: John i. 12, 'To as many as received him, to them gave he power to become the sons of God'; to the penitent: Acts ii. 38, 'Repent, and you shall receive the Holy Ghost'; to the obedient': He is become the author of salvation to all that obey him'

2. The one superaddeth to the other. Not the privilege without the qualification; that is sufficiently done by the word; not the conscience by discourse, and the Spirit immediately; no, they concur to produce the same conclusion. The Spirit's testimony superaddeth certainty, authority, and overpowering light: 1 Cor. iv. 4, 'For I know nothing by myself, yet am I not hereby justified; but he that judge th me is the Lord;' and Rom. ix. 1, 'I say the truth in Christ, I lie not, my conscience also bearing me witness in the Holy Ghost.' As the influences of the heavens work strongly, but imperceptibly, while they mingle themselves with the motions of the creatures; so doth the Spirit with our spirit; it fortifieth and strengthened the testimony of a man's own heart; and so doth with more authority and power persuade us that we are the children of God.

3. The necessity of this to our full comfort.

[A.] We cannot pray without it. For the text is brought to prove that they have a spirit within them, which inclineth them to cry, Abba, Father. Surely it is a great advantage in prayer, to be able to say, Isa. lxiii. 16, 'Doubtless thou art our father;' and again, Isa. lxiv. 8, 'But now, Lord, thou art our father.' But how will you do, unless you be God's children? And how will you know you be God's children, but by the Spirit bearing witness to, and with your spirits? I know all God's children have not the comfort of the Spirit, but they have the Spirit of comfort, and in some measure can come to God as a father.

[B.] We cannot apply the promises without it, for the promises are children's bread. Unless we be the children of God, what comfort can we take in the promises, unless we have an interest in them? Privileges have their conditions annexed: the right is suspended till the condition be performed; that is, till we know ourselves to be true believers, the promises are in vain and of no effect. If to all, you deceive the most; for though some are of God's family, the whole world lieth in wicked ness; the most are the children of the devil. If to some, they have their characters, which occasioneth the restraint; and you are told here, this is known by the Spirit's bearing witness to our spirits.

But what shall poor creatures do, that have not yet this clear testimony?

(1.) Disclaim all other confidence. When you cannot, apply Hos. xiv. 3, 'Asshur shall not save us, we will not ride upon horses: neither will we say any more to the works of our hands, ye are our gods: for in thee the fatherless findeth mercy'

(2.) Own God in the humbling way; creep in at the back door of the promise, 1 Tim, i. 15, 'Jesus Christ came into the world to save sinners.' If Christ came to save sinners, I am sinner enough for Christ to save. Luke xv. 18, 19, 'I will arise and go to my father, and wilt say unto him, Father, I have sinned against heaven, and before thee; and am no more worthy to be called thy son; make me as one of thy hired servants'

(3.) Come to him, as the God and Father of our Lord Jesus Christ: Eph. iii. 14, 'For this cause I bow my knees unto the Father of our Lord Jesus Christ.' Certainly God will love and accept all those that come to him by Christ.

 (4.) There is a child-like inclination, when there is not a child-like familiarity and boldness. The soul cannot keep away from God, and that is an implicit owning of him as a father: Jer. iii. 19, 'Thou shalt call me father, and shalt not turn away from me'. We call him father; unspeakable groans discover the spirit of adoption, as well as unutterable joys; we own him by way of option and choice, though not by actual assurance of our special relation to him, and interest in his fatherly love; there may be a child-like love to God, when we have no assurance of his paternal love to us.

(5.) There is a child-like reverence and awe, when not a child-like confidence. Their heart standeth in awe of (as the Rechabites), their father's command, dare not displease him for all the world; these in time will overcome. In short, God hath a title to our dearest love, when we cannot make out a title to the highest benefit.

SERMON XXIV

If children, then heirs, heirs of God and joint heirs with Christ; if so be that we suffer with him, that we may also be glorified together.

Romans VIII. 17.

THE Apostle had showed, ver. 13, that if we through the Spirit do mortify the deeds of the body, we shall live. He proveth it by this medium and argument; that as many as obey the sanctifying motions of the Spirit, are children of God; and children may look for a child's portion. He proveth they are children, because the Spirit accompanieth the dispensation of the new covenant, whereby we are adopted into God's family; and this Spirit acts suitably, as is evident by his impression, ver. 15, by his testimony and witness, ver. 16. Now he goeth on further, and proveth, that if we be children, we are heirs; and that we shall live, if we mortify the deeds of the body, is more abundantly proved, for our inheritance is eternal life and glory, 'And if children then heirs' &c. In the words observe,

1. A dignity—inferred from our adoption.

2. The amplification of it—from the excellent nature of this inheritance, 'Heirs of God, and joint heirs with Christ.'

3. It is applied as a comfort against adversities. 'If so be that we suffer with him, that we may also be glorified together'

promises; that is, the thing promised, spiritual and eternal blessings and rewards.

1. The dignity inferred is, that we are heirs. The inheritance belonging to children, *jure nascendi*, all children are not necessarily heirs, but only males, and among them the first born; but *jure adoptionis*, they that are adopted, are adopted to some inheritance. So here, 'if children, then heirs'; be they sons or daughters, begotten to God sooner or later, male or female; are all one in Christ: Gal. iii. 18; they are not debarred from the inheritance.

2. The amplification of it, or the greatness and excellency of this inheritance, in two expressions, 'Heirs of God, and joint heirs with Christ.' The first expression heightens the privilege in our thoughts; as the party adopting is, so is the privilege more or less glorious in our thoughts. Adoption is in all free, and in some, glorious. If a mean man adopt another's child, it is an act of free favour; but if adopted to a great inheritance, suppose many lordships, or to the succession of a crown, it doth enhance the benefit. So here, this giveth a right to the everlasting goods of the heavenly father. Secondly, The other expression, 'joint heirs with Christ' This heritage giveth us a communion with the only begotten Son of God; what the Son of God by nature enjoyeth, that the children of God by adoption enjoy also, so far as they are capable; we together with Christ enjoy God for ever more. He is his God and Father, and our God and Father: John xx. 17; he is glorified, and we are glorified together with him.

3. It is applied as a comfort against adversities and afflictions': If so be that we suffer with him, that we may be also glorified together.' The latter clause we may look upon as propounded, 1. As a concession, 2. As a condition.

[A.] A concession; seeing that we suffer with him, that we may be glorified together. Though we shall hereafter have communion with Christ in glory, yet for the present we may have communion with him in afflictions. This doth not infringe our privilege, but confirm it rather: I Pet. iv. 13, 'Rejoice, inasmuch as ye are partakers of Christ's sufferings; that when his glory shall be revealed, ye may be glad with exceeding joy'. Those that suffer for Christ, do also suffer with Christ; they are brought into a nearer conformity to him in his state of humiliation, that afterwards they may be conformed to him in glory.

[B.] In the way of condition. We must submit to the condition of afflictions as necessary to obtain glory; for there must be striving before crowning: 2 Tim. ii. 5, 'If a man strive for masteries, yet he is not crowned except he strive lawfully'; that is, if any man would enter into the lists in any of the Olympic games, he must observe the rules in running, wrestling, &c.; he must submit to the laws of the game, or exercise. He applieth this similitude, ver. 12, 'If we suffer with him, we shall reign with him'; that is, we must suffer for Christ, and we shall be rewarded with the participation of his glory; so here, we would all have our privileges; but before we enjoy the full of them, we must be conformed to him, suffer for him, and with him; that in imitation of our head and chief, we may come to glory the same way that Christ did, by sufferings: Heb. ii. 10. 'For it became him, for whom are all things, and by whom are all things, in bringing many sons unto glory, to make the captain of their salvation perfect through suffering.' But you will say, all are not called to the afflictions of the gospel; is this condition indispensable? Then none but martyrs are glorified.

Answer, (1) All have not Abel's cross, do not run the hazard of their lives; but usually they will have Isaac's cross: Gal. iv. 29, 'He that was born after the flesh persecuted him that was born after the Spirit'; meaning thereby those cruel mockings and scoffings which Isaac endured from Ishmael, Gen. xxi. The children of God living upon an unseen God, and an unseen world, sensual men mock at their interest in God, and labour to shame them from their confidence in promises yet to come.

(2.) Though all suffer not, yet all must be prepared and contented to suffer: Mat. xvi. 24, 'Then said Jesus unto his disciples, If any man will come after me, let him deny himself, and take up his cross and follow me' God knoweth at what rate our sincerity must be tried; yet everyone should make Christ a good allowance; and our alienation from the world must be so great, and our resignation to God so full, that nothing we enjoy here, not life itself, may be an impediment to our fidelity to Christ.

(3.) When God seeth it fit, we must actually suffer the loss of all things and obey God at the dearest rates: 1 Pet. iii. 17, 'If the will of God be so, that ye shall suffer for well doing'; *affirmativa praecepta non ligant ad semper*, affirmative precepts do not bind at all times, as negatives do. We must never do anything against the truth, but we are not always tied to suffering; but when we come to a necessity of either suffering or sinning, then God manifesteth his will to his people, that they should suffer; and then if we suffer with him, we shall also be glorified together. No creature could have brought us to this necessity, without God; it is plainly God's will that we should suffer; and remember it is his will that we should also reign with him.

Doctrine That all God's children are heirs of a blessed and glorious inheritance. I shall show you,

1. The agreement between common heirs and them.

2. The difference.

3. Those properties which show the greatness of the inheritance. First, The agreement; in these things:

1. There is an inheritance provided. We have a right to all the good things God hath promised, especially eternal life; therefore the people of God are called 'heirs of salvation,' Heb. i. 14'; heirs of the kingdom,' Jam. ii. 5; and the heavenly estate is called 'the inheritance of the saints in light' Col. i. 12. Those excellent things which are to be enjoyed by us in the other world are in the nature of an inheritance.

2. The conveyance is by promise and covenant; as other heritages are conveyed by formalities of law, so is this. The covenant is so offered by God, and so it must be accepted by us: Ps. cxix. Ill, 'Thy testimonies I have taken as an heritage forever' As we say a man's estate lieth in bills and bonds, so are God's testimonies our heritage; not the promises, but the things promised. And so it is said, Heb. vi. 12, that God's holy ones did through faith and patience inherit the

3. Our tenure is by sonship. [A.] It is free; for the inheritance is not purchased by us, but freely bestowed upon us. A child's tenure differeth from a servant's; the one earneth his wages, and the other hath his estate from his father's bounty and free gift; so is ours the gift of God, Rom. vi. 23, in opposition to works; called therefore 'the reward of inheritance,' Col. iii. 24. Though servants earn what they receive from men, yet from the Lord Christ, whatever they receive for faithfulness in their calling, it is a free retribution; though they are servants to men, yet they are sons to God, for all are children and heirs in heaven; there is no distinction of servants and sons there. In short, whatever is promised to any work of ours, it is not from any worth in the work, but from God's free grace. [B.] It is full; for the inheritance is more than a legacy. God showeth his goodness to all his creatures, but to his children he giveth the inheritance. As Isaac had the inheritance from Abraham, but to his sons that he had by concubines he gave gifts, and sent them away, Gen. xxv. 5, 6. All men taste of his common bounty, but his saints have their inheritance reserved for them; which showeth that we should put a distinction between our heavenly inheritance, and those earthly enjoyments which flow in the channel of common providence. Alas! That far exceedeth anything we enjoy here; all things here are but mean and fading in themselves, and liable to spoil and devastation from others; but this is our eternal and durable estate, which the wicked shall not partake of, whatever gifts God bestoweth on them now.

4. There is a time between right and possession; and in the meantime the heirs live by hope, till the inheritance fairly descendeth to them; so here: Titus iii. 7, c Being justified by faith, we are made heirs according to the hope of eternal life' We are heirs, but it is little that we enjoy now; God's sons and heirs make no fair show in the flesh; to outward appearance there is little difference between their condition, and the condition of the men of the world.

For God will not distinguish the heirs of promise from others by their outward condition, but internally. There is hope of a better estate, and surely to expect such great things, and not be affected with them, argueth a dead and stupid heart. Is a right nothing before possession? Or is the expectation so grounded, a vain fancy? Surely a Christian is or will be a great man. Is the heir nothing better than a slave, because he doth not as yet come to the enjoyment of what is provided for him? A right and a hope should give us more joy than usually we find in ourselves; if it were a vain expectation, and not grounded upon a right, it were less; but being it is so, we should be more affected with it.

5. As an heir hath not only assurance of the inheritance, but present supply and maintenance, and other demonstrations of love to support his expectation from him that adopted him, that all the estate falleth to him; so in the meantime God's children have the pledges of his love, the possession of the heavenly inheritance is begun here in the kingdom of grace; and is afterwards completed in the kingdom of glory. The Spirit now with his comforts and graces is set forth under a double notion of earnest, and first fruits, Eph. i. 14, 'The earnest of inheritance' 'First fruits,' Rom. viii. 23. There are two acts of a Christian, to look, and long for this estate: look for it, because it is sure; and long for it, because it is good. God giveth us a pledge and earnest, to show how sure; a taste, to show how good; thus far they agree.

Secondly. Wherein they disagree.

L It is an inheritance not lessened by the multitude of co-heirs: God is an infinite portion that cannot be divided, and sufficeth the whole world. In other heritages many a fair stream is drawn dry, by being dispersed into several channels; but here the more company, the greater the privilege; what a happiness is it to enjoy God among all the saints! The company is ever propounded as a blessing: Mat. viii. 11, 'Ye shall sit down with Abraham, Isaac, and Jacob, in the kingdom of heaven'; and Heb. xii. 22, 23, 'Ye are come to an innumerable company of angels,' &c. When God is all in all, he will fill up every vessel. As when the same light is seen by all, the same speech is heard by all, the one doth not see less, nor the other hears less, because another seeth and heareth with him. In the world we straiten others, the more we are enlarged ourselves; but not then.

2. In other inheritances the father must die, before the son can inherit. *Haereditas est successio in totum jus defuncti*; death taketh away the father, that the son may succeed him. God hath heirs, but no successors; we do not possess after our Father's death, but with our Father; he liveth forever, and we live forever with him; we die that we may go to the living God; 'When strength faileth, and heart faileth, thou art my portion forever' Ps. lxxiii. 26. When others must leave their inheritance, we go to ours, then it beginneth.

3. In other heritages, the heirs are designed by name, but here by character. Men are contentious; everyone would say, he is meant in the description; but here the heirs are not named, but described by certain qualifications, which must be tried by ourselves, warranted by the Spirit, judged and examined by Christ at the last day. Sometimes they are termed the called: Heb. ix. 15, 'That they that are called may receive the promise of eternal inheritance;' by which is meant those which are effectually called, and converted unto God. Sometimes

this privilege is settled upon believers, John i. 12, such as do heartily and thankfully accept of Christ, and his grace; and sometimes the sanctified, as Col. i. 12; arid Acts xx. 18; such as are dedicated to God, and live as a people set apart for him. All these are sons; therefore made heirs, qualified, and made capable of this blessed inheritance.

Thirdly, The properties of this inheritance, which set forth the greatness of it.

1. It is a glorious inheritance: Eph. i. 18, 'That ye may know what are the riches of the glory of the inheritance in the saints.' That inheritance which is appointed for those who are renewed by the Spirit of God, is a glorious inheritance. There is nothing in heaven but what is glorious; the object of it is the glorious God, whom we shall see, as we are seen: 1 Cor. xiii. 12, especially as he shineth forth in the glorious person of our Redeemer: John xvii. 24, 'Father, I will that those whom thou hast given me may be where I am, that they may behold my glory.' The state of our bodies and souls shall be glorious, Phil. iii. 21; the place shall be glorious, the upper paradise, 2 Cor. xii. 4; the company glorious, all the glorified saints and angels; our employment glorious, Rev. vii. 12, blessing, and praising, and glorifying of God, for ever and ever.

2. It is an eternal and undefiled inheritance: 1 Pet. i. 4, 'To an inheritance incorruptible, and undefiled, that fadeth not away, reserved in heaven for you.' I gather from that place, that it is a celestial and incorruptible inheritance, and so doth exceed all worldly possessions which come from fathers to their children. The things of this world are both defiling and perishing; they pollute us, *omnis turpitudo est a mixtura*; when our hearts cleave to the things of this world, they are debased by them to something beneath themselves. But this celestial inheritance doth not corrupt, but purify affections; these things below make us worse, but cannot make us better; they are perishing as well as fading: for they decay in our hands; like flowers they wither in our hands while we smell at them; but this endureth for ever; we shall not fail, and to be sure the ever-living God will not fail us.

3. It is a blessed inheritance, the expression in the text, 'heirs of God, and joint heirs with Christ.' First, heirs of God. The inheritance is the Lord himself, blessed forever, to be enjoyed by the saints to all eternity. He is the inheritance of his people now: Ps. xvi. 5, 6, 4 The Lord is the portion of mine inheritance, the lines are fallen to me in a pleasant place'; Ps. cxix. 57, 'Thou art my portion, Lord'; and Lam. iii. 24, 'The Lord is my portion, saith my soul, therefore will I hope in him'; see what conclusions are drawn thence, duty, and hope. Much more then will God be our all-sufficient portion: Kev. xxi. 7, 'He that overcometh shall inherit all things; and I will be his God, and he shall be my son'; all things equivalently, all things immediately in God; God is instead of all, infinitely supplying and filling up the room of all, riches, honours, contentment, and comforts. If we have God, nothing shall be missed, nothing wanted to make the state of those that enjoy it completely happy. God is all immediately from himself: 1 Cor. xv. 28; God shall be all in all, who filleth all the desires, and perfecteth all the powers of our souls, of himself, without the intervention of means. Secondly, joint heirs with Christ, we enjoy it by him, and we enjoy it with him.

[A.] By him, for Christ is the heir of all things; and we can have no title but by and through him. He hath the whole inheritance in his power, and the absolute disposing of all the good things which belong to it: John xvii. 2, 'Thou hast given him power over all flesh, that he should give eternal life to as many as thou hast given to him.' He hath power of condemning and absolving; unless we sincerely and cordially come to him, and accept him upon God's offer, and obey him, we have no right.

[B.] We enjoy it with him. Christ as mediator hath a double inheritance. (1.) Of life and glory. (2) Of dominion and power.

(1.) Of life and glory. For we read, 1 Tim. iii. 16, that he is 1 received up into glory' and there he liveth forever at the right hand of God. Now Christ will not be there alone; he cannot satisfy himself unless he have his people with him; for we do with Christ enjoy God, and live with him for evermore. Christ will have his people sharers in the same life and glory: John xii. 26, 'If any man will serve me, let him follow me, and where I am, there shall my servant be: if any man serve me, him will my Father honour.' His people shall fare as he doth, if they will serve him and follow him; that is, not take it ill to be no better used than he was. He will be with them in trouble, and they shall be with him in glory; in their eternal estate they shall have constant, intimate, and nearer fellowship with him.

(2.) An inheritance of dominion and power: Eph. i. 21, 'God raised him far above all principality, and power, and might, and dominion, and every name that is named, not only in this world, but in that which is to come.' Christ as mediator was exalted to the highest degree of glory, next to God in heaven; far above that fading power of rulers and potentates by whom he was put to death; yea, above the highest degree of angelical power. But doth any of this fall to our share? See what Christ saith: Rev. iii. 21, 'To him that overcometh, I will grant to sit with me on my throne, even as I also overcame, and am sat down with my Father in his throne.' He that persevereth in spite of all temptations, shall partake of that honour to which my Father hath exalted me unto, after my sufferings. He shall reign with Christ, and sit down with Christ on the right hand of the majesty of God; not the same methods used towards him, to bring him 'to a glorious eternity; but invested in the same power as Christ the head: Ps. xlix. 14, 'The upright shall have dominion in the morning.'

Use 1. Is information of several truths.

1. That our heavenly inheritance cometh to us not by our own purchase and procurement, or merit; but by virtue of our sonship. For so the apostle reasoneth, 'If sons, then heirs.' It is given by the mercy of God, or the bounty of our Father: Luke xii. 32, 'Fear not, little flock, it is your Father's good pleasure to give you a kingdom.' It is purchased by Christ; indeed the Scripture doth not expressly say *in terminis*, that Christ purchased it for us, but the merit of his death reached that effect; the immediate end of Christ's death was to expiate our transgressions; Heb. ix. 15, 'For this cause is Christ the mediator of the new covenant, that by means of death, for the redemption of the transgressions under the first covenant, they which are called might receive the promise of eternal inheritance' His death removed sin, and the eternal penalties due to it; and the new covenant, which is so full of heavenly promises, is thereby introduced; none but such whose sins are expiated, can be heirs; and yours could not be expiated without the death of the mediator. Therefore take away this death, and there can be no new covenant, no inheritance; this death satisfied the justice of

God, and merited his favour. Again, we are purchased; though it be not said heaven is purchased, Eph. ii. 14. Once more, it is said he gave himself, Eph. v. 25, 26, 27; all the benefits depend on the blood of Christ; and 1 Thes. v. 9, 10, 'For God hath not appointed us to wrath, but to obtain salvation by our Lord Jesus Christ, who died for us, that whether we wake or sleep, we should live together with him.' The price of this purchase then is Christ, is Christ's death and blood. Christ having purchased it, hath left it in legacy: John xvii. 24, 'Father, I will that those thou hast given me may be where I am'; Luke xxii. 22, 'This is the new testament in my blood, which is shed for you'. What are the legacies? Pardon and life, Mat. xxvi. 28, 29; and Christ liveth for ever to be executor of his own testament, Heb. vii. 25. We then adopted believers, are designed heirs of salvation and eternal glory, out of mere grace, not out of any merit of ours.

2. It informeth us that it is a safe way upon the observation of the saving effects of God's Spirit in ourselves, to conclude that we are in an estate of grace, even the adopted children of God. For so doth the apostle reason in this place: They are children of God; how is it known? By the work and witness of the Spirit within us; thence we conclude, 'if sons, then heirs'; the like: Gal. iv. 6, 'Because ye are sons, he hath sent forth the Spirit of his Son, crying, Abba, Father. Wherefore thou art no more a servant, but a son; and if a son, then an heir of God through Christ'. Which teacheth us how to come to a conclusion in soul debates. Have I a child-like inclination, and sense and confidence that God hath adopted me into his favour, and have I the sanctifying of the Spirit upon my heart? I may be bold then to enter my claim.

3. It informeth us that the privileges of believers are so linked together, that where one of them is, there are all the rest. Therefore if we enjoy one, then we must collect and infer that the rest do belong to us also; if sons, we must not rest there'; then heirs, heirs of God, and joint heirs with Christ' One link of the golden chain draweth on another; there is a great deal of profit in these collections and inferences; our minds are usually taken up with trifles and childish toys; surely the privileges of a Christian are not so much considered as they should be. The benefit of it is this: partly, it keepeth our hearts in a way of praising God, and constant rejoicing in God; if we did more consider the excellency of our inheritance: 1 Pet. i. 3, 4, 'Blessed be God, who hath begotten us to a lively hope, to an inheritance incorruptible, undefiled.' Our thoughts are too dead and cold till we revive the memory of our excellent privileges by Christ. Partly, as it keepeth us in a constant and cheerful adherence to the truth, whatever it cost us; we slight all temporal things, how grievous or troublesome soever they be: Rom. viii. 18, 'For I reckon that the sufferings of the present life are not worthy to be compared with the glory that shall be revealed in us' Rom. v. 3, 'We glory in tribulation, as knowing that tribulation worketh patience' Partly, To help us to despise the pleasures of sin which are but for a season, while eternal things are in view: 2 Cor. iv. 18, 'While we look not to the things which are seen, but to the things which are not seen; for the things which are seen are temporal; but the things which are not seen are eternal' And partly, To digest the labours of duty and obedience, all the pains of the holy life, 2 Cor. v. 9. 'Wherefore we labour, whether present or absent, that we may be accepted of the Lord' What shall we not

do for such a father, that hath provided such an inheritance for us, that we may enjoy him and be accepted with him? Therefore we should stock our minds with these thoughts.

4. That we should not question our estate, because we are under grievous pressures and afflictions. For the words are an anticipation of an objection If sons of God, and heirs of glory, why are we then so afflicted? He inverteth the argument, You are so afflicted, that you may have the inheritance. It is rather an evidence of our right than an infringement of it, especially if patiently endured for God's sake, seeing thereby you are conformed to the Son by nature: Rom. viii. 29, 'He hath predestinated us to be conformed to the image of his Son'. We have communion with Christ and his sufferings; and if we be like him in his estate of humiliation, we shall be like him in his estate of exaltation also.

Use 2. Is exhortation.

1. To believe this blessed inheritance which is reserved for the children of God. It is a great happiness, but let not us therefore suspect the truth of it; for it is founded in the infinite mercy of the eternal God, and the everlasting merit of a blessed Redeemer; and we are prepared and qualified for it by the almighty operation of the conquering Spirit; it is an happiness that lieth in another world, and we cannot come at it but by death. But is there no life beyond this? Where then shall the good be rewarded, and the wicked punished? It is unseen, but it is set before us in the promises of the gospel, which God hath confirmed by miracles, and sanctified to the conversion and consolation of many souls throughout all successions of ages. And were the best and wisest of men that ever the world saw, deceived with a vain fancy? Or can a lie or delusion be sanctified to such high and holy ends? Therefore do you believe it? John xi. 26, 'Whosoever liveth and believeth in me shall never die; believest thou this?' If you believe your reconciliation with God by the death of Christ, why not your salvation by his life? If your adoption into his family, why not the inheritance? Both privileges stand by the same grace.

2. Let us live always in the desire of it; that desire that will quicken you to look after it, Phil. iii. 14, and to seek after it in the first place, Mat. vi. 33; that desire that will quicken you to long for the enjoyment of it, Phil. i. 23.

3. To comfort yourselves with the hope of it: Rom. v. 2, 'And rejoice in hope of the glory of God' It is the glory of God; God giveth it, God is the solid part of it; and can we expect shortly to live with God, and upon God, and not rejoice in the hope of it? Is a deed of gift from God, the security of infallible promises, nothing? Is the title nothing before possession? When this estate is so sure and near, we should more lift up our heads, and revive our drooping spirits.

4. Let us walk worthy of it:

[A.] Despising Satan's offers, Heb. xii. 16. Be not a profane person, as was Esau; 1 Kings xxi. 3, 'The Lord forbid that I should part with the inheritance of my father.' Be chary of your inheritance; keep the hopes clear, fresh, and lively.

[B.] Wean your hearts from the world: Col. iii. 1,2. If ye be risen with Christ, seek the things that are above, set your affections above, and not on the earth.' There is your Father, your head, your Christ, your patrimony; it is reserved for you in the heavens.

[C.] Live in all holy conversation and godliness, 1 Pet. iii. 7; living heirs of the grace of life, in all duties to God, love to one another, as heirs in the grace of life, in all duties to God, love to one another, fidelity in all our relations. We that shall live in the clear vision and full fruition of God in Christ, should be other manner of persons.

[D.] In an heavenly manner: Phil. iii. 20, 'But our conversation is in heaven'; either acting for it, or living upon it, or solacing ourselves with it. With delightful thoughts of heaven sweeten your pilgrimage here; be willing to suffer afflictions, if God call us thereunto, patiently. You suffer with Christ; Christ takes it as done to himself: Acts ix. 'Why persecutest thou me? 'Fill up your share of the sufferings providence hath appointed for Christ mystical: Col. i. 24, 'Who now rejoice in my afflictions for you, and fill up that which is behind of the afflictions of Christ in my flesh, for his body's sake, which is the church'; 2 Cor. i. 6, 'And whether we be afflicted it is for your consolation and salvation'; and Phil. iii. 10, 'That I may know him, and the power of his resurrection, and the fellowship of his sufferings, being made conformable unto his death.'

SERMON XXV

For I reckon that the sufferings of this present time are not worthy to be compared with the glory that shall be revealed in us.

Romans VIII. 18.

IN this chapter the apostle speaketh first of bridling lusts, and then of bearing afflictions; both are tedious to flesh and blood. The necessity of taming the flesh is deduced throughout that whole discourse, which is continued from ver. 1. to the end of ver. 17, where he maketh patient enduring afflictions a condition of our glory; 'if we suffer with him, we shall also be glorified together.' He now showeth us a reason, why we should not dislike this condition; because the good which is promised is far greater than the evil which we fear. Two things nature teacheth all men; the first is to submit to a lesser evil, to avoid a greater; as men will cut off an arm or a leg to save the whole body; the other is, to undergo a lesser evil to obtain a greater good than that evil depriveth us of. If this principle were not allowed, it would destroy all the industry in the world; for good is not to be obtained unless we venture somewhat to get it; upon this principle the apostle worketh in this place, 'For I reckon' &c. In the words take notice of

1. The things compared; *The sufferings of the present life* and *the glory to be revealed in us.*

2. The inequality that is in them; *They are not worthy.*

3. The conclusion or judgment of the apostle upon the case; *I reckon*

1. The things compared. On the one side, 'the sufferings of the present time.'

[A.] Mark that, sufferings plurally, to comprise all of the kind, reproaches, strifes, fines, spoiling of goods, imprisonment, banishment, death. Again of the present time, to distinguish them from the torments of hell, which maketh up a part of the argument; for if to avoid tem poral evils we forsake Christ, we shall endure eternal torments; but the apostle speaketh of temporal evils.

[B.] On the other side, 'The glory that shall be revealed in us.' Every word is emphatical. (1.) Our reward is called glory; in our calamity we are depressed and put to shame; but whatever honour we lose in this mortal life, shall be abundantly supplied and recompensed to us in heaven': If any man serve me, him shall my Father honour' John xii. 26. An afflicted, persecuted people are usually misrepresented and scandalized in the world; but there is a life and state of glory prepared for them in heaven; men cannot put so much disgrace upon them, as God will put marks of honour and favour. (2.) It shall be revealed. This glory doth not appear for the present, it is not seen; it is not conspicuous to the eyes of men; therefore some believe it not, others regard it not'; it doth not yet appear what we shall be; the world knoweth us not, as it knew him not': 1 John iii. 1,2,' Therefore the world knoweth us not, because it knew him not. Behold, now we are the sons of God, and it doth not yet appear what we shall be; but we know, that when he shall appear, we shall be like him, and see him as he is.' But it shall be seen, because of God's decree and promise; for the glory is prepared, though it be not revealed. (3.) In us, or upon us, when we shall be raised immortal, incorruptible, and we shall be so highly favoured and honoured by Christ, as we shall be at the day of judgment, then this glory is revealed upon us; that is, we shall be possessors of it; we have the right now, but then the possession.

2. The inequality between them: 'They are not worthy to be compared'; not worthy to future glory, not worthy to be set the one against the other, as bearing no proportion.

3. The conclusion or judgment of the apostle in this case. The word *logizomai* is emphatical, and implieth that he had weighed these things in his mind; after the case was well traversed, he did conclude and determine upon the whole debate; *rationibus bene subductis colligo et statuo*. The apostle speaketh like a man that had cast up his accounts, well weighed the matter he speaketh of; and then concludeth, resolveth, and determineth, that the sufferings which are to be under gone for Christ are nothing, considering the glory and blessedness which shall ensue.

Doctrine That every good Christian, or considerate believer, should determine that the happiness of his glorified estate doth infinitely outweigh and exceed the misery of his present afflictions. I shall open the point by these considerations:

1. That counterbalancing temporal things with eternal, is the way to clear our mistakes, or prevent the delusions of the flesh. The apostle observeth this method here and elsewhere: 2 Cor. iv. 17, 'This light affliction, which is but for a moment, worketh for us a far more exceeding and eternal weight of glory'; and it is necessary; for all our mistakes come by reckoning by time, and not by eternity; but looking to eternity sets us right again: 2 Cor. iv. 18, 'Looking not to the things which are temporal, but to the things which are eternal.' The flesh is importunate to be pleased with present satisfactions; it must have something seen and at hand; and this tainteth our minds, so that present things bear a big bulk in our eye, but things to come are as a vain fancy; therefore nothing will scatter this mist and cloud upon our understandings, but a due sight of eternal things, how real they are, and how much they exceed for greatness and duration. Then we shall find that time to eternity, is but as a drop lost or spilt in the ocean; as a point to the circumference; and that the honours and dignities of the world, which dazzle men's eyes, are vain and slippery; that riches, which captivate their hearts, are uncertain and perishing; that pleasures, which enchant their minds, are sordid and base, and pass away as the wind; that nothing is great but what is eternal. If wicked men did but consider the shortness of their pleasures, and the length of their sorrows, they would not be so besotted as they are; and if holy men did but consider the shortness of their afflictions, and the length of their joy and glory, it would animate and encourage them to carry it more patiently and cheerfully in all their tribulations.

2. This may be done four ways:

[A.] Comparing temporal good things with eternal good things, that we may wean and draw off our hearts from the one to the other, and so check the delights of sense; as wealth with heavenly riches: Heb. x. 34, 'Ye took joyfully the spoiling of your goods, as knowing in your selves that ye have in heaven a better and a more enduring substance.' Eternal bliss in heaven is the most valuable and durable kind of wealth; all other treasure cometh more infinitely short of it, than wampompeage, or the shells which the Indians use for money, doth of our coin and treasure. So to wean us from our sensual delights, the scripture propoundeth to our consideration that eternal and solid joy which resulteth from the immediate fruition of God, Ps. xvi. 11. So to wean us from vain glory, and that we may be contented with the glory that comes from God only, it telleth us of the honour and glory of the saints, John v. 44. All the sensual good things we dote upon are but a may-game or painted show in comparison of what we shall enjoy there.

[B.] Temporal bad things with eternal bad things; so to defeat the terrors of sense. All the sufferings of the world are but as the scratch of a pin or a flea-biting, to that woe, wrath, and tribulation that abideth for every soul that doth evil; no fire like the fire of hell, nor pains like the pains of the worm that never dieth: Luke xii. 4, 5, 'Fear not them that kill the body, and after that have no more that they can do; but I will forewarn you whom ye shall fear; fear him, which after he hath killed, hath power to cast into hell' Men threaten prisons, God threateneth hell; they can mangle the body, but when they have cut it all in pieces, they cannot reach the soul; if we sin to avoid trouble in the world, we escape at a dear rate. As a nail driveth out a nail, so doth one fear drive out another; temporal sufferings are nothing to eternal: Heb. xi. 35. 'They accepted not deliverance, looking for a better resurrection'; the general resurrection is better than present remission of torments.

[C.] Temporal good with eternal evil. Many succeed well in a way of sinning here, live without any remarkable blast and stroke of God's judgment; but how is it with them in the other world? *Momentum est quod delectat, eternum quod cruciat*[36] Heb. xi. 25, 'The pleasures of sin are but for a season'; but the punishment of sin is forever; if we compare the pleasures of sin with the pains of hell, it may be a means to reclaim us from the sensual life. This short pleasure is dearly bought.

[D.] Temporal bad things, with eternal good things. This here, and 2 Cor. iv. 17, 'For our light afflictions, which are but for a moment, worketh for us a far more exceeding and eternal weight of glory.' A due sight of eternity will soon show us the smallness of all that we can suffer here; and so our afflictions are not matters much to be stood upon, or accounted of; the comparison must be rightly stated, and weighed, and improved by proper considerations.

3. In this last comparison these things are considerable

[A.] Our sufferings come from men, but our glory cometh from God; now as the agent is, so is the effect; man afflicts as a finite creature, but God rewardeth us as an infinite and eternal being; man showeth himself in his wrath, and God in his love; man in his anger: Isa. li. 12, 'Who art thou, that thou shouldest be afraid of a man that shall die, and of the son of man who shall be as grass?' Men soon perish and are gone, and the effects of their anger cease with them; they can do no more than God pleaseth, and their time is limited; they can rage

---

[36] delights last a moment, pain for eternity

no longer than God pleaseth. But as man showeth himself as man, God showeth himself as God. It is intimated in the genera] expression of the covenant, 'I will be your God,' be such a benefactor as a God should be; do us good so as becometh an infinite eternal power; thence are those reasonings: Mat. xxii. 32, 'I am the God of Abraham, and the God of Isaac, and the God of Jacob; God is not the God of the dead, but of the living'; Heb. xi. 16, 'But now they desire a better country, that is an heavenly; wherefore God is not ashamed to be called their God, for he hath prepared for them a city'. He will give us somewhat like himself; now what comparison between the wrath of man and the bounty of God?

[B.] Our sufferings are earthly, but our glory is heavenly. As the place is, so is the estate; here both the good and evil is partial, but there both are complete; for here we are in the way, there *in termino*, in our final estate; here a believer's spiritual condition will counter balance all his outward troubles; his consolation exceed his afflictions: 2 Cor i. 5, 'For as the sufferings of Christ abound in us, so our consolation doth abound by Christ'; much more his eternal estate. For now we are but in part acquainted with God, but there he is all in all, 1 Cor. x. 28; here we see him in a glass, but there face to face, 1 Cor. xiii. 12. Here we have the earnest, there the whole bargain; here a taste, there a full feast; here the beginning, there the consummation.

[C.] Our sufferings are but short, but our glory eternal: 1 Pet. i. 6, 'For a season, if need be, ye are in heaviness through manifold temptations'; the trouble is but of short continuance; so 1 Pet. v. 10. 'He hath called you to eternal glory by Jesus Christ, after you have suffered a while.' It is but a little time that we suffer; for God knoweth our spirits are soon apt to fail; he considereth we are but dust. Indeed the Lord useth a difference with his children; some have shorter trials, some longer; but they are all but for a season. If they should last for our whole lives, they are but momentary, if compared with eternity. But it is not credible that our lives should be altogether calamitous; there is no instance either in scripture, or the records of time; there are intervals of rest, and our enemies cannot trouble us, but when it is permitted of God. But if there were no intermission, yet this life itself is but for a moment, compared with eternity. If you consider that which in these afflictions we most dread, and beyond which the power of the most cruel adversaries cannot reach, death itself; it is but for a moment; in the twinkling of an eye we are in eternity; death cometh in a moment, and it is gone in a moment; after that, we enjoy eternal rest and peace. Therefore though in our way to heaven we should endure the most grievous calamities, yet since they are but short and momentary, we should submit to them, that we may enjoy so great a good as the vision and fruition of God. *Toleramus brevia, expectamus eterna*; the sufferings are temporal, the glory is eternal, because it dependeth upon the will of an immutable God, and the everlasting merit of a glorious Redeemer: when either of these foundations fail, your blessedness will be at an end. But these can never fail; and therefore our glory will be everlasting. Well then, the pain and suffering will be short; within a little while you will feel it no more than if it had never been; if the pain be remembered, it will be but to increase your joy.

[D.] As they are short, so they are light. *Leves et breves*. The scripture often joineth them together: 2 Cor. iv. 17, 'This light affliction which is but for a moment.' They are light, just so they are short in compari son of eternal glory; as of short continuance if compared with eternity, so of small weight if compared with the reward; eternity maketh them short; and the greatness of the reward maketh them easy. There are degrees in our troubles; some of the saints get to heaven at a cheaper rate than others do; but yet the afflictions of all are light, if we consider the unspeakable glory of the world to come. Indeed we do but prattle when we presume fully to describe it; for it doth not appear what we shall be, and it hath not entered into the heart of man to conceive the great things which he hath prepared for them that love him. But the scripture expressions everywhere show it shall be exceeding great, and also by the beginnings of it. The world is ignorant and incredulous of futurity, therefore God giveth us the beginnings of heaven and hell in this world, in a wounded spirit and the comforts of a good conscience; these things we have experience of; we know not exactly what our future condition will be, but the hopes and fears of that estate are very affective; the fears and horrors of eternal torment, which are found in a guilty conscience, do in part show what hell will be, or the nature of that woe and anguish which abideth for the impenitent: Prov. xviii. 14, 'The spirit of a man will sustain his infirmity; but a wounded spirit who can bear?' The salve for this sore must come from heaven only. So the joys of a good conscience, which are unspeakalle and glorious, 1 Pet. i. 8, show that the happiness appointed for the saints will be exceeding great; for if the foretaste be so sweet, the hope and expectation be so ravishing, what will the enjoyment be? Besides, God moderateth our sufferings, that they may not be over-long, or over-grievous: 1 Cor. x. 13, 'But God is faithful, who will not suffer you to be tempted above that you are able; but will with the temptation also make a way to escape, that ye may be able to bear it.' If the trial be heavy, he fortifieth us by the comfort and support of the Spirit, and so maketh it light and easy to us. To a strong back that burden is light which would crush the weak and faint, and cause them to shrink under it; but though God moderateth our afflictions, he doth not abate our glory; that is given without measure: 'A far more exceeding weight of glory'

[E.] The sufferings are in our mortal bodies, but the glory is both in soul and body. It is but the flesh which is troubled and grieved by affliction; the flesh which, if delicately used, soon becometh our enemy; the soul is free, and not liable to the power of man. Now it becometh a man, much more a believer, to look after the soul: Heb. x. 39, 'We are not of them who draw back to perdition, but of them that believe to the saving of the soul'; the Greek here signifies that they that are tender of flesh are apostates in heart; if not actually and indeed so, yet in the practice; but those which will purchase the saving of the soul at any rates, are the true and sound believers. The world, which gratifieth the bodily life, may be bought at too dear a rate; but not so the salvation of the soul; they that are so thirsty of the comforts and interests of the bodily life, will certainly be prodigal of their salvation. But a believer is all for the saving of his soul; that is the end of his faith, and labours, and sufferings, and his self-denial. The end of his faith is to save his soul, 1 Pet. i. 9. So much as God is to be preferred before the creature, heaven before the world, eternity before time, the soul before the body; so much doth it concern us to have the better part safe. But yet this is not all; that which is lost for a while, is preserved to us forever; if the body be lost temporally, it is secured to all eternity. If we lose it by the way, we are sure to have it at the end of the journey, when the body shall have many privileges bestowed upon it; but this above all the rest, that it shall be united to a soul fully sanctified, from which it shall never any more be separated, but both together shall be the eternal temple of the Holy Ghost.

[F.] Sufferings do mostly deprive us of those things which are without a man; but this is a glory which shall be revealed in us. By sufferings we lose estate, liberty, comfortable abode in the world among our friends and relations. If life itself, which is within us, it is only as to its capacity of outward enjoyments; for as to the fruition of God and Christ, so it is true he that loseth his life shall save it, Mat. x. 39, and shall live though he die, John xi. 25; it is but deposited in Christ's hands. But this glory is revealed in us, in our bodies in their immortality, agility, clarity, and brightness; in our souls by the beatifical vision, the ardent love of God, the unconceivable joy and everlasting peace and rest which we shall have when we shall attain our end. Now if we be deprived of things without us; if we be denied to live in dependence on the creature, that we may immediately enjoy God, should we grudge and murmur?

[G.] Our sufferings dishonour us in the sight of the world, but this glory maketh us amiable in the sight of God. For having such a near relation to God, and being made like him, we are qualified for a perfect reception of his love to us; we love God more in the glorified estate, and God loveth us more, as appeareth by the effects; for he communicateth himself to us in a greater latitude than we are capable of here. Now is the hatred of the world worthy to be compared with the love of the Father? Or should their frowns be a temptation to us, to divert us from that estate wherein we shall be presented 'holy, and unblamable, and irreprovable in his sight?' Col. i. 22. When perfectly sanctified, we love God more, and are more beloved by him.

[H.] The order is to be considered. For look; as to the wicked, God will turn their glory into shame; so as to the godly, he will turn their shame into glory. It is good to have the best at last; for it is a miserable thing to have been happy, and to have had experience of a better condition, and to become miserable: Luke vi. 24. 'Woe to you rich, for you have received your consolation'; and Luke xvi. 25, 'Son, in thy life time thou receivedst thy good things, and Lazarus evil things; but now he is comforted, and thou art tormented.' The beggar had first temporal evils, and then eternal good things; but the rich man had first temporal good things, and then eternal evil things; as many that do well here in the world, fare ill in the world to come. But now it is otherwise with the godly: John xvi. 20, 'Your sorrow shall be turned into joy.' Our last and final portion is most to be regarded; the Christian by temporal trouble goeth to eternal joy; the worldling by temporal glory to eternal shame; a Christian's end is better than his beginning, he is best at last; a man would not have evil after experience of good.

4. The comparison, though it be rightly stated and weighed by us, yet it will have no efficacy unless we have faith, or a deep sense of the world to come. For unless we believe these

things, they seem too uncertain, and too far off to work upon us. It is easy to reason down our bodily and worldly choice, and to show how much eternal things exceed temporal; but this taketh no hold of the heart, till there be a firm belief of the glory reserved for God's people: Heb. xi. 1, 'Faith is the substance of things hoped for, and the evidence of things not seen'; and 2 Pet. i. 9, 'He that lacketh these things is blind, and cannot see afar off.' To draw us from things that we see and feel, we need a clear light about things we see not; men are sharp sighted enough in things that concern the present world, but beyond it we can see nothing, but by the perspective of faith; and therefore reason as long as we will, yet the consideration of the other world doth nothing prevail with us, without a lively faith.

5. This faith must be often exercised by serious meditations, or deep and ponderous thoughts. For the greatest truths work not, if we do not think of them. Faith showeth us a truth, but consideration is the means to improve it, that we may make a good choice, and our hearts may be fortified against all temptations; we must often sit down, and count the charges with ourselves, what it will cost us, what we shall lose, and what we shall get: Luke xiv. 28, 29, 30. The Spirit of God will not help us without our thoughts; for he dealeth not with us as birds do in feeding their young, bringing meat to them, and putting it into their mouths, while they lie still in their nest, and only gape to receive it; but as God giveth corn while we plough, sow, weed, dress, and with patience expect his blessing. No, here the apostle was reasoning and weighing the case within himself.

6. There is, besides sound belief and serious consideration, need of the influence and assistance of the Holy Spirit. For besides his giving faith, and exciting and blessing meditation, to dispose and frame our hearts to bide by this conclusion, the influence of the Holy Ghost is necessary. For God is the chief disposer of hearts; it is not enough notionally to know this, but we must be practically resolved, and the heart inclined; it is a new enlightened mind and a renewed heart that is only capable of determining thus, that we may live by it; and that is by another spirit than the spirit of the world, which naturally possesseth us, even the Spirit of God, 1 Cor. ii. 12, which is promised to his children, and inclineth us to place our happiness, not in worldly things, but in Christ and his benefits. In short, sense is too strong for reason without faith; and faith cannot do its office without the Spirit; the flesh seeketh not reason, but ease; unless the heart be changed, and otherwise biased and bent, all is lost.

Use. Now I must show you the use of this doctrine.

First. Certainly it is useful for the afflicted in any sort, whatever their troubles and afflictions be.

1. For common evils:

[A.] Are you pained with sickness, and roll to and fro in your bed, like a door on the hinges, for the weariness of your flesh? In heaven you shall have everlasting ease, for that is a state of rest, Heb. iv. 9. We are apprehensive of present pain, but not of the greatness of the ease, peace, and glory that shall succeed; though the pains be acute, the sickness lingering, and hangeth long upon you, yet present time is quickly past; but eternity shall have no end.

[B.] Must you die, and the guest be turned out of the old house? 'You have a building with God, eternal in the heavens'. 2 Cor. v. 1. You do but leave a shed to live in a palace, and forsake an unquiet world for a place of everlasting repose.

2. It is especially to be applied to those that suffer for righteousness' sake. Shall we shrink at sufferings for Christ, when we shall be in glory with him for evermore? How short is the suffering? How long the reward? For a greater good, we should endure a lesser evil. A traveller endureth all the difficulties of the way, for the sake of the place where he is going unto; so should we. What is the evil threatened? Are you cast out by man as unworthy to live in any civil society? You shall be received by the Lord into an everlasting abode with him: 1 Thes. v. 17, 'And so shall we be ever with the Lord'. Have you lost the love of all men, for your sincerity and faithfulness? You shall everlastingly enjoy the love of God, Rom. viii. 39. Are you reproached, calumniated in the world? Then you shall be justified by Christ, and your faith found to honour, praise, and glory, 2 Pet. i. 7. Are you cast into prison? You shall shortly be in your Father's house, where there are many mansions, John xiv. 2. Are you reduced to sordid poverty? You may read in the scripture of the 'riches of the glory of the inheritance of the saints' Eph. i. 18. In short, are you tempted, opposed, persecuted? Consider, much of your journey is past away; you are nearer eternity than you were when you first believed, Rom. xiii. 11. They that both tempt and persecute cannot give so much to you, or take so much from you, as is worthy to be compared with your great hopes. Immortal happiness is, most desirable, and endless misery most terrible; therefore be you faithful to the death, and you shall have the crown of life, Kev. ii. 10. Is life itself likely to be forced out by the violence of man? The sword is but the key to open heaven's door for you; surely this hope will make the greatest sufferings to become light, turn pain into pleasure, yea, and death itself into life.

Secondly. It is useful for all, if only for the afflicted. None is exempted, and you must hear for the time to come; but every good Christian should be of this temper and spirit, and wholly fetch his solaces from the world to come, else he is not possessed with a true spirit of Christianity, which warneth us all to prepare for sufferings, and calleth for self-denial. Besides, this is a great means to mortify worldly affections, which are the great impediment of the heavenly life. When we once learn to despise the afflictions of the world, our affections to the delights thereof die by consent; both are rooted in the same disposition and frame of heart; such a dead and mortified temper, as hath learned to contemn earthly things; and they are both fed and maintained by the same considerations, a looking to the end of things, which maketh us wise, Deut. xxxii. 29. If our hearts be often in heaven, it will lessen all worldly things in our eyes; and it will make us not only patient and contented in sufferings, but diligent in holy duties, fearful of sinning. For all those pleasures which tempt us to neglect duty, or to make bold with sin, are no more worthy to be compared with the glory which shall be revealed in us, than our sufferings are; yea, the argument holdeth stronger against them; if the greater sufferings should not deter us from our duty, certainly vain pleasures should not. They that cast off" the profession and practice of godliness out of indulgence to carnal delights or some worldly hope, are less to be pitied, because they involve themselves in a more heinous sin than they that shrink from it out of some great fear. For torment and death, which are the chiefest things we fear, are destructive of our nature; therefore we have a natural shunning and abhorrence of them; but those other things are such things as nature may easily, and without greater inconvenience, want; such as preferment, splendor of life, sottish pleasures. They are enticed by their mere lust, which is not so pressing as fear.

SERMON XXVI

For the earnest expectation of the creature waiteth for the manifestation of the sons of God.

Romans VIII. 19.

THE apostle's intent in this paragraph is to set forth the excellency of that glory which shall be revealed in the children of God. The argument is, because when this is brought to pass, there shall be a general renovation of all things. It is figuratively expressed; all things are by a natural inclination carried to their most perfect estate; so are the creatures to this renovation and restoration, as if they did wait and long for it'; for the earnest expectation' &c.

In the words—(1.) Who waiteth? The creature. (2.) How it waiteth? With earnest expectation; as it were looking attentively for the time. (3.) For what, or the term of its waiting? For the manifestation of the sons of God:

First. Let us explain these circumstances. Secondly. Consider how much they suit with the apostle's scope.

First, For explication.

1. Who waiteth? The creature: but what creature? Some understand man, designed elsewhere by this appellation, creature: Mark xvi. 15, 'Preach the gospel to every creature,' that is, to all mankind; so here they understand man, because there are affections and dispositions attributed to the creature here spoken of, which are only proper to such a creature as is reasonable; but they are metaphorically to be understood; they do, as it were, long for and expect. Well then, let us see what creature is intended. Not the good angels; for they are not subject to vanity, and they are in possession of this glory: Mat. xviii. 10, 'They always behold the face of our heavenly Father'. Not devils or evil angels; they do not earnestly expect these things, but tremble at them: Mat viii. 29. Not men, not the wicked, the reprobate world, for they care not for these things, yea, they scoff at them: 2 Pet. iii. 3, 'There shall come in the last days scoffers, walking after their own lusts, saying, Where is the promise of his coming? 'Not the saints and believers; for they are distinctly spoken of by themselves, ver. 23, and are opposed to this expecting, groaning creature, 'And not only they, but we ourselves also' Not the beasts, for they are incapable of a prospect of futurity, and are made to be taken and destroyed. Therefore it is meant of the whole frame of the universe, heaven, and earth, and the creatures in them; they do, as it were, expect the time when they shall be restored to the primitive state of their creation. The whole frame of the universe was first made in a beautiful state for the glory of God, and the use of man; it is subject to many changes, and at length to destruction. The earth and the elementary bodies shall be burnt up as a scroll, but they shall be renewed and restored when the children of God come to their glorious estate; the deformation of the creature began with man's sin, and the reformation with his complete happiness.

2. How it earnestly expecteth and waiteth? The word signifieth, it expecteth with head lifted up, and stretched out. The same word is used, Phil. i. 20, 'According to my earnest

expectation.' When a man longingly expecteth anything, he lifts up the head, sendeth his eyes after it, that he may see it afar off: As Judges v. 28, 'The mother of Sisera looked out of a window, and cried through the lattice, Why is his chariot so long a-coming?' But how can this be applied to the creature, which is without reason and sense? I answer, By a metaphor it is translated from man to them; because there is something analogous, as they are directed and inclined to such an end; as in the scripture the floods are said to clap their hands for joy, and the mountains and hills leaping and skipping like rams. And in the desolation, the city of Jerusalem is said to 'weep sore in the nights; her tears are on her cheeks'; and again, Lam. ii. 18, 19. The wall is said to 'cry in the night.' Yea, our Lord himself speaketh to the sea, as if it had ears: Mark iv. 39, 'He said to the sea, Peace be still! 'So the apostle speaketh of the creature as if it had will, desire, hope, sorrow, and groaning.

3. For what? The manifestation of the sons of God. Manifestation is the discovery of something which before was obscure and hidden; and by sons, the subject for the adjunct, is meant the right and privileges of God's children. That is, that the glory prepared for them may visibly appear, when they shall be set forth with splendour and majesty, becoming the sons of God; for 'the righteous shall shine like the sun in the kingdom of the Father,' Mat. xiii. 43. And it is said 'sons,' comprehending all of that sort; Christ is not excluded, and all believers are included; your happiness dependeth on the glory of Christ: Col. iii. 4, 'When Christ, who is our life, shall appear, then shall ye also appear with him in glory'; 1 John iii. 2, 'But we know, that when he shall appear we shall be like him, for we shall see him as he is.' And the creature is said to expect it, because their perfect estate dependeth on our happiness: Acts iii. 21, 'Whom the heavens must receive until the time of the restitution of all things.' 'We look for new heavens, and new earth, 2 Pet. iii. 12, 13, wherein dwelleth righteousness'.

Secondly. How it suiteth with the apostle's scope? I answer: The apostle intendeth. three things, 1. To set forth the excellency of our hopes. 2. To raise up expectation. 3. To persuade the necessity of patience in the meantime. The present argument is serviceable to all these uses.

1. It showeth that there is an excellent state of happiness, far beyond what we do now enjoy, provided for the people of God. This is seen, partly because all things tend to it, as to their great end and state of perfection; there is a tendency in the inanimate creatures. And partly, because the glory is so great that there must be a dissolution of the present world, and a pure estate of things, before we can have our happiness. We admire the splendour of the present world; are taken with earthly things; too apt to place our happiness in them; but this world must be purged and refined by fire before it can be capable to suit with that blessed estate of things which God hath appointed for hi? People. God denieth not the splendour of the world, as too good for his people, but as too bad and base to be their portion; the delights of wicked men shall be burnt up before their eyes, when he bestoweth their true happiness upon them. There would not be else a harmony in all the parts of the world to come, if there were not new heavens and a new earth. This polluted state is not

consistent with that happiness; therefore when the saints are perfected, the world is restored.

2. To quicken earnest expectation. All things are carried to their end; the little seed will work through the dry clods, that it may come into stalk and flower. The whole universe is directed and inclined to a more happy estate; so should we look after our most perfect state; the creatures by inclination wait for it, and shall not we who are to have the chief part therein?

3. To persuade the necessity of patience, during our sufferings in the meantime. We live in a groaning world, and such as shall be first destroyed, and then restored. As the frame of the sublunary world being now in disorder, and at length to be dissolved, groaneth after a restoration; so, though we be harassed with afflictions, and must at length die, and this animated body be turned into a rotten carcass, yet at length shall be raised up in glory.

The points are three. (1.) That the glorious privileges of God's children are manifested at the last day. (2.) That the state of the creatures is renewed, when God's children come to be manifested in their glory. (3.) That this estate of things Bought earnestly to be desired and expected by us.

For the first point, That the glorious privileges of God's children are manifested at the last day. It supposeth—

First, That their estate and happiness is hidden for the present but—

Secondly. Then manifested.

First. Here we must enquire. 1. How they are hidden? 2. From whom? 3. Why they are hidden? *Secondly*. How they are manifested then; and so we shall the better understand how the word is used in opposition to the present estate.

[A.] They are hidden as to their persons. [B.] Their life is hidden. [C.] As to their privileges and glorious estate.

[A.] Hidden as .to their persons. Now, it is little known who are God's children; Christ himself was not known in the world: 1 John iii. 1, 'The world knoweth us not, because it knew him not;' much less are his people known; for he did more to distinguish himself than they possibly can do. But it shall be in time manifested who are God's children: Mai. iii. 18, 'Then shall ye return, and discern between the righteous and the wicked; between him that serveth God, and him that serveth him not.' Some pretend to be his children and servants; others really are so. It is not exactly known in the winter, when the roots lie in the earth we cannot tell what will appear in the spring; but when the sun shineth in its strength and warmth, the bosom of the earth, things hidden, then discover themselves. As Moses told the rebels in Num. xvi. 6, 'Tomorrow the Lord will show who are his;' so in the morning of the resurrection, the natural and only begotten Son is known; Christ will appear in all his royalty and glory as the great God and Saviour of the world, Titus ii. 13. So all the children of God are known; they now lie hid among multitudes and swarms of sinful men; but then Christ shall 'gather all nations and he shall separate the one from the other, as a shepherd divideth his sheep from the goats' Mat. xxv. 32. There shall be an eminent and sensible distinction of the one from the other, beyond all power of mistaking.

[B.] Their life is hidden: Col. iii 3, 'Our life is hidden with Christ in God' Hidden not only in point of security, as maintained by an invisible power; but in point of obscurity; there is a veil upon it. How so? Partly, because the spiritual life is hidden under the veil of the natural life; it is a life within a life; the spiritual life is nothing else but the natural life sublimated, and overruled to higher and nobler ends: Gal. ii. 20, 'I live, yet not I, but Christ liveth in me; and the life which I now live in the flesh, I live by the faith of the Son of God.' They live in the flesh, but they do not live after the flesh. The children of God eat, and drink, and sleep, and marry, and give in marriage, as others do; for when they are converted they do not divest themselves of the interests and concernments of flesh and blood; but all these things are governed by grace, and carried on to eternal ends; the grace now, or vital principle that ruleth this life is not seen, though the effects appear. Partly, Because of the veil of afflictions, outward meanness, and abasement, Heb. xi. 37, 38. The world was not worthy of them; yet they wandered about in sheep-skins and goat-skins, and the dens and caves of the earth. Who would think that so much worth should lie hid under a base outside? Would any judge that these lived in the highest favour of God, and constant communion with him, who had so little of his protection and common bounty? That they should have so near a relation to God, and yet be so miserably poor and destitute? That those that want bread should be heirs of a kingdom? Jam. ii. 5. That they that feel the hand of God upon them so heavy and smart sometimes, should have so much of his heart? Partly under the veil of reproaches and calumnies: 1 Pet. iv. 6, 'They are judged according to men in the flesh, yet live to God in the spirit.' They are presented in the world as a company of dissemblers and hypocrites, and yet in the meanwhile are the sincere servants and children of God: 2 Cor. vi. 8, 'As deceivers, and yet true'; the world counteth them deceivers, but God counteth them faithful. By the reproach of the world, as husbandmen by soil and dung, God maketh his heritage the more fruitful; those that have a mind to hate will take Tip every prejudice against the people of God, and will not easily be dis possessed of it. And partly, because there is another veil upon good Christians, and that is the veil of infirmities, by which they often quench the vigour arid obscure the glory of that life which they have, whilst they show forth too much of Adam and too little of Jesus. And so the spiritual life is carried on darkly, and in a riddle: Jam. iii. 2, 'In many things we offend all.' Certainly if our privileges be hidden, yet our graces should appear in their fruits and effects. Little of our happiness will be seen in this world, yet our holiness should be apparent and visible: 2 Thes. i. 11, 12, 'Wherefore also we pray always for you, that our God would count you worthy of this calling, and fulfil all the good pleasure of his goodness, and the work of faith with power; that the name of our Lord Jesus Christ may be glorified in you, and ye in him, according to the grace of our God, and the Lord Jesus Christ. 5 If your condition be obscured and darkened by afflictions, it should not be obscured and darkened by sins; a perpetual tenor of happiness we cannot expect in a changeable world; yet by a constant course of holiness, we should plainly distinguish ourselves from those that will perish in the common apostasy and defection of mankind. But alas! God's children are not so cautious but that they border too near the world; and though there should be such a broad difference that the children of God may be manifestly distinguished from the children of the devil, 1 John iii. 10, yet too much of the influence of the evil spirit remaineth with us, and is bewrayed[37] by us upon all occasions. Yet there is a generation of men that row against the stream of flesh and blood: 1 Pet. iv. 4, 'Wherein they think it strange that you run not with them into the same excess of riot.'

[C.] Hidden as to their privileges, and the glory of their estate. Many of God's children being mean, and low, and indigent, oppressed by the world, harassed with sundry calamities and afflictions, it doth not appear that we have such a great and glorious Father. Now we are stained with sin, blackened with sufferings, there is no visible appearance of our great dignity and prerogative. There must be a distinction between earth and heaven; our filiation in the world to come is another thing to what it is in this world; for then their glory shall be manifest: Col. iii. 4, 'When Christ, who is our life, shall appear, then shall ye also appear with him in glory' For the present, our glory is spiritual and future: First, it is spiritual, and maketh no fair show in the flesh, as the image of God is an internal thing; as 'the king's daughter is glorious within,' Ps. xlv. 13. It lieth not in great revenues and pomp of living, but a plentiful participation of gifts and graces; their comforts are spiritual, known by feeling rather than by report: Phil. iv. 7, 'The peace of God, which passeth all understanding,' Rev. ii. 17, 'To him that overcometh will I give to eat of the hidden manna, and will give him a white stone, and in the stone a new name written, which no man knoweth saving he that receiveth it.' God's children are not utterly abandoned and left to the will of men; the protection of God's providence is a mystery and riddle to the world, that must have all things under the view of sense: Ps. xxxi. 20, 'Thou shalt hide them in the secret of thy presence from the pride of man; thou shalt keep them secretly in a pavilion from the strife of tongues;' and Ps. xci. 1, 'He that dwelleth in the secret place of the Most High, shall abide under the shadow of the Almighty'; Job. xxix. 4, 'As I was in the days of my youth, when the secret of God was upon my tabernacle.' God keepeth them, and maintaineth them, nobody knoweth how; there is a secret and visible blessing goes along with them; as others are blasted by an invisible curse. And secondly, it is future. The time of our perfection and blessedness is not yet come, and we cannot for the present judge of it, nor the world imagine what it shall be; they do not consider the end of things, but look all to the present; for the present they find the saints miserable; and those that are dead, the world taketh them for lost: 1 Cor. xv. 19, 'If in this life only we have hope in Christ, we are of all men most miserable' They that are worse used by other men, have little advantage by Christ now; their sonship entitleth them to a miserable portion in the world's estimation, who know not, consider not things to come.

2. From whom they are hidden. Not from God, who 'knoweth those that are his,' 2 Tim. ii. 19; not from Christ, who died for them, and hath their names graven upon his breast and shoulders, and is mindful of them upon every turn: John x. 14, 'I am the good shepherd, who know my sheep, and am known of mine.' Christ hath a particular and exact knowledge of all the elect, their individual persons, who they are, where they are, and what they are, that

---

[37] divulged

shall be saved; he taketh special notice of them, that he may suitably apply himself to them. They are not altogether unknown to the good angels, for they are their charge: Heb. i. 14, 'Are they not all ministering spirits, sent forth to minister for them who shall be heirs of salvation?' And they shall gather them from the four winds at the last day, Mat. xxiv. 31. From whom then are they hidden?

[A.] From the world. The world knoweth us not, as they knew him not; they are hid from the world, as colours from a blind man; they have no eyes to see; they are blinded by the delusions of the flesh, and cannot judge of spiritual things, because they are to be spiritually discerned, 1 Cor. ii. 14; as a beast cannot judge of the affairs of a man. It is a life above them; these things are out of their sphere, for they value all things according to the interest of the flesh; and being blinded with malice and prejudice, they censure this estate perversely, and so malign and oppose it: 1 Pet. iv. 4, 5, 'They think it strange you do not run with them into the same excess of riot, speaking evil of you; who shall give an account to him who is ready to judge the quick and the dead.' They are unwilling any should put a disgrace upon their fleshly course of life; therefore if they cannot draw others into a fellowship of their sins, they labour to blacken them with censures, or root them out with furious oppositions and persecutions. But their perverse judgment should be no discouragement to us; let us rather pity their ignorance, than be troubled at their malice; it is enough for us that we have the favour of God, and our hopes lie elsewhere.

[B.] In a great measure from ourselves. What with corruptions within, and temptations without, we have much ado to be persuaded that God is our father, and we his children; our condition being so unsuitable, and our conversations so much beneath our rights and privileges; so that it needeth to be cleared by the Spirit of adoption; no less agent or witness will serve the turn: Rom. viii. 16, 'The Spirit itself beareth witness to our spirits that we are the children of God' When that is done, yet the glory intended to be revealed in us is not sufficiently known; we have not now an heart to conceive of it, 1 Cor. ii. 9; and prophecy is but in part, 1 Cor. xiii. 9; and the apostle when rapt up in paradise, heard *arreta remata,* 2 Cor. xii. 4. Heavenly joys cannot be told us in an earthly dialect; the scripture is fain to lisp to us, and to speak something of it, as we can understand and conceive of things to come by things present; therefore our glory is in a great measure unknown, and will be till the day of manifestation; and then there shall be a crown of glory prepared for us.

3. Why this glory is hidden?

[A.] Because now is the time of trial, hereafter of recompense. Therefore now is the hiding time; hereafter is the day of the manifestation of the sons of God; if the glory were too sensible, there were no trial, neither of the world, nor of the people of God. Christ himself might be discerned by those who had a mind to see him; yet there was obscurity enough in his person to harden those that were resolved to continue in their prejudices; therefore it is said, Luke ii. 39, 'This child was set for the rise and fall of many in Israel.' So if the whole excellency of a Christian's estate were laid open to the view of sense, there would be no trial; Christ had his bright side and dark side; a glory to be seen by those whose eyes were anointed with spiritual eye- salve: John i. 14, 'And the Word was made flesh, and dwelt among us, and we beheld his glory, as the glory of the only begotten of the Father'; and affliction and meanness enough to harden those who had no mind to see. So God hath his chosen ones in the world, who keep up his honour and interest; and he hath his ways to express his love to them, but not openly; they are called his c hidden ones' Ps. lxxxiii. 3. They are under his secret blessing and protection, but not visibly owned, but in such a way as may be best for their trial, and the trial of the world. The Lord Jesus came not with external appearance; his divine nature was hidden under the veil of his flesh; and his dignity and excellency under a base and mean outside; in the outward estate there was nothing lovely to be seen by a carnal eye: Isa. liii. 2, 'He hath no form and comeliness; and when we shall see him, there is no beauty that we should desire him; yet in himself, he was 'the brightness of the divine glory, and the express image of his person,' Heb. i. 3.

[B.] God hath chosen this way to advance his glory, that he may perfect his power in our weakness, 2 Cor. xii, 9. By wants and weak nesses his fatherly love appeareth to us, more than in an absolute and total exemption from them. God would not so often hear from us, nor would we have such renewed experiences to revive the sense of his fatherly love and grace, which would otherwise be dead and cold in our hearts, were it not for these wants and afflictions during our minority and nonage.

[C.] To wean and draw us off from things present to things to come; that we may be contented to be hidden from, and hated by the world, if the course of our service expose us to it. For we must not look upon things as' they are, or seem to be now, but what they will be hereafter. Now is the trouble, then the reward; present time is quickly passed; and therefore we should be dead to present profits, and present pleasures, and present honours; and look to eternity, that is to come: 2 Cor. iv. 18, 'While we look not to the things which are seen, but at the things which are not seen; for the things which are seen are temporal, but the things which are not seen are eternal.' how glorious will the derided, vilified believer be then! It should be our ambition to look after this honour; it is the day of the manifestation of the sons of God. Though the wicked have a larger allowance by the bounty of God's common providence, yet you have his special love. We think God doth not place his hands aright; no! God doth not misplace his hands; as Joseph thought of his father, Gen. xlviii, when he preferred Ephraim before Manasseh. What a poor condition was the only be gotten Son of God in when he lived in the world! When you are poorer than Christ, then complain; though you do not enjoy pleasures, honours, riches, esteem, yet if you enjoy the favour of God, it is enough; though mean, yet if heirs of glory, Jam. ii. 5. God doth not esteem persons according to their outward lustre: 1 Sana. xvi. 7, 'Look not on his countenance, or the height of his stature; for the Lord seeth not as man seeth; for man looketh upon the outward appearance, but the Lord looketh on the heart.'

Secondly. How manifested? Their persons shall be known and owned: Rev. iii. 5, 'But I will confess his name before my Father, and before his angels' It is no litigious debate then; no more doubt when owned, not by character, but by name; they shall be manifested to themselves, and their glory also revealed to the world by the visible marks of favour Christ will put upon them, when others are rejected: Isa. lxvi. 5, 'But he shall appear to your joy, and they shall be ashamed.' Yea, the world shall stand wondering: 2 Thes. i. 10, 'When he shall come to be glorified in his saints, and to be admired in all them that believe'

Doctrine 2. That the state of the creatures shall be renewed, when God's children come to be manifested in their glory; for he saith, 'the whole creation groaneth and waiteth'

1. This is clear, that heaven and earth, that is, the lower heavens and the elementary bodies, as well as the earth, shall suffer some kind of change at the last day; for it is said: Ps. cii. 26, 'As a vesture shalt thou change them, and they shall be changed' He will change them, quite from the condition wherein they now are.

2. That this change of the world and the heavenly and elementary bodies shall be by fire: 2 Pet. iii. 7, 'The heavens and the earth which are now are reserved unto fire against the day of judgment, and the perdition of ungodly men.'

3. That notwithstanding this fire and universal destruction, rational creatures shall subsist to all eternity, in their proper place assigned to each of them; the godly in heaven, the wicked in hell: Mat. xxv. 46, 1 These shall go away into everlasting punishment, but the righteous into eternal life'

4. It is probable that the brutes and plants, and all such corruptible bodies as are necessary to the animal life, but superfluous to life everlasting, shall be utterly destroyed.

5. That the world and elementary bodies shall be refined and purged by this fire, and not utterly destroyed. This is the design of the scripture, and therefore this general conflagration seemeth not to turn all things into nothing in regard of their substance, but change of qualities; and to change them with a perfective, not a destructive change; to change the matter, not reduce it into nothing; for that which is made matter of desire or hope, cannot be simple and total destruction or annihilation, as it is by the apostle here; and it is compared with the deluge, where the form of the world was destroyed, not the substance: 2 Pet. ii. 6, As the world that was overflowed by water, perished; so shall the world perish, which is consumed with fire; not by annihilation, but a change of qualities; only for the better, as that was for the worse.

6. What use this restored world serveth for, we need not anxiously enquire; whether to be a perpetual monument of the wisdom, power, and goodness of the creator (the creating of the world served for this end, so may the renewing of it); or whether it shall be an habitation for the just during the judgment, which is by some conceived to last for a thousand years; and at first consumed by a purging fire, and afterwards utterly destroyed by a consuming fire; we shall enquire in the following verses.

Doctrine 3. That this estate of things ought earnestly to be desired and expected by us. For to this end the apostle mentioneth the earnest expectation of the creature, and the day principally concerneth us; and therefore it is the duty of God's children to look for this day. There are two choice scriptures that describe the communion of the church with Christ, and the dispensations of Christ to the church; and they both conclude with a desire of his coming. One is Cant. viii. 14; the other is Rev. xxii. 20. The first place, 'Make haste my beloved, and be like a young hart or roe upon the mountains of spices' Christ is not slack, but the church's affections are strong; "make haste," my beloved; that is the bride's last and great suit to the bridegroom, his coming in glory to judge the world. The wanton prostitute would have her husband defer his coming; but the chaste spouse thinketh he can never come soon enough; they that go a-whoring after the world, and are wholly taken up with the world, neither desire his coming, nor love his appearing: but the spouse would have all things hastened, that he may return; either come down to them, or take them up to himself; it is that day only can perfect a believer's consolation; they do what they can to have the blessed and longed-for meeting hastened. In the other place Christ saith, 'Surely I come quickly'; and the church like a quick echo, saith, 'Even so, come Lord Jesus, come quickly.' It taketh the word out of Christ's mouth. There is the same Spirit in Christ and the church; for it is Christ's Spirit which resideth in the church; and therefore Chrst speaketh in a way proper to him, 'Behold I come quickly' in a way of promise; and the church, in a way proper to her, 'Even so come.' And Christ's voice and the Church's voice are unisons; our acclamation answereth to his proclamation: Christ saith, 'I come' as desiring to meet with us'; even so come' as desiring his fellowship and company. The saints look for his coming, Titus ii. 13, by faith and hope; and long for his coming, love his appearing, 2 Tim. iv. 8, in a way of love.

Now his coming must be desired by us:

[A.] With earnestness and hearty groans: 2 Cor. v. 2, 'For this we groan earnestly'

[B.] With constancy, not for a fit. The Spirit in the bride saith, 'Come' Rev. xxii. 17. The new nature stirreth up these desires in us; as soon and as long as he worketh in us, there is a bent this way; we should always stand ready to meet him.

[C.] With patience. Here is earnest desire and waiting in the text: 1 Thes. i. 10, 'We wait for his Son from heaven'

Use 1. Is to reprove those that never look after this estate.

[A.] That have nothing to incline them to look higher than the world; that are under the power of a carnal nature, that wholly bendeth them to earthly things, Phil. iii. 19; that are well enough satisfied with the happiness of beasts, to enjoy pleasures without remorse; have not sense and care of the world to come. Those whose happiness is terminated on things of the present life are so far from Christians, that they are scarce men.

[B.] That have much to divert them from it; namely, unpardoned unmodified sin. If thieves and malefactors might have liberty to choose whether there should be an assizes, would they give their vote that way? Would they look and long for the time? They are not fire-proof, or such as may abide the day of refining: 2 Pet. iii. 11, 'Seeing all these things must be dissolved, what manner of persons ought we to be in all holy conversation and godliness? 'They are riot at peace with God, ver. 14.

Use 2. To press believers to live in the constant expectation of this glorious day; to make us heavenly: Phil. iii. 20, 'But our conversation is in heaven, from whence we look for the Saviour.' Live as if it were always present, which by faith we look for; this will make us faithful, 2 Tim. iv. 7; persevere to the end, 1 John ii. 24; make us press forward, and make us long to be at home: 2 Cor. v. 8, 'For we are confident, I say, willing rather to be absent from the body, and to be present with the Lord.

SERMON XXVII

For the creature was made subject to vanity, not willingly, but by reason of him who hath subjected the same in hope.

Romans VIII. 20.

HERE is the reason why the creature waiteth with earnest expectation for the consummate state of the faithful: because it is for the present in a disordered estate, subject to vanity. In the words three things:

1. The present state of the creature.

2. The manner how it came into that estate.

3. The hope of getting out of it.

Doctrine The creature is made subject to vanity for man's sin.

Here I shall enquire,

First, In what sense the creature is made subject to vanity.

Secondly, The manner how it came into it.

Thirdly, The reason why the innocent creature is punished for man's sin.

First. In what sense the creature is made subject to vanity. In several respects:

1. It is put by the order of its natural estate, or much of that harmonious and perfect condition wherein God disposed it. The perfection and harmony of the world is often now disturbed by tempests, inundations, distempered weather, pestilential airs, and noxious fogs and vapours; whence come plagues, and famine, and murrains, and other diseases. The world is a theatre whereon much sin and many changes have been acted for thousands of years; not only among men, but much destructive enmity is to be found among elements themselves, and a mutual invasion of one another; for the confederacies of nature tire in a great measure loosened, though not altogether dissettled. This is the vanity of disorder. It is very observable, that when God cometh to punish a people or a nation for their sins, the prophets express it as if the whole creation were to be put into a rout and disorder; as when Babylon's destruction is threatened: Isa. xiii. 13, 14, 'I will shake the heavens, and the earth shall remove out of its place in the day of his fierce anger; and it shall be as a chased roe, and a sheep whom no man taketh up'; so Isa. xxxiii. 9, 'The earth mourneth and languisheth; Lebanon is ashamed and hewed down; Sharon is like a wilderness; Bashan and Carmel shake off their fruits'; so Isa. xxxiv. 4, when God threateneth the Idumeans and other enemies of the church, it is said, 'All the host of heaven shall be dissolved, and the heavens shall be rolled together as a scroll, and all their host shall fall down as a leaf falleth off from the vine, and as a falling leaf from the fig-tree; for my sword shall be bathed in heaven; it shall come down upon Idumea, and upon the 'people of my curse, to judgment. It was but a particular judgment, yet the expressions carry it as if the whole universe were to be put into a disorder; for by the sin of man came all those mutations which we see in the world. On the contrary, you shall see in the promises the scripture speak as if the whole creation were to

be restored when man is reduced to God. I shall only instance in that: Isa. li. 16, 'I have put my words in thy mouth, that I may cover thee in the shadow of mine hand, that I may plant the heavens, and lay the foundations of the earth, and say unto Zion, Thou art my people'; implying, that if mankind were better, the marks and prints of the curse would cease and be quite extinguished; there would not be such disorder in the creature as now appeareth; but it would seem to be planted again; man's reestablishment in a state of obedience to the creator would be a reestablishment of the order of the world.

2. There is the vanity of corruption. It is put into a corruptible condition; the creature is now frail and fleeting, and still decaying: Eccles. i. 2, 'Vanity of vanities, all is vanity'; not only vain, but vanity itself; and vanity of vanities, is extreme vanity; thus not only some things, but all things are thus fluid and vain, because of their inconstancy and mutability: so Ps. xxxix. 5, 6, 'Verily every man in his best estate is altogether vanity; surely every man walketh in a vain show; surely they are disquieted in vain' The uncertainty, weakness, and emptiness of all earthly things is soon discovered, and within a little while the most shining glory is burnt to a snuff. We vain creatures trouble ourselves about these transitory nothings, as if they would continue with us to all eternity, and had some solid, durable enjoyment and satisfaction in them; whereas they wither like flowers while we smell at them.

3. Vain in regard of its final dissolution and last change, when 'the heavens shall pass away with a great noise, and the elements shall melt with fervent heat, and all the works that are therein shall be burnt up' 2 Pet. iii. 10. 'As a vesture shalt thou change them, and they shall be changed' Ps. cii. 26. Though this change be not an abolition, an annihilation, yet a great waste it will be, and an utter destruction of many things in the world.

4. Vain in regard of its end and use. There is a double end and use:

[A.] Nextly and immediately. This sublunary world was made to be a commodious habitation for man: Ps. cxv. 16, 'The heaven, even the heavens, are the Lord's; but the earth hath he given to the children of men.' By an original grant, God gave the use of all his creatures upon earth unto man; indeed all things here below were either subject to our dominion, or created for our use. Some things are not subject to our dominion, as sun, moon, and stars, with their influences, yet created for our use; therefore David in his night-meditation, Ps. viii. 3, 4, 'When I consider the heavens, the work of thy fingers, the moon and the stars, which thou hast ordained; what is man, that thou art mindful of him? And the son of man, that thou visitest him?' That all this should be made for the comfort of man, it is God's great goodness to us: but other things were not only created for man's use, but also subject to man's dominion: Gen. i. 26, 'Let them have dominion over the fish of the sea, and over the fowls of the air, and over the cattle, and over all the earth, and over every creeping thing that creepeth upon the earth'; this was God's charter to man as a deputy- god and vice-king in this lower world. Man enjoy eth the benefit of those things which are not under his command, as sun, moon, stars, clouds, winds; all in their course do us service, to give us light, heat, and influence, and rain, by which they drop down fatness on the earth; but the other creatures we have a dominion over them, and they are to be subdued by us; the earth by habitation and culture; the sea by navigation and fishing; but above all the rest, the cattle are most at our command, to afford us food and clothing, and do us a voluntary kind of homage, in their labours submitting to our direction and government. Well then, the inferior globe of earth, and air, and sea, to have the dominion and use of the creatures that are therein, were all made and given for man's use and comfort. As God hath provided the highest heavens for his own place and court of residence, so he hath made the earth for a commodious habitation for man. But when was this given to man? In innocency; for by rebellion against God we forfeited this lordship of ours; and till it be restored by Christ, we have no comfortable right to exercise it (as by and by). And in part, this was manifested in renewing this patent to Noah, saved out of the waters in the ark, which was a type of Christ: Gen. ix. 1, 2, 'God blessed Noah, and said unto him, The fear of you, and the dread of you, shall be upon every beast of the earth, and upon every fowl of the air, and upon all that moveth upon the earth, and upon all the fishes of the sea; into your hand they are delivered.' This was the next end for which the creature was made.

[B.] Ultimately and terminatively they were made for God. For God 'made all things for himself,' Prov. xvi. 4; and the creatures are called his servants: Ps. cxix. 91, 'They continue to this day according to thy ordinance; for all are thy servants'. Man was but a fellow- creature with the rest of the world, and could not challenge a lordship over them by his own right, without God's free gift. We could not claim a dominion over that which had no dependence on us, either by creation, or by present sustentation; for dependence is the foundation of all subjection and sovereignty. Now that which necessarily dependeth upon the gift of another, must be used to the ends for which it is given; God never gave the creatures so to man as to dispossess himself. The supreme right still remaineth in him; and our grant was not a total alienation from God; for that is impossible, unless the creature were put into an absolute state of independency. No, God reserved an interest still, that all these things should be used for his glory. To pass over this right any other way, is inconsistent with the wisdom of God, and the nature of the creature: Rom. xi. 36. 'All things are of him, and through him, and to him; to whom be glory for ever and ever.' This quit-rent God reserveth to himself for all his bounty, that we should honour him and acknowledge him in all that we are, have, and do: 1 Cor. x. 31, 'Whether ye eat and drink, or whatever you do, do all to the glory of God.' Well then, these things being premised, we shall the better state the vanity to which the creature is made subject for man's sin: *vanum est quod excidit fine suo*; that is vain which faileth in its use. Now the use is to serve man innocent, and to promote God's glory; therefore the creatures, if they had reason, it would be a grief to serve God's enemies, and to such vile uses as they abuse them.

(1.) It is a part of their vanity that they are made to serve man in a state of corruption, and the most wicked of the kind, that refuse to come out of the apostasy and defection from God. The creatures naturally take the part of the creator, are to be accounted friends or enemies to us, as God is; for the scripture speaketh of them as involved in his league and covenant; yet they are forced to serve those whom they are appointed to punish. God causeth his sun to shine on the good and the evil; and causeth his rain to fall upon the just and unjust; to serve wicked men's turns with whom they are at no peace. It is an old and a vexed question, What right and interest wicked men have in the creatures? As much as needeth to be now spoken to it may be comprised in these propositions:

First, man never had the right of an absolute and supreme lord, but only of a steward and a servant. The supreme original right was in the creator, but the subordinate and limited right was in man, who had nothing absolutely his own, but was to use all for God, to whom he was accountable. All things are ours for God; nothing is properly and ultimately our own.

Secondly, upon the fall, man lost the right of a servant; for when the first charter was broken, the rights that accrued thereby were lost, and by lapse forfeited into the hands of the true owner again.

Thirdly, though the right of a servant was forfeited and lost, yet God was pleased out of his patience and indulgence to continue fallen man the use and benefit of the creature, and some kind of right to them, a civil right and providential right. First, a civil right; as Nabal's sheep were said to be his sheep, 1 Sam. xxv n 4, and he is a thief that should have stolen them from him. A man is a thief before God and man that robbeth a wicked man; still we have such a right to the creatures that our fellow-servants may not take from us without our Lord's consent. Secondly, a providential right; as God puts them into our hands by the fair allowance and disposure of his providence: Ps. xvii. 14, 'They have their portion in this life: thou fillest their bellies with thy hid treasure.' So Jer. xxvii. 5, 'I have given it to whom it seemeth meet unto me'; corn, houses, lands, goods, cattle. He that hath an absolute right and interest in the creature may dispose it at his pleasure.

Fourthly, though they have a civil and providential right, yet they have not a filial and evangelical right; for that is by Christ. In him all things are ours: 1 Cor. iii. 22, 'All things are yours, and you are Christ's, and Christ is God's;' and with him he hath given us all things, Rom. viii. 32; and it is said, 1 Tim. iv. 3, 4, that 'every creature of God is good,' and created c to be received with thanksgiving of them that believe, and know the truth' These are heirs of promise who have right by Christ.

Fifthly. The evangelical right is that which sanctifieth the creature to us; and so thereby the creature may more comfortably serve us, our right being restored by Christ: 1 Tim. iv. 4, 'The creature is sanctified by the word and prayer' The more we believe and acknowledge God in Christ, the more comfortable use of the creature; whereas unregenerate men, who have forfeited the right of a steward, use the creature as if they had the right of a lord; use goods, lands, moneys, us their own, and given to them for themselves, and not for God; and this is a part of the vanity the creature is subject unto.

(2.) The creatures are often employed as instruments to fulfil our lusts, which in their original use were intended for God's glory; and so God is dishonoured rather than glorified by them. Some abuse the creatures to pride in apparel, some to gluttony and drunkenness, some to base sparing; whereas those that would be good stewards for God should use wholly what God hath put into their hands for God's glory; that the creature may not be turned from the end and use for which it was first made, as it is when the provisions of this life are used, not for strength, but for surfeiting and drunkenness; our clothes not for warmth, but for pride and wantonness; and the remainder and overplus of our estates employed in pomp, not in charity. But now, when this is little minded, the creature is abused to our vain ends.

Secondly. The manner how it came into this state of vanity. It is expressed negatively and positively.

1. Negatively; not willingly, that is, by its own natural propension. Voluntariness is attributed to the senseless creature by translation from man; and what is against the natural inclination of the creature, or the use for which it was ordained by God, it is said to be done unwillingly. The first institution of the creature was for God's glory and the benefit of man; and all creatures were fitted for the use for which they were made; and if it be put by its natural use, it hath a resemblance of violence. Therefore if you take vanity for the disorder or perishing of the creature; you may say, not wittingly; for all things tend naturally to their own preservation; and so what tendeth to its destruction cannot be said to be done willingly. Or if you take it for falling from its end and use, as the service of wicked men in their lusts; the creature is not subject to this bondage willingly, but forced to submit to it, as the world is now constituted.

2. Positively. God by his judgment hath subjected the creature to this curse for man's sin; man as the meritorious, and God the efficient cause of this vanity which is brought upon the creature; so that it is brought upon them by man as a sinner, by God as a judge.

[A.] First, by man as a sinner; that brought the hereditary and old curse. As the lower world was created for man's sake, so by the just judgment of God the curse came upon the whole earth for man's sake: Gen iii. 17, 18, 'Cursed is the ground for thy sake; in sorrow shalt thou eat of it all the days of thy life; thorns and thistles also shall it bring forth unto thee'. This was the original curse. So for the actual curse: Ps. cvii. 33, 34, 'He turneth rivers into a wilderness, and the water springs into dry ground; a fruitful land into barrenness, for the wickedness of them that dwell therein.' Barrenness or fertility is not a natural accident, but ordered by God for the punishment of man's sin. Therefore we should lift up our eyes above all natural causes, and fix them upon God, who chastiseth men for their unfruitfulness towards him, and punisheth countries whose plenty hath been infamously abused, and spent upon their lusts.

[B.] Secondly, by the will and power of the creator; he it is who hath the sovereign disposal of the creature, and to order it as he pleaseth with respect to his own glory.

(1.) Herein we see God's justice, who by the vanity of the creature would give us a standing monument of his displeasure against sin. Creatures are not as they were made in their primitive institution; the enmities and destructive influences of the several creatures had never been known, if we had not rebelled against God; we should never have been acquainted with droughts, and famines, and pestilences, and earthquakes; these are fruits of the fall, and introduced by our sin; and by these God would show us what an evil thing sin is: Jer. ii. 19, 'Thine own wickedness shall correct thee, and thy backslidings shall reprove thee; know therefore and see that it is an evil thing and bitter, that thou hast forsaken the

Lord thy God, and that my fear is not in thee, saith the Lord of Hosts' We being in a lower sphere of understanding, can only know causes by the effects; here is an effect; it hath brought misery upon us and upon the whole creation. When God looked upon the whole creation, all the creatures were good, Gen. i. 31, 'very good'; but when Solomon had considered them, all was vanity, very vain. What is the reason of this alteration? Sin had interposed.

(2.) The power and sovereignty of God. All the creatures are subject to the will of God, even in those things which are contrary to their natural use and inclination; for therefore he employeth them to destroy one another, and man who hath brought this disorder upon them. If God bid the fire burn, however kindled, what can withstand its flames? If he bid the earth cleave and swallow up those who had made a cleft in the congregation of the Lord, the earth presently obeyeth: Num. xvi. 31, 'As he had spoken these words, the ground clave asunder that was under them, and the earth opened her mouth, and swallowed them up.' So if God bid the sea stand up like a mountain and wall of congealed ice, it will do so, and afford passage for his people; and return again to its wonted course and fluidness and drown the Egyptians, it will do it: Exod. xiv. 28, 'The waters returned, and covered the chariots.' So for other things: Job xxxvii. 6, 'He saith to the snow, Be thou upon the earth; and likewise to the great rain, Be thou upon the earth.' Not a drop of rain falleth from the clouds but by God's per mission; so verse the 12, 'The clouds are turned about by his counsels, to do whatever he commandeth them upon the face of the earth' Nothing seemeth to be more casual than the motion of the clouds, or at least to arise from mere natural causes; yet still are at the direction of God; for it followeth, ver. 13, 'He causeth it to rain for the correction of a land, or for mercy' Sometimes it is sent in mercy, and sometimes in judgment; this bridle God keepeth upon the world, to check their licentiousness, and awe them into obedience to himself.

(3.) His mercy during the day of his patience. In the midst of judgment he remembereth mercy. Though there be much vanity in the creatures, yet there is still a usefulness in them to mankind. Though the air might poison us, and the earth swallow us up, and the mouth of the great deep vomit forth an inundation of waters, and the fire scorch up the earth, yet it is great mercy that God hath so bound up the creatures by a law and decree, that the earth is still a commodious habitation to man; that many of the changes and commotions in the elementary and lower world conduce to our benefit, but especially the stated course of nature; that the earth doth bring forth its fruits in due season, and the sun rejoiceth to run its course; all this is goodness to poor creatures, while God offereth pardon of sin and restitution by Christ; we still enjoy the blessings we have forfeited; though with some diminution and abatement, we are restored to the use of the creatures; but these are subject to vanity. We have our lives, but not that perfect constitution of body which Adam enjoyed before his fall. Creatures are not so useful and serviceable to us as they were in their first creation. In the inward righteousness and holiness restored to man, there is a mixture of corruption. It was needful there should be some continual remembrance of sin, that we might be the more abased in ourselves, and more sensible of God's mercy; and yet for the honour of God some monument should be left of his benignity and bounty to his creature.

Thirdly, The reasons why the innocent creature is punished for man's sin.

1. To destroy the image of jealousy, or the great idol that was set up against God. Man's great sin was his forsaking the creator, and seeking his happiness in the creature: Jer. ii. 13, 'For my people have committed two evils; they have forsaken me the fountain of living water, and hewed them out cisterns, broken cisterns, that will hold no water.' He forsook God by distrust, and betook himself to the creature out of necessity; for man cannot subsist of himself, but must have somewhat to lean unto. The first temptation did entice man from God to some inferior good more pleasing to his fleshly mind. Man was made for God, to serve him, love him, and de light in him, and to use all the creatures in order to God, for his service and glory; he was to use nothing but with this intention. But by sin, all that man was capable of using was abused to please his flesh. Now as Satan, the tempter, aimed at this, that by depending on the creature we might have no cause to look back upon God any more, as when they break off a treaty of marriage, they set another match a-foot; or rather, as those that endeavour to draw away a man's heart from his own wife, entangle him in the love of a strange woman; so God, to counterwork Satan, blasts the creature, and much of the beauty and virtue of it is lost, that we may think of returning to him: Hos. ii. 7, 'I will return to my first husband; for then it was better with me than now.' Disappointment in the creature sendeth many to God, who otherwise would never think of him; for they are made the more sensible of their disadvantage in forsaking him.

2. The creature is still made an instrument of sin, and therefore is involved in God's curse, as to the disorder, ruin, and destruction of many of the parts of it. For if we use these creatures contrary to their nature and end, and to the wrong of their proper lord and owner, no wonder if he blasted what is so abused. The creatures are sometimes abused as objects of worship and trust, to the alienating men's hearts from God, as in gross idolatry': They worshipped the queen of heaven,' meaning the sun, whom they made a female, Jer. xliv. 18. And the Lord complaineth, Ezek. xvi. 16, 17, 18, 19, that they decked their high places with gold and silver, and did set oil and incense before them. So still we set up the creature for our end and happiness, as if it were more attractive and amiable than God, and fitter to con tent and delight the soul; use so much of the world as is within our grasp and reach, against God and our true happiness. Besides brutish wickedness, how many sacrilegious morsels do men offer to an intemperate appetite, and abuse other things by their sinful desires, meat to surfeiting, drink to excess, apparel to pride; wealth, power, and interest to serve their revengeful minds?

3. In the curse on the creature, man is punished. His blessings cursed, Mai. ii. 2. Those things which were made for our use and service, become first instruments of our sin, and then of our punishment. It is just with God not only to punish us in our persons, but in the things belonging us; as demolishing the houses and castles of a rebel is taken to be a part of his punishment among men. Pharaoh's house was smitten for Sarah's sake: Gen. xii. 17, 'And the Lord plagued Pharaoh and his house for Sarah's sake'; and Num. xvi. 32, 'The earth

swallowed them up, and their houses, and their goods' So God brought vanity on the creature for man's sake; murrain on the beasts and cattle; blasts upon corn and vines, and other fruits of the earth. We have interest in them, and our subsistence is by them; yea, the king himself is served by the field; their destruction is our loss; as mercy to the earth is mercy to men.

Use 1. To teach us the evil of sin. Man by sin brought a curse upon himself, upon his posterity, and upon all the creatures; that is it we are upon; sin disordered the whole world; therefore let us work our hearts to a detestation and abhorrence of it. We see how highly God is displeased with it; the creator, who out of his overflowing bounty created all things, and delighted in them when he had made them, yet was provoked to curse what he had created, when once man had sinned; and so sin hath made a great change in the world. But because these are ancient things, and do little move us, see the judgments of every age and time, which are the fruit of this vanity, which is brought upon the creature. If a nation sin: Deut. xxviii. 22, 23, 'The Lord thy God shall smite thee with fevers, and with the sword, and with blasting, and mildew, and consume thee until thou perish. The heaven that is over thy head shall be brass, and the earth under thee, iron; the Lord shall make the rain of thy land powder and dust; from heaven shall it come down upon thee, until thou be destroyed.' So ver. 38, 39, 40, 'Thou shalt carry much seed into the field, and shalt gather but little in, for the locusts shall consume it; thou shalt plant vineyards and dress them, but shalt neither drink of the wine nor gather the grapes; for the worms shall eat them; have olive trees, but the olive shall cast its fruits.' These are things often fulfilled before our eyes; so Isa. xxiv. 4, 5, 6, 'The earth mourneth and fadeth away; the world languisheth and fadeth away; the earth also is defiled under the inhabitants thereof; they have transgressed the laws, changed the ordinance, broken the everlasting covenant. Therefore hath the curse devoured the earth, and they that dwell therein are desolate; therefore the inhabitants of the earth are burned, and few men left.' So for our persons, it is our sin that bringeth the curse of God on all that we enjoy. Thus God by the vanity and perishing of the creature, would show how angry he is with man for sin.

Use 2. Do not cast a greater burden upon the creature; you have already brought in too much disorder and confusion upon the world. But how do we cast a greater burden upon the creature? When you sin with and by the creature; as by injustice, unmercifulness, oppression, because you have much filthy excess; by these and such-like you make the creature the object and occasion of sin; especially opposition to God, oppressing his servants, dealing cruelly and unmercifully with men, hoping your greatness should bear you out in any of these cases.

1. Consider how the creature will cry to God for revenge: Hab. ii. 11, 'For the stone shall cry out of the wall, and the beam out of the timber shall answer it'; the very materials of their buildings and unjust acquisitions shall witness against them; James v. 3, 'The canker and rust of your gold and silver shall witness against you.'

2. Those that put a burden upon the creature shall have the creature's burden put on them. By your sin they are subjected to vanity, and by their vanity you are subjected to wrath; they

are ready to revenge God's quarrel, if he do but hiss for them, Isa. vii. 18; he can make 'thistles grow instead of wheat, and cockle for barley,' in heritages gotten by oppression, Job xxxi. 40.

3. The creature shall be delivered; but those that abuse the creature shall not. It is subjected in hope, but their worm dieth not, their fire goeth not out.

Use 3. Is to persuade us to turn our hearts from the creature to God; for the creature is made subject to vanity. They change, but he changeth not. 1 John ii. 17, 'The world passeth away, and the lusts thereof.' There is no true happiness to be found under the sun. Surely they that can see no vanity, nothing but glory and goodness in outward things, Satan hath bewitched them, Mat. iv. 8. Shall we fix our minds on a reeling world, ever subject to changes? Ps. lxxxiii. 13, 'my God, make them like a wheel, as the stubble before the wind'; those things are continually rolled and turned upside down, as a wheel is turned and turned, never standeth still in a declivity. The creature is vain, and made more vain by our confidence: Ps. xxx. 6, In my prosperity I said, I shall never be moved;' therefore if we love the creature, let it be after God, and for God; not in comparison with God. If the heart be set uponworldly things, it is stolen from better: Ps. lxii. 10, 'Trust not in oppression, become not vain in robbery; if riches increase, set not your heart upon them' God is impatient of a corrival[38]; 'I am married to you.' Jer. iii. 14. Not in exclusion of God; as when we rejoice in the creature apart from God, an heart divided from him, Luke xii. 19. Not in opposition to God; as if by the creature we were able to make our party against him.

Use 4. Let us seek after restitution by Christ. The covenant made with God in Christ doth secure us against the hurt of the creature: Job v. 23, 'For thou shalt be in a league with the stones of the field, and the beasts of the field shall be at peace with thee'; and Hosea ii. 18, 'And in that day I will make a covenant for them, with the beasts of the field, and with the fowls of heaven, and with the creeping things of the ground' They are included in God's covenant, who concerneth himself in all our affairs; the new creature suiteth with the new world: Rev. xxi. 5, 'And he that sat upon the throne said, Behold, I make all things new' 2 Cor. v. 17, 'Whosoever is in Christ, is a new creature'; their mercies are sweet; come not in anger, but purchased; we have a covenant-right restored.

Use 5. Is hope. If inanimate creatures are delivered from vanity, much more saints. Let us bear our burden with patience; the crea ture was subject to vanity, but it was not their fault, but ours; obedientially God subjected them; but God would not leave the world under a perpetual curse.

---

[38] rival, competitor

SERMON XXVIII

Because the creature itself also shall be delivered from the bondage of corruption into the glorious liberty of the children of God.

Romans VIII. 21.

IN this verse the apostle showeth what hope was appointed by God for the creature, which for a while was subject to vanity; 'Because the creature,' &c.

In the words observe

1. The deliverance asserted: 'Because the creature itself also shall be delivered.'

2. The terms of this deliverance explained: (1.) *Terminus a quo*. From the bondage of corruption. (2.) *Ad quem*, Into the glorious liberty of the children of God.

1. Asserted, *Oti* may be taken causally, as giving a reason of the hope mentioned; so we render it because; or specificative, as showing what kind of hope they have: 'subjected the same in hope that the creature itself also shall be delivered from the bondage of corruption'; for the word *elentherotheseian*, asserted into freedom; for it is now in bondage, as the following words declare.

2. Explained. First, the *terminus a quo*; that which he called vanity before, he now calleth 'bondage of corruption'; therefore this *douleia phthoras* must be explained as the vanity was, that signifieth either disorder or alteration, and corruption or dissolution, or perversion from its use, as it serveth wicked men, especially as it is abused by them to the fulfilling of their lusts; all this vanity, and all this bondage is an heavy yoke to the creature, and from all this it shall be freed. The term to which': Into the glorious liberty of the children of God.' But here a doubt ariseth. Shall the senseless creatures be made par takers of the same glory with God's children? That is absurd to be conceived. To solve this, Chrysostom thinketh *eis* is put for *dia*, as these particles are often exchanged; so *eis ten eleuthesian* should be rendered 'by the glorious liberty'. Others, to prevent this absurdity, make it not the term of the change, but the term of expectation, when the children of God are advanced into their glory; then, and not till then, shall the creatures be freed from the bondage of corruption. But the apostle's words do signify not only time, but estate; not at, but into; it is no such absurdity to say that the creature shall in its kind and manner partake of the glorious estate of the saints; for there is somewhat common to them both, and that is incorruption, 1 Cor. xv. 42. So the meaning is, it shall be translated from a state of corruption to a state of incorruption, and such a measure of beauty and glory doth agree thereunto.

Two points I shall observe from this verse:

Doctrine 1. That the creatures shall be freed from corruption, and be made partakers of a better estate than now they have.

Doctrine 2. That the liberty to which God's children are reserved is a glorious liberty.

First, let me speak of the restoration of the creature, and then of the glorious liberty of the saints.

Doctrine 1. For the first, let me state it, how far the creatures shall be delivered from the present vanity and misery, and for what reasons. We must keep to scripture generals, lest we run into curiosities; that rule of Augustine is good, *Melius dubitare de occultis, quam litigare de incertis*; it is better to doubt of what is hidden, than to contend about what is uncertain. We may define things with danger, but we may be ignorant of them without danger; therefore as to creatures that shall be restored, and not restored, we must not be too nice and inquisitive. Possibly this is one of those difficulties mentioned by St. Peter, 2 Pet. iii. 16, that in his beloved brother Paul's epistles, there are *dusnoeta tina*. I am sure these concern the matter there treated of.

First, for things that are not to be restored.

1. Whatever came in by sin, will be utterly destroyed; as thorns, thistles, poisonous weeds: Gen. iii. 17, 18, 'Cursed is the ground for thy sake, thorns and thistles shall it bring forth to thee.' The reason is, when the cause is taken away the effect ceaseth. If the curse of God upon the earth be a part of man's punishment; then upon man's deliverance the creature is delivered also. Now it continueth for a mark of God's displeasure, and our humiliation, because man is restored but in part; but upon our full deliverance, no more of this is found.

2. All creatures that arise out of corruption and putrefaction; as toads, mice, flies, bats. As they were not in the first creation, so they shall not appear in this restitution of all things at the coming of the Lord.

3. All living creatures which perish before, or at the end of the world. It is probable these shall not be renewed and restored again; partly, because these serve only for the use and the sustenance of the earthly life; but in glory freed from this necessity: 1 Cor. vi. 13, 'Meats for the belly, and the belly for meats; but God shall destroy both it and them.' In this life the body hath an absolute necessity of them; but in the next life the meat itself, as well as the eating or desiring of meat, shall be taken away. Partly, because, if these should be restored, there must be a resurrection of them, which is only promised to men. And the apostles when they speak, restrain it to mankind, who have reasonable souls living to God, while their bodies are rotting in the grave; but the soul of the beasts goeth downward, Eccl. iii. 21; that is, perish with their bodies, which are buried in the ground.

4. All artificial works done by the hand of man, as cities, castles, houses, gardens. They shall all be burnt up, and be extant no more; for though these things are useful during the earthly life, yet then they are all consumed, as being defiled by the inhabitants thereof: 2 Pet. iii. 10, 'The earth also, and the works which are therein, shall be burnt up'; that is, which men have made, and built thereupon; which should turn our hearts from our affecting those things, or fixing upon the creature which is passing away, whilst we neglect God, who is the same, that passeth not.

Secondly. That which shall be restored is the fabric of heaven and earth; not the highest heavens; they need no purifying fire, no unclean things entering there; but the lower heavens and this earth; the state of things after the dissolution is often called a 'world to come.' Now *world*, in the sacred dialect, comprehendeth the visible heavens and earth;

meaning by heavens, the airy and starry heaven; and by earth, dry land and waters. Well then, heaven and earth, sun, moon, and stars, which had a being in the creation, and undergo the purging- fire at the dissolution, shall be restored as gold that hath been melted and refined in the fire. If you ask for what use? We must refer that to the event; the scripture in the general, 2 Pet. iii. 13, "We expect, according to his promise, new heavens and a new earth, wherein dwelleth righteousness'; wherein righteous men shall have a firm place, and always dwell therein, and exercise righteousness; whereas this earth is full of wicked and unrighteous men, which then shall be all in hell. But the difficulty is about the use of this lower world.

1. What if God restore it as a monument of his wisdom, goodness and power? An object wherein by the great beauty of the creature, the just shall see God by reflection?

2. What if for the exercise of our delight and gratitude? To delight the eyes and minds of the saints, the creatures having a glory and brightness put upon them, somewhat proportionable to their own glorious estate? God will make a proportion between the heir and the inheritance, the lord and the servants, the habitation and the inhabitant; as the church is altered, so must her dwelling; there shall be nothing in nature displeasing to the eyes of God's children, but all delightful to all eternity.

3. What if to be a trophy of the final abolition of death, the last enemy that shall be destroyed? The world is now a monument of sin, and then of our redemption, that all the fruit of sin is done away both in us and the world.

4. What if to complete the first grant of dominion to man over the creatures? This grant must some time or other take place: Ps. viii. 6, 'Thou madest him to have dominion over the work of thine hands; thou hast put all things under his feet' It is not done here; therefore in the world to come, as the apostle speaketh: Heb. ii. 5, 'For unto the angels hath he not put in subjection the world to come'; which world to come concerneth the state of the church under Christ, and the state of glory after the resurrection. Now we have the right, then the possession; an eternal kingdom over all creatures. For it is said of the saints, that they shall have dominion in the morning, and that they 'shall reign with Christ for ever and ever,' Rev. xxii. 5; and of the new heavens and the new earth, Rev. xxi. 7, 'He that overcometh shall inherit all things,' which beareth some sense.

Use. It showeth us three things:

1. The certainty of our hopes. There is hope that the creature at length shall be delivered into a state agreeing with the future glory of God's children. Therefore much more is their deliverance to be hoped for by the children of God themselves. For if these dumb insensible things be made partakers of a better estate than they have now, will not God take care for the recompence of his people?

2. The excellency of our hopes. It appeareth hence, what excellency of glory is reserved for the children of God, since all the world shall be refined and restored for their sakes; and seeing the glory of that state requireth the creature should be -changed before it can suit with it.

3. It showeth us the manner of entering into our hopes. As the creature must be freed from the state of corruption, before it can par take with God's children in any degree of their glorious liberty, so must we be changed before we are capable of it. How changed? First, By grace. Secondly, By death. We must be changed by grace, and freed from the corruption of sin: Eph. v. 5, 'For this we know, that no whoremonger, nor unclean person, nor covetous man who is an idolater, hath any inheritance in the kingdom of Christ and of God'. Common knowledge will easily show us, that those that impenitently persist in gross sins, are incapable of any right unto, and never shall come to the possession of that blessed estate of eternal glory. We have a larger catalogue, Gal. v. 20, 21; and the apostle concludeth, that they that do such things shall not inherit the kingdom of God; there is no mixture of godly and ungodly in the kingdom of heaven. Nay, we may go further, not only exclude them who live in gross sin; but every unregenerate person: John iii. 3, 'Except a man be born again, he cannot see the kingdom of God'; and in the 5th verse it is explained, 'he cannot enter into it.' Every man in his natural estate, be e to appearance better or worse, is unmeet for glory; and there must be a change wrought in him; he must be delivered from the bondage of sinful corruption, or he cannot enjoy the glorious liberty of the children of God. Not only an epicure[39], or drunkard, or whoremonger is excluded; but a painted pharisee, as long as his heart is corrupt and unrenewed, hath no right, and never shall have possession; he must be changed from a state of corruption to a state of holiness; and the image of God, in which he was created, must be restored in him.

2. Changed by death. The saints being mortal, must be changed before they can inherit eternal life. All that we derived from old Adam must be laid and left in the grave: 1 Cor. xv. 50, 'Flesh and blood cannot inherit the kingdom of God; neither doth corruption inherit incorruption.' These earthly frail bodies of ours cannot be received into heaven, till they be changed and immortalized: ver. 53, 'This corruptible must put on incorruption, and this mortal must put on immortality.' As a man to build his house better, razeth it to the very bottom; so God will have the body resolved into dust, before he will set it forth in this new fair edition. As the creature is dissolved, that is, delivered from the bondage of corruption; first the creature is set free, and discharged from being obnoxious to change and alteration; so we must first die, then be raised in incorruption; which should make us the more ready and willing to submit to the appointed course, and not only even dare to die, but to be willing to die, since death puts an end to sin, and all our calamities, and is the gate and entrance by which we pass into glory.

Doctrine 2. That the liberty to which God's people are reserved is a glorious liberty.

Here I shall first speak of the liberty of God's children in this life; secondly, the glorious liberty in the world to come. For the one is a step to the other. For it is called, 'a glorious

---

[39] one devoted to sensual pleasure

liberty,' to distinguish it from the liberty of God's children here in this world, which is not glorious, but gracious, to show how it exceedeth this estate in glory. Therefore I must show

First, What is the liberty of God's children in this world.

Secondly, What in the world to come.

First, What is the liberty of God's children in this world. There are three practical notions in which man is greatly mistaken, misery and happiness; wisdom and folly; liberty and bondage. Misery and happiness: men count none miserable but the afflicted; none happy but the prosperous; because they judge by the present ease and commodity of the flesh. Wisdom and folly: We all affect the repute of wisdom, Job xi. 12; please ourselves with a false show of wisdom, neglecting what is true and solid, which is to be wise to salvation. Liberty and bondage: man accepteth of a false liberty rather than none; every man would be at his own dispose, live as he list; whereas the true liberty must be determined by our condition as creatures; by our end, as creatures that are in pursuit of true happiness. To think the only true liberty is to be at the command and control of none above ourselves, or to live at large according to our hearts' desire, is to affect a thraldom and bondage instead of liberty; therefore it concerneth us to state exactly what is the liberty of God's children now. It either relateth to our duty, or to our felicity.

1. To our duty; and so our liberty must be stated by these four things.

[A.] It must be such a liberty as becometh a creature who is in subjection to God. It is not a power to live as we list, but a power to live as we ought. To affect a power to live as we list, and to be accountable to none, is to revive the arrogancy of Adam, and to sup up again the poison of the old temptation, 'ye shall be as gods' Gen. iii. 5. It was man's original ambition to be at his own dispose, and lord of his own actions; to think, and speak, and do as he pleaseth: Ps. xii. 4, 'Our tongues are our own, who is lord over us? 'And the rebellion of the libertine world is set forth by casting off the yokes and cords of duty: Ps. ii. 3, 'Let us break their bands asunder, and cast away their cords from us,' meaning there, the laws of God and Christ, who are impatient of any restraint. 'But this is a liberty cannot be justified; for since man hath principium et finem, a principle upon which he dependeth in his being and operations, and an end unto which he is appointed, he must wholly give up himself to the will of another, and his liberty lieth in a readiness to comply with God's commands, who is his proper lord, to whom he is to subject himself, and to give an account of all his actions. So that man's true liberty is God's service: Ps. cxix. 45, 'I will walk at liberty, for I seek thy precepts.' To will and do things pleasing to our creator is the only liberty proper to us.

[B.] It must be such a liberty as will leave us in a capacity to pursue our chief good, and last end. For all creatures are by natural instinct carried to their last end; and, the more fettered and restrained from this, the more they are in bondage; the less, the more free; which holdeth good in all creatures; but principally in the reasonable. Certainly the reasonable nature is dishonoured, and debased, and under a defect, as it is disabled from the fruition of God, or seeking after it; we are in bondage as we are captivated and entangled with the love of inferior things, and so perverted and diverted from the pursuit of true happiness. The restraining of our irregular desires is not bondage, but the gratifying of them, for that is a snare to us. Men live in sin with as much delight as fishes in their own element; yet they are in bonds still, as they are detained from God, and turned aside from him; our liberty is our power over inferior things; and our bondage is their power over us. 1 Cor. vi. 12. When we love God with all our hearts, and serve him with all our minds, we are free. Liberty in the root implieth an inclination to God, as the supreme object of our love. In the first act, in a power of choosing the means whereby we may enjoy him; in the second act, in an exercise of this power, or in an actual pursuing the end by these means. The elective power, and a governing our actions in order to our great end, is our liberty; the angels that immutably and indeclinably adhere to their last end are freer than us, who may err from it. Well then, none are such slaves as they that cannot use the means which should make them happy; but employ their whole time in seeking after pleasures, and honours, and profits; like dissolute servants, who being sent by their masters to a mart or fair to buy commodities, spend their time and money in some inn or house of entertainment by the way, and neglect their fair or mart, to which they were sent to employ their money to the best advantage. So we are enslaved by the way, and neglect our main business.

[C.] It must be such a liberty as will suit with the dignity of a rational creature, as man is. For that is the liberty of a man, when he acteth with a condecency to the reasonable nature. Man was at first made to be happy; his happiness consisted in the fruition of God; and his subjection to him was no captivity and restraint, but rather a part of that blessedness. But we became bondmen, not only by breaking the law of God, but by disordering the constitution of our souls; by submitting conscience and reason to our lusts; so suffering the beast to ride the man; for the rule of the apostle is of immutable equity, Rom. vi. 11, 'His servants you are, to whom ye yield yourselves to obey.' Now man giving up reason to appetite becometh a very slave; as a country is enthralled when the base prevail above the honourable, and beggars get on horseback, but the princes are on foot. Such a deordination there is, when reason is put out of dominion, and lusts prevail; our bondage is described by the apostle, Tit. iii. 3, 'Serving divers lusts and pleasures.' Our lusts urge us to an eager pursuit of inferior things; reason or the leading part of the soul reclaimeth, but it hath no force; besides our dependence upon God, which cannot be shaken off. If since our apostasy from him, we had a perfect understanding to guide us, the danger would not be so great; but in this corrupt estate, the mind is blinded by our passions and appetites; and therefore to be left to the dispose of our brutish affections is the greatest judgment that can be: Ps. lxxxi. 12, 'So I gave them up to their own hearts' lusts, and they walked in their own counsels.' This is the greatest thraldom that can befall such a creature as man is; it leaveth us no power to dispose of ourselves; men often see what they should do, but cannot do it, being drawn away by their own lusts; and though we have some kind of remorse from the remainders of reason, especially being assisted by the Holy Spirit, as to some common help; yet we foully miscarry still, till it hath brought us to misery, as it did Samson the strongest, Solomon the wisest of men. Then therefore is a man at liberty, when reason and conscience are again put into dominion, and a man is fitted to please God, and seek after his true happiness, with the con tempt of all worldly things.

[D.] It must be such a liberty as bringeth us nearest to the state of innocency, which is man's first estate; and the state of glory, which is his last and most perfect state. Now this doth consist in a freedom from the power of sin; the liberty of innocency was posse non peccare; Adam might not have sinned; the liberty of glory will be non posse peccare, they cannot sin; as not with a moral cannot, it is absurd, that may be obtained here: 1 John iii. 9, 'He can not sin, because he is born of God;' but with a natural cannot; it is impossible; the soul doth indeclinably adhere to God as the chiefest good; therefore now the nearer we come to this, the will of man is best disposed, and the more to be accounted as free. Divines usually consider man in a fourfold estate: *In statu institute*, in a state of integrity, and so man might not have sinned. *In statu destitute*, in a state of corruption, so he can do nothing else but sin; that every imagination of the thoughts of his heart was only evil continually, Gen. vi. 5. *In statu restituto*; and so he hath an inclination partly to good by the Spirit of grace dwelling in him; partly to evil, by reason of the relics of sin; and is only so far freed from the bondage of corruption, as that it shall not reign in him, Rom. vi. 14. *In statu praestituto*, in the state to which he is appointed; in the state of glory, in which he can will nothing but what is good; a blessed necessity it is, and our highest liberty; for liberty is not opposite to necessity, but obligation or impulsion; we are never more free than when we are past all possibility of sinning.

2. As it relateth to our felicity; and so it implieth two things: (1.) Our immunities and privileges; (2.) Our rights and prerogatives.

[A.] The immunities and privileges of God's children. We are de livered from much misery by Christ. First, From the slavery of sin: Rom. vi. 18, 'Being made free from sin, ye became the servants of righteousness.' Though sin still dwelleth in us, yet the guilt is remitted, the damning power gone: Rom. viii. 1, 'There is no condemnation to them that are in Christ'; the reigning power broken: Rom. vi. 14, 1 For sin shall not have dominion over you' and so it is more and more mortified in us, by the grace of regeneration, till at length it be abolished by death. And so the being is gone, and our enthralled spirits are in some measure set free, to know, serve, and love God, and delight in him as our lord, and life, and end, and all. Secondly, from death, as the curse of the law; and so from those everlasting torments which the wicked must endure. The second death hath no power over such; and though we are obnoxious to the first death, yet the venom -and sting of it is gone: 1 Cor. xv. 56, 57, 'death, where is thy sting? grave, where is thy victory?' And of an enemy it is made a friend: 1 Cor. iii. 22, 'Death is yours'; it is made the gate and entrance into eternal rest. Thirdly, From the bondage that did arise in us from the fear of eternal death. Where sin is entertained, it bringeth another inmate along with it, and that is the fear and terror of death and damnation, which ariseth from the consciousness of sin. Now to be free from the accusations of a guilty conscience, and those self-tormentings which in the wicked are the foretastes of hell, is surely a great mercy; and this is the privilege of God's people: Heb. ii. 14, 15, 'To deliver them who through fear of death are all their life-time subject to bondage'

And sinners are such bond-men, that they dare not call themselves to an account for the expense of their time, and course of their employments, which all wise men should do; and think seriously of God, and the day of judgment, and the world to come; therefore it is a great mercy to have a quiet well settled conscience. Fourthly, From the tyranny and power of Satan, as a deceiver, and enemy, and executioner of the wrath of God; who thereby taketh wicked men captive at his will and pleasure. He cannot totally prevail against the elect: Mat. xvi. 18, 'Upon this rock I build my church, and the gates of hell shall not prevail against it'; though he vex and tempt them continually. He hath a kind of right to apostate souls: Eph. vi. 12, 'Ruler of the darkness of this world'; but his power is much broken as to the elect; they are daily exercised by him, but they overcome, and stand steadfast in the faith. Fifthly, They are freed from the law and covenant of works, which requireth that which to us is become impossible; and also from the burdensome task of useless ceremonies imposed on the church in the times of infancy and darkness. And the apostle biddeth us stand fast in the liberty wherewith Christ hath made us free, Gal. v. 1. The ceremonial law was a bondage, by reason of the great trouble, expense, and pain to the flesh which did attend the observation of it, especially in its use, a bond confessing the debt; and Christ hath purchased this freedom and liberty to the church, and we should stand to the defence of it. Sixthly, An immunity from such temporal judgments as might hinder our salvation, and the service of God: 1 Cor. x. 13, 'There hath no temptation taken hold of you, but such as is common to man. But God is faithful, who will not suffer you to be tempted above that you are able, but will with the temptation also make a way to escape, that ye may be able to bear it;' and Rom. viii. 28, 'All things shall work together for good to them that love God' No ab solute immunity from troubles; God hath reserved a liberty to his wisdom and justice to afflict us as he shall see cause: Ps. lxxxix. 32, 'Then will I visit their transgressions with the rod, and their iniquity with stripes' but will preserve us to his heavenly kingdom, 2 Tim. iv. 17, 18.

[B.] Their rights and prerogatives. First, They have a right to serve God with a ready and free will, and on comfortable terms: Luke i. 74, 75, 'That being delivered out of the hands of our enemies, we might serve him without fear, in holiness and righteousness before him, all the days of our lives;' Ps. li. 12, 'Restore unto me the joy of thy salvation, and uphold me by thy free Spirit'; and Rom. viii. 15, 'For we have not received the spirit of bondage again to fear, but we have received the spirit of adoption, whereby we cry, Abba, Father' Secondly, A liberty of access to God. A large door is opened to us, for communion with him: Eph. iii. 12, 'To whom we have boldness and access with confidence;' Heb. iv. 16, 'Let us come with boldness to the throne of grace, that we may have grace, and find mercy in a time of need'; and Heb. x. 19, 'Having therefore, brethren, boldness to enter into the holiest by the blood of Jesus'; 1 John iii. 21, 'Beloved, if our hearts condemn us not, then have we boldness toward God' Thirdly, A free use of all the creatures which fall to our share and allowance by God's fatherly providence: 1 Tim. iv. 3, 4, 'Forbidding to marry, and commanding to abstain from meat, which God hath created to bo received with thanksgiving of them that believe and obey the truth. For every creature of God is good, and nothing to be refused, if it bo received with thanksgiving;' 1 Cor. iii. 22, 23, 'Whether Paul, or Apollos, or Cephas, or the world, or life, or death, or things present, or things to come; all are yours, and ye are Christ's, and Christ is God's.' With good conscience we may use the creatures, and get them sancti fied to us by the word and prayer. Fourthly, A right to eternal life: Tit. iii. 7, 'That being justified by his grace, we should be made heirs according to the hope of eternal life'; Rom. viii. 17, 'If children, then heirs, heirs of God, and joint-heirs with Christ; if so be we suffer with him, that we may be also glorified together.' Though we have not the possession, yet a title sure and indefeasible; so that you see (and yet I have told you little of it) it is valuable. But it is a glorious liberty we are to speak of:

Secondly. Our glorious liberty in the world to come. That is a liberty which implieth the removal of all evil, and the affluence of all good; and may be considered either as to the soul, or to the body.

1. As to the soul. We are admitted into the blessed sight of God; and the perfect fruition, and pleasing of him in perfect love, joy, and praise, to all eternity: 1 Cor. xiii. 12, 'For now we see through a glass darkly, but then face to face; now I know in part, but then shall I know even also as I am known'; 1 John iii. 2, 'But we know that when he shall appear we shall be like him, for we shall see him as he is;' Ps. xvi. 11, 'Thou wilt show me the path of life; for in thy presence is fulness of joy, and at thy righthand pleasures forevermore'; Ps. xvii. 15, 'As for me, I will behold thy face in righteousness, I shall be satisfied when I awake with thy likeness.'

2. As to the body, it is in a state of immortality and incorruption, wholly freed from death, and all the frailties introduced by sin; and because the body remaineth behind when the soul is in glory, our deliverance and redemption is said to be yet behind: Eph. i. 14, 'Which is the earnest of our inheritance, until the redemption of the purchased possession'; Eph. iv. 30, 'And grieve not the Holy Spirit, whereby ye are sealed to the day of redemption'; and that in respect of the body: Rom. viii. 23, 'Waiting for the adoption, to wit, the redemption of our body.' In short, this glorious liberty may be somewhat understood by the liberty which we have now.

[A.] Our liberty now is imperfect and incomplete, but then it is full and perfect. It is but begun now, and our bonds loosed in part; but our complete deliverance is to come from sin at death, from all misery when our bodies are raised up in glory. Sin dwelleth in the saints now, but in death it will be utterly abolished; therefore they groan and long for it: Rom. vii. 24, 'wretched man that I am, who shall deliver me from the body of death? 'Yet with hope, ver. 25' I thank God, through Jesus Christ our Lord; so then, with the mind I myself serve the law of God; but with the flesh the law of sin' Our bodies now are subject to corruption and diseases, as others are; but Phil. iii. 21; God will then perfectly glorify his children in body and soul.

[B.] Spiritual liberty is consistent enough with corporal bondage. Paul was in prison when Nero was emperor of the world; many that are taken into the liberty of God's children are not freed from outward servitude: 1 Cor. vii. 21, 22, 'Art thou called being a servant? Care not for it; but if thou canst be made free, use it rather' The condition of a slave is not incompetent with Christianity; Joseph was a slave in Egypt, but his mistress was the captive, as she was overcome by her own lusts; servants may be the. Lord's freemen, and freemen may be Satan's slaves.

[C.] All the parts of liberty are quite other than now.

(1.) First, as to duty, we are not so free from the power of sin as to be able to govern our own actions in order to eternal happiness: Rom. vii. 25, 'With my mind I serve the law of God, with my flesh the law of sin' There is law against law, mutual conflicts and mutual opposition; though grace gets the mastery, not absolute freedom. Our present estate is but a convalescency, a recovery out of sickness by degrees.

(2.) As to felicity:

(a.) Immunity: First, from the curse of the law, and the wrath of God. We have alright, but the solemn and actual judgment is not passed, nor the case adjudged; but at the last day, when the condemning sentence is passed upon the wicked, our sins shall be blotted out, Acts iii. 19. Secondly, death remaineth on the body, but then the last enemy shall be quite destroyed, 1 Cor. xv. 26. Thirdly, Satan doth still trouble us, and vex us, winnow us as wheat; but then he shall be trodden under our feet, Rom. xvi. 20. Fourthly, From the afflictions of the world; they do not now endanger salvation, but then wholly gone: Rev. xxi. 4, 'Then God shall wipe all tears from our eyes; then no more sorrow and crying'; that is, because of oppression and violence.

(b.) For rights and prerogatives. Now we serve God at a distance by some service, then immediately minister before the throne; here we come to God now and then, but then we shall be ever with him; we have now a right to use creatures, then we shall need none; now a title to heaven, but then possession, made actual partakers of eternal blessedness; therefore there cannot be a greater liberty than the children of God have at the last day.

Use 1. Is to admire the goodness of God to poor afflicted creatures. We have this glorious liberty from God's bounty, Mat. xxv. 34; Christ's love, he purchased it; it is the Son of God hath made us free, John viii. 36; it is applied to us by the Spirit: Rom. viii. 2, 'The Spirit of life in Christ Jesus hath made us free from the law of sin and death' The Roman captain said, 'With a great sum obtained I this freedom' Acts xxii. 28; to us it cometh on mere favour.

Use 2. Have you interest in this blessedness? Is the liberty begun? Hath he sealed you to the day of redemption? Eph. iv. 30. You will find the comfort and benefit of his sealing. On that day God will own those whom he hath stamped and marked with his own seal; that is, whom the Spirit hath formed for God, by impressing his image upon them in righteousness and true holiness. After that day no more place will be left for doubts and fears; but till that day this is our warrant and assurance, till full possession; the seal of the Spirit is an holy frame of heart, fitted to serve, please, and enjoy God.

SERMON XXIX

For we, know that the whole creation groaneth and travaileth in pain together until now.

Romans VIII. 22.

THE apostle had showed how the creature waiteth for its future perfect estate; now, what sense it hath of its present condition. In the words we have,

1. The certainty, 'We know.'

2. The agony of the creature, 'It groaneth and travaileth in pain.'

3. Their consort and agreement in this groaning, 'The whole creation groaneth,' etc.

4. The duration and continuance, 'Until now'

1. The certainty of what is asserted, 'We know.' But how do we know? First, we see by our sense, that the whole creation is under vanity and corruption. Secondly, we know by faith that it came by sin; so that partly from sense, and partly by faith, we conclude that the creature is under a burden.

2. The great agony of the creature; it 'groaneth and travaileth in pain'; groaneth as a man under an heavy burden; travaileth in pain, as -a woman in child-bearing; the creature would fain be disburdened of this estate. Some think that this last metaphor implieth that the issue will be comfortable, for the pain of travail ends in joy: John xvi. 21, 'A woman when she is in travail hath sorrow, for her hour is come; but as soon as she is delivered of the child, she remembereth no more the anguish, for joy that a man-child is born into the world.' It may be so here; only I find this metaphor used for bitter pangs and sorrows, without any respect to the end and issue; as Mat. xxiv. 8, 'All these are the beginning of sorrows'

3. The consort and harmonious agreement that is between all the parts of the world; 'the whole creation' collectively, or every creature distributively; they all groan together, and travail in pain together.

4. The duration and continuance, 'until now'; that is, from the time that sin entered into the world unto this present time.

Doctrine That the whole creation groaneth under the burden of our sins.

First. What is this groaning of the creature; or in what sense the creature is said to groan.

Secondly. How we are concerned in these groans.

Thirdly. How we know it; for who ever heard the groaning of the whole creation?

First. What is this groaning of the creature? Or how can that be ascribed to things without reason, sense, and life? There are two causes of groaning in sensitive creatures, labour and pain; that which answereth to labour is unwearied motion; that which answereth to pain is corruption and decay.

1. Labour and motion. So we may say the creature is worn out with hard labour to serve the uses of man; because it is in continual motion. The sun moveth from east to west in the day, and in the night from west to east again: Eccles. i. 5, 'The sun also ariseth, and the sun goeth

down, and hasteth to his place, where he arose;' the Hebrew, panteth, as pressing forward to be at his appointed place; to give man light to go about his labour. How many thousands of miles hath it- travelled to come to us again, since we went to bed? So Job xxxvii. 11, 'By watering he wearieth the thick cloud, and scattereth the bright clouds; it is turned about by his counsels'. He speaketh of the clouds as things that could be wearied, being hurried hither and thither, to serve the earth in divers places, and spendeth itself in that service. The earth is digged, and rent, and torn with the plough, seldom suffered to enjoy its sabbaths, that it may bring forth fruit to man; the rivers flow, and the sea hath its ebbs and tides; all things in the lower world are full of labour; and so the creature is wearied and worn out to serve even rebel man, to whom God continueth this favour.

2. That which answereth to pain, is their passing away by corruption; the four elements being contrary one to another, are still wasting one another, till all fail; heat against cold, and moisture against dry- ness; all things being compounded of these four elements do in the end return to them again by dissolution and corruption. And besides, by God's judgment the creature is often blasted in its greatest glory and beauty. Look, as in a fruitful season the valleys are said to laugh with fatness, Ps. lxv. 12, 13; and the flourishing of the spring is as it were nature's smile; it is a pleasant sight to behold when the earth is blessed of God with increase and variety of fruits; the creatures do as it were rejoice in God's bounty, and invite us to rejoice with them; so on the other side, when these things are taken away, it doth as it were mourn, and look sorrowful- like under the judgment; as they laugh in their kind, so they mourn and groan in their kind: as Jer. xii. 4, 'How long shall the land mourn, and the herbs of the field wither, for the wickedness of them that dwell therein? 'Isa. xxiv. 4, 'The earth mourneth and fadeth away; the world languisheth and fadeth away'; Isa. xxxiii. 9, 'The earth mourneth and languisheth, Lebanon is ashamed'; Jer. xxiii. 10, 'Because of swearing the land mourneth;' Joel i. 10, 'The field is wasted, the land mourneth, for the corn is wasted, the new wine is dried up, the oil languisheth.' In all these places, and many more, the earth is said to mourn when it lieth waste, stripped and despoiled of its wonted verdure and bravery in grass, corn, plants, fruits, wherewith it was once clad and adorned. Now this may come to pass, partly, by external drought, as when the grass was burnt up, that there was no fodder for the beast, 1 Kings xviii. 5. Partly, by storm and tempest, which maketh spoil and havoc of it: Prov. xxviii. 3, 'A sweeping rain leaveth no food.' Partly, by vermin: Joel i. 4, 'That which the palmer-worm hath left> the locust hath eaten; that which the locust hath left, the canker-worm hath eaten; that which the canker-worm hath left, the caterpillar hath eaten.' Sometimes by the irruption and invasion of an enemy: Isa. i. 7, 'Your country is desolate; your cities are burnt with fire; your land, strangers devour it in your presence; and it is desolate, as over thrown by strangers.' Sometimes by murrains and pestilential diseases, which hinder all cultivation and tillage: Amos iv. 10, 'I have sent among you the pestilence after the manner of Egypt; your young men have I slain with the sword, and have taken away your horses; I have made the stink of your camp to come up into your nostrils.' God hath variety of ways to punish man in blasting the creature; and on all the occasions the land appeareth as in a mourning weed; and the barren parched ground and withered fruits

of the earth are, as it were, the groaning of the creature under man's sin. These things premised, we may see in what sense the creature is said to groan.

[A.] In a way of supposition. If they had any life, sense, or reason, they would groan, or be thus affected; being wearied with labour, liable to destruction, and perverted from their natural use; often blasted by God's judgment. If God should open the mouth of the creature, as he did that of Balaam's ass, it would rebuke our madness, groan under their hard servitude: 2 Pet. ii. 16, 'Balaam was rebuked for his iniquity; the dumb ass, speaking with man's voice, rebuked the madness of the prophet.' So if the creature could speak with man's voice, and had man's affections, they would loudly groan in the ears of the Lord of Hosts, and blame us for our disobedience and unthankfulness to God.

[B.] By analogy. There is some proportion and suitableness between our affections, and the inclinations of the creature; there is something in them which is as it were sense and reason, that is, a shadow and resemblance of it. The grass groweth as if it grew by art, and knew how to grow; and the corn sprouteth forth as regularly as if it were under direction; every creature acteth by a rule from which it swerveth not; a stone in descending, falleth by a straight line as if it had reason to pick it out; all the art of man cannot draw a straighter line, than that by which a stone falleth down, when it is thrown up into the air. Every creature hath an obediential instinct to glorify God, as if it obeyed by reason. The creation did. as it were, mourn at the crucifying of Christ; for nature seemed to be routed into a disorder; the rocks were rent, the earth quaked, the sun was struck blind with astonishment. There is an intellective assistance, which runneth along with the creature; that is, the wise and powerful providence of God leadeth them, and governeth them, and directeth them to a better estate; so that they do in their kind groan under their present burden, till they be delivered from it.

Secondly. How are we concerned in these groans? Very much.

1. They are upbraiding groans, as they upbraid us of our security and unthankfulness. We that have reason are more senseless than the creatures; the creature groaneth, and we are stupid, neither affected with our sin or misery: Jer. xii. 14, 'The land mourneth; yet they say, he shall not see our last end'; that is, no evil shall come unto us; they thought all would be well enough. So, 'For swearing, and lying, and stealing, and adultery, the land mourneth,' Hos. iv. 2, 3; but doth the swearer mourn, the adulterer mourn? 'The vines howl, and the fig tree languisheth' Isa. xxiv. 7; but doth the drunkard mourn, because God is provoked by his filthy excess? It is very observable that the prophets do often turn from men, and speak to creatures; as Lam. ii. 18, 'wall of the daughter of Zion, let thy tears run clown as a river day and night; let not the apple of thine eye cease.' He calls on the wall, either because no men left to mourn, or no men had an heart to mourn, or for both reasons. So Micah vi. 1, 2, 'Hear, ye mountains, the Lord's controversy, and the strong foundations of the earth, hear the word of the Lord;' so Jer. xxii. 29, 'earth, earth! 'as if it were in vain to speak to men. Insensible creatures are more fit to be spoken to, than an incredulous, and self-willed, and obdurate people; they keep still their obediential subjection to their creator, and do tremble when he threateneth, and groan when he afflicteth; and therefore the creature is brought in

groaning here, as in our stead; the earth groaneth, which hath not sinned, but only suffercth for sin, to upbraid the hardness of our hearts, because we who are the criminal parties groan not.

2. They are awakening groans. It is spoken hyperbolically to quicken our consideration, and to represent the more emphatically the great misery the creatures are in while they serve sinful man, especially in fulfilling his lusts. Carnal men do not think of these things, and so have no ear to hear these groans; the creatures speak by our thoughts, and they groan by our affections; namely, as they excite and stir us up to sigh and long for a better estate than is to be had in this reeling and uncertain world, where sin hath introduced so many changes. Job saith, chap. xii. 7, 8, 'Ask now the beasts, and they shall teach thee; the fowls of the air, and they shall tell thee; or speak unto the earth, and it shall teach thee; and the fishes of the sea, and they shall declare unto thee.' What was the point he had then in hand? That by the providence of God wicked men may prosper; not only as these things do most serve the wicked, but the strong keep under the weak, and the great devour the less. But how do the creatures speak, or tell, or declare? even the mute fishes, that scarce make any sound or noise? We ask them by our study and meditation, and they answer us by our own thoughts, by the convictions and conclusions we draw from them; there is a great deal of morality in the bosom of nature, and much wisdom to be learned from the creature, if we would pick it out, and seriously employ our thoughts that way. This is one lesson among the rest; the creature hath something to say to us concerning the vanity and decay of all things, and a better estate to come; we hear the creature groaning, as it offereth matter to us to sigh, and groan, and long for a better estate, that we may be at home with God, and free from the miseries of the present world.

3. They are instructive groans; for they teach us many good lessons.

[A.] They teach us the vanity of the creature, which is now often changed, and must at length be dissolved. To a common eye this world seemeth to be in its highest splendour and beauty, because worldly men judge of things by their carnal affections: Ps. xlix. 11, 'Their inward thought is, that their houses shall continue forever, and their dwelling places to all generations' They think their heritages and honours shall forever continue in their name and family, and carry themselves accordingly; their carnal complacency possesseth them with vain conceits; and when their posterity are swept away and shifted, new comers that are established in their room are as vain as they. But now, if we bring the word to the creature, and God by his Spirit giveth us an heart to observe these things, we shall see that all is passing and perishing, that the whole world hath a great evil that burdens it, and will at length prove its destruction; namely, sin; that the groaning universe doth in effect say to us, 'Arise, depart, this is not your rest' Micah ii. 10. It is spoken to the Jews; the land of Canaan was given for a rest at first, but by their sin it had lost much of that use; the frequent changes of estate they met with there for their sins was a summons to remove and look higher. It is true of all the world, it is not our resting-place, since it was defiled by sin; therefore the groaning creature should wean us from the world, and inflame us with a desire of heaven, where is perfect and eternal happiness.

[B.] It teacheth us the evil of sin; it is the burden of the whole creation, of which it would fain be eased. All the vanity that is upon the creature, and all annoyance which we have from the creature, is the fruit of our rebellion against God; which should make us more humble for sin past, and more cautious for the time to come. So much sin as you introduce, so much you disturb the harmony of the creation, and are accessary to the many destructive changes wrought in the world.

[C.] It readeth us a lecture of patience. We live in a groaning world, and must expect to bear our share in the common concert; the world is a valley of tears. Now to seek for joy in a valley of tears, to affect an exemption from groaning, it is to be singular, and be out of tune from the rest of the creation. What is in Ps. lxxxiv. 6, c the valley of *Bacha*, the *Septuagint* renders 'the valley of weeping'; it means the scorched weeping ground they passed through; and because their going to Jerusalem to worship was a figure of our progress or journey towards heaven, therefore many apply it to the world, resembled by a valley, as heaven is by a mountain, like Mount Sion; and a valley of tears, because we frequently meet with mourning occasions. Now it should not trouble us to be put upon groaning in a groaning world. We have company with us in our mourning; . not only our fellow saints; the apostle urgeth, 1 Pet. v. 9, 'These things are accomplished in your brethren which are in the world.' Every one of God's children have their share of hardships in the world; we think no sorrow like to our sorrow, and that none are so hardly dealt with as we are; others have their sorrows and hardships; the measure and weight of others' sorrows we know by guess, but our own by feeling. All things considered, you will find your lot no harder than the saints of God who went to heaven before you. But here is more company offered; the whole creation groaning for a burden brought upon them, not by their fault but ours; yet submitting to that appointed service till it be the will of God to ease them.

[D.] A lecture of long suffering; which is patience extended. When we are oppressed with many persecutions and afflictions, and these continue long, and we see no end, we despond': The creature groaneth and travaileth in pain until now'; that is, from the time sin entered into the world until the whole be dissolved. The continuance of the universe is much longer than the continuance of our lives; therefore let us not repine at so short a time, for the creature hath been in a groaning condition these six thousand years, or thereabout. Surely the softness and delicacy of our flesh is too great, if we must see the end of our troubles as soon as we enter into them. If the creature is obedient to the creator in bearing the burden he lays on it, though it groan under it, then surely we should submit to his disposing will, so long as he will have us in a suffering condition: Jam. i. 4, 'Let patience have its perfect work'.

[E.] A lecture of repentance and solemn humiliation. If the creature groan under original vanity and corruption, brought upon it by the first sin, sin being wonderfully increased, the world is ready to sink under the weight of it; therefore when sin increaseth, it is a groaning time; the multitude of the wicked are a burden to the countries where they live. The heathens would call a wicked man, 'the burden of the earth'; the word of God showeth it more plainly; therefore when the wicked increase and walk on every side, and they increase in wickedness, it is time to look about us, and seriously and heartily humble ourselves before God: Lev. xviii. 25, 'And the land is defiled, therefore I do visit the iniquities thereof upon it; and the land itself vomiteth out her inhabitants'; Micah ii. 10, 'Because it is polluted, it shall destroy you with a sore destruction; t and Jer. ix. 19, 'Our dwellings have cast us out.' The land doth as it were loathe to bear and feed them that so grossly dishonour God.

[F.] A lesson of hope in long sorrow. We should keep up hope and expectation; the creature groaneth till now; yea, but still it expecteth its final deliverance. It is an expression of great rebellion, distrust, and contempt, to say, 'Why should I wait on the Lord any longer?' 2 Kings vi. 33. God can bring the bitterest condition to a most comfort able issue. Consider how he dealeth with other creatures; the creature groaneth and travaileth in pain, but the birth will ensue; the groaning of the creature is like a travailing in birth, and so the calamities of the saints: John xvi. 21, 22, 'A woman when she is in travail hath sorrow, because her hour is come; but as soon as she is delivered of the child, she is no more in anguish, for joy a man is born into the world; and ye now are in sorrow, but I will see you again, and your hearts shall rejoice, and your joy no man taketh from you.' The throes of our sorrow may be very sharp and bitter; but the birth will occasion joy enough to countervail the tediousness of it.

4. They are complaining, accusing groans. The apostle saith, Jam. v. 4, 'Grudge not one against another'; groan not one against another; that is, give not occasion to one another to com plain against you to God. It is sad when one Christian complaineth against another for his froward, and perverse, and unbrotherly carriage; much more of near relations, husbands and wives, ministers and people. The apostle saith it is not profitable when they give their account with grief and not with joy, Heb. xiii. 17. This groaning of the creature must be interpreted by the standard of this notion: the creature groaneth not with us, but groaneth against us; because of the slavery we put them unto they groan for vengeance and destruction; not in fellow-feeling with thee, but in indignation against thee, if thou be a wicked man. There is a groaning by way of sympathy and compassion, as we are bidden, Horn. xii. 15, to 1 rejoice with them that rejoice, and weep with them that weep'; and there is a groaning by way of accusation and appeal, for revenge against those that have wronged us. We have abused the creature; the groan of a worm in the ear of the Lord of Hosts will be heard; so James v. 2, 3, 'Your riches are corrupted, your garments are moth-eaten, your gold and silver is cankered, and the rust of them shall be a witness against you, and shall eat your flesh as it were fire; you have heaped up treasure together for the last days.' In the Day of Judgment, the groans of the creature and the circumstances of our sinful actions shall be brought forth as witnesses against us; the moth-eaten garments, the cankered silver shall be produced. So Hab. ii. 11, 'The stone shall cry out of the wall, and the beam out of the timber shall answer it;' that is, the materials of the house built by oppression shall come as witnesses. There is a kind of antipathy between them therein represented. The stones of the wall shall cry, Lord we were built up by rapine and violence; and the beam shall answer. True, Lord, even so it is. The stones shall cry, Vengeance, Lord, upon our ungodly ones; and the beam shall answer, Woe to him, because he built his house with blood! Conscience is a

terrible remembrancer; the very creatures which sinners abused will be brought in testimony against them to their conviction and condemnation. You will say, what is this to the restoration of the universe, or those elementary bodies in this lower world, to which you seem to confine this restoration? These creatures shall be consumed in the last fire; how then brought into the judgment?

Answer,

(1.) The elementary bodies do concur to the increase and preservation of these things. Lands gotten by violence are made fruitful by sun, air, and rain j the sun now shineth upon these wicked men, and the rain falleth upon their fields; the creatures abused to excess come from both the sunshine and the earth's fertility, which is the mother of all wealth.

(2.) Though many of these creatures shall be consumed in this last fire, yet they shall have an *esse cognitum*, in the memory and conscience of the sinner, though not an *esse rei*, an actual existence. And thus the wine abused to drunkenness may witness against the drunkard; the sacrilegious morsels which the glutton alienated from the poor, and devoted to lust and appetite, shall witness against the glutton. *Memoria praeteritorum* is one of the punishments in hell: Luke xvi. 25, 'Son, remember that thou in thy life-time receivedst thy good things' The very clothing by which they did manifest their pride, shall witness against the proud; the lands, goods, and houses of worldlings, Isa. v. 8, shall witness against the worldling; the gold and silver which they preferred before everlasting riches, shall wit ness against the carnal; the place, the room, the bed wherein men committed filthiness and lewdness, shall witness against the unclean; when conscience shall be forced to the review, all these things shall come into his mind. To this also may be referred that passage j Josh. xxiv. 27, 'And Joshua said unto all the people, Behold this stone shall be a witness unto us, for it hath heard all the words of the Lord, which he spake unto us; it shall be there for a witness to you, lest you deny your God.' How could the stone which he had placed under a great oak, which was very near the sanctuary of the Lord, hear or give witness? Partly by God's appeal, and partly i>y their memory and conscience. It was a monument to put them in mind of this solemn covenant; and so might serve to convince them of their sin. Thus hearing is ascribed to a senseless stone, because it was a circumstance that might be produced in the judgment.

Thirdly, how we know it? For who ever heard the groaning of the whole creation?

1. By sensible experience we know the vanity of the creature. Ocular demonstration is enough to tell us all that things are frail and perishing: Ps. cxix. 96, 'I have seen an end of all perfection.'

2. The word affirmeth, First, that this came in by man's sin; and the common apprehension of mankind attesteth it, that wicked men are unprofitable burdens of the earth, and bring a judgment on the place where they live. Secondly, that God having repaired the world by Christ, there is a better estate appointed for man; and so by con sequence for the creatures, which are an appendage to him: Isa. xi. 6, 7, 8, 9. The enmity of the creature shall cease there, as in Noah's ark.

3. The Spirit improveth it, both the vanity of the creature, and our mortality, and the hopes of restoration. God must teach us the plainest lessons: Ps. xc. 12, 'Lord, teach us to number our days, that we may apply our hearts unto wisdom.' Deut. xxix. 2, 3, 4, 'Ye have seen all that the Lord did before your eyes in the land of Egypt, unto Pharoah, and unto all his servants, and unto all his land; the great temptations which thine eyes have seen, the signs and the great miracles, yet the Lord hath not given you an heart to perceive, and eyes to see, and ears to hear, unto this day' And the hopes of restoration: faith is his mere gift and production: Eph. ii. 8, 'For by grace ye are saved, through faith; and that not of ourselves, it is the gift of God.'

From the whole take these corollaries:

1. That sinful man is an enemy to all the creatures, as well as to himself. He hath brought misery upon himself, and all the world which was his place to dwell in. The creation was a well-tuned instrument, upon which man might make music to the praise and honour of God; but the strings of the harp are 'broken; and there is nothing but jarring instead of harmony, and groans for praise. Yea, man himself, who is the mouth of the creation, is very dumb and tongue-tied in the praises of God.

2. That every particular land fareth the worse for wicked men. Man hath brought a burden on the creation, and the increase of wicked men showeth the ruin of any people or country: Prov. xi. 10, 11, 'When it goeth well with the righteous, the city rejoiceth; and when the wicked perish, there is shouting. By the blessing of the upright the city is exalted: but it is overthrown by the mouth of the wicked.' The meaning of these two proverbs is, that the godly bring on a blessing on the land where they live, and the wicked a curse. The godly bring on a blessing by their prayers and holy example, God's providence, and respect thereunto; but the wicked a curse by their abuse of the creatures. The corrupt world think otherwise, that all their dishonour, their judgments, come from suffering the godly to live amongst them. 'It is not for the king's profit to suffer them to live,' Esth. iii. 8.

3. That we must not ascribe the alterations and changes of the creature to chance or fortune, but to God's providence punishing man's sin. Some do not see the hand of God; as ignorant, stupid, and careless persons: Ps. xxviii. 5, 'They regard not the work of the Lord, nor the operation of his hand'. And some care not to see: Isa. xxvi. 11, 'When thy hand is lifted up, they will not see'; they put all judgments upon the ordinary course of second causes; either a chance, 1 Sam. xiv. 9; or attribute it to some natural thing: John xii. 29, they said it thundered, when God spake from heaven to own Christ. Some see, but are in part blinded with malice and prejudice; which is to be seen by their making perverse interpretations of providence: 2 Sam. xvi. 8, 'The Lord hath returned upon thee all the blood of the house of Saul.'

4. You see a reason why a righteous man should be merciful to his beast: Prov. xii. 10, 'A righteous man regardeth the life of his beast; but the tender mercies of the wicked are cruel.' There is burden enough already upon the creature, under which he groaneth; he would bring on no more than needeth; he will not use them unmercifully, nor wear them out with too great and continual labours; but giveth them that food, rest, and refection

which is necessary. In the destruction of Nineveh God had respect to the beasts: Jonah iv. 11, 'There was much cattle in that city'

5. The wonderful dullness and dead-heartedness of man in case of sin and misery; so that the creatures are fain to supply our room. Few are sensible of this burden; we should all groan, but do not. Surely we ought to be excited to groan for sin and misery, and long for the happiness of the saints; so ver. 23, 'And not only they, but we ourselves also, which have the first fruits of the Spirit, even we ourselves groan within ourselves, waiting for the adoption, to wit, the redemption of our bodies.'

6. The great need there is to draw off our hearts from the inordinate love of the creature, and to lay up treasure in heaven. What can we expect from a groaning creature, which will soon come to an end, but that only we wholly trust sense, and judge according to present appearance? Otherwise we would say with the apostle, we know and look further than the compass of this world, to that place where all is firm and stable; but we seldom improve these thoughts.

7. How unsuitable sensual rejoicing is unto the state which we are now in. It is a groaning world, and here we seek all our pleasures and contentments. It is a charge against sensualists, Jam. v. 5, 'Ye have lived in pleasure upon earth' the place of our exile, the place defiled with man's sin, the place subjected to a curse for man's sake. Moderate contentment is allowed us during our pilgrimage, as appears both by the dispensation of God's providence and covenant; but our full joy is reserved for hereafter; his providence alloweth many natural comforts; and his covenant many perpetual blessings.

SERMON XXX

And not only they, but ourselves also, who have the first fruits of the Spirit, even we ourselves groan within ourselves, waiting for the adoption, the redemption of our bodies.

Romans VIII. 23.

IN these words the apostle pursueth his main scope, which is to direct believers patiently to wait for their final happiness. He doth it by comparing the disposition of the children of God with the inclination of the creatures, spoken of in the former verses: 'and not only they,' &c.

There is a comparison,

1. Between persons and persons.

2. Between actions and actions.

1. Between persons and persons; the whole creation, and those that have the first fruits of the Spirit. The one is a feigned, the other a real person; therefore this groaning and expectation is attributed to the children of God, with greater propriety of speech. The creatures are said to groan and wait, upon supposition if they had sense and reason they would groan and wait; we, by certain knowledge and true desire; the creatures groan as they are assisted and directed by God to a better state; we, by voluntary inclination; the creatures groan by others, as they excite our thoughts to consider their vanity and vicissitudes; the saints by themselves, and in themselves; others cannot perform it for them; they expect by God's direction, and groan by our meditation; but we properly, and without a figure.

2. Actions and actions. There are two ascribed to the creature: waiting, ver. 10, groaning, ver. 22. They groan, and we groan; they wait, and we wait; the groaning is amplified by the manner, and the waiting by the object.

[A.] The groaning is amplified by the manner. It may be rendered, among ourselves; the whole church of God groaneth, as well as the whole creation; or rather, in ourselves, *ex imo corde*; these groans came from the bottom of the heart.

[B.] The waiting is amplified by the object or matter which they wait for: 'For the adoption, the redemption of our bodies' The last expression explaineth the former, our full adoption and redemption, which shall be accomplished at the general resurrection.

Doctrine That those that have received the first fruits of the Spirit, do groan and wait for a better estate than they now enjoy. I shall speak of this point, *First*, By way of explication; *Secondly*, By way of confirmation.

First, For explication.

1. The description of the persons, 'We that have the first fruits of the Spirit.' The expression alludeth to the customs of the law, where the offering of the first fruits sanctified the whole heap: Rom. xi. 16: 'For if the first fruits be holy, the lump also is holy'. Thence it is applied to any such beginnings as are a pledge of more to ensue; as here, the first fruits of the Spirit are the pledges and beginnings of eternal life. What are they? The graces and comforts of

the Spirit: First, the graces. Salvation is begun in our new birth: Titus iii. 5, 'But according to his mercy he saved us, by the washing of regeneration, and the renewing of the Holy Ghost;' and sanctifying grace is called an immortal and incorruptible seed, 1 Pet. i. 23; and they that are made partakers of it are implied to have eternal life abiding in them, 1 John iii. 13, because the life is now begun, which shall be perfected in heaven. For the present there is an eternal principle in them which carries them to eternal ends. Secondly, The comforts which are consequent upon the graces. For the Spirit is first a sanctifier, and then a comforter; he worketh holiness; and by holiness, peace, joy, and comfort, which are some foretastes of that sweetness which is in heaven. This peace and joy is raised in us, partly, by the life and exercise of faith and love; 1 Pet. i. 8, 'Whom having not seen ye love; in whom, though now ye see him not, yet believing, ye rejoice with joy unspeakable, and full of glory;' and Rom. xv. 13, 'Now the God of hope fill you with all joy and peace in believing.' And partly, by the apprehension of God's love and favour to us: Ps. iv. 6, 7, 'Lord, lift up the light of thy countenance upon us. Thou hast put gladness into my heart, more than in the time when their corn and wine increased' And also, by our approaches to him in the word and prayer, where God doth most familiarly manifest himself to his people: Isa. lvi. 7, 'I will bring them into my holy mountain, and make them joyful in the house of prayer' These comforts of the Spirit they meet with in God's sacred ordinances: Ps. lxxxiv. 10, 'For a day in thy courts is better than a thousand elsewhere.' Thus I have shown you what they are; now for to what use they serve? Answer, They are an earnest and a foretaste; an earnest, to show how sure: Eph i. 13, 14, 'In whom also, after ye believed, ye were sealed with the Holy Spirit of promise, which is the earnest of our inheritance, until the redemption of the purchased possession'; 2 Cor. v. 5, 'Now he that hath wrought us to the self-same thing is God, who also hath given us the earnest of the Spirit,' a begun, possession. Secondly, a foretaste, to show how good: 1 Pet ii. 3, 'If so be ye have tasted that the Lord is gracious' As the clusters of Canaan grapes were carried before them to animate the Israelites, and the Italian grapes the Gauls; so the graces are pledges of our future perfection; and the comforts, tastes of our future happiness.

2. The acts mentioned are two, groan, and wait; the one doth more directly respect our present, the other our future estate. We groan because of present miseries; we wait because of our future happiness. Or rather both acts respect both estates compounded; as groaning, our present and future happiness; for there are groans that come from sorrows; and groans which come from hope and desire: 2 Cor. v. 2, 'In this we groan, earnestly desiring to be clothed upon with our house which is from heaven'; and ver 4, 'We groan being burdened' Grief at our present state, the burden of sin and misery, and desire of future deliverance: Prov. xiii. 12, 'Hope deferred maketh the heart sick, but when the desire cometh, it is as a tree of life' On the other side, waiting importeth two things, an earnest and desirous expectation of what is to come, and a patient submission to God for the present.

[A.] An earnest and desirous expectation of what is to come; there fore said to look and long for it: Tit. ii. 13, 'Looking for the blessed hope;' and Heb. ix. 28, 'To them that look for him' 2 Tim. iv. 8, 'And to them also that love his appearing'.

[B.] A patient submission to God for what is present. 'Patience of hope' 1 Thes. i. 3; and Ps. xxxvii. 7, 'Rest on the Lord, and wait patiently for him'. Our happiness is delayed, and in the meantime, we have many trials; our estate to come is excellent and glorious, and our present estate is miserable and despicable. It is offered to us upon sure and gracious terms, therefore we wait; but in the meantime, we conflict with difficulties, and therefore we groan. So that as these two duties respect our different estate, so they chiefly express our apprehension and respect to our sinful estate: it is earnest, it is patient and submissive. First, it is earnest; for we groan, as a woman with child doth exactly count her time; or the Israelites in bondage did wait for the year of jubilee; or the hireling when his covenanted time will expire. Secondly, with patience and submission to God's pleasure and leisure, possessing their souls in meekness. And observe the motive; this waiting is earnest and desirous; for the godly have not only a sense and feeling of the miseries and calamities of this life, but a fervent desire of the joys of heaven. The miseries and troubles of the present world are matters of sense; we need not scripture to tell us that we are burdened, and pained, and conflict with diverse evils; our flesh feeleth it; and we know it to our grief, that here is little else but disquiet and vexation. Sense can discover what should drive us from the world; but sense cannot discover what should draw our desires after a better estate; that we learn by faith; the joy is set before us in the promises of the gospel: Heb. vi. 18, 'That we might have strong consolation, who have fled for refuge to lay hold on the hope that is set before us'; and Heb. xii. 2, 'Looking unto Jesus, the author and finisher of our faith, who endured the cross, despised the shame, and is set down at the right hand of the throne of God' The promises set it in our view, that we may eye it much, that we may often look upon it, press earnestly towards it. Groaning is stirred up by sense, waiting by faith.

3. This better estate is called adoption, and the redemption of our bodies.

[A.] It is called adoption. We are now taken into God's family; but our present adoption is imperfect, and inconspicuous. First, it is imperfect, as all our privileges by Christ are. We have not yet our full liberty from the bondage of corruption, nor possession of our blessed inheritance; then we shall be coheirs with Christ, ver. 17; brought into 'the glorious liberty of the children of God' ver. 21. Secondly, it is inconspicuous: 1 Joh. iii. 1,2,' Therefore the world knoweth us not, because it knew him not. Behold, now we are the sons of God, and it doth not yet appear what we shall be; but we know that when he shall appear, we shall be like him'; and Rom. viii. 19, 'waiteth for the manifestation of the sons of God' It then appeareth to all the world who are the children of God, and what happiness is provided for them.

[B.] The redemption of our bodies. By redemption is meant our full and final deliverance; and it is applied to the body, because death remaineth upon that part until God redeemeth us from the hand of the grave, Ps. xlix. 15. But more distinctly, redemption is taken either for the impetation, or application. First, the impetration[40] is by the merit of Christ, and so we were redeemed when the ransom and price was paid for us, Heb. ix. 12; not for the soul only, but for the body also, as appeareth, 1 Cor. vi. 20, 'For ye are bought with a price, therefore glorify God in your body, and in your spirit, which are God's.' Secondly, the application is our actual deliverance and freedom by virtue of that price, which is either begun or perfected. Begun, when our bonds are in part loosed: Eph. i. 7, 'In whom we have redemption through his blood, the forgiveness of sins'; and perfected in the other world. Therefore the day of judgment is called 'the day of our redemption' Eph. iv. 30; when the last enemy is destroyed, namely, death, and our bodies are raised up in glory; then we are actually free from all evil. And because this is done by virtue of that price and ransom which Christ paid for us, it is called redemption; and the redemption of our bodies, because the body, which was sown in corruption, is raised in incorruption; and that which was sown in dishonour is raised in glory; and that which was sown in weakness is raised in power, 1 Cor. xv. 42, 43. Though the price was paid long ago, the full fruit is not enjoyed till then; for then we have our final and complete deliverance from all sin and misery, vanity and corruption. In this life we are not free from those things which lead to corruption, that is, from sin, misery, and afflictions; at death, the soul is made perfect, but the body is in the power of the grave; but then the body enjoy eth a glorious resurrection.

Secondly. By way of confirmation: Why we should groan and long for this estate. The reasons concern either this life, or the next.

1. For this life: I shall prove, [A.] That there is cause or matter for groaning, and desiring a better estate. [B.] That those that have the first fruits of the Spirit are more apprehensive of this misery than others are or can be.

[A.] The pressures and miseries of this life call for this groaning; 'being burdened' saith the apostle, 'we groan'. We have an heavy burden upon us, both of sin and misery.

(1.) Of sin. To a gracious heart and waking conscience it is one of the heaviest burdens that can be felt: Rom. vii. 24, 'wretched man that I am, who shall deliver me from the body of death?' Paul was whipped, imprisoned, stoned, in perils by land and sea, persecuted by enemies, undermined by false brethren; but afflictions did not sit so close to him as sins; the body of death was his sorest burden, therefore did he long for deliverance. A beast will leave the place where he findeth neither food nor rest; it is not the troubles of the world only, which set the saints a-groaning, but indwelling corruption; this grieveth them, that they are not yet rid of sin; that they serve God with such apparent weakness and manifold defects; that they are so often distracted and oppressed with sensual and worldly affections; they cannot get rid of this cursed inmate, and therefore desire a change of states. By the grace of God they have got rid of the guilt of sin and reigning power of sin; but the being of it is a trouble to them, which will still remain till this tabernacle be dissolved; then sin shall

---

[40] The act of obtaining by petition or entreaty.

gasp its last; and the saints are groaning and longing for the parting day, when by putting off flesh they shall put off sin, and come and dwell with God.

(2.) Of misery. This burden is a partial cause of the saints' groaning, 'for they have not divested themselves of the feelings of nature, nor grown senseless as stocks and stones; they are of like passions with others, and love their natural comforts as others do; human nature is the same thing in all that are made of flesh and blood: Job vi. 12, 'Is my strength the strength of stones, or is my flesh of brass?' They feel pain as everyone doth, which will extort complaints from them. Now a Christian's misery may be reckoned from three things: 1. Temptations from Satan. 2. Grievous persecutions from the world. 3. Sharp afflictions from God himself. All these concur to wean a Christian from the world.

(a.) Temptations from Satan; who seeketh all advantages, either to withdraw us from God, or to distract us in his service, and make it tedious and wearisome to us: 1 Pet. v. 8, 9, 'Your adversary the devil goeth about, seeking whom he may devour.' All these things are accomplished in your brethren in the flesh; they are all haunted with a busy tempter, who is restless in his endeavours to ensnare their souls; this world is Satan's walk, the devil's circuit, who goeth up and down to destroy unwary creatures; and therefore his assiduous temptations are one of the Christian's burdens.

(b.) Bitter and grievous persecutions; which sometimes make them weary of their lives, that they may be freed from their hard task- masters. As Elijah was weary of the trouble he had by Jezebel's pursuits, that he durst not trust himself in the land of Israel and Judea, but goeth a day's journey into the wilderness, and sat down under a juniper tree, and requested for himself that he might die; 'for,' saith he, 'I am not better than my father's house,' 1 Kings xix. 4, 5. Surely the troubled will long for rest.

(c.) Sharp afflictions from God himself, who is jealous of our hearts, because we are not watchful over them. We are too apt to take up with a worldly happiness, and to root here; looking no further, whilst we have all our comforts about us; our hearts saying, it is best to be here, till God by his smart rod awaken us out of our drowsy fits. We are so pleased with our entertainment by the way, that we forget home; therefore the Lord is fain to embitter our worldly portion, that we may think of a remove to some better place and state, where all tears shall be wiped from our eyes. We would sleep and rest here, if we did not sometimes meet with thorns in our bed; 'All the days of my pilgrimage,' saith holy Jacob, Gen. xlvii. 7, 'are -few and evil.' Our days are evil, and it is well they are but few; that in this ship wreck of man's felicity we can see banks and shores, and a landing place, where we may be safe at length. Here most of our days are sorrow, grief, and travail; but there is our repose; our heart would fail, were there not some hopes mingled with our tears.

[B.] That those who have the first fruits of the Spirit are more apprehensive of this misery than others are or can be.

(1.) Of misery and afflictions. Partly, because grace intendereth the heart; they look upon afflictions with another eye than the stupid world doth; they look upon them as coming from God, and as the fruit of sin, and they dare not slight any of God's corrective dispensations. There are two extremes, slighting, and fainting, Heb. xii. 5. Affliction cannot be improved if we have not a sense of it; we owe so much reverence to God, as to tremble at his anger, Num. xii. 14; when he crosseth and disappointeth us, it must not be slightly passed over. Look as in the flood, Gen vii. 11; when the windows of heaven were opened from above, and the fountains of the great deep were broken open from below, the flood increased; so when nature and grace concur to heighten the afflictions, the children of God must needs have a greater and more tender sense of it than others have. As those that are of a delicate constitution are more capable of pain than the stubborn and robustious[41]; and the tender flesh of a child will sooner feel the lash than the thick skin of a slave; so the children of God, who have a more serious apprehension of things, and a more tender spirit, soonest feel the burden of their Father's displeasure, and do more lay it to heart, than careless spirits, who laugh out their cross, and drink away their sorrows. And partly, because they are more exercised with afflictions; the world hateth them because they are so good, and God chastens them because they are no better': Many are the troubles of the righteous,' Ps. xxxiv. 19. There is more squaring, and hewing, and cutting used about stones, which are to be set in a stately palace, than those which are placed in an ordinary building; the vine is pruned, when the bramble in the hedge is not looked after; the child is put under discipline when the bastard liveth more at large. God meaneth to destroy those, whom by a just judgment he permitteth to go on in their sins, to their eternal undoing.

(2.) They are more sensible of sin as a burden: Ps. xxxviii. 4, 'Mine iniquities are gone over my head; they are a burden too heavy for me.' That sins are a burden to a wounded conscience is evident by their complaints; if a millstone fall upon them, it is not so heavy and bruising, as one spark of God's wrath lighting upon the conscience for sin; but they are also a burden to a tender conscience. And partly, because they have more light than others, and see more into the heinous nature and evil of sin: Jer. xviii. 31, 'After I was instructed, I smote upon the thigh'; and Rom. vii. 9, 'When the commandment came, sin revived, and I died.' And partly, because they have more love than others have; and they that love much, will mourn most for sin, Luke vii. 47; she wept much, because she loved much. The more holy any are, the more they are troubled about offending 'God than others are, or themselves were before. What is the reason? It is not from the increase of sin, but the increase of light and love; they see more and more into sin than formerly they did, or could do; as in a glass of pure water the least mote is soon espied. And partly, because they have more heartily renounced sin; therefore the relics of it are a greater burden to them. Elements burden not in their own place; wicked men are in their own element; it is a sport to them to do evil; for 'fools make a mock of sin.' But it is otherwise with the children of God; sin is that they hate, and pray down, and strive against; they are aspiring after a better estate; and it is a trouble to them, they find so little of it while they are in the body.

---

[41] rowdy, unruly, or out of control

2. The other sort of reasons concern the other life. A Christian here is unsatisfied, and waiteth for a better and purer estate, a state of constant felicity, and exact conformity to God; and that for four reasons.

[A.] By the first fruits of the Spirit he is confirmed in the belief of the certainty of this estate; for the Holy Ghost openeth his eyes to see the reality of the world to come: Eph. i. 17, 18, 'That the God of our Lord Jesus Christ, the Father of glory, may give unto you the Spirit of wisdom and revelation in the knowledge of him; the eyes of your understanding being enlightened, that ye may know what is the hope of his calling, and what the riches of the glory of the inheritance of the saints in light.' 1 Cor. ii. 12, 'Now we have not received the spirit of the world, but the Spirit which is of God, that ye may know the things that are freely given us of God.' Faith is the eye of the soul, Heb. xi. 1; and an eagle-eye it is, that helpeth us to look above the mists and clouds of the lower world, and see eternity at the back of time, and glory following shame, and rest labour. Now affections follow persuasion: Heb. xi. 13, 'Being persuaded of these things, they embraced them' They that see there is another world, a life infinitely more desirable than that which we now enjoy, will find their affections stirred towards it; an estate so blessed, if it were soundly believed it would be earnestly desired; and certainly men do not believe this blessedness, if they be coldly affected towards it.

[B.] By the first fruits of the Spirit, they do in part know the excellency of it. Surely it is no slight and vain thing which is so desired, groaned after, and waited for by all the saints. They find somewhat in themselves which makes them to value and esteem it; if the first fruits be rich and glorious, what will the whole harvest be? If the taste be so ravishing, what will the whole feast prove? Surely it will wholly swallow us up with joy. The joys of the Spirit are unspeakable things, 1 Pet. i. 8; but 'at his right hand there is fulness of joy for evermore' Ps. xvi. 11. The refreshings we meet with by the way doth mightily support us; what comfort shall we have when we come to our journey's end, and enjoy what we have heard of? And what we have heard is little to the enjoyment. The saints would not part with their communion with Christ here for all the world; what will it be when our union and communion is full and perfect? To get a glimpse of Christ, as he showeth himself through the lattice, doth much revive the drooping soul; but there we shall see him with open face; here we get a little from him in his ordinances, and that little is as much as we can hold; but there he is all in all, and we are filled up with the fulness of God. Christ in us now is the hope of glory, Col. i. 27; but Christ in us then is glory itself; the Spirit in us now is a well springing up, but then the water groweth not only into a stream, but into ocean; holiness here is called the seed of God, but then it is the life of God; grace tendeth to the place whence it cometh, as a spark of fire tendeth to the element of fire; there it is in its perfect estate. In short, look what difference there is between the spring-head and the out-fall of the water into the sea; such difference there is between our enjoyment of God now, and hereafter.

[C.] By the first fruits of the Spirit, we are prepared and fitted for that blessed estate. We read in the scripture, that as heaven is prepared for the saints, so the saints are prepared for heaven: Rom. ix. 23, 'Vessels of mercy, which he hath aforehand prepared unto glory; Col. i.

12, 'Who hath made us meet to be partakers of the inheritance of the saints in light.' Now we are prepared by the Spirit's sanctifying body and soul, and fitting us for the heavenly estate; it is said, 2 Cor. iii. 18, 'We are changed into his image from glory to glory.' As grace increaseth, glory hasteneth on; every degree is a step nearer; we grow more meet to dwell with God, as we grow more like God. Now this argument holdeth good on God's part and ours. When God hath formed us and fitted us for any estate, he will bring us to it; as the apostle telleth us, 2 Cor. v. 6, 'Now he that hath wrought us to this selfsame thing is God, who hath given us the earnest of the Spirit' This piece of workmanship was never designed to be left always here in the world, but suited to a better place, to which it shall be translated. It is the wisdom of God to bestow all things in apt places; every creature hath its element, and a peculiar nature, which carrieth it thither; as fishes desire to live in the water, and fowls in the air; it is answerable to the nature which God hath put into them. The new creature hath a suitableness to the glorious estate to come here after; therefore the New Jerusalem is the only convenient place to the new creature; and they that have a divine nature, must live in the immediate presence of God. On their part, God's word telleth them of a better life than this, and their hearts incline them to it, they being formed and fitted for it; for the more a thing is formed for the end, the more vehemently it tendeth towards it. God will not carry us to heaven against our will; therefore there is not only a preparation, but an earnest expectation, which is the fruit of it; they long to enjoy their God, to see their Redeemer, to enter upon that blessed estate for which God hath prepared them, whereof in part he hath assured them. No man is unwilling to be happy, and to attain his end. Certainly a Christian out of heaven is out of his proper place; we are like fish in a paddle-trunk, or small vessel of water, which will only keep us alive; we would fain be in the ocean.

[D.] By the first fruits of the Spirit our title and right is assured. For it is compared to a seal, to warrant our present interest: Eph. iv. 3, 'Ye are sealed with the Holy Spirit of promise'; to an earnest, to secure our future enjoyment: 2 Cor. iv. 22, 'Who hath also sealed us, and given us the earnest of the Spirit in our hearts.' This blessed state belongeth only to those who have the first fruits of the Spirit; their title is clear; for God will own his seal and impress, will never take back his earnest, but it remaineth with us till there be no place left for doubts and fears. Now who, being secured of a better estate, and for the present burdened with sorrow and temptations, would not groan and long after it?

Use. [A.] Is information. It informeth us of the certainty of blessed ness to come. If there were any perfect estate in this life nothing would sooner bring us to it than a participation of the Spirit; but this doth not; for they that are partakers of the Spirit groan, wait, and are not satisfied with their present estate, but long for a better, breathe after something greater, and beyond what they here enjoy. Therefore certainly God hath reserved for them a better estate in another world. We prove another life by the disposition and instinct of nature towards happiness in the general, yea, eternal happiness; all would be happy; they grope and feel about after eternal good, Acts xvii. 26. This being the universal desire of all mankind, it is an argument that there is such a thing as eternal good, for natural desires are not frustrate; for nature doth nothing in vain. But the desires of the sanctified do much more prove it; for these act more regularly, direct their desires and groans to a certain scope and end; and those are excited by the Holy Spirit of God; he imprinteth the firm persuasion of this happiness in them, and stirreth up these groans after it, and that usually in our gravest and severest moods, when we are solemnly conversing with God in his holy worship; then he doth raise up these affections towards heavenly things, by the word, prayer, and sacraments, and leaveth this heavenly relish upon our hearty as the present reward of our duties. And the more serious and holy any are, the more do they feel of this. Now this is a greater argument; for holiness was never designed for our torment; and these desires being of God's own planting, they will not be disappointed.

[B.] That none but those who have the first fruits of the Spirit will groan and hope for eternal life. Others have no warrant, for they have not God's earnest; and God never giveth the whole bargain, but he first giveth earnest; for 'without holiness no man shall see God.' Others have no inclination; for most men's thoughts are not busied about this, but rather go after worldly things; they are for serving their lusts, and pleasing their fleshly appetites and fancies; whereas the apostle biddeth us be sober, and truss up the loins of our minds, 1 Pet. i. 13, if we would hope to the end, for the grace that is to be brought unto us at the revelation of Jesus Christ. It is true, death is the ordinary refuge for embittered spirits, and the back-door we seek to get out at in our discontent. In passion men will desire to die; when beaten out of the world, heaven is their retreat; but no serious groans, and desires of heaven.

[C.] That we must so groan under the present misery, that we may wait for deliverance with patience. Hope is not only made up of look ing and longing, but waiting also: Heb. vi. 12, 'Be ye followers of them who through faith and patience inherit the promise'

[D.] That one great means to support our faith and patience is the hope of the redemption of our bodies. (1.) Because the man cannot be happy till the body be raised again; for the soul alone doth not consummate the man, neither was it made to live eternally apart from the body, but is in a state of widowhood till it be united to it again, and live with its old mate and companion. The man is not happy till then. (2.) It is the body is most pained in obedience, and endured all the troubles and labours of Christianity; there it hath part in the reward as well as the work; Heb. xi. 35, 'Not accepting deliverance, that they might obtain a better resurrection.' (3.) It is the body which seemed to be lost. Some of the bodies of the faithful were devoured by wild beasts, others consumed in the fire; some swallowed up in the sea; all resolved in dust. Therefore because here the temptation lays the smart or destruction and torture of the body, the cordial is suited; Christians do not only desire the blessed immortality of the soul, but the resurrection of the body. The body is weak, frail, subject to aches and diseases, stone, gout, strangury, death itself, tumbled up and down, and tossed from prison to prison; but then redeemed from all evil and misery.

Use 2. Is exhortation. To rouse up our languid and cold affections, that we may more earnestly groan and long for heavenly things. If we look to this world, the pleasures of it are dreams and shadows; the miseries of it many and real; we find corruption within, temptations without, grievous afflictions, oppressing the bodily life; but above all, we do too often displease and dishonour God. If to the other world, the pleasures of it are full, glorious, and eternal. God is fain to drive us out of this world, as he did Lot out of Sodom, yet loath to depart. Have we not smarted enough for our love to a vain world? sinned enough to make us weary of the present state? If heaven be not worth our desires and groans, it is little worth. There is the best estate, the best work, and the best company.

Question. But how shall we do to get up our hearts from this world to a better? These things are necessary:

[A.] The illumination of the Spirit, that the mind be soundly persuaded: 2. Cor. v. 1, 'For we know that if our earthly house of this tabernacle were dissolved, we have a building of God, an house not made with hands, eternal in the heavens.'

[B.] Strong inclination, or an heart fixed on heavenly things: Mat. vi. 21, 'For where your treasure is, there will your heart be also.' Col. iii. 1, 'If ye be risen with Christ, seek those things which are above, where Christ sitteth at the right hand of God. Set your affections upon things above, and not upon the earth.'

[C.] Love to Christ: Phil. i. 23, 'For to me to live is Christ, and to die is gain.' They that love Christ will desire to be with him; they delight in his presence, count it their honour to be miserable with him, rather than happy without him.

[D.] Some competent assurance of our own interest: 2. Tim. iv. 8, 'Henceforth there is laid up for me a crown of righteousness, which the Lord, the righteous judge, will give me at that day, and not unto me only, but unto all that love his appearing.'

[E.] Some mortification, that the heart should be dead to the world, weaned from the pleasures and honour thereof: Gal. vi. 14, 'God forbid that I should glory, save in the cross of our Lord Jesus Christ, by whom the world is crucified unto me, and I unto the world.' While our hearts are set upon worldly profits and pleasures, and gratify the vices and lusts of the body, we are loath to depart: 'They have their portion in this life' Ps. xvii. 14.

Use 3. Do we groan and wait? If so

[A.] There will be serious waiting, and diligent preparing: 2 Pet. iii. 14, 'Wherefore, beloved, if ye look for such things, be diligent that you may be found of him in peace, without spot, and blameless.'

[B.] It will frame our lives: Phil. iii. 20, 'For our conversation is in heaven.'

[C.] It will put us upon self-denial. That maketh the Christian labour and suffer trouble and reproach; desire is the vigorous part of the soul: 1 Tim. iv. 10, 'For therefore we labour and suffer reproach, because we trust in the living God.'

SERMON XXXI

For we are saved by hope, but hope that is seen is not hope: for what a man seeth, why doth he yet hope for?

Romans VIII. 24.

IN this verse the apostle giveth a reason why believers do groaningly expect the adoption, the redemption of their bodies, and so, by consequence, salvation because yet they had it not. And in this reason there is secretly couched a prolepsis, or an anticipation of an objection; as if the apostle had said, If any shall object, We are adopted already, redeemed already, saved already, this I would answer him: We are not actually saved, but in right and expectation only; salvation indeed is begun in the new <birth; but is not complete till body and soul shall be glorified in the day of judgment; then we are redeemed or saved from all evils, and then do presently enter into the actual possession of the supreme happiness or glory which we expect. He proveth it by the nature of hope, because hope is of a future thing: 'For we are saved by hope; but hope,' &c.

In the words two things: 1. An account of the present state of a believer; 'For we are saved by hope'

2. The proof of it by two reasons. The first is taken from the nature of hope': For hope that is seen is not hope.' The second from the absurdity of the contrary; 'For what a man seeth, why doth he yet hope for?'

1. An account of the present state of a believer, 'We are saved by hope' A Christian is already saved; but he is only now saved by hope, *spe, non re*[42]; he hath complete salvation, not in actual possession, but earnest expectation; that is the apostle's drift here. He doth not show for what we are accepted at the last day, but how saved now; he doth not say we shall be saved by hope, but we are saved by hope, which expecteth the fulfilling of God's promises in our salvation.

2. The proof.

[A.] By a reason taken from the nature of hope; it is conversant about things unseen: 'Hope that is seen is not hope'; *elpis blepomene*[43] is the thing hoped for; the act is put for the object; as also Col. i. 5, 'The hope which is laid up for you in heaven' Hope is wrought in our hearts, but the thing hoped for is reserved in heaven for us. 'Is not hope'; there it is taken for the act of hoping is not hoped for. The meaning is, things liable to hope are not visible and present, but future and unseen; for vision and possession do exclude hope.

[B.] From the absurdity of the contrary supposition'; for what a man seeth, why doth he yet hope for it'; that is, things enjoyed are no longer looked for. To see is to enjoy; as also 2 Cor.

---

[42] Hope, does not matter
[43] Hope that is seen

v. 7, 'We walk by faith, and not by sight'; that is, we believe now, but do not enjoy. So here, where the thing hoped for is possessed already, it is said to be seen. Otherwise if you take seeing properly, a man may hope for that which he seeth, as the wrestler or racer hath the crown in view; but whilst he is wrestling and racing he hopeth to have it, but hath not yet obtained it. Well then, the apostle's meaning is, who would look for that which he hath in his hands? It is foolish to say he hopeth for it, or looketh for it, when he doth already enjoy it.

Doctrine Hope is one of the graces necessary to obtain the great salvation promised by Christ.

First. For explication:

1. Hope is a desirous expectation of some promised good. The act is a desirous expectation; the object is some promised good. Of the act I shall speak afterwards; the object I shall consider now. It is some good; for evil is not hoped for, but feared. And a good promised; for hope, the grace, is grounded upon the word of God: Ps. cxxx. 5, 'I have hoped in thy word' And the apostle telleth us that the heirs of promise being secured by two immutable things, God's word and God's oath, do fly for refuge to lay hold upon the hope set before them: Heb. vi. 18. The promise doth both declare and assure; declare what we may hope for; the apostle saith it is set before us; not before our senses, or the eyes of the body, but before our faith, the eyes of our minds, in the gospel; and withal doth assure us in hoping; for we have the word of God, who is the supreme verity, that neither can deceive nor be deceived; and the promises of the gospel are ratified by the solemnity of an oath; the more to excite our drowsy minds to consider upon what sure grounds we go upon. Well then, there is some word of promise assented unto by faith, before we expect the good promised. Promises are the holdfast we have upon God, and the sure grounds of raising hope in ourselves, or pleading with God in prayer. We may plead them to ourselves if we would have strong and solid consolation: Ps. lvi. 4, 'In God I will praise his word; in God have I put my trust; I will not fear what man can do unto me.' Thus did David rebuke his fears. The fidelity of God in his promises is matter of firm confidence and hope to us. Only we must not make promises to ourselves, lest we become false prophets to ourselves, and build up our own dreams. So in pleading with God we have free leave to challenge God upon his word: Ps. cxix. 45, 'Remember the word unto thy servant, wherein thou hast caused me to hope.' Our necessities lead us to the promises, and the promises to Christ, in whom they are yea and amen; and Christ to God, as the fountain of grace; there we put these bonds in suit, and turn promises into prayers.

2. The promises do concern either this life or that which is to come: 1 Tim. iv. 8, 'Godliness is profitable to all things, having the promise of the life that now is, and that which is come.' There are supplies necessary for us during our pilgrimage; therefore God hath undertaken not only to give us heaven and happiness in the next world, but to carry us thither in a way best pleasing to himself, and conducible to our good; that we may serve him with comfort and peace all the days of our lives. Therefore there is an hope in God's promises for what we stand in need of by the way; and God delighteth to train us up in a way of faith and hope in

expecting our present supplies, that by often trying and trusting him for these things, we may the better hope for the great salvation; as men practise swimming in the shallow brooks before they venture in the deep ocean. But temporal things are only promised so far as it may be for God's glory and our good; we must not set God a task to provide meat for our lusts, or imagine that his providence will lacquey[44] upon our humours[45] and vain fancies. It is the ordinary practice of his free grace and fatherly love to provide things comfortable and necessary for his children: Mat. vi. 3, 'For your heavenly Father knoweth that ye have need of all these things.' There is a common bounty and goodness which reacheth to all his creatures, even to the preservation of the smallest worm; how much more will he provide for us whom he hath adopted into his family, and to whom he hath made promises that he will never leave us to insupportable difficulties? You would count him an unnatural father that feedeth his dogs and hawks and lets his children die of hunger. Certainly we may hope in God that he will do what is best, all things considered.

3. The great promise, and so the principal object of our hope, is salvation by Christ, or eternal life: 1 John ii. 25, 'This is the promise' and so the principal object, which he hath promised us, eternal life.' Christ hath promised other things too, but this is the promise. It is the great end of Christ's mediation to bring us to God: 1 Pet. iii. 18, 1 For Christ also hath once suffered, the just for the unjust, that he might bring us to God'; and that is not fully done till we live with him in heaven; this is the end of our faith, 1 Pet. i. 9; this is the prime benefit offered to us in the gospel, to which all others tend. By justification our incapacity is removed; by sanctification eternal life is begun; by the mercies of daily providence we are preserved in our duty and motion towards this happy estate'; Kept blameless to the heavenly kingdom,' 2 Tim. iv. 8. From hence we fetch our comfort during the whole course of our pilgrimage, this we look upon as the recompense of all our pains and losses; and upon the hopes of it the life of grace is carried on, and the temptations of sense defeated; and therefore hope is described in scripture by this object more than any other thing. Called thence, 'The hope of salvation'; and all other hopes are in order to this: Rom. xv. 4, 'Whatever things were written aforetime, were written for our learning, that we through the patience and comfort of the scriptures might have hope'; that is, by submitting and waiting upon him in variety of providences here in the world we might still keep up the hope of eternal life.

4. Eternal life must be expected in the way God promiseth it. We must not take that absolutely which God promiseth conditionally; God promiseth it to them that believe in Christ: John vi. 40, 'This is the will of him that sent me, that everyone which seeth the Son, and believeth on him, may have everlasting life, and I will raise him up at the last day' Those that saw him with the eyes of the body, and were not offended at his despicable

---

[44] To attend to as a lackey
[45] Oddities; quirks

appearance, but could own him as the Messiah, as Lord and Saviour: those that see him with the eyes of the mind, see such worth and excellency in him, as to be content to run all hazards with him, and count all things but dung and dross, that they may be found in him, that they may venture their souls and all their interests in his hands. Sometimes to the obedient, Heb. v. 8; sometimes to them that persevere notwithstanding temptations, Rom. ii. 7; sometimes to the mortified, Rom. viii. 13. No; you must consider not only the grant or the benefit contained in the promise, but the precept, the condition required. The benefit or privilege offered, expresseth God's grace; the condition required points out your duty, and by consequence your right; for we are not duly qualified according to promise, and the gift is suspended till we fulfil the condition. But when you have done that which the promise requireth, then your title to heaven is incomparably more sure than any man's title to his possessions, and the inheritance to which he was born; and you will find the saints, in fixing and raising their hopes, do not only look upon what is promised, but their own qualification: Ps. cxix. 166, 'Lord, I have hoped for thy salvation, and done thy commandments'; so Ps. xxxiii. 18, 'The eye of the Lord is upon them that fear him, that hope in his mercy'; so Ps. cxlvii. 13, 'The Lord taketh pleasure in them that fear him, that hope in his mercy.' They so believe in God, as they fear to offend him; and the hope of salvation goeth hand in hand with a care of keeping the commandments; we must not look to one side of the covenant only, the privileges and benefits; but also to the duties and qualifications of those that shall be saved the penitent believer, the mortified saint, the heavenly-minded, self-deny ing Christian. All this is shown, that it is not enough to expect eternal life, but it must be expected in God's way.

5. The expectation is certain and desirous. It is certain; for it goeth upon the promise of the eternal God; it is desirous, because the thing promised is our chief happiness; all the pomp and glory of the world is but a May-game to it. With respect to these two proper ties different effects are ascribed to hope:

[A.] It is patient and earnest. Patient: 1 Thes. i. 3, 'Remembering without ceasing your work of faith, and labour of love, and patience of hope'; and in the verse next the text': And if we hope for it, then do we with patience wait for it'; and earnest: ver. 39,' For the earnest expectation of the creature waiteth for the manifestation of the sons of God' The emblem in the resemblance of it is the earnest expectation of the creature; and 2 Pet. iii. 12, 'Looking for and hasting unto the coming of the Lord.' It is patient, because it is sure; it is earnest, because it is good. When the soul therefore is possessed with the truth and worth of these things which we hope for, it looketh and longeth, because they are such glorious blessings; but tarrieth God's leisure, because his word is sure, though he doth delay our happiness, and how smart and heavy soever his hand be upon us for the present.

[B.] There is another pair, rejoicing and groaning. Rejoicing: Rom. v. 2, 'Rejoicing in the hope of the glory of God'; and groaning: 2 Cor. v. 2, 'In this we groan, earnestly desiring to be clothed upon with our house which is from heaven.' We groan because of present burdens, and our desire is delayed; but we rejoice that our affection may be somewhat answerable to the greatness of the thing hoped for, which is the vision and fruition of the ever-blessed

God. When we seriously consider what we shall have to do hereafter, how can a Christian choose but rejoice? It must needs possess his mind with a delight. It is, without question, a comfortable thing to him to think that he shall see the glory of God, and be filled with his love, and be exercised in loving, lauding, and praising him for evermore. Where this is soundly believed and earnestly hoped for, it will breed such a joy as supports us under all discouragements, fears, cares, and sorrows; and on the other side, weigheth down all the pleasures and riches of the world; in short, sweeteneth our lives and maketh religion our chiefest delight.

Secondly, Reasons to prove that hope is a necessary grace, I shall prove,

1. For the state of a believer in this world. We are not so saved by Christ as presently to be introduced into the heavenly inheritance, but are kept a while here upon earth to be exercised and tried. Now while we want our blessedness, and there is such a distance between us and it, in the meantime we encounter with many difficulties; there is need of hope, since the believer's portion is not given him in hand; he hath it only in hope; things invisible and future cannot else be sought after. As our understandings are cleared by faith to see things to come, otherwise invisible, our wills are warmed by love, that we may be earnestly carried out after the supreme good; so our resolutions and inclinations must be fortified by hope, that we may seek after it, and not be diverted either by the comfortable or troublesome things we meet with in the world. This is the difference between the children of God in their war fare and in their triumph; in their way and in their home; they that are at home are rejoicing in what we expect and are in possession of that supreme good which we hope for, they are entered into the joy of their Lord, and have neither miseries to fear nor blessings to desire beyond what they do enjoy; they see what they love and possess what they see; but the time of our advancement to these is not yet come, and therefore we can only look and long for it; the glorified are distinguished from us by fruition, and we are distinguished from all others by hope. We are distinguished from pagans who have no hope: Eph. ii. 12. 'Having no hope and without God in the world'; 1 Thes. iv. 13, 'Sorrow not -as -others which have no hope.' We are distinguished from temporaries: Heb. iii. 16, 'If we hold fast the confidence and rejoicing of jiope firm to the end.' The temporary loseth his taste and comfort, and so either casteth off the profession of godliness or neglecteth the power and practice -of it; the other is diligent, serious, patient, mortified, heavenly, holy, because he keepeth the rejoicing of his hope; the end sweeteneth his work.

2. From the new nature, which is not entire without hope. This is one of the constitutive graces which are essential to a Christian: 1 Cor. xiii. 13, 'And now abideth faith, hope, and charity, these three; but the greatest of these is charity'; he opposeth the abiding things, the necessary graces, to the arbitrary gifts, and among these he reckoneth hope. It is the immediate fruit of the new birth: 1 Pet. i. 3, 'Begotten to a lively hope' The new nature presently discovereth itself by a tendency to its end and rest; which is the fruition of God in heaven; now the new creature cannot be maimed and imperfect because it is the immediate production of God.

3. From the use for which it serveth.

[A.] It is necessary to quicken our duties. Hope sets the whole world a-work; the husbandman plougheth in hope, and the soldier fighteth in hope, and the merchant tradeth in hope; so doth the Christian labour and serve God in hope: Acts xxvi. 7, 'Unto which promise, our twelve tribes, instantly serving God day and night, hope to come.' Certainly a man that hopeth for anything will be engaged in the earnest pursuit of it, and follow his work close day and night; but where they hope for no great matter they are sluggish and indisposed. The principle of obedience is love, but the life of it is hope: Acts xxiv. 15, 16, 'I have hope towards God, that there shall be a resurrection of the just and unjust'; 'and herein' or thereupon, or in the meantime, 'do I exercise myself to keep a conscience void of offence towards God and towards men'.

[B.] To vanquish temptations, which are either on the right hand or on the left, but both are defeated by hope. On the right hand when some present delight is ready to invite us to sin; on the left hand when some present bitterness is likely to draw us from the ways of God; in both cases the hopes of future joys outweigh that pleasure and allay that bitterness. If the temptation be the comforts of the world, or the delights of sin, he that sincerely hopeth for heaven, dareth not think so slightly of it as to lose it, or put it to hazard for a little carnal satisfaction; it is noted high profaneness in Esau to sell the birthright for a morsel of meat, Heb. xii. 16. Sin cannot offer him things so good, but he must forego better, and so the heart riseth in indignation against the temptation': Shall I leave my fatness, my sweetness, to rule over the trees? 'If the temptation be some grievous inconvenience or affliction: Rom. viii. 18, 'For I reckon that the sufferings of this present time are not worthy to be compared with the glory that shall be revealed in us'; and 2 Cor. iv. 17, 'For our light affliction, which is but for a moment, worketh for us a far more exceeding and eternal weight of glory'. This is the language of one that hopes for salvation; all is but a flea-biting to him that hath his heart in heaven.

[C.] To comfort us in all our tribulations. There are many difficulties that intervene and fall out between hope and having; between our first right to eternal life and our full possession of it. In our journey to heaven, we meet with trials and sufferings by the way; now it is hope carrieth us through, and therefore it is compared to an anchor, Heb. vi. 19; to an helmet, 1 Thes. v. 8. As we would not go to sea without an anchor, nor to war without an helmet; so neither must we think of carrying on the spiritual life without hope. Nothing else will compose the mind or keep it stable in the floods of temptation; therefore it is an anchor. Nothing else will cause us to hold up head in our daily conflicts and encounters with afflictions but this helmet. Without this anchor we are in danger of spiritual shipwreck; without this helmet our heads are exposed to deadly blows from sin, Satan, and worldly discouragements.

[D.] That we may die peaceably, and with comfort. We need hope while we live, but we most need it when we come to die, and shoot the gulf of death. They that are destitute of the hope of salvation are then in a dangerous, woeful, and most lamentable case: Job xxvii. 8, 'What is the hope of the hypocrite, if he hath gained, when God taketh away his soul?' They may be full of presumption and blind confidence while they live, but what hope have they when they come to die? All their worldly advantages will then yield them no solid comfort. We live in a presumptuous dream that all shall be well; but then they die stupid and senseless, or else despairing; and their hopes fail when they have most need of them. But then a lively hope of eternal life sustaineth the hearts of the faithful; they are going to possess what they expected; and when they resign their souls to Christ they can commit their bodies to the grave in hope: Ps. xvi. 9, 10, 'My flesh shall rest in hope, for thou wilt not leave my soul in hell, nor suffer thine holy one to see corruption'; God will not utterly forsake that dust that is in covenant with him, nor suffer his servants totally to be extinguished, or finally to perish.

Use 1 is Information.

1. That the great reward of a Christian lieth not in things seen, but unseen; not in the good of this world, but of another; because hope is one of the graces requisite to his constitution, and hope is about future things. Much to blame then are they who place all their happiness in present things which are so transitory. God hath reserved us to a future estate, because he bestoweth graces that suit with it, and nothing so opposite to it as the spirit of the world: 1 Cor. ii. 12, 'For we have not received the spirit of the world, but the Spirit which is of God.'

2. The cognation and kin that is between faith and hope. The one is the evidence of things not seen, Heb. xi. 1; the other is the earnest desire and expectation of things not seen; the one is an assent, the other an appetition. Faith differeth from hope

[A.] In the order of nature. Faith goeth before, as the cause is before the effect; first there is a firm persuasion of good things to come, and then a certain expectation of them in the way which God hath ap pointed. Faith assents to the truth of the promise, and hope looketh for the accomplishment of it.

[B.] In the object there is some difference. First, in the latitude of the object. The object of faith is larger; faith is of things past, present, and to come; as by faith we believe the creation of the world, Heb. xi. 4; the present existence of God, Heb. xi. 6; and the truth of heavenly joys, Heb. xi. 1; hope is only of things to come. So again, we believe some things that we hope not for, as the torments of the damned; for hope is an expectation of good to come, and the pains of hell are matter of fear, not of hope. Secondly, in the formal consideration of the object. Faith looketh to the word promising, verbum rei, hope to the thing promised, *rem verbi*. Faith considereth the veracity or truth of God in making the promise; hope the benignity and goodness of God in making so great a promise as eternal life and salvation by Christ. Faith respects the person giving, his fidelity; hope, the persons receiving, their benefit. Faith persuadeth us there is salvation; hope, that we shall, or at least may, obtain it.

[C.] There is a difference in the subject. Faith, as it is an assent, is in the mind; hope is in the affections, as reflecting upon the goodness of the thing promised; so that though there be some difference between faith and hope, yet they are much of a like nature.

3. It informeth us of the excellency of hope. Faith saveth, Eph. ii. 8; and hope saveth, as in the text; which is to be regarded, because our thoughts run so much upon faith that we

overlook hope; and we do so altogether regard our present reconciliation with God through the merits of Christ, that we forget our eternal fruition of him in glory, and what is necessary thereunto, as if the whole drift of the new covenant were only to comfort us against the guilt of sin. Now a Christian should mind both, not only his peace with God, but his going off from the world; and must believe, not only to the pardon of sins, but also to eternal life: 1 Tim. i. 16, 'For this cause I obtained mercy, that in me first Jesus Christ might show forth all long- suffering, for a pattern to them that should afterwards believe on him to everlasting life' There is the final and ultimate object of faith, which must be first thought of; for all things are influenced by the last end. When we are invited to Christ, we are invited by this motive, that sinners shall not only be pardoned, but glorified. Therefore a true and well-grounded hope of eternal life is a more weighty point than we usually think of; and a great part of religion lieth in drawing off the heart from things visible and temporal to those that are in visible and eternal. The great effects of faith, which are love to God and victory over the world, are more easily produced when faith hath the assistance of hope, or this lively expectation of the world to come. Therefore we must not only consider the death of Christ as it hath procured for us the pardon of sin, or the promise of pardon; but as he died for us, that we might live forever with him, 1 Thes. v. 9; that so the soul may more directly and expressly be carried to God and heaven.

It informeth us that none can be saved without hope of salvation. A Christian, as soon as he is made a Christian, hath not the good things promised by Christ; but as soon as he is made a Christian he expecteth them; as an heir is rich in hope, though he hath little in possession. Take any notion of applying grace. As soon as we are justified, we are 'made heirs according to the hope of eternal life' Tit. iii. 7; as soon as we are converted and regenerated we are 'begotten to a lively hope' 1 Peter i. 3; and as soon as we are united to Christ: Col. i. 27, 'Christ in you the hope of glory.' And without hope how can a man act as a Christian? Since the whole business of the world is done by hope, certainly the whole spiritual life is quickened by this grace: Tit. ii. 12, 13, 'For the grace of God that bringeth salvation hath appeared unto all men, teaching us that, denying all ungodliness and worldly lusts, we should live soberly, righteously, godly, in the present world; looking for the blessed hope, and the glorious appearing of the great God and our Saviour Jesus Christ;' and Phil. iii. 20, 21, 'For our conversation is in heaven, from whence we look for the Saviour, the Lord Jesus Christ, who shall change our vile body, that it may be fashioned like unto his glorious body'.

But then here ariseth a great doubt, how far every man is bound to hope for salvation? For those that have no assurance of their own sincerity, and cannot unquestionably make out their propriety and interest, how can they hope for salvation?

Answer, To solve this doubt, we must consider a little the several states of men as they stand concerned in everlasting life. Some have but a bare possibility; others have a probability; a third are gotten so far as a conditional certainty; others have an actual certainty, or firm persuasion of their own right and interest.

(1.) To some the hope of heaven is but a bare possibility, as to the careless Christian who is yet entangled in his lusts; but God continueth to them the offer of salvation by Christ; they may be saved if they will accept this offer; it is brought home to their doors, and left to their choice. It is impossible indeed in the state in which they are, but their hearts may be changed by the Lord's grace: Mark x. 27, 'With men it is impossible, but not with God; for with God all things are possible'; he can make the filthy heart to become clean and holy, the sensual heart to become spiritual and heavenly; there are many bars in the way, but grace can break through and remove them. This possibility checketh scruples, and aggravateth their evil choice; for they 'forsake their own mercies' Jonah ii. 8; by their vain course of life they deprive themselves of happiness which might be theirs. It is their own by offer, for God did not exclude them; but not their own by choice, for they excluded themselves, judge themselves 'unworthy of eternal life,' Acts xiii. 46. This possibility is an encouragement to use the means: Acts viii. 22, 'Pray, if perhaps,' or, if it be possible, 'the thought of thine heart may be forgiven thee.'

(2.) Others have a probability, or a probable hope of eternal life; as when men begin to be serious, or in some measure to mind the things of God, but are conscious to some notorious defect in their duty, or have not such a soundness of heart as may warrant their claim to everlasting blessedness; as we read of 'almost Christians' Acts xxvi. 28; and 'not far from the kingdom of heaven' Mark x. 24. And such are all those which have only the grace of the second or third ground; they receive the word with joy, but know not what trials may do; they have good sentiments of religion, but they are much choked and obstructed by voluptuous living, or 'the cares of the world' Luke viii. 14. Yea, some such thing may befall weak believers; they dare not quit their hopes of heaven for all the world, but cannot actually lay claim to it, and say it is theirs. Now probabilities must encourage us till we get a greater certainty; for we must not despise the day of small things; and it is better to be a seeker than a wanderer.

(3.) A conditional certainty, which is more than possible or probable. That is, when we adhere to God's covenant, and set ourselves in good earnest to perform the conditions required in the promises of the gospel, expecting this way the blessings offered. As for instance, the hope is described by Paul, Acts xxiv. 15, 16. 'And have hope towards God, which they themselves also allow, that there shall be a resurrection of the dead, both of the just and the unjust; and herein do I exercise myself, to have always a conscience void of offence towards God and towards men.' There is such a dependence upon the promise as breedeth an hope, and this hope puts upon strict and exact walking; such a conditional certainty is described in Rom. ii. 7, 'Who by patient continuance in well-doing seek for glory, honour, immortality, and eternal life.' I am sure to find salvation and eternal life, if I self-denyingly and patiently continue this way, and by the grace of God I am resolved so to continue. Now there is much of hope in this; partly because this is the hope which is the immediate effect of regeneration, the hope that is the fruit of experience, and belongeth to the seasoned and tried Christian who hath approved himself; hearsay is another thing, Rom. v. 4. And partly because this suiteth with God's covenant, or the conditional offer of eternal life, according to the terms of the gospel, where the benefits are offered to invite us to walk in the way of life. Now here is faith believing, hope expecting, and resolution to take God's way; even to deny ourselves, sacrifice our interests, and heartily to exercise ourselves unto godliness. And partly because much of the life of Christianity lieth much in this conditional hope and certainty, it being absolutely necessary to all acts of grace. And partly that we may have much comfort by it, for we are making out our claim. I do not doubt, or considerably doubt, of the reward of godliness ex parte Dei; no, I know they are sure and steadfast by the promise; but my own qualification is not so sensible and clear that I can positively determine my own right; but I have support and comfort in this way: 1 Cor. ix. 26, 'Kun not as one uncertain'; for I have reward in my eye.

(4.) There is actual certainty of our interest, as being qualified. Which admits of a latitude; for it may be full or not full, firm or not firm: Heb. vi. 14, 'And we desire that every one of you do show the same diligence, to the full assurance of hope to the end'; it may be interrupted or continued; the full hope removeth all doubts and fears; that which is not full hath some doubts accompanying it; but the certainty prevaileth, and is more than the doubting. This is comfortable, to sail to heaven with full sails, rather than make an hard shift to get thither by many doubts and fears; and it is a blessed thing when we can say, 2 Cor. v. 1, 'For we know that if our earthly house of this tabernacle were dissolved, we have a building of God, an house not made with hands, eternal in the heavens'; 2 Tim. iv. 8, 'Henceforth there is laid up for me a crown of righteousness.' In short, the more we address ourselves to our duty, the more we put ourselves in the way to receive the promise.

SERMON XXXII

For we are saved by hope; but hope that is seen is not hope; for what a man seeth, why doth he yet hope for?

Romans viii. 24.

2. WE must distinguish of hope. There are several kinds of hope. (1.) There is an hope in the creature, and (2.) an hope in God.

First, All things besides God are false confidences. Carnal men hope for that in the creature which is only to be found in God; dream of an uninterrupted tenor of worldly felicity in present enjoyments; therefore their hopes are compared to a spider's web, which is gone with the turn of a besom, Job xiii. 13, 14. They lay their designs in their minds as curiously as the spider's web is woven; but the besom of providence cometh, and spider and web are both swept away, and trodden under foot. By the prophet Isaiah it is compared to a dream: Isa. xxix. 8, 'As when an hungry man dreameth, and behold he eateth; but he awaketh, and his soul is empty; or as a thirsty man dreameth, and behold he drinketh; but he awaketh, and behold he is faint, and his soul hath appetite'. A false hope is but a waking dream, which faileth in extremity, and giveth but an imaginary refreshment and satisfaction. This may befall God's children who fall asleep in the midst of worldly prosperity: Ps. xxx. 6, 'In my prosperity, I said, I shall never be moved'. It is hard to keep from sleep when we lean our heads upon a soft carnal pillow, and in our sleep we have many fantasies and dreams; this is hope in the creature.

Secondly, But then there is an hope in God, whose immutable mercy and truth maketh him a fit object for hope: Ps. cxxx. 7, 'Let Israel hope in the Lord'; so Ps. xlii. 5, 'Hope thou in God, for I shall yet praise him.' He hath the sovereign command of all things; and in vain do we look for good apart from him; if the creature say yea, and God no, all the promises of the creature prove but a lie. Hope in God is that which we press as our respect to him as God; for faith, hope, and love are duties of the first commandment; negatives include their positives; if no other god is before him, then we own the true God for our God. The positive duties of the first commandment are *cultus naturalis, non institutes*; such as these are our duty to God as God, though he give no direction about them; if God be our God, then hope in him: Lam. iii. 24, 'The Lord is my portion, saith my soul; therefore will I hope in him'; that is, expect all my happiness from him.

Hope in God is twofold, either irrational and groundless, or a rational hope that is built upon solid grounds.

1. There is a vain and groundless hope, which is irrational, such as is in carnal and careless sinners, who say they hope well; but their hope will one day leave them ashamed, Rom. v. 5. For it is not an hope built on the word of God; though they live in their sins, yet they hope they shall do well, enough, though they be not so strict and nice as others are. Like condemned men in bolts and irons, that dream of crowns and sceptres when they are near unto, and ready for their execution; so they hope for heaven with as much confidence as the holiest of them all, though God hath told them, Heb. xii. 14, that 'without holiness, no man

shall see the Lord. 'This hope is but a vain dream, and an awakening time will come; this hope is not only without faith, but against faith; this hope is nothing else but a confidence that God will prove a liar; so that it is a blasphemy, rather than an act of worship; a believing Satan rather than God; or hoping in God, who hath declared the flat contrary in his word: 1 Cor. vi. 9, 10, 'Know ye not that the unrighteous shall not inherit the kingdom of God? Be not deceived; neither fornicators, nor idolaters, nor adulterers, nor effeminate, nor abusers of themselves with mankind, nor thieves, nor covetous, nor drunkards, nor revilers, nor extortioners, shall inherit the kingdom of heaven'

2. There is a rational hope, which is built upon solid grounds, probabilities, or certainties.

[A.] There is a rational probable hope. For hope is sometimes taken for a probable expectation: 1 Cor. xi. 7, 'Hopeth all things. 'It mean- eth there, not a divine, but a charitable, prudential hope; we hope well of others whose hearts we know not, as long as nothing appeareth to the contrary; charity goeth upon probabilities, therefore hopeth all things: 2 Cor. i. 7, 'Our hope of you is steadfast, that as you have been partakers of the sufferings of the gospel, so shall ye be also of the con solation'; so towards God: 1 Cor. ix. 10, 'He that plougheth, plougheth in hope'; a man hath no promise of a good crop; but the ordinary providence of God giveth him a probable hope of success. In temporal things, when we know not what the event will be, such a kind of hope we have. There is no express promise; but such is the Lord's power and goodness commonly exercised in his providential government, that we have no reason to despair, and say it shall not be; yea, much reason to believe that God will give success to our endeavours, for his glory in the world, considering what hath usually befallen his servants in like cases; though we cannot draw a firm and certain argument from thence, yet it is probable, for the most part it is so. But in matters that concern eternal life, somewhat of this hope may be observed; as before conversion, when we begin to be serious and seek after God, we cannot say certainly God will give us converting and saving grace; we must follow God, though we know not what will come of it, as Abraham did, Heb. xi. 8. There the rule in such cases is, I must do what he hath commanded; God may do what he pleaseth; yet it is some comfort that we are in a probable way. Nay, after conversion, such hope men may have as to their own interest in eternal salvation; they cannot say heaven is theirs, or that God will certainly keep them to his heavenly kingdom; yet they dare not quit their hopes of heaven for all the world, nor cease to walk in the way of salvation; it is probable they are God's children.

[B.] There is a firm and certain hope, when we have assurance of things hoped for, by the promises and offers of the gospel: as Acts xxiv. 15, 'I have hope towards God that there shall be a resurrection both of the just and unjust.' Without this hope a man cannot be a Christian.

We must certainly expect the promised blessing to be given to those that are capable and duly qualified; and all that are enlightened by the Spirit do see it and expect it, and positively conclude, that 'verily there is a reward for the righteous', Ps. lviii. This hope is the life of religion, and doth excite us to look after it by due and fit means; their eyes are enlightened with spiritual eye-salve, that they get a sight of the world to come: Eph. i. 18, 'The eyes of your understanding being enlightened, that ye may know what is the hope of his calling, and the riches of the glory of his inheritance in the saints'; and if they believe the gospel, it cannot be otherwise. I am certain there is such a thing: Col. i. 5, 'For the hope which is laid up for you in heaven, whereof ye heard before in the word of the truth of the gospel.' There this truth is made known; all that close with the gospel receive it, and by it is this blessed hope of glory wrought in us.

3. There is a twofold certain hope; one sort necessary, the other very profitable, but not absolutely necessary to the life and being of a Christian; the first sort is the fruit of faith, the second the consequent of assurance. The first grounded merely upon the offers of the gospel, propounding the chiefest good to men, to excite their desires and endeavours; the other is grounded on the sight of our own qualification, as well as the offers of the gospel; the one is antecedent to all acts of holiness, the other followeth after it. An antecedent hope there must needs be, before the effect of the holy life can be produced; for since hope encourageth and animateth all human endeavours, no man will engage in a strict course displeasing to flesh and blood, but he must have some hope; and this hope the conditional offers of the gospel doth beget in us, and all serious creatures have it that mind their proper happiness. Rejoicing in hope is the same with *archen upostaseos* Heb. iii. 6, 14; it is the first taste we have of the pleasures of the world to come. Keep up this gust and taste, and you are safe.

But then there is another hope, that is grounded upon the evidence of our sincerity, and is the fruit of assurance, when we can make out our own claim and title to eternal life, which is not usually done without (1.) Much diligence: Heb. vi. 11, 'And we desire that every one of you do show forth the same diligence, to the full assurance of hope, unto the end' (2.) Much sobriety, and weanedness from the world, 1 Peter i. 13. (3.) Much watchfulness, that we be not moved away from the hope of the gospel, Col. i. 23; that our hopes of eternal life begotten in us by the gospel be not weakened and deadened in us; it is not enough thankfully at first to embrace the conditional offer, but we must keep up this hope in life and vigour. (4.) Much resolution in our conflicts with the devil, world, and flesh, 1 Thes. v. 8. Lastly, some experience, Rom. v. 4, of God's favour and help in troubles, and our sincerity therein. When we are seasoned and tried, our confidence increaseth; the frequent experience of God's being nigh to us, and honouring us in sundry trials, is a ground for hope to rest upon, that he will not leave us till all be accomplished: Phil. i. 20, 'According to my earnest expectation and my hope, that in nothing I shall be ashamed; but that with all boldness, as always, so now also, Christ shall be magnified in my body, whether it be by life or death.' Paul gathereth his confidence for the future from former experience. Now these two sorts of hope must be distinguished; for the first hope may be accompanied with some doubts of our own salvation, or the rewards of godliness *ex parte nostri*[46], at least; not *ex*

---

[46] From our part

parte Dei[47], for there all is sure and steadfast, and to doubt there is a sin; it would detract from the goodness, power, and truth of God; but when our qualification is not evident, this doubting may do us good, as it may quicken us to more diligence to make our title more clear and explicate; especially when we are conscious to ourselves of some notorious defect in our duty, and have a blot upon our evidences; indeed the rather, when more godliness might be expected from us, as having more knowledge or helps, or obliged by calling and profession to greater integrity and holiness of life. Doubting is right when it ariseth from a right and true judgment of our actions according to the new covenant; and we cannot truly say who hath the greatest interest in us, God or the world, sin or holiness. Would you have men muffle their consciences, and think that they have more grace than -they have, or judge their condition to be better than it is, absolutely safe, when they are not persuaded of their sincerity? Indeed, when conscience judgeth erroneously, and a man thinketh he hath not that godliness which is necessary to salvation, which indeed he hath, he overlooketh God's work, his judgment of himself is erroneous, and therefore culpable; though it be not unbelief, or a distrust of Christ.

Well then, as to these two hopes

(1.) That hope which ariseth from faith must every day be more strengthened; for though there be no fallibility in God's promise, yet our faith may be weak or strong according to our growth and improve ment; and in some temptations God's children for a while may question articles of religion of great importance, and the eternal recompenses, not their own interest only; as David: Ps. lxxiii. 13, 'Verily I have cleansed my heart in vain, and washed my hands in innocency.' As if he had said, What reward is there of holiness, mortification, patience, and self-denial? In the lower world, where God is unseen, our great hopes yet to come,' the flesh being importunate to be pleased, and the things of the world necessary for our use, and present to our embraces, Christians are not certain and past all doubts of the truth of their everlasting hopes, else there would be no weak faith nor faint hope. Did not the disciples in a great temptation doubt of an article of faith? Luke xxiv. 21, 'But we trusted that it had been he which should have redeemed Israel'; and ver. 25, 'ye fools, and slow of heart to believe all that the prophets have spoken! 'To doubt of what the prophets spake was not to doubt of their own salvation, but of the constant state of their souls. All the godly are persuaded of the truth of the gospel, that ordinarily they have no considerable doubts about it, but that still they resolve to cleave to God and Christ, looking for their reward in another world, whatever it cost them here, and in some measure can sell all for the pearl of price.

(2.) As to the hope which ariseth from your assurance.

First, Make your sincerity more clear and unquestionable, and every day your hope and your confidence will increase upon you. To believe and hope that you yourselves shall be saved is

---

[47] From God's part

very desirable and comfort able; but then you must do that which assurance calleth for 'give diligence to make your calling and election sure' abound in the love and work of the Lord, grow more indifferent to temporal things, venture all in Christ's hands; for while your faith and repentance is obscure, you will not have such full comfort, though you are confident of the truth of God's promise to all penitent believers.

Secondly, This latter or consequent hope, which dependeth on the assurance of our interest, admits of a latitude it may be full or not full: Heb. vi. 11, 'To the full assurance of hope'. That is full which casteth out all fear; that is not full which is accompanied with doubts; but the certainty prevaileth: Mark ix. 24, 'Lord, I believe, help thou mine unbelief'; Cant. v. 2, 'I sleep, but my heart waketh' Now we should labour to go to heaven with full sails, or 'abound in hope' Rom. xv. 13; and 2 Peter i. 11, 'For so an entrance shall be ministered unto you abundantly, into the everlasting kingdom of our Lord and Saviour Jesus Christ' with hearts full of comfort.

Thirdly, When it is full, it may be interrupted, or continued to the end; or at sometimes it may be full, or not full at another: 1 Peter i. 13, 1 Hope to the end.' If we continue in our duty with diligence, affection, and zeal, our full hope may be continued; if we abate our fervour, grow remiss and cold in the spiritual life, we lose much of the comfort of our hopes.

Fourthly, The hope which followeth after experience and much exercise in the spiritual life may result from an act of ours, and from an impression of the comforting Spirit. (a.) From an act of ours. From our considering the truth of God's promises, or his wonderful mercy in Christ, and his grace enabling us in some measure to fulfil the conditions of the new covenant, when thereupon we put forth hope: Phil, iii. 20, 21, 'For our conversation is in heaven, from whence we look for the Saviour, the Lord Jesus Christ, who shall change our vile body, that it may be fashioned like unto his glorious body. (b.) Or some impression of the comforting Spirit supporting and relieving us in our distresses, or rewarding our self-denial and obedience; as Rom. v. 5, 'Hope leaveth not ashamed, because the love of God is shed abroad in our hearts by the Holy Ghost given unto us.' The one is an act of godliness, the other one of God's internal rewards; the one is a duty, the other a felicity. '

Use 2. Is to press us to get, and act hope. Hope implieth two things

First, Certain persuasion. *Secondly*, An earnest expectation. The certainty is seen in the quiet and pleasure of the mind for the present; the earnestness in the diligent pursuit after the thing hoped for by all holy means. Now we must look to both acts of hope.

First, To strengthen the certain expectation. There we must often revive the grounds of hope, which are these

1. The mercy of God, which hath made such rich preparation for our comfort in the gospel. The first ground of hope to the fallen creature is the undeserved grace, mercy, and goodness of God: 2 Thes. ii. 16, 'He hath given us everlasting consolation, and good hope through grace.' And therefore it is our great invitation to hope: Ps. cxxx. 7, 'Let Israel hope in the Lord, for with the Lord is mercy and plenteous redemption.' Apply yourselves to God as a God of mercy; otherwise, such were our undeservings and our ill deservings, there were

no hope for us; so Ps. xiii. 5, 'I have trusted in thy mercy; my soul shall rejoice in thy salvation'; let others trust in what they will, I will trust in thy mercy. The serious remembrance of God's mercy maketh hope lift up the head; so Jude 21, 'Looking for the mercy of the Lord Jesus unto eternal life'; there is our best and strongest plea to the very last. Therefore the heirs of promise are called, Rom. ix. 23, 'vessels of mercy'; because from first to last they are filled up with mercy.

2. The promise of God, which cannot fail: Tit. i. 2, 'The hope of eternal life, which God that cannot lie hath promised before the world began.' He promised it to Christ in the covenant of redemption, and he hath promised it to us in the covenant of grace; that before time, this in time. Now God will not fail to do what he hath promised; when he made the promise, he meant to perform it. For what need had God to court his creature into a false hope, or to flatter him into a fool's paradise? To tell them of a happiness he never meant to give them? And if he meant it, is he not able to perform it? Men break their word out of weakness; they cannot do all that they would; their will exceedeth their power: or out of imprudence; they cannot foresee what may happen: or out of levity and inconstancy, for all men are liars; but none of these things can be imagined of God. We have God's word and oath, Heb. vi. 18; we have his seal, the Spirit, who hath wrought miracles without, to confirm this hope and assure the world: Heb. ii. 4, 'God also bearing them witness, with signs arid wonders, and with divers miracles and gifts of the Holy Ghost'; within, preparing the hearts of the faithful for this blessed estate: Eph. iv. 30, 'And grieve not the Holy Spirit, whereby ye are sealed to the day of redemption'; and giving them some beginnings of it, as an earnest: 2 Cor. i. 22, 'Who hath sealed us, and given us the earnest of the Spirit.' Now since we go not upon guesses, but sure grounds, the promise of the eternal God thus sealed and confirmed, should not we hope?

3. Our relation to God. He is our God and Father: John xx. 17, 'I ascend to my Father and your Father, and to my God and your God'. As our God, he will give us something like to himself; something better than the world yieldeth, something fit for a God to give; or else he could not with honour take that title upon him: Heb. xi. . 16, 'Wherefore God is not ashamed to be called their God, for he hath prepared for them a city.' As our Father, he will give us the heavenly inheritance: Luke xii. 32, 'Fear not, little flock, it is your Father's pleasure to give you the kingdom.' If God were a judge only, we might fear how it would go with us in the day of trial; but if he will dignify us with the title of children, we may expect a child's portion: Rom. viii. 17, 'And if children, then heirs; heirs of God, and joint- heirs with Christ; if so be we suffer with him, that we may be also glorified together.' Be sure that you be adopted, justified, taken into the family.

4. Christ's merit and passion: Rom. v. 10, 'For if, when we were enemies, we were reconciled by the death of his Son, much more, being reconciled, we shall be saved by his life' Surely the blood of God was given for some other thing than that little happiness and .sorry pittance of comfort which we enjoy here. Do men that understand themselves give vast sums for trifles? When wise men lay a broad and large foundation, we expect a building suitable; if Christ be abased, we may be exalted; if he was apparelled with our flesh, we may

be clothed with his glory. That which keepeth hope alive is the consideration of that ransom which Christ paid to reconcile us to God, that we might be capable of the highest fruits of Christ's death, an assurance of his love, even eternal life.

5. His resurrection and ascension: 1 Peter i. 21, 'God hath raised him from the dead, and gave him glory, that your faith and hope might be in God' Christ confirmed his mediatorship, and herein he is a pattern to us; taken possession of heaven in our name and nature; he did in our nature rise from the dead and ascend into heaven, to give us a real and visible demonstration of a resurrection and a life to come, that we might look and long for it, whilst we follow him in obedience and sufferings. Christ is entered into his glory, and shall we be kept out? Some saw him after he was risen, and some saw him ascending; we have certain testimony of it, that he is gone to heaven before us; he that came to be an example of duty is also a pattern of felicity.

6. His potent intercession. He is sat down on the right hand of majesty, that he may apply his purchase, and bring us into possession of that happiness which he hath procured for us. We have a friend at God's right hand, who cannot satisfy himself to be there without us: John xvii. 24, 'Father, I will that they whom thou hast given me may be where I am, and may behold my glory.' He is gone to heaven as our forerunner: Heb. vi. 19, 20, 'Which hope we have as an anchor of the soul, both sure and steadfast, and which entereth into that within the veil, whither the forerunner is for us entered; even Jesus, made an high priest for ever after the order of Melchisedec'; gone ashore, whither we seek to land: Micah ii. 13, 'The breaker is come up before them.' He hath taken all impediments out of the way, and prepared a safe landing-place for us.

7. All our former experience of God. He hath ever borne us good will, never discovered any backwardness to our good; he purposed it in Christ before the world was; sent his Son to die for us before we were born or had a being in the world; called us when we were unworthy; warned us of our danger when we did not fear it; offered this happiness to us when we had no thought of it; and lest we should turn our backs upon it, followed us with an earnest and incessant importunity, till we came to have anxious thoughts about it, till we began to make it our business to seek after it; by the secret drawings of his Spirit, inclined us to choose him for our portion. How many contra dictions and strugglings of heart were there ere we were brought to this. Ever since he hath been tender of us in the whole conduct of his providence, afflicted us when we needed it, delivered us when we were ready to sink; he pardoned our failings, visited us in ordinances, supported us in troubles, helped us in temptations, and is still mindful of us at every turn, as if he would not lose our hearts. And shall we not hope in him to the last? Hath he forgotten to be gracious? As they said, Judges xiii. 23, 'If the Lord were pleased to kill us, he would not have received a burnt-offering and a meat offering at our hand, neither would he have showed us these things'; so if God had no mind to save us, he would not use such methods of grace about us.

8. The greatness of the gospel covenant. For that allayeth a great many fears, to remember that we are to interpret our qualification according to the covenant of grace and the sweet terms thereof; and though there be many failings, we may be accepted with the Lord, who

will not impute to his people their frailties and sins of infirmity. Not perfection, but sincerity, is our claim; we have indeed a faith too weak, and mingled with doubtings, too little love to God, and self-love too prevalent; our desires of grace too cold, our thoughts often distracted; but yet where the heart is set to seek the Lord, he will accept us, and our infirmities shall be forgiven us for Christ's sake. When he justifieth, who shall condemn? Rom. viii. 23. He will answer for the imperfection of our holy things; every sin is not a sign of death, some are consistent with a state of grace and hopes of glory. There are some sins which every one that truly repenteth ceaseth to commit them: Prov. xxviii. 13, 'He that covereth his sins shall not prosper; but whoso confesseth and forsaketh them shall have mercy;' there are other sins which they that repent do hate, but they too frequently return: Rom. vii. 15, 'What I hate, that do I'; as, the imperfection of our graces, many vain thoughts and inordinate passions, too much deadness and coldness in holy duties; these are forgiven, and consist with life; these are causes of child-like humiliation, but not of judging ourselves ungodly, or cast out of the favour of God.

Secondly, to breed earnestness, and this desirous expectation.

1. Think often of the sinfulness and misery of the present evil world, even the better part of it, that which is incident to the people of God, which are to be considered either singly or collectively. Singly; each saint and servant of God findeth enough to drive him off from the world, and to make him long for heaven, a great deal of sin to make him long for his perfect estate. Here in many things we offend, all of us, and the best of us, James iii. 2; but above, there are the spirits of just men made perfect. A great deal of misery, unless we are in love with distress, and prefer vanity and vexation of spirit before our rest and quiet repose. Why should we not desire to be at home with the Lord, which is much better for us? Phil. i. 23. We had been more in danger to forget heaven if all things had suited to our desires, and our way had been strewed with worldly flowers and delights; but God hath more wisely ordered it, that our temptation to abide here should not be too strong; or when the world appears to us in too tempting a garb and posture, a valley of tears and snares, a world full of sins, crosses, and pains, should make us look out after a better estate. Consider them collectively as a church, here it is quite different from what it will be hereafter. Alas! how often is it like a ship in the hands of a foolish guide, who knoweth not the right art of steering; spotted with calumnies of adversaries, or the stains and scandals of its own children; sometimes rent and torn with sad divisions, every party impaling and enclosing the common salvation, and confining it to their own bounds, unchristianing and unministering all the rest, and many times, in the pursuit of these contentions, unmanning themselves, while they seek to bear down all that stand in their way, Though it is better to dwell in the courts of the Lord than in the tents of wicked ness, yet truly a tender spirit will groan under these disorders, and long to come to the great council of souls, to the spirits of just men made perfect, who with perfect harmony are lauding and praising God for evermore.

2. Remove impediments, which are sensuality and addictedness to worldly things. Some seek all their delights and happiness in the things of this world, and so set more by earth than heaven, and will do more for it. Certainly when we fall into the snare of worldly hopes,

and are laying designs for greatness here, it is a troublesome interruption to think of a remove, and their great change cometh upon them unawares, unthought of and unlocked for: Luke xxi. 34, 'Take heed to yourselves, lest at any time your hearts be overcharged with surfeiting and drunkenness, and the cares of this life, and so that day come upon you unawares' See also Luke xii. 17-20, 'And he thought within himself, saying, what shall I do, because I have no room to bestow all my fruits and goods? And he said, This I will do, I will pull down my barns, and build bigger; and say to my soul, Thou hast much goods laid up for many years, take thine ease, eat, drink, and be merry. But God said unto him, This night thy soul shall be required of thee'; Ps. cxlvi. 4, 'His breath goeth forth, he returneth to his earth, in that very day his thoughts perish.' Certainly the cares and pleasures of this world steal away the heart from the life to come; worldly delights make us unwilling to remove.

3. Meditate often on the worth of this blessedness: Col. iii. 1, 'If ye be risen with Christ, seek those things which are above, where Christ sitteth at the right hand of God.' Are you unwilling to come to God, the object of your everlasting joy and love? To Christ, your blessed redeemer and saviour, who hath done so much for you, to bring you home to himself? To the innumerable company of saints and holy angels, and those peaceful regions that are above? Surely if you hold your eye open upon the mark, you will press on with the more diligence, Phil. iii. 14.

4. The more earnestly you look for these things, the more doth heaven come to you before you come to it: Phil. iii. 20, 'But our conversation is in heaven'; living for heaven, or upon heaven here, by earnest hope, the joy of the Lord entereth into you; Rom. xv. 13, 'Now the God of hope fill you will all joy in believing'; the more our hearts are exalted to look after it; but usually we are taken up with toys and trifles.

Use 3. Have we this hope? You may be contented with a pre sumptuous conceit or idle expectation, and call it hope; it is not a slight thinking of heaven; no, but a certain and desired expectation of the promised blessedness, according to the terms of the new covenant; the true hope is neither groundless nor fruitless.

1. A groundless hope is a false hope, which buildeth on false promises; you cannot render *logon* or an account of it, 2 Peter iii. 5. As David asked the reason of his doubts, so we of our hopes: Ps. xlii. 15, 'Hope thou in God.' They think if they have confidence, though without holiness, they shall see God; they hope to be saved without regeneration, and so hope for that which God never promised; think to be saved while unsanctified; these build on false evidences; James i. 21; build on the sand, Mat. vii. 24; build on false experiences, God's patience, the blessings of this life, deliverance only: their cry from imminent danger, Ps. lxxviii. 38; vanishing tastes, Heb. vi. 5.

2. It is not fruitless.

Use 4. Is direction in the Lord's Supper. This duty was appointed to raise and confirm our hope, for it is a seal of the covenant, and the principal covenant blessing is eternal life. Three things are consider able: the acting of hope, the receiving new pledges of God's love, the binding ourselves to pursue everlasting life.

1. The acting of hope. We come to take Christ and all his benefits, which are pardon and life. He is drinking 'new wine in his Father's kingdom,' Mat. xxvi. 29. We come to think of the happiness of the blessed; some are gotten to heaven already; we are of the same family: Eph. iii. 15, 'Of whom the whole family of heaven and earth is named.' It is but one household; some live in the upper, some in the lower room: those on earth are of the same society and community with them in heaven: Heb. xii. 23, 'To the general assembly and the church of the firstborn, which are written in heaven'. They have gotten the start of us, and are made perfect before us, that we may follow after; we are reconciled to the same God, by the same Christ, Col. i. 20; we expect our portion from the bounty of the same Father, Luke xii. 32. He that hath been so good to that part of the family which is now in heaven, will he not be as good to the other part also that remain here upon earth? Therefore they that are working out their salvation with fear and trembling may and should encourage themselves, and look upon this felicity as pre pared for them, though not enjoyed by them, and will one day be their portion, as well as of those others who have passed the pikes, and are now triumphing with God. The apostle telleth us, 1 Cor. xi. 26, 'As often as ye eat this bread, and drink this cup, ye show forth the Lord's death till he come'; and he cometh to bring us up to those blessed mansions which are in his Father's house. When we show forth the Lord's death, we are to think of those that are in our Father's house: John xiv. 3, 'I will come again, and receive you to myself, that where I am, there you may be also.' To keep afoot this promise in the church, and to keep it alive in our hearts, we come to the Lord 's Table.

2. Our business is to receive new pledges of God's fatherly love and our blessed inheritance, which are represented under a double notion: as an earnest, to show how sure; as first-fruits, to show how good.

[A.] Earnest. Hope is not built upon promises alone, but we have earnest also; the promise is given us in the word, the earnest is given in our hearts, 2 Cor. i. 22. Though God be truth itself, and promiseth nothing but what he meaneth to perform, yet he will give us earnest of his promises. The outward pledges are the elements; the inward pledge is the earnest of the Spirit; his comfort and graces are a part of the promised felicity. He would not weary and burden us altogether with expectation, but giveth us somewhat in hand, light, life, grace, joy, peace; one drachm of these is more precious than all the world, yet these are but an earnest. This is the confirmation that we have in the midst of our doubts and fears; they expect the full sum.

[B.] First-fruits. We come to get a taste of these things to deaden our taste of other things, which would divert us from these hopes, which are vain delights of the flesh, 1 Peter i. 13. Bodily pleasures are put out of relish by these choice and chaste delights; these are our songs in the house of our pilgrimage.

3. To bind ourselves to the more earnest pursuit of these hopes. Our journey is not ended, nor our warfare and conflicts; therefore here we bind ourselves to continue our race, and finish the good fight of faith; as the Israelites in their first passover had their loins girt and their staves in their hands, as resolving on a journey to Canaan, the land of rest; so we

profess ourselves strangers and pilgrims; let us therefore resolve on our journey towards heaven, and bind ourselves to the performance of it.

SERMON XXXIII

But if we hope for that we see not, then do we with patience wait for it.

Romans viii. 25.

IN this verse the former doctrine is improved to the main end of this discourse, which is to persuade to a patient waiting for glory to come, in the midst of the sufferings and troubles of this life. The apostle goeth to work by way of supposition and inference.

First, The supposition, 'If we hope for that we see not'

Secondly, The inference thence deduced, 'Then do we with patience wait for it'

From the first, observe that hope is conversant about what we see not. Hope may be taken for a natural affection, or for a spiritual grace; the one will help to explain the other.

1. The object of hope as it is a natural affection. It is a good, future, possible, and hard to be obtained.

[1.] A good it must be, for hope is one of the affections of prosecution, not aversation; man hath an irascible and concupiscible faculty, called by the apostle passions and lusts,; a desiring or eschewing faculty; the one is con versant about good, the other about evil; for evil is not hoped for, but feared; herein the affections and the grace agree; they both aim at good, but the object of the Christian hope is *summum bonum*, the best and chiefest good, which is the vision and fruition of God, in comparison of which all the good things of the earth are but trifles, and poor, inconsiderable vanities.

[2.] A good future; for when anything is possessed, it ceaseth to be hoped for; when the thing desired is seen and enjoyed, hope hath no more to do; herein also the two hopes agree; the object of Christian hope is something future, not yet received or enjoyed. In this lower world our God is unseen, our blessedness is yet to come, and lieth in another world, which we cannot come at till we shoot the gulf of death; therefore the Christian hope needeth to be more strong and fixed.

[3.] It is possible; for the serious and regular desires of nature can never be carried to that which is impossible. A man may wish for mountains of gold, and please his fancy with chimeras of strange things; but his reason and will is only affected with things feasible, and such as probably may be obtained, and lie within his grasp and reach; the industrious hope is only of things possible.

[4.] It is not only possible, but difficult, not to be procured without some industry and labour; for things easy to be compassed are as if they were already enjoyed. These two last qualifications of the object of hope show that it is a middle thing between despair and presumption; despair only looketh at the difficulty, and leaveth out the possibility, and so taketh off all endeavours; as Paul's companions (Acts xxvii. 20, 'When all hope they should be saved was taken away') ceased striving, and let the ship go whither it would. Men will not labour for that which they despair to obtain; it holdeth good in spirituals; when men despair of mending their condition, they give over all care about it; as those wretches, Jer. xviii. 12, 'And they said, There is no hope, but we will walk after our own devices, and we will every one do the imagination of his evil heart.' We have a saying, 'Past cure, past care.' On the other side, presumption never considereth the difficulty, but only pleaseth itself with a loose and slight reflection upon the possibility; and therefore do unreasonably imagine to obtain their end without setting themselves to use the means, or bestowing that cost and pains by which all worldly good is obtained. Now presumption is most incident to young men, who are not acquainted with the world, and promise themselves great things without considering what may be said to the contrary, or what is needful to obtain them; difficulty there is in every business; if only considered, it breedeth despair; if overlooked, it breedeth presumption; but hope between both apprehendeth such difficulty as calleth for diligence, and such possibility as every cross accident may not make us give over the attempt. It holdeth good in religion; the difficulties must be sufficiently under stood, for Christ will have us sit down and count the charges; and yet not so regarded as to discourage us in our duty; we must stand all hardships as good soldiers of Jesus Christ; and press towards the mark of our high calling in Jesus Christ, whatever it costs us.

2. As it is a spiritual grace. There the object of hope is some good, future and unseen. But other qualifications are necessary beyond these already mentioned.

[A.] It must be something promised by God. [B.] Believed by us, before we can hope for it.

[A.] Such future things as God hath promised to bestow upon us. These are the matter and object of our faith and hope; the promise giveth us notice, and the promise giveth us assurance. (1.) Notice. We can have no other certain knowledge of their futurity but by God's promise. The light of nature or reason giveth a shrewd guess at a future estate, but the certain knowledge we have by God's word; there life and immortality is brought to light: 2 Tim. i. 10, 'He brought life and immortality to light through the gospel.' There we have the clear prospect of it. The heathen had nothing but the light of nature to guide them, spake doubtfully of a future estate; like men travelling on the hills, and see the spire of a steeple at a distance, sometimes they have a sight of it, and presently they lose it, and so cannot certainly tell whether they saw it, yea or no; but all is clear, full, and open in God's promise. (2.) Certainty and assurance; for it conveyeth a right to us upon certain terms; for he that believeth on the Son of God hath everlasting life, John iii. 36; hath it in the offer and promise of God, if he will fulfil the condition required; not only shall have it at the close of their days, but they have the grant already, and therefore wait for the fruition. As we are fulfilling the conditions, we gain more security and confidence that we shall have it: 1 Tim. vi. 12, 'Fight the good fight of faith, lay hold on eternal life;' ver. 19, 'Laying up in store for themselves a good foundation, that they may lay hold on eternal life;' the meaning is, challenge it for theirs. In short, our expectation must be grounded on some promise, or else it is but a fancy and presumption.

[B.] The thing hoped for must be believed by us, for there can be no expectation of things not seen till there be faith, which is 'the evidence of things not seen'. Heb. xi. 1. First, there is a firm assent by faith; we are as confident in some measure of those things, as if we saw them with our eyes, or as we are of those things which we daily see. Then after this assent there followeth earnest expectation; for hope maketh the assent practical. Though God promise never so much, yet if we believe him not, we expect nothing; therefore faith is necessary. Look as to bodily sight, there needeth an object to be seen, and an eye by which we see; so in spiritual sight, the promise sets the object before us: Heb. xii. 2, 'Looking unto Jesus'; and Heb. vi. 18, 'Lay hold of the hope set before us' But the eye is faith, which, though it cannot give us sight, itgiveth us foresight; we have heard of it, though yet we have not seen it, and see it by the eyes of the mind as it is contained in the promise of the everlasting God, though we do not, aad cannot see it with the eyes of the body. Com pare it with reason. By reason we apprehend more than we see, for we see effects in their causes, but that is but probable foresight, for many things intervene between the cause and the effect. By faith we foresee the blessing in the promise; by reason we see things beyond sense, so far as natural probabilities will carry us; by faith we see things beyond reason, so far as the promises of good invite us to a better hope.

But how can we surely hope for that we see not, which neither sense nor reason can inform us of?

Answer 1. This glory is not a fancy; it is seen by many in our nature that now possess it, and by the word of God you are invited to follow them in the same course of holiness and godliness, that you may in time see it also: Heb. vi. 12, 'Be ye followers of them who through faith and patience have inherited the promises'; propound the same noble end and the same holy course, and matters of faith will in time become matters of sense. Now, though the end be unknown, the way is so good and holy and justifiable by reason, that we should venture the imitation of them, not their holiness only, but their faith, Heb. xi. 13; they lived and died in this faith; their life was holy, and their death was happy, that are gone into the other world. But you will say, If we could talk with any of these that are gone into the other world: Luke xvi. 30, 31, 'And he said, Nay, Father Abraham, but if one went unto them from the dead, they would repent: and he said unto him, They have Moses and the prophets, and if they will not hear them, neither will they be persuaded if one should come from the dead.' They are out of the sphere of our commerce; their testimony is not convenient for the government of God, who will not govern the world by sense, but by faith; and besides, you have better hopes, Moses and the prophets; there is more reason to persuade a man the scriptures are true, than to believe a message brought him from one among the dead.

2. One that hath seen, and is an infallible witness, hath testified to us of the truth of these things we hope for: John i. 18, 'No man hath seen God at any time; the only-begotten Son, which is in the bosom of the Father, he hath declared him.' Christ perfectly saw and knew all that he hath told us of God and the world to come: John iii. 11, 'Verily, verily, I say unto thee, We speak that which we know, and testify that we have seen, and ye receive not our witness;' so that our faith and hope goeth on sure grounds; so ver. 32' What he hath seen and heard he testifieth, and no man receiveth his testimony.' A good man, whose testimony is valuable, that hath been in a strange country, and testifieth what he hath seen there of it, would not we believe him? Christ, that came from the other world, and told us of the blessedness of it, deserveth the credit of a good man; he used a faithful plainness: John xiv. 2, 'If it were not so, I would have told you.' But more of a teacher sent from God, who

confirmed his message by miracles, and laid down a doctrine holy and good; and shall not we receive his testimony concerning these things he had perfect knowledge of, assured us of the truth of them? Shall we not receive his testimony?

3. Those that saw him and conversed with him were not only authorised by him to show us the way to eternal life, but saw so much of it themselves as the mortal state is capable of, yet enough to prove the reality of the thing: 1 John i. 1-3, 'That which was from the beginning, which we have heard, which we have seen with our eyes, which we have looked upon, and our hands have handled of the word of life (for the life was manifested, and we have seen it, and bear wit ness, and show unto you that eternal life which was with the Father, and manifested unto us); that which we have seen and heard declare we unto you'; Acts iv. 20, 'For we cannot but speak the things which we have seen and heard;' they had it not by hearsay, but some kind of sight. There being fidelity in the witnesses, there should be faith in those that hear and read. The apostles had sensible confirmation of what they did declare. If they say that they heard, saw, and handled that which they never did, then they were deceivers; if they only imagined they did see and hear those things, then they were deceived; if what they saw and heard will not amount to a proof of eternal life, then their testimony is not sufficient. But their downright simple honesty and great holiness showeth that they had no mind to deceive, and the nature of the things they relate showeth that they could not be deceived; for they were eye-witnesses and ear-witnesses, and always conversing with Christ: the proof is sufficient. If such miracles, such resurrection, ascension, such a voice from the excellent glory, will not prove another world, what will?

4. There is care taken that we also may have a sight of these things so far as is necessary to a lively and quickening hope; for the Spirit is given to refine our reason and elevate our minds, and raise them above sensible things, that we may believe these supernatural truths, and hope to enjoy this blessedness in the way of Christianity: Gal. v. 5, c For we through the Spirit wait for the hope of righteous ness by faith.' Interpret it not only of the righteousness of faith, but the hope built thereupon; it doth assure us of bliss and glory for all that are obedient to the faith, and believe those endless joys which are prepared for Christians, John i. 17, 18.

5. If we see not these things by faith, it is because we are blinded by lusts and brutish affections, which misbecome the human nature: 2 Cor. iv. 3, 4, 'If our gospel be hid, it is hid to them that are lost, whose eyes the God of this world hath blinded' It is because worldly advantages Lave seduced and perverted their affections, which enchain their minds, that these sublime truths make no impression upon them, nor have any influence upon their hearts; so 2 Peter i. 9, 'He that lacketh these things is blind, and cannot see afar off.' They have not that purity of heart which should enable them to believe this doctrine, or see things that should contradict or check their lusts; and being wedded to present things, have no prospect of things to come.

Use 1. For confutation of those that will not believe or hope for anything which they see not. They think Christians a company of credulous fools; that nothing is sure that is invisible; that the promises of the gospel are but like a dream of mountains of gold, or pearls dropt from the sky; and all the comforts thence deduced are but fanatical illusions; that nothing so ridiculous as to depend upon unseen hopes that4ie in another world; they make the life of faith a matter of sport and jesting: Ps. xxii. 7, 8, 'All they that see me laugh me to scorn; they shoot out the lip and shake the head, saying, He trusted in God that he would deliver him; let him deliver* him, seeing he delighted in him'; 1 Tim. iv. 10, 'We therefore labour and suffer reproach, because we trust in the living God.' Christians thought their reward sure, and endured all things; atheists and infidels therefore scoff at them, persecute them. To these I shall propose two things.

1. Is nothing to be believed and hoped for that is not seen? Reason will show you the contrary. Country people obey a king whom they never saw, but only know his power by the effects in his laws and officers of justice; and doth not sense teach us the same concerning God? If we transgress his laws by omitting a duty or committing a sin, we hear from him though we see him not: Horn. i. 18, 'For the wrath of God is revealed from heaven against all ungodliness and unrighteousness of men'; and Heb. ii. 2, 'For if the word spoken by angels was steadfast, and every transgression and disobedience received a just recompense of reward.' And for hope; do not men venture their estates in foreign countries in the hands of persons whom they never saw nor knew? And shall we venture nothing on the promises of God? It is true, God liveth in another world, and our hopes lie there also; but doth he not manifest himself from thence, to be concerned in our actions, whether they be good or evil? And if he be concerned in them, will he not punish the evil and reward the good? Hath not natural conscience a sense of these things? And therefore it is unreasonable to question these things.

2. They think good people are credulous and easy of belief; their own experience of these good people evidenceth the contrary, that they are too slow of heart to believe what God hath revealed con cerning the other world, and that by the use of all holy means it is with difficulty accomplished. But what if we prove that none so credulous as the atheist or infidel?

[A.] You are not sure there is no such life; it is impossible they should ever know or prove the contrary; it may be, without question, the Lord that made this world can make a world to come, and the same persons to exist there in ignominy, contempt, and shame, that lived wicked here, and bestow honour on the godly and holy. The question between the downright infidel and the Christian is not so much whether there be a world to come, but whether we can prove there is none. The belief of the positive, that there is a God, that there is everlasting life, is necessary to our hope; but to their conviction let them infallibly prove there is none; they can never do that; you cannot disprove the reality of the Christian hope, or by any sound argument evince that there is no heaven or hell. For aught you can say or know, there are both; and if we should go on no further, it were best to take the surer side; especially when you part with no more than a few base pleasures and carnal satisfactions that are not worth the keeping. In a lottery, where there is but a loose possibility of gaining, men will venture a shilling, or a small matter, for a prize of a hundred pounds; so, be there no heaven or hell, or be there one, you part with no more than the vain pleasures of a fading life; but if it should prove true, in what a woeful case are you then, when, to gratify a brutish mind, you run so great an hazard? The heathens granted it an hypothesis conducing to virtue and goodness.

[B.] To the atheist and infidel, bating all scripture, it may be proved that it is a thousand to one but it is so. Natural reason will persuade us of the immortality of the soul, and the fears of guilty conscience are shrewd presages of eternal punishment; the tradition and consent of barbarous nations, as well as the civilised, doth attest it, desires of happiness are so natural. So that these bravadoes, that would outface the religion they are bred in, showeth; none so credulous as they that will hearken to every fond suggestion of their own carnal hearts or atheistical companions, and prefer the brutish conceits of their own frothy wit before the common reason of mankind, or that rational evidence wherewith the doctrine of eternal life is accompanied.

Use 2. Is to reprove the sensual part of mankind, who are altogether for the present world: 2 Tim. iv. 10, 'Demas hath forsaken us, and embraced the present world.' They must have present delights, present fruition; a little thing in hand is more than the promises of those great things which are to come. The worldling's comfort wholly lieth in those things that are seen; they live by sense, as the Christian liveth by faith; they must have something in the view of sense, or have nothing to live upon lands, honours, pleasures; when these are out of sight, they are in darkness; but a Christian looketh to things future and unseen, secured to him by the promise of God.

Use 2. is to exhort us to seek after the happiness we never saw. We shall see it in time, but now we hope for it; and it is no vain and uncertain hope; the things we hope for are sure and near. [A.] They are sure. God's truth is as certain as truth itself can be, and believers so account it in the holy word: Job xix. 25, 26, 'I know that my Redeemer liveth, and that he shall stand at the latter day upon the earth; and though after my skin worms destroy this body, yet in my flesh I shall see God, whom I shall see for myself, and mine eyes shall behold, and not another, though my reins be consumed within me'; 2 Cor. v. 1, 'For we know that if our earthly house of this tabernacle were dissolved, we have a building of God, an house not made with hands, eternal in the heavens' To a believer it should not be a conjecture, but a point of faith and certainty. [B.] It is near. Things at a distance move us not, though they be never so great; it will not be long ere our great change come about, and therefore we should have more effectual thoughts about the world wherein we shall shortly live, and make what preparations are necessary thereunto; as 2 Tim. iv. 6, 'The time of my departure is at hand'; therefore we should watch, and be always ready; we must be gone hence ere long; therefore do not set objects of faith at a greater distance than God hath set them, lest your time be stolen from you, and you step into the other world before you thought of it, or prepared for it.

Use 3. Do we hope for that which we see not?

[A.] It may be known by the victory and overruling influence of these hopes, if they govern the design and business of our lives. If they do, then these things will take up more of our time and hearts and care than things sensible and visible: 2 Cor. iv. 18, 'While we look not at the things which are seen, but at the things which are not seen; for the things which are seen are temporal, but the things which are not seen are eternal'. If your hope be not powerful and effectual to overcome your inclinations to things seen, and break the force of them, it is but a slight hope.

[B.] If we hope for things unseen, they will be the life and joy and solace of our actions. Some have no other joys and sorrows than what are fetched from fleshly and sensible things, and speak of nothing so comfortably and so seriously as of this worldly life; the pleasures of the flesh revive them, but they take little comfort in the joys of the other world. But where the eye of the soul is opened to behold the glory of the world to come, it lets in an abundance of heavenly pleasure: Rom. v. 2, 'And rejoice in the hope of the glory of God'.

[C.] More eager desires and diligent seeking after this blessedness. For hope is an industrious affection: Col. iii. 1, 'If ye be risen with Christ, seek those things which are above'; Mat. vi. 33, 'First seek the kingdom of God and his righteousness' His great business is to get what he hopeth for; his endeavours are serious and constant, and the course of his life is for heaven.

Secondly, The inference thence deduced, 'Then do we with patience wait for it'.

Doctrine They only hope for eternal life who continue in the pursuit of it with patience. As hope is bred by faith, so is patience bred by hope. It is sometimes made the fruit of faith, or a steadfast reliance on God's promises; as Heb. vi. 12, 'But followers of them who through faith and patience inherit the promises'; sometimes of hope: Horn. xii. 12, 'Rejoicing in hope, patient in tribulation'. The great work of hope is to provide us patience to endure the hardships which at present lie upon us.

1. Let me speak of the kinds of patience. There is a threefold sort of patience.

[A.] The bearing patience, which is a constancy in adversity, and worketh constancy and perseverance, notwithstanding the difficulties and trials that we meet with in our passage to heaven: Heb. x. 36, 'Ye have need of patience, that after ye have done the will of God, ye may receive the promise'. A child of God cannot be without patience, because he cannot be without troubles and molestations in the flesh; a man would think that he that hath done the will of God, and been careful in all things to keep a good conscience, should have nothing else to do but go and take possession of his blessed hopes; but it is not enough to do good, but before we can go to heaven we must suffer evil; God hath something to do by us, and something to do with us. Now we must be pre pared to do all things rather than fail of our duty, nor desert a good way because it is difficult to follow it; but suffer the greatest evils, and suffer long and constantly, even to death, and that readily and willingly. And this is patience.

[B.] There is the waiting patience, to tarry God's leisure. Evil is present, and good is absent, and to come; a trouble may arise from the absence of the good we hope for, and the long delay of it, as well as from the evil that we endure; in the meantime, therefore, the scriptures recommend to us 'the patience of hope,' 1 Thes. i. 3, or waiting the good pleasure of God, till our final deliverance be accomplished: Lam. iii. 36, 'It is good to hope and quietly wait for the salvation of God.' Time is certainly determined in God's purpose, and it will not be long ere it come about; and it is not only decreed and determined, but promised. We must undergo death before we can have life; and we are not lords of our own lives, but guardians to keep them for God, and he will in time deliver the soul into a state of light, life, and glory. This waiting patience is delivered to us under the similitude of an husbandman, James v. 7, who 'waiteth for the precious fruit of the earth, and hath long patience for it, till he receive the early and latter rain.' The husbandman cannot look for a present harvest; but the seed that is cast into the ground must endure all weathers before it can spring up into a blade and ear; so must we expect our season.

[C.] The working patience, which is going on with our self-denying obedience, how tedious soever it be to the flesh. Thus we are told that the good ground 'bringeth forth fruit with patience,' Luke viii. 15. The others are hasty, must have present satisfaction, or else grow weary of religion. All evils come from impatience; they could not tarry till God gave crowns and pleasures, therefore they miscarried by their inclinations to vain delight. So the heirs of promise are described to be those that continue with patience in well doing, Rom ii. 7. And to the church of Ephesus, God saith, Kev. ii. 2, 'I know thy works, and thy labour, and thy patience.' The business of religion is carried on with great diligence and painfulness; it is not an idle and sluggish profession; lusts are not easily mortified, neither do graces produce their perfect work with a little perfunctory care; no, but much labour is required. Now, to abound in the work of the Lord requireth a fervent hope to sweeten it.

2. The qualification of that hope which produceth this patience: it is well grounded, and it is lively.

[A.] It is a serious and well-grounded hope. When we first gave up ourselves to Christ, we reckoned and allowed for labours and troubles; the Lord telleth us aforehand, Mat. vii. 14, 'Strait is the gate and narrow is the way that leadeth unto life, and few there be that find it.' The entrance and the progress is dis pleasing to the flesh, or the carnal nature in us; so Mat. xvi. 24, 'Then said Jesus unto his disciples, if any man will come after me, let him deny himself and follow me'; and Luke xiv; if we will make war with the old serpent, build for heaven. Your hope is groundless if you hope for eternal life and are unwilling to undertake any difficulty for Christ's sake; you must reckon upon displeasing the flesh, offending the world, if you would enter into life.

[B.] It is lively; it is not the cold and superficial, but the earnest and effectual hope. The desires of a lively hope are vehement; we long for enjoyment, and would fain attain the end; but they are also submissive, and we will quietly wait God's leisure; as Paul had a desire to depart, yet was willing to abide in the flesh if he might do God any service, Phil. i. 23, 24. Though the way be long, the difficulties great and many, yet we must be content to be without our reward till our work is finished, and without our crown till our war fare is ended, and suffer evil things, and not forsake good things, which are the way also to obtain better; as long as God will prolong life, though it be to endure more troubles, we must submit.

3. How this hope produceth patience; with respect to the object, and the subject

[A.] With respect to the object. This patience ariseth from the certainty and goodness of the things hoped for; it is a sure and great reward. First, The certainty; it is not a vain hope, such as is built upon the promise of a deceitful man, but the word of the ever-living God: Job xiii. 15, 'Though he slay me, yet I will trust in him.' The holy obstinacy of hope cometh from the certainty of the promise. Secondly, the greatness of the things promised. They are rare and excellent, worth the waiting for. It promiseth rest for labour, Kev. xiv. 13; your troublesome work will not last long, but be over in a little time, and you shall have joy and delight for pain and sorrow and all the sad things of the present life: 1 Peter iv. 13, 'But rejoice, inasmuch as ye are par takers of Christ's sufferings, that, when his glory shall be revealed, ye may be glad with exceeding joy.' And glory for shame: Heb. xii. 2, 'Looking unto Jesus, the author and finisher of our faith, who for the joy that was set before him endured the cross, despising the shame.'

[B.] The subject. First, it breedeth courage and fortitude, and strengtheneth our resolutions for God and heaven; the spirit of power is hope, 2 Tim. i. 7. Secondly, it breedeth joy and comfort. All the pleasures of the world doth not give that quiet content and rest to the soul, which the hope of glory doth to a believer: Mat. v. 12, 'Rejoice, and be exceeding glad, for great is your reward in heaven'.

Use 1. To persuade us to this patience of hope. The things hoped for are to come, at a great distance; many things must be done, many things suffered, and we must make our way through the midst of dreadful enemies, if we would attain our end. It is with us as with David, he was promised a kingdom, and at length he had it, but in the meantime liable to many troubles. Remember, David had his troubles; so it is with you, many are the troubles of the righteous, but you must do nothing unworthy of our great hopes; we expect great things, therefore we should contemn low things and endure hard things; all the pleasures of the world are mean and low, and the hardships carry no comparison or proportion with our hopes. What great evils will men endure to obtain worldly gain, rise early go to bed late, eat the bread of sorrows, run from one end of the world to the other! Our hope is not sound unless it breedeth this patient waiting. If we have a true hope, we not only ought in point of duty, but shall; it is the property of hope so to do, to submit with patience to all things which God sendeth in the meantime, and comfort ourselves with the glory that shall ensue.

SERMON XXXIV

Likewise the Spirit also helpeth our infirmities; for we know not what toe should pray for as we ought; but the Spirit itself maketh intercession for us with groanings which cannot be lettered.

Romans viii. 26.

IN the context you have several arguments to persuade to patience under affliction; those two that are of chief consideration are, the hope of glory to come, and the help of the Spirit for the present. This latter is in the text.

In this verse, 1. The help of the Spirit is generally asserted.

2. The reason evidencing the necessity of that help.

1. The Author. 2. The manner of the Spirit's assistance. 3. The particular assistance, where we have

1. The help of the Spirit is generally asserted 'Likewise the Spirit also helpeth our infirmities' By infirmities he meaneth afflictions, and the perturbations occasioned thereby, as fretting or fainting; or more generally any sinful infirmities, as ignorance, distrust, &c. For afflictions, see 2 Cor. xii. 9, 10, 'And he said unto me, My grace is sufficient for thee, for my strength is made perfect in weakness; most gladly therefore will I rather glory in my infirmities, that the power of Christ may rest upon me. Therefore I take pleasure in infirmities, in reproaches, in necessities, in persecutions, in distresses, for Christ's sake; for when I am weak, then am I strong. 'For sins, see Heb. v. 2, 3, 1 Who can have compassion on the ignorant, and on them that are out of the way, for that he himself also is compassed with infirmities; and by reason hereof he ought, as for the people, so also for himself, to offer for sins'. The word for help is notable, *ounantilambanetai*, helpeth our infirmities (a Mark ix. 24, 'Lord, I believe, help my unbelief' help me against it); which we render, 'he helpeth also' joineth in relieving, helpeth us under our infirmities, goeth to the other end of the staff, and beareth a part of the burden with us; the word signifieth to lift up a burden with another. In afflictions we are not alone, but we have the Holy Ghost as our auxiliary comforter, who strengtheneth and beareth us up when we are weak and ready to sink under our burden.

2. The reason evincing the necessity of that help'; for we know not what we should pray for as we ought'. In which there is—

[A.] Something intimated and implied; that prayer is a great stay in afflictions. James v. 13, 'If any among you be afflicted, let them pray' God doth afflict us not that we may swallow our griefs, but vent them in prayer. We have no other way to relieve ourselves in any distress, but by serious addresses to God; this is the means appointed by God to procure comfort to the distressed mind, safety to those that are in danger, relief to them that are in want, strength to them that are in weakness; in short, the only means for obtaining good and removing evil, whether temptations, dangers, enemies, sin, sorrows, fears, cares, poverty, shame, sickness. God is our only help against all these, and prayer is the means to obtain relief from him; yea, all grace and strength, and the greatest mercies that we desire and stand in need of.

[B.] That which is expressed, that we know not how to conceive our prayers aright, either as to matter or manner. It is said of Zebedee's children, 'Ye know not what ye ask' Mat. xx. 22; and it is true of all others also; we often beg a mischief to ourselves instead of a blessing. In those times they were subject to great persecutions, and therefore prayed for an exemption from them; which not happening according to desire, they were troubled. Therefore the apostle telleth them, 'We know not what we should pray for as we ought'; we know not what is absolutely best for us till the Spirit enlighten and direct us. There is a darkness and confusion in our minds; we consult with the flesh, and ask what is most easy, and what is most advantageous. The Spirit of God knoweth what we most stand in need of, and is best for our turn, health, wealth, honour; or sickness, poverty, and disgrace. There is need of great consideration when we pray, more than good men commonly think of; that we may neither ask things unlawful, nor lawful things amiss, James iv. 3. We know not what spirit we are of, Luke ix. 55; we count revenge, zeal; therefore the Holy Ghost doth instruct and direct our motions in prayer, 2 Cor. xii. 8, 9.

[3.] The particular assistance we have from him is mentioned 'But the Spirit maketh intercession for us with groans which cannot be uttered.' Where observe

(1.) The author of this help and assistance'; The Spirit itself maketh intercession for us'; not that the Spirit prayeth, but sets us a-praying. As here the Spirit is said to pray in us, so elsewhere we are said to 'pray in the Holy Ghost' Jude 20. He prayeth, as Solomon is said to build the temple; he did not do the carpenter's or mason's work, but he directed how to build, found out workmen, and furnished them with money and materials. Neither doth the Spirit make intercession for us as Christ doth, Rom. viii. 34, 'Who is at the right hand of God, and maketh intercession for us'; presenting himself to God for us. The drawing up of a petition is one thing, the presenting it in court is another; the Spirit as a notary inditeth our requests, and, as an advocate, presenteth them, and pleadeth them in court.

(2.) The manner of his help and assistance. He stirreth up in us ardent groans in prayer, or worketh up our hearts to God with desires expressed by sighs and groans. *Stenagmois alaletois*, may be rendered unuttered groans, as well as unutterable, and so some take it here; and indeed that way it beareth a good sense. That the virtue of true prayer doth not consist in the number and artifice of words, as those that thought they should be heard for their vain babblings and much speaking, Mat. vi. 7. Alas! the greatest command and flow of words is but babbling, without these secret sighs and groans which the lively motions of the Spirit stirreth up in us. There may be this without words; as Moses cried unto the Lord though he uttered no words, Exod. xiv. 15. Or unutterable; whatsoever proceedeth from a supernatural motion of the Spirit, its fervour and efficacy and force cannot be apprehended or expressed: 1 Peter i. 8, 'Ye rejoice with joy unspeakable and full of glory' and Phil. iv. 7, 'The peace of God which passeth all understand ing shall keep your hearts and minds' In short, the sum of all is this: we have no reason to faint under afflictions, since there is help in prayer; and these prayers are not in vain, being excited by the Spirit dwelling in us; we are ignorant, and he teacheth us what to pray for, and assisteth us by his holy inspirations; we are cold and backward, and he inflameth us, and exciteth us to pray with fervour, and holy sighs and groans. The points from this verse are three

1. That the Holy Spirit doth strengthen and bear us up in our weaknesses and troubles, that we may not faint under them.

2. That prayer is one special means by which God's Holy Spirit helps God's children in their troubles and afflictions.

3. That the prayers of the godly come from God's Spirit.

Doctrine For the first point, that the Holy Spirit doth strengthen and bear us up in our weaknesses and troubles, that we may not faint under them.

The sense of this doctrine I shall give you in these four considerations

1. That it is a great infirmity and weakness if a Christian should faint in the day of trouble. The two extremes are slighting and fainting: Heb. xii. 5, 'My son, despise riot the chastening of the Lord, nor faint under it'; so Prov. xxiv. 10, 'If thou faintest in the day of trouble, thy strength is small'. Partly because there is so little reason for a Christian's fainting. Who should be more undisturbed in the world than he who hath God for his God, Christ for his saviour, and the Spirit for his comforter, and heaven for his portion? Partly because there is so much help from God. Either he hath already obtained strength from God which he doth not improve, or may obtain strength from God which he doth not seek after. God, prayed unto, giveth deliverance or support: Ps. cxxxviii.; . 3, 'In the day when I cried thou answeredst me, and strengthenedst me with strength in my soul'. And partly because of the mischiefs which follow this fainting. There is a twofold fainting—

[A.] There is a fainting which causeth great trouble, perplexity, and dejection of spirit: Heb. xii. 3, 'Lest ye wax weary, and faint in your minds'. Weariness is a lesser, fainting an higher degree of deficiency; in weariness the body requireth some rest or refreshment, when the active power is weakened, and the vital spirits and principles of motion dulled; but in fainting the vital power is contracted, and retireth, and leaveth the outward parts lifeless and senseless. When a man is wearied, his strength is abated; but when he fainteth, he is quite spent. These things, by a metaphor, are applied to the soul or mind. A man is wearied when the fortitude of his mind or his spiritual strength is broken or beginneth to abate, or his soul sits uneasy under sufferings; but when he sinketh under the burden of grievous, tedious, and long afflictions, then he is said to faint; the reasons or grounds of his com fort are quite spent. Now this is a great evil in a child of God; for the spirit of a man, or that natural courage that is in a reasonable creature, will go far as to the sustaining of foreign evils: Prov. xviii. 14, 'The spirit of a man will sustain his infirmity' And it is supposed of a Christian that his spirit is sound and whole, being possessed of the love of God; and therefore, though his natural courage be spent, which goeth on probabilities, yet his faith and hope should not be spent, which goeth on certainties, nor be overmuch perplexed about worldly troubles, as if his mercy were clean gone, or his promise would fail. Therefore a Christian should strive against this: Ps. lxxvii. 7-10, 'Will the Lord cast off forever? Will he be favourable no more? Is his mercy clean gone forever? Doth his promise fail for evermore? Hath God forgotten to be gracious? Hath he in anger shut up his tender mercies? And I said, This is my infirmity; but I will remember the years of the right hand of the Most High.'

[B.] There is a fainting which causeth dejection and falling off from God. Surely this worse becometh the children of God: Kev. ii. 3, 'Thou hast borne and hast patience, and hast laboured and hast not fainted.' This maketh us cast off our profession and practice of godliness, and so cuts us- off from all hope of reward: Gal. vi. 9, 'Ye shall reap in due time, if ye faint not.' It is not taken there for some weariness, or remiss- ness, or perplexity, which may befall God's children, but a total defection. When troubles discourage us in our duty, it is a step towards it, and tendeth to apostasy, which Christians should prevent in time: Heb. xii. 12, 13, 'Wherefore lift up the hands which hang down, and the feeble knees, and make straight paths for your feet, lest that which is lame be turned out of the way.' We often begin to faint, and lag in heaven's way, being wearied and vexed with the oppositions of the carnal world, reproaching, threatening, and persecuting us; but when we begin to waver, we should look to it betimes, and rouse up ourselves, that we may resolve to go on and finish our race, and not lose the benefit of our former labours and sufferings.

2. Consideration, That in this weakness, if be we left to ourselves, we cannot support ourselves. This appeareth, partly because they that have but a light tincture of the Spirit give up at the first assault: Mat. xiii. 21, 'When tribulation ariseth because of the word, by and by he is offended.' Offers of pardon of sins and eternal life affect them for a while, and engage them in the profession of godliness; but when once it cometh to prove a costly business, they give it over presently. And partly because the most resolved, if not duly possessed with a sense of their own weakness, soon miscarry, if not in whole, yet in part; witness Peter, Mat. xxvi. 33-35. Christ had warned them that such afflictions should come, as the stoutest should stumble at them, and fall for a time; but Peter, being conscious to himself of his own sincerity, could not believe such weakness to be in him; but God will soon confute confidence in our own strength, as the event of his fearful fall did evidently declare. Partly because they that seem to be most fortified, not only by resolution, but strong reasons, may yet overlook them in a time of temptation. As Eliphaz told Job, chap. iv. 3-5, 'Behold, thou hast instructed many, and hast strengthened the weak hands; thy words have upholden him that was falling; and thou hast strengthened the feeble knees. But now it is come upon thee, and thou faintest; it toucheth thee, and thou art troubled.' It is one thing to give counsel, and another to practise it; and there is a great deal of difference between trial apprehended by our judgment and felt by our sense: John xii. 27, 'Now is my soul troubled; and what shall I say? Father, save me from this hour; but for this cause came I to this hour.' When well, we easily give counsel to the sick; they that stand on shore may direct others when struggling with a tempest. And besides, we know many things habitually which we cannot actually bring to remembrance, being overcome with the sense of present evils; and grace that seemeth strong out of trial is found weak in trial, and faileth when we should most act it. And partly because those that do not wholly despond, but are yet wrestling, are plainly

convinced that they cannot conquer by their own strength: Jer. viii. 18, 'When I would comfort myself against my sorrow, my heart fainteth within me.' The tediousness of present pressures doth so invade their spirits, that they find themselves much too weak to grapple with their troubles; they essay to do it, but find it too hard for them. Now after all these experiences of the saints, where is the man that will venture in his own strength to compose his spirit and overcome his own infirmities?

3. That when we cannot support ourselves through our weakness, the Spirit helpeth us. We speak not of the necessity of the Holy Spirit to our regeneration, but confirmation. After grace received, worldly things set near and close to us, and the love of them is not so quite extinct in us but that they have too great a command over our inclinations and affections, that we cannot overcome our infirmities without the assistance of grace, which Christ dispenseth by his Spirit. And it is not enough for us to stand upon our guard and defend ourselves, but we must implore the divine assistance, which is engaged for us: Eph. iii. 16, 'That he would grant unto you, according to the riches of his glory, to be strengthened with might by his Spirit in the inner man'; 1 Peter i. 5, 'Who are kept by the power of God through faith to salvation;' 1 Cor. x. 13, 'There hath no temptation taken you but such as is common to man; but God is faithful, who will not suffer you to be tempted above what you are able, but will with the temptation also make a way to escape.' The Spirit that enlighteneth a Christian fortifieth him, and the same grace which he sheddeth abroad in the soul filleth us both with light and strength, and as a spirit of strength and counsel doth enable us to bear all the afflictions which otherwise would shake and weaken our resolutions for God and heaven.

4. They that rouse up themselves, and use all means, are in a nearer capacity to receive influences from the Spirit than others. For the apostle's word is, 'He helpeth also'; we have been at the work, reason ing and pleading, but he maketh our thoughts effectual: Ps. xxvii. 14, 'Wait on the Lord, be of good courage, and he shall strengthen thy heart; wait, I say, on the Lord.' If we do not exercise faith and hope, how can we look for the assistance of the Holy Ghost? If we give way to discouragement, we quit our own comfort; but when we strive to take courage from the grounds of faith, it is followed with strength from God to undergo the trouble; so Ps. xxxi. 24, 'Be of good courage, and he shall strengthen your heart, all ye that hope in the Lord.' When we arm ourselves with constancy and fortitude, there is no doubt of God's seasonable relief; but if you, out of love of the ease and contentment of the flesh, give way to difficulties, and despond, how can you expect God's assistance? You banish it from you.

Use 1. Is comfort to the children of God. For the Lord is not a spectator only of our troubles, but an helper in our conflicts We are set forth as a spectacle to God, men, and angels, 1 Cor. iv. 9; therefore we should see how we acquit ourselves. But our comfort is that he is the strength of our souls, that we are engaged in his cause, and by his power and strength. God will not desert us, or deny to support us, unless we give him cause by our negligence and grievous sins; no, if you wait upon him, strength will be renewed to you: Isa. xl. 31, 'They that wait on the Lord shall not faint, but renew their strength.' In our weakness he maketh his strength and power to appear, and can enable his servants to do and endure anything rather than quit his cause; they shall have a new supply of strength, when they seem to be clean spent, and overcome all difficulties in the way to heaven.

Use 2. Is direction. To ascribe our standing to the Spirit. We are weak creatures of ourselves, able to do nothing; but through the Spirit of Christ, all things, Phil. iv. 13; that is, go through all conditions. We owe all that we are and all that we do to the Holy Spirit; we live by his presence, understand by his light, act by his power, suffer by the courage he inspireth into us. We are ungrateful to the Holy Spirit if we ascribe that to ourselves as authors, whereof we are scarce servants and ministers. Paul more humbly acknowledges, 1 Cor. xv. 10, 'But by the grace of God I am what I am.'

Use 3. Is exhortation. Let us not faint under our troubles. There are many considerations.

1. Sinners are not discouraged by every inconvenience occasioned by their sins, but can deny themselves for their lusts' sake. And shall we be discouraged in God's service? Every lesser inconvenience that befalleth us in the way of our duty is taken notice of, but the great evils of sin are not regarded. When you see sin's martyrs walk about the streets, or carried to their execution, it should be a shame to Christians. Some whose flesh is mangled by their sin, impoverished by their sin, brought to public shame by their sin, die for their sin; and are we so weak when we suffer for Christ?

2. Others have borne far heavier burdens, and yet do not sink under them. The Lord Christ, Heb. xii. 3, 'endured the contradiction of sinners,' and many of his precious servants: Heb. xi. 35, 'They accepted not deliverance, looking for a better resurrection.' They might, upon certain conditions, have been free from their cruel pains and tortures, but these conditions were contrary to the law of God, therefore would not by indirect means get off their trouble. Now, shall we praise their courage and not imitate it? That is to be Christians in speculation.

3. God promiseth to moderate the afflictions and sweeten the bitter ness of them, lest we should faint: Isa. lvii. 16, 'I will not be wroth[48] forever, and contend always; for so the spirit should faint, and the soul which I have made.' God hath great consideration of man's infirmity and weakness, and how unable they are to hold out under long and grievous troubles; therefore he stayeth his hand, will not utterly dis hearten and discourage his people. A good man will not overburden his beast. If you be satisfied in the wisdom and faithfulness of God's providential government, you have no reason to faint, but keep up your dependence upon him.

4. When reason is tired, faith should supply its place, and we should hope against hope, Horn. iv. 18. Faith can fetch water not only out of the fountain, but out of the rock; when other helps fail, then is a time for God to work.

---

[48] angry

5. Give vent to the ardour of your desires in prayer: Luke xviii. 1, Christ taught men to 'pray always, and not to faint.' Keep up the suit, and it will come to an hearing-day ere it be long: Jonah ii. 7, 'When my soul fainted within me, I remembered the Lord, and my prayer came unto thee into thy holy temple'. When our infirmity cometh to a degree of faintness, then it is a time to be earnestly dealing with God.

6. What will you get by your fainting, but the creature for God? Heb. iii. 12, 'Take heed, brethren, lest there be in any of you an evil heart of unbelief in departing from the living God.' Murmuring for prayer? Lam. iii. 39, 40, 'Wherefore doth a living man complain, a man for the punishment of his sins? let us search and try our ways, and turn to the Lord.' Unlawful shifts for duty? Isa. xxviii. 15, 'For we have made lies our refuge, and under falsehood have we hid ourselves.' This is overmuch haste; will you choose God for your enemy to escape the enmity of man? And perdition for salvation? Heb. x. 39, 'But be not of them who draw back unto perdition, but of them that believe to the saving of the soul' Will you run into hell for fear of burning?

7. The Holy Spirit blesseth these considerations, and doth further comfort the saints, partly by shedding abroad the love of God in their hearts, Rom. v. 3-5; God's smiles are infinitely able to counterbalance the world's frowns; and partly by a clearer sight of their blessedness to come. Remember your eternal blessings, and how far your afflictions prepare you for them: 2 Cor. iv. 16, 17, 'For this cause we faint not; but though our outward man perish, yet the inward man is renewed day by day. For our light affliction, which is but for a moment, worketh for us a far more exceeding and eternal weight of glory'. The greatest trouble cannot make void this hope; yea, it doth prepare you for it; your spiritual estate is bettered by them.

Doctrine 2. That prayer is one special means by which the Holy Spirit helpeth God's children in their troubles and afflictions.

1. Troubles are sent for this end, not to drive us from God, but to draw us to him: Ps. 1. 15, 'And call upon me in the day of trouble, I will deliver thee, and thou shalt glorify me. Trouble in itself id a part of the curse introduced by sin. When God seemeth angry, we have a liberty to apply ourselves to him. In trouble we are apt to think God an enemy, and that he putteth the old covenant in suit against us, but then God expects most to hear from us.

2. Prayer is a special means to ease the heart of our burdensome caves and fears: Phil. iv. 6, 'Be careful for nothing, but in everything by prayer and supplication let your requests be made known unto God' When the wind is got into the caverns of the earth, it causeth earth quakes and terrible convulsions till it get a vent; we give vent to our troublesome and unquiet thoughts by prayer, when we lay our burden at God's feet.

3. It is a special means of acknowledging God as the fountain of our strength and the author of our blessings. First, As the fountain of our strength and support; we have it not in ourselves, and therefore we seek it from God; he is able to keep us from falling, therefore we pray to him: 1 Peter v. 10, 'But the God of all grace, who hath called us to his eternal glory by Jesus Christ, after that ye have suffered a while, make you perfect, stablish,

strengthen, settle you' Secondly, As the author of our deliverance: 2 Tim. iv. 18, 'He shall deliver me from every evil work'

Use 1. Is to exhort us to prayer. First, He delights to give out blessings this way: Jer. xxix. 11, 12, 'For I know the thoughts that I think towards you, saith the Lord, thoughts of peace, and not of evil, to give you an expected end. Then shall you call upon me, and ye shall go and pray unto me, and I will hearken unto you'; and Ezek. xxxvi. 37, 'Thus saith the Lord God, I will yet for this be inquired of by the house of Israel, to do them good.' And our Lord Christ, as mediator, was to ask of the Father: Ps. ii. 8, 'Ask of me, and I will give thee the heathen for an inheritance, and the uttermost parts of the earth for a possession' Secondly, All mercies come the sweeter to us as they increase our love to God and trust in him: Ps. cxvi. 1, 2, 'I love the Lord, because he hath heard my voice and my supplication; because he hath inclined his ear unto me, therefore will I call upon him as long as I live'

Use 2. Is information. If we would have the Spirit's help, let u pray. There we have most sensible feeling of his assistance; our strength lieth most in asking; and when we are at a loss what to do, your hearts are more eased in prayer than in any other work. Every condition is sanctified when it bringeth you nearer to God; if crosses bring us to the throne of grace, they have done their work; your trouble is eased.

Doctrine 3. That the prayers of the godly come from God's Spirit.

That the Spirit hath a great stroke in the prayers of the saints, is evident by many other scriptures besides the text; as Jude 20, 'Praying in the Holy Ghost'; that is, by his motion and inspiration. Look, as we breathe out that air which we first suck in, so the prayer is first breathed into us before breathed out by us; first inspired, before uttered; so Zech. xii. 10, 'I will pour upon them a spirit of grace and supplications'; a spirit of grace will become a spirit of supplications. Where he dwelleth in the heart, he discovereth himself mostly in prayer; so Gal. iv 6, 'Because ye are sons, God hath sent forth the Spirit of his Son into your hearts, crying, Abba, Father' The Spirit's gracious operations are manifested especially in fitting us for, and assisting us in, the duty of prayer. Affectionate and believing prayers are, ascribed unto him 'God hath put forth the Spirit of his Son, crying,' &c. Here I shall inquire

First, In what manner the Spirit concurreth to the prayers of the faithful.

Secondly, What necessity there is of this help and assistance.

Thirdly, Caution against some abuses and mistakes of this doctrine.

For the first, these three things concur in prayer, as different causes of the same effect the spirit of a man, the new nature, and the Spirit of God. First, there is the spirit of a man, for the Holy Ghost makes use of our understandings for the actuating of our will and affections; the Spirit bloweth up the fire, though it be our hearts that burn within us. Secondly, The new nature in a Christian is more immediately and vigorously operative in prayer than in most other duties; and the exercise of faith, love, and hope in prayer doth flow from the renewed soul, as the proper inward and vital principle of these actions; so that we, and not the [Spirit of God, are said to repent, believe, and pray. Well then, there is the heart of man, and the heart renewed and sanctified; for the Spirit, as to his actual motions, doth not blow upon a dead coal. But then there is the Spirit of God, who createth and preserveth these gracious habits in the soul, and doth excite the soul to act, and doth assist it in acting according to them; as, for instance, the natural spirit of man out of self-love willeth and desireth its own good, and its own felicity in general, and is unwilling of destruction and apparent misery, or whatever may occasion it. But then, as we are renewed, this will to good is sanctified, that God is chosen as our portion and felicity, or as the principal good to be desired by us. Faith seeth that the favour and fruition of God in a blessed immortality is our true happiness, and love desireth it above all things, and on the contrary, shunneth damnation and the wrath of God, and sin as sin, and all the apparent dangers of the soul. Hope waiteth and expecteth the fruition of God, and the good things which leadeth to him. Accordingly, we address ourselves to God, and put forth and act this faith, love, and hope in prayer this our renewed spirit doth; but the Holy Ghost himself is the principal cause of all, who doth create this faith, love, and hope, and still preserve it, and order and actuate it. The soul worketh powerfully and sweetly by an earnest motion and inclination towards God.

SERMON XXXV

Likewise the Spirit also helpeth our infirmities; for we know not what we should pray for as we ought; but the Spirit itself maketh intercession for us with groanings which cannot be uttered.

Romans viii. 26.

WE now come more distinctly to show what the Holy Ghost doth in prayer.

1. He directeth and ordereth our requests so as they may suit with our great end, which is the enjoyment of God. For of ourselves we should pray only after a natural and human affection, which sets up itself instead of God, and self is considered as a body rather than a soul, and so asketh bodily things rather than spiritual, and the conveniences of the natural life rather than the enjoyment of the world to come. Let a man alone, and he will sooner ask baits and snares and temptations, than graces and helps, a scorpion instead of fish, and a stone rather than bread. We take counsel of our lusts and interests when we are left to our own private spirit, and so would make God to serve with our sins, and employ him as a minister of our carnal desires; as it is said of them in the wilderness, Ps. lxxviii. 18, 'They tempted God in their hearts by asking meat for their lusts'; our natural will and carnal affections will make us pray ourselves into a snare. In the text it is said, 'We know not what to pray for as we ought'; and in ver. 27, 'He maketh intercession for the saints according to the will of God.' *Kata theos*, according to God; not only with respect to Lis will, but his glory and our eternal good; so that human and carnal affection shall neither prescribe the matter nor fix the end. To pray in a holy manner is the product of the Spirit, and the fruit of his operation in us. Faith and love and hope are more at work in a serious prayer than human and carnal affection, which referreth all its desires and inclinations to the bodily life.

2. He quickeneth and enliveneth our desires in prayer. There is a holy vehemency and fervour required in prayer, opposite to that care less formality and deadness which otherwise is found in us; these are the 'groanings which cannot be uttered' spoken of in the text. Groaning noteth the strength and ardency of desire, when there is a warmth and a life and a vigour in prayer. Oh! How flat and dead are our hearts oftentimes, when we want these quickening motions! A flow of words may come from our natural temper, but these lively motions and strong desires from the Spirit of God. It is notable that the prayer which is produced in us by the Spirit is represented by the notion of a cry; twice it is said, teaching us to cry, Abba, Father; not with respect to the loudness of the voice, but the earnestness of affection. Crying for help is the most vehement way of asking, used only by persons in great necessity and danger. A prayer without life is as incense without fire, which sendeth forth no perfume or sweet savour. The firing of the sacrifices was a token of God's acceptance; so when warmth of heart cometh from heaven, God testifieth of his gifts.

3. He encourageth and emboldeneth us to come to God as a father. This is one main thing twice mentioned in scripture: Rom. viii.] 5, 'We have received the spirit of adoption, whereby we cry, Abba, Father'; and Gal. iv. 6, 'Because ye are sons, God hath sent forth the Spirit of his Son into your hearts, crying, Abba, Father.' A great part of the life and comfort

of prayer consisteth in coming to God as a reconciled father. Now this is seen in two things [A.] Child-like confidence; [B.] Child-like reverence.

[A.] Child-like confidence, or a familiar owning of God in prayer, when we come to him as little children to their father, for help in their dangers and necessities. Christ hath taught us to say, 'Our Father,' and in every prayer we must be able to say so in one fashion or another; not with our lips, but with our hearts; by option and choice, if not by direct affirmation: Luke xi. 13, 'If ye, then, being evil, know how to give good gifts to your children, how much more shall your heavenly Father give the Holy Spirit to them that ask it?' We forget the duty of children, but God doth not forget the mercies of a father. Let it be the voice of our trust and hope rather than of our lips.

[B.] With child-like reverence, in an humble and aweful way. God, that hath the title of a father, will have the honour and respect of a father, Mai. i. 6. If this should breed fear and reverence in us at other times, it should much more when we immediately converse with him: 1 Peter i. 17, 'If ye call on the Father, who without respect of persons judgeth every man' God will be sanctified in all that draw nigh unto him, Heb. x.; so Phil. iii. 11, 'Serve the Lord with fear, and rejoice with trembling.' Our familiarity with God must not mar our reverence, nor confidence and delight in him our humility; and serious dealing with God in prayer is wrought in us by the Spirit, in whose light we see both God and ourselves, his majesty and our vile- ness, his purity and our sinfulness, his greatness and our nothingness.

Secondly, the necessity of this help and assistance.

1. The order and economy of the divine persons showeth it. In the mystery of redemption God is represented as our reconciled God and Father, to whom we come; Christ as the mediator, through whom we have liberty and access to God as our own God; and the Spirit as our guide, sanctifier, and comforter, by whom we come to him. God is represented as the great prince and universal king, into whose presence- chamber poor petitioners are admitted; Christ openeth the door by the merit of his sacrifice, and keepeth it open by his constant intercession, that wrath may be no hindrance on God's part, nor guilt on ours; for otherwise, 'God is a consuming fire' Heb. xii. 29, and sin divides, and separates between God and us, Isa. lix. 2. Then the Spirit doth create, preserve, and quicken and actuate these graces, in the exercise of which this access is managed and carried on; otherwise, such is our impotency and averseness, that we should not make use of this offered benefit: Eph ii. 18, 'For through him we both have an access by one Spirit unto the Father'. The enjoyment of the fatherly love of God is the highest happiness, in which the soul doth rest content. Christ is the way by which we come to the Father, and the Spirit our guide, which causeth us to enter in this way, and goeth along with us in it. We cannot look aright to the blessed Father, but we must look to him through the blessed Son, and we cannot look upon the Son but through the blessed Spirit, and so we come a-right to God.

2. That prayer may carry proportion with other duties. All the children of God are led by the Spirit of God, Rom. viii. 14; as in their whole conversation, so especially in this act of prayer. Look, as in common providence, no creature is exempted from the influence of it; for in him they all live, move, and have their being. Exempt any creature from the dominion of

providence, and then that creature would live of itself; so as to gracious and special providence, you cannot exempt one action from the Spirit's influence; for 'we live in the Spirit and walk in the Spirit' Gal. v. 25; we sing with the Spirit, and hear in the Spirit, and serve God in the Spirit; so we pray in the Spirit only. There is a special regard to this duty, because here we have experience of the motions of the renewed soul directly towards God, and so of the comforts and graces of the Spirit, more than in other duties.

3. Because of our impotency. We cannot speak of God without the Spirit, much less to God: 1 Cor. xii. 3, 'No man can say that Jesus is the Lord, but by the Holy Ghost'; that is, believe on him as the Messiah and redeemer of the world. It was a deadly state the Redeemer found us in. To lessen man's misery was to lessen the grace of Christ; so we must not extenuate the honour of our sanctifier; we can neither live, nor work, nor walk, nor pray, without the Spirit. The help is not need less, if we consider what we are, and what prayer is; what we are, who are enemies to our own happiness and holiness; and prayer, which requireth such serious work. Surely the setting of our hearts and all our hopes upon an invisible glory, and measuring all things thereunto, is a work too hard for a carnal, sensual creature that is wedded to present satisfactions. And without this there is no praying in a spiritual manner. They that love sin will never heartily pray against it; and they that hate a holy, spiritual, heavenly life, can never seek the advancement of it. Now this is our case: we may babble and speak things by rote, or we may have a natural fervency when we pray for corn, wine, and oil, and justification and sanctification in order there unto; we may have a wish, but not a serious volition of spiritual and heavenly things, which is the life and soul of prayer.

4. With respect to acceptance: Ps. x. 17, 'When thou preparest the heart, thou bendest the ear'; Rom. viii. 27, 'He knoweth the mind of the Spirit, because he maketh intercession for the saints according to the will of God'. God knoweth what is a belch of the flesh, and what is a groan of the Spirit; every voice but that of his Spirit is strange and barbarous to him. He puts us upon holy and just requests; he hath stirred them up in us, as a father teacheth a child to ask what he hath a mind to give him.

Thirdly, Cautions against some abuses and mistakes in prayer.

1. This is not so to be understood as if the matter and words of prayer were immediately to be inspired by the Holy Ghost, as he inspired the holy men of God in their prophesying and penning the holy scripture. We read, 2 Peter i. 21, that 'holy men spake as they were moved by the Holy Ghost'; and we may say, holy men pray as they are moved by the Holy Ghost But yet there is a great deal of difference between both these; partly because they were immediately moved and infallibly assisted by the Spirit, so moved and extraordinarily borne through, that they could not err and miscarry; they were free from any fault, failing, or corruption in the matter, form, or words wherein this was expressed; all was purely divine. But in our prayers we find the con trary by sad experience. Partly because it had been a sin in the prophets not to have delivered the same message which they received of the Lord, both for matter, manner, and method; but it is no sin in a child of God against the guidance and governance of God's Spirit, to use another method than he used; to contract and

shorten, or to lengthen and enlarge his prayers, as opportunity serveth. And yet the prayer is the prayer of the Spirit, that is directed, ordered, and quickened by the Spirit.

2. This is not to be understood as if we should never pray till the Spirit moveth us. The prophets were not to prophesy till moved by an extra ordinary impulse; for they were not bound by the common law of God's servants or children to see visions, or to prophesy. But we are not to stay from our duty till we see the Spirit moving; but to make use of the power we have as reasonable creatures: Eccles. ix. 10, 'Whatever thy hand findeth to do, do it with all thy might'; and to stir up the gifts and graces that we have as believers: Isa. lxiv. 7, 'And there is none that calleth upon thy name, that stirreth up himself to take hold of thee'; 2 Tim. i. 6, 'Wherefore I put thee in remembrance that thou stir up the gift of God which is in thee;' and in the way of duty to wait and cry for the necessary influences of the Lord's Spirit: Cant. iv. 16, 'Awake, north wind! and come, thou south wind! blow upon my garden, that the spices thereof may flow forth; let my beloved come into his garden, and eat his pleasant fruits.' And to obey his sanctifying motions: Ps. xxvii. 8, 'When thou saidst, Seek ye my face, my heart said unto thee, Thy face, Lord, will I seek'.

3. We cannot say we have not the spirit of prayer, because we have not such freedom of words as may give vent to spiritual affections. If there be a sense of such things as we mainly want, that is, Christ and his graces, and an affectionate desire after them, and we address ourselves to God with these desires in the best fashion we can, that we may have help and relief from him, and you are resolved not to give him over till you have it, you have the spirit of grace and supplications, though it may be you cannot enlarge upon these things with such copiousness of expression as others do. Therefore let us consider what is the spirit of prayer, and how far doth he make use of our natural faculties. I conceive it thus. A man is convinced that his happiness lieth in the enjoyment of God; that there is no enjoyment of God but by Christ, till he be justified and sanctified, and walk in holy obedience to him. The Spirit of God upon this changeth his heart, and it is set within him to seek after God in this way: 1 Chron. xxii. 19, 'Now set your heart and your soul to seek the Lord your God;' and Ps. cxix. 36, 'Incline my heart unto thy testimonies' Now, because the will without the affections doth not work strongly, but is like a ship without sails affections are the vigorous and forcible motions of the will, without which it would lie sluggish and idle, or like a chariot without wheels and horses, or a bird when her wings are clipped therefore the Holy Ghost stirreth up these affections, and our heart within us makes us willing, and this bringeth the soul to God. For no other can give us satisfaction, but he alone; and the difficulties of salvation are so many that we cannot overcome them but in his power and strength. Now sense of wants, and an earnest desire of a supply, will ordinarily put words into a man's mouth, and affections beget expressions; yet because many accidental reasons may hinder it, the weight of prayer is not to be laid so much upon the expression as the affection. If there be a strong and an earnest desire after grace, it will make us express ourselves to God in the best manner that we can. As long as you pray for necessary graces, and other things in subordination thereunto, and can heartily groan and sigh to God for what you want with respect to your great end, the prayer is well performed. There may be a great petulancy and

extravagance of words where there is not a good and an honest heart vain babblings, without faith, or feeling, or spiritual affections.

4. It is not to be understood as if all that pray graciously had the Spirit in a like measure, or the same persons always in the same measure. No, the wind bloweth where it listeth, John iii. 7, and he giveth us to will and to do. We cannot find the assistance at our own pleasure; some have it in a more plentiful, others in a scanty measure, though all have it. Jesus Christ himself, though he had not the Spirit by measure, yet he exercised and acted the spirit of prayer more at one time: Luke xxii. 44, 'And being in an agony, he prayed, *ektenesteron*, more earnestly'; his love to God was always the same, but the expression of it different. So God's children seek heavenly things with a weaker degree of desire, and sometimes with a stronger; at sometimes we have the directing work of the Spirit, and are not sensible of those earnest and inexpressible groans; that is to say, we put up our requests for things lawful and useful, and most necessary for us at the time, but not with that ardour and fervency that we do desire. We cannot say that the Holy Ghost doth not assist these prayers, as sometimes the assistance is given us more largely as to the groaning part, and men are all in a flame. Strong and passionate affections do most bewray themselves, sometimes as a spirit of confidence and holy liberty with our Father, and faith is clearly predominant in prayer; at other times repentance and child-like reverence and fear are altogether in action in the prayer, and there is a great seriousness, though not such life and vigour or strength of faith as grief for sin, bemoaning our failings.

5. Gifts are more necessary when we join with others, and are their mouth to God; but the spirit of prayer is of most use when we are alone, and we have nothing to do but to set ourselves before the searcher of hearts, and draw forth our desires after him; when, without taking in the necessities of others, we present our personal requests to God, and lament the defects of our own hearts and the plague of our own souls. When we pray alone, it is good to observe the workings of our own hearts; surely whatever prayer we make to God, we should find it in our hearts: 2 Sam. vii. 27, 'Therefore hath thy servant found in his heart to pray this prayer unto thee.' Having a deep sense of our wants, a real desire of the blessing, we ask exercising grace rather than memory and invention; pouring out our very souls to God, with sighs and groans rather than words; we are at liberty there to use or not use the voice, to continue speech and break it off, and lift up the heart by strong desires to God.

Use 1. It informeth us—

First, What kind of help we have from the Spirit of God in prayer; his work is to guide and quicken you.

First, to guide you in prayer, that you may pray to God in a holy manner; we know not what to pray for as we ought, on a fourfold reason; [A.] As blinded with self-love; [B.] As discomposed by trouble; [C.] As struck dumb by guilt; [D.] As straitened by barren ness and leanness of soul.

[A.] As blinded by self-love. Oh! what strange prayers will men put up to God, if they take counsel of their lusts and interests! As the disciples that called for fire from heaven; Christ told them, 'Ye know not of what manner of spirit ye are of', Luke ix. 55. Self-love so blindeth us that if we be led by it, we shall rather beg our ruin than our salvation; for we know not what is either profitable or prejudicial to us; so that it would be an argument of God's anger to grant our requests. The ambitious, if he should pray from the passion that possesseth him, would only ask honour and worldly greatness; the covetous, only that God would double his worldly portion, and enlarge his estate according to his vast desires; the sensual, the ability and opportunity of glutting his brutish inclinations; the vindictive, that he may interest God in his quarrels; all sinners would serve him only to serve their carnal turns. Whatever words we use to God in. prayer, if we serve him to these ends, and hope that by praying they shall be the better gratified, our prayer is turned into sin; but he that is guided by the Spirit entreateth nothing of God but what is pleasing to him, and suiteth with his glory. We come to our Father which is in heaven when we pray; and our welfare in the world must be subordinated to our eternal and heavenly estate. And we come in the name of Christ; now to ask honours in his name who was born in a stable and died on a cross, pleasures in his name who was a man of sorrows, is utterly incongruous. No; God's glory, kingdom, will, must be preferred before our inclinations; other things asked with reservation and submission.

[B.] Our minds are discomposed by trouble, that we scarce know what to do or say: 2 Chron. xx. 12, 'Lord, we know not what to do, but our eyes are unto thee' Our Lord Christ: John xii. 27, 'My soul is troubled, what shall I say? 'In great grief, Christ himself was at a loss; the great teacher of the church, who hath so much to say for our comfort and counsel in such cases, yet was amazed, and at a nonplus; and David, Ps. lxxvii. 4, 'I am sore troubled, I cannot speak.' Our words stoppeth the mouth. Now when our thoughts are thus confounded, we scarce know what to pray for; the Spirit teacheth us what to say. Look, as in the case of the fear of men: Luke xii. 12, 'For the Holy Ghost shall teach you in the same hour what you shall say'; so in our perplexities, when we are scarce able to open our mouths to God.

[C.] When struck dumb by some newly contracted guilt, as David kept silence and grew shy of God, Ps. xxxii. 3. The Spirit urgeth us to penitent confession and humble suing out our pardon, ver. 5, with that brokenness of heart which becometh a sinner.

[D.] When straitened by barrenness, and leanness of soul; would fain pray, but are dry and barren of matter. It is because we use not meditation and serious recollection: Ps. xlv. 1, 'My heart is inditing[49] a good matter, my tongue is the pen of a ready writer.' One that is well acquainted with God and himself cannot want matter. First, the Holy Ghost puts us upon the serious consideration of these things; and then when we come to speak to God, a man will

---

[49] writing

copiously enough be supplied out of the abundance of his heart: Mat. xii. 34, 'Out of the abundance of the heart the mouth speaketh.' If the mind be stocked and furnished with holy thoughts and meditation, it will break out in the lips.

2. His next office is to quicken you, or raise your affections and holy desires, which are the life of prayer. The prayer continueth no longer than the desires do; therefore groans are more prayer than words. Weeping hath a voice: Ps. vi. 8, 'The Lord hath heard the voice of my weeping.' Tears have a tongue, and a language which God well enough understandeth. Look, as babes have no other voice but crying for the mother's breast, that is intelligible enough to the tender parent; so when there are earnest and serious desires after grace, God knoweth our meaning.

Secondly, it informeth us that the motions of the Spirit are a help in prayer, not the rule and reason of prayer. Many will say they will pray only when the Spirit moveth them; now he helpeth in the performance, not in the neglect of the duty. We are to make conscience of it. God giveth out influences of grace according to his will or good pleasure; but we must pray according to his will of precept. The influence of grace is not the warrant of duty, but the help; we are to do all acts in obedience to God's command, whatever cometh of it, Luke v. 5. God is sovereign; disposed or indisposed, you are bound. Our impotency is our sin. Now our sin cannot excuse us from our duty, for then the creature were not culpable for his sinful defects and omissions. The outward act of a duty is commanded as well as the inward; though we cannot come up to the nature of a perfect duty, yet we should do as we can. *Tota actio*[50], and *totum actionis*[51], falleth under the command of God: Hosea xiv. 2, 'Take with you words'; ay, and also take with you affections. Though I cannot do all, I must do as much as I can, bring such desires as I have. God's Spirit is more likely to help you in duty, than in the neglect of it. You quench the Spirit that must assist you by neglecting the means; when the door is bolted, knocking is the only way to get it open. Present yourselves before God, and see what he will do for you. By tacking about, men get the wind, not by lying still; there is many times a supply cometh ere we are aware: Cant. vi. 11, 12, 'Or ever I was aware, my soul made me like the chariots of Amminadib.' We begin with much deadness and straitness; by striving against it, rather than yielding to it, we get enlargement afterwards; God assists those that will be doing what he commandeth; when we stir up our selves, he is the more ready to help us.

Use 2. Is caution. See that your prayers come from the Spirit; there are some prayers it is a reproach to the Holy Spirit to father them upon him.

1. An idle and foolish loquacity. When men take a liberty to prattle anything in God's hearing, and pour out raw, tumultuous, and in digested thoughts before him: Eccles. v. 2, 'Be not hasty to utter anything before God'; it is a great irreverence and contempt of his

---

[50] All activity
[51] All activities

majesty. Surely the Spirit is not the author of ignorant, senseless, and dull praying; nothing disorderly cometh from him. The heathen are charged with vain babbling and heartless repetitions: Mat. vi. 7, 'They think to be heard for their much speaking.' Shortness or length are both culpable, according to the causes from whence they come; shortness out of barrenness and straitness, or length out of affectation, or ingeminating the same thing, without savour or wisdom, or a mere filling up the time with words.

2. A frothy eloquence and affected language; as if the prayer were the more grateful to God, and he did accept men for their words rather than their graces, and were to be worshipped with fine phrases and quaint speeches. No, it is the humble exercise of faith, hope, and love, which he regardeth; and such art and curiosity is against God's sovereignty, and doth not suit with the gravity and seriousness of worship. If we would speak to God, we must speak with our hearts to him rather than our words; and the more plain and bare they are, the better they suit with the nature of duty. Moses was bid to put off his shoes in holy ground, to teach us to lay aside our ornaments when we humble ourselves before God. It is not words, but spirit and life; not a work of oratory, but filial affection. Too much care of verbal eloquence showeth our hearts are more conversant with signs than things, words than matter; and it hath a smack of the man, and smelleth of the man, but savoureth not of the Spirit: Ps. cxix. 26, 'I declared my ways, and thou heardest me'

3. Outward vehemency and. loud speech. The heat which ariseth from the agitation of bodily spirits, and vehemency of speech, differeth from an inward affection, which is accompanied with reverence and child-like dependence upon God. It is not the loud noise of words which is best heard in heaven; the fervent affectionate cries of the saints are those of the heart, not of the tongue: Ps. x. 17, 'Lord, thou hast heard the desire of the humble;' and Ps. xxxviii. 9, 'O Lord, all my ways are before thee, and my groaning is not hid from thee' The vehemency of the affection may sometimes cause the extension of the voice; but without it, we are but as tinkling cymbals.

4. Natural fervency, when instant and earnest for some kind of blessings, especially when we are oppressed with grievous evils, and would fain get rid of them; yet they cannot be looked upon as a motion of the Spirit; partly because it is the temporal inconvenience they mind more than the removal of sin; and cry more to get ease of their troubles than repentance for their sins which procured them; and the supply of their necessities which they mind, and not the favour of God; and therefore the Holy Ghost calleth it howling, Hos. vii. 14, like the moans of the beasts for ease. Partly because they have no more to do with God when their turns are served, and they are delivered from their troubles: Jer. ii. 27, 'In the time of their trouble they will say, Arise, and save us'; Exod. x. 17, 'Entreat the Lord, that he may take away this death only'; so that all cometh from mere self-love. Partly because those relentings which they have for sin go not deep enough to divorce their hearts from it: Ps. lxxviii. 36, 37, 'Nevertheless, they did flatter with their mouth, and they lied to him with their tongues; for their heart was not right with him, neither were they steadfast in his covenant.' Even then, when they sought God right early, and remembered that God was their rock, and the high God their redeemer, the judgments of God had some slight effect

upon them, reduced them to some degree of repentance and good behaviour and temper for a while; but all this while they were but like ice in yielding weather, thawed above, and hard at bottom. Partly because, if they pray for spiritual things, it is but a dictate of conscience awakened for the time, not the desires of a renewed heart, seconded with constant endeavours to obtain what we ask of God; and so, 'The soul of the sluggard desireth and hath nothing' Prov. xiii. 4; they are not urging desires that quicken to diligence.

But what prayers, then, come from the Spirit?

[A.] When there is something divine in them, such as are suited to the object to whom we pray, and looketh like worship relating to God; when it hath the stamp of his nature upon it. We apprehend in God two sort of attributes, some that belong to his mercy and goodness, some to his majesty and greatness. Now his mercy and goodness is seen in the joy of our faith and confidence, his majesty and greatness in our humility and reverence; both prompt us to serious worshipping.

[B.] When there is something beyond the work of our natural faculties; and prayer is not the fruit of memory and invention, but of faith, hope, and love. A man, by the help of memory and invention, may frame and utter a prayer which his heart disliketh.

[C.] Whatever prayers are according to the will of God: ver. 27, 'And he that searcheth the heart knoweth what is the mind of the Spirit, because he maketh intercession for the saints according to the will of God'.

Use 3. Is to exhort you to get this spirit of prayer and supplication.

1. Beg the Spirit of God from his fatherly love: Luke xi. 13, 'If ye then, being evil, know how to give good gifts to your children, how much more shall your heavenly Father give the Holy Spirit to them that ask him?

2. Beg it as purchased by Christ; as one of his disciples, as one that hath consented to the covenant of grace, which is a dutiful and obediential acceptance of Christ Jesus as our alone remedy. So doth Paul pray for it: Eph. i. 17, 18, 'That the God of our Lord Jesus Christ, the Father of glory, may give unto you the spirit of wisdom and revelation in the knowledge of him; the eyes of your understanding being enlightened, that ye may know what is the hope of his calling, and what the riches of the glory of his inheritance in the saints.' So doth God offer it.

3. Obey the Spirit in other things, and then he will help you in prayer: Rom. viii. 14, 'For as many as are led by the Spirit of God are the sons of God.' That implieth that he not only directs, but we follow his direction; therefore make it your business to obey his motions when he would restrain you from sin: Rom. viii. 13, 'If ye through the Spirit mortify the deeds of the body, ye shall live.' When he inviteth and leadeth you into communion with God, which is called by the apostle walking in the Spirit, Gal. v. 25, obey him speedily, for delay is a plausible denial; thoroughly doing all that he requireth of you constantly, not sometimes only, when generally you neglect him. The Spirit is a stranger to you in prayer, when you neglect his other motions. There is a grieving the Spirit: Eph. iv. 30, 'And grieve not the Holy Spirit, whereby ye are sealed to the day of redemption'; a resisting the Spirit:

Acts vii. 51, 'Ye stiff-necked and uncircumcised in heart and ears, ye do always resist the Holy Ghost'; and there is a quenching the Spirit: 1 Thes. v. 19, 'Quench not the Spirit.'

4. Do not pride thyself with the assistance he giveth: Ps. xci. 15, 'He shall call upon me, and I will answer him, and will be with him in trouble, and I will deliver him.' Simon Magus would fain have the power to work miracles: Acts viii. 19, 'And when Simon saw that through the laying on of the apostles' hands the Holy Ghost was given, he offered them money, saying, Give me also this power, that on, whomsoever I lay hands, he may receive the Holy Ghost.

SERMON XXXVI

And he that searcheth the hearts knoweth what is the mind of the Spirit, because he maketh intercession for the saints according to the will of God.

Romans viii. 27.

IN these words the former privilege is amplified. He had spoken of the assistance we have from the Spirit; now, acceptance. Those sighs and groans which are stirred up in us by the Spirit are not without fruit and success, for they are taken notice of and accepted by the Lord. If they were confused and unintelligible groans or hasty sighs, that die away and are gone like a puff of wind, the privilege were not so much; no, they are of greater regard than so; they are observed and rewarded by God 'And he that searcheth,' &c.

In the words we have

First, A property of God mentioned, that he searcheth the hearts.

Secondly, An inference thence, or an application to the matter in hand—He knoweth the mind of the Spirit.

Thirdly, A reason why those groans are not unprofitable—Because he maketh intercession for the saints according to the will of God. God knoweth the meaning of them, and accepteth what is agreeable to his will.

First, Let us consider the property of God which is here mentioned 'He that searcheth the hearts'. God needeth no search, but knoweth all things by simple intuition; but it is spoken after the manner of men, who inquire and search into those things which they would know more accurately and exactly; and so it sets forth the infinite know ledge of God.

Doctrine They that come to worship God had need have their hearts deeply possessed with a sense of his omnisciency.

I shall prove two things—

1. That God is omniscient, and in particular doth know the hearts of men.

2. That those that would worship before the Lord must soundly believe and seriously consider this.

1. That the hearts of men lie open to the view of God is a truth often inculcated in scripture, as in that speech of God to Samuel the prophet, 1 Sam. xvi. 7. When Eliab, Jesse's eldest son, was brought before Samuel, surely the. Lord's anointed is before him'; And the Lord said, Look not on his countenance, nor on the height of his stature, for I have refused him. The Lord seeth not as man seeth; for man looketh on the outward appearance, but the Lord looketh on the heart.' Man seeth things slightly and superficially, and judges of all things according to the show and outside, for his sight can pierce no deeper; but God searcheth the heart and reins, knoweth who is, and will continue to be, a faithful instrument of his glory: 1 Chron. xxviii. 9, 'And thou, Solomon, my son, know thou the God of thy father, and serve him with a perfect heart and a willing mind: for the Lord searcheth all hearts, and understandeth all the imaginations of the thoughts.' A man cannot sincerely frame himself

to the service of God unless he doth first believe him to know all things, even our very thoughts, yea the imaginations of the thoughts; the first motions of the soul which set on men to do what they do; so Prov. xv. 11, 'Hell and destruction are before the Lord, how much more the hearts of the children of men? 'He compareth two things which are most unknown to us, the state of the dead, and the hearts of men. God knoweth all those that are in Sheol, the state of the dead, though they are unknown or forgotten by the most of men. We know not what is become of the bodies or souls of men, the number of the damned or the blessed; but God keepeth an exact account of all, he knoweth where their souls are, and their bodies also, what is become of their dust, and how to restore to every one their own flesh. And as he knoweth who are in the state of the dead, so what are the thoughts and hearts of men now alive. The thoughts of the heart are hidden from us till they be revealed by word or action. Who can know our thoughts? What more swift and sudden? What more various, what more hidden, than our thoughts? Yet he knoweth them, not by guess or interpretation, but by immediate inspection; he seeth them before they are manifested by any overt act; he knoweth with what hopes and confidences and aims we are carried on, in whose name we act, and upon what principles and ends. Again, Jer. xvii. 9, 10, 'The heart of man is deceitful and desperately wicked; who can know it? I the Lord search the heart, and try the reins, even to give every man according to his ways, and according to his doings' The heart of man is altogether unknown to others, and very hard and difficult to be discovered by ourselves; there are so many sleights and shifts and circuits and turnings to conceal and colour our actions. But there is no beguiling of God, who hath an eye to discover the most secret motions and inward intentions, and will accordingly deal with men according to their deserts. But the scripture doth not only assert, but argue this point—

[A.] From the immensity and greatness of God; God is in all, and above all, and beyond all; nowhere included, nowhere excluded. And so his omnipresence doth establish the belief of his ommsciency: Jer. xxiii. 23, 24, 'Am I a God at hand, and not a God afar off? Do not I fill heaven and earth? Can any hide himself where I shall not see him? 'God is everywhere, here where you are; nearer and more intrinsic to us than our very souls. Therefore all we think, speak, or do, is better known to him than it is to ourselves; we do all as in his sight, speak all as in his hearing, think all as in his presence; that which can be absent is not God; you may be far from him, but he is not far from every one of you.

[B.] From creation. He hath made our hearts, and therefore knoweth our hearts: Ps. xciv. 9, 10, 'He that planted the ear, shall not he hear? He that formed the eye, shall not he see?' Surely he that made man knoweth what is in man, and observeth what they do. The same argument is urged, Ps. cxxxix. 13, 'Thou hast possessed my reins, for thoa hast covered me in my mother's womb'; and again, Ps. xxxiii. 15, 'He fashioneth their hearts alike, he considereth all their thoughts'. He that hath so much wisdom to give you the power to think, knoweth the acts; if he hath given knowledge to the creatures, he himself hath it in a more eminent degree. Nothing can be concealed from him who hath creating power; as he hath created all alike, he is able to discern them severally one by one, and to understand all the operations of their very hearts.

[C.] From God's government, which is twofold. First, powerful, by his effectual providence, as he governeth all creatures; secondly, moral, by his laws, as he governeth the reasonable creature. Both infer the point in hand.

(1.) The government of his effectual providence, which is necessary to all our actions; 'for in him we live, move, and have our being,' Acts xvii. 28. All things move as he moveth them, in their natural agency; the creature can do nothing without him, and actually doth all things by him; his wisdom guideth, his will intendeth, his power moveth and disposeth all. This is urged, Ps. cxxxix. 10, his hand leadeth us, his right hand holdeth us up wherever we go; that is, we are still supported by his providential influence, and therefore we cannot be hidden from him. Doth God support a creature whom he knoweth not, in an action he understandeth not? Therefore he is not regardless of thy thoughts, words, and ways.

(2.) His moral government. He hath given a law to the reasonable creature, and he will take an account whether it be kept or broken. And therefore, since all persons and causes are to be judged by him, he doth perfectly understand them, and every one of us is clearly and fully known to God, both as to our hearts and actions, or else he were in capable to judge us. This is often urged: Ps. xciv. 10, 'He that chastiseth the nations, shall not he correct? He that teacheth men knowledge, shall not he know? 'He that giveth laws to men demandeth exact obedience to these precepts, and will chastise and punish men's disobedience.' So Heb. iv. 13, 'All things are naked to the eyes of him with whom we have to do'; that is, in the judgment.

2. That they that would worship God aright had need be deeply possessed with this.

[A.] From the nature of worship in general, which is a converse with God, or a setting ourselves immediately before the Lord. In solemn duties we come to act the part of angels, and to behold the face of our heavenly Father; as in prayer we come to speak to God, and in the word we come to hear God speak to us, in the Lord's Supper to be feasted at his table. God is everywhere with us, but we are not always and everywhere with God; we profess to be with him when we come to worship, to turn back upon all other things, that we may stand before the throne of God. Prayer is the most familiar converse with God that we are capable of while we dwell in flesh, called therefore a visiting of God, and an acquainting ourselves with him, a drawing nigh to him, a calling upon God. It is unnecessary to cite places. Now none of this can be done unless we believe him to be present and conscious to all that we do or say, for all else is but an empty formality; therefore, when we pray, we must remember that we converse with him that searcheth the heart, and knoweth what and how we ask; as 1 Kings viii. 39, 'Hear thou in thy dwelling-place, and forgive, and do to every man according to his ways, whose heart thou knowest; for thou, even thou only, knowest the hearts of all the children of men.' All the faith, the seriousness, the comfort of prayer, dependeth upon the belief of this; for who would call upon him of whom he is not persuaded that he heareth him, or be serious in a duty, that knoweth not whether God regardeth, yea or no? Or what comfort can be taken in having prayed and made known his desires to God, unless he be persuaded those prayers come unto the ears of the Lord of Hosts. So for hearing the word, that which bindeth us to reverence is that we are in the sight of God: Acts x. 33, 'We are all here present before the Lord, to hear all things which are commanded thee of God'; otherwise men will come to see and be seen rather than to be taught and instructed. God is everywhere, but he is especially there where his ordinances are. And we are to be so seriously attentive as if God himself did speak to us by oracles, when his message is brought to us; otherwise it will have no effect upon us: 1 Thes. ii. 13, 'Ye received it not as the word of men, but, as it is in truth, the word of God, which effectually worketh also in you that believe'; 2 Cor. v. 20, 'As though God did beseech you by us.' We lift up our hearts to him, and set him before our eyes, as having to do with God himself; this only begets seriousness in hearing. So for the Lord's Supper, which is a middle duty between the word and prayer, and compounded of both; we hear God tendering his covenant, assuring us of his blessings promised, and commanding us to fulfil the requisite duties, that we may be capable of them. We, promising and praying, by resolving and promising testify our consent to the covenant thus stated; by prayers and groans, our dependence. Now there is no covenanting with one that is absent. You will say he is present in his institution; he is so, and that is a help to faith; therefore visible signs are appointed to be an instance of God's presence with us, but all his internal work is immediately transacted between our souls and God himself. We look on him as present that seeth and heareth all, Deut. x. 12. It is to the soul God speaketh, I am thy God: Ps. xxxv. 3, 'Say unto my soul, I am thy salvation'; and the soul spake unto God, 'Thou art my portion, saith my soul.' Either as to promise of obedience, Ps. cxix. 57, or dependence, Lam. iii. 24. Two outward witnesses are conscious to what is done between God and our souls; so Ps. xvi. 2, 'my soul, thou hast said unto God, Thou art my God'. Upon this inward soul-covenanting do all our privileges depend; and if God knoweth not all things, nor engageth his heart to draw nigh unto him, how can this be?

[B.] From the danger of dissembling with God in acts of worship, or putting him off with feigned pretences. The scripture sets forth three phrases a mocking of God, a lying to God, and a tempting of God. A mocking of God: Gal. vi. 7, 'Be not deceived, God is not mocked'; that is, *impune*; there is no escaping the accurate search of the all-seeing God. Ananias and Sapphira's sin was hypocrisy in keeping back part of what was devoted; they would seem liberal and pious as others who were joined to the church, and so, by a part of godliness, seek to be excused from the whole. And whilst they observe externals, neglect internals, own religion when profession is not costly, put on a garb of devotion at times, but lay it aside ordinarily; do what is plausible to men, but neglect what is acceptable to God; now this is called a lying to the Holy Ghost, Acts v. 3. Why to the Holy Ghost, rather than the Father and the Son? Because of his special precedency and inspection over church affairs: Acts xx. 28, 'Take heed therefore unto yourselves, and to all the flock over which the Holy Ghost hath made you overseers'; Acts xv. 28, 'For it seemed good unto the Holy Ghost, and to us, to lay upon you no greater burden than these necessary things.' They pretended to do it by his instinct; as all Christians that pray, profess or pretend to pray by the Holy Ghost. Oh! Observe this. Many make a false confession of faith, or promise of obedience; this is called a lying, not to men, but to God, Acts v. 4. Oh! Then we should be exceedingly fortified against hypocrisy in worship; it is to think to deceive God, whom we profess to be omniscient; nay, it is a tempting of the Spirit of the Lord: ver. 9, 'How is it that ye have agreed together to tempt the spirit of the Lord?', putting it to the proof whether he will discover us or no. Now, rather than run this hazard, it concerneth us greatly and thoroughly to be possessed of this truth, that God searcheth the heart.

[C.] There can be no true worship unless we be deeply possessed with a thorough sense of the infinite knowledge of God.

(1.) There can be no faith unless the worship be performed and tendered to God as an all-seeing spirit: Heb. xi. 6, 'Without faith it is impossible to please God; for he that cometh to God must believe that he is, and that he is a rewarder of them that diligently seek him' If God know me not, nor in what manner I serve him, it is all one whether I serve him religiously, or with a cold, faint, formal worship; for he seeth not with what heart I go about it. If we pray, and think to be never the better for praying, there can be no life in prayer; for a persuasion to be heard and accepted must be at the bottom of all duties; therefore all that would serve him diligently must believe that he is omniscient, and knoweth all things.

(2.) There can be no reverence; for it is all one to pray to an idol, and to a God that heareth not and seeth not; yea, it is worse, for they were persuaded of a virtue or a divine power belonging to their idols; therefore all your worship will be but a conformity to the common custom and fashion: Ezek. xxxiii. 31, 'They come before thee as thy people cometh, and sit before thee as thy people; and they hear thy words, but they will not do them; for with their mouth they show much love, but their heart goeth after their covetousness'; it is but a show of devotion.

Use 1. Is comfort to sincere worshippers.

1. God knoweth their persons; that there is such a man in the world, the desires of whose soul are to the remembrance of his name. It is an usual temptation which haunteth the children of God, that in the throng of his creatures he forgetteth us: Isa. xl. 27, 'My way is hid from the Lord, and my judgment is passed over by my God;' God looketh not after me, taketh no notice of those things which concern me, or regardeth not my cause and complaint. How doth God know all things, and not know you? All things are under a providence, but his people are under a special providence. Christ saith of the sparrows, Luke xii. 6, 'Not one of them is forgotten before God;' and are his children forgotten? No, 'Christ knoweth his sheep by name' John x. 3; and to Moses, Exod. xxxiii. 12, 'I know thee by name' A father cannot forget how many children he hath, though his family be never so large and numerous.

2. He knoweth their condition, and wants, and weaknesses: Mat. vi. 32, 'Your heavenly Father knoweth that you have need of these things; 7 and ver. 8, 'Your Father knoweth what things ye have need of before you ask him' Yet asking is necessary, solemnly to act your faith and dependence; but he will not neglect or forget us; his omnisciency giveth all that have interest in him that hope.

3. Our prayers are heard, though never so secret: Mat. vi. 6, 'Thy Father which seeth thee in secret shall reward thee openly' though confined within the closet of the heart: Acts ix. 11, 'And the Lord said unto him, Arise, and go into the street which is called Strait, and inquire in the house of Judas for one called Saul of Tarsus, for behold, he prayeth.'

4. Our prayers shall be rightly understood. There are many good motions known to God which we either will not or cannot take notice of in ourselves; as many times large affection to God overlooketh that little good which is in us, but God doth not overlook it. It is well when we can say as Peter, John xxi. 17, 'And he said unto him, Lord thou knowest all things, thou knowest that I love thee.' But he owneth sincerity where we can scarce own it; and many a serious soul hath his condition safe before God, when he cannot count it so himself. This is implied in this place.

Use 2. Caution. Let us take heed of all hypocrisy in prayer, or putting ourselves into a garb of devotion when the temper of our hearts suiteth not; let not your lips pray without or against your hearts.

[A.] Without your hearts. That may be done two ways—

(1.) When you pray words by rote, and all that while the tongue is an utter stranger to the heart; as some birds will counterfeit the voice of a man, so many men do that of a saint, saying words pre scribed by others or invented by themselves, without life and affection; this is to personate and act a part before God, complaining of burdens we feel not, and expressing desires we have not. In these is verified that of our Saviour: Mat. xv. 8, 'This people draweth nigh unto me with their mouth, and honoureth me with their lips, but their heart is far from me'; or that of the prophet: Jer. xii. 2, 'Thou art near in their mouth, and far from their reins'; they do but compliment God with empty formalities.

(2.) When we pray cursorily, or use a few general words that serve all turns and persons alike, but are not suited and fitted to our case. Unless all your confessions and desires be particular, they do not affect the heart; for generals are but notions, and pierce not very deep: 1 Kings viii. 38, 'What prayer and supplication shall be made for any man, or by all the people, which shall know every man the plague of his own heart'; that is the sin whereby his own conscience and heart is smitten, and thereby moved to pray. It is easy to spend invectives against sin in the general; this doth not come close enough to stir up deep compunction and holy desires. We pray of course, but do not bemoan ourselves, and draw forth our earnest requests for the things we stand in need of. Names are prized when we hate the thing, and names are hated when we love the thing.

[B.] Against the heart; when you are loath to leave the sin which you seem to pray against; or ask that grace which you have no mind to have: Ps. lxvi. 18, 'If I regard iniquity in my heart, the Lord will not hear me'. He that asketh for that grace he would not have, doth but lie to God.

Now, to quicken you to this caution, take these considerations—

(1.) No wandering thought in prayer is hidden from God: Job xlii. 2, 'No thought can be withholden from thee;' from his notice and knowledge: Ps. cxxxix. 2, 'Thou knowest my thoughts afar off;' your thoughts are as visible to God as your words are audible to men.

(2.) God most abhorreth our prayers when we pray with an idol in our hearts: Ezek. xiv. 3, 'These men have set up idols in their hearts, should I be inquired of them? saith the Lord'. They were resolved what to do, yet would ask counsel of God; as many now would keep their lusts, yet pray against them; as if the very complaining were a discharge of their duty, without detesting, without endeavouring.

(3.) Above all things, God looketh to the spirit, what the poise and bent of the heart is: Prov. xvi. 2, 'God weigheth the spirit' The Spirit puts us in the balance of the sanctuary; therefore look to principles, ends, and aims.

(4.) That in covenanting with God there may be a moral sincerity where there is not a supernatural sincerity: Deut. v. 28, 29, 'I have heard the words of this people, which they have spoken unto thee; they have well said all that they have spoken. Oh that there were such an heart in them that they would fear me, and keep all my commandments always!' They dissembled not for the time, which may happen in two cases by some impendent or incumbent judgment, as when people are frightened into a little religiousness, or in a pang of devotion or solemn worship. Now this should make us cautelous[52]. Bring to God the best desires and purposes that you have, but rest not in them, but get them strengthened yet more and more, that our sincerity may be verified and evidenced.

Secondly, I come now to the second thing God 'knoweth the mind of the Spirit'.

Doctrine That it is a comfort to God's children that the Lord knoweth what kind of spirit is working in prayer.

Here I shall do three things

1. Show the different spirit that worketh in prayer.

2. In what sense God is said to know the mind of the Spirit.

3. Why this is such a comfort to God's children.

1. The different spirit that may work in prayer. I shall take notice of a fourfold spirit

[A.] The natural spirit of a man, seeking its own welfare, which is not a sin; for God put it into us; and such an inclination there was in Christ himself: Mat. xxvi. 39, 'my Father! If it be possible, let this cup pass from me; nevertheless, not as I will, but as thou wilt'; and John xii. 27, 28, 'Father, save me from this hour; but for this cause came I to this hour' There was the innocent desire of his human nature to be freed from the burden; but his greater respect to God's glory and the public benefit of mankind made him submit to it. His human nature was to show a reasonable aversation from what was destructive to it; but his resolved will was to

---

[52] Cautious, wary. Possibly crafty, cunning

submit to God, and overcome all impediments. Take the instance lower. Nature prompted Paul to ask freedom from the thorn in the flesh; but grace taught him to submit to God's will. Paul sinned not in having or giving vent to the natural inclination; but the spiritual instinct must guide and overrule it. So when we ask natural conveniences we sin not, but yet this is not the spirit which God heareth in prayer. 'Christ was heard, in that he feared' Heb. v. 7; yet the cup did not pass away, but he was supported; so Paul was heard, not for the removal of the thorn in the flesh, but for sufficient grace: 2 Cor. xii. 9, 'And he said unto me, my grace is sufficient for thee, for my strength is made perfect in weakness.'

[B.] There is a carnal, sinful spirit, which may be working in prayer; as when the disciples called for fire from heaven, Christ telleth them, Luke ix. 55, 'Ye know not of what spirit ye are of.' Men often miscarry in prayer, being blinded either by an erring judgment, or their carnal passions.

(1.) By an erring judgment. They put their false conceits and opinions into their prayers, and so would engage God, as Balaam sought by building altars, against his own people. This kind of praying, it is a begging of God to do the devil's work, to destroy his own kingdom, and suppress his most serious worshippers to gratify the faction that opposeth them. Nothing is so cruel and bloody but false and partial zeal will put men upon, if their judgments be once tainted; they think the killing of others is doing God good service, John xvi. 2. Their devotions will be soon tainted also; for men that follow a blind con science will hallow and consecrate their rage and cruelty by prayer and solemn worship: Isa. lxvi. 5, 'Your brethren that hate you, that cast you out for my name's sake, said, Let the Lord be glorified'; thence the old by word, *In nomine Domini incipit omne malum*[53]; prayer is made a preface to cruelty. Now it is a comfort to the faithful that God will not hear these prayers; he knows what is the mind of the Spirit.

(2.) By carnal passions and desires. Fleshly interest breedeth partiality; and men think God should hear them in their worldly requests. The motions of the flesh are very earnest, for corrupt nature would fain be pleased: James iv. 3, 'Ye ask and have not, because ye ask amiss, that ye may consume it upon your lusts'; it is the flesh prayeth, and not the spirit 'You ask meat for your lusts,' Ps. lxxviii. 18. When their wants were abundantly supplied, yet they remained querulous and unsatisfied; they must have dainties as well as necessaries, as if God's providence must serve their carnal appetites. In these and such like cases the flesh prayeth, and not the spirit; but Christ will not put this dross into his golden censer, nor perfume our lusts with his sweet incense.

[C.] The new nature, called also spirit, which inclineth us to God heaven: Zech, xii. 10, 'I will pour upon them the spirit of grace and supplication.' This prompteth and urgeth us to ask spiritual and heavenly things; and such kind of requests are most pleasing to God, 1 Kings iii. 10; those things which are necessary to God's glory and our salvation. There is what the

---

[53] In the name of the Lord all evil begins.

flesh savoureth and what the spirit savoureth. The wisdom of the flesh perverteth and diverteth hearts from God and heaven to base, low things, such as the good things of this world pleasures, riches, honours. But the spirit, or the renewed part, savoureth other things. What is the savouring of the spirit? What the new nature would be at, or chiefly desireth. And it is a truth that the same spirit which is predominant at other times will work in prayer; for the desires follow the constitution and frame of the heart: Rom. viii. 5, 'For they that are after the flesh do mind the things of the flesh; but they that are after the Spirit the things of the spirit.' As their constitution is, so will their gust be; and this taste and relish will show itself in all things, even in their prayers and devotions; and whatever their words be, the working of their hearts are according to their universal bent and temper.

[D.] The Holy Spirit of God: Jude 20, 'Praying in the Holy Ghost'. His assistance is necessary to prayer, not only to sanctify our hearts, but to excite our desires and direct our addresses to God; so that we are enabled and raised to perform this duty with more ardency and regularity than we of ourselves could attain unto. A Christian hath both flesh and spirit in him, and they remain in him as active principles, always lusting against each other, Gal. v. 17. In prayer we feel it; for the saints speak sometimes in a mixed dialect, half the language of Ashdod and half of Canaan, both of the flesh and of the spirit, only the one overruleth the other by the power of the Holy Ghost. Take it in either property of prayer confidence, or fervency of desire.

(1.) For confidence: Jonah ii. 4, 'I said, I am cast out of thy sight; yet I will look again to thy holy temple.' There is a plain conflict between faith and unbelief; unbelief's words are first out, as if we were utterly rejected out of God's care and favour; yet faith will not suffer us to keep off from God, and therefore corrects and unsaith again what unbelief had said before'; Yet I will look again to thy holy temple,' try what God will do for me. So Ps. xciv. 18, 'When I said, My foot slippeth; thy mercy, Lord, held me up'; yet there is relief in God when all their own confidence and courage faileth them.

(2.) In point of fervency. The flesh valueth, esteemeth, earnestly craveth temporal mercies; fancieth a condition of health, wealth, liberty, and worldly conveniencies, as best for us. We admire carnal happiness, Ps. cxliv; but the spirit corrects the judgment of the flesh. There is a higher and better happiness; and that we should mainly seek after, and all our worldly interests should be subordinated there unto. Now it is not merely the spirit or new nature in us which doth hold out in these conflicts, but the new nature assisted by the Spirit of God, who helpeth us in all our infirmities, and to whom religious manners showeth we must ascribe all that we have and do. All our faith and fervency cometh from him; and without his assistance we should either sink under the difficulties, or be cold and careless in our requests.

2. In what sense God is said to know the mind of the Spirit.

[A.] By way of distinction.

[B.] By way of approbation.

[A.] By way of distinction. God perfectly knoweth the mind and intention of those groans which the Spirit exciteth in his own children; he knoweth what cometh from the *natural*, what from the *carnal*, what from the *divine* Spirit; to what principles these motions belong. For he 'weigheth the spirits,' Prov. xvi. 2; that is, he doth so exactly know them, as if they were put into a balance; what principles, motives, and aims we are acted by; and observeth not only the matter of the prayer, but the disposition of the petitioner; whether the frame of his heart be Christian and gospel-like; humble, holy, and heavenly; or else it hath a carnal bias upon it.

[B.] He knoweth by way of approbation, that he doth regard and accept the groans of the spirit; for words of knowledge imply allowance, respect, approbation; as Ps. i. 6, 'God knoweth the way of the righteous, but the way of the wicked shall perish'; approveth, favoureth, prospereth, as the opposite clause manifesteth. As Christ's not knowing the wicked implieth their rejection, Mat. vii. 23: so he knoweth the mind of the Spirit, he doth regard and accept of what is of the Spirit in prayer. The groans of believers are more than the pompous petitions of hypocrites; it is not luscious eloquence which God regardeth, but serious devotion; if there be holy breathings after communion with him; if your prayers be not senseless, without a due feeling of your necessities and wants; nor heartless, without a desire of the graces and mercies you stand in need of, God will accept you.

3. Why this is such a comfort and benefit to the children of God.

[A.] God's knowledge by way of distinction between the moans of nature and the groans of the Spirit.

(1.) Because sometimes they do not speak in prayer, but join with others; you make it your prayer if you accompany it with your sighs and groans; it is not the speaker only, but all that consent by the serious motions of their hearts. When the gifted prayed in the primitive church, the *idiotes*, the private person—we translate it 'the unlearned'—was to say amen, 1 Cor. xiv. 16; and then it was his prayer as much as the prayer of him that spake; their hearty amen was *signaculum fidei, et votum desiderii*, a hearty assent to the prayer, or a hearty expression of their earnest desire.

(2.) Sometimes they cannot speak and put their desires into a language, as oppressed with troubles. God knoweth the secret groans of our hearts, when you cannot give them the vent of expression: Ps. xxxviii. 9, 'Lord, all my desire is before thee; my groaning is not hid from thee.' The soul is so confounded that we cannot put our desires into distinct thoughts and words; but yet they are as formal speech before God, for he can interpret the most secret motions of our hearts: Exod. ii. 24, 'God heard their groans, and remembered his covenant'; Ps. xii. 5, 'For the oppression of the poor, for the sighing of the needy, now will I arise, saith the Lord'; Ps. vi. 8. 'For the Lord hath heard the voice of my weeping. 'Such sighs, groans, tears, have an intelligible language in heaven. .

(3.) Sometimes they dare not speak. For the prophet telleth us of an evil time when 'the prudent will keep silence' Amos v. 13; and another prophet speaketh when a man cannot 'trust in a friend' and must 'keep the door of his mouth from her that lieth in his bosom'

Micah vii. 5; when they dare not speak against that which they cannot mend, scarce dare peep or mutter or bemoan themselves, or plead with God. Such is the iniquity of the times, the guard is put upon them; then God knoweth the desires of their hearts, and smothered griefs and concealed complaints.

(4.) Sometimes they are slandered when they speak ^by the scoffing atheist or carnal world, who know not the Spirit and his holy motions, because their heart is wholly devoted to sensual and earthly things; the best strains of devotion are mocked at, and all that suiteth not with their carnal way is counted folly: 1 Peter iv. 4, 'Speaking evil of you'; and ver. 14, 'On their part the Spirit is evil spoken of.' The world, when they hear of believers praying in the Spirit, they scoff at it; as those, Acts ii. 13, when the Holy Ghost came upon the apostles, some 'mocked, saying, These men are full of new wine'; so when anything of God more than ordinary appeareth in them, they deride it. They are not skilled in the motions of the Spirit when they are earnest. 'Festus thought Paul mad, and beside himself', Acts xxvi. 24. The wisdom of the flesh is enmity against God, and cannot judge aright of his ways and motions. But now it is a comfort that God will put another kind of construction upon the Spirit's working than the world doth; they call evil good, and good evil; but God can distinguish; they are incompetent judges, having no savour and relish of these things. Many things suit not with the corrupt sense of men, that are yet agreeable to God's holy will; and that which is slandered in the world is owned by God; and how much soever they are contradicted and scoffed at, yet they enjoy sweet and real communion with him. Though the world knoweth not this Spirit, yet God knoweth and owneth it, as the event declareth.

(5.) Sometimes they themselves find it hard to interpret their duty, and judge what is flesh and what is spirit, but yet God knoweth the mind of the Spirit; and when they set themselves to converse with God in the best fashion they can, the Lord granteth the desires of their hearts: Ps. lxvi. 19, 'Verily God hath heard, he hath attended to the voice of my prayer'. We find our prayers are not rejected by God; he hath some doubt of it, as appeareth in the verses before and after; and so took it as a token of his sincerity. God, who cannot patronise any sin, had been pleased to give him his approbation.

(6.) The saints that are little satisfied in their work plead their desires: Nehem. i. 11, 'Lord, I beseech thee, let now thine ear be attentive to the prayer of thy servant, and to the prayer of thy servants who desire to fear thy name'; and Isa. xxvi. 9, 'With my soul have I desired thee in the night; yea, with my spirit will I seek thee right early.'

(7.) The children of God may be the better satisfied in his providence and favours to them; for God will hear so much of the prayer as cometh from the Spirit. We ask natural conveniences to a certain end; God will not always give the means, but the end shall be promoted; he knoweth whether the means will prove a mercy, yea or no, or the end be promoted by these means or other. Now they desire the spirit may be heard, not the flesh. Abraham would have the promise fulfilled, and pitcheth on Ishmael: Gen. xvii. 18, 'Oh that Ishmael might live before thee! 'But God intended a better way by Isaac. If he give us our will, it is in anger; that is our prayer; but the Spirit's prayer is to glorify God, and according to the will of God. God's answer is according to the mind of the Spirit.

[B.] God's knowing by way of approbation, that he will accept and regard the prayer stirred up in us by his Spirit. The reason is given in the text, 'because he maketh requests for the saints according to the will of God'. In which clause we have—

1. The work—'he maketh intercession'

2. The persons for whom—'for the saints.'

3. The rule, nature, or kind of intercession—*kata theos*, 'according to the will of God.'

Let us, *1st*, Open these things, *2dly*, Consider why the prayer so made must needs be acceptable and pleasing to God.

1. The work of the Spirit—'he maketh intercession'; that is, exciteth and directeth us to pray; he employeth and maketh use of our faculties, mind and heart and tongue; yea, of our graces, faith, hope, and love. Of faith to believe God's being and providence, both as to his present government, internal or external, or as to the future and eternal recompenses. This faith is the life of prayer; for 'how shall they call on him in whom they have not believed?' Rom. x. 14, and Heb. xi. 6 Of our hope; looking for these things, we ask of him according to his will; otherwise prayer is but a wearisome, fruitless task: Mai. iii. 14, 'It is in vain to serve God; what profit is it to call upon him?' When we expect what we ask, there is more life in asking: Ps. cxxx. 5, 'I wait for the Lord, my soul doth wait, and in his word do I hope'; that is the posture of the soul in prayer. And for love; for here we come to show our hearty groans after everything which will bring us nearer to God. Surely they that call upon God aright are they which 'delight themselves in the Almighty' Job xxvii. 10. The duty is an act of love; and the life of the duty cometh from the fervency of our love, for it is a solemn expression of our desires. If God be our portion, we will thirst after him, and express our desires after what conduceth to communion with him. Thus the Spirit maketh use of our faculties and graces; he strengtheneth our faith, quickeneth our love, and stirreth up our hope; so that, as it is said, Mat. x. 20, c It is not ye speak, but the Spirit of your Father that speaketh in you'; when he doth enable us to speak what is fit and proper before the tribunals of men. So he maketh intercession when he enableth understanding creatures to speak what is fit and proper before the throne of grace, what will become faith, hope, and love.

2. The persons for whom he prayeth 'for the saints' for two reasons

[A.] Because the saints only are acquainted with these operations: 1 Cor. ii. 14, 'The natural man receiveth not the things of the Spirit'; and John xiv. 17, 'Whom the world cannot receive, because they know him not and see him not'. They do not regard his motions and operations, but have their eyes fixed upon this world, and the sins and vanities thereof; they have no mind to employ him, though he offereth himself to them, but the saints cannot live without him.

[B.] These are only fit to converse with God in prayer. The persons are qualified for audience and acceptance with God, and may obtain whatsoever in reason and righteousness we can ask of him: 1 John iii. 22, 'And whatsoever we ask we receive, because we keep his commandments, and do what is pleasing in his sight.' None else are in grace and favour with God, and in a receiving posture, according to the terms of the promise; none but such as are justified, sanctified, and live in obedience to him: Prov. xv. 8, 'The sacrifice of the wicked is an abomination to the Lord, but the prayer of the upright is his delight'; John ix. 31, 'God heareth not sinners; but if any man be a worshipper of God, and doth his will, him he heareth'; and James v. 16, 'The fervent effectual prayer of a righteous man availeth much;' and Ps. lxvi. 18, 'If I regard iniquity in my heart, the Lord will not hear me'; so Prov. xxviii. 9, 'He that turneth away his ear from hearing the law, even his prayer is an abomination'; these, and many more places, show who are they who have God's ear. The saints, and none but they; who are careful to avoid all known sin, and make conscience of per forming all known duty. Then you will have a large share in his heart and love; and he will be near you when you call upon him, to counsel, quicken, and direct you, and, give you answers of grace upon all occasions.

3. The rule, nature, or kind of this intercession he puts us upon; *kata theos* is the same with *katho dei*, ver. 26, 'according to the will of God,' for matter and manner, and ask lawful things, to a holy and lawful end.

[A.] The matter of the prayer: 1 John v. 14, 15, 'And this is the confidence that we have in him, that if we ask anything according to his will, he heareth us.'

What is the meaning of that, 'According to his will'?

Answer (1.) With conformity to his revealed will. (2.) With due submission to and reservation of his secret will.

(1.) With conformity to his revealed and commanding will: that we ask nothing unjust and unholy, as if we would have God to bless us in some unlawful purpose, or, being biased by envy, revenge, or any corrupt and carnal affection, ask anything contrary to piety, justice, charity, or that holy, meek spirit which should be in Christians. Unlawful desires vented in prayer are a double evil, as they are contrary to God's commanding will, and as they are presented to him in prayer to accomplish what we desire by his help, as we would have him accommodate his providence to fulfil our lusts.

(2.) With a due reservation of and submission to his secret and decreeing will. The things we ask of God are of three sorts—First, barely lawful; so is every indifferent thing, as when Moses would fain enter into Canaan. We cannot say God will give us such things; God denied it to Moses'; Let it suffice thee, speak no more of this matter, Deut. iii. 22. God would only give him a Pisgah[54] sight. Secondly, not only lawful, but commanded, such a thing as may fall within the com pass of our duty; as when parents ask the conversion of their children, or children beg the continuance of their parents' life, it is not only lawful, but commanded; yet God disposeth of the event as it pleaseth him. Thirdly, somethings are absolutely good and necessary for us, as the gift of the Holy Spirit, Luke xi. 13. Such God will give. But in the two former things we must use the means, but refer the event to God, who

---

[54] The mountain from which Moses viewed the Promised Land, not being allowed to enter it.

can best dispose of us to his own glory; for though the thing be lawful, though it be good, yet it beareth these exceptions First, If it be not contrary to any decree of God, and cross not the harmony of his providence. Would we have God rescind and disorder his wise counsels for our sake? Secondly, If it be not inconvenient and hurtful for us; but of that God will be judge. Some present temporal good may be a cause of future inconvenience; and something bitter now, may be afterward found wholesome. God knoweth whether life or death be best, a present riddance of troubles or a continuance of them; therefore it followeth, ver. 28, 'All things shall work together for good to them that love God.' That which is apprehended as evil may turn to good; therefore these things should not be peremptorily asked, but with limitation and exception of God's will; as our Lord Christ, Mat. xxvi. 39, 'And he went a little farther, and fell on his face and prayed, saying, my Father! If it be possible, let this cup pass from me; nevertheless, not as I will, but as thou wilt.' It is one thing to believe for certain that God will grant our petition with this condition, if the grant be for his glory and our good, and another thing to believe absolutely that he will not deny the particular thing we ask of him, without such exception and reservation. It is not for us to determine what is most conducing to God's glory and desirable for us; we must commit and submit to God, to our heavenly Father, who is never backward to our good, and will certainly guide all things for the best.

[B.] The manner.

(1.) With faith. What faith have we in prayer? With respect to God, that he is able and willing to help his people; that we need not run to other shifts, and be divided between God and carnal means, James i. 6-8. As to the acceptance of our persons, we must pray that we do not weaken our confidence by any allowed sin: 1 John iii. 20, 21, 'For if our hearts condemn us, God is greater than our hearts, and knoweth all things; if our hearts condemn us not, then have we confidence towards God'; we sin away our peace, and then cannot come cheerfully to God. As to the particular blessings asked, necessary, that are absolutely promised, must be absolutely expected. But the promise of the common blessings of this life is not absolute; these things are dispensed as shall be for God's glory and our good. The saints themselves express themselves with some hesitancy about these things, though inclined to hope the best; as David, 2 Sam. xii. 22, 'Who can tell whether the Lord will not be gracious to me, that the child may live? 'God knoweth what we most really want, and what is most agreeable to our desires, being able to choose for us better than we can for ourselves: Joel ii. 14, 'Who knoweth if he will return and leave a blessing? '

(2.) With fervency, or that life and seriousness which will become addresses to God: Mat. vii. 7, 'Ask, seek, knock'; we are not in good earnest unless we set ourselves to seek the Lord, Dan. ix. 3. Christ taught us to pray in two parables; one for the Spirit, Luke xi., by a man coming to his friend for loaves at midnight; for right done to the church, Luke xviii. 1, in the parable of the widow and unjust judge. Persevere till prayer be answered, Mat. xv. 26, 27; keep wrestling and striving with God: Rom. xv. 30, < Now I beseech you, brethren, for the Lord Jesus Christ's sake, and for the love of the Spirit, that ye strive together with me in your prayers to God for me.'

(3.) With humility; we must come as 'less than the least of his mercies,' Gen. xxxii. 10; Ezra ix. 6, 'O my God, I am ashamed, and blush to lift up my face to thee my God'; as the publican, Luke xviii. 13, 'God be merciful to me a sinner;' as Abraham, Gen. xviii. 27, 'Behold now I have taken upon me to speak unto the Lord, who am but dust and ashes.'

(4.) With holy ends, that God may be glorified: John xiv. 13, 'And whatsoever ye shall ask in my name, that will I do, that the Father may be glorified in the Son;' in the Spirit, John xvi. 14, 'He shall glorify me, for he shall receive of mine, and shall show it unto you'; Ps. cxv. 1, 'Not unto us, O Lord, not unto us, but unto thy name give glory;' Joel ii. 14, 'Who knoweth if he will return and repent, and leave a blessing behind him, even a meat offering and a drink offering unto the Lord our God? '

2dly, The reasons why the prayers so made must be acceptable to God.

1. Because here all the divine persons concur. We pray according to God's will, in Christ's name and mediation, by the motion and instinct of the Spirit. Everyone is a ground of hope; therefore it will not be lost labour, or breath poured out into the air: 2 Sam. xiv. 1, 'When Joab perceived that the king's heart was towards Absalom, 'he makes use of the advantage. Christ's merit breeds confidence: Heb. x. 19, 'Having therefore, brethren, boldness to enter into the holiest by the blood of Jesus.' And then the Spirit's motion; God accepteth what cometh from himself: Ps. x. 17, 'Lord, thou hast heard the desire of the humble, thou wilt prepare their heart, thou wilt cause thine ear to hear' what is excited and stirred up in us by his Spirit.

2. On man's part, the person is qualified, the petition just, the end right, and the heart excited.

Use. Is to show us what prayers are heard; such as (1.) cometh from God, and (2.) are made to God. Certainly such shall be dealt with as friends; God will bestow marks of abundant favour upon them, and reward their love and obedience by hearing their prayers; he delights to do great things for their sakes, and will have it known that their supplication is acceptable to him. Oh! Pray thus by the Spirit.

1. Is your prayer such a prayer as cometh from God? Such a prayer as is inspired by the Spirit, holy and fervent? Holy, for he is a holy and heavenly spirit, and puts us mainly upon holy and heavenly things; things that always make us better, not worse; and in other things referring our choices to God, what he liketh and thinketh best for us, not what we do for ourselves: 'not my will, but thine be done.' Then fervent, *deesis energoumene*: James v. 16, 'The fervent effectual prayer of a righteous man,' when it looketh like wrestling with God.

2. To God. Like worship relating to God, it hath the stamp of his nature upon it. Some of his attributes relate to his mercy and goodness, some to his majesty and greatness; the one is seen in the joy of our faith and confidence, by our delight to converse with him; the other in our humility and deep reverence of God, when we come to him as poor undone creatures without his grace.

SERMON XXXVII

And we know that all things work together for good to them that love God, to them who are the called according to his purpose.

Romans viii. 28.

IN the former verse the apostle telleth us how the Spirit maketh intercession for the saints, what God liketh and thinketh best for them, not what they like themselves most profitable, though not most pleasing. Green fruit is most pleasing to the appetite of the child, but the parent knoweth it is not so wholesome; on the other side, medicinal potions are bitter, but they tend to health; therefore, though the afflictions continue, God may hear our prayers, for we find this best for us in the issue, 'And we know' &c.

In the words

First, a privilege. *Secondly*, the persons qualified.

In the privilege, observe First, The certainty of it—and we know. Secondly, The nature of it; and there—

[A.] The extent of it—All things; prosperity, adversity, all the varieties of conditions we pass through.

[B.] The manner of working—Work together, with the Spirit say some, *cooperantur, non per se operantur*. This is a truth, but not of this place. The poisonous ingredients which are used in a medicine do good, not of themselves, but as ordered and tempered by the skill of the physician. Rather 'work together' *omnia semel adjumenta sunt*, as Beza paraphrastically rendereth it; singly they are against us, if we look upon providences by pieces, as there is no beauty in the scattered pieces that are framed for a building till they are all set together; so men look upon God's work by halves.

[3.] The end and issue; for good. Sometimes for good temporal, for our greater preservation; but rather for good spiritual, the increase of grace; chiefly for eternal good, to fit us and prepare us for the blessedness of the everlasting estate: this is the privilege.

Secondly, A description of the persons who enjoy it.

1. By their act towards God—To them that love God, believing his mercy and goodness in Christ. They love him above all things, and are willing to hazard and venture all things for him.

2. God's act or work upon them; they are effectually called—To them who are the called according to purpose. There is a distinctive term by which God's purpose is intended; they are called; not obiter, by the by, as they live within the hearing and sound of the gospel, but according to God's eternal purpose, and the good pleasure of his grace.

I begin with the privilege.

Doctrine That all things that befall God's children in this life are directed by his providence to their eternal happiness.

First, I shall explain this point with respect to the circumstances of the text. Secondly, Give a more general state of the case. The first will be done

1. By opening the nature of the privilege.

2. The certainty of it.

1. The nature of it; and there we begin with

[A.] The extent 'All things.' It must be limited by the context, which speaketh of the afflictions of the saints.

(1.) All manner of sufferings and trials for righteousness' sake, such as reproaches, stripes, spoiling of goods, imprisonment, banishment, death, all such kind of things. Reproaches are as dung cast upon the grass, which seemeth to stain it for a while, but afterwards it springeth up with a fresher verdure[55]. Stripes are painful to the flesh, but occasion greater joy to the soul; as Paul and Silas after they were scourged sung at midnight in the stocks, Acts xvi. Spoiling of goods stirreth up serious reflections on a more enduring substance; the hopes whereof we have in ourselves, Heb. x. 34. Imprisonment doth but shut us up from temptations, that we may be at liberty for a more free converse with God; as Tertullian telleth his martyrs—'You went out of prison when you went into prison, and were but sequestered from the world for more intimacy with the Holy Ghost.' So banishment; every place is alike near to heaven, and the whole earth is the Lord's, and the fulness thereof. They know no banishment that know no home here in the world; but because we have an affection to our natural comforts, especially to the place of our service, God is wont to recompense his exiles with an increase of spiritual blessings; as John had his revelations when banished to Patmos, Rev. i. 9. Death doth but hasten our glory; if the guest be turned out of the old house, you 'have a building of God, eternal in the heavens,' 2 Cor. v. 1, and so do but leave a shed to live in a palace. Though your life be forced out by the violence of men, the sword is but the key to open heaven's doors for you, and you are freed from hard task-masters to go home to your gracious Lord.

(2.) Ordinary afflictions incident to men. Are you pained with sick ness, and roll to and fro on your bed, like a door on the hinges, through the restless weariness of the flesh? Many times we are best when we are weakest, and the pains of the body help to the invigorating and renewing the inward man, 2 Cor iv. 16. In heaven you shall have ever lasting ease, for that is a state of rest. Have you lost children? If God give you a better name than sons and daughters, you have no cause to complain, Isa. lvi. 5. It is honour enough to you that you are children of God; if poor and destitute, yet if rich in the gifts and graces of the Spirit, it is made up to you: Rev. ii. 9, 'I know thy poverty, but thou art rich' But it is not expedient to name all cases; whatever the calamity and affliction be, God knoweth how to turn it to

---

[55] lush green vegetation

good, so that though we restrain 'all things 'to the context, it is large enough for our consolation.

But is there not more in it? For men are always given to over-gospeling and enlarging their privileges—doth it not comprehend sin?

Answer, No, not in the intention of the apostle. God hath not made a promise that all the sins of believers shall work for their good. It is true God made advantage of the sins of the world for the honouring of the grace in Christ, Rom v. 16, 17. It should be our care that Satan may be a loser, and Christ have more honour by every sin we commit. True repentance can draw good out of sin itself, to be a means of our hatred and mortification of it; so love and gratitude to our Redeemer: Luke vii. 47, 'Her sins, which are many, are forgiven, for she loved much; but to whom little is forgiven, the same loveth little' Sin doth not do good as sin, but as repented of; it is not the sin, but the repentance. But for the proof of this 1. Then it would destroy the qualification mentioned in the text 'Those that love God.' Our love is a love of duty; none love God but those that obey him and keep his commandments. 2. To assure us aforehand that our sins would turn to our good would open a gap to looseness, and is contrary to the usual methods of God in his word, who commands obedience, with a promise of increase of grace, and threateneth disobedience, and punisheth it also, by hardness of heart, and a tradition, or giving us up to vile affections. Now there would be no reconciling these passages if God assured us by promise that our sins should turn to good, and yet sins be punished with blindness of mind and hardness of heart. 3. If any should object, they mean infirmities, not grievous and heinous sins; yet even then they see a reason to limit this universal particle, *panta*, and so have lost the advantage. But whether they limit it enough, let us see. It is one thing to say they shall not hurt us; it is another to say they shall conduce to our good, or are means appointed to that end. 4. If God make use of our infirmities for our good, it is to be ascribed to his grace, who bringeth good out of so great an evil; as David by his fall got wisdom, Ps. li. 6; it was the Lord's mercy that made him thereby more sensible of his duty, watchful over a naughty heart. But this is no natural effect of sin; and to say God hath promised it, it would tempt us to omit our caution, and so we should lose this benefit. God, of his wonderful grace, may do many things which he does not think fit to assure us of by promise. 5. We see many Christians fall from some degrees of grace which they never afterwards recover again, though preserved in the state of grace for the main. God will not vouchsafe to them such a liberal portion of his Spirit as they had before. Jehoshaphat is said, 2 Chron. xvii. 3, to have 'walked in the first ways of his father David'; his first ways were his best ways, when he kept himself free from those scandalous crimes he fell into in his latter time.

But doth it not imply that our prosperity shall turn to good, as well as adversity?

Answer, Though it be not formally expressed in this place, which speaketh only of sufferings and afflictions, yet it is virtually included. For, 1. God keepeth off, or bringeth on the cross as it worketh for our good; and all providences wherein the elect are concerned are over ruled by his grace for their good: Cant. iv. 16, 'Awake, north wind, and come, thou south, blow upon my garden, that the spices therein may flow out.' Out of what corner soever the wind bloweth, it bloweth good to the saints, the sharp north wind or the sultry south wind. 2. It is a threatening to them that do not love God, that their prosperity tendeth to their hurt: Ps. lxix. 22, 'Let their table become a snare, and that which should be for their welfare become a trap' Their worldly comforts serve to harden their hearts in sin. 3. The sanctifying of their prosperity is included in a Christian's charter: 1 Cor. iii. 21-23, 'All things are yours, life or death, the present world and the future world, because you are Christ's, and Christ is God's'; their prosperity cometh from the love of God, and tendeth to their good. Therefore let this be included, though afflictions are chiefly spoken of in the context.

[B.] The manner of bringing it about 'They work together' Take anything single and apart, and it seemeth to be against us. We must distinguish between a part of God's work and the end of it. We cannot understand God's providence till he hath done his work; he is an impatient spectator that cannot tarry till the last act, wherein all errors are reconciled; as Christ told Peter, John xiii. 6, 7, 'What I do thou knowest not now, but thou shalt know hereafter.' We are much in the dark; we look only to present sense and appearance; his purposes are hidden from us; for the agent is 'wise in counsel and excellent in working.' His way of working is under a veil of contraries, and unperceivable to an ordinary eye; he bringeth something out of nothing, light out of darkness, meat out of the eater. His end is not to satisfy our sense and curiosity, but try our faith, John vi. 6, to exercise our submission and patience, as in the case of Job, and our dependence and prayer. God knoweth what he is a-doing with you, when you know not: Jer. xxix. 11, 'For I know the thoughts that I think towards you, saith the Lord; thoughts of peace, and not of evil, to give you an expected end' When we view providence by pieces, and see God rending and tearing all things in pieces, we are perplexed; therefore we must not judge of God's providence by the beginnings, till all work together. When we apprehend nothing but ruin, God may be designing to us the choicest mercies: Ps. xxxi. 22, 'For I said in my haste, I am cut off from before thine eyes; nevertheless, thou heardest the voice of my supplication'; so Ps. cxvi. 11, 'I said in my haste, All men are liars'—Samuel, and all that had told him he should enjoy the kingdom. Haste never speaketh well of God and his promises, nor maketh any good comment on his dealings; we must stay till all causes work.

[C.] The end and issue 'For good'

1. Sometimes to good temporal, or our better preservation during our service: Gen. 1. 20, 'But as for you, ye thought evil against me, but God meant it unto good, to bring it to pass as it is at this day, and to save much people alive'. Both the Egyptians and themselves had wanted a preserver, if he had not been sold and sent into Egypt. We often find by experience that God ordereth our disappointments for good. Suppose a man's heart were much set upon a voyage to sea, but he is hindered by many impediments, and before he cometh the ship is gone; and afterwards he heareth that all that were in the vessel were drowned: this disappointment is for good. Crassus's rival in the Persian war, when he heard how that army was intercepted and cut off by the craft of the barbarians, had no reason to stomach his being refused. Many of us, whose hearts are set upon some worldly thing, have cause to say we had perished if we had not perished, and suffered more if we had suffered

less. In the story of Joseph there is a notable scheme and draught of providence; he is cast into a pit, there to perish; thence, upon second thoughts, drawn forth to be sold to the Ishmaelites; by them brought into Egypt; sold for a slave again. What doth God mean to do with poor Joseph? While a slave, he is tempted to adultery; refusing the temptation, he is falsely accused, kept a long time in ward and duress; all this is against him. Who would have thought that in the issue all should have turned to his good? Who would have thought that the prison had been the way to preferment? that by the pit he should come to the palace of the king of Egypt? that he should exchange his party coloured coat for the royal robes of a king's court? Thus in temporal things we gain by our losses; and God chooseth better for us than we could have chosen for ourselves.

(2.) Spiritual good. So all affliction is made up and recompensed to the soul; it afflicts the body, but bettereth the heart: Ps. cxix. 71, 'It is good for me that I have been afflicted, that I might learn thy statutes.' There is more to be learned in affliction than in the vastest libraries; no book will teach us so much as experience under God's discipline. Madmen are kept in the dark, and under hardship, to bring them to their wits again; so God is forced to use us a little hardly to cure us of our spiritual frenzy. Thou darest not pray, Lord, let me have my worldly comforts, though they damn me; let me not be afflicted, though it do me good; and if thou darest not pray so, wilt thou murmur when God ordereth it so? If a man break an arm or a leg in pulling us out of the water, wherein otherwise we should certainly be drowned, would we be angry with him? And shall we fret against the Lord when he takes away the fuel of our lusts, which will certainly drown us in perdition and everlasting destruction? Is it not a good exchange to part with outward comforts for inward holiness? Certainly that will be of more gain to us than all the affliction, pain, and loss which we suffer will do us hurt. Certainly we lose nothing but our rust by scouring. If God will take away our peace, and give us peace of conscience our worldly goods, and give us true riches, have we any cause to complain? If outward wants may be recompensed by an abundance of inward grace, and we have the less of the world that we may have more of God, and be kept poor and destitute that we may be rich in faith, James ii. 5, who is the loser? If we have a healthy soul in a sick body, as Gaius had, 3 John 2, and an aching head maketh way for a better heart, doth not God deal graciously and lovingly with us? In short, afflictions are compared to fire, that purgeth away the dross, 1 Peter i. 7; to the fan that driveth away the chaff, Mat. iii. 12; to pruning, that cuts off the luxuriant branches, and maketh the other that remain the more fruitful, John xv. 2; to physic, that purgeth away the sick matter, Isa. xxvii. 9; to ploughing and harrowing the ground, that fitteth it to receive the good seed, Jer. iv. 3. And shall we be troubled when God cometh to make use of this fire to purge out our dross? this fan to winnow away our chaff? this pruning to lop off the luxuriances of our souls? this plough to break up our fallow ground, to destroy the weeds that are in our hearts? this sharp medicine to cure our sick souls? Should we not rather rejoice that he will not let us alone in our corruption, but refine us as metal is by the fire? and fan and winnow us, that we may be pure grain? and prune us, that we may be fruitful in holiness? and use medicine, to cure those distempers which otherwise would destroy us? and suffer the ploughers to make long furrows upon our backs, that we may enjoy the richer crop? This is for good.

(3.) For our eternal good. Heaven will make us complete amends for all that we suffer here: 2 Cor. iv. 17, 'Those light afflictions which are but for a moment worketh for us a far more exceeding and eternal weight of glory'; these afflictions are so far from infringing our happiness, that they do promote it. How promote? and how work? Partly as the patient enduring doth secure our interest. God will not fail to reward them that patiently suffer for his sake, or submit to his discipline; for these transitory light afflictions and sufferings are so accepted by him, that they are sure to be rewarded by him: Mat. v. 12, 'Great is your reward in heaven;' and James i. 12, 'Blessed is the man that endureth temptations, for when he is tried he shall receive the crown of life, which God hath promised to them that love him' Partly as they are a means which God useth to draw us off from the love and esteem of the world, and to awaken in us an earnest desire and serious pursuit after heavenly things, Gal. vi. 14. They conduce to mortification, and kill the gust of the flesh; so that our title is not only more secured, but our hearts prepared. Partly because here is the full recompense, the good that answers all objections; if cast out by men, you are received by the Lord; if calumniated by the world, approved by God; if you have lost the love of all men for your faithfulness and sincerity, you shall enjoy the love of God; if imprisoned, you shall shortly be in your Father's house. There all your fears and sorrows will be at an end, your desires accomplished, and your expectations satisfied; it is heaven that turneth pain into pleasure, death into life. And partly because, though we fail in particular conflicts, yet God secureth our everlasting estate. *Romani praelio saepe victi, bello nusquam*[56]. So Christians. We cannot say that always there is such sensible benefits by afflictions; but this is the sense of the place, as the following verses show, that the general issue of things is determined and put out of controversy by it. The infallibility of God's conduct cannot be discerned by every particular event; for a Christian may not gain by every trouble he falleth into, but by all together his eternal estate is promoted; they all are means to preserve us till we come to heaven. Thus you see how he that could turn stones into bread, water into wine, can extract a blessing out of our saddest miseries and afflictions, and make the bitterest herbs to yield honey to the saints.

2. The certainty of this—'We know.' Not by an uncertain and fallible conjecture, but upon sure grounds. What are they?

[A.] The promise of God, by which he hath secured the salvation of his people, notwithstanding their troubles: Heb. vi. 17, 18, 'Wherein God, willing more abundantly to show unto the heirs of promise the immutability of his counsel, confirmed it by an oath, that by two immutable things, in which it was impossible for God to lie, we might have strong consolation, who have fled for refuge to lay hold of the hope set before us.' God's resolved

---

[56] The Romans were often beaten in battle, never in war.

purpose declared in his covenant cannot be altered; his promises in time are his eternal purpose before time; he hath undertaken by promise and oath to be their God, the God of their salvation.

[B.] By the experiences of the saints, who have found it so: Ps. cxix. 67, 'Before I was afflicted I went astray, but now I learn thy statutes;' they have been persuaded of it: Phil. i. 19, 'I know that this shall turn to my salvation' All the troubles he endured should be so ordered by God, as they at length turn to his eternal happiness.

[C.] From the nature of the thing.: Two considerations enforce it

(1.) All things are at God's disposal, and forced to serve him. Men, devils, crosses, and comforts, nothing can fall out against or without his will. Angels, devils, men, have no power to null and frustrate his decrees, for he is the supreme and universal lord: Ps. xxxiii. 11, 'The counsel of the Lord standeth for ever; the thought of his heart to- all generations;' and therefore he blasts and frustrateth all the devices- of the wicked, and what he decreeth shall immutably come to pass.

(2.) His special care over his people. He hath carried them in the womb of his decrees before the foundation of the world; he loveth them more than a mother loveth her tender infant: Isa. xlix. 15, 'Can a woman forget her sucking child, that she should not have compassion on the son of her womb? yea, they may forget, but I will not forget thee.' If the mother be so tenderly affected to the child whom she carried in her womb for some few months, will not God much more? He is as tender of them as the apple of his eye, Zech. ii. 8. He hath secured his covenant-love by promise: 1 Cor. x. 13, 'But God is- faithful, who will not suffer you to be tempted above that you are able'; he will never leave you to insupportable difficulties.

Secondly, To give a more general state of the case.

1. This good is not to be determined by our fancies and conceits, but by the wisdom of God; for God knoweth what is better for us than we do for ourselves. We judge according to present appearance,, but he hath a sight or inspection of our hearts, and a prospect or fore sight of all future events; and therefore his divine choices are to be preferred before our foolish fancies; what he sendeth or permitteth to fall out is fitter for our turn than anything else. Could we once be persuaded of this, a Christian would be prepared for a cheerful entertainment of all that should come upon him. Besides, he is a God of bowels, and loveth us more dearly than we do ourselves; therefore we should be satisfied with his dispensations, whatever they are. Should the shepherd or the sheep choose his pastures? the child be governed by his own fancy or the father's discretion? the sick man by his own appetite or the physician's skill? It is necessary sometimes that God should displease his people for their advantage: John xvi. 6, 7, 'Because I have said these things to you, sorrow hath filled your heart; nevertheless, I tell you the truth, it is expedient for you that I go away' We are too much addicted to our own conceits; Christ's dealing is expedient and useful, yet very unsatisfactory to his people. He is to be judge of what is good for us, his going or tarrying, not we ourselves, who are short-sighted, distempered with passions, whose requests many times are but ravings, and ask of God we know not what. Peter said,

Mat. xvii. 4, 'Master, it is good for us to be here;' he was well pleased to be upon Mount Tabor, but little thought what work God had to do by him elsewhere. So Jer. xxiv. 5, the basket of good figs was sent 'into the land of the Chaldeans for their good' What good in a dispersion! but God foresaw worse evil would befall the place where they then lived. The selling of Joseph for a slave was to appearance evil, but God meant it for good, Gen. 1. 20. God may keep us low and bare, expose us to difficulties, prejudices, reproaches, bitter sufferings, yet all is for good.

2. Good is to be determined by its respect to the chief good or true happiness. Now what is our chief happiness but the vision and fruition of God? It consists not in outward comforts— riches, liberty, health, honour, or comfortable relations, but our acceptance with God; other things are but appendages to our felicity: Mat. vi. 33, *prostethesetai*, 'But first seek the kingdom of God, and these things shall be added unto you.' Affliction taketh nothing from our solid and essential happiness, rather helpeth us to the enjoyment of it as we increase in grace and holiness. That is evil that separateth us from God, that is good which bringeth us nearer to him; sin separateth us from God, therefore always evil, Isa. lix. 2. But afflictions are not always evil, but make us more earnestly to seek after him, Hos. v. 15; and so to be trained up under the cross, in a constant course of obedience and subjection to God, is good: Lam. iii. 27, 'It is good that a man bear the yoke from his youth' because it keepeth him modest, humble, and sober.

3. This good is not always the good of the body, or of outward prosperity; and therefore our condition is not to be determined by the interest of the flesh, but the welfare of our soul. If we had the world at will, we cannot be said to be in a good condition if the Lord should deny us spiritual blessings; we are more concerned as a soul than a body: Heb. xii. 10, 'He verily for our profit, that we may be par takers of his holiness.' He doth not call the good things of this world, that pelf which all desire, profit, but the participation of the divine nature. Affliction is good if it be sanctified; holiness wrought by affliction should be more to us than all our outward comforts.

4. It is not good presently enjoyed and felt, but waited for; and therefore our condition must not be determined by sense, but faith, Heb. xii. 11. Affliction for the present is not pleasing to natural sense, nor is the fruit for the present evident to spiritual sense; but it is good because in the issue it turneth to spiritual good. While under the affliction, we feel the smart, but do not presently find the benefit; physic must have time to work; that which is not good may be good; though it be not good in its nature, it is good in its use; faith should determine so, though we feel it not: Ps. lxxiii. 1, 'Yet God is good to Israel.'

5. A particular good must give way to a general good, and our personal benefit to the glory of God and the advancement of Christ's kingdom. It was good, yea, much better, for Paul to be in heaven; yet if it was needful for the saints to continue in the flesh, he submitteth, Phil. i. 24. We must not so desire good to ourselves as to hinder the good of others; all elements will act contrary to their particular nature for the conservation of the universe; that may be good for the glory of God which is not good for our personal contentment and ease: John xii.

27, 28. The sense of our duty, and the desire of glorifying God, should overcome our natural inclination.

6. In bringing about this good we must not be idle spectators, but assist under God. When we are diligent to exercise ourselves unto godliness, then evil is turned into good, and all crosses and afflictions into means of salvation. Besides the elective love of God at the bottom of all, there is the actual power and influence of the Spirit, and prayer on our part: Phil. i. 19, 'Through your prayer, and the supply of the Spirit of Christ Jesus;' and Heb. xii. 11, 'Now no chastening for the present seemeth to be joyous, but grievous; nevertheless, after wards it yieldeth the peaceable fruit of righteousness to them that are exercised thereby' It is not the bare nature of the cross doth it; we must labour for that we look for; the saints are not only passive objects, but active instruments, of providence; there is an exercise on our parts; we are to make use of all things, then God will bless us.

7. If it be true of particular persons, it is much more true of the church; all is for good: Ps. lxxvi. 10, 'Surely the wrath of man shall praise thee, and the remainder of wrath shalt thou restrain' Christ many times gets up on the devil's shoulders; all providence is for the elect's sake: 2 Tim. ii. 10, 'Therefore I endure all things for the elect's sake, that they may obtain salvation by Christ, with eternal glory' The sufferings of the apostles conduced to the good of true Christians; God considered the good of the whole church.

Use 1. Is information.

1. That the exception against God's providence from the evils that abound in the world is vain and frivolous. It was an old doubting question, If there be a God, how are there evils? If there were not a God, how is there good? One part answereth the other; the text more fully; he turneth evil unto good. That there are devils: God knoweth how to make use of them, to punish the wicked and exercise the godly. That there is sin: if there had been no sin, no Christ. That there are miseries: if no miseries, many graces would be lost; there would be no fortitude, no patience, no earnestness in prayer. That there are wicked men: it showeth God's distinguishing mercy, that when so many are drowned in the common shipwreck of mankind, it is the greater mercy that we escape; if others are bad, let us bless God that made us better. Lastly, that there is death, that there might be a passage out of this world, and a period to our labours and sorrows.

2. It teacheth us how to interpret prayers. We have prayed for the continuance of a blessing, and lost it; for the riddance of a trouble, yet it continueth upon us. This is the very case here; if God heareth them, how come they to suffer such hard things? The Spirit teacheth us to pray. Now the denial of either suit turneth to good. We often come to God with carnal requests, which being interpreted, sound but thus, Give me that wherewith I may offend thee, or have my flesh pleased, or lusts fed. God findeth us doting on the creature, and we take it ill to be interrupted in our whoredoms. We must distinguish between what is really best for us and what we judge best; other diet is more wholesome for our souls than what our sick appetites craveth; we are best many times when weakest, worst when strongest.

3. It giveth us a reason of waiting. Though we do not presently know why everything is done, let us wait. Providence doth not work without a cause; we see it not now, but we shall see it when God turneth it to good. We must not judge of God's work by the beginning; God seemeth an adversary for a while to them that indeed enjoy his eternal love. Let patience have its perfect work, and when providence is come to a period, you will know more.

4. What reason to trust God with events. Some things fall under our duty, others are a mere event. Our care is about events rather than duty, and so we take God's work out of his hands; and so it is not care, so much as carking; we inquire what shall become of us, rather than what we shall do. Do you your duty, and God knoweth how to turn all things for good, Phil. iv. 6, 7. Nothing can go amiss to him that is found in the way of duty.

5. It informeth us of the happiness of God's children. We may put in for a share; when we are sanctified to God, all things are sanctified to us; and things that otherwise would be snares prove helps, and discouragements prove furtherances. The creature is as if it were another thing to the saints; if they are advanced, their hearts are enlarged to God: 2 Sam. vii. 2, 'And the king said unto Nathan the prophet, See, now I dwell in an house of cedar, but the ark of God dwelleth within curtains'; Nehem. i. 11, 'O Lord, I beseech thee, let now thine ear be attentive to the prayer of thy servant, and to the prayer of thy servants who desire to fear thy name; and prosper, I pray thee, this day thy servant, and grant him mercy in the sight of this man; for I was the king's cup bearer'; meaning he had improved this place for God. When they are afflicted, they do not fret or faint, but humble themselves under the mighty hand of God, and so meet him at every turn. Oh! What a blessed thing is it to be under the special care of God, and to have all things about us ordered with respect to our eternal welfare! It is not so with the wicked; if God make Saul a king, Judas an apostle, Balaam a prophet, their preferment will be their ruin; Haman's honour, Achitophel's wit, Herod's applause, turned to their hurt. If in prosperity they contemn God, in adversity they deny and blaspheme God 'This evil is from the Lord, why should I wait on him any longer? 'As the salt sea turneth all into salt water, so a man is as the constitution of his heart is.

Use 2. Is caution. 1. Against misconstruction of providence; 2. Against non-improvement.

1. Against misconstruction of providence. There may be a seeming harshness in some of God's dealings, but, all things considered, you will find them full of mercy and truth, Ps. xxv. 10. If there be a seeming contradiction between his word and providence, you must not always interpret the word by providence, but providence by the word: Ps. lxxiii. 17, 'Until I went into the sanctuary of God, then I understood their end.'

2. Against non-improvement. Let us not lose the benefit by our negligence and folly; let us observe how we may profit of everything; God would not send this affliction, did he not know how it would be good for me. Therefore to this end—

[A.] Take these motives.

[B.] Consider what profit is to be gotten by afflictions.

[A.] Motives.

(1.) It is not enough to be good in the affliction, but we must get good by the affliction. Carnal men are somewhat good in the affliction; more modest when God's hand is heavy upon them, and they are somewhat disabled or discouraged from following their lusts; yea, and may make great promises of reformation when God hath them under; but as soon as they are delivered, they encourage themselves in the practice of their old sins; as metals are melted while they are in the furnace, but as soon as they are taken out they return to their natural hardness again. But the godly are the better afterwards; they cannot forget their old smart by sin: Josh. xxii. 17, 'Is the iniquity of Peor too little for us, from which we are not cleansed unto this day?' They remember what was—the great burden in their troubles, and what was the great comfort and support under them, and are the better all their lives. But others are of another temper: Ps. lxxviii. 34, 'When he slew them, then they sought him, and inquired early after God'. The sense of present smart, and the terror of an angry God, may frighten them into a little religiousness for the present, or drive them into a temporary repentance and seeking friendship and favour with God, and they leave off their sins for a time; but as soon as they are delivered, are as bad as ever. When affliction produceth temporary repentance, we are good in it; but when it produceth constancy of obedience, then we get good by it; it hath but some weak effect on us when we are good in it, but a saving effect when good by it.

(2.) The affliction cometh as a blessing where it is improved to good. It is a great advantage to observe whether our afflictions come as a cross only, or as a curse. Where they leave us worse rather than better, they are the beginnings of sorrows either in this life or the next; sometimes in this life, the cross goeth with a mind to return, or else some worse thing cometh in its place: John v. 14, 'Sin no more, lest a worse thing come unto thee.' God, that letteth a sinner escape one trouble, can easily reach him again, if he neglect God and his soul's good. If when the smart of the rod is gone, we return again to our old vanity, the Lord can easily put us into a worse condition than before; he can heat the furnace seven times hotter, and that which cometh after is the most grievous. But especially in the next world, when God sendeth eternal punishments instead of temporal; as sometimes God breaketh up the course of his medicinal discipline, letteth a people go uncorrected and unreclaimed for their greater condemnation: Isa. i. 5, 'Why should you be stricken anymore? ye will revolt more and more;' that is, it is in vain to seek to amend you by chastisements. When men wax the worse for all their afflictions, and will riot be brought home to God, they are given over as incorrigible; a brand is put upon Ahaz: 2 Chron. xxviii. 22, 'In the time of his dis tress did he trespass yet more against the Lord; this is that king Ahaz 'mark him for an obstinate and obdurate sinner. Now such God leaveth to themselves: Hosea iv. 17, 'Ephraim is joined to idols, let him alone.' They are desperate and irrecoverable, and reserved for eternal torments; this is the sorest judgment, to be given up to our own ways, without any check from divine providence. On the other side, God doth correct us in love, not in anger, when he doth bring good out of it and by it; if it produce a thorough repentance and change, it is a pledge of God's love, and our eternal glory. God's faith fulness may be then observed: Ps. cxix. 75, 'I know, Lord, that thy judgments are right, and that thou in faithfulness hast afflicted me; 'that he is pursuing his covenant-love, and carrying on your salvation, though by a way not so pleasing to the flesh.

(3.) That it is your part to get benefit by the affliction, but God's to remove it. For the getting benefit by the affliction falleth within the compass of our duty, but the removing the affliction is a bare event belonging to God's providence. We must do what is our part, and then God will do what is his; not but that God helpeth us in the improvement, for we obtain this grace by prayer, and the supply of the Spirit of Christ; but the removal is wholly God's work, and must be referred to him. Therefore your inquiry should be, What am I obliged unto in such a condition? and charge yourselves with you own proper work. Elihu telleth you what reflections you should have: Job xxxiv. 31, 32, 'Surely it is meet to be said unto God, I have borne chastisement, I will not offend anymore; that which I see not teach thou me: if I have done iniquity, I will do no more.' This is work proper for us: what sins will God have to be mortified? what vanities left? what duties more effectually performed? what graces strengthened? and then let God alone to take off the trouble when it hath done its errand; for surely he delights not to grieve and displease his people further than is for their profit, and he would not continue the affliction if he had not more work to do; his pity moveth him to spare the wicked when they relent under his strokes, much more to deliver the godly when they seriously profit by it.

(4.) If the constitution of our hearts were right, we would desire to profit by the affliction rather than to get rid of it. This is everywhere represented as the temper of the godly: 2 Cor. iv. 16, 'For which cause we faint not; but though our outward man perish, yet the inward man is renewed day by day'; 2 Cor. xii. 10, 'I will rejoice in infirmities.' Surely spiritual and heavenly things should be valued above earthly and carnal, not by a bare speculative approbation, but by a practical esteem. Now a practical esteem is manifested by three solid effects: by our caring or seeking for the one rather than the other: Mat. vi. 33, 'But first seek the kingdom of God and his righteousness, and all these things shall be added unto you;' by quit ting the one for the other when necessity so requireth: Mat. xiii. 45, 46, 'Again, the kingdom of heaven is like unto a merchant-man seeking goodly pearls , who, when he hath found one pearl of great price, he went and sold all that he had and bought it'; by our submission to God's dispensation, when he blasteth and taketh away the one, to promote the other. We should be glad that it goeth well with the inward man, by the loss and decay of the outward; the lowest degree of sincerity is that the loss of outward concernments should trouble us the less; but surely if grace be in any good degree of strength, we should rejoice and be abundantly satisfied that God thinketh fit to take away earthly things, that thereby he may make us more mindful of that which is heavenly, and doth lessen us in the world, that he may thereby excite us to a more lively exercise of grace, and retrench the interests of the flesh, that the spirit may be enlarged and kept in good plight. Therefore to a child of God an exemption from troubles is not so good as an improvement of them. Our Lord, when he taught us to pray, would have us indeed deprecate the temptation; but our chief request by way of reserve: Mat. vi. 13, 'And lead us not into temptation, but deliver us from evil;' so in his prayer: John xvii. 15, 'I pray not that thou shouldest take them out of the world, but that thou shouldest keep them from the evil'; teaching us our desires should be not so much to be delivered from the world as the evil of the world, from sins rather than afflictions, and that we should seek grace rather than deliverance. The deliverance is a common mercy, the improvement a special mercy; carnal men may escape out of affliction, but carnal men have no experience of grace in sanctifying afflictions; and bare deliverance is no sign of special love, but improvement is. Paul rejoiced in this, that God would deliver him from every evil work, 2 Tim. iv. 18. Therefore we should submit to endure the evil of chastisement that we may escape the evil of the sin; it is worse to be sinful than miserable, to be unclean than to be sick, to be voluptuous than to be poor; and so the affliction bringeth greater good than it taketh from you. Therefore Christians should be careful that they murmur not against God's dispensations, for there are two evils that we bewray thereby (1.) A despising of God; (2.) A despising of holiness; and a Christian should be tender of either.

First, A despising of God, as if he knew not what was fittest and best for you, and would send any trouble upon you that he knoweth not how to turn to good: Job xxxiv. 33, 'Should it be according to thy mind? He will recompense it, whether thou refuse or whether thou choose'. Should our condition be at our own disposal? and should God ask of us whether we like it or no? Is it not better to be satisfied in his will, and say, Surely God would not send this affliction if he did not know how it should be good for me? We would carve out our own condition, and have our will in everything; but is this wise or just? must God be subject to our passions and affections? No, whether we will or no, he will take his own way.

Secondly, It is a lessening the value of holiness, as if this profit did not countervail our loss. We profess we esteem grace more than wealth, and spiritual things more than carnal; but when we are put to the trial, we little regard holiness, but only mind the ease of the flesh, and therefore are so hardly reconciled to the cross. Surely that which doth us good should not be entertained with such impatient resentment; it is worse in Christians, who are more obliged to count all things dung and dross: Phil. iii. 7-10, 'But what things were gain to me, those I counted loss for Christ. Yea doubtless, and I count all things but loss for the excellency of the knowledge of Christ Jesus my Lord: for whom I have suffered the loss of all things, and do count them but dung, that I may win Christ, and be found in him, not having mine own righteousness, which is of the law, but that which is through the faith of Christ, the righteousness which is of God by faith; that I may know him, and the power of his resurrection, and the fellowship of his sufferings, being made conformable to his death.' But we may say as Moses to God, 'Behold, the children of Israel have not hearkened unto me, how then shall Pharaoh hear me? 'We cannot hope to convince a worldly man of this, that loss of estate or poverty is good; the ambitious man, that it is good to be despised and contemned; and the voluptuous man, that pain is sometimes better than ease, and sickness, that checketh the desires of the flesh, is better than health, that gratifieth them. Alas! the children of God are hardly convinced that mortifying affliction is better than carnal prosperity; how then will the world believe it?

[B.] What profit is there to be gotten by afflictions? It is hard to instance in all particulars, because God hath several ends in our afflictions, according to the distempers that need cure; but the usual profit of afflictions is seen in these things—

(1.) That the time of affliction is a serious thinking time: 1 Kings viii. 47, 'If they shall bethink themselves in the land of their captivity.' We have more liberty to retire into ourselves, being freed from the attractive allurements of worldly vanities; and for the present there is some restraint on the delights of the flesh, which use to besot the mind, and hinder better thoughts. Adversity maketh men serious; the prodigal came to himself when he began to be in want, Luke xv. 17. Sad objects make a deeper impression on our souls than delightful do; they help us to consider our ways, and God's righteous dealings, that we may behave ourselves wisely, and suitable to the dispensation we are under: Eccles. vii. 14, 'In the day of adversity consider' See from what hand it cometh, to what issue it tendeth, what is thy duty under it, how little thou canst mend thyself without submitting to God, that to hope to escape by ill means is but like an attempt to break prison. It is better to make supplications to our judge; these providences are not to be lightly passed over; the author of them is God, the occasion sin, the end repentance.

(2.) It is an awakening, quickening time. Some are awakened out of the sleep of death, and are first wrought upon by afflictions. This is one powerful means to bring in souls to God, and opening their ears to discipline, Job xxxvi. 10; they had still slept in their sins if God had not awakened them by the smart discipline of the cross. But others are quickened and awakened to more carefulness of their duty, more watchfulness against sin; and the graces of the Spirit, which lay dormant in us through neglect, are more set a-work. Sense-pleasing objects deaden the heart; God's best children sleep when they have a carnal pillow under their heads: Ps. xxx. 6, 'And in my prosperity I said, I shall never be moved.' But now, because they do not stir up themselves, God stirreth them up by a smart rod, that faith may be working, love fervent, hope lively, prayers carried on with warmth and zeal; prayers otherwise are dead, thoughts of heaven cold, or none; wherein all these graces are acted: Isa. xxvi. 16, 'Lord, in trouble they have visited thee; they poured out a prayer when thy chastening was upon them;' and Hos. v. 15, 'I will go and return to my place till they acknowledge their offence, and seek my face; in their affliction they will seek me early.' When our gust and taste of spiritual and heavenly things is recovered, then we are awakened and in good earnest.

(3.) It is a learning time. This the scripture witnesseth everywhere: Ps. cxix. 71, 'It is good for me that I have been afflicted, that I might learn thy statutes'; Ps. xciv. 12, 'Blessed is the man whom thou chastenest, Lord, and teachest him out of thy law' God teacheth us, though he teach us as Gideon did the men of Succoth, with briars and thorns; and we read of Christ Jesus himself, Heb. v. 8, 'He learned obedience from the things which he suffered'; he did experimentally understand what obedience was in hard and difficult cases, and so could the better pity and help sinners when they obey God at a dear rate. In affliction we have an experimental knowledge of that of which but a notional knowledge before. We come by experience to see how false and changeable the world is, what a burden sin is, what sweetness there is in the promises, what a reality in the world to come, how comfortable an interest in God is. Luther said, *Qui tribulantur sacras scripturas melius intelligunt securi et fortunati eas legunt sicut Ovidii carmen*—'The afflicted see more in the scriptures than others do; the secure and fortunate read them as they do Ovid's verses.' Certainly, when the soul is humble, and we are refined and purified from the dregs of sense, we are more tractable and teachable, our understandings are clearer, and our affections more melting. Now spiritual learning is a blessing that cannot be valued enough. If God write his law on our hearts by his stripes on our backs, we have no reason to complain.

(4.) It is a repenting time, to stir up the hatred of sin by the bitter effects of it: Jer. ii. 19, 'Now know what an evil and bitter thing it is that thou hast forsaken the Lord thy God, and that my fear is not in thee.' Weigh with thyself what hath brought all these evils upon thee. Experience teacheth fools: so Lam. iii. 39, 'Wherefore doth a living man complain, a man for the punishment of his sin?' He hath no reason to murmur against God, when he considereth his own deserts, and that he suffereth nothing but what he hath produced to himself by his sins; and therefore we ought to have deep shame and sorrow for our former miscarriages. It conduceth to breed true remorse to consider our folly, and the misery brought upon us thereby: Jer. xxxi. 18, 'Surely I have heard Ephraim bemoaning himself thus, Thou hast chastised me, and I was chastised, as a bullock unaccustomed to the yoke: turn thou me, and I shall be turned; thou art the Lord my God. Surely after that I was turned, I repented; and after that I was instructed, I smote upon my thigh; I was ashamed, yea, even confounded, because I did bear the reproach of my youth.'

(5.) It is a weaning time, from the pleasures and conveniences of the present world. First, The pleasures of the world. Pleasure is the great sorceress that hath enchanted all mankind; they all court plea sure, though in different shapes; it is deeply engrained in our nature, and the cause of our many miscarriages: Titus iii. 3, 'Serving divers lusts and pleasures'; and because we have divers pleasures, God sendeth divers afflictions. The soul is almost so sunk in flesh that it ceaseth to be spirit, John iii. 6. Pleasure is that which draweth us off from God, and engageth us in the creature: James i. 14, 'But every man is tempted when he is drawn away of his own lust, and enticed' Now, among the divers afflictions, diseases are natural penances which God hath put upon us to reclaim us from vain pleasures. The gust of the flesh would be too strong, if God did not check it by embittering our portion in the world. Secondly, The conveniences of the present life—riches, honours, friendships. Afflictions are sent to cure our carnal complacency, and increase the heavenly mind. Riches: Heb. x. 34, 'And took joyfully the spoiling of your goods, knowing in yourselves that ye have in heaven a better and an enduring substance.' Relations, possessions: 1 Cor. vii. 29-31, 'The time is short; it remaineth that both they that have wives be as though they had none, and they that weep as though they wept not, and they that rejoice as though they rejoiced not, and they that buy as though they possessed not, and they that use this world as not abusing it; for the fashion of this world passeth away.' Friendship, John xvi. 32. Doting on the creature is spiritual adultery: James iv. 4, 'Ye adulterers and adulteresses, know ye not that the friendship of the world is enmity with God? Whoever, therefore, will be a friend of the world is the enemy of God' If an image of jealousy be set up, God will blast it; he turneth the world loose upon us, so that friends prove as broken reeds. It is easy for God to prosper his people in the world, and suit all things to their own desires; but he knoweth our proneness to carnal love, and how easily our heart is enticed from himself. Our temptations would be too strong if the world did appear in an over-amiable, tempting dress; therefore he doth exercise us sometimes with the malicious, envious world; sometimes with the cares, griefs, pains, disappointments, which are incident to the present life; and will show us what a restless, empty world we have here, that we may the more earnestly look after those peaceful regions which are above.

(6.) It is a time of increasing our love to God, upon a twofold account.

First, Affliction showeth us that nothing is worthy of our love but God; whatsoever robbeth God of it soon proveth matter of trouble and distress to us. Our hearts are the more averse from God because they are inclined to the creature: Jer. ii. 13, 'For my people have committed two evils: they have forsaken me, the fountain of living water, and hewed them out cisterns, broken cisterns that will hold no water.' Men bestow their hearts on something beneath the chief good, which becometh an idol and false god to them, and which they respect and love more than God. Now the love of God cannot reign in that soul where the love of the world and fleshly lusts reigneth: 1 John ii. 15, 'If any man loveth the world, how dwelleth the love of the Father in him? 'It is not in him. Now the great work of grace is to cast out the usurper, and to give God the possession of what is his own; and therefore the heart must be circumcised before it be true to God: Deut. xxx. 6, 'The Lord thy God will circumcise thy heart, and the heart of thy seed, to love the Lord thy God with all thy heart, and with all thy soul, that thou mayest live.' First the foreskin and fleshliness that sticketh so close to us must be taken off, before we can adhere to God as our proper and chief happiness. Now this is God's own work by his internal grace; but yet he useth external means, and amongst the rest sharp afflictions, to wean us from the creature, and to show us that we do but court our own trouble and infelicity when we bestow our affections elsewhere; for hereby God plainly demonstrateth that he is our all-sufficient and indeficient God. All-sufficient, as answering all our necessities and desires; indeficient, our never-failing good, when all things fail about us: Hab. iii. 18, 'Yet I will rejoice in the Lord, and joy in the God of my salvation' And thus, by desolating the creature, doth he drive our foolish hearts to himself, that we may have the solid delights of his love.

Secondly, This love of God is the comfort by which we are supported in all our distresses. The servants of God have never so much of the joy in the Holy Ghost as in their great sufferings; their delight in God is then purest and unmixed. God comforteth them when they have nothing else to take comfort in: Job. xvi. 20, 'My friends scorn me, but mine eye poureth out tears to God.' When all friends forsake us but one, that one is sweeter to us than ever. Humble moans to God giveth us ease and comfort, notwithstanding the neglect and contempt of man; and when the world undervalueth, it is enough that God approveth. Our delights in God are often corrupted by a mixture of sensual delights, so that we cannot tell what supporteth us, God or the creature, our remaining comforts, the help or pity of friends, or God alone. Therefore, that the affliction may pierce the spirit, the Lord causeth it to be sharpened and pointed by the scorn and neglect of men, and their strange carriage towards us, that we may fetch our supports from him alone. That still we are not barred from access to the throne of grace, there is our cordial; that we have a God to go to, to whom we may make our moan, and from whose love we may derive all our comforts; so David speaketh feelingly in deep afflictions: Ps. lxiii. 3, 'Thy loving- kindness is better than life'. This supplieth all his wants, and sweeteneth all his troubles, and giveth more comfort than what is most precious and desirable in the creature. I will show you how it helpeth to raise our love to God. There are two acts of love desire after him, and de light in him; for we love a thing when we desire to enjoy it, and find contentment in it, being enjoyed.

(a.) Desire is the pursuit of the soul after God, *desiderium unionis*. The great act of love is an affecting of union with the thing beloved. Now, because of our imperfect fruition of him in this life, love mainly bewrayeth itself by desires of the nearest conjunction with God that we are capable of; and the motions of grace tend to this end, to conjoin us to God, or to bring God and us together; and to this end tend faith and hope, and ordinances and means, the word and prayer; and so sacraments, that we may get more of God. When a house is a-building, there are scaffolds and poles and instruments of architecture used; but when the house is finished, all these are taken away. So here are many means to bring us to God there is faith and hope and ordinances; but when we come to the vision and fruition of him, all these cease, and love only remaineth. In the heavenly Jerusalem love is perfect, because there God is all in all. But while the distance pontinueth, see how the hearts of the saints worketh: Ps. lxiii. 8, 'My soul followeth hard after thee!' All acts of the spiritual life are a further pursuit after God, that we may meet him here and there, and .we may find more of him in every duty, and be united to him in the nearest way of communion that we are capable of: Ps. xxvii. 4, 'One thing have I desired of the Lord, and that will I seek after; that I may dwell in the house of the Lord all the days of my life, to behold the beauty of the Lord, and inquire in his temple.' This was David's great desire, above all earthly desires whatsoever. But have the saints always this ardent and burning desire? No, it is mightily quenched by the prosperity of the flesh; when they have something on this side God to detain their hearts, they forget him, suck on the breasts of worldly consolation. You will find their desires are most earnest in affliction; as David, when in a wandering condition: Ps. xlii. 1, 2, 'As the hart panteth after the water-brooks, so panteth my soul after thee, God; my soul thirsteth for God, yea for the living God; when shall I come and appear before thee?' Naturalists tell us that the hart is a thirsty creature, especially when it hath eaten vipers; they are inflamed thereby, and vehemently desire water. This emblem David chooseth to express his affection thereby, and his longings after God, and the means to enjoy God when he was in his troubles; so the prophet Isaiah, Isa. xxvi. 9, 'With my soul have I desired thee in the night; yea, with my spirit will I seek thee right early.' He speaketh this in the person of the church during the time of their troubles. When God's judgments are abroad in the earth, then they had continual thoughts of God, and their endeavours were early and earnest. At other times you will find the church flat, cold, and more indifferent as to the testimonies of his favour: Jer. ii. 31, 32, 'O generation, see ye the word of the Lord; have I been a wilderness unto Israel? A land of darkness? Wherefore say my people, We are lords, we will come no more unto thee? Can a maid forget her ornaments? Or a bride her attire? Yet my people have forgotten me days without number'. They had something whereon to live apart from God; therefore afflictions are necessary to quicken these desires.

(b.) The other affection whereby love bewrayeth itself is by a delight in God; the cream of it is reserved for heaven, but now it is pleasing to think of God, if the soul be in good plight: Ps. civ. 34, 'My meditation of him shall be sweet, I will be glad in the Lord.' It is the solace of their hearts to entertain thoughts of God; to speak of him and his gracious and wondrous works, is the contentment and pleasure of their souls: Eph. v. 4, 'Neither filthiness, nor foolish talking, nor jesting, which are not convenient, but rather giving of thanks' There is their jesting, to draw nigh to him: Ps. cxxii. 1, 'I was glad when they said unto me, Let us go into the house of the Lord! 'This is their heaven upon earth, to obey him and serve him: Ps. cxii. 1, 'Praise ye the Lord: blessed is the man that feareth the Lord, that delighteth greatly in his commandments!' Now this delight is flagged, and we even grow weary of God and weary of well doing. We dote upon the world, and grow estranged from God and cold in his service, till we are quickened by sharp afflictions; then we begin to mind God again, and a serious religiousness is revived in us. The hypocrites never mind God but in their troubles; Job xxvii. 10, 'Will he always call upon God?' But the best saints need this help, and would grow dead and careless of God were it not for sharp corrosives. Well now, seeking after God and delighting in God being our great duties, we should observe how these are promoted by all the troubles that befall us.

SERMON XXXVIII

To them that love God.

Romans viii. 28.

Now we come to the character and notification of the persons to whom this great privilege doth belong. First, Their carriage towards God—*To them that love God.*

Doctrine The elect are specified by this character, that they love God. Here I shall show you—

1. What is love to God.

2. Why this is made the evidence of our interest.

1. What is love to God? Love in the general is the complacency of the will in that which is apprehended to be good. The object is good, and love is a complacency in it. The object must be good, for evil is the object of our displicency[57] and aversion[58]. And apprehended as good, for otherwise we may turn from good, as evil to us. Now love to God is the complacency of the will in God, as apprehended to be good. And therefore we must consider

[A.] The object.

[B.] The act.

[C.] The properties.

[A.] The object. We consider God as good. There is a double motive in the object to excite us to love God: because he is good, and doth good, Ps. cxix. 68, from his nature, and from his work.

(1.) The excellency of his nature—he is good. There is a threefold goodness in God

(a.) His essential goodness, which is the infinite perfection of his nature.

(b.) His moral goodness and holiness, which is the infinite perfection of his will.

(c.) His beneficial goodness, which is the infinite propension that is in him to do good to the creature. All these are the object of our love.

(a.) His essential goodness should make him amiable to us; partly because the glorious perfections of his nature are the object of our esteem, and esteem is the ground of love we affect what we prize and value, or else we do not really esteem, prize, and value it; and partly because they are the object of our praise now we praise God for his excellences, to increase our love to him and delight in him; otherwise our praise is but an empty compliment; and partly because the angels and blessed spirits do admire and adore God for the excellences of his nature, not only for the benefits they have received by him, but as he

---

[57] dissatisfaction, aversion, discontent
[58] aversion

is an infinite and eternal being, of glorious and incomprehensible majesty; they are represented as crying out, Isa. vi. 3, 'Holy! Holy! Holy! Lord God of Hosts!' Now God must in some measure be served on earth as he is in heaven. Surely we should not speak, or think, or worship the infinite eternal God, without some act of love, holy delight, and pleasure: Ps. cxlvii. 1, 'Praise ye the Lord; for it is good to sing praises to our God, for it is pleasant, and praise is comely'; so Ps. xcv. 1, 'Come let us sing unto the Lord, let us make a joyful noise to the rock of our salvation '(and all this is the acting of love), 'for the Lord is a great God, and a great King above all gods '(there are the motives); Ps. v. 10, 'Let them that love thy name be joyful in thee' So that you see it is a great duty to delight ourselves in God's essential perfections.

(b.) His moral goodness, or his righteousness and holiness. Surely this is an amiable thing, and therefore the object of our delectation. I prove it thus First, If holiness be lovely and pleasant in the creature, why not in God? In the saints holiness doth attract our love: Ps. xvi. 3, 'My delight is in the saints, the excellent ones of the earth'; and Ps. xv. 4, 'In whose eyes a vile person is contemned; but he honoureth them that fear the Lord'. We are to love saints as saints, reduplicative; why not God as holy and righteous? We are to love the law of God as it is pure, Ps. cxix. 140; therefore we are to love God, a copy of whose holiness the law is; the same reason that doth enforce the one doth enforce the other. Secondly, I argue, We are to imitate his holiness and righteousness, therefore we are to love and delight in it: Eph. v. 1, 'Be ye followers of God, as dear children;' and 2 Cor. iii. 18, 'But we all, with open face beholding as in a glass the glory of the Lord, are changed into the same image from glory to glory.' Now love begetteth likeness; it is the greatest demonstration of God's love to us to make us like himself, and the greatest expression of our love to God to desire it, to endeavour after it, to value and prize it as our happiness; see Ps. xvii. 15, 'As for me, I will behold thy face in righteousness; I shall be satisfied when I awake with thy likeness'.

(c.) His beneficial goodness or benignity: Ps. c. 5, 'For the Lord is good; for his mercy is everlasting'; therefore all his saints should love him. We are first led to the Lord by our own interest, and the benefits we have, or may have, by him: Ps. lxxxvi. 5, 'Thou, Lord, art good, ready to forgive, and plenteous in mercy unto all that call upon thee.' This doth first attract the heart of guilty sinners to seek after God, but afterwards we look upon him as a lovely object in himself. While we look upon benignity as a moral perfection in God, without the fruits which flow thence to us, it is an engaging thing; as it was observed heretofore that Caesar's virtues were more amiable than Cato's virtues. Caesar's virtues were clemency, affability, liberality; Cato's virtues, rigid justice and fidelity in his dealings: both were amiable, but the one more taking than the other. There is somewhat a like observation, Rom. v. 7, 'Scarcely for a righteous man would one die, but for a good man one would even dare to die' By the righteous man is meant one of a severe and rigid innocency; by a good man, a man bountiful and useful. To apply it: God's benignity is a thing amiable, though it be considered but as an attribute in God, not exercised and acted on us. Because this most suiteth the necessities of the indigent and fallen creature, therefore the scripture doth much insist upon it, to move us to return and seek reconciliation with him.

(2.) He doth good, or hath been good to us.

(a.) As in creation; he made us out of nothing, after his own image, we must remember him as a creator, so as to consider the obligations which lie upon us to love, please, and serve him: Eccles. xii. 1, 'Remember thy creator in the days of thy youth.' All that we are and have, we have it from God and for God.

(b.) In redemption, where we have the greatest representation of the goodness of God; 1 John iv. 10, 'Herein is love, not that we loved God, but that he loved us, and sent his Son to be a propitiation for our sins'; it is the signal instance; and Rom. v. 8, 'Herein God commended his love, that while we were yet sinners Christ died for the ungodly;' the fullest discovery.

(c.) In the mercies of daily providence: Deut. xxx. 10, 'Thou shalt love the Lord thy God; for he is thy life, and the length of thy days.' Especially in his tender care about his people: Ps. xxxi. 33, 'Oh! Love the Lord, all ye his saints, for the Lord preserveth his saints, and plentifully rewardeth the proud doer' His hearing prayer is one instance: Ps. cxvi. 1, 'I will love the Lord, because he hath heard my voice and my supplications'

(d.) In the rewards of the other world, which are provided especially for them that love him: 1 Cor. ii. 9, 'Eye hath not seen, nor ear heard, neither hath entered into the heart of man, the things which God hath prepared for them that love him'; and 1 John iii. 1, 2, 'Behold what manner of love the Father hath bestowed upon us, that we should be called the sons of God. Behold now we are the sons of God, and it doth not appear what we shall be; but we know that when he shall appear we shall be like him, for we shall see him as he is' Thus God is an object of our love.

[B.] The act. It is the complacency and well-pleasedness of the soul in God as an all-sufficient portion. This implieth—

(1.) A desire or earnest seeking after God in the highest way of enjoyment we are capable of here; and so those mercies are most valued which are nearest to himself, and show us most of God, and do least detain us from him, his favour, and image; or to mention but one, his sanctifying grace and Spirit; and therefore his saints are described to be those that hunger and thirst after righteousness, Mat. v. 6; they earnestly desire to be like God in purity and holiness. And his sanctifying Spirit is the surest pledge of God's love: Rom. v. 5, 'Because the love of God is shed abroad in our hearts by the Holy Spirit given us'; and doth most help us to love him again: Rom. viii. 15, 'And have received the spirit of adoption, whereby we cry, Abba, Father' Other gifts, that conduce to please the flesh may keep us from him, as wealth, honour, and pleasures; but saving grace, as it cometh from God, so it carrieth us to him.

(2.) A delight in him. So far as they enjoy God, they delight in him: Ps. iv. 6, 7, 'Lord, lift up the light of thy countenance upon us; thou hast put gladness in my heart more than in the time when their corn and wine increased.' His favour is life, his displeasure as death to their soul c Thou didst hide thy face, and I was troubled' Ps. xxx. 7. They look upon God reconciled as the best friend, and God displeased as the most dreadful adversary.

(3.) It is their comfort and solace that they shall more perfectly see him and be like him in the other world to which they are tending, when they shall behold their glorified Redeemer, and their own nature united to the Godhead, and their persons admitted into the nearest intuition and fruition of God they are capable of, and live in the fullest love to him and delight in him: Rom. v. 2, 'We rejoice in hope of the glory of God.'

(4.) They are so satisfied with this that their great business is to please God and be accepted with him: 2 Cor. v. 9, 'Wherefore we labour, that whether present or absent, we may be accepted with him.'

[C.] The properties of this love.

(1.) It is not a speculative, but a practical love. Some please themselves with fancies and airy religion that consists in lofty strains of devotion, and fellow-like familiarity with God; but the true love is seen in obedience: John xiv. 15, 'If ye love me, keep my commandments'; and 1 John v. 3, 'For this is the love of God, that we keep his commandments.' Our love is a love of duty; we have such a deep sense of the majesty of God, such an esteem of his favour, that we dare not hazard it by doing anything which may be a breach of our duty, or a grief to his Spirit, or a dishonour to his name.

(2.) It is not a transient, but a fixed love; not a pang of zeal for the present, but a radicated inclination towards God, or a deep impression left upon the heart, which disposeth it to seek his glory and do his will; the bent of the mind is to God and heaven. They do not choose him for their portion only, but cleave to him; all their desire and endeavour is to please, glorify, and enjoy God. Some have good inclinations, but they are as unstable as water, being divided between God and the world, James i. 8; but these allow no rival and competitor with God in the soul: Ps. lxxiii. 25, 'Whom have I in heaven but thee? And there is none on earth that I desire besides thee'

(3.) It is not a cold, but a fervent love. We are not to love God after any sort, remissly, coldly, but with the greatest vigour and intension of affection; so it runneth, Mat. xxii. 37, 'Thou shalt love the Lord thy God with all thy heart, and with all thy soul, and with all thy might' Many words are heaped together to increase the sense that our love may be a growing love, quickened and heightened to a further degree.

(a.) It is God that is loved, not the creature. Thou shalt love thy neighbour as thyself, but God with all thy heart. In a moral consideration there are three beings God, neighbour, self. There is a law that you should love God, and a law that you should love your neighbour; but where is the positive law that you should love yourselves? Turn over the scriptures, and you will find nothing of this. There are laws to restrain self-love, none to excite it; in this we need no teacher; there is something in our bosoms to prompt us to love our selves, therefore it is rather supposed than enforced. Paul's adverbs are emphatical, Titus ii. 12, 'that we should live soberly, righteously, and godly.' What is it to live godly, but to esteem, love, reverence, and serve God with all our heart and all our strength? And to live justly as to our neighbour, what is it but to love our neighbour as ourself? 'What ye would that men should do unto you, do ye the same to them' What is it to live soberly as to ourselves, but that our self-love should be moderated, that we should abstain from all unlawful and superfluous pleasures, and use the lawful ones sparingly, as meat, drink, clothing, recreation, unless we would have our souls choked or snared? Self-love hath so filled the hearts of men that there is no room, or little room, left for the love of God or our neighbour; but yet there is a measure set how we should love our neighbour, but we cannot over-love God; there all the heart, all the soul, all the might; it is *modus sine modo, mensura sine mensura, et terminus sine termino*; here no excess or hyperbole hath any place.

(b.) The nature of the object loved. God is infinitely and eternally good, therefore we must love God without any exceptions and restrictions. As the object of love is goodness, so the measure of the goodness is the measure of the love: a greater good must be loved more, and a lesser good must be loved less. Somewhat besides God may be good, but it is finite and limited; the creature is a particular good, and our love to it is a particular limited love. God only is a sea of goodness without banks and without bottom; therefore our love to God is not limited 'by the object, but the narrowness of the faculty. God in this life is seen darkly, and so also loved, for our love doth not exceed our knowledge. That is our defect: God deserveth more.

(c.) God is loved *ut finis*, as the last end, and all other things *ut media ad finem*. Now common reason will tell us that the end is desired without measure, and the means in a certain respect and proportion to the end. As, for instance, when you are sick you send for the physician, the end is health; the medicaments and prescriptions are the means; the end you intend absolutely, but the means you would have used in a just measure, and with respect to the end. Fasting is prescribed in measure, and blood-letting in measure; the potions neither too bitter nor too strong, nor in too great quantity. You do not fear to be made too well, or too healthy, or too strong; this is your end. A man that giveth up himself to a scholar's life, his end is learning, he doth not fear to be too learned; yet too much reading is a weariness to the flesh, and dulleth the mind. There is a greater largeness about the end than about the means. Now God is the chief good, and so the last end; therefore all the heart and all the soul and all the mind. Surely not a cold, but a high and strong love is due to him.

(d.) Because of the wonders of his love towards us. The highest angel doth not love God with such a love as he loveth the meanest saints; and shall we love him coldly and faintly who hath loved us at so high a rate? I will not speak of his love which he showed us in creation, when as yet we had no being: he made us after his own image, and lords of the visible world, with bodies so exactly contrived, and souls endowed with such excellent faculties; but I will speak of the wonders of his love in our redemption, that when we were enemies he sent his Son to die for us. I urge this, I press this; this is enough for my purpose: God so loved the world, so much above the conception or thought of men and angels, that his Son came in the similitude of sinful flesh, and died for us. Now, as one fire kindleth another, so should this love beget a like love in us 'We love him, because he loved us first,' 1 John iv. 19.

(4.) I need scarce add that it must be a superlative love that God must be loved above all other things; above the creature, above our selves; not to be respected as an inferior good, nor merely as equal unto any, but above all, or else we do not at all love him. We cannot love him so much as he deserveth to be loved, for so God only loveth himself; we cannot love him so much as the glorified saints and angels love him, for we are not yet perfect; we do not love him as some eminent saints in flesh, because we, it may be, are novices, or because of our negligence; but we must love him more than any other thing is loved; we must love him above all, and all in and for God, or else we are not sincere: Mat. x. 37, 'He that loveth father or mother more than me is not worthy of me.' Some have a partial half-love to God when they have a greater love to other things; then religion will be an underling, and God's interest least minded. If anything be nearer and dearer to us than God, and the advantages we expect from men are preferred before the conscience of our duty to him, we cannot be upright and faithful to Christ.

2. Why is this made the evidence of our interest in this privilege? Why those that love God, rather than those that believe in him, especially since faith is the immediate fruit of effectual calling?

I answer,

[A.] The apostle speaketh of the children of God, and children will love their father. What more natural? what more kindly? They are regenerated and sanctified by the Spirit for this end: Gal. iv. 6, 'Because ye are sons, God hath sent forth the Spirit of his Son into your hearts, crying, Abba, Father.' An heart inclined to God cannot keep away from him.

[B.] Of children that belong to the gospel dispensation. Now they that love God are the only gospel Christians, being deeply possessed with that love which God hath showed to us in Christ: 1 John iv. 19, 'We love him because he loved us first' Now we see greater reasons of loving God, and are taught a more perfect way of loving God. We know God more, and feel more and taste more of his love: Luke vii. 47, 'Wherefore I say unto thee, Her sins, which are many, are forgiven, for she loved much; but to whom little is forgiven, the same loveth little'.

[C.] This gospel estate we enter into by faith. Now faith is such a believing of God's love to us in Christ as giveth us a lively sense of it in our souls. It is not a bare apprehension, a hearsay-knowledge, but a taste that we have by faith: 1 John iv. 16, 'And we have known and believed the love that God hath to us'; and 1 Peter ii. 3, 'If so be ye have tasted that the Lord is gracious.' Whatever of the love of God faith apprehendeth and feeleth, begetteth love again, Gal. v. 6. Knowledge and faith and hope are but the bellows to keep in this holy fire, to work our hearts to love God.

[D.] This faith is the fruit of effectual calling, which is a great expression of God's love to us who were so unworthy, 2 Tim. i. 9, and passing by thousands and ten thousands who were all as good as we, and we as deep in the common pollution as they, and in outward respects were far better and more considerable, great, wise, and learned: 1 Cor. i. 26, 'Ye see your calling, brethren, that not many wise men after the flesh, not many noble, are called.' And called us to such dignity and honour and blessedness: 1 Peter iii. 9, 'Knowing that ye are thereunto called, that ye should inherit a blessing'; 1 Thes.ii. 12, 'That ye would walk worthy of God, who hath called us to his kingdom and glory' It was not our will nor our worth that moved him, but his own love. Now this love calleth for love again: God loveth first, best, and most; but yet we should love as we can, love to our utmost; that which was begun in love on God's part should be accompanied with love on ours.

[E.] This effectual calling is the fruit of God's eternal purpose, which he purposed in himself, to save us by Christ. Vocation is actual election, the first eruption and breaking out of his eternal purpose. For as God distinguished us from others who lay in the same polluted mass of mankind by the purpose of his grace before time, so he actually calleth us out from others in time, to be a people to himself; therefore vocation is called election, John xv. 19. Now in God's free election we have the* clearest view of his love and our great obligations to God. And therefore what should more excite our love and gratitude? This was ancient love before we or the world had a being; it was the design God travailed with from all eternity. And who are we that the thoughts of God should be taken up about us so long ago? It is love purposed and designed; his heart is set upon it to do us good; it was not a thing of chance, but foreordained. If one doth us a kindness that lieth in his way, and when opportunity doth fairly invite him, he is friendly to us; but when he studieth to do us good, it is more obliging. This is a feast long in preparing, to make all things ready for our acceptance, therefore this calleth for love.

[F.] This purpose is followed with his watchful and powerful providence, guiding and ordering all things, that it may not miscarry and lose its effect, which is as great and sensible an argument of the love of God as can be propounded to us: Job vii. 17, 18, 'What is man, that thou shouldest magnify him? And that thou shouldest set thine heart upon him? And that thou shouldest visit him every morning, and try him every moment?' If a prince should form the manners of a beggar's child, and watch him at every turn, it would be a great condescension. When others are spilt on the great common of the world by a looser providence, they are a peculiar people, who have a special interest in his love and care, and his charge. Now the scripture delighteth to suit qualifications and privileges: Ps. xxxi. 14, 'I trusted in thee, Lord; I said, Thou art my God'; Isa. lviii. 13, 14, 'If thou turn away thy foot from the sabbath, from doing thy pleasure on my holy day, and call the sabbath a delight, the holy of the Lord, honourable, and shalt honour him, not doing thine own ways, not finding thine own pleasure, not speaking thine own words; then shalt thou delight thyself in the Lord, and I will cause thee to ride upon the high places of the earth, and feed thee with the heritage of Jacob thy father, for the mouth of the Lord hath spoken it'; Ps. xci. 1, 'He that dwelleth in the secret place of the Most High shall abide under the shadow of the Almighty.' So here, God's love, expressed in his mindfulness and vigilancy over our affairs, should excite our love to him again, and our love will be highly recompensed by his care and mindfulness of us.

[G.] These believers and called ones are considered as afflicted, and his purpose is to arm them against the bitterness of the cross. Nothing so fit for this use as love; if we did love

God, the burden of afflictions would be light and easy to be borne, because it is from God it cometh, John xviii. 11. Love is the fittest grace to bring the heart to submit to God. Love God once, and nothing that he saith or doth will be unacceptable to you; his commands will not be grievous, nor his providences grievous; our desires will be after him when his hand is most smart and heavy upon us; and when sense representeth him as an enemy, yet we cannot keep off from him: Isa. xxvi. 8, 'In the way of thy judgments, Lord, we have waited for thee: the desire of our soul is unto thee, and to the remembrance of thy name.'

[H.] Not only with ordinary afflictions, but troubles for their fidelity to Christ; love will endure much for God, as well as receive much from him: James i. 12, 'Blessed is the man that endureth temptations; for when he is tried, he shall receive the crown of life, which he hath promised to them that love him.' Mark, it is not said to them that fear him or trust in him, but them that love him; because it is love that maketh us hold out in temptations, love that engageth us to zeal and constancy, that overcometh all difficulties and oppositions for God's sake. *Nihil est quod non tolerat, qui perfecte diligit*; he that loveth much, will suffer much. He cordially adhereth to God with courage and resolution of mind, and is not daunted with sufferings: Cant. viii. 7, 'Many waters cannot quench love, neither can the floods drown it; if a man would give all the substance of his house for love, it would utterly be contemned' Love is not bribed nor quenched. Where love prevaileth upon the heart, we shall esteem nothing too much or too dear to be parted with for God's sake. As in these troubles God's love is best known and discovered to us, so our love to God is best known and discovered also; the more we love God, the more sensible do we find it, and are persuaded that all things shall work together for good; your title is clearer, experience greater: 1 Cor. viii. 3, 'If any man love God, the same is known of him'; that is, owned by him in the course of his providence. If we are sanctified to God, all things would be sanctified to us. It is otherwise with hypocrites: if God endow them with gifts, they prove a snare to them; but if you love God above all, count his favour your happiness, and make pleasing of God your constant work, and resolve to obey him at the dearest rates, you will soon find this testimony of God's love; then all the influences of his eternal love and grace shall be made out to you, and his external providence doth help you on in the way to heaven; for a man that loveth God as his chief good shall never be a loser by him.

[I.] This is a sure and sensible note of effectual calling; for as sincere faith is the immediate fruit of it, so true faith cannot be severed from love. This is that which maketh us saints indeed; but without it, whatever gifts and parts we have, whatever knowledge and utterance, we are nothing, 1 Cor. xiii. 1-3. There may be many convictions, and purposes, and wishes, and good meanings in those who are yet but under a common work; but till there be a thorough fixed bent of heart towards God, as our last end and chief good, we have not a sure evidence of grace, or that our calling home to God is accomplished. Many a thought there is of the goodness of God, the necessity of a saviour, the love of Christ, and the joys of heaven; yet after all this, the heart may be unrenewed and unsanctified till this addictedness and devoted- ness to God; for it is not every wish or minding of Christ, but a hearty, sincere affection, which is required of us as to our title: Eph. vi. 24, 'Grace be with all them that love our Lord Jesus Christ in sincerity'; not for a time, not with an ineffectual love, or upon some foreign motives, but have this habitual love which constituteth the new heart. Well then, this is a sure mark of one that hath interest in the love of God, and one of those marks which is best known to the person that hath it; for love to Christ cannot be well hidden, but will be easily discerned.

Use, To inform us that these are for the present excepted out of this privilege that do not sincerely love God, and love him above all.

They are of two sorts

1. Some have a weak and imperfect motion of their wills a wish, a faint desire to please God in all, and above all things; but being overcome by their own lusts, they do not simply and absolutely desire it, 'and had rather please their fleshly lusts than please God; at least the event doth so declare it. You give God nothing, if you do not give him all the heart. We are so to love God and seek his glory and do his will when it is cross to our carnal interest; his favour must be valued as our happiness, and the pleasing of him made our greatest work; and for his sake we must be content to suffer anything, though nover BO hard and difficult and contrary to our nature. Let not such say they love God that cannot deny a lust for him, nor will not for his sake venture the loss of anything that is dear to them, either goods, or liberty, or favour of men, or preferment, or credit. Pilate was loth to venture the Jews' displeasure; the Gadarenes would part with Christ rather than their swine; surely if we put the love of God to hazard upon light occasions, we do not love him, nor count his favour our supreme- happiness.

2. Others have a deliberate resolution, and seem for the present absolutely and seriously to please God in all things, and keep his commandments; but they do not verify it in their conversations. Their purposes and resolutions are not dissembled for the present, but yet soon changed; they neither keep the commandments of God nor study to please him; there is a moral sincerity in them, but not a super natural sincerity. Wherein differ they? The moral sincerity is a dictate of conscience, but the supernatural sincerity is a fruit of heart-changing grace. What shall we do, then? Beg such a heart of God: Deut. v. 29, 'Oh that there were such a heart within them, that they would fear me, and keep my commandments always' God showeth what we should do; convinced conscience showeth what purposes and resolutions we should make, but a converted heart is only able to keep- them. That must be sought of God, and all good means must be used that these purposes that we conceive to be sincere may be found to be so. And God will not fail the striving and endeavouring soul that seeketh to persevere in its holy will and purpose to obey and please God; but by internal grace and external providence will help us onward in our course to heaven. But if we depend upon our purposes and resolutions made in solemn duties, with a clear conscience, and with a deliberate and seemingly resolved will, without those subsequent endeavours which evidence they come from a renewed heart, alas! They will soon come to nothing.

Use 2. To exhort us to the love of God. The more you love him your title is the clearer, experience greater, hopes of eternal life stronger.

1. Consider these two things God is lovely in himself, and hath loved us.

[A.] That God is lovely in himself, because of his wisdom and greatness, as well as because of his benignity. We are, or may be, soon persuaded that we ought to love him as the fountain of all goodness; but the other attributes should attract and draw our hearts also. I shall add this argument to all the rest: Whatever engageth us to adhere to God as an all-sufficient portion, that is certainly a motive of our love; for love is nothing else but a delightful adhesion to God. Now his infinitely glorious essence, dominion, and power, engage us to adhere to him; therefore we must press you to consider the excellency of his nature, evidenced in the absolute dominion of his providence and holiness of his laws. We would have you consider neither with the exclusion of the other; not his greatness without his goodness, nor his benignity and goodness without his greatness, neither of both without his holiness; all maketh our love more strong and regular.

[B.] He hath loved us in what he hath done already, in what he hath prepared for us.

(1.) In what he hath done already in Christ, which showeth that God is love: John iii. 16, 'God so loved the world, that he gave his only-begotten Son'; 1 John iv. 10, 'Herein is love, not that we loved God, but he loved us, and sent his Son to be a propitiation for our sins'

(2.) In what he will do. He hath greater benefits to give us than what he hath already given: James ii. 5, 'God hath chosen the poor of the world, rich in faith, and heirs of a kingdom which he hath promised to them that love him'; not to learned, rich benefactors, but to them that love him, and are willing to do and suffer anything for his sake: 1 Peter ii. 9, 'But ye are a chosen generation, a royal priesthood, a holy nation, a peculiar people; that you should show forth the praise of him who hath called you out of darkness into his marvellous light'.

2. That love runneth a-wasting on the creature. That is ruinous and destructive, this conduces to our good; if we suffer loss here, we will be recompensed by a greater benefit.

I come now to the last clause—*Who are called according to purpose.*

Doctrine The effectually called are those that love God, and are beloved by him. Let me speak—

1. Of the several kinds of calling.

2. The properties of effectual calling

3. The ends of it.

First, Let us distinguish the several kinds of calling

1. There is a twofold calling proper and improper.

[A.] The improper call is the general and common invitation of all men in the world, by the works of creation and providence, by all which God inviteth men to seek after him. The work of creation, Acts xvii. 27. All God's works have a tongue, and a voice proclaiming and crying up an infinite and eternal power, who is the fountain of our being and happiness; so Rom. i. 20, 'The invisible things of God, from the creation of the world, are clearly seen, being understood from the things which are made'; Ps. xix. 1, 'The heavens declare the glory of

God, and the firmament showeth his handiwork.' No man can look seriously upon the works of creation, but this thought will arise in his mind, that all this was made by a powerful, wise, and good God. He telleth us, ver. 3, 'There is no speech and language where their voice is not heard'; though it be not an articulate, yet it is a very intelligible voice. They in effect speak to every nation in their own language, that there is an eternal God, who must be sought after and worshipped and served. And as the works of creation, so the works of providence, whether for good or evil. Good: Acts xiv. 17, 'Nevertheless, he left not himself without witness, in that he did good.' The comfortable passages of providence are a pregnant, full, and clear testimony that the government of the world is in the hands of a good God. So afflictive providences; some of God's works have a louder and more distinct voice than others: Micah vi. 9, 'The Lord's voice crieth unto the city, and the man of wisdom shall see thy name; hear ye the rod, and who hath appointed it'; or if you suppose that concerneth the church, take Rom. i. 18, 'For the wrath of God is revealed from heaven against all ungodliness and unrighteousness of men.' God doth discipline and instruct the world by his judgments, that he is holy, just, and true. God's works speak to us, only we must take heed of a deaf ear; non-attentiveness to God's providence made way for the prevalency of atheism and idolatry in the world. There are two propositions, that, if well minded and improved, would preserve a lively remembrance of God in the hearts of men that all good cometh from God: James i. 17, 'Every good and perfect gift is from above, and cometh down from the Father of lights'; and all evil from God: Amos iii. 6, 'Shall there be evil in a city, and the Lord hath not done it?' And that any notable effect in either kind is a sign and witness of an invisible power. If men would not look upon all things that befall them as mere chances, they could not sleep so securely in their sins; but God would have a greater testimony in every man's bosom that he hath a care of human affairs, and is a rewarder of such as please him, and an avenger of such as do offend him. The question about this improper calling is, What is the use of it? Or whether it be sufficient to salvation?

(1.) Though the works of creation and providence reveal a God, yet these natural apostles, sun, moon, and stars, say nothing of Christ, and there is salvation in no other, Acts iv. 12. They did teach the world that there is a God, and that this God must be served, and will be terrible to those that serve him not; and possibly that God was placable[59], or willing to be appeased, because of the continuance of the creation, and the manifold mercies we lost or forfeited by our apostasy and defection from him. The apostle saith it is an invitation to repentance, Rom. ii. 4. Yet the knowledge of Jesus Christ the Son of God, and of redemption purchased to lost sinners through him, is a mystery which the greatest wits in the world could not understand but by God's revealing it in his word.

---

[59] easily calmed; gentle and forgiving.

(2.) The use of this call to those that have no other, but barely it, is to leave men without excuse, Rom. i. 20; and that it might prevail to work some restraint of sin, and to promote some external reformation in the world, for the good of mankind, Rom. ii. 14.

(3.) Those who have a louder call in the word are the more obliged to regard this call and invitation by the works of God's creation and providence. The call by the word is more perfect and more pressing, and suited more to work upon our thoughts, the object being more clearly and fully propounded to us. Yet this latter call is not privative, but accumulative; it doth not null the duty of the former call, or make it wholly useless to us, but helps us to interpret it the better, and we need all helps. Faith doth not withdraw itself from natural knowledge, and make it useless to us. Though we are to exercise ourselves in the law of God day and night, yet we must not overlook the works of creation and providence, and whilst we study his word, neglect God's works; for they are a confirmation of our faith, and a great occasional help to our love, as appeareth by the instructions which the holy men of God gather thence; witness David's night meditation, Ps. viii., 'Thy moon and thy stars'; and his morning meditation, Ps. xix., 'The heavens declare the glory of God.' The glories of God which we read of in the word are visible in the creation; and though David preferreth the book of scripture, yet he doth not lay aside the book of nature. We must use the world as a glass, wherein to see the glory of God. He hath not the heart of a man in him who is not stricken with admiration at the sight of these things the glory of the heavenly bodies, and the wonderful variety of all creatures; and besides, there is none so good, but he needeth the mercy and direction of God to invite him to a more frequent remembrance of him. How happy are they that have such a God for their God 1 How miserable they that make him their judge and avenger!

[B.] The proper calling is the voice of God in the word of his grace inviting sinners to Christ. This is called distinctly his calling: Eph. i. 18, 'That ye may know what is the hope of his calling'; and the 'high calling of God in Jesus Christ' Phil. iii. 14; and again, 'That our God would count you worthy of his calling', 2 Thes. i. 11; and explained, 1 Cor. i. 9, 'Faithful is he which hath called you into the fellowship of his Son Jesus Christ our Lord.' Now this is a more close and full discovery of God than is to be found elsewhere; God calleth and inviteth some by the creatures only, others by his grace in Christ.

But this being calling most properly taken, why is it not vouchsafed to all? I answer—

(1.) God is not obliged to send the gospel to any; it is his free dispensation: Rom. xi. 35, 'Or who hath first given to him, and it shall be recompensed to him again?' God doth not send the gospel by necessity of nature, or any pre-obligation on the creature's part, but merely of his own grace, which worketh most freely, and sendeth it where it pleaseth him.

(2.) All have more knowledge of God by nature than they make good use of: Rom. i, 21, 'When they knew God, they glorified him not as God.' And till men improve a lower dispensation, why should they be trusted with a higher? If a vessel will not hold water, you will not trust wine, or any more precious liquor in it.

2. God's gracious invitation of lost sinners to Christ, which properly is his calling them, is either external or internal; external by the word, internal by his Spirit.

[A.] External, by the commands and promises of the word, requiring such duties from them, and assuring them of such blessings upon obedience. Thus Wisdom's maidens are sent forth to invite guests to her palace, Prov. iv. 2; and the king's servants to call them to the marriage-feast, Mat. xxii. 9; and so far they prevail in their message, that many present themselves. God would not leave us to a book, but hath appointed a living ministry, 2 Cor. vi. 10.

[B.] Internal, not only by the word, but by his Spirit, and the checks of their own conscience, which is a nearer approach of his grace and power to us. By the motions of his Spirit; how else could it be said, Gen. vi. 3, 'My Spirit shall not always strive with man'? And Acts vii. 51, 'Ye do always resist the Holy Ghost'? And also by their consciences soliciting them to the performance of their duty, and challenging them for the neglect of it. It is natural duty: Rom. ii. 14, 15, 'The Gentiles do by nature the things contained in the law; these, having not the law, are a law to themselves, which show the works of the law written in their hearts; their consciences also bearing witness, and their thoughts in the meanwhile accusing or excusing one another.' And for acceptance of the gospel-covenant: 1 John iii. 20, 21, 'If our heart condemn us, God is greater than our heart and knoweth all things; if our heart condemn us not, then have we confidence towards God'.

3. This external and internal calling may be ineffectual or effectual.

[A.] The ineffectual call consists in the bare tender and offer of grace, but is not entertained. God may knock at the door of the heart that doth not open to him; knock by the word, knock by the motions of the Spirit and checks of conscience; so, 'many are called, but few are chosen', Mat. xxii. 14. There is not the fruit of election, nor are these the called according to purpose.

[B.] The effectual call is when God changeth the heart, and bringeth it home to himself by Jesus Christ. We are not only invited to Christ, but come to him by the strength and power of his own grace: John vi. 44, 'No man can come to me, except the Father, which hath sent me, draw him' When we yield to the call; as Paul, who was extra ordinarily called, saith, Acts xxvi. 19, 'I was not disobedient to the heavenly vision;' we have his consent and resignation recorded: Acts ix. 6, 'Lord, what wilt thou have me to do?' He yieldeth up the keys of his heart, that Christ may come and take possession. In an ordinary call: 2 Cor. viii. 5, 'They first gave themselves to the Lord;' it is in other places expressed by our receiving or embracing Christ, John i. 12, both are implied our thankful accepting of Christ, and our giving up ourselves to him; they both go together, and where the one is, the other is also. In every covenant there is *ratio dati, et accepti*, something given and something required: Christ and his benefits, and what we have, are, and do, both are an answer to God's call.

Secondly, The properties of effectual calling.

(1.) It is a holy calling: 2 Tim. i. 9, 'Who hath called us with an holy calling'; and it is also a heavenly calling: Heb. iii. 1, 'Partakers of the heavenly calling:' because we are called to duties and privileges, these must not be severed; some are forward to the privileges of the calling, but backward to the duties thereof. A good Christian must mind both, the privileges to take him off from the false happiness, and the duties that he may return to his obedience to God; the one is the way and means to come to the other; for it is said, he hath 'called us to glory and virtue,' 2 Peter i. 3; meaning by glory, eternal life, and by virtue, grace and holiness. In the way that God offereth it we embrace it; we heartily consent to seek after eternal glory in the way of faith and holiness; and so by it the heart is turned by Christ from the creature to God, from sin to holiness.

Thirdly, The ends of effectual calling, both on God's part and the creature's.

(1.) On God's part, that God may show his wisdom, power, and goodness.

(a.) His wisdom is seen partly in the way and means that God taketh to convert sinners to himself. There is a sweet mixture of wisdom and power; there is no violence offered to the will of the creatures, nor the liberty of second causes taken away, and yet the effect is obtained. The proposal of good to the understanding and will, by the secret power of the Lord's grace, is made effectual; and at the same time we are taught and drawn: John vi. 44, 45, 'No man can come to me, except the Father, which hath sent me, draw him; as it is written in the prophets, They shall all be taught of God; every man therefore that hath heard, and learned of the Father, cometh to me.' There is opening blind eyes, and turning a hard heart, Acts xxvi. 18. He worketh strongly like himself, sweetly with respect to us, that he may not oppress the liberty of our faculties; and the convert, at the same time, is made willing by his own choice, and effectually cured by God's grace; so that Christ cometh conqueringly into the heart, and yet not by force, but by consent. We are transformed, but so as we prove what the good and acceptable will of the Lord is, Rom. xii. 2. The power of God and the liberty of man do sweetly consist together; and we have at the same time a new heart and a free spirit, and the powerful efficacy of his grace doth not destroy the consent and good liking of the sinner. The will is moved, and also changed and renewed. In the persuasive and moral way of working, God taketh the most likely course to gain the heart of man, discovering himself to us as a God of kindness and mercy, ready to pardon and forgive: Ps. cxxx. 4, 'But there is forgiveness with thee, that thou mayest be feared;' for guilty creatures would stand aloof off from a condemning God. No, God hath laid the foundation of the offer of his grace in the highest demonstration of his love and goodness that ever could come into the ears of man to hear, or could enter into the heart of man to conceive viz., in giving his Son to die for a sinful world: 2 Cor. v. 19, 20, 'To wit, that God was in Christ, reconciling the world to himself, not imputing their trespasses unto them, and hath committed unto us the word of reconciliation. Now then, we are ambassadors for Christ, as though God did beseech you by us; we pray you in Christ's stead, be ye reconciled to God'. And not only in the offers of pardon, but eternal life and blessedness, so infinitely beyond the false happiness that our carnal self-love inclineth us unto, that it is a shame and disgrace to our reason to think that these things are worthy to be compared in any serious debate, or that all the pleasures and honours and profits we dote upon should come in competition with that blessed immortality and life which is brought to light in the gospel, 2

Tim. i. 10. And powerful grace goeth along with all this, to make it effectual, partly in the time of conversion, taking us in our month, and that season which is fittest for the glory of his grace. Some are called in the morning, some at noon, some in the evening of their age; as Mat. xx. 3-6, &c., some were hired to go into the vine yard at the third, some the ninth, some the eleventh hour. That any believe in Christ at all is mercy; that some believe in him sooner, some later, is the Lord's wise ordering. He that is called betimes may consider God's goodness, which broke out so early, before he longer provoked him, and contracted a habit of evil customs, and that God instructed him betimes to take heed of sin, and spending his fresh and flowery youth in the service of the devil; whereas, otherwise, lost days and months and years would have been a perpetual grief to him. He that is called at the latter end of his days, having so many sins upon him, may be quickened to glorify God, that he would not refuse him at last, nor despise him for all his rebellions, nor remember against him the sins of his youth, that a long and an old enemy should be taken into favour. God knoweth how best to gain upon every heart. And partly in the means and occasions which God useth to convert us. It is many times dispensed in a contrary way to human expectation: Paul when pursuing the people of God, some when scoffing and mocking, at least when they dreamt of no such matter. But of that here after.

(b.) In this effectual calling God showeth forth his love and grace.

(i.) That the rise of all was his elective love. None are in time effectually called but those that before all time were chosen to life; for it is said here, 'called according to purpose' From all eternity he had a purpose to be thus gracious to us. Those that were in the corrupt mass of mankind are distinguished from others in his eternal purpose before the foundations of the world, and were in time called out from others; and vocation is but election broken out, therefore called election. Trace the stream till you find the well-head, and you will discern that you can ascribe your calling to nothing else, but 1 even so, Father, because it pleased thee,' Mat. xi. 26. God before time elected us; in the fulness of time Christ gave a ransom to provoked justice for us; and in due time the effects of God's eternal love and Christ's purchase are applied, and so we come to have a right to the blessedness we were chosen unto and was purchased for us. Oh! Admire this grace!

(2.) God needed us not; he had an only Son to delight in, Prov. viii. 31; millions of angels to serve him, Dan. vii. 10. What loss would it be to him if the world of mankind had been destroyed? Acts xvii. 25, 'God is not worshipped with men's hands, as if he needed anything' No, to the fulness of his happiness nothing can be added.

(3.) He was highly provoked and offended by us, for we had cast off the mercies of our creation, and from his creatures were become his rebels. And then, 'in due time Christ died for the ungodly' Rom. v. 6; and upon his death and propitiation is the offer grounded. Sinners are called to repentance, Mat. ix. 13.

(4.) Great was our misery we fell into by reason of sin: Eph. ii. 3, 'Children of wrath' Indeed we were senseless of our misery, careless of our remedy, loth to come out of that wretched estate into which we had plunged ourselves: John iii. 19, 'And this is the condemnation, that light is come into the world, and men love darkness rather than light, because their deeds were evil.' Oh! What mercy was this! That God had such pity and compassion upon us, when we had none upon ourselves. How freely then did he love us! How powerful did he work upon us! Calling and conquering, ruling and overruling all matters wherein we were concerned, that he might convert us to himself.

(5.) That he should call us who were so inconsiderable, when others were left to perish in sins: 1 Cor. i. 26, 'Ye see your calling, brethren, how that not many wise men after the flesh are called' When so many were passed by who are before us in outward respects, learned, great, and wise, and God showed mercy to us, we were as deep in the common pollution as they, and for many natural abilities and perfections came far short of them, surely this is merely the love and good pleasure of God.

(6.) This calling bringeth us into such an estate as entitleth us to the peculiar and special protection of God. We are his charge, that he may guide all things about us for his own glory and our good. This is intimated in the text. When once you believe God's offers, and yield hearty obedience to them, you are a peculiar people. Why? Because called out of darkness into his marvellous light, 1 Peter ii. 9. All his creatures are the work of his hands, and under the disposal of his providence; but you have -a special propriety and peculiar interest in his love and care, whom he will maintain, and never forsake.

(7.) By this calling you are interested in his kingdom and glory to be had hereafter; for it is said, 1 Peter iii. 9, 'You are called to inherit a blessing;' that is, a blessedness, which consists in the clear vision and full fruition of God. Surely they that were naturally under the curse should be more apprehensive of this great privilege.

[C.] It is an act of power: Rom. iv. 17, 'Even God, who quickeneth the dead, and calleth those things which be not as though they were' God only can work so great a change by his creating power, which spake all things out of nothing. Certainly, he that can do what he will both in heaven and in earth, Ps. cxxxv. 3, can subdue the heart of man when he pleaseth. The will of man, though never so deeply engaged in a course of sin and wickedness, cannot resist it, but yieldeth to it: Ps. ex. 3, 'They shall be a willing people in the day of thy power;' of graceless they become gracious, of unwilling, willing. And God showeth more power in this than in his other works, for here is a principle of resistance; as to break a skittish horse is more than to roll a stone.

2. The ends with respect to man. It is a great mercy, this external, internal, and effectual calling, take it all together.

[A.] It giveth us notice of the remedy provided for us by the propitiation of Christ, and the covenant founded thereupon. Light is come into the world, John iii. 19 a sure way to direct us to true happi ness; without it the world had been a dark dungeon, wherein guilty malefactors are for a while permitted to live.

[B.] This calling bringeth home this grace to us, and layeth it at our doors, and leaves it upon our choice; if we will accept it, well and good: Acts xiii. 26, 'To you is the word of salvation sent.' What say you to it? God hath sent a gracious message to you in particular, will you accept or refuse? And Acts iii. 20'; And he shall send Jesus Christ, which before was preached unto you.' It doth excite us in particular to look after the remedy of our lapsed estate.

[C.] This calling is our warrant, plea, and claim, which giveth us leave to apply these privileges, if we consent to the duties required; as the apostle saith of an office, so it is true of the dignity of being Christians, which is a spiritual priesthood: Heb. v. 4, 'And no man taketh this honour upon himself, but he that is called of God, as was Aaron' For a man to take or receive to himself honour and privilege which doth not belong to him, is usurpation, which will succeed ill with him; but by calling we have God's consent; or as those, Mat. xx. 7, 'Why stand ye here idle all the day? No man hath hired us.' Before we can with any tolerable satisfaction to conscience assume such great privileges, we must produce our warrant. It was encouragement to the blind man to come near to Christ, 'Arise, the Master calleth thee' Mark x. 49. The same hath the trembling sinner: the Master calleth thee, and wilt thou draw back?

[D.] The internal effectual call giveth us a heart to come to Christ; for the power of God disposeth us to accept of his offer, and not only encourageth, but inclineth us to come to him, for his calling is sanctifying and changing the heart: Rom. ix. 25, 'I will call them my people which were not my people'; that is, make them to be so.

Use 1. Hearken to this calling.

1. From the benefit. Doth God call thee to thy loss? Or do thee any wrong when he disturbeth thy sleep in sin, and invites thee to partake of the riches of his grace in Christ? No, he calls thee to the greatest happiness thou art capable of: 2 Thes. ii. 14, 'He hath called you by our gospel to the obtaining of the glory of our Lord Jesus Christ.' God seeketh to advance you to the greatest honour can be put upon mankind; it is a blessed estate: 1 Peter v. 10, 'He hath called you to his eternal glory by Jesus Christ'; that glorious happiness forever.

2. The great misery, if we refuse this call. 'None of those that were bidden shall taste of my supper' Luke xiv. 24. They are not only excluded from happiness, but are under extreme wrath and misery: Prov. i. 24-26, 'Because I have called, and ye refused, I have stretched out my hand, and no man regarded, but ye have set at nought all my counsel, and would none of my reproof, I will also laugh at your calamity, I will mock when your fear cometh'

Use 2. Is to press you to make your calling and election sure, 2 Peter i. 10. It cannot be more sure than it is in itself, but it may be more sure to us. This may be known by these signs

1. Doth the word of God come to you with power, so as to produce its effect? It is a sign of election when the gospel cometh to us not in word only, 2 Thes. i. 4, 5. The Spirit accompanieth it, that this calling may have its effect, and convert you to God.

2. By your obedience to this call; attendancy, choice, and pursuit.

[A.] A deliberate weighing, in order to choice: Acts xvi. 14, 'The Lord opened the heart of Lydia, so that she attended unto the things which were spoken of Paul.' A deep and serious consideration of the offers of pardon and life by Christ, this maketh way for other things: Mat. xiii. 19, 'When any one heareth the word of the kingdom, and understandeth it not, then cometh the wicked one, and catcheth away that which was sown in his heart' &c.; Mat. xxii. 5, 'But they made light of it,' &c. Non-attendancy is the bane of the far greatest part of the world; a flash of lightning cometh into their minds, and is soon gone.

[B.] A thorough choice; as Lydia is commended for attending, so Mary for choosing: Luke x. 42, 'But one thing is needful, and Mary hath chosen that good part which shall not be taken away from her.'

[C.] A constant and earnest pursuit. A choice made in a sudden pang and humour may be as soon retracted: Phil. iii. 12, 'Not as though I had already attained, or were already perfect; but I follow after, if that I may apprehend that for which also I am apprehended of Christ Jesus.' Seeking these things in the first place, Mat. vi. 33. That pursuit which is the fruit of calling must be speedy: Gal. i. 15, 16, 'But when it pleased God, who separated me from my mother's womb, and called me by his grace, to reveal his Son in me, that I might preach him among the heathen, immediately I conferred not with flesh and blood' &c. The call of God must be obeyed without delay: Heb. iii. 7, 8, 'Wherefore, as the Holy Ghost saith, To-day, if ye will hear his voice, harden not your hearts, as in the provocation, in the day of temptation in the wilderness' The case is uncertain, we know not whether we shall ever get again such an offer; and our indisposition is the greater. And then it must be earnest: Phil. iii. 14, 'I press towards the mark, for the prize of the high calling of God in Christ Jesus.' It must be our scope and business, and accompanied with self-denial and dependence on God: Heb. xi. 8, 'By faith Abraham, when he was called to go out into a place which he should after receive for an inheritance, obeyed, and he went out, not knowing whither he went.

[D.] By walking worthy of it: Eph. iv. 1, 'I, therefore, the prisoner of the Lord, beseech you that you walk worthy of the vocation wherewith ye are called'; 1 Thes. ii. 12, 'That ye walk worthy of God, who hath called you unto his kingdom and glory.' That ye behave yourselves so as may beseem the duties and hopes of Christians more holy, more heavenly. God is a holy God, and the happiness he hath called you unto a glorious estate; labour to get the heavenly mind and holy conversation; be deeply possessed with God's love in calling you, that you may love him again; it is not our will nor our worth, therefore it could not begin with us.

(1.) Not our will. Besides a simple want of good-will, there is in us a carelessness yea, an' averseness, in closing with his gracious offers, Mat. xxiii. 37. If it did depend on the choice of our will, we would refuse to be gathered, and would live and die estranged from God; when all things are ready, we are not ready.

(2.) Not our worth. There is nothing in the elect more than in the reprobate to move God to bestow this blessing on us yea, much why he should abhor us, Ezek. xvi. 6. Only, where sin abounded grace did much more abound, Rom. v. 20. The worthiest have no claim but grace.

We come now to the last clause—To them who are the called according to his purpose. The limiting term of this calling must be now considered—'According to purpose.' Surely it is not meant of our good purpose and resolution to turn to God, which is none at all, till God work it in us; and calling is God's act, and therefore it is meant of his purpose. And presently his foreknowledge and predestination is spoken of: nothing plainer can be said to signify God's purpose, which he purposed in himself. But if God's purpose be meant, some think it is only his purpose concerning the way of salvation, or the saving of mankind by Christ, or the gospel-way: Eph. i. 9, 'Having made known the mystery of his will, according to his good pleasure, which he purposed in himself;' and Eph. iii. 11, 'According to the eternal purpose which he purposed in Christ Jesus our Lord.' The gospel was firmly resolved upon by God according to his eternal purpose. But this is not all, the word relateth to a degree concerning those persons in particular whom he intended to save by Christ. His revealed will holdeth forth the way of our duty, or the course agreed upon and purposed by him; but there are some persons whom he determineth to call to grace and glory. The word is often elsewhere applied to persons: 2 Tim. i. 9, 1 Who hath called us with an holy calling, not according to our works, but according to his own purpose and grace;' and Rom. ix. 11, 'That the purpose of God according to election might stand;' and Eph. i. 11, 'In whom also we have obtained an inheritance, being predestinated according to the counsel of his own will'; and so it suiteth with the text, which applieth this to persons. Three words are here used purpose, foreknowledge, and predestination. Because there is wisdom in this decree, therefore it is called foreknowledge; because there is an ordination of means to a certain end, therefore it is called predestination; because it is fixed and unchangeable, therefore it is called purpose.

Many notes might be observed in this clause.

1. We are beholding to God's eternal election and purpose for all the good that we get by affliction and other providences; for God's purpose is the supreme reason assigned in the description of the per sons who have an interest in this privilege. We love God because we believe his goodness in Christ; we believe his goodness in Christ because he hath called us; and he hath called us because of his eternal purpose; and thence it is that all this good cometh to us.

2. The purpose of God concerning our eternal salvation is manifested in our being called: that is the first eruption of God's elective love; we are in the dark before.

3. Those that continue in their final unbelief and impenitency are called only by the bye; the elect, with a purpose to save them. God raineth on the rocks as well as on the new-mown grass.

But I will content myself with one point—That there are certain persons before all time elected of God according to his mere good pleasure and grace, that in time they may be effectually called and saved.

For some persons here are said to be the called according to purpose. Let me explain, and then confirm it.

1. The object of this purpose are certain definite and individual persons; Jacob, not Esau; Peter, not Judas; man by man, or by head and poll they are known to God, 2 Tim. ii. 19. Put into the hands of Christ, that he may redeem them, and give an account of them at the last day: John xvii. 6, 'I have manifested thy name unto the men which thou gavest me out of the world; thine they were, and thou gavest them me, and they have kept thy word'; John vi. 40,

'And this is the will of him that sent me, that every one that seeth the Son, and believeth on him, may have everlasting life, and I will raise him up at the last day' And they do all believe, and are infallibly converted: John vi. 37, 'All that the Father giveth me shall come to me; and him that cometh to me I will in nowise cast off.'

2. The reason of this purpose is only the Lord's grace and good pleasure. Christ, debating the matter, giveth no other account of the gospel's being hid from the wise and prudent, and revealed unto babes, but this only: Mat xi. 25, 'Even so, Father, for so it seemeth good in thy sight.' The cause is only God's pleasure; the reason of this can be found nowhere else, but only in the bosom of God himself. There is nothing before, or above, or without his purpose, as the first cause of all that good which cometh to us; he doth not foresee any merit or motive in us; as Christ telleth his disciples, John xv. 10, 'I have chosen you, you have not chosen me'; his choice is antecedent to ours. The persons that are singled out to be objects of this special grace were a part of lost mankind, by nature the same that others are, some of the world that lay in wickedness; but when God had all Adam's posterity under the prospect of his all-seeing eye, he chose some, and passed by others; he found all guilty, but doth not punish all, but spare some; and found nothing in the creature to cast the balance of his choice, or to determine it to one more than to another. Others were as eligible as they, God created them all; all were alike obnoxious to him. The prophet argueth, Mai. i. 2, 'Was not Esau Jacob's brother?' It was grace alone did put the difference.

3. This purpose noteth the sure and powerful efficacy of this grace. God will not be disappointed in his purpose, for there is nothing that can be imagined that should occasion the alteration of it. Men are forced to alter their purposes, either out of a natural levity that is in them, or some impediment falleth out which they foresaw not, or through defect of power they cannot do what they intend to do; but none of these things are in God, no levity and unstability, for he is Jehovah that changeth not, Mai. iii. 6. And the apostle speaketh of the immutability of his counsel. God's purpose is both an act of his understanding, and therefore called counsel, and also his will, therefore called his decree; and therefore being once set, it cannot be altered or revoked; no cause of revocation can be imagined either in God or out of God; not in God, nothing can fall out but what God foresaw at first; nor can be frustrated for any defect of power, for he is almighty, angels, devils, and men being subject to him as the supreme and universal Lord.

4. This grace is brought about in a way most convenient for the honour of God and the good of the creature: in a way of faith and holiness. Faith: John iii. 16, 'God so loved the world, that he gave his only-begotten Son, that whosoever believeth on him should not perish, but have everlasting life' Holiness: Eph. i. 4, 'According as he hath chosen us in him before the foundation of the world, that we should be holy and without blame before him in love.' Now faith is his gift: Eph. ii. 8, 'We are saved by grace through faith; and that not of ourselves, it is the gift of God.' And holiness is wrought in us by the Spirit of sanctification, and that with a respect to his election: 2 Thes. ii. 13, 'He hath chosen you to salvation through the sanctification of the Spirit, and belief of the truth.' God did not choose us because he did foresee that we should be believers, or would be holy, but that we might believe, and might

be holy; he could not foresee any faith or holiness in us but what was the fruit of his own grace and elective love to us; all is still according to his purpose and grace, which was given us in Christ before the world began. Faith and holiness is the way and means of bringing about his purpose, not the foreseen cause and reason, or the end; the fruit of it, not the motive to induce God to show us mercy.

5. To promote this faith and holiness, and to preserve them till their glorified estate, God's providence about them is very remark able.

[A.] He contriveth means to bring them into the world. Many of their parents may be wicked, and deserve to be cut off for their sins, but because there is a blessing in some of the clusters, they are not destroyed. Many times a slip may be taken from an ill stock, and grafted into the tree of life; though the grace of the covenant runneth most kindly in the channel of the covenant 'How much more shall these, which be the natural branches, be grafted into their own olive- tree? 'Horn. xi. 24. But yet God will show the liberty of his counsels, and choose some out of families very opposite to his ways; and therefore many wicked men are spared, that they may be a means to bring into the world those that afterwards shall believe: Ahaz is let alone to beget Hezekiah, and a wicked Ammon Josiah; and there was one in the house of Jeroboam who made Israel to sin, one child only, in whom was found some good thing towards the Lord God of Israel, 1 Kings xiv. 13, a godly young man that had in his heart the true seeds of religion.

[B.] When they are born, God hath a special care of them, that they may not die in their unregenerate condition; from the womb the decree beginneth to take place and be put in act: Gal. i. 15, 'It pleased God, who separated me from my mother's womb, and called me by his grace'; Jer. i. 5, 'When thou earnest out of the womb, I knew thee.' He took special notice that that child was a vessel of mercy, and to be employed for his glory, and used for such and such purposes as he had designed themselves unto; to fit them with such a constitution of body and mind, as might best serve for that use. If a man would trace the progress of providence, he would plainly see that God still hath been pursuing his choice; and that that antecedent love, which is the fountain of all our mercies, is it which rocked you in your cradles, suckled you at your mother's breast, trained you up, and took care of your non-age, visited you with his early mercies, disposed of several providences for your safety and preservation. It is said in heaven 'We shall know as we are known' 1 Cor. xiii. 12; compare Gal. iv. 9, 'But now, after that ye have known God, or rather are known of God.' Then we shall understand how many several circumstances concurred to bring us home to God, and how the goodness of God hath gone along with you from time to time, to preserve you till the time of grace was come, rescued you in imminent dangers, when the thread of your life was likely to be fretted asunder.

[C.] The dispensation of means, and the directing of means to such a place and people, where, and among whom, the course of your life fell. Not only the doctrine, but the journeys of the apostles were ordered by the Spirit: Acts xvi. 7, 'They assayed to go into Bithynia, but the Spirit suffered them not'; Acts xiii. 26, 'To you is this word of salvation sent;' not brought by us, but sent by God; not only in regard of his institution, but providential direction.

Certainly there is a special providence goeth along with ordinances, and they are ordered and directed with respect to God's elective love; he sendeth, furnisheth, continueth able instruments: Acts xviii. 10, 'I am with thee, and no man shall set on thee to hurt thee, for I have much people in this city.' Wherever God lighteth a candle, he hath some lost groat[60] to seek. He had much people belonging to his election in Corinth. God doth not say, Because there are much people (though it is good casting out the net where there is store of fish), but, 'have much people'. He understandeth not the Corinthians which were converted already; so there were few or none at that time in Corinth, but to be converted. They were God's people, elected and redeemed by him, though as yet wallowing in their sins. Therefore the first moving-cause of all this business was the election of God, or his purpose to call them; the persons never thought of seeking means for themselves, and have not a heart to entertain them for a long time; but God is at work for their good, when they intended no good to themselves. We read of saints in Nero's household, Phil. iv. 22. Who would look for saints in the family of so bloody a persecutor? Yet the gospel could find its way thither, and seize on some of his menial servants; for God had strange ways and methods to convert those that belong to his grace. I cannot say to them, but to some others, Christ was made known to them by Paul's defence: 2 Tim. iv. 17, 'Notwithstanding the Lord stood with me, and strengthened me, that by me the preaching might be fully known, and that all the Gentiles might hear.'

[D.] In blessing the means, quite besides the purpose and intention of the parties that receive benefit by them, as appeareth by the circumstances of their conversion and first acceptance of Christ; many times they come where they may hear of God and Christ, with careless and slight spirits, or drop in by chance, as Paul's infidel: 1 Cor. xv. 24, 25, 'There cometh in one that believeth not' How many do thus stumble upon grace unawares to themselves, not minding or desiring any such matter; but God directeth a serious word that pierceth into their very hearts. Sometimes God calleth them, when opposing and persecuting, as Paul, Acts ix.. Many, when they came to scoff, have felt the mighty power and majesty of God in his ordinances; and what begun with scoffing ended in a more serious work: Isa. lvii. 18, 'He went on frowardly in the way of his own heart: I have seen his ways, and I will heal him' The officers that came to attack Christ, John vii. 46, said, 'Never man spake like this man' Sometimes men have been loath to come, drawn with much importunity against their inclination and prejudices: John i. 46, 'Can any good come out of Nazareth?', saith Nathanael to Philip. 'Come and see'; and there he met with Christ. The Galileans were a ruder part of the Jews, a gross and blockish sort of people. It was generally conceived no prophet was of that country where Jonah was; thus Nathanael held off out of a prejudicate[61] opinion. Many of these things which come as it were by chance to us, and

---

[60] any of various medieval European coins, in particular an English silver coin worth four old pence, issued between 1351 and 1662
[61] to affect in a prejudicial manner

without our foresight, are well foreseen and wisely ordered by God; as Augustine was carried besides his purpose, that God's purpose might come to pass in the conversion of Firmus a Manichee.

[E.] In suiting all his dealings with them, so after conversion, that they may be kept blameless to his heavenly kingdom, John x. 3. Christ calleth his sheep by name; knoweth all his flock particularly; taketh notice of all their persons and conditions; hath a special affection to them and care of them; so Ps. i. 6, 'The Lord knoweth the way of the righteous'; knoweth their necessities, straits, hopes, burdens, and temptations. His business in heaven is to order his providence for their good, 2 Chron. xvi. 9; sometimes giveth seasonable correction: Ps. cxix. 75, 'I know, Lord, that thy judgments are right, and that thou in faithfulness hast afflicted me'; 1 Peter i. 6, 'Now for a season, if need be, ye are in heaviness'; sometimes to lessen the affliction or remove it: Ps. cxxv. 3, 'For the rod of the wicked shall not rest upon the lot of the righteous, lest the righteous put forth their hands to iniquity'; and 1 Cor. x. 13, 'But God is faithful, who will not suffer you to be tempted above that you are able, but will also with the temptation make a way to escape, that ye may be able to bear it' God considereth who needeth chastening, and who needeth protection and deliverance: thus I have stated it.

Secondly, I shall give you an argument or two to confirm it 1. That there is a difference between man and man is plain and obvious to sense; some are good and holy, others are naught and wicked; some understand the gospel, others are ignorant of it; some scoff, others believe; some have a dead faith, others a lively and deep sense of the world to come, and make preparation accordingly. Ask the reason of this difference, whence is it? You will say their choice and inclination: some choose the better part, others abandon themselves to their lusts and brutish satisfactions. True; but whence cometh this different choice and inclination? Experience showeth us that man from his infancy and childhood is very corrupt, and more inclinable to evil than to good, to things earthly than heavenly, carnal than spiritual; and you may as well expect to gather grapes from thorns, and figs from thistles, as that man of his own accord should become good and holy, and that we should be able to bring our own hearts to love God and delight in God: Job xiv. 4, 'Who can bring a clean thing out of an unclean? Not one.' Well, then, since all are not good, but some are, whence cometh the difference? Is it from a better temper and constitution of body? That is a benefit and gift of God; but this is not the whole cause. Many besot brave wits, and spoil an excellent temper and constitution of body, by their intemperance and incontinency; and, on the other side, many of crabbed and depraved tempers master their natural inclination by grace; and God doth often choose beams and rafters for the sanctuary of the most crooked timber. Is it education, and setting their inclinations right from their infancy? It is, I confess, a great advantage to be brought up in the nurture and information of the Lord, in a course of virtue and religion: Prov. xxii. 6, 'Train up a child in the way that he should go, and when he is old he will not depart from it.' The first infusions stick by us, and conduce, if not to conversion, yet to conviction; but many wrest themselves out of the arms of the best education, and turn the back upon all those godly counsels and instructions which are instilled into them. Is it the ordinances and means of grace? These certainly have great force and efficacy this way. God knoweth what keys will fit the wards of the lock; if anything, the doctrine of the gospel will do it. But they have not all believed: Rom. x. 16, 'For Isaiah saith, Who hath believed our report?' We see the same seed that thriveth in the good and honest heart is lost in highway, stony, thorny ground; the difference is not in seed, but soil; whatever means and helps you can imagine, all is nothing till God puts a new heart into us. Is it a good temper and disposition of mind, so that grace is represented to us congruously, so that it findeth us fitly prepared? Certainly seasons should not be over-slipped, but yet this is not the adequate cause of conversion, that some believe, others not, because we are so happy to find them in a disposition of mind to obey the word. We see that many that come with an ill disposition and temper of soul to hear the word of God, yet God taketh them by the heart. People should bring a prepared mind, free from distractions and prejudices. But that is not all that is necessary: we are to use the means, but the success is from God, who will take his own time. Chris tians, when they think themselves best prepared, find not that efficacy in the word they could desire.

2. All good is of God: 1 Cor. iv. 7, 'Who maketh thee to differ? And what hast thou, that thou hast not received?', and Jer. xxiv. 7, 'I will give them a heart to know me.' It is his grace maketh the difference: Mat. xiii. 11, 'It is given you to know the mystery of the kingdom of heaven, but to them it is not given.' The cause of putting a difference between the one and the other is in the will of God the giver; the advantages in the means of better temper, better ministry, somewhat there is in that: Acts xiv. 1, 'They so spake, that a great multitude of Jews and Greeks believed.' All this is to be imputed to God's external providence. One way of preaching may be more apt to convert souls than another; a dart, headed and feathered, and sent out of a strong bow will pierce deeper than falling of its own weight; pure solid doc trine, rationally enforced, is more likely to do the deed; but yet the thorough cause of the difference is internal grace changing the heart, and powerfully inclining it to God: Acts xi. 21, 'The hand of the Lord was with them, and a great number believed and turned to the Lord.' It is God's mighty power maketh the difference.

3. Whatever God doth in time, he purposed to do before all time; for God doth nothing rashly and by chance, but all by counsel and predestination. It is according to his purpose, especially in man's salvation; nothing is done but what he decreed to be done; even the least circumstance, time, means, and occasion, it is all according to purpose, not of yesterday, but from all eternity: Acts ix. 11, God's sending Ananias to Paul, and was not that foreknown and determined?

Use. Is to press us to admire grace. Nothing moved God to let put his love upon us but his free, eternal, distinguishing love; nothing keepeth the heart so right with God as a due sense of his free grace and love; for the gjpry of his grace was the great thing God. aimed at in all his dealings with us: Eph. i. 6, 12, 'To the praise of the glory of his grace, wherein he hath made us accepted in the beloved; that we should be to the praise of his glory who first trusted in Christ'; Rom. ix. 23, 'And that he might make known the riches of his glory on the vessels of mercy, which he had afore prepared unto glory.' This is the study of the saints:

Eph. iii. 18, 19, 'May be able with all saints to comprehend what is the breadth and length, and depth and height, and to know the love of Christ, which passeth knowledge.' It is the great excitement to duty: 2 Cor. v. 14, 'The love of Christ constraineth us'; Rom. xii. 1, 'I beseech you by the mercies of God'; 1 John iv. 19; Titus ii. 11, 12. It breedeth a good spirit if love is at the bottom of all our duties.

2. We have the truest view of our obligations to God in his elective love; *dulcius est ipso fonte*[62]. Nothing will so much excite our love and gratitude as to consider—

1. That God all-sufficient, who needeth nothing, should choose us. He might have possessed himself if he had never created anything without himself. If you remove all creatures from him, you detract nothing from God; if you add all to him, you increase nothing in God. It is the creature's indigent condition that maketh him go without his own compass for the happiness of his being. Man cannot be happy in loving himself, nor be satisfied in his own intrinsic perfections, therefore seeketh supplies from abroad; but God's happiness is to love himself and delight in himself.

2. That when God would look abroad among the creatures, he would choose us whom he found in the polluted mass of mankind, and make us objects of his grace, and when he came to call us, found us entangled in other sins, as Abraham, the father of the faithful, an idolater, Joshua xxiv. 2; every one that looketh into himself will find they were in temper to choose anything rather than Christ, unless the Lord had prevented us by his goodness, and turned our crooked wills. And if we consider why we taken and others left: Jer. iii. 14, 'I will take you one of a city, and two of a family.' And lastly, if we consider this powerful prosecution of his eternal purpose, this certainly will excite our love and gratitude.

---

[62] Sweet is the fountain

SERMON XXXIX

For whom he did foreknow, he also did predestinate to be conformed to the image of his Son, that he might be the first-born among many brethren.

Romans viii. 29.

HERE is a reason why all afflictions work together for good to the called according to purpose, because they were predestinated to be like Christ in all manner of likeness in sufferings, holiness, felicity. In sufferings; they must be afflicted as Christ was; he had his share, and they have their share: Col. i. 24, 'I rejoice in my sufferings, that I may fill up what is behind of the sufferings of Christ in my flesh' Christ mystical is to suffer so much; he was appointed, and they are appointed: 1 Thes. iii. 3, 'That no man should be moved by these afflictions; for yourselves know that we are appointed thereunto' Holiness: we are to be holy as he is holy, as well as afflicted as he was afflicted, 1 Peter i. 15. And again for felicity: his sufferings had a good end, so shall ours; he bore afflictions, and passed through them to eternal glory 'The captain of our salvation was made perfect by sufferings,' Heb. ii. 20; so in us, the cross maketh way to the crown; we can go no other way to heaven than Christ did. Therefore the conclusion out of all is, that afflictions work for good; they do not infringe our holiness, but promote it rather, if we be humble, meek, and patient as Christ was; they do not infringe our happiness, for still it fareth with us as it did with Christ. As he was a pattern in bearing afflictions holily and courageously, so in the crown of glory to be obtained after the victory; he was the leader of a patient and obedient people to everlasting happiness. So that here is a double argument why all afflictions must turn to good: because our afflictions fall not out besides the purpose of God; as not in Christ, so not in us; the head was to bear his share, and the members their share: and because the cross and sufferings are a means conducing to conformity to Christ in holiness and happiness— 'For whom he did foreknow' &c. In the words observe

1. The way God took in bringing his children unto glory, by conformity to Christ, in these words—*To be conformed to the image of his Son.*

2. The grounds of this conformity, set forth by two words, foreknowledge and predestination—*Whom he did foreknow, he also did predestinate.*

3. The reason of this conformity to Christ That he might be the first-born among many brethren; that is, that he might have the privilege of the elder son, or the true and proper heir. The elder son was to be the head of the family, and lord of all the rest of the brethren. Let us explain these things.

[A.] The way and end aimed at: to conform us to the image of his son; that is, in resemblance to Christ, that we might enter into glory the way by which Christ entered, by a life of sufferings and hardness.

[B.] The grounds of this conformity God's foreknowledge and pre destination. The first of these terms implieth his gracious purpose to save us; foreknowing here is choosing, or taking them for his own from all eternity: 1 Peter i. 2, 'Elect according to the foreknowledge of God;' that is, according to the eternal purpose of his love to them. For having all Adam's posterity in his eye and view, he freely chose them; they were in a sort present to God, and in his eye, before the foundation of the world; so that his foreknowledge is his purpose to do them good. The other word, predestination, is his appointing them to come to glory by the way of faith and holiness; for to destinate is to appoint, or order means to a certain end, and to predestinate is to appoint aforehand. And this predestinating is used of God's act, because when man willeth, or chooseth, or ordereth anything, it presupposeth an antecedent goodness in the things which he willeth or chooseth, or an antecedent convenience in the thing ordered to the end to which it is appointed, which is prudent destination; but when God chooseth, or willeth, or ordereth anything, he causeth this good ness or convenience to be in it; and therefore it is properly called pre destination. Well then, observe, not things but persons are here spoken of 'Whom he did foreknow, he also did predestinate.' His foreknowledge implieth his favour and his choice: John x. 14, 'I am the good shepherd, that know my sheep, and am known of mine'; and ver. 27, 'I know them, and they follow me.' And his predestination is his appointing them to come to such an end by convenient means; sometimes it is applied to privileges, sometimes to duties. To privileges; because of the convenience of antecedent and subsequent privileges, so Eph. i. 5, 'He hath predestinated us to the adoption of children.' It is fit we should be made children before we have a right to a child's portion; therefore God, by predestinating us to the adoption of children, maketh us fit to obtain the inheritance. Sometimes to duties; as to-faith: Acts xiii. 48, 'As many as were ordained to eternal life believed;' and in the text, to holiness 'He did predestinate us to be conformed to the image of his Son'; that is, by predestination he bringeth it to pass that in time they do resemble Christ. The order and course of God's saving the elect must not be broken; he hath decreed, and forecasted by what means he will bring them to glory. In short, foreknowledge and predestination agree in that both are eternal, but they differ in the formality of the notion; foreknowledge noteth his choice, or the purpose of his love, predestination his decree to bring things to a certain end by certain appointed means; and so he did foreordain and design them, by conformity to Christ in life and suffering, to come to celestial glory; and thus by foreknowing he did predestinate, and by predestinating he did foreknow.

[C.] The reason of this conformity to Christ—'That he might be the first born among many brethren'; that is, that he might have the honour due to the first-born. The first-born was lord of the rest of the family: Gen. xxvii 31, 'I have made him thy lord, and the rest of his brethren have I given to him for servants.' The first-born gave to the rest of his brethren a share of his father's goods, reserving to himself a double portion, Deut. xxi. 17. Now this is applied to Christ, who is Lord of the church, or head of the body, Col. i. 18, 'and heir of all things' Heb. L 2. And by virtue of this relation to the church, he must *proteuein*, first it in all things; or, as we translate it, he must in all things have the pre-eminence, Col. i. 18; in our conflicts and trials he is the captain of our salvation, Heb. ii. 10; in holiness he is our pattern or copy, 2 Cor. iii. 18, *primum in unoquoque genere est mensura et regula ceterorum*; in our glory and blessedness he is our forerunner, Heb. vi. 20, having actually taken possession of that felicity and glory which he spake of to his followers; so that Christ's honour is reserved, and believers are comforted, whilst they follow their head and leader in every state and condition.

Doctrine That the elect are in time distinguished from others by being conformed to the image of Christ.

1. Wherein this conformity to Christ consisteth.

2. Why this is the distinction between the elect, or called according to purpose, and others.

First, Wherein this conformity to Christ consisteth. I answer, in three things.

1. In sufferings and afflictions, in our passage to a better estate. As by the bounty of God we taste somewhat of the world to sweeten our pilgrimage, so also somewhat of the evil of the world to make us hasten our journey; and herein we are made conformable to Christ, who was a man of sorrows, Isa. liii. 3. This must be expected by us; for John xv. 20, 'The servant is not greater than the lord; if they have persecuted me, they will persecute you also.' Art thou poor? None of us is so poor as Christ was. Hast thou many enemies? He had more, and was pursued with greater malignity. It must be patiently endured by us: 1 Peter ii. 21, 'Because Christ also suffered for us, leaving us an example that we should follow his steps 'we that look for his glory must bear his cross. Now he calleth us to no harder lot than he himself endured, or to go in any part of rough way that he hath not trod before us. Surely they that fancy to themselves an easy life, free from all kind of sufferings and molestations, must seek another leader: 2 Tim. ii. 11, 12, 'If ye be dead with him, ye shall also live with him; if we suffer with him, we shall also reign with him'; we must be like him whom we have chosen for our head and chief in every state. What do we with Christianity if we refuse to be like Christ? We must be holy as he was holy, and afflicted as he was afflicted: 2 Cor. iv. 10, 'Always bearing about in our body the dying of the Lord Jesus.' When name dieth, and interests die and languish; when we are scorned and reproached, despitefully used for righteous ness' sake, we carry up and down with us the lively resemblance of the sufferings of Christ, and so we begin to look like Christians; and however this seemeth to be troublesome and distasteful to those who are blinded with the delusions of the flesh, yet a believer should count it his glory, honour, and happiness, as Paul reckoneth it among his gain and great advantages he had by Christ: Phil. iii. 10, 'That I may know the fellowship of his sufferings, and be made conformable to his death, and count all things but loss and dung in comparison of it.' The bitter cross should be made lovely to us, because hereby we are made more like our Lord and Master. If our sufferings go on to death, we have the same issue that Christ had, and must endure it on the same comforts: Heb. xii. 2, 'Looking to Jesus, the author and finisher of our faith; who, for the joy set before him, endured the cross, and despised the shame, and is set down at the right hand of God.' Death itself is a passage to life, therefore is Christ called 'the first- begotten from the dead' Kev. i. 5. Well then, afflictions come not by the will of man, nor the bare permission of God, but his special decree; we are 'predestinated to be conformed to the image of his Son'

2. In righteousness and holiness. God hath appointed his chosen ones to be like his own Son in holiness; this the scripture doth everywhere witness: Phil. ii. 5, 'Let the same mind be in you that was in Jesus'; and Mat. xi. 29, 'Learn of me, for I am meek and lowly'; John xiii. 15, 'I have given you an example, that you should do as I have done;' Col. iii. 13, 'Forgiving one another, as Christ forgave you' and in many other places. Many reasons there are for it, why this part of the conformity should be most regarded.

[A.] This is the end of conformity to him in our afflictions: Heb. xii. 10, 'That we may be partakers of his holiness'; that we may live a life of patience and holiness and contempt of the world, for otherwise God would not afflict but for our profit; he doth not grieve his children willingly, but as there is need and cause.

[B.] This is the way to conformity to him in glory. We that look for immaculate felicity in the other world must be like him for eximious[63] sanctity in this world: 2 Cor. iii. 18, 'We are changed into his image and likeness, from glory to glory'; it is begun here and perfected there. Eternal glory is little else but holiness perfected, and spiritual life issueth into the heavenly as the rivers lose themselves in the ocean; therefore we shall never be like him in glory unless we be like him in grace first; this is the pledge of our beatitude.

[C.] This is a sign of our communion with Christ: 1 John ii. 6, 'He that saith be abideth in him ought also to walk as he walked.' If his Spirit be precious to you, is his example of no regard? Do you value his benefits and slight his holiness? It is a sign you esteem him for your own turns. You love Christ the saviour and hate Christ the sanctifier; you would abide in him to have his happiness, but you would not abide in him to imitate his obedience; this is perverse and unthankful dealing; no, you must mind both if you would justify your pretensions of adhering to Christ.

[D.] This will give us boldness in the judgment: 1 John iv. 17, 'We have boldness in the day of judgment; because as he is, so are we in the world.' That day may be considered in *esse rei* or in *esse cognito*[64]. In *esse rei*, the day itself, when a perfect distinction is made between the sheep and the goats, elect and reprobate; now you shall stand in the judgment, for Christ will own his own image acknowledge his mark. In *esse cognito*, in our present apprehensions of it, that when we think of it, we may have boldness. This giveth you joy and confidence for the present; sincerity breedeth confidence. When we are like Christ, our consciences are emboldened against the terrors of judgment to come.

3. In felicity and glory. Conformity to Christ showeth us not only what we should do, but what we may expect; the scripture speaketh of this conformity to him in glory, both as to the body and as to the soul. The body: Phil. iii. 21, 'Who shall change our vile body, that it may be fashioned like unto his glorious body,' And the soul: 1 Cor. xv. 4, 'As we have borne the image of the earthly one, we shall also bear the image of the heavenly'; 1 John iii. 2,

---

[63] Choice, excellent
[64] To be aware

'When he shall appear, we shall be like him'; and Ps. xvii. 15, 'But as for me I will behold thy face in righteousness, I shall be satisfied when I awake with thy likeness' Our blessedness standeth in communion with God and conformity to him, or the vision and fruition of him; when we are thoroughly changed into his likeness, we are in our perfect estate. Holiness for the present standeth in the intuition and sight of God, which we have by faith, and that communion we have with him in the duties of obedience. God is a holy and happy being; our conformity to his holiness is more exact; our communion with him as the fountain of all happiness is more full; we are in a capacity for a more perfect reception of his benefits.

Secondly, Why this is the distinction between the elect and others, this conformity to the image of his Son.

1. This suiteth with God's design of recovering man out of his lapsed estate, by setting up a pattern of holiness and happiness in our nature. To evidence this, I will show

[A.] That our primitive glory was God's image 'Let us make man after our image and likeness,' Gen. i. 26. This was our perfection, which made us amiable in the sight of God, and was bestowed upon man as a special and eminent favour; this was the ornament and crown of glory which he would put upon a creature, which was his masterpiece, and the most excellent of all his works; and indeed what greater perfection can be in a creature than the nearest resemblance to his creator? Now this being lost by sin, to, have this restored is the true glory of man: 2 Peter i. 4, 'That we may be made partakers of the divine nature.' We read, Prov. xii. 26, 'That the righteous is more excellent than his neighbour'; namely, as he hath more of the image of God upon him. It is not the rich, the honourable, the powerful man, but the righteous man is more excellent; he hath more of God, and more of a divine spirit in him, than all the rest of the world have. Tae saints are called 'vile persons,' Ps. xv. 4. Wickedness maketh a man base and vile, as holiness puts honour and glory upon them; therefore, this is the greatest excellency we are capable of, to come as near to God as we can in wisdom, purity, and holiness.

[B.] When this glory was lost none was fit to restore it but Jesus Christ, the Son of God incarnate, or made man; for thereby the glory of the Father was again visible in him in our nature: Col. i. 18, 'He is the image of the invisible God'; Heb. i. 3, 'The brightness of his Father's glory, and the express image of his person' He was made flesh, that the perfections of the Godhead might once more shine forth in human nature. In an image there must be similitude and likeness, and deduction, or a means of conveying that likeness; therefore, to make us like God, there must be a fit means. God is a pure spirit; we are creatures that indeed have an immortal spirit, but it dwelleth in flesh; therefore, to make us like God, the word was made flesh, and dwelt among us, and we beheld his glory as the glory of the only-begotten Son of God,' John i. 14. So by this means was this likeness deduced, and the image of God restored to lost man, and man restored to God's favour, and made capable of happiness; therefore all the heirs of promise are predestinated to be conformed to the image of his Son, or to God appearing in their nature.

2. Because they are all called after Christ's name, Christians from Christ. Now all that are called after Christ's name should be framed after his image, otherwise they will be called

Christians to the disgrace of Christ. The apostles never transferred their names to their disciples. They were of several factions, that said, one, I am of Paul; another, I am of Apollos; another, I am of Cephas; and I, of Christ, 1 Cor. i. 12. No, we are all of Christ, and called Christians because we par take of his purity and holiness. Surely, then, we ought to transcribe Christ's life, and live as if another Jesus Christ were come into the world 'Let everyone that nameth the name of Christ depart from iniquity,' 2 Tim. ii. 19. He that nameth the name of Christ, that calleth himself by Christ's name, or undertaketh the profession of the faith of Christ, must depart from iniquity, as Christ did.

3. Because all that are elected by God and redeemed by Christ are sealed by the Spirit. And what is the seal of the Spirit, but conformity to the image of Christ? It is often spoken of in scripture: Eph. i. 15, 'Ye are sealed by the Holy Spirit of promise;' and Eph. iv. 30, 'And grieve not the Holy Spirit, whereby ye are sealed to the day of redemption'; 2 Cor. i. 22, 'Who hath sealed us, and given us the earnest of the Spirit'. What is it, but the image of Christ impressed upon the soul by his Spirit? A seal prints upon the wax that which is engraven upon itself; princes stamp their own image on their coin; so doth the Holy Ghost form Christ in us, or imprint the image of God upon our souls. Now they that are thus sealed have God's mark, and are his peculiar treasure, and the first-fruits of his creatures; chosen out from others to be a people to serve, please, glorify, and enjoy God; so that if a man be to examine and judge his own estate, this is that which he is to look after, whether he be conformed to the image of Christ, yea, or no: 2 Cor. xiii. 5, 'Examine yourselves whether you be in the faith; prove yourselves; know ye not your own selves that Jesus Christ is in you, except ye be reprobates? 'That is it your observation and search must fix upon, whether Jesus Christ be in you or no.

[A.] Christ may be in you objectively, as he is apprehended and embraced by faith and love; the object is in the faculty. Things we often think of and love are in our minds and hearts; that is not it, or not all you seek after.

[B.] Again, Christ is in you effectively, as a principle of a new and heavenly life by his Spirit: Gal. ii. 20, 'Christ liveth in me' That indeed is more.

[C.] Christ is in you representatively, or by way of conformity: Gal. iv. 19, 'Till Christ be formed in you'. Whether his nature and graces be there, whether you do resemble him in nature and life, this is that you seek after, as the fruit of the former.

4. Because Christ was an example; this hath great force. I take it for granted that it is a great advantage not only to have a rule, but a pattern and example; because man is so prone to imitate, an example in our nature maketh it the more operative; therefore Christ came to be an example of holiness and patience and happiness to us.

[A.] By this example our pattern is the more complete. There are some graces wherein we cannot be said to resemble God, as in humility, patience, obedience; these things imply inferiority and subjection, and God is inferior to none. But there are other graces, as knowledge, wisdom, justice, mercy, purity, wherein we resemble God. But in the other we have pattern from Christ: humility, Mat. xi. 29; obedience, Heb. v. 8; patience, 1 Peter i. 21.

These are hard duties, go against the bent and hair; but when the Son of God will submit to them, and give us the example, shall we refuse to live in that manner and by those laws the Son of God chose to live by? Besides, it is the more likely he will pity and help us, because he knoweth what it is to obey in these cases.

[B.] This example showeth that a holy life is possible to those who are renewed by grace. Christ hath humbled himself, and obeyed God in our nature, and so had the interests of flesh and blood to gratify as well as others; therefore all these things may be done by those that have not divested themselves of flesh and blood. To assure us the more of this; Christ chose a life that might minister instruction to all men; rich and poor, bond and free, may imitate him, persons retired and solitary, and those that live abroad in the world, learned and unlearned. Had he lived deliciously, and conquered kingdoms, and acted as a free monarch and potentate, the poor might have been disheartened; but the meanest may learn of him; and the others need not be discouraged if they have a heart to subordinate all to God; Christ sanctifieth a free life.

[C.] This example showeth what will be the issue and success of a life spent in patience and holiness. Christ, when he had fulfilled all righteousness, and suffered what was necessary for our redemption, went home to God, and entered into that glory he spake of, and was received up into heaven as the reward of his obedience: 1 Peter i. 21, 'God gave him glory, that our faith and hope might be in God.' That this might be a visible demonstration to the world what shall be the end of a life spent in holiness and obedience.

Use 1. Is information.

First, what little hopes they have to get to heaven who are no way like Christ.

1. So unlike him in holiness. When Christ spent whole nights in prayer, they either pray not at all in secret, or put off God with the glance of a short compliment; it was as meat and drink to Christ to do his Father's will, and it is their burden; Christ was humble and meek, they proud and disdainful; Christ went about doing good, and they go about doing mischief; Christ was holy and heavenly, they vain and sensual; darkness is as much like light as they like Christ. Instead of showing forth the virtues of the Redeemer, they are of their father the devil, and his lusts will they do, 1 Peter ii. 1, compared with John viii. 4.

2. So unlike him in patience and courage under sufferings. Christ obeyed God at the dearest rates, and they are drawn from their duty by a small interest, a weak temptation, a shameful pleasure, a slight injury; the greatest things that can befall us are, in comparison of eternal glory, but a light affliction, which is but for a moment. Our sufferings cannot be long, for the chains which unite the soul to the body are soon broken.

Secondly, it informeth us how we should be satisfied in our good estate, or know whether we have the true holiness; viz., when we are such in the world as Christ was in the world. Some are satisfied, and content themselves with this, they are not as other men, who are beasts in man's shape: Luke xviii. 11, 'God, I thank thee that I am not as other men, extortioners, unjust, adulterers, or even as this publican.' This is a sorry plea, when we have nothing to bear up our confidence but the badness of others. Others seek for virtue among the heathens, and think their perfection lieth in imitating the pagan gallantry; but alas! Their virtue was but a shadow; self-love was the principle, pride the soul, and vain-glory the end thereof; besides, it was stained with many notorious blemishes. Alexander was valiant, but in his anger often dyed his hands in the blood of his friends; Pompey wise, but ambitious; Cato generous, and stiff for public liberty, but many times drank somewhat too liberally; Caesar was merciful, but lascivious. No, it is not these, but the Son of God we must look upon, who hath established the genuine holiness. Others look no higher than the people who are in reputation for goodness among whom they live: but remember, they have their blemishes; either they sit down with low degrees of holiness, whereas we are to be 'holy as he is holy,' 1 Peter i. 15, 'pure as Christ is pure' 1 John iii. 3, or else are tainted with some of their errors; for good people have their failings, which are authorised to the professing world by their example; as sheep go out at the gap where others have gone out before them: 2 Cor. xi. 1, 'Be ye followers of me, as I am of Christ'. Alas! Otherwise to follow the best men will mislead us. Others bolster up themselves by the failings of the saints, whose miscarriages are recorded in the word of God. *Si David, cur non et ego?* If David, why not I? No, Christ must be the copy that must ever be before our eyes; you must be holy as he is holy, and pure as he is pure.

Use 2. Is exhortation; to persuade you to look after conformity to the image of his Son. All men would be like God in glory and felicity, but not in righteousness and holiness. Satan's temptation to our first parents was, 'Ye shall be as gods'; Gen. iii. 5, not in a blessed conformity, but a cursed self-sufficiency; but this is no temptation we bring to you, but a remedy to recover the loss you incurred by that temptation, and a remedy not invented by ourselves, but decreed by God, and brought about in the most solemn way that can be imagined. The Son of God became one of us that we might be made like him: Phil. ii. 7, 'He was made in the likeness of men'; Rom. viii. 3, came 'in the similitude of sinful flesh,' took man's nature and punishment upon him, that he might purchase grace to conform us to that holy life which he carried on in our nature; this is that we persuade you unto. Now for directions.

1. The foundation is laid in the new birth, and the change wrought in us by regeneration. The Son of God was conceived by the operation of the Holy Ghost; so are we born of water and the Spirit, John iii. 5. In the birth of Christ it was said, Luke i. 35, 'The Holy Ghost shall come upon thee and the power of the Highest shall overshadow thee; therefore also that holy thing which shall be born of thee shall be called the Son of God.' The Holy Ghost was the dispenser of this mystery, who formed the body of the Word incarnate, and gave him life; now thus we are conformed to the image of his Son. It is the Holy Ghost that begets us unto God, and maketh us new creatures; we owe our birth to him, that birth whereby we become the children of God.

2. Christ, being formed in the Virgin's womb by the Holy Ghost, devoteth himself to God; for he saith, Heb. x. 7, 'A body hast thou prepared me: for lo, I come to do thy will'; 1 Cor. iii. 23, 'Christ is God's'; he came into the world as God's. Such a resignation there must be of ourselves to God, that we may do his will whatever it costs us, and suffer whatever he

imposeth upon us: 1 Cor. viii. 5, 'They first gave themselves to the Lord, and to us by the will of God.'

3. When we are dedicated to God, the Holy Ghost is the same to Christians that he was to Christ, a guide and comforter. He that giveth life giveth conduct and motion; you find Christ still guided by the Spirit. If he retire into the deserts: Mat. iv. 1, 'Jesus was led by the Spirit into the wilderness;' when he went back again: Luke iv. 14, 'Jesus returned by the power of the Spirit into Galilee.' So Christians are still guided by the Spirit, led into, and out of conflicts, Rom. viii. 14. So a comforter: John i. 32, 'Upon him shalt thou see the Spirit descending and remaining on him'; so 1 John iii. 24.

4. There is a conformity of life necessary, that we be such to God and man as Christ was to God, seeking his glory 'I seek not mine own glory,' John viii. 50; pleasing God, ver. 29; obeying his will, John vi. 38; delighting in converse with him, for Christ spent much time in prayer; was subject to his natural parents, Luke ii. 51; subject to rulers, Mat. xvii. 27; good to all: Acts x. 38, 'Went about doing good'; humble to inferiors, John xiii. 3, 4.

5. Eye your pattern much, Heb. xii. 2. Christ told the Jews, John viii. 12, 'I am the light of the world; he that followeth me, shall not walk in darkness'; his doctrine, his example. You must often examine what proportion there is between the copy and the transcript.

6. Shame yourselves for coming short, Heb. iii. 12-14. It is not an arbitrary thing: so much as you are unlike Christ, so much you lose of your evidence of election before time, and glory in time; you should look upon yourselves as under a spiritual engagement to be more like Christ every day. A man is much under the command of his design, and the scope of his life.

7. A religious use of the means of communion with him, especially the Lord's Supper. Natural means communicate their qualities to us; we are changed into them when they are assimilated unto us. Nero sucked the milk of a cruel nurse; Achilles was valiant, his master nourished him with the marrow of a lion. Those creatures bred amongst rocks are more rough and savage; those that live in the fertile plains are more tractable. This holy food changeth our inclinations, and promotes holiness in us; by eating Christ's flesh and drinking his blood at this ordinance, we are inclined to live the life of Christ, and that is nourished and strengthened in us by it.

SERMON XL

Moreover, whom he did predestinate, them he also called; and whom he called, them he also justified; and whom he justified, them he also glorified.

Romans viii. 30.

HERE is a further declaration of the last argument, represented by a gradation or chain of causes, beginning at election and ending in glory. Those whom God hath appointed unto salvation he doth not presently put in possession of it, but by degrees, with respect to his eternal purpose; he offereth grace to them in Christ, which they accepting, are justified. Then God dealeth with them as justified, beginning a life in 4ihem which shall be perfected in heaven. All which proveth that God by an infallible decree doth guide all things to the good of the elect. Moreover, whom he did predestinate, &c.

In the words observe this general point—

That those whom God electeth before time he effectually calleth, justifieth, and sanctifieth in time, and will finally glorify when time shall be no more.

In handling this point I shall not speak of the nature of these acts of grace, but only of their connection and relation to one another, which I shall represent to you in these propositions

1. That God's eternal purpose, will, or decree, is the first rise of all things; for the apostle beginneth with predestination, or his fore-appointing, and fore-ordaining certain persons to come to salvation. Something there is besides God, or without God, as sense teacheth us. Now how came it to be translated from the state of pure possibility into the state of futurition[65] and being, but only by the will of God? Else something would exist whether God would or not. Surely all things are of God; and being of God, they are first conceived in the womb of his everlasting purpose and decree, before they have any natural existence in the world. I say his everlasting purpose, for there can be no new thought, intent, and purpose in God; and if all things, surely the most necessary things, the disposal of man to his eternal estate; he doth nothing therein but what he purposed and decreed to do from all eternity; therefore all things must be reduced hither as to their proper spring and fountain. That all things are of God, no Christian will deny; that they are not besides, or against his will, is as evident as the former. That this will of God is eternal, and dependeth not upon emergencies of occasion from the creature, is as evident as that. I shall prove out of the scriptures that nothing is made or done without the will of God; not the world: Kev. iv. 11, 'Thou hast created all things, for at thy pleasure they are and were created' If the world were not created at his will, why was it not created sooner? Or why this world and no more? So men, that these and no others. There is not one man more that liveth upon the earth than God pleaseth, from Adam to the end of the world; he hath determined their number, fixing the times and places in great order: Acts xvii. 26, 'He hath made of one blood all nations of men,

---

[65] the state or condition of being about to exist

to dwell on the face of the earth, and hath determined the times before appointed, and the bounds of their habitation.' If there were any creature in the world whom God willed not, he would be independent of God, and exempted from his providence. The dispersion of all mankind into all quarters of the earth is from his will and purpose; he did decree and fore-appoint from all eternity that such men should live here and there, so many and so long, in such places. Again, that some should have more means of knowing their creator, others less, it is all from the mercy and will of God: Ps. cxlvii. 19, 20, 'He showed his word unto Jacob, his statutes and judgments to Israel; he hath not dealt so with any nation.' His church hath a privilege and an advantage above other nations in the world; the Jews had above the heathens, and Christians above the Jews; and no other reason can be assigned but his eternal love, as many people that have the means. All the difference between them and others cometh from God's will, as the rise of it: 2 Tim. ii. 18, 'The Lord knoweth who are his.' Now the will of God reacheth to the smallest and least matters, even to the contingent motions of second causes. In the least things the scripture plainly witnesseth: Mat. x. 29, 30, 'Are not two sparrows sold for a farthing? And one of them shall not fall to the ground without your heavenly Father. But the very hairs of your head are all numbered'. The least things are not left to blind chance or the will of man, but God determineth the smallest matters. Surely God hath the knowledge and care and overruling of them, and of the brute creatures that are made to be taken and destroyed. Much more of man; for it is said, Acts xvii. 28, 'In him we live, and move, and have our being.' Our life dependeth upon God, as the sounding of the pipe dependeth on the breath of the musician; and we move, as the divers tunes of the pipe dependeth on the modulation of his breath or the motion of his fingers. 'Have our being;' there the similitude faileth. A pipe, though it cannot sound without the breath of a musician, or sound to a tune unless he play upon it; yet it may be, whether he breathe in it or play upon it, yea or no. But we have life and breath and all things from God; for if he should suspend his providential influence, we do not only cease to live and move, but also to be. Now God doth not only rule and govern these things, but doth rule and govern them with respect to his decree, or his eternal purpose. I will prove it, because (1.) He foreknew all things before they came to pass; (2.) That God determineth all these things that they may come to pass. God foreknew them: Acts xv. 18, 'Known unto God are all his works from the beginning of the world.' Things that come not to pass till long afterward were fore seen by God; he is not surprised by any event. If anything could fall out which God foresaw not, his wisdom were not infinite and eternal. Arid how could he foretell things to come, if he did not know them? Isa. xliv. 7, 'Who, as I, shall call, and shall declare it, and set it in order for me, since I appointed the ancient people, and the things that are coming, and shall come?' That is, who can tell aforehand what shall befall a people in after times, and relate the constant course and tenor of my dispensations? But how doth God foreknow things? From the nature of the thing, or from his own decree? Certainly God hath not his prescience from the nature of future things, but all things have their futurity[66] from God's decree. Because it was the purpose of God to do this or permit that; therefore he knoweth that this or that will come to pass: Acts ii. 23, 'Him being delivered by the determinate counsel and foreknowledge of God;' so that God determineth as well as foreknoweth. Many will say that God doth foreknow what men will do in tune by their own free will, but hath not determined; but the scripture teacheth us that nothing is done in time, by rational or irrational agents, but it was by the determination of God working the good and permitting the evil: Acts iv. 28, 'For to do whatsoever thy Hand and thy counsel determined before to be done' God foreseeth nothing as certainly future but what he hath before determined shall be, nothing good but what he hath decreed to work in us, nothing bad but what he hath decreed to permit, and serve his providence of it, and so it will certainly come to pass; so that all the difference between us and others cometh merely from God, and is to be ascribed to him: 1 Cor. iv. 7? 'Who made thee to differ?'

2. That what God so willeth and purposeth doth infallibly come to pass. Certainly what God intendeth to do, he will not cease till he hath done it; for what should hinder? Any change in God himself, or any impediment without? No change in God himself; no, for he is Jehovah, that changeth not: Mai. iii. 6, 'For I am God, I change not;' Job xxiii. 13, 'But he is in one mind, and who can turn him? And what his soul desireth, even that he doth; for he performeth the thing that is appointed for me' Certainly God is unchangeable in himself, and also in his mind, and in the purpose of his love towards his children; and he carrieth on the pleasure of his own will by his efficacious providence, without controlment. It is spoken by Job in his vexation; but it is usually observed that in that whole book there are good doctrines, though sometimes misapplied by the speakers. If God himself should change his purpose, it must be either for the better, that reflecteth on his wisdom, or for the worse, and that reflecteth on his goodness. Nothing without God can hinder God, when he applieth himself to the performance of what he hath purposed; for all creatures are at his beck, can do nothing without him, much less against him: Ps. cxv. 3, 'But our God is in the heavens, he hath done whatsoever he pleased'. None can resist the counsel of his will, seconded by his almighty power, or the work of his hands. Men may wish things, but God effecteth them. Nothing is faulty, nothing is wanting, when he will work; therefore his purpose, backed with almighty power, cannot be disappointed.

3. Whatever so cometh to pass is brought about in the most convenient order. The purpose of his will is also called the counsel of his will: Eph. i. 11, 'He worketh all things according to the counsel of his will'; not that God deliberateth or consulteth as men consult, out of ignorance or doubtfulness of what is most convenient; but God's will is called counsel, because there is depth of wisdom to be seen in what he doth. The creation showed his wisdom, for the world is established in an excellent order: Ps. civ. 24, 'Lord, how manifold are thy works! In wisdom hast thou made them all.' God hath disposed variety of

---

[66] renewed or continuing existence

excellences in the world by a wise contrivance, which striketh the heart of man with reverence whenever he beholdeth them. So for his providence; there is an excellent contexture of occurrences, which maketh the whole frame the more beautiful: Eccles. iii. 11, 'He hath made everything beautiful in its time.' There is at first a seeming con fusion in the government of the world, and the events that happen in it; but when we see all in their frame, when his whole work is done, it is full of order. So in the work of redemption, and all the means to bring the effect of it about, there is much more a great deal of wisdom to be seen. It is said, Eph. i. 8 (in the dispensation of his grace by Christ), 'He hath abounded towards us in all wisdom and prudence.' Means are fitly ordered to bring God's purpose about with honour to himself and benefit to us, and are so set, as links in a chain, that not one of them can be left out, and so as no violence is offered to the creature, and the liberty of second causes is not taken away. For though the decree be fixed and absolute, yet the dispensation thereof is conditional; for whom he hath predestinated, them he hath called. God will not discover his eternal differencing intent to any person before the actual application of Christ by faith; our particular election cannot be known till we do believe. All to whom the gospel cometh are children of wrath, Eph. ii. 3, in the sentence of his law, whatever they may be in the purposes of his grace; and so they can only look upon themselves as all alike in sin, and so all alike in danger of condemnation; and so God proceedeth with them in such a way as is most agreeable to a reasonable creature, by persuasion and proposal of arguments to come out of this wretched estate; and the outward dispensation being alike to elect and reprobate, the one having no more favour than the other, those that are passed by are found without excuse for their unbelief. Jesus Christ is propounded to them as an all-sufficient saviour, and also a promise that whosoever believeth shall be saved. More than this, in respect of external means, is not tendered to the elect, nor less than this to reprobates; though the elect's receiving be the fruit of special grace, the others rejecting is without excuse. God indeed giveth to the one a heart to receive, yet the external offer is made to both; and if they embrace it not, it is long of themselves. This then is the wisdom of God, that his absolute fixed purpose taketh place by an efficacious, conditional dispensation.

4. That God doth not find this order in causes, but maketh it; for all good is the fruit and effect of predestination, not the motive and cause of it, otherwise it would be a post-destination, not a predestination. Effectual calling and justification and glory are effects of God's eternal purpose, and flow from it as streams out of a fountain; and herein differeth the purpose of God to do good from the purpose of man. Something is presented to us as good and convenient, that moveth our will to purpose and choose, and inclineth us for its own goodness to seek after it, and set about the means whereby we may obtain it; but nothing in the creature can move God. What is the effect of the decree cannot be the motive of it. Indeed God willeth one thing in order to another, as effectual calling in order to justification, and both in order to glory; but then these are co-ordinate causes. His will and good pleasure is the original of this order, and the free grace of God is the only supreme and fountain-cause of our salvation: 2 Thes. ii. 13, 14, 'Because God hath from the beginning

chosen you to salvation, through sanctification of the Spirit, and belief of the truth; whereunto he called you by our gospel, to the obtaining of the glory of the Lord Jesus Christ.' The cause is our election; the means of execution are the sanctification of the Spirit and our belief of the truth; the end is our eternal salvation, or our obtaining the glory of our Lord Jesus Christ. And mark, he saith they were chosen from the beginning, as elsewhere it is said this grace was given us in Christ before the world was, 2 Tim. i. 9; and he hath chosen us before the foundation of the world, Eph. i. 4; so that from this pre ordination all cometh. Well then, God hath of his mere grace put his eternal purpose in that model and mould wherein we now find them; he that is the efficient cause of all things is also the dirigent[67] cause, appointing in what order grace and mercy should be dispensed.

5. This order of causes is so settled and joined together, that none can separate them. , The chain is indissoluble, and one link draweth on another; none are glorified but those that are sanctified and jus tified, and none are justified but those that are effectually called, and none are effectually called but those that are predestinated according to the purpose of his grace; and, on the other side, whoever is effec tually called, justified, and sanctified, may be assured of his predes tination to eternal life, and his future glorification with God. This connection must not be, cannot be disturbed; which is to be noted, because some, upon the vain presumption of the infallibility of God's purposes, think it needless to be serious, diligent, and holy; if I be elected, I shall be saved. No, God hath linked means and ends together; his decree establisheth the duties of the gospel, and checketh all thoughts of dispensation from them; never think that this order shall be broken or disturbed for your sakes. Drunkards and gamesters may as well imagine that God will break the ordinance of day and night, by turning day into night and night into day for their sakes, as the unholy soul to think to be justified and glorified till they be effec tually called and sanctified. No, you must be holy, or conclude that you shall have no saving benefit by Christ; for they who are fore ordained are a chosen generation, a distinct society and community of men, who are called out of darkness into his marvellous light, to show forth the virtues of God, 1 Peter ii. 9; made objects of his special grace and love, that they may show forth the distinction God hath made between them and others, by the choiceness of their spirits and conversations; their carriages must be suitable to their privileges.

6. The method is to be observed, as well as the connection.

[A.] The first effect of predestination is effectual calling. Certainly all that are chosen before time are called in time: Rom. i. 7, 'Beloved of God, called to be saints.' First beloved, then called; so 2 Peter i. 10, 'Make your calling and election sure.' By making our calling sure, we make our election sure; for that is the first eruption of God's eternal love. You may know God hath distinguished you from others, when you are recovered from the devil, the world, and the flesh, to God: John v. 19, 'We know we are of God, and the whole world lieth in

---

[67] directing

wickedness.' When there is a conspicuous difference between us and others, we may trace the stream to the fountain, and know God hath made- a difference before the world began, and distinguished you from them that perish. Once you were as vain, sensual, worldly-minded as others, till God called you out of the lost world, to be a peculiar people to himself; but this act of grace cometh from on high. Vocation is the fruit of election; the first grace found you in the polluted mass of mankind, as having found you entangled in many foolish and hurtful lusts. Now this is a mighty engagement upon us; if God hath made such a difference, oh! do not unmake it again, and confound all again by walking after the course of this world, for you do in effect set yourselves to disannul his decree. Conformity to the world is a confusion of what God hath separated; God made the difference when none was, and by the power of his grace you must keep it up.

[B.] The next step is, 'Whom he hath called, them he hath justified.' Calling is chiefly by the gospel, and the next end of that is faith in Christ, or conversion to God; and certainly none are justified, but those that are called, and all that are called are justified: Acts xxvi. 18, 'To turn them from darkness to light, and from the power of Satan to God.' When we are turned from Satan to God, we receive the forgiveness of sins: Mark iv. 12, 'Lest at any time they should be converted, and their sins should be forgiven them'; where forgiveness of sins is mentioned as a consequent of their conversion and turning to the Lord; so when we are brought into the kingdom of Christ, then we have redemption by his blood, the remission of sins, Col. i. 13, 14. Till we become Christ's subjects, we cannot have the privileges of Christ's kingdom; this is the order set down here, of conveying to us the benefits of Christ's death: first called, then justified. They that are yet under the power of sin are under the guilt of it; as in the fall there was sin before there was guilt, so in our recovery there must be conversion before remission; a new nature or life from Christ, then a new relative estate. When we are regenerated, we are justified, and adopted into God's family: Heb. viii. 10-12, 'For this is the covenant that I will make with the house of Israel after those days, saith the Lord, I will put my laws into their mind, and write them in their hearts, and I will be to them a God, and they shall be to me a people, and they shall not teach every man his neighbour, and every man his brother, saying, Know the Lord, for all shall know me from the least to the greatest, for I will be merciful to their unrighteousness, and their sins and their iniquities I will remember no more.' It is fit God's turn should be served before ours, that we should be willing to return to our obedience before we have our discharge.

[C.] The next step is, 'And whom he justified, them he also glorified'

But you will say, Doth the apostle, in the several links of the golden chain, omit sanctification?

I answer, No, it is included, as to the beginning, in vocation; as to the continuance and further degree, it is included in glorification. This, therefore, is the order; God doth first regenerate, that he may pardon; and he pardoneth that he may further sanctify, and so make us ever lastingly happy. Now regeneration is included in vocation; for his calling us is all one with his begetting us by the word of truth, James i. 18. But his further sanctifying, which is consequent to justification, is implied in the word glorified; as grace is glory begun, so glorification is sanctification consummate and completed: 2 Cor. i. 22, 'Who hath sealed us, and given us the earnest of the Spirit in our hearts,' which is *centesima pars*. Here our happiness standeth in loving God and being beloved of him; there, in the most perfect act of love and reception of his benefits: this love is here enkindled by faith, there by vision; here so far like God that sin is mortified, there nullified.

[D.] Those that are sanctified are glorified in part, there are fully glorified. The apostle speaketh of it as past; he will certainly and infallibly glorify them as if they were in heaven already 'Hath eternal life' John v. 24. Hath it in the promise, hath it in the pledge, the gift of the sanctifying Spirit. We have small beginnings and earnests and foretastes of everlasting blessedness in this life; by faith we may foresee what God will be forever to his saints. Now by being sanctified we are put into a capacity of eternal life 'Without holiness we cannot see God.' Heb. xii. 14. But holiness maketh us more fit; and as it is increased in us, so we are nearer to glory, and are more suited to it.

Use 1. Is information. It informeth us of divers truths necessary to be observed by us.

1. In all this order and chain of causes there is no mention 1 of merits, but all is ascribed to grace and God's free favour, choosing, calling, justifying, sanctifying, glorifying us; from the first step to the last it is all grace; our best works are excluded from having any meritorious influence upon it: Rom. ix. 11, 'Before the children had done either good or evil, it was said, Jacob have I loved, and Esau have I hated, that the purpose of God, according to election, might stand' Mark, there was a *voluntas*, and *voluntas miserendi*: 2 Tim. i. 9, 1 Not according to works, but according to his purpose and grace, which was given us in Christ before the world began.' Works are still excluded, as they stand in opposition to God's free mercy and goodness; it is a free act of his disposing, to which only God was induced by his own love.

2. That predestination is most free, not depending upon foreseen works and faith. We are chosen to faith and holiness, but not for it; the scripture saith, to faith: 2 Thes. ii. 13, 'Because God hath from the beginning of the world chosen you to salvation through sanctification of the Spirit, and belief of the truth 'and to holiness: Eph. i. 4, 'According as he hath chosen us in him before the world, that we should be holy' But we are not chosen because we believed and were holy, or because God did foresee it, but that we might believe and be holy; faith and holiness are only fruits and effects of God's grace in us; there was no foreseen cause in us to move God to bestow it upon us.

3. That predestination to glory doth not exclude the means by which it is brought about: such as Christ's gospel, ministry, faith, holiness, the cross. No, a conditional dispensation is subordinate to an absolute decree; God that hath predestinated will yet call before he will justify; God giveth the condition, taketh away the heart of stone, worketh faith and holiness in us; God's purpose is that such and such shall be called and saved by faith in Christ. Now this maketh an absolute connection between faith and salvation; now the elect, till they are called and do believe, know nothing of this, but it is their duty to fulfil the condition.

4. The greatness of our obligation to God. Here are the several steps and degrees whereby his eternal love descendeth to his chosen, or the several acts and effects by which he

bringeth them to their purposed blessedness, and do all infer a new obligation, that he was pleased to choose us who were equally involved in misery with others, and call us with a holy calling, passing by thousands and ten thousands in out ward respects much before us, and justify us freely by his grace, forgiving us so many offences, and bestowed upon us the gift of the sanctifying Spirit, by which we are regenerated and fitted for everlasting glory; see here the great love of God. God's love in time cannot be valued enough, but God's love before all time should never be forgotten by you; there you have the rise and fountain of all the benefits done unto us; this was ancient love before we or the world had a being; It was the design God travailed with from all eternity; and who are we, that the thoughts of God should so long be taken up about us? It is love managed with wisdom and counsel; his heart is set upon it to do us good. Those benefits came not by chance, but were fore-laid and fore-ordained by God. If one do us a kindness that lieth in his way, and when opportunity doth fairly invite him, he is friendly to us; but when he studieth to do us good, we know his heart is towards us: God sets all his wisdom and grace a-work. This was a feast long in preparing, that it might be the more full and ample, and all things be ready if we be ready, and our remedy at hand before our misery took effect. This is a distinguishing love, differencing us from others all along, by choosing, calling, justifying, glorifying, that one should be taken and the other left.

5. The blessedness of a Christian: they are predestinated, called, justified, and glorified: all which are special grounds of comfort and patience under the cross, whatever may befall a Christian in this world. God hath predestinated and singled us to be objects of his grace and instruments of his glory in this world, and to be conformed to the image of his Son, ver. 29, (and we can fare no worse than Christ did), .and that the Lord should call us in due time out of the corrupt and miserable state of mankind to the faith of Christ (and shall not we suffer for it?), and then justify us, and free us from the curse of the law, and absolve us from the guilt and eternal punishment of all our sins, and moderate the temporal punishment of them (surely the cross may be the better borne); and then a life begun which shall not be quenched. Blessed is that soul who hath these privileges.

6. See the way how we get assurance of God's love and our own salvation. We know the purposes of God's grace by the effects by which he witnesseth his love to his elect ones. By vocation our pre destination is manifested, by justification we feel the comfort of it, so climb up to glory by degrees. Those whom God hath predestinated from all eternity, and will glorify in the world to come, he doth power fully call. The scripture promiseth salvation, not to the named, but described persons; here, then, is your way of procedure. Would you know your election of God? Are you called, sanctified, brought home to God? Begin to live in the Spirit.

Use 2. Do not know these things in vain, nor reflect upon them merely to satisfy curiosity, or to keep up a barren, speculative dispute, but to cherish the love of God, holiness, patience, and become more serions in the work of salvation.

What effects have you of this predestination?

1. Love to God. From everlasting to everlasting he is God, Ps. xc. 2, Ps. ciii 17; and from everlasting to everlasting his mercy is to them that fear him. We see his love in his purposes and performances; the one before the world began, the other when the world shall have an end. And so two eternities meet together, eternal glory arising from purposes of eternal grace; so that whether we look backward or forward, you see the everlasting love of God. Oh! Then, let God be yours first and last; let the everlasting purposes of his grace be your constant admiration, and the everlasting fruition of God in glory be your fixed end, which is always in your eye; and let the sense of the one and the hope of the other quicken all your duties. God's mercy, you see from all eternity it began, and to eternity it continueth. We adjourn, and put off God, as if we had not sinned enough, and dishonoured his name enough: hereafter will be time enough to return to our duty. If we begin ever so soon, God hath been aforehand with us; some make early work of religion, as Josiah, Samuel, Timothy; some are called sooner, some later; but though all are not called so soon as others, they are loved as soon as others, for these benefits were designed to us from all eternity.

2. Holiness. That we might hate sin more, and prize holiness more. Holiness is inferred out of election, as a special fruit of this predestination: Eph. i. 4, 'He hath chosen us to be holy'. It is inferred out of calling, for 'he hath called us with an holy calling' 2 Tim, i. 9. The calling is from misery to happiness, from sin to holiness. It is inferred out of justification: sanctification is the inseparable companion of it. God freeth us *a malo morali*[68], that freeth us *a malo naturali*[69]; impunity followeth uprightness, our recovery were not else entire. Our case is like that of a condemned malefactor, sick of a deadly disease, who needs not only the skill of the physician to heal him, but the pardon of the judge. And it is inferred out of glorified; none shall enjoy everlasting glory after this life but such as are holy here; and if they be not sanctified and renewed by the Spirit, they shall never enter into the kingdom of God; for we cannot have one part of the covenant while we neglect another: it is not only the way, but part of glory.

3. Patience under afflictions. The same notions are used of afflictions which are used of your privileges by Christ: 1 Thes. iii. 3, 'Ye are appointed thereunto.' You should look to that in all that befalleth you; he that appointed you to the crown, appointed you to the cross also. Called: 1 Peter ii. 21, 'For even hereunto were ye called.' We are called to the fellowship of the cross; we consented to these terms: Mat. x. 38, 'He that taketh not up his cross, and followeth after me, is not worthy of me.' Justified; the comforts of it are most felt then: Rom. v. 1, 'Being justified by faith, we have peace with God.' Glorified; take it for degrees of holiness; holiness is promoted by affliction: Heb. xii 10. 'We are chastened, that we might be partakers of his holiness.' Final blessedness: 1 Peter iv. 13, 'Rejoice, inasmuch as ye are par

---

[68] From evil morals
[69] From evil nature

takers of Christ's sufferings, that when his glory shall be revealed, ye may be glad with exceeding joy.' Christ's last day is a glad day to you.

4. More seriousness in the work of salvation: 2 Peter i. 10'; Give all diligence to make your calling and election sure;' 2 Peter iii. 14, 'Wherefore, beloved, seeing that ye look for such things, be diligent, that you may be found of him in peace, without spot, and blameless.'

SERMON XLI

What shall we then say to these things? If God be for us, who can be against us?

Romans viii 31.

We are now come to the application of these blessed truths, and the triumph of believers over sin and the cross; yea, over all the enemies of our salvation. It is begun in the text— 'What shall we then say?' The words contain two questions—

1. One by way of preface and excitation.

2. The other by way of explication, setting forth the ground of our confidence. So that here is a question answered by another question.

First, Let us begin with the exciting question, What shall we then say to these things?

Doctrine When we hear divine truths, it is good to put questions to our own hearts about things.

There are three ways by which a truth is received and improved by sound belief, serious consideration, and close application. Sound belief: 1 Thes. ii. 13, 'For this cause also we thank God without ceasing, because when ye received the word of God, which ye heard of us, ye received it not as the word of men, but (as it is in truth) the word of God, which effectually worketh also in you that believe' Serious consideration: Deut. xxxii. 46, 'Set your hearts unto all the words I testify among you this day'; Luke ix. 44, 'Let these sayings sink down into your ears.' Close application: Job v. 27, 'Lo! This it is, we have searched it out; know thou it for thy good.' Now these three acts of the soul have each of them a distinct and proper ground; sound belief worketh upon the clearness and certainty of the things asserted; serious consideration on the greatness and importance of them; close application on their pertinency and suitableness to us; see all in one place, 1 Tim. i. 15, 'This is a faithful saying, and worthy of all acceptation, that Jesus Christ came into the world to save sinners, of whom I am chief.' These are all necessary to make any truth operative. We are not affected with what we believe not; therefore, to awaken diligence, the truth of things is pleaded: 2 Peter i. 5, 10, 16, 'And besides this, giving all diligence, add to your faith virtue, and to virtue knowledge' &c.'; Wherefore the rather" brethren, give all diligence to make your calling and election sure,' &c.; 'For if ye do these things, ye shall never fall; for we have not followed cunningly devised fables, when we made known unto you the power and coming of our Lord Jesus Christ'. So for consideration: Heb. iii. 1, 'Wherefore, holy brethren, partakers of the heavenly calling, consider the apostle and high priest of our profession, Jesus Christ'. The weightiest things lie by, and are as if they were not; sleepy reason is as none, and the most important truths work not till consideration make them lively. So for application, what concerneth us not is passed over; unless we hear things with a care to apply them, we shall never make use of them: Eph. i. 13, 'After ye heard the word of truth, the gospel of your salvation.' It is not enough to know the gospel to be a doctrine of salvation to others; but we must look upon it as a doctrine that bringeth salvation to our own doors, and leaveth it upon our choice. A plaster doth not heal at a distance, till it be applied to the sore; truths are too remote till we set the edge and point of them to our own hearts. Now this question in the text relateth to all three.

1. It challengeth our faith 'What shall we say to these things? 'Do we believe them, and assent to them as certain verities? The apostle doth in effect demand what we can reply or say to these things. The unbelieving, dark, and doubtful heart of man hath many things to say against divine truths; let God say what he will, the heart is ready to gainsay it; yet it is good to press ourselves thoroughly with the light and evidence of truths, to compel the heart to bring forth its objections and scruples. If any mind to contradict, have we any solid arguments to oppose? Truth wanteth its efficacy when it is received with a half conviction; and doubts smothered breed atheism, irreligion, and gross negligence. Certainly the weighty truths of Christianity are so clear, that the heart of man hath little or nothing to say against them; therefore follow it to a full conviction. Doth any scruple yet remain in our minds? It is good thoroughly to sift things, that they may appear in their proper lustre and evidence: John xi. 26, 'Believest thou this?' Pose your hearts.

2. This question doth excite consideration or meditation. We should not pass by comfortable and important truths with a few glancing and running thoughts; it is one part of the work of grace to hold our hearts upon them: Acts xvi. 14, 'Whose heart the Lord opened, that she attended to the things that were spoken.' Otherwise, in seeing we see not, and in hearing we hear not, when we see and hear things in a crowd of other thoughts; as when you tell a man of a business, whose mind is taken up about other things. No, your minds must dwell upon these things till you are affected with them; a full survey of the object showeth us the worth of it. 'What shall we say to these things?' That is, what can be said more for our comfort and satisfaction? Or what do we desire more? How should we be satisfied with this felicity and love of the ever-blessed God to his people?

3. It awakeneth application to ourselves, that we may make use of these things for our own good. Application is twofold, direct or reflexive; and the question may be explained with respect to both.

[A.] Direct application: as when we infer and bind our duty upon ourselves, from such principles as are laid down; so, 'What shall we say to these things?' That is, what use shall we make of them? Christianity is not a matter of speculation only, but of practice; therefore, when we hear the truth of it enforced, we must commune with ourselves. What doth this call for at our hands, but serious diligence? 2 Peter iii. 11, 'Seeing then that all these things shall be dissolved, what manner of persons ought we to be in all holy conversation and godliness?' The truths of the gospel are not propounded that we may talk at a higher rate than others do, but to live at a higher rate. If I should be negligent, indifferent, careless, what will become of me?

[B.] Reflexive application is when we consider our state and course, and judge of it by such general truths as are propounded to us. Direct application is by way of practical inference; reflexive, by way of discovery; and to this sense may this question be interpreted, 'What shall we say to these things?' Doth heart and practice agree with them? Do I live answerable to these comforts and privileges? What, am I one called and sanctified, and one that continueth with patience in well-doing upon the hope of eternal life? 2 Cor. xiii. 5, 'Know ye not your own selves, how that Jesus Christ is in you, except ye are reprobates?' If Christ be formed in his people, is he formed in me? Thus things must be brought home to the heart, and laid to the conscience, if we would make a profitable use of them.

Use. Is to awaken this self-communing; to make our assent more strong, our consideration more deep and serious, and our application, either by way of inference or discovery, more close and pungent Do we assent? Is this a truth to be lightly passed over? If this be true, what must I do? Or what have I done? Now this you should do upon these occasions

1. When you are tempted to unbelief. There are some points which are remote from sense, and cross the desires and lusts of sensual men, and we either deny them, or doubt of them, or our hearts are full of prejudice against them; and also the devil doth inject thoughts of blasphemy, or doubts about the world to come, into the hearts of people; especially in those that take religion upon trust, or are secretly false to that religion they have received upon some evidence. Now, to prevent all this, it is good r r to commune with ourselves, that we may be well settled in the truth; therefore see with what evidence the great things of the other world are represented unto us in the word of God, and what a just title they have to our firmest belief. Faith will not be settled without serious thoughts, and it soon withereth there where it hath not much depth of earth, Mat. xiii. 5, 6; no thoughts in the highway ground, slight thoughts in the stony ground. Faith is a child of light, and given upon certain grounds: Luke i. 4, 'That thou mightest know the certainty of those things wherein thou hast been instructed'; and Acts xvii. 11, 12, 'They searched the scriptures whether those things were so'; therefore many of them believed. But presumption and slight credulity is a child of darkness, the fruit of ignorance and incogitancy; therefore it is good in those truths that need it most to ask, What say we to these things?

2. When you are in danger of fulness, deadness, and neglect of Christ and his salvation, so that your hearts need quickening and exciting to duty. Sometimes a coldness in holy things, and a sluggish ness creepeth on the best, and you may find you begin to grow care less and customary; the conscience becometh sleepy, the heart dead, the affections cold. A lively inculcation is then necessary; you must rouse up yourselves by putting questions to your hearts: Heb. ii. 3, 'How shall we escape, if we neglect so great salvation?' Both by way of assent: Is it not true that there is a heaven and a hell? And is the gospel a fable? And by way of consideration: What trifles and paltry vanities do you neglect Christ for? And application, by way of inference: Must not I work out my own salvation with fear and trembling? By way of discovery: Is this a flight from wrath to come, and a pursuit after eternal life? That, serving God instantly day and night, we may attain to the blessed hope; that, giving diligence, we may be found of him in peace.

3. When strong lusts tempt you to sin in some scandalous and unworthy manner, what will ye do to relieve yourselves, but by such, kind of questions? Gen. xxxix. 9, 'How shall I do this great wickedness, and sin against God?' Rom. vi. 21, 'What fruit have you in those things whereof you are now ashamed?' And your hearts should rise in indignation against the temptation or carnal motion, Shall I lose my fatness to rule over the trees? If of profit: Mat.

xvi. 26, 'What is a man profited if he shall gain the world, and lose his own soul? 'If of pleasure, What! Lose the birthright for one morsel of meat?

4. In a time of sorrow and discouragements; when affliction breaketh us, and lieth heavy upon us day and night. Suppose continual poverty or sickness, or else when we are wearied with a vexatious and malicious world; then should we revive our hopes and comforts, expostulate with ourselves about our drooping discouragements: Ps. xlii. 5, 'Why art thou disquieted, my soul? And why art thou cast down within me? Still hope in God.' We must cite our affections before the tribunal of sanctified reason. This is the drift of this question in the text 'What shall we say to these things? 'This were enough to comfort the most distressed and afflicted. Who will be so much grieved for what he knoweth is for his good? Yea, so great a good as eternal salvation?

5. Whenever any message of God is sent to you, go home and practise upon it speedily, whether any duties are pressed upon you in the name of Christ, or sins reproved 'What shall we say to these things? 'Is it not a duty? or that a sin? A weighty duty, or a heinous sin? Do I perform this duty, or avoid this sin? or, What do I mean to do for the future? If upon the first opportunity, as soon as the message is brought to us, we did fall a-working of the truth upon our hearts, more good would be done, our Christianity would be more explicate and serious; whereas the impression that is left upon us in hearing is soon defaced, and all for want of such serious reflections and self-communings: James i. 22-24, 'But be ye doers of the word, and not hearers only, deceiving your own souls: for if any be a hearer of the word, and not a doer, he is like a man that beholdeth his natural face in a glass; for he beholdeth himself, and goeth his way, and straightway forgetteth what manner of man he was'; they forget how much they were concerned in the truths delivered.

Second question by way of explication If God be for ws, wlio shall be against us f There observe two things

1. The ground supposed—'If God be for us.'

2. The comfort built upon it—'Who shall be against us? '

From both observe—

That if God be for us, we need not be troubled at the opposition of those that are against us.

[A.] I shall explain the words of the text, both concerning the ground laid and the comfort thence inferred.

[B.] Show you the reasons of it.

[A.] To explain the words, and there the ground supposed—'If God.' It is not *dubitantis*, but *ratiocinantis*; not the *if* of doubting, but of reasoning. The meaning is, this being taken for granted, the other must needs follow. In the supposition, two things are taken for granted

(i.) That there is a God.

(ii.) That he is with, and for his children.

(i.) For the first: it is some comfort to the oppressed, that there is a God, who is the patron of human societies, and the refuge of the oppressed; who will take notice of their sorrows, and right their wrongs: Eccles. v. 8, 'If thou seest the oppression of the poor, and the violent perverting of judgment in a province, marvel not at the matter; for he that is higher than the highest regardeth, and there be higher than they'; so Eccles. iii. 16, 'Moreover, I saw under the sun the place of judgment, that wickedness was there; and the place of righteous ness, and that iniquity was there. I said in my heart, God shall judge the righteous and the wicked.' Man, that should be as a god to his neighbour, proveth oftentimes as a devil or wild beast to him, making little use of his power, but to do mischief. And many times God's ordination of magistrates is used as a pretence to their violence; and tribunals and courts of justice, which should be as sanctuaries and places of refuge for wronged innocence, are as slaughter-houses and shops of cruelty. Now this is a grievous temptation; but it is a com fort that the Lord will in due time review all again, and judge over the cause, that he may right his people against their oppressors. There is a higher court to which we may appeal: all things are governed by a holy and wise God, who will right his people, and vindicate their innocency.

(ii.) That he is with, and for his children, 'If God be with us'. But when is God with us? This must be stated with respect to the forementioned acts of grace. Worldlings judge God's presence by wrong rules; they measure his love and favour altogether by the outward estate; if their mountain stand strong, if their houses be filled with the good things of this world, then they conclude God is with them. No, we must determine it by the context; and we begin—

(a.) With predestination. God is with his people, not by a wavering will, but a constant, eternal decree. There are some that belong to the election of his grace: 2 Tim. ii. 19, 'The foundation of the Lord standeth sure.' See that reasoning: Luke xviii. 7, 8, 'And shall not God avenge his own elect, which cry day and night unto him? Though he bear long with them, I tell you that he will avenge them speedily' Now election is for awhile a secret; but we have the comfort of it when we make our calling and election sure. Certainly God loveth his people with a dear and tender love, since he hath carried them in the womb of his decree from all eternity.

(b.) Effectual vocation is the eruption of this purpose. God is not with us, but in us. When we are made partakers of a divine nature, we have a pledge of his being with us in our own heart. We dwell in God, and God in us, 1 John iii. 24. The new creature is under his special care and protection, and he is very tender of them, 1 Cor. i. 9.

(c.) Justification is another act of his grace. We often give God occasion to withdraw from us; but his pardoning mercy maketh up the breach. Woe unto us if God depart from us! We often banish, and drive away our own mercies: Isa. lix. 2, 'But your iniquities have separated between you and your God; and your sins have hid his face from you, that he will not hear.' But he multiplieth to pardon, and accepteth us in the beloved, to the praise of his glorious grace. And so his favour and gracious presence is continued with penitent believers that cry for mercy.

(d.) It endeth in glory. The God of our salvation discontinueth not his care over us till he hath brought us into his immediate presence. Here God is with us while we dwell in houses of clay; there we are with God for ever in his glory. If he be with us here, we are to be with him there for ever; for we do not part company, but go to him whom we love and serve.

(e.) God is with us with respect to his particular care and providence, ver. 28, guiding all things for good. Now God's providence is either external or internal.

1st. God's external providence is seen in blessing our affairs: Gen. xxxix. 2, 'The Lord was with Joseph, and he was a prosperous man;' and ver. 21, 'The Lord was with Joseph, and gave him favour in the sight of the keeper of the prison'; Acts vii. 9, 'And the patriarchs, moved with envy, sold Joseph into Egypt, but God was with him.' This was most eminently fulfilled in our Lord Christ; he had such great success because God was with him: Acts x. 38; and John iii. 2. 'Nicodemus said, no man can do these miracles that thou dost, except God be with him.' But in their measure it is fulfilled in the saints also. God was with Christ; he driveth away the devil from him by a word, Mat. iv. They ask leave of him to enter into the herd of swine, Mark v. 12. So in Christians; God is with them, to give them success, even to wonder, against Satan and his instruments. So God is with us when he loveth us, defendeth us, and blesseth our endeavours.

2nd. His internal providence, in a way of comfort and support, and sanctifying their troubles. Thus God was with Paul 'when all forsook him:' 2 Tim. iv. 16, 17, 'The Lord stood by him and strengthened him.' And so he comforts his people: Isa. xli. 10, 'Fear not, for I am with thee'; so Isa. xliii. 2, 'When thou passest through fire and water, I am with thee;; not only to keep them from fire and water, but to be with them in fire and water. A Christian is never alone, though all forsake him. Well then, the meaning is, since God will fulfil his eternal purpose, to justify, sanctify, glorify, what can hinder our eternal salvation? We that were predestinated when we were not, called when we were averse, justified when guilty, sanctified when unholy, and glorified, though now miserable, what cause have we to fear?

2. The comfort built upon it—'Who can be against us?' Let us state the meaning of this clause.

[A.] The whole world seemeth to be against those that believe in Christ. There are but two sides in the world, God and Satan. The whole world is Satan's kingdom: if God be with us, all else but 'God and his confederates will be against us. All is divided into two seeds and two kingdoms: the saints fight under Christ's conduct, the world under the devil's. We were listed as soldiers in baptism, under the captain of our salvation, and we renew our military oath in the' Lord's supper, wherein we are afresh engaged against Satan; therefore 'Who can be against us?' doth not imply an exemption from troubles and opposition, but only that the victory is secured. There will be many against us: the army of wicked men is employed to uphold Satan's kingdom, to maintain what he hath gotten, and to hinder the redemption and delivery of his captives. We cannot expect none will be against us; but we need not fear them. Who are they that are against us, but vanquished enemies? We serve under a captain who hath already conquered, John xvi. 33; a captain whom Satan feareth, and who is able and willing to help us. This then is the first consideration: there will be enemies, but we need not fear them.

[B.] Though they be against us, yet they shall not do us any considerable hurt. See the like question, 1 Peter iii. 13, 'Who is he that will harm you, if you be followers of that which is good? 'God is with and for the sanctified and justified; the devil, the world, and the flesh, are against them; yet they cannot make void God's purpose; for if God be a friend, all tendeth to our good. So that the meaning of the question is, who will be against us so as to harm us? God's help is our safety and security.

[C.] Let us see how far they may harm us. The devil and wicked men are the enemies to Christ's kingdom and subjects; the devil desireth their spiritual, the wicked their temporal ruin. The devil useth the latter, in subserviency to the former, to shake their faith, by fines, imprisonments, exile, torture, death; but God is with them, standeth for them, helpeth them, strengtheneth them, protects them, many times giveth them safety in the midst of danger, bread in the midst of penury and want, joy in the midst of sorrow; if they kill the body, he will save the soul, and raise up the body at the last day. Let us see, then, how far the harm may extend.

(1.) Our conquest is not always nor principally by a visible prosperity, nor worldly greatness and dominion. God's protection is a secret: Job xxix. 4, 'The secret of the Lord is upon their tabernacle;' the special favour and providence of God, which the world knoweth not of, nor can discern. There is an insensible blessing goeth along with them; as the wicked are eaten out by an insensible curse, though they have great revenues. God can put a very great blessing in the compass of a very little means: so Ps. xxxi. 20, 'Thou shalt hide them in the secret of thy presence from the pride of man.' They find sure refuge and defence in God, whatever proud and contentious men design against them: so Ps. xci. 1, 'He that dwelleth in the secret place of the Most High' It is a riddle to the carnal world how they subsist; but the Lord, by the invisible conduct of his providence, taketh care of them, provideth for them, and protecteth those that love, fear, serve, and put their trust in him.

(2.) Sometimes God permitteth that they shall harm us in our temporal interests, but not eternal. Alas! Many times the people of God suffer many hard things: Heb. xi. 37, 'They were stoned, they were sawn asunder, they were slain with the sword, they wandered about in sheep-skins, and goat-skins, being destitute, afflicted, tormented.' The meaning is not, who shall be against us to take away our lives and liberties? God will sometimes glorify himself in his people's sufferings, and in the general will have us perform to him a tried obedience: James i. 12, 'Blessed is the man that endureth temptations; for when he is tried, he shall receive the crown of life, which the Lord hath promised to them that love him;' make us perfect as Christ was by sufferings, Heb. ii. 10. But if we keep our innocency, the worst they can do is to send us to heaven, and so make us par takers of that which we desire most, Luke xii. 4. When they have killed the body, they can do no more. If they cut it to bits and parcels, they cannot find out the immortal spirit; and however they molest and mangle the flesh, they cannot hurt the soul, or hinder our eternal salvation, or take us out of Christ's hands, John x. 28. And a Christian upon these terms should be content, that by conformity to Christ he may be brought to eternal glory.

(3.) Christians are to be considered, not only in their personal capacity, but also in their community. They may prevail as to single persons, to kill and burn them, but not as to root out the church: Ps. cxxix. 1, 2, 'Many a time have they afflicted me from my youth, may Israel now say: many a time have they afflicted me from my youth; yet they have not prevailed against me.' God hath still preserved his church from age to age, notwithstanding the many hostile attempts against it. His people have been severely chastised, but yet in mercy delivered: the 'gates of hell shall not prevail against it' Mat. xviii. 18. The wit and policy, the power; and strength of enemies, shall not utterly destroy the Christian church. Their arms and weapons were usually kept over the gates, and there they were wont to sit in council. As not particular faithful believers eternally, so as it considereth the congregation and society of Christian professors, it shall never perish totally and irrecoverably; but whatsoever changes it undergoeth in the world, it shall again lift up the head.

[B.] The reasons why we need not be troubled at the opposition of those that are against us.

(1.) Because of the infinite power of God; take it for his sovereignty, or his ability and sufficiency, or strength.

(a.) If you take it for his sovereignty: all things are under his dominion, and are forced to serve him, both angels and men, good or bad of either kinds, they are all his hosts; therefore he is called the Lord of Hosts, who is the God of Israel. Whatever you fear is something under the dominion of God, and you need not fear the sword, if you do not fear him that weareth the sword: Ps. ciii. 19, 'His kingdom ruleth over all'; not only over all men' but all things, and those not only actually existent, but possible: 1 Chron. xxix. 11, 'Thine is the kingdom, Lord, and thou art exalted as head above all.' The most potent and most opposite creatures are not exempt from his subjection: he created them at his pleasure, and disposeth of them at his pleasure; they have a perpetual dependence upon him both for being and operation; their rebellion against him doth not diminish his dominion over them. Now this is a mighty comfort to God's people, that whatever creature they are in danger of, that creature is subject to this kingdom and dominion of God, be it angels or devils, man or beasts, sea or wind, sickness or disease, Mat. viii. 7, 8, fire, wild beasts, &c.

(b.) For ability or sufficiency. All the ability of the creature lieth either in wit or strength. For the first: will they resist him with wit and policy? Can any creature outwit God? Compare two places, Prov. xxi. 30, 'There is no wisdom, nor counsel, nor understanding against the Lord,' with Job xii. 13, 'With him is wisdom and strength; he hath counsel and understanding.' Both man's wisdom and God's wisdom is set forth by three words, understanding, counsel, wisdom. Let us see what is in the Lord, and what is against the Lord? Is there wisdom against the Lord? In the Lord there is the same; only against him there is the wisdom, the counsel, and understanding of the creature; in him, of the creator. Surely the creature can do nothing without him or against him, for it is dependent. Whatever the creature hath, it cometh from him; otherwise our understanding is but ignorance, our counsel rashness, our wisdom folly. Pharaoh thought to go wisely to work, but that wisdom cost him dear, when he intended to suppress God's interest, Exod. i. 10. Ahab, when God threatened to cut off his posterity, begets seventy sons, and disposeth and placeth them in the most strong and fenced cities: 2 Kings vii. 8, 'And it came to pass, when the letter came to them, that they took the king's sons, and slew seventy persons.' Herod would go wisely to work to destroy him that was born king of the Jews in the cradle; but Christ was preserved for all that. The synagogue of Satan is still hatching crafty counsels to destroy the spouse of Christ, but with what effect? Antichrist is consumed more and more. We are afraid of our subtle enemies. Are we ever in such straits but God knoweth how to bring us out? They cannot overwit the Lord by whatever is plotted in Home or hell. God knoweth all, for he hath understanding; counterworketh all, for he hath counsel; in the issue they will but play the fool, for he hath wisdom.

(c.) Strength. If any have the courage to oppose God's people and interest in the world, the attempt will be fruitless; the malice of men and devils will be fruitless; he only that can overcome God can hurt us. Our enemies are strong, ourselves weak; but how strong is God? They are nothing, nothing in comparison with God. So God saith, 'I am, and there is none else' Isa. xl. 17. All nations before him are as nothing: as the stars differ in glory, but when the sun ariseth, the inferior lights are obscured, and their difference unobserved. Nothing, by way of exclusion of God; as the sunbeam is nothing when the sun withdraweth, the sound in the pipe nothing when the musician taketh away his breath: Ps. civ. 29, 30, 'Thou hidest thy face, they are troubled: thou takest away their breath, they die, and return to their dust: thou sendest forth thy Spirit, they are created; and thou renewest the face of the earth.' Nothing, by way of opposition to God, and his cause and interest in the world: Isa. xli. 11, 'Behold all they that are incensed against thee shall be ashamed and confounded; they shall be as nothing.' Usually we feel them something in the effects of their rage and malice; yet they are as nothing to faith: and therefore faith should wink out all the terror of the creature: Isa. li. 12, 13, 'Who art thou, that thou shouldst be afraid of a man that shall die, and the son of man, that shall be made as grass, and forgettest the Lord thy maker? 'Let God's favour and displeasure be well weighed and compared with man's favour and displeasure, and you will find little cause and temptation to divert you from your duty. We have a God of might to depend upon, who can preserve us, notwithstanding the malice of enemies; therefore why should we bewray any fear or apprehensions of dangers?

(2.) Because of God's love to his people. If he had never so great power, yet if he were not willing and ready to help them, we could not draw any security from thence. But we have no more reason to doubt of this than of the former. God, that is wise enough and powerful enough to defeat all opposition, is also good enough to do it. First, He knoweth their persons, and their wants, and all their dangers and necessities: Mat. x. 29-31, 'Are not two sparrows sold for a farthing? And one of them shall not fall to the ground without your Father; but the very hairs of your head are all numbered. Fear ye not, therefore, ye are of more value than many sparrows.' It is spoken to the disciples, when Christ had first sent them forth upon his message. What is the comfort? The malice of men can extend no further than the providence of God seeth fit to permit and order; God hath the knowledge, care, and government of the least things that belong to his people; their lives are dearly valued by God, and shall not be destroyed by any negligence and oversight of his, or prodigally wasted. He that taketh. knowledge of the least creatures will much more take care of his servants; so Ps. lvi. 8, 'Thou tellest my wanderings; put thou my tears in thy bottle; are they not in thy book? 'David at that time had been long from home, flitting up and down from wilderness to wilderness, and cave to cave; but was God ignorant of his condition during the days of his exile? No; this was particularly known and considered by him, as if God had laid up all the tears that dropped from him, and kept a sure record and register of all his sorrows. Well then, since God knoweth all that befalleth them, will he be an idle spectator, or make a party with them to help and deliver them? Secondly, how tender he is of them: Zech. ii. 8, 'He that toucheth you, toucheth the apple of his eye.' The eye is a tender part; nature hath much guarded and fenced it. Now to meddle with them is to touch the apple of his eye. The troubles of his people go near his heart. Certainly they that are against God's people are against God himself; benefits and injuries as done to them, God taketh it as done to him: Mat. xxv. 40, 'And the king shall answer and say unto them, Verily I say unto you, Inasmuch as ye have done it to one of the least of these my brethren, ye have done it unto me;' and Acts ix. 4, 'And he fell to the earth, and he heard a voice saying, Saul, Saul, why persecutest thou me? 'The Jews have a proverb, 'What is done to a man's apostle is done to himself.' Thirdly, it is his usual practice in the dispensations of his providence, namely, to regard them, and intend their good: 2 Chron. xvi. 9, 'The eyes of the Lord run to and fro throughout the earth, to show himself strong in the behalf of those whose hearts are perfect with him'; there is a description of providence, and the persons that have benefit by it. Providence is described by the eyes of the Lord; as the Egyptians in their hieroglyphics did set forth providence by the picture of an eye. God is all eye; and those eyes are not represented as shut up or closed by sleep, but as open, to note his vigilance, and in motion, as running to and fro, prying into every corner of the whole earth, to note the particularity of his providence. And the persons who have benefit by it are those whose hearts are perfect with him. The world shall know that they are under the protection of an almighty and all-sufficient God. As to knowledge he is all eye, so as to power all hand, which is the great comfort of his people. He will show himself strong, manifest this almighty power in preserving and protecting them. Fourthly, it is not only the ordinary practice of his love and free grace, but it is secured by promise and covenant: Gen. xv. 1, 'I am thy shield, and thy exceeding great reward'; and Ps. lxxxiv. 11, 'For the Lord God is a sun and a shield; the Lord will give grace and glory, and no good thing will he withhold from them that walk uprightly.' As to positive blessings, he is a sun; as to privative blessings, he is a shield. As to way and end: by the way he is more a shield, till we are *exobeleis*: hereafter more a reward, and an exceeding great reward when our sun is in the high noon of glory. Well now, then it is blasphemy to say that either God cannot or will not help us. If he cannot save us, he is not God; if he will not save us, he is not our God: if he cannot, he is impotent, and so unfit to be God; if he will not, he is false, and must break his covenant; which are blasphemies to be abhorred by every Christian.

(3.) The great foundation that was laid for God's being with us in the incarnation of the Son of God. Jesus Christ is the true Emmanuel, God with us, Mat. i. 23. There we see God in our nature, and so drawing nearer to us, and coming within the reach of our commerce. In and by him, we are made nearer to God, who stood more aloof from us before. Since our nature dwelt with God in a personal union, first, there is a way opened for access: Heb. x. 20, 'By a new and living way which he hath consecrated for us through the veil; that is to say, his flesh'; and Eph. iii. 12, 'In whom we have boldness, and access with confidence, through the faith of him.' Certainly it is a great advantage to think how near God has come to us in Christ, and how near he hath taken the human nature to himself. This maketh our thoughts of God more sweet and comfortable. Secondly, not only access, but reconciliation: 2 Cor. v. 19, 'God was in Christ, reconciling the world to himself.' There was not only a distance between us and God by reason of impurity, but a difference by reason of enmity. God is a God of glorious majesty, and we are poor creatures; God is a God of pure and immaculate holiness, and we are sinful creatures, lapsed and fallen under the guilt of sin, and desert of punishment. There was our great trouble and grievance, and nothing comfortable could we expect from him. But when God is willing to come among us, and take our nature, and die for a sinful world, there is a foundation laid for his being with us, to help us, and bless us upon all occasions. The wonderful marriage which the divine nature hath made with the human doth help us against the thoughts of distance; but his death and sufferings, as the price of our atonement, doth make up the quarrel and breach between us and God. In his person, God manifested in our flesh, way is made for access; for in Christ God doth condescend to man, and man is encouraged to ascend to God; but in his sufferings the distance is taken away, and the guilty fears appeased which most do alienate us from God. God hath 'set him forth to be a propitiation through faith in his blood,' Rom. iii. 25. Now after such a foundation laid, will the Lord be strange to his people, as if the breach still continued? It cannot be. Thirdly, God in our nature hath taken upon him an office to defend and help his people, which he manageth both in heaven and in earth. In heaven by his constant intercession: Heb. viii. 1, 2, 'We have such a high priest who is set on the right hand of the throne of the Majesty in the heavens: a minister of the sanctuary, and of the true tabernacle, which the Lord hath pitched, and not man'; and Heb. ix. 24, 'For Christ is not entered into the holy places made with hands, which are the figures of the true, but into heaven itself, now to appear in the presence of God for us.' We have a friend in court, Jesus the true and great high priest, who hath the names of his people graven upon his breast and shoulder, to show how much they are in his heart, and to represent them and their necessities to God. On earth, 1. Externally, by his powerful providence; for all judgment is put into his hands, John v. 22, that he may defend his church and people. 2. Internally, by his Spirit: Mat. xxviii. 20, 'Lo, I am with you always unto the end of the world.' Into that part or age of the world our lot falleth, Christ is ready with his protection and blessing. Now would Christ take such an office, to be head over all things to the church, and neglect the duty of it? No; the head of the church is also 'the saviour of the body' Eph. v. 11. The whole body, and every member of it, is dear to him, as united to him in the sacred mystical body; and he will take care of them. And upon these accounts we may pray for, and expect 'grace to help in a time of need': Heb. iv. 16, 'Let us come with boldness to the throne of grace, that we may obtain mercy, and find grace to help in a time of need'.

Objection But you will say, If there be such a power and goodness in God, and thus secured by the mediation of Christ and his blessed covenant, how cometh it that they are reduced to such great exigencies? Judges vi. 13, 'If the Lord be with us, why then is all this befallen us?'

Answer

1. It is supposed you are Christians, and have not the spirit of a worldling, that liveth upon and seeketh his main happiness in the creatures apart from God. A true Christian is one that is dead to the world, but alive to God; one that hath laid up his treasure above the reach of all enemies: Mat. vi. 19-21, 'Lay not up treasure for your selves upon earth, where moth and rust doth corrupt, and where thieves break through and steal; but lay up for yourselves treasures in heaven, where neither moth nor rust doth corrupt, and where thieves do not break through nor steal; for where your treasure is, there will your heart be also.' Otherwise we cannot deal with you, for it is a vain attempt to hope to reconcile Christianity with your carnal affections; but if you be such, though the feelings of nature "be not altogether quenched in you, you will not be greatly moved as long as your main happiness is safe; that is, while God's love to you is not lessened, while your communion with him is as free as it was before, while you lose no degree of grace, and your hopes of glory suffer not any eclipse; for your solid happiness lieth in these things, other things are but appendages to sweeten our pilgrimage; and though a Christian hath a value for his natural comforts, yet it is a value and an esteem that is sub ordinated to higher enjoyments, that he hath something of value to esteem as nothing for Christ.

2. Temporal protection and prosperity is not excluded from the compass and latitude of this privilege, but included so far as God seeth fit, so far as it is good to have peace and liberty. Heretofore the blessings of God's presence were visible and sensible; as they observed of Abraham, Gen. xxi. 22, 'God is with thee in all that thou dost'; so it is promised to Isaac: Gen. xxvi. 3, 'I will be with thee, and bless thee;' to Jacob: Gen. xxxv. 3, 'God was with me in the way that I went;' to Moses: Exod. iii. 17, 'I will be with thee;' to Israel: Deut. ii. 7, 'The Lord thy God hath been with thee 'Josh. i. 5, 'I was with Moses, and I will be with thee;' to David, 2 Sam. vi. 18. So that we cannot say that he will not own and bless us in the course of his providence; but communion with him, and the enjoyment of his gracious presence, is that which the godly desire most: Exod. xxxiii. 5, 'If thy presence go not along with us, carry us not up hence.'

3. Though temporal happiness be not altogether excluded, there must be trial; for there is no crowning without striving, nor can a reward be expected for sitting still: 2 Tim. ii. 5, 'He must strive' according to the laws of the exercise, to put in for the prize in the Olympic games, and to refuse to run or wrestle, was ridiculous; so it is to think of heaven and do nothing for it, or run no hazard for it; partly because we need afflictions, that the inner man may be renewed, and we be more prepared, dispositively fitted for glory, being weaned from the world, and mortifying the flesh: 2 Cor. iv. 16, 'For which cause we faint not, but though our outward man perish, yet the inward man is renewed day by day;' 1 Peter i. 6, 'Wherein ye greatly rejoice; though now for a season, if need be, ye are in heaviness through manifold temptations.' We suffer to quicken us in our drowsiness and refine us

from our dross. Partly to conform us to Christ, that we may overcome the world; he overcame it by suffering, to show us that by suffering we shall overcome it, which is a nobler victory than if we had overcome it by the sword: Horn. viii. 37, 'Nay, in these things we are more than conquerors' It is for the honour of God that it should be known that God hath a people that love him, and are dearly beloved by him.

4. In these trials God is with us; and so if he save you not from afflictions, he will save you in and by afflictions. How is God with us in deep and pressing afflictions? Partly in bridling the rage of men; if you be in your enemies' hand, your enemies are in God's hand: whatever power they have is given them from above, John xiv. 11, and they cannot do anything but as God permitteth. Partly by the effects of his internal government (1.) Supporting them: Ps. cxxxviii. 3, 'In the day when I cried, thou answeredst me, and strengthenedst me with strength in my soul;' 2 Cor. xii. 9, 'And he said unto me, My grace is sufficient for thee'; Phil. iv. 13, 'I can do all things through Christ which strengtheneth me.' If we have his supporting presence, though we have not his delivering presence, it is enough. (2.) His comforting presence: Ps. xci. 15, 'I will be with him in trouble' God is most with his afflicted people (as the blood runneth to the wronged part), as the mother is with the sick child, even to the envy of the rest. Then we are most prepared for the comforts of his Spirit, being refined from the dregs of sense. (3.) His sanctifying presence, blessing the affliction for an increase of grace: Heb. xii. 10, 'But they verily for a few days chastened us after their own pleasure, but he for our profit, that we might be partakers of his holiness' Now these experiences show that he is still with us.

Use. Is information.

1. It informeth us of the misery of wicked men in general. By parity of reason, if God be against us, it is no matter who is for us. How soon are all things blasted when God is against a people! They make little reckoning of God's help, or securing their greatness by God's protection; therefore the ruin is the more speedy: Ps. Hi. 7, 'Lo, this is the man that made not God his strength, but trusted in the abundance of his riches, and strengthened himself in his wickedness' Alas I how soon can God blast all their confidences. Man is the mere product of his maker's will, and all that supports his being is the fruit of his bounty; surely he that blew up this bubble can as soon crush and dissolve it. They look upon the godly as the most afflicted creatures, because the hatred of the world is usually upon them; but sure they are the most miserable: though they have all the world on their side, yet if they have God against them, they have cause to fear; there is a wall between them and heaven. Certainly wicked men have stronger enemies than the people of God have or can have; they have God himself for an enemy, and he will overcome.

2. What reason the enemies of God's people have to be afraid, and to stop their fury and rage against his cause and interest. It is fruit less and vain to curse those whom God will bless; Balaam could teach them this: Num. xxiii. 8, 'How shall I curse whom God hath not cursed? Or how shall I defy those whom God hath not defied?' It is ruinous; to allude to Acts xxii. 27: they that set themselves against his people set themselves against God: Isa. xxxvii. 23, 'Whom hast thou reproached and blasphemed? Against whom hast thou exalted thyself,

and lifted up thine eyes on high? Even against the Holy One of Israel.' Men do not know and consider who is their party, and with whom they have to do, that breathe out nothing but threatenings and destruction against the servants of the Lord. Are you a match for God? He is their second, and engageth against you; and he can soon tread out this smoking flax, and with the wind of his displeasure scatter this dust that flieth in the faces of his people.

3. That a Christian is, or may be, above all opposition; and the fear of man, which is a snare to others, should be none to him, for he hath God's favour and almighty protection to support his courage and fortitude. There are two things trouble us, an inordinate respect to worldly happiness as our end, or an inordinate respect to man as the author or means of procuring it; cure these two evils, and what should trouble or perplex a Christian?

[A.] An inordinate respect to temporal happiness: that must be cured in the first place. What is your first and chiefest care? To secure your temporal interests, or to save your souls? To cure our cares and fears, Christ directeth us, Mat. vi. 33, 'First seek the kingdom of God and his righteousness, and all these things shall be added unto you.' He promiseth us a kingdom, Luke xii. 32. And the apostle describeth the true Christian, Heb. x. 39, to be one that believeth to the saving of his soul. Now if you will be Christians indeed, stand to this, that whatever becometh of other things, your business should be to save your souls, and then your trouble about worldly accidents is plucked up by the roots; for it is our affections to them cause our afflictions by them. Can men take away the privileges of God's kingdom from you? Or cast you into hell, and prohibit your entrance into heaven? No; but you would save your stake? Agreed, so it be consistent with your duty and fidelity to Christ; but if it cannot be, venture it in God's hands. Heaven is worth something; and it is a question whether they desire it or not that will venture nothing for it; therefore this must be determined and fixed as your resolution in the first place, that you will get to heaven whatever it cost you, and will obey God at the dearest rates.

[B.] An inordinate respect to man, as if he did all in the world. Sense seemeth to tell us so, but faith must teach us better; therefore, to cure this, consider who is most able to help or hurt you, and whether it be better to have God a friend or an enemy. If you will take the judgment of the people of God, you shall see

(1.) That they always profess that God's presence, to whom all things are subject, is their great security: Ps. xlvi. 7, 'The Lord of Hosts is with us; the God of Israel is our refuge, Selah.' They think themselves safe enough with God, though all the world should be against them.

(2.) They have been confident of his presence with them, and fatherly love and care over them, in the saddest condition: Ps. xxiii. 4, 'Though I walk in the valley of the shadow of death, I will fear none evil, for thou art with me' When death and they walk side by side, yet they are still confident of God's favour and presence; God doth not forsake his people, though he permitteth them to be exercised with divers calamities, Heb. xi. 35, 36.

(3.) Upon this ground they defy the creature: Ps. xxvii, 1, 'The Lord is my light and salvation, whom shall I fear? the Lord is the strength of my life, of whom shall I be afraid?', so Ps. cxviii. 6, 'The Lord is on my side, I will not fear what man can do unto me'. It argueth great pusillanimity to yield to temptation when God is with us and for us, and to doubt of the sufficiency of his protection; for they must first prevail against God before they can against you.

(4.) Will you believe the judgment of your own reason? Then consider what is man and what is God, and set the one against the other his wisdom against their policy, his power against their weakness, his love and mercy against their malice and cruelty. What do we believe God to be and man to be? Man, compared with God, is a sorry, feeble, worthless thing, a puff of wind or a pile of dust, nothing, less than nothing, and vanity. Surely God is infinite in wisdom, power, and goodness; man, a poor creature, that in point of wisdom would give anything to know futurity, and the event and success of his enterprises, and is often cut off in the midst of his designs: Ps. cxlvi. 4, 'He returneth to his earth; in that very day his thoughts perish' leaveth his projects and contrivances: Ps. ii. 12, 'And ye perish from the way' while in the course and heat of their under takings. We do not tell you what is in the other world, what is matter of faith, but what is obvious and sensible here. In point of power, how fain would men do more than they could, but that they are in the chains of providence, and under the restraints of God's invincible power! It is in their thoughts to cut off and destroy; but there is a higher power that disposeth of all circumstances: all is in your Father's hands. So his love and mercy against their malice and cruelty: Ps. lxxvi. 10, 'Surely the wrath of man shall praise thee the remainder of wrath shalt thou restrain': the frustration of their attempts. God often ordereth this.

(5.) How much it concerneth us to be in such a condition that we can say, God is with us; then you need not desire the best things in the world, nor fear the worst. But when can we say, God is with us? Three things are necessary.

(a.) That the person be right, that he be renewed by the Spirit of God, and be reconciled to him; for called and justified are the privileges between the two eternities in the context, and the sure evidence of our interest in both. Then God taketh us into his special charge and protection, when regenerated by the Holy Ghost, and reconciled by the blood of Christ; for the new creation are his family: James i. 18, 'Of his own will begat he us with the word of truth, that we should be a kind of first-fruits of his creatures'; Titus ii. 14, 'Who gave himself for us, that he might redeem us from all iniquity, and purify unto himself a peculiar people, zealous of good works'. These are the peculiar people. With others, God is no more present than he is with the rest of his creatures, in a way of common preservation. Therefore, if you would be certain of God's favour, and that your peace is made with him, you must look to this, that you be in an estate of pleasing God, that you are sanctified by the Spirit, and, being justified by faith in Christ, are at peace with God, Rom. v. 1. If you be renewed, and God reconciled, you need fear nothing. The evidence of both, and so of our interest in his providence, is our unfeigned dedication to God; for if we be for both, God will be for us. If you have given a hearty consent to his covenant, then you shall have the privileges of it: he will be your sun and shield, and then we need fear nothing.

(b.) As to our cause, it must be good. Take God's side against Satan and his instruments: 2 Chron. xv. 2, 'The Lord is with you while you be with him; and if ye seek him, he will be found of you'; 2 Chron. xiii. 9, 10, 'With them are golden calves, and with us is the Lord our God'. God is there where his ordinances and worship are consume thee in the way.' Therefore, lest God depart, we must be tender.

(c.) Our conversation must be holy, for wilful sin and guiltiness breed fears of God's displeasure. It is our sins that give our enemies advantage against us: Judges iii. 12, 'And the Lord strengthened Eglon, the king of Moab, against Israel, because they had done evil in the sight of the Lord.' We read often in Scripture that their shadow was gone from them: Numb. xiv. 23, 'Because you are turned away from the Lord, the Lord will not be with you'. We banish away God's presence from us, because he cannot with honour own, such a people: Amos v. 14, 'Seek good, and not evil; so the Lord, the God of hosts, shall be with you.' If, after we have devoted ourselves to God, we retain our former sins, we lose the mercy and comfort of his favourable presence. We do but dream of God while we continue in sin. If we would have God to be with us, we must carry ourselves as in his presence, and be dutiful and obedient to him, seek him, rely on him, and keep his way.

Use 2. Is to press you to lay up this truth in your hearts; for it is the ground and foundation of all religion.

1. This is the ground of close adherence to God, when we cease from man, and cleave to God alone; then you live as those that from their hearts do believe that there is a God, and that he is a 'rewarder of those that diligently seek him' Heb. xi. 6, which are the fundamental principles which are at the bottom of all Christian practice; and the more you live upon them, the more cause you will see to stick to God, and please God rather than man. They that trust in him, and do stand or fall to him alone, they are the best Christians; you so far withdraw yourselves from God as you look to man. If once man get the pre-eminence of God, and be set above him in your hearts; that is, be loved, trusted, obeyed before God, so far your hearts grow dead to God, and religion presently withereth and decayeth: Prov. xxix. 25, 'The fear of man bringeth a snare, but he that trusteth in God shall be safe.' The soul that cannot entirely trust God, whether man be pleased or displeased, can never long be true to him; for while you are eyeing man, you are losing God, and stabbing religion at the very heart.

2. This keepeth us from shifting and helping ourselves by unlawful means: Gen. xvii. 1, 'I am God all-sufficient, walk before me, and be thou upright.' Were we soundly persuaded that his power is above all power, and his wisdom above all wisdom, and his goodness arid fidelity invincible, it would save us from many sinful miscarriages and unlawful means that we take for our own preservation. We often lose ourselves by seeking to save ourselves without God, and because we cannot depend upon his all-sufficiency. Well then, since it hath such an universal influence upon all our conversations, we should get it rooted and settled in our hearts, that we may not be tossed up and down with the various occurrences of this life; God is our happiness, and not the creature.

3. This filleth us with courage and magnanimity in the most desperate cases: Dan. iii. 17, 18, 'Nebuchadnezzar, we are not careful to answer thee in this matter; our God whom we serve is able to deliver us from the fiery furnace; but if not, we will not serve thy god, nor worship

the golden image which thou hast set up' This is true fortitude, to look to God alone; he will deliver from death, or by death; he can save us from trouble; or if not, he will hasten our glory. Yet we must resolve to stick close to him, however he determine the event.

4. This maketh us live quietly from cares and fears, when we can commit and submit all to God: Phil. iv. 6, 7, 'Be careful for nothing, but in everything by prayer and supplication, with thanksgiving, let your requests be made known unto God; and the peace of God, which passeth all understanding, shall keep your hearts and minds through Jesus Christ.' It is a blessed frame, questionless, to be careful for nothing. This is to be had by ceasing from man, and trusting in the Lord, who hath the government and disposal of all things.

Directions—

1. Let the will of God be your sure rule. For God must institute that religion which you expect he should accept and reward. None trust in the Lord but those that keep his way: Ps. xxxvii. 34, 'Wait on the Lord, and keep his way, and he shall exalt thee to inherit the land'

2. Let the favour of God be your happiness. Be quieted in his acceptance, whether man be pleased or displeased: 2 Cor. v. 9, 'Wherefore we labour, that whether present or absent, we may be accepted of him'. Let God be enough to you, without and against man.

SERMON XLII

He that spared not his own son, but delivered him up for us all, how shall he not with him also freely give us all things?

Romans viii. 32.

THE apostle had been speaking of God's eternal decree, which is his hidden love; now he speaketh of redemption by Christ, which is his open and declared love. In predestination his love was conceived in his own heart; in redemption it is manifested in the effects and com mended to us: that was the rise, this the visible demonstration. In the former verse the apostle reasoned a causa; here is *argumentum a signo*. Once more: the former question is a comfort against that trouble which may arise *ex praesentia mali*, this against our trouble which may arise *ex absentia boni*. The covenant notions by which God is ex pressed are two, suitable to the two sorts of blessings we have by him, positive and privative; that he is a sun and a shield: Ps. lxxxiv. 11; and Gen. xv. 1, 'Fear not, Abraham, I am thy shield, and thy exceed ing great reward' Do you fear evil? God is our shield; and 'if God be with us, who can be against us?' That is, so as to procure our utter and eternal ruin. Do you want good? God is our sun, and our exceeding great reward. There is blessing enough to be had in God. The argument of the text showeth it—'He that spared not his own Son' &c.

In the words we have two things God's former and after bounty.

1. A foundation, or

2. An inference.

First, The foundation and ground- work of the argument is propounded

1. Negatively—*He spared not his own son*.

2. Positively—*But delivered him up for us all*.

Secondly, the inference is considerable, both for the matter and the form.

[A.] In the matter, take notice of a gift resulting from the death of Christ; where

(1.) The extent of the gift or donation all things.

(2.) The freeness of the gift.

(3.) The method and order.

[B.] The form. It is an appeal to our reason and conscience—*How shall he not?* As if it were said, Can any man be so absurd and illogical, so little skilled in the art of reasoning? How is it possible to imagine that he that gave us Christ will deny us anything that is good for us?

Doctrine That in the death of Christ God hath laid a broad foundation for a large superstructure of grace, to be freely dispensed to all those that have an interest in him. Let me here show you

1. How the death of Christ is here expressed.

2. What a superstructure of grace is built thereupon.

3. The strength and force of the inference.

4. Who have interest in Christ, and may more expressly take com fort in it, and reason thus within themselves.

First, How the death of Christ is here expressed, as to God's act about it.

1. Negatively 'He spared not his own Son' where we have the act and object of it.

[A.] God's act is intimated in that expression, 'He spared not' There is a twofold not-sparing, either in a way of impartial justice, or in a way of free and eminent bounty.

(1.) In a way of impartial justice; so it is said, 2 Peter ii. 4, 5, 'God spared not the angels that sinned'; and again, 'He spared not the old world'; that is, would use no clemency, but gave them their deserved punishment. So many would interpret this, *ouk epheisato*, he spared not Christ, but stirred up all his wrath against him, when he took upon him to satisfy for our sins. When he took upon him to satisfy for our sins, divine justice would not abate him one farthing: Zech. xiii. 7, 'Awake, sword, against my shepherd, and against the man that is my fellow, saith the Lord of hosts; I will smite the shepherd, and the sheep shall be scattered'

(2.) In a way of eminent and free bounty. So we are said to be sparing of those things which are most dear and precious to us; but upon great occasions we part with them. In this sense, when the elect had need of Christ, God did not spare him, but came off freely with him: John iii. 16, 'God so loved the world, that he gave his only-begotten Son' parted with him out of his bosom, gave him to die for our sakes.

[B.] The object—'His own Son'; that is, not an adopted son, but only begotten. What dearer to parents than their children? Parents will part with their all to redeem their children, especially if they have but one, and that dearly beloved. But God's love to Christ is not to be measured by an ordinary standard; all is infinite between the Father and him; therefore this heighteneth his grace to us, that he spared not his own Son. Let us consider what might have moved God to spare his Son.

(1.) The incomparable worth and excellency of his person. Things which are rare and excellent use to be spared, unless upon great necessity. Now the Lord Jesus was so the Son of God that he was co-equal with him in divine honour and glory. Thus did the Jews understand him when he called himself the Son of God: John v. 18, 'The Jews sought the more to kill him, not only because he had broken the sabbath, but said also that God was his Father, making himself equal with God.' And they were not mistaken in it; for Christ was indeed so the Son of God as to be equal in essence, power and glory with the Father. Their fault was that they denied this title to be due to Christ. The apostle explaineth it: Phil. ii. 6, 'Who being in the form of God, thought it no robbery to be equal with God' It was no blasphemy, no usurpation of divine honour; Christ was not thrust down from heaven for robbery and usurpation, as the sinning angels were, but was sent down. The divine honour did justly and rightly belong to him. Now that God spared him not on this occasion is the great demonstration and condescension of his love.

(2.) The singular and infinite love between God and Christ. He is called his dear Son: Col. i. 13, *uiou agapes*. The Father loved him dearly; and we are chary of what we tenderly love; therefore the only begotten Son is said to be in the bosom of the Father, John i. 18, which intimateth not only his co-existence with him from all eternity, but the mutual familiarity, delight, and complacency which the divine persons have in one another, which is also set forth, Prov. viii. 30, 'Then was I by him, as one brought up with him; I was daily his delight, rejoicing always before him'; as two mates or companions of suitable dispositions, always bred up together, and rejoicing in one another. Thus is Heaven fain to lisp to us in our own dialect, to set forth the intimacy, oneness and delight that is between the Father and the Son; yet God spared him not.

(3.) Though he had no equal or advantageous exchange. Christ is more worth than a thousand worlds, as the people could say of David 'Thou art worth ten thousand of us'. 2 Sam. xviii. 3. How much more may it be said of Christ? What could God gain that might be an equal recompense for the death of Christ. All the world set against God is nothing, less than nothing, Isa. xl. 17. Now no man doth give much for what is but little esteemed; but God gave his own Son to recover the perishing world of mankind.

2. Positively 'But delivered him up for us all.' Mark—

[A.] The person who did it.

[B.] The act, what he did—delivered.

[C.] The persons for whom—for us all

(1.) The person who—'God spared not his own Son, but delivered him up for us all.' This word is used of several agents; Judas delivered him: John xix. 11, 'He that delivered me unto thee hath the greater sin'; Pilate delivered him to be crucified, John xix. 16; the high priests delivered him to Pontius Pilate, Mat. xxvii. 2; the people delivered him up to be scourged and crucified by the Gentiles, Mat. xx. 19; yea, Jesus Christ delivered up himself: Rom. iv. 25, 'Who was delivered for our offences'; and here, 'God delivered him up for us all.' One word is used, but the act proceeded from several causes; the people delivered him out of ignorance and inconsiderate zeal, Judas out of covetousness and treachery, the high priests out of malice and envy, Pilate out of a faulty compliance with the humours of the people, and to preserve the reputation of his government, Christ out of obedience to God, God himself to show his infinite love to us. It is for our comfort to observe God's act in this tradition. If it had been done without God's knowledge and consent, nothing had been done for our salvation; God doth nothing rashly or unjustly. Therefore, since Christ was delivered by the determinate counsel of God, Acts ii. 23, the reason must be inquired into; it was out of his love to recover a lost world, that he might make satisfaction to provoked justice for our wrongs and offences: so that Christ died, not by the mere wickedness of man, bat the righteous and wise ordination of a gracious God; and so it is a great argument of God's love, and a ground both of gratitude and confidence to us. We must look to the Father's act, to whom we make our prayers, with whom we would fain be reconciled, whose judgment we fear, whose favour we seek after. Now he appointed his own Son to do the office of a mediator for us. The law which condemneth us is the law of God; the wrath and punishment which we fear is the wrath of God; the presence into which we come is the presence of God; and the fountain of all the blessings we expect is the favour of God; and God spared not his own Son, but delivered him up for us all, to assure our comfort, peace, and hope; his hand is chief in it.

(2.) The act, what he did—'He delivered him up' not only to be made flesh for us, John i. 14, which was a state of being at the greatest distance from his nature, who was a pure spirit. But God, who is a spirit, was made flesh that he might be nearer to us, and within the reach of our commerce, and took a mother upon earth that we might have a father in heaven, which maketh all the promises of God more credible to us; for the exaltation of man is a thing of more easy belief than the abasement of the Son of God; if he will assume flesh, we may reasonably expect to be appareled and clothed upon with his glory. But also made sin for us, 2 Cor. v. 21. Sin is taken in scripture sometimes for a sacrifice for sin, or a sin-offering, by a metonymy of the adjunct for the subject, as *piaculum* in Latin is both a sin and a sacrifice for sin; so the priests in the prophet's reproof are said to eat the sins of the people, Hosea iv. 8, that is, the sacrifices, when they minded nothing but to glut themselves with the fat of the offerings, part of which was the priest's portion; and so Christ was made sin for us, that is, an expiatory sacrifice for our sin. So in the beginning of this chapter, Rom. viii. 3, 'God, by sending his Son in the similitude of sinful flesh, hath by sin condemned sin in the flesh'; that is, by the sufferings of Christ, or his becoming a sin-offering, hath put an everlasting brand upon sin, to make it odious and hateful to the saints. Once more: made a curse for us, Gal. iii. 13, to note the pain and shame of his death, and to show that Christ was appointed to bear that curse of the law and punishment which belongeth to us, which was so grievous and terrible as that his human nature staggered and recoiled a little, by a just abhorrence of the great evil which he was to undergo; and when he was under it, his soul was exceeding sorrowful and heavy unto death, so that it extorted from him tears and strong cries; yet God spared not his Son, but delivered him up to these penal and dreadful evils! God might be . said not to spare his Son if he had only used him as an *internuncius*, and messenger; but when he used him as a redeemer, as one that was to pay a ransom for us, it may be much more said so.

(3.) 'For us all 'the persons for whom; for the cursed race of fallen Adam, who had no strength to do anything for themselves; who had cast away the mercies of our creation, and were senseless of our misery and careless of our remedy; had abused the goodness of his bounty and patience, and were utterly lost to God and themselves. The whole time that we lived in the world showed God's sparing us, but yet he spared not Christ. Every moment we lived after the committing of sin was the fruit of God's indulgence; the arrow is upon the string, only God respiteth execution, and took this way of redemption by Christ that we might be discharged, not only from the hurt, but the fear of his wrath and curse due to us.

Secondly, God having laid this foundation, let us see what a super structure of grace is built thereon. He doth freely give us all things; all good things are the gift of God, James i. 17. And whatever God giveth, he giveth freely, for there can be no pre-obligation upon him: Rom. xi. 35, 'Who hath given him first?' But here the chief thing considerable is the largeness of the gift, he will give all things. This comprehensive and capacious expression includeth much comfort in its bosom. Let us explain it a little; both the creature and the creator, from God to the poorest thing in the world, through Jesus Christ all is ours: Rev. xxi. 7, 'He that overcometh shall inherit all things, and I will be his God, and he shall be my son.' God himself maketh over himself to his children, who is all in all; he doth enjoy God, and all things besides which may be a blessing to him. He is ours that hath all things and can do all things; and what can the soul desire more?

2. This 'all things' reacheth to the two worlds; heaven and earth are laid at the foot of a believer: 1 Tim. iv. 8, 'But godliness is profitable to all things, having the promise of the life that now is, and of that which is to come.' Here God is not wanting to his people, but the gift and grace promised is eternal life.

3. This 'all things' concerneth the whole man the body and the soul. The body is in covenant with God as well as the soul, and therefore it is provided for by the covenant. We feel not only the comfort of it at the last day, when it is raised up as a part of Christ's mystical body, but for the present; the bodily life exposeth us to manifold necessities; but Mat. vi. 33, 'First seek the kingdom of God, and his righteousness, and all these things shall be added unto you'. He that hath any place or office hath the perquisites of the place or office. Now for the soul: 2 Peter i. 2, 'The divine power hath given us all things necessary to life and godliness'; meaning by life internal grace, and by godliness the fruit of it, a holy conversation. There is not only the remote inclination, but the actual readiness, yea the final accomplishment, will, and deed, Phil. ii. 13.

4. All things that are for our real advantage, of what nature soever they be: 1 Cor. iii. 21, 'All things are yours'; ordinances, providences, death, the connection between both the worlds, whatever belongeth to our happiness, and will further us to the kingdom of glory, for God is engaged 'No good thing will he withhold', Ps. lxxxiv. 11. Well then, is not a Christian, completely provided for that hath God and the creature, heaven and earth, pardon and life, grace and glory that is, reconciled to God by the death of Christ, and saved by his life protection and maintenance, and a sanctified portion in this world, and the happiness of the life to come? A Christian, that is safe among friends and enemies, that liveth in communion with God here, and shall dwell forever with him hereafter, is he not well provided for?

Thirdly, The strength and the force of the inference. Certainly this broad and ample foundation will support the building, though the top of it mount above the clouds, and be carried so high as the glory to come.

1. Because the giving of Christ is a sign and pledge of his great love to us. And what will not love, and great love, do for those whom it loveth? John iii. 16, 'God so loved the world, that he gave his only-begotten Son.' He doth not tell you how, but leaveth you to admire and rejoice at so unspeakable and unconceivable love; and 1 John iv. 10, 'Herein is love, not that we loved God, but God loved us, and sent his Son to be a propitiation for our sins.' The apostle awakeneth our drowsy thoughts 'Herein is love,' here is a full, manifest, real proof of his love; it is commended to us, set before our thoughts, Rom. v. 8. Christ's love resteth not in good wishes, or the kind affection of his heart, but breaketh forth into action and evidence, and real performance. Nay, it is not only real, but glorious; things may be demonstrated as real which yet are not commended or set forth as great. Sometimes God

professeth his love to a people—'I have loved you'; but because they were afflicted and miserable, they expostulate with this bold reply, Mai. i. 2, 'Wherein hast thou loved us? 'Now here is a full and clear demonstration of it 'He spared not his own Son' Now what may not we promise ourselves from this great love? Hereby we see how much his heart is set upon our salvation; therefore no fear but he will carry it through. God is in good earnest with you, or he would never have made such provision; in short, he would never have given up Christ to be betrayed and sentenced and crucified, and to die for a sinful world, if he had not been in good earnest in his love.

2. Because Christ is the greatest and most precious gift; and surely God, that hath given so great a benefit as his own Son, will he stick at lesser things? He that hath given a pound, will he not give a farthing? Hath he given Christ, and will he not give pardon to cancel our defects, and grace to do our duty? comfort to support us in our afflictions? supplies to maintain and protect us during our services? and finally, will he not reward us after we have served him? Reconciliation by his death is propounded as a more difficult thing than salvation by his life, Rom. v. 10. Two things breed confidence: the fidelity of God, and his liberality; his liberality in his gifts, and his fidelity in his promises. His giving up Christ to die for us is a pledge of both: this was the greatest promise, the exhibition of the Messiah; and this was the greatest gift; all other gifts fall short of this, and do not beget such a confidence and hope. In creation God gave you a reasonable nature, such a life as is the light of man; but in redemption, to make way for a divine nature, he hath given us his Son, and giveth us many outward blessings in his daily providence, which are in their kind beneficial to us, and tokens of his goodness; but they are not assurances of his special love: Eccles. ix. 1, 'No man knoweth love or hatred by all that is before him.' I have riches, honour, esteem, food, raiment; I cannot! Therefore conclude God loveth me: I am poor and afflicted, therefore God hateth me; these are weak and ill-grounded conclusions. He hath given me his Son, and washed me in his blood, and pardoned my sins, and healed my nature; therefore he hath loved me. This is the right arguing; in short, other benefits may be comprehended, we know their worth, nature, benefit, and use; but this surpasseth knowledge, we cannot express nor conceive sufficiently the value and greatness of it. In other benefits we stand indebted to God for some outward gifts corn, and wine, and oil, great parts, understanding. Here, *Deum debemus*, we stand in debted for a person of the Godhead.

3. It is a gift in order to other things; and therefore he will complete that gift. Christ cometh not to us empty-handed; his person and benefits are not divided. He came to purchase all manner of bene fits and blessings for us, not only to raise our wonder and astonishment by this great act of his condescending love, but to procure the favour of God, the image of God, the everlasting fruition of the glory of God. Now, will God by an antecedent bounty lay the foundation so deep, and withhold the consequent bounty, which is the upper building, for which this foundation was intended? Shall so great a price be paid, and we obtain nothing? It is said of the foolish builder, after he had laid the foundation 'This man began to build, and was not able to finish,' Luke xiv. 29, 30. Surely the wise God will finish what he hath begun, if we be qualified, and do not *ponere obicem*, shut up the way by our incapacity. God

may now do us good without any impeachment of honour. His justice and holiness is sufficiently demonstrated: Rom. iii. 25, 26, 'Whom God hath set forth to be a propitiation through faith in his blood, to declare his righteousness, for the remission of sins; to declare, I say, at this time his righteousness, that he might be just, and the justifier of him that believeth in Jesus'. The authority of his law is kept up: Gal. iv. 4, 5, 'But when the fulness of time was come, God sent forth his Son, made of a woman, made under the law, to redeem them that were under his law, that we might receive the adoption of sons.' The truth of his threatening doth not altogether fall to the ground: Gen. ii. 17, 'In the day thou eatest thereof thou shalt surely die.' Therefore all is made easy and commodious[70] to our thoughts, and we can with the more confidence wait for what God hath promised.

4. Because the giving of Christ showeth how freely God will give all things to us: he gave Christ unasked, and unsought too. In this instance we see not only his infinite and great love, but his free and undeserved love: Rom. v. 8, 'God commended his love towards us, in that, while we were yet sinners, Christ died for the ungodly;' and v. 10, 'When we were enemies.' *Non invocantibus, sed provocantibus Deus sese offert*, saith Bernard. When the world had corrupted their way and cast off God, then Christ died for us, even for them that were neither loving nor lovely; a consideration to support our confidence, notwithstanding the sense of our un worthiness.

Fourthly, Who have an interest in Christ, and may reason thus within themselves; something seemeth to be implied in that 'Shall he not also together with him give us all things?' They that have an actual interest in Christ; others have but the offer upon condition, they are invited, but you may be assured.

1. Those to whom God giveth Christ. In the scripture we read sometimes of Christ given for us, and sometimes of Christ given to us. His being given for us noteth the impetration, and the purchase of the benefits; his being given to us, the application of them. The one speaketh the love of God to lost man, obnoxious to sin and misery; the other, God's love to us in particular: Gal. i. 10, 'It pleased God to reveal his Son in me'; Rev. i. 5, 'Loved us, and washed us in his blood.' The first gift is Christ: John v. 12, 'He that hath the Son hath life;' and Heb. iii. 14, 'Partakers of Christ;' 2 Cor. xiii. 5, 'Christ in you.' We receive his person, and with him his Spirit, to work life in us. We do not live in the body till we be united to the head; nor till we have Christ, do we receive the saving effects of his grace; clear that once, and shall he not with him give us all things? God offereth him to all, but he giveth him to you when you believe.

2. Those that give up themselves to Christ: 1 Cor. iii. 22, 'All things are yours,' because 'ye are Christ's, and Christ is God's.' If you be to Christ what Christ was to God, a dedicated servant, ever to do the things that please him; when you enter into covenant with him, and devote yourselves to his use and service, that to you 'to live is Christ,' Phil. i. 21. As God

---

[70] ample or adequate for a particular purpose

giveth Christ to you, you live in Christ; as you give yourselves to Christ, you live to him. God giveth us Christ, and all things with him, and we give up ourselves, and every interest and concernment of ours, to Christ, to be used for his glory. If you be sincere and hearty in this, you need not doubt of a plentiful allowance.

Use 1. Is to press us to admire the love of God, who spared not his own Son, but delivered him up for us all.

1. In that he spared not Christ. The Lord telleth Abraham: Gen. xxii. 12, 'Now I know that thou lovest me, since thou hast not withheld thy son, thine only son, from me.' So here is a full demonstration; certainly God loved Christ better than Abraham loved Isaac; and God was not bound by the command of a superior, but did it voluntarily. Oh, get your hearts deeply possessed with this love! Lord, we see how much thy heart is set upon the recovery of lost man!

2. That all this was done that he might spare us; for that is the fruit of it: Mai. i. 17, 'I will spare them, as a man spareth his own son that serveth him.' The indulgence of God to us is set forth by two amplifications propriety, and towardliness or obedience. Propriety: his own Son. A faulty child is a child still, and therefore not easily turned out of the family. But it is not a prodigal, or a rebellious son, but a good child; his Son that serveth him. Now, if we consider what God is, the purity of his nature, the strictness of his law, that sin is an act of disloyalty to God, and what we are, our manifold defects, surely it is love, great love that he would spare us. If God should be strict on the best of us, what would become of us?

Use 2. To improve it.

1. To confidence and hope. A man that wants not Christ cannot want anything; when the elect had need of God's own Son, he did not spare him; and when given us his Son, will he not give mercy and grace to help in every time of need? He that stood not on the greatest benefit, will he stand upon a less? There are two grounds of hope (1.) The cause; (2.) The merit. The fountain-cause is the infinite love of God; an emperor's revenue will pay a beggar's debt; the same good- will that moved him to give his Son will move him to give other things that we stand in need of, and may tend to our good. The other is the merit of Christ's sacrifice. God, that is not sparing of his Son, will not be sparing of what is purchased by his Son, surely his purchase will be made good. Christ sitteth at the right hand of God to see that it be done: Heb. x. 12, 'But this man, after he had offered one sacrifice for sins, for ever sat down at the right hand of God' That one offering hath done the work.

2. Improve it to obedience. God spared not his own Son, and shall we spare our lusts? There is a twofold argument in it. First, an argument of gratitude; let us not spare ourselves, neither body, nor soul, nor life, nor liberty, nor strength, nor time, nor anything that is near and dear to us, so we may glorify God. The apostle saith not barely, he gave his Son for us, but he spared not to give him. We have thoughts, and to spare, shall not God have them?

We have time—we bestow many hours in vanity—shall we not bestow some on God? But surely it should be as a wound to our hearts that we should be so unwilling not to spare our lusts, that which is not worth keeping. The other argument is from fear: if we spare our sins,

God will punish them: Job xx. 13, 'Though he spare it, and forsake it not, but keep it still within his mouth'; Deut. xxix. 21, 'The Lord will not spare him.' I may reason as the apostle— 'If God spare not the natural branches, take heed also lest he spare not thee,' Rom. xi. 21. Christ was -only a surety for sinners, thou art an obstinate and unreclaimed sinner.

3. Improve this to patience under poverty. If God hath dealt spar ingly with us in the matters of this world, yet he hath been bountiful in his Son; more in your souls, though less in your houses. 'He that spared not his Son, doth with him freely give us all things.' So under affliction by death, the death of friends, thou art apt to say, I cannot spare such a child, or yoke-fellow, or relation, when God seemeth to be about to take them away; God will not spare them, though you cannot or will not; but you cannot say God doth not love us or them; God loved Christ, yet will not spare him.

4. And especially should this be improved to give us great boldness and encouragement in prayer.

[A.] Because God loveth us. Usually when we come to God in prayer, we draw an ill picture of him in our minds, as if he were all wrath and vengeance, and unwilling to be reconciled to man, or brought to it with much difficulty; therefore it concerneth us to obviate this prejudice, and to conceive of God in prayer as one that loveth us. We have gained a great point when we can come with this thought into his presence, I am now praying to a God that loveth me, and will do me good. Yes, you will say, if I could come to that, I had gained a great point indeed. But what hindereth, when Christ came on purpose to show the love and loveliness of God to us? for our redemption came first out of the bosom of God, and Christ's mission into the world, and dying for sinners, was the fruit of his love; and mainly it served for this end, to give us a full demonstration of the love of God and his pity to the lost world of sinners, that when our guilt had made him frightful to us, we might not fly from him as a condemning God, but love him and serve him and pray to him as one willing to be reconciled to us. Light and heat are not more abundant in the sun than love is in God. What hindereth then, but that you come with this thought? But how shall I know that he loveth me? What things may assure me of it? What saith the text? 'God spared not his own Son, but delivered him up for us all.' There is, I confess, a twofold love his general love and his special love: his general love, which intendeth benefits to us; and his special love, which putteth us in possession of them; his general love to the lost world, and his love and mercy to us in particular, giving us the saving benefits purchased for us, and intended to us.

(1.) His general love to the lost world; that is a great thing. The devil seeketh to hide the wonderful love of God revealed in our redeemer, that we may still stand aloof from God, as more willing to punish than to save; and many poor dark creatures gratify his design and aim, are still seeking signs and tokens of God's love, or something in themselves to warrant them to come to God by Christ, and to persuade us that we shall be welcome if we do so; and because they cannot find anything in themselves that he will admit them, they are troubled, but all this while they are but seeking the sun with a candle. What greater evidence of God's willingness to receive you than the death of Christ, than the invitations of the gospel? This is alone above all evidences of his love, 'He spared not his own Son, but delivered him up for us all.' But herein we are like the Jews, who when they had seen many wonders wrought by Christ, would still have a new sign. The greatest sign is given already, Christ's dying for a sinful world. Men and angels cannot find out a sign, pledge, and confirmation of the love of God above that. Yet if that be not enough, we have another sign, the promises and invitations of the gospel, which show his willingness to welcome sinners. Salvation is offered not to named, but described persons; therefore, if we are willing to come under these hopes upon Christ's terms, these must satisfy our scrupulous minds that there is no bar put to us, but what we put to ourselves by our refusing the grace, as God offereth it. Certainly God's love and mercy to mankind is our first motive, and his willingness to impart good things to them on his own terms; and surely he is well pleased with our acceptance of them. It is true it is said, 1 John iv. 19, 'We love him because he loved us first.' But the first motive to draw our hearts to him is not his special elective love to us above others, for that we cannot know till we love him; but his common love and mercy to sinners, and that was manifested in Christ's being sent as a propitiation for our sins, and not for ours only, but for the sins of the whole world, 1 John ii. 2. This is that which is propounded to us to recover and reconcile our alienated and estranged affections to God: 2 Cor. v. 19, 'God was in Christ, reconciling the world to himself'. This grace God offereth to us as well as to others, namely, that God for Christ's sake will pardon our sins, if we will but forbear further hostility, and enter into his peace. None are bound to believe that God especially loveth them but those that are especially beloved by him, for none are bound to believe a falsehood; and a falsehood it is to us till we have the saving effects and benefits; and therefore it is not the special but the general love of God which draweth in our hearts to him; yea, his saints, after some testimonies received of God's special love, make this to be the great engaging motive: Gal. ii. 20, 'I live by the faith of the Son of God, who loved me, and gave himself for me.'

(2.) There is a special love when this grace is applied to us: Eph. ii. 4, 5, 'But God, who is rich in mercy, for his great love wherewith he loved us, when we were dead in trespasses and sins.' He did not begin to love us when we were converted, that is of a more ancient and eternal rise; but then he did begin to apply his love to us; and this no ordinary, but great love. When God was angry with us, and pronounced death on us in the sentence of his law, then he quickened us and reconciled us to himself, when his law represented him as an enemy, and in the course of his providence he appeared as an enemy, and the apprehensions of our guilty fear bespeak him an enemy; then did God for Christ's sake bestow his converting grace upon us. Now it is a great advantage to draw nigh to God as a reconciled father, and actually in covenant with us; surely this is and will be the object of our everlasting love and joy, Horn. v. 18; and a notable prop of confidence in prayer. Could we once believe that he dearly loveth us, and is actually reconciled to us, and taketh us for his children, and delighteth in our prosperity, oh, how cheerfully should we come into his presence 1 John xvi. 27, 'The Father himself loveth you, because you have loved me, and believed that I came out from God.' We have then not only his own intercession, but the Father's especial love, as the ground of our audience and acceptance. Now this particular interest dependeth on something wrought in our souls by the Holy Spirit; our Lord inentioneth two things, their faith in Christ, and love to God, or a thankful acceptance of him as our Lord and Saviour; love to God, or a thankful obedience to him, John xiv. 22, 23. We cannot perceive our special interest in the love of God, but by the evidences of our sincerity; when we see God's love tokens in our hearts, faith and love wrought in us by his Spirit, then we may know that he loveth us by his special love. The question is, Doth God love me? Hath he given his Spirit? How shall 1 know that? Answer, By the effects. Do you believe in Jesus Christ? How shall I know my faith is sincere, and the faith of God's elect? Doth it work by love? Gal. v. 6. How shall I know that I love God? The acts of sincere love are seeking after God and delighting in him; if you cannot find the latter, the former is a comfortable evidence: Prov. viii. 17, 'I love them that love me, and they that seek me early shall find me' The *desiderium unionis*, the desirous seeking love, if it be serious and earnest, it is sincere, though you find not such delightful apprehensions of his grace to you; clear this once, and when you come to pray, you may know that God loveth you with a special love. The dearest friend we have in the world doth not love us the thousandth part so much as he doth; nay, as Valdesso saith, the highest angel doth not love God so much as he loveth the lowest saint. God loveth like himself, becoming the greatness and infiniteness of his own being; and with this persuasion pray to him.

[B.] God's love is not a cold and ineffectual love, that consists only in raw wishes, but an operative and active love, that issueth forth, to accomplish what he intendeth to us, though by the most costly means, and at the dearest rates. God is good, and doth good, Ps. cxix. 68. He hath a love to us, and will do good to us. Our love many times goeth no further than good wishes and good words be warmed, be clothed but give not those things which are needful for the body, James ii. 26. Our Lord resteth not in kind wishes, but giveth a full demonstration of his love; if Christ be needful for the saints, they shall have him, 'God spared not his own Son'

[C.] It is a great love, such as may raise our wonder and astonishment, and so may enlarge our expectations and capacities for the reception of other things: Eph iii. 18, 19, 'That ye may with all saints comprehend what is the height and breadth, the length and depth, and to know the love of Christ, which passeth knowledge, that ye may be filled with all the fulness of God.' There is such an infiniteness and immensity in this love of God in Christ, as raiseth our desires and hopes to expect all other things from him which belong to our happiness. If God will do this, what will he not do for those whom he loveth? He that hath given a talent, will not he give a penny? We confidently go to one with a request who hath done some great thing for us already. What greater thing could there be than his giving his Son to die for a sinful world? John xv. 13, 'Greater love hath no man, than that he lay down his life for his friends.' We were not friends in state, but only friends in his purpose; nay, we were actual enemies, but reconciled and brought into friendship by his death. No man can express greater love to his dearest friends than to adventure to die for them. This did Christ for us.

[D.] It was a love expressed to us when our case was not only difficult, but desperate and remediless, as to any other agent: Isa. lvi. 16, 'And he saw that there was no man, and wondered that there was no intercessor; therefore his own arm wrought salvation for us'; Ps. xl. 8, 'The redemption of the soul is precious, and ceaseth for ever'. Like perplexities often occurring in the church's case: 2 Chron. xxii. 12, 'our God, wilt thou not judge them? for we have no might against this great company that cometh against us, neither know we what to do, but our eyes are unto thee'; and Esther iii. 14, when the writing was signed and sent abroad by all posts for the destruction and extermination of the Jews, the city Shushan was perplexed.

[E.] Though we cannot absolutely determine of the success as to particular events, yet this giveth good hope and confidence towards God.

1st. As to particular events, no absolute certainty; for (1.) God promiseth not all that you desire, or think that ye want in bodily things. (2.) Many things are necessary to serve the order and harmony of his providence in the communities and societies wherein we live; and God may deliver his people in such a way, and by such means as they never dreamt of; as Paul's going to Rome; therefore, for the way, his wisdom must be the judge, not our partial conceits. (3.) As to temporal events. We must pray with submission: 1 John v. 14, 'And this is the confidence that we have in him, that if we ask anything according to his will, he heareth us'. It is not always necessary for us that we should have love and respect from men, and never be tried and exercised with want, or pain, or suffering.

2nd. This giveth good hope. (1.) Because it is for Christ's sake that he fulfilleth all promises to us, and so giveth us deliverance in any strait or present exigence. (2.) Because we are heard in what we ask for God's glory and our own good; so our prayers are accepted. (a.) God's glory. But he must choose the means; the end is granted; the prayer is not lost, but rewarded as an act of our sincerity. (b.) For our good, that is the chiefest good: Rom. viii. 28, 'All things shall work together for good to them that love God.' The great promise is eternal salvation, all things else subordinated to it. If you beg ease for the flesh, merely for its own sake, or worldly prosperity to please the flesh, you bespeak your own denial; Christ puts no such dross in his golden censer.

Use 3. Is to persuade you to get an actual interest in Christ, by receiving him when God offereth him, and is willing to give him to you, John i. 12. Faith is a broken-hearted and thankful acceptance of Christ, and a giving up ourselves to him by an entire and unbounded resignation, 2 Chron. xxx. 8. Yield up yourselves to the Lord, to be sanctified and governed by him.

SERMON XLIII

Who shall lay anything to the charge of God's elect? It is God that justifieth.

Romans viii. 33.

WE have done with the general triumph of believers, and considered what supported them against the fear of evil and the fear of death viz., the hope of good. Now the apostle descendeth to particulars; and the first ground of a believer's trouble is sin, the guilt of which raiseth many doubts and fears within us, all which are removed by justification. Now justification is opposite to two things, accusation and condemnation: the one maketh way for the other; for those that are justly accused are also condemned. As it is opposite to accusation, so to justify is the part of an advocate; as to condemnation, so to justify is the part of a judge. A believer is upon good terms in both respects; there are no accusers before God that we need to be afraid of, and they may with comfort appear before the bar of their judge. If we are impleaded, we may stand in the judgment; as to accusation here, and as to condemnation hereafter, accusation may seem to infringe our present comforts, condemnation make void our future hopes. But things present and to come are both ours.

The apostle beginneth with the accusation in this verse, and speaketh of condemnation in the text—*Who shall lay anything*, &c.

In which words observe

1. A question, or bold challenge of faith Who shall lay anything to the charge of God's elect f

2. The reply, or answer, it is God that justifieth. The question or interrogation intimateth the matter of our trouble, something that may be laid to our charge; the answer, the ground of our support and comfort, which is God's free justification by Christ. In the challenge, or question, first, what is denied, having anything laid to our charge; secondly, the persons concerned, God's elect. Both must be explained.

First, The question implieth a denial, not simple and absolute, but in some respects; not as if no accuser, for the devil accuseth us: Rev. xii. 10, he is called 'The accuser of the brethren, who accuseth us before God day and night' And the world accuseth us: it accused Jeremiah, Jer. xxxvii. 13, as a revolter to the Chaldeans; Amos vii. 10, as a mover of sedition; Paul as a pestilent fellow, and a mover of sedition, and, in general, all Christians: 2 Cor. vi. 8, 'As deceivers and yet true.' Our own consciences accuse us: Rom. ii. 15; 1 John iii. 20, 'For if our hearts condemn us'; and David, Ps. xxv. 7, saith,

'Remember not the sins of my youth.' Nor is it to be understood as if there were no ground for the accusation. The devil is *katigoros*, not a whisperer or a slanderer, but an impleader in a court of justice, before the tribunal of God, *antidikos*, that is, an adversary in law, one that joineth with us in plea of law; he may slander us, as he did Job, that he was a mercenary man, though perfect and upright, Job i. 8, 11. But too often there is too much ground for the accusation. The world accuseth us, but we often give them too great occasion: 2 Cor. xi. 12, 'That I may cut off occasion from them that desire occasion.' Our hearts accuse us for committing and omitting many things contrary to the law of God: James iii. 2, 'In many things we offend all'; so that it is not an absolute denial of a legal accusation. How then can the apostle say, 'Who shall lay anything to our charge?' I answer, it is to be interpreted as to the success; they cannot prevail in the plea; if they charge, God will discharge. The devil is often a slanderer, the world raileth, conscience may give a wrong judgment; but when the accusation cannot be wholly denied, yet there is a remedy for the penitent believer: it is in vain to accuse those whom God upon just reasons acquitteth. God is not in danger to be mistaken by false accusation, or to do us an injustice; but when our real guilt is before our face, and the malice of Satan will seek thereupon to procure our condemnation, yet there are just reasons to be presented before him to procure our pardon.

2. The persons 'God's elect,' who in justification are considered, not as elect, but as effectually called; for the order is set down, ver. 30, 'Whom he did predestinate, them he called; and whom he called, them he justified.' Those whom God hath chosen before the foundation of the world, and now truly believing in Christ, these are justified, for otherwise they are condemned already, John iii. 18; children of wrath as well as others, Eph. ii. 3; for we must consider the elect as to the purpose of his grace, or the sentence of his law; for till the elect are effectually called and justified they are children of wrath as well as others.

Secondly, the reply and answer 'It is God that justifieth' This implieth two things: (1.) his finding out a way to acquit them, according to the terms of the gospel, as when all men were *upodikoi theo*, obnoxious to God's vengeance; but now a clear and sure way of pardon: Rom. iii. 19-22, 'Now we know that whatsoever things the law saith, it saith to them that are under the law, that every mouth may be stopped, and all the world may become guilty before God. Therefore by the deeds of the law there shall no flesh be justified in his sight, for by the law is the knowledge of sin; but the righteousness of God without the law is manifested, being witnessed by the law and the prophets; even the righteousness of God which is by faith of Jesus Christ unto all and upon all that believe.' There is mercy for all penitent believers, to accept and bless them.

(2.) He doth actually acquit all those that submit to these terms: Eph. i. 6, 'Who hath accepted us in the beloved, to the praise of his glorious grace.' The covenant setteth down the terms, and by per forming them we are capable of this benefit of absolution.

Doctrine That no charge or accusation will take effect, to prejudice the acceptation of them whom God justifieth.

1. What is justification? It consisteth in two things first, in the pardon of all our sins; secondly, in the acceptation of us as righteous in Christ.

[A.] The first is necessary, for God doth not vindicate us as innocent, but pardoneth us as guilty; those that are impleaded before his tribunal are all sinners, and sinners are not vindicated, but pardoned; and the apostle describeth justification by the pardon of sin: Rom. iv. 6, 7, 'As David describeth the blessedness of the man to whom the Lord imputeth righteousness without works, saying, Blessed are they whose iniquities are forgiven, whose sins are covered'. God, in justifying his people against the imputations of the world, doth bring forth their righteousness as the noon-day; but in justifying them against the accusations brought before his own tribunal, doth not vindicate our innocency, but show his own mercy in a free discharge of all our sins. This is sometimes set forth in scripture by the blotting out of all our transgressions; as Isa. xliii. 25, 'I, even I, am he that blotteth out thy transgressions for my own name's sake, and will remember thy sins no more'; as we are no more charged with what is cancelled or blotted out of a debt-book; so Isa. xxxviii. 17, 'Thou hast cast my sins behind thy back,' as men cast behind them such things as they list not to look on; and Micah vii. 19, 'Thou wilt cast our sins into the depth of the sea.' As that which is cast into the sea is lost, forgotten, and cannot be recovered; so sin shall not be brought into the judgment against the pardoned sinner.

[B.] In accepting us as righteous in Christ, who died for our sins to reconcile us unto God; and therefore sometimes he is said to be 'made righteousness to us'. 1 Cor. i. 30, and we are said to be 'made the righteousness of God in him,' 2 Cor. v. 21; that is, we have the effect of his sufferings, as if we had suffered in person; for they were under gone in our stead, and for our sakes, and the fruit of it given to us by God himself.

2. How many ways doth God justify? Four ways especially [A.] By way of constitution; [B.] estimation; [C.] sentence; and [D.] execution.

[A.] Constitutively, by his gospel-grant, or the new covenant in the blood of Christ. The covenant of grace is God's pardoning act and instrument by which we know whom, and upon what terms, God will pardon and justify namely, all such as repent and believe the gospel. We are constituted just and righteous, and exempted from the curse and penalties of the law. We may know the true way of justification by its opposition to the false or pretended way: Acts xiii. 38, 39, 'Through this man is preached unto you the forgiveness of sins; and by him all that believe are justified from all those things, from which they could not be justified by the law of Moses'. The Jews expected to be justified by the law of Moses, but we are justified by the law of Christ; that is, this constituteth our right. And herein justification and sanctification differ, God sanctifieth by his Spirit, but justifieth by the sentence of his word, or promise of the gospel. Our right immediately results thence, as by an act of indemnity we are freed from all the penalties which otherwise we might incur, without any further act of the magistrate. We are constituted righteous by his deed of gift in the gospel, but made holy by his Spirit; but if any quarrel at this term, and say that God by the new covenant doth declare who are justifiable, but doth not justify, I answer further, we are justified—

[B.] By way of estimation, whereby God doth determine our right, accept or deem and account them righteous who fulfil the terms of the gospel, and actually convey to them the fruits of Christ's death. This is spoken of, 1 Cor. vi. 11, 'And such were some of you; but ye are washed, but ye are sanctified, but ye are justified'; once vile sinners, now washed, sanctified, and justified. As soon as they believe they are put into a state of acceptation, that is, justifying; he continueth to justify them unto the death, and he keeps them in that estate wherein they have exemption from the punishment of sin, and a right to eternal life.

[3.] By way of sentence. This is in part done here, when God interpreteth our righteousness and sincerity: Job xxxiii. 23, 24, 'If there be a messenger with him, an interpreter, one among a thousand, to show unto man his uprightness, then he is gracious unto him, and saith, Deliver him from going down to the pit; I have found a ransom;' and doth by the Spirit of adoption assure us more and more of the pardon of our sins; but more solemnly at the last day, when the judge doth, sitting upon the throne, pronounce and declare us righteous before all the world, and as those who are accepted unto life: Acts iii. 10, 'That your sins may be blotted out when the times of refreshing shall come from the presence of the Lord.' Then the sentence is solemnly pronounced by the judge sitting on the throne; and we are justified before God, men, and angels. There are two parts of judgment to condemn, and to absolve or justify: Mat. xii. 36, 37, 'But I say unto you, that for every idle word that a man shall speak, he shall give account thereof at the day of judgment; for by thy words thou shalt be justified, and by thy words thou shalt be condemned;' then every man's doom shall be pronounced.

[D.] By way of execution, when the sentence is executed. This is in part done here, as God taketh off the penalties and fruits of sin, either in the way of his internal or external government, and giveth us many blessings as the pledge of his love; and above all, the gift of the Holy Spirit, whereby he sanctifieth us more thoroughly, and worketh in us that which is pleasing in his sight. This he giveth as the God of peace, as reconciled to us in Christ: Heb. xiii. 20, 21, 'Now the God of peace, that brought again- from the dead our Lord Jesus, that great shepherd of the sheep, through the blood of the everlasting covenant, make you perfect in every good work, to do his will, working in you that which is pleasing in his sight, through Jesus Christ;' 1 Thes. v. 23, 'And the very God of peace sanctify you wholly: and I pray God your whole spirit and soul and body be preserved blameless unto the coming of our Lord Jesus Christ; faithful is he that calleth you, who will do it'; but more fully at the last day, when we enter into everlasting glory, and the wicked are turned into hell with the devil and his angels: Mat. xxv. 46, 'And these shall go into everlasting punishment, but the righteous into life eternal' Then is the full and final execution, a perfect freedom from all misery, and a possession of all happiness.

3. How it can stand with the wisdom, justice, and holiness of God, to justify a sinner. It is a great crime to take the unrighteous to be righteous; and to pronounce the wicked justified seemeth to be against the word of God: Prov. xxiv. 24, 'He that saith unto the wicked, Thou art righteous, him shall the people curse, nations shall abhor him;' Prov. xvii. 15, 'He that justifieth the wicked, and he that condemneth the just, even they both are an abomination unto the Lord. Now what is an abomination unto the Lord is surely contrary to his nature: Exod. xxxiv. 7, 'He will by no means clear the guilty.'

Answer There is no abating the force of these objections, if there were not good ground for God's absolution, or sentence of justification. I shall mention three: Christ's ransom, the covenant of grace, and our faith or conversion to God.

1. Christ's ransom maketh it reconcilable with God's justice, and the honour of his law and government. Job xxxiii. 24, 'Then he is gracious unto him, and saith, Deliver him from going down into the pit; I have found a ransom;' Rom. iii. 25, 'Whom God hath set forth to be a

propitiation through faith in his blood, to declare his righteousness for the remission of sins'
There is full satisfaction given to God's wronged justice.

2. His covenant reconcileth it with his wisdom. God is not mistaken in judging us righteous
when we are not; for we are constituted righteous, and then deemed and pronounced so;
made righteous, as the apostle speaketh, Rom v. 19. Our right is founded in Christ's
obedience, but resulteth from the promise. The constitution is by covenant. God doth first
put us into a state of favour and reconciliation, and then treateth and dealeth with us as
such; constituteth us righteous by his covenant, and then in his judgment accepteth us as
righteous. He will not acquit them in judgment whom his covenant doth not first pardon.

3. Effectual calling, or the conversion of man, reconcileth it with his holiness; for a sinner, as
a sinner, is not justified, but a penitent believer. It is true, it is said, 'God justifieth the
ungodly,' Rom. iv. 5; those that were once so, but not those that continue so. Certainly he
sanctifieth before he justifieth: Acts xxvi. 18, 'To open their eyes, and turn them from
darkness to light, and from the power of Satan to God, that they may receive forgiveness of
sins, and inheritance among them that are sanctified by faith that is in me'; and in many
other places. No man is freed from the guilt of sin, which render eth us obnoxious to God's
wrath, who is not freed from the filth of sin, which tainteth our faculties; for Christ is made
to us both 'righteousness and sanctification' 1 Cor. i. 30. By losing God's image, we lost his
favour; and in the order wherein we lost it, we recover it. God regenerateth that he may
pardon and justify, and restoreth first our holiness, and then our happiness. It is not
consistent with God's holiness to give us pardon, and let us alone in our sins. A man would
not put a toad in his bosom. But more fully to give you a prospect into this matter, let us
take notice of the several things which are mentioned in scripture as belonging to our
justification, as, for instance, sometimes we are said to be justified by grace, as Rom. iii. 24,
'Being justified freely by his grace;' sometimes by the blood of Christ, as Rom. v. 9, 'Being
justified by his blood, we shall be saved from wrath through him;' sometimes by faith, as
Rom. v. 1, 'Being justified by faith, we have peace with God through our Lord Jesus Christ;'
some times .by works: James ii. 24, 'Ye see then how that by works a man is justified, and
not by faith only'. All these things concur to our justification, and do not contradict, but
imply one another. The first moving cause of all is grace; the meritorious cause is Christ's
blood; the means of applying, or the condition on our part upon which we are capable at
first of receiving so great a privilege, is faith; and the means of continuing in our justified
estate is by good works, or new- obedience. I say, our first actual pardon, justification, and
right to life, is given upon condition of our first faith and repentance; but this estate is
continued to us both by faith, Rom. i. 17, and new obedience; these fairly accord. The grace
of God will do nothing without the intervention of Christ's merits; and Christ's merits doth
not profit us till it be applied by faith; and sound believers will live in a course of new
obedience. Let us consider them severally—

[1.] The first moving cause that inclined God to show us mercy in our undone and lost estate
was merely his grace. God might have left us obnoxious to the curse without any offer of
peace, as he did the fallen angels; but such was his grace, that he thought of the way of our

recovery, how we might be redeemed, renewed, and justified; surely all this is of grace: Titus iii. 5-7, 'Not by works of righteousness which we have done, but according to his mercy he saved us, by the washing of regeneration, and the renewing of the Holy Ghost; which he shed on us abundantly, through Jesus Christ our Saviour, that, being justified by his grace, we should be made heirs according to the hope of eternal life.' The rise of all is the love and goodwill of God.

[B.] We are justified by the blood of Christ. Blood is not exclu sive of the other parts of his obedience, but doth imply them rather, as the consummate act thereof: Phil. ii. 7, 'He became obedient unto death, even the death of the cross.' It is by the merit of his sacrifice and obedience, God took this course to exalt the glory of his justice, as well as his grace; and in the mystery of our salvation there is such a temperament of both, that they shine with an equal glory.

[C.] We are justified by faith: Acts xiii. 39, 'And by him all that believe are justified from all things, from which ye could not be justified by the law of Moses.' Certainly none are justified in a state of impenitency and unbelief; it is not enough to look to the first moving cause, the grace of God, or the impetration of it by the blood of Christ, but how it is applied to ourselves, and what right we have; for the righteousness of Christ is none of ours, till we do repent and believe. Let us see how our title doth arise: When we thankfully, seriously, and broken-heartedly accept Christ as our Lord and Saviour, then we are found in him, not having our own righteousness.

[D.] We are justified by works, and not by faith only, by which are meant the fruits of sanctification. For true faith and true holiness will show itself by good works; faith giveth us the first right, but works continue it, for otherwise a course of sin would put us into a state of damnation again; therefore at the last judgment these are considered: Kev. xx. 12, 'And the dead were judged out of those things which were written in the books, according to their works;' Mat. xxv. 35, 36, 'For I was an hungry, and ye gave me meat; I was thirsty, and ye gave me drink; I was a stranger, and ye took me in; naked, and ye clothed me; I was sick, and ye visited me; I was in prison, and ye came unto me.' Faith is our consent, but obedience verifieth it, or is our performance of what we consented unto, the one as covenant-making, the other as covenant-keeping; we are admitted by covenant-making, but continued in our privileges by covenant- keeping: Ps. xxv. 10, 'All the paths of the Lord are mercy, and truth, unto such as keep his covenant.'

But yet a little more must be said to reconcile the two apostles. Paul saith, 'A man is justified by faith, without the deeds of the law,' Rom. iii. 28; and James saith, chap. ii. 24, 'Ye see then how by works a man is justified, and not by faith only.' There is a twofold charge commenced against us; as sinners and breakers of the law, as hypocrites and unsound believers. To the first we have nothing but the merits of Christ to plead; to the second, a fruitful obedience; or else, Paul, in the opposition between works and faith, meaneth by works legal observances, by faith true Christianity. The Jews boasted of their legal observances, to the rejection of the faith of Christ. And James by faith, a dead faith; and by works, Christian duties, or acts of obedience to God; not external observances of the law of man.

4. Why no charge or accusation can lie against them whom God justifieth.

[A.] Because God is the supreme law-giver, to -appoint the terms and conditions upon which we shall be justified; and when he hath stated them, and declared his will, who shall reverse it or revoke it? Heb. vi. 17, 18, 'Wherein God, willing more abundantly to show unto the heirs of promise the immutability of his counsel, confirmed it by an oath, that by two immutable things, in which it was impossible for God to lie, we might have strong consolation.' No cause of revocation can be imagined in God or out of God. Within God: not want of wisdom, for nothing can fall out but what he foresaw at first: Ps. ex. 4, 'The Lord hath sworn, and will not repent'; not inconstancy of will, 'for he is not as man, that he should repent' 1 Sam. xv. 29. Nor can his will be frustrated through any defect of power, for he is almighty. Nothing without God: neither devils, nor angels, nor men, have power to null and frustrate the force of his constitutions. The new covenant is his resolved will and purpose, not to be altered. Surely in making it, God determineth of his own, and not another's right It is in his power to absolve or condemn, upon what terms he pleaseth. Therefore if out of his sovereign will he hath put our justification in such a course, who can reverse it?

[B.] Because the promise of justification is built upon Christ's everlasting merit and satisfaction, and therefore it will hold good for ever: Heb. x. 14, 'By one offering he hath perfected forever them that are sanctified' Christ procured these promises for us, and that by his death; therefore everlastingly they hold good: 2 Cor. i. 20, 'For all the promises of God in him are Yea, and in him, Amen' and called the everlasting covenant. It is even become the interest of God to justify us, that he may not lose the glory of his grace, and the merit and oblation of Christ: Isa. liii. 11, 'By his knowledge shall my righteous servant justify many, for he shall bear their iniquities.' He that hath borne our sins, all this cost would be in vain if he should not pardon and justify. There is such a value in the death and obedience of Christ, that the scripture puts a *pollo mallon* upon it, comparing it with the influence of Adam, as a common root: Rom. v. 17, 18, 'For if by one man's offence death reigned by one, much more they which receive abundance of grace, and of the gift of righteousness, shall reign in life by one, Jesus Christ: therefore as by the offence of one judgment came upon all to condemnation, even so by the righteous ness of one the free gift came upon all men unto justification of life;' and with the legal sacrifices: Heb. ix. 13, 'For if the blood of bulls and goats, and the ashes of an heifer, sprinkling the unclean, sanctifieth to the purifying of the flesh; how much more shall the blood of Christ?' &c. There is the same reason in both; besides institution and appointment, there is an intrinsic value.

[C.] Because it is conveyed by the solemnity of a covenant. Now God by his covenant hath made it our right; his justice is engaged: 1 John i. 9, 'If we confess our sins, he is faithful and just to forgive us our sins'; 2 Tim. iv. 8, 'Henceforth there is laid up for me a crown of righteousness, which the righteous judge shall give me at that day.' By solemn promise you convey a right to another in the thing promised; so doth God.

[D.] When we believe, God, as the supreme judge, actually determineth our right, so that a believer is rectus in curia, hath his *quietus est*: Rom. iv. 1, 'Being justified by faith, we have peace with God, through our Lord Jesus Christ.' And then, who can lay anything to our charge, to reverse God's grant?

[E.] The Lord, as the sovereign disposer of man's felicity, doth many times uncontrollably give us the comfort of it in our own consciences: Job xxxiv. 29, 'When he giveth quietness, who can trouble? and when he hideth his, face, who then can behold him? whether it be done against a nation, or against a man only.' None can obstruct the peace which he giveth. God's dispensations, whether for good or evil, are effectual and irresistible. You may depend on the good he under- taketh to do; though this peace be assaulted, yet it will stand. God's manifesting, or hiding his face, is enough to make a creature happy or miserable.

Use 1. Is information. To show us—

1. The misery of wicked men. They are not justified by God; and therefore the charge of God's broken law lieth heavy upon them, and the weight of it will sink them to the nethermost hell. It may be the world may flatter and applaud them, and they may absolve and acquit themselves at an easier rate; but 'there is no peace, saith my God, to the wicked,' Isa. lvii. 20. It is not our security, delighting ourselves to sing lullabies to our own souls; for we are never upon sure terms till God justifieth us. Many absolve themselves upon easy terms, either because they sit still, and cry God mercy, or upon the account of their superficial righteousness, as the pharisees justified themselves. No, we must judge ourselves, but it is God must justify us; till we have our discharge from him, we are never safe; therefore it concerneth us to consider upon what terms we stand. Are we troubled in mind? or at peace? If troubled in mind, take God's remedy. If we be at peace, whence cometh it? Is it warranted by the covenant of God? That granteth no pardon, no justification, but to those that repent and believe.

2. The happiness of the godly. It is in vain to accuse those whom God acquitteth; you need not fear an accuser, not because innocent, but because justified. Though the world revileth you, the devil would stir up legal fears, revive your old bondage. When your hearts condemn you for many defects, you must stick to this, God justifieth. For the reproaches of the world, you need not be troubled at them; when they accuse you falsely of pride, hypocrisy, covetousness, you may say as Job: chap. xvi. 19, 'My witness is in heaven, and my record is on high'. He that is the judge of all men is a witness and observer of their ways, and will acquit those whose hearts are upright with him from the censures of the world. God will not ask their vote and suffrage. When Satan would revive our bondage by the thoughts of death, and the consequences of it, consider wherefore did Christ come into the world, and die for sinners, but to free us from those tormenting fears? Heb. ii. 14, 15, 'Forasmuch as the children are partakers of flesh and blood, he also himself took part of the same, that through death he might destroy him that had the power of death, that is, the devil; and deliver them who, through fear of death, were all their life time subject to bondage.' But when our hearts condemn us, especially for some wounding sin, the case is otherwise. God by conscience writeth bitter things against you, Job xiii. 26. We must not smother our sin,

nor deny our guiltiness, but appeal from court to court: Ps. cxxx. 3, 4, 'If thou, Lord, shouldest mark our iniquities, Lord, who shall stand? But there is forgiveness with thee, that thou mayest be feared'; and Ps. cxliii. 2, 'Enter not into judgment with thy servant, for in thy sight shall no man living be justified.' If it be from the general view of sin, or the remembrance of some special sin, sue out your pardon in Christ; your justification is not nullified; you are still under a pardoning covenant, and the actual pardon on repentance is granted to you.

Use 2. Is to press us to get into this blessed condition, that you may say, It is God that justifieth. Consider the weight of the case; it concerneth damnation or salvation, whether you are under the curse, or heirs of promise. And all this is depending before God. To justify is God's act; but man must fulfil the condition. Well then, let us sup pose a judiciary process; there will be such at the last day certainly— 'For we must all stand before the tribunal seat of Christ'. Rom. xiv. 10. Our cause lieth before God now, and our qualification must be tried and judged now, in order to our reconciliation with God, as hereafter in order to our everlasting fruition of him in glory. Well then, the judge is God: Gen. xviii. 23; and Ps. xciv. 2, 'Lift up thyself, thou judge of the earth!' The judge accepteth the godly while they are in the body: 2 Cor. v. 9, 'That whether we are present or absent, we may be accepted with him'; but 'he is angry with the wicked every day,' Ps. vii. 11. The witnesses are Satan and conscience; the plea in traverse is about our guiltiness, according to a double rule, the law of works or grace If according to the law of works, alas! none of us can stand in the judgment. There we plead, not innocent, but guilty; Christ could say, John viii. 46, 'Which of you convinceth me of sin? 'but here it is otherwise: Rom. iii. 19, 'All the world is become guilty before God.' Here is no denial, no extenuation, all are become corrupt'; none doth good, no, not one.' Now Christ was made sin, and underwent the curse for us. To the second, the law of grace, there must be, first a hearty acceptance of an offered Saviour, and a consent, both of subjection and dependence. Secondly, sincere obedience: Rom. viii. 1, 'They walk not after the flesh, but after the Spirit.' He liveth as one turned from the world and the flesh to God. The more sensible we are of our own vileness, the more we see the necessity of a redeemer.

SERMON XLIV

Who is he that condemneth? It is Christ that died, yea rather, that is risen again, who is even at the right hand of God, who also maketh intercession for us.

Romans viii. 34.

IN the former verse, justification is considered as opposite to accusation; now, as opposite to condemnation; there, 'Who shall lay anything to our charge?'; here, 'Who is he that condemneth?' With respect to both, we must look upon Christ as our advocate, and God as our judge. Somewhat in this verse concerneth our exemption from the danger of accusation, namely, all the acts of Christ's mediation here mentioned; somewhat in that verse concerneth the question propounded here about condemnation, namely, the sentence of God as our judge. For the answer given there must be repeated, 'Who is he that condemneth? It is God that justifieth.' We need not fear an accuser, because we have an advocate; we need not fear to be cast in the judgment, because we have a favourable judge, who will not justify and condemn too. Thence ariseth this part of the triumphant song which the apostle puts into the mouth of a believer, 'Who is he that condemneth? it is Christ that died,' &c. In the words we have—

1. A triumphant challenge—*Who is he that condemneth?*

2. The ground of it. It is Christ's mediation—*It is Christ that died*, &c.

1. The challenge—'Who is he that condemneth?' It is meant with respect to God's judgment. In the world the saints have been, and often are condemned, not only to death: James v. 6, 'Ye have condemned and killed the just, and he doth not resist you;' but some, if they had their wills, would adjudge them to the bottom of hell: John xvi. 2, 'They will put you out of the synagogues, as well as kill you;' that is, curse, and condemn you to hell, which is the second death. But their rash censures are not ratified in heaven; their cursing hurts no more than their absolution benefiteth us; therefore this is riot the meaning. The words relate to the supreme court. What fear is there of condemnation by God, when he declareth his mind concerning the justification of such as believe in Christ? Now God hath expressly said 'that he that believeth shall not come into condemnation'; and who dareth to contradict his sentence? False teachers may deny this comfort to the penitent believers, and make their hearts sad whom God would not have made sad, but God will not retract his grant; and the sentence of any judge on this side God needeth not to be stood upon. It is on their part presumption, and usurpation of the throne of God, and their act cannot do us harm; we stand or fall to our own proper lord and master.

2. The ground of the challenge. We are acquitted from condemnation on Christ's account. This blessing runneth in the channel of his mediation; four branches of it are here mentioned (1.) Christ's death; (2.) Resurrection, with a 'yea rather'; (3.) His exaltation at the right hand of God; (4.) His intercession for us; all which would be in vain, and lose their effect, if any condemnation were to be feared by us. From the whole observe—

Doctrine 1. That freedom from the fears of condemnation is one great privilege of true and sound believers.

Doctrine 2. That our triumph over the fears of condemnation ariseth from the several acts of Christ's mediation.

Doctrine 1. For the first point, that freedom from the fears of condemnation is one great privilege of true and sound believers.

What a great privilege it is, will appear—

1. By the dreadfulness of the sentence.

2. The difficulty to get rid of these fears.

3. The sure and solid grounds of a believer's peace.

1. The dreadfulness of the sentence. To condemn is to adjudge to punishment; and for God to condemn is to adjudge us to everlasting punishment. The final sentence is set down, Mat. xxv. 41, 'Depart from me, ye cursed, into everlasting fire, prepared for the devil and his angels.' In the general they are pronounced cursed; but in particular there is—

[A.] The *poena damni*[71], the loss of God's favour and presence and glory. They depart from God, who made them at first after his image; from the Redeemer, whose grace was offered to them, but slighted by them; from the Holy Ghost, who strove with them to sanctify them, and reduce them to God, till they quenched all his motions, and expelled him out of their hearts. The disciples wept when Paul said, 'Ye shall see my face no more'; but what anguish will fill the hearts of the reprobate when God shall say to them, Ye shall never see my face more; you are now cut off from all hopes and possibility of salvation forever. Wicked men banish God out of their company now: Job xxi. 14, 'Depart from us; for we desire not the knowledge of thy ways' God will then be even with them, and banish them out of his presence; not from his essential presence, for that is with them to their everlasting misery; but from his gracious presence, which is the everlasting delight of the saints, and from all possibility of acceptance with him.

[B.] *Poena sensus*[72], 'into everlasting fire, prepared for the devil and his angels.' (1.) Into fire, not purifying, but tormenting; for so hell is a place of torment, and a state of torment: Luke xvi. 24, 'I am horribly tormented in this flame;' and ver. 25, 'He is comforted, and thou art tormented;' ver. 29, 'That they come not into this place of torment.' (2.) It is for duration, everlasting fire. It had a beginning, but will never have an end. The saints in all their troubles can see both banks and bottom; they never met with any such hard condition, but it had an end; but here there still remaineth a fearful looking for more fiery indignation from the Lord. The glory which they refused is everlasting glory, and the torments which they incur are everlasting torments. (3.) It is said, 'Prepared for the devil and his angels.' This showeth the

---

[71] Penalty of loss
[72] Penalty of sense

greatness of the misery of the wicked. The devil and his angels must be their everlasting companions; they who entertained his suggestions in their hearts shall then remain forever in his company and society. As Christ with his blessed angels and saints make one kingdom or family, living together in perpetual blessedness; so the devil and his angels, and the wicked, make one society, living together in perpetual misery. This is the sentence of condemnation the Christian notion of it.

2. The difficulty to get rid of these fears.

[A.] We all deserve condemnation upon many accounts, both upon the account of original sin: Rom. v. 18, 'As by the offence of one judgment came upon all to condemnation, so by the righteousness of one the free gift came upon all to justification of life.' Our actual offences make it more our due; for 'the wages of sin is death,' Rom, vi. 23. The second death as well as the first.

[B.] In our natural estate we were actually condemned by the sentence of the law, which is confirmed by the gospel, if we refuse the offered remedy: John iii. 18, 19, 'He that believeth not, is condemned already;' and ver. 12, 'This is the condemnation, that light is come into the world, and men love darkness rather than light, because their deeds are evil'

[C.] Our consciences own it, that where there is guilt there will be condemnation; and therefore 'our own hearts condemn us,' 1 John iii. 20. And unless this condemnation be reversed, and that upon good grounds, we can have no firm and solid peace within ourselves. Conscience speaketh aloud this truth, and is the more to be regarded; partly because—

(1.) The fears of the guilty creature are founded in the nature of God, his holiness and justice. His pure holiness: Hab. i. 13, c Thou art of purer eyes than to behold iniquity.' It is a natural truth that sin is displeasing to God, and maketh the sinner hateful and loathsome to him, and worthy to be cast off and punished by him. God's holiness is at the bottom of all our fears. We fear his wrath, because it is armed with an almighty power; we fear his power, because it is set a- work by his justice; we fear his justice, because it is awakened by his holiness, which cannot endure sin and sinners: 1 Sam. vi. 20, 'And the men of Bethshemesh said, Who is able to stand before this holy Lord God?' So also on the other hand, all men's security ariseth from a misprision of God's nature, as if he were not so holy: Ps. 1. 21, 'Thou thoughtest that I was altogether such an one as thyself,' not much offended with sin. Now, for the justice of God: Rom. i. 32, They knew the just judgment of God (dikaioma, his righteous dealing,) that they that do such things, are worthy of death' He hath revealed his wrath from heaven against all ungodliness and unrighteousness of men. Men are convinced in their own consciences, that they are liable to his condemnation and judgment. The barbarous people of Melita had a sense that divine vengeance followed sinners: Acts xxviii. 4, 'He is a murderer, whom, though he hath escaped the sea, vengeance suffereth not to live.' Therefore till God's justice be appeased a man can have no satisfaction in him.

(2.) The next reason, because of the deepness of the impression. The conscience of sin is not easily blotted out; man is conscious to himself that he hath offended God, and deserved his wrath; and this trouble and fear is not easily appeased, nor the wounds of conscience healed. The apostle still goeth upon this argument against the Jews, that the sacrifices could not make the worshipper perfect as appertaining to the conscience, Heb. ix. 9, that is, perfectly remove the guilt, or the fear of condemnation and punishment, Heb. x. 2. The worshippers were never so purged as to have no conscience of sin; so that the expiation and purging out of sin is no slight thing.

(3.) After grace received much of our old bondage remaineth with us; for 'all their life-time they are subject to bondage,' Heb. ii. 15. We carry these shackles with us to heaven's gates. Which cometh to pass, partly through the imperfection of our graces: 1 John iv. 17, 18, 'Herein is our love made perfect, that we may have boldness in the day of judgment, because as he is so are we in the world. There is no fear in love, but perfect love casteth out fear, because fear hath torment: he that feareth is not perfect in love.' It is possible a man may be justified; but because his love doth not prevail to a greater obedience to God or conformity to Christ, therefore some of that fear which hath torment in it yet remaineth, and we have not that confidence which may embolden us against the fears of condemnation, or the terrors of the judgment. As faith worketh by love, and love produceth its effect, which is obedience to God and conformity to Christ, the fear of being condemned is cast out, and the conscience is more soundly established. And partly because God seemeth to revive these condemning fears by many harsh corrections, which look very wrath-like. An instance we have, 1 Kings xvii. 18. The woman of Sarepta, when her only son died, said to Elisha, 'What have I to do with thee, thou man of God? art thou come to call my sin to remembrance, to slay my son?' She thought that that providence intimated that God began to reckon with her about her sins; this may be a mistake, for God's providence must be expounded by his word. The grievous bitterness is intended for good, not for evil; to prevent condemnation, not establish it as the concluded determination and sentence of our judge: 1 Cor. xi. 32, 'We are chastened of the Lord that we may not be condemned with the world.' However, you see these fears are soon revived in us by bitter and grievous providences, which make us unravel all our hopes, and question whatever God hath done for us. And partly too, God may do it by some judicial impression on the con science: Job xiii. 26., 27, 'Thou writest bitter things against me, and makest me possess the iniquities of my youth; thou puttest my feet into the stocks, and lookest narrowly unto all my paths; thou settest a print upon the heels of my feet.' He speaketh there as if God did pursue him as one that was not justified. The wounds of a healed con science may bleed afresh, and sins long ago committed may be raked out of their graves, and like walking ghosts stare in the face of con science; and they may be apt to suspect all is wrong, and that they are still liable to the condemnation of God. God may permit this upon new provocations, when we walk not humbly and cautiously with him, and do not cherish the fervency of our love to him, and the tenderness of our consciences. Now all this showeth how hard a matter it is to get rid of the fear of condemnation. Before justification there is guilt, law, conscience against us the law condemneth, hearts condemn, and God himself seems to condemn us; after justification, imperfection of grace, sharp afilictions, and sad thoughts about past sins, these seem to condemn us.

3. The sure and solid grounds of a believer's peace. Before our conscience can be established these three things must be done

[A.] God's honour secured.

[B.] The law satisfied.

[C.] The conditions of the gospel fulfilled.

[A.] God's honour secured by a fit demonstration of his justice and holiness, which are the two attributes which do revive our guilty fears. His justice concerneth the rewarding of the obedient, and punishing the transgressors according to his law. The government of the world is secured by keeping up the honour of his justice: Gen. xviii. 25, 'Shall not the judge of all the earth do right?' and Rom. iii. 5, 6, 'Is God unrighteous who taketh vengeance? God forbid; how then shall God judge the world?' Certainly the government of the world is not provided for if there be not a means to keep up the honour of his justice; for God is not to be looked upon as a private party wronged, but the governor and judge of the world, who must have satisfaction, or declare his righteousness. His holiness must be demonstrated also, or his displeasure against sin, which is sufficiently done by the sufferings of Christ, which put an everlasting brand upon sin: Rom. viii. 3, 'God sending his own Son, in the likeness of sinful flesh, and for sin, condemned sin in the flesh'. At Golgotha we have the truest sight of sin.

[B.] His law satisfied, and the authority thereof kept up: Gal. iv. 5, 6, 'Christ was made under the law, to redeem them that were under the law, that we might receive the adoption of sons.' Christ was made under the law moral, which all are subject unto; as obedience unto natural parents, Luke ii. 51; positive and ceremonial, which the Jews were bound to obey, Mat. iii, 15; more particularly, the law of a redeemer and saviour; so he was obliged to die for us: Ps. xl. 6-8, 'Sacrifice and offering thou didst not desire; my ears hast thou opened: burnt offering and sin-offering hast thou not required. Then said I, Lo, I come; in the volume of the book it is written of me: I delight to do thy will, my God; yea, thy law is in my heart.' This was the noblest piece of service, or the highest degree of obedience, that ever could be performed to God: Rom. v. 19, 'By the obedience of one shall many be made righteous'; Phil, ii .8, 'And being found in fashion as a man, he humbled himself, and became obedient unto death, the death of the cross;' and Heb. v. 8, 9'; Though he was a son, yet learned he obedience by the things which he suffered; and being made perfect, he is become the author of eternal salvation unto all that obey him'; and was carried on with such humility, patience, and self-denial, resignation of himself to God, faith on him, and charity and pity to men, that such an act of love, and such a piece of service or obedience, cannot be done by men or angels. Then for the penalty and curse c He was made a curse for us,' Gal. iii. 13. Our curse and condemnation is legible in what Christ endured for us, the loss in his desertion, pain in his agonies and bloody sweat, and painful and shameful death. They were not light things which Christ endured, but such as extorted prayers, tears, and strong cries,

[C.] The conditions of the gospel are fulfilled.

(1.) I take it for granted that the gospel maketh sufficient provision against the condemnation of believers: John v. 24, 'Verily, verily, I say unto you, He that heareth my word, and believeth in him that sent me, hath everlasting life, and shall not come into condemnation, but hath passed from death to life.' This being the great result of the gospel, Christ prefixeth his Amen, Amen; implying that it is a truth worthy to be respected and credited. And this is the truth, that the penitent believer, when God cometh to judge of men, shall not fare ill in the judgment.

(2.) That this is done upon condition that we take God's remedy; so it is propounded: Mark xvi. 16, 'He that believeth and is baptized shall be saved, and he that believeth not shall be damned' The gospel hath a sanction as well as the law, both promise and threatening, and all upon the condition which God hath imposed.

(3.) That the promise doth consist of something the party is willing of; and the condition of what the promiser will have, but the receiver is not so ready to perform. The accepting the benefit promised is not so great a matter in ordinary contracts; but in God's covenant, being not a matter of sense, it is somewhat to be willing to accept: Isa. lv. 1, 'Ho, every one that thirsteth, come ye to the waters, and he that hath no money: come ye, buy and eat; yea, come, buy wine and milk without money and without price: Kev. xxii. 17, 'And the Spirit and the bride say, Come; and let him that heareth say, Come; and let him that is athirst come; and whosoever will, let him take of the water of life freely.' But God, besides the benefit of the creature, respects his own glory, and the recovery of the creature to himself from the devil, world, and flesh, which the creature is most backward unto. Every man would be freed from condemnation, and saved from hell. Now God hath promised that which we would have, that we may yield to that which naturally we would not have; we would have pardon, but God will have subjection; therefore it is said, Heb. v. 9, 'And being made perfect, he became the author of eternal salvation unto them that obey him.' We would have the second death to have no power over us; but God will have us holy, and that we should consent to our duty. We would not be condemned, but God will have us walk, not after the flesh, but after the Spirit, and so hath granted non-condemnation to such, Rom. viii. 1; those that are true Christians, and consent to the duty of the new covenant. The honour of God is concerned in our subjection to him, and the honour of Christ, who redeemed us to God, Kev. v. 8, as our comfort is concerned in being exempted from the fears of condemnation.

(4.) The more explicitly the condition is fulfilled, the more is our comfort and assurance, and the more may we make the bold challenge of faith; that is, the more clearly we obey the sanctifying motions of the Spirit, and mortify the desires of the flesh: 1 John iii. 21, 'If our hearts condemn us not, we have confidence towards God'; Gal. v. 18, 'If we be led by the Spirit, we are not under the law,' i.e., the condemning sentence thereof. Where worldly lusts bear a sway, a man is under the law, not under grace. He that liveth in a state of sin carrieth his sting and wound about him, and hath the matter of debts 1 and fears in his own bosom, and cannot attain to the true courage and boldness of the saints. As the flesh and spirit are at war in our hearts, so are law and grace; as the spirit prevaileth against the flesh, so doth grace prevail against our law-fears. The same was intimated, Rom. viii. 14, 15. Well then, if we would depend on the everlasting merits of Christ, we must accept the blessed covenant, wherein God hath promised to discharge the sincere and upright from condemnation, and look to the sureness of our claim, that we do not allow ourselves in any voluntary disobedience to Christ.

Use, is information.

1. It showeth us the bad condition of wicked men, who have within themselves an accusing conscience, and above themselves a condemning judge; and thence it is they dare not look inward or upward. They dare not look inward; all their pleasures are but stolen waters, and bread eaten in secret, Prov. ix. 17, delights gotten by stealth, when they can get conscience asleep; as servants feast themselves in a corner when they can get out of their master's sight. Nor upward; they dare not entertain themselves with serious thoughts of God: their hearts condemn them, and they look upon him as one that doth ratify, and is ready to execute the sentence; and therefore every remarkable dispensation of God puts them in a fright: Job xv. 2, 'And fill his belly with the east wind'; ver. 21, 'A dreadful sound is in his ears' Now this is a miserable condition, when we have no sound peace and quiet within ourselves. If they do not always feel the stings of con science, they are always subject to them; for the present, a stupid conscience is their disease, the benumbing lethargy of the soul; if they make a shift to shake off these thoughts, death will revive their fears, and that may surprise them in an instant: 1 Cor. xv. 56, 'The sting of death is sin.' Oh, how much better is it with the sound and serious believer, who preserveth most tenderness of conscience, and yet hath most peace, hath a higher sense of his duty than others have, and yet can, with greater satisfaction than others do, depend on the merit of Christ, and look for acceptance with God!

2. It showeth us what course to take, in case our heart doth condemn us. What must we do? Sit down in despair and die? No; but examine the matter seriously.

[A.] Conscience must not be despised, partly for its nearness to us; it is God's spy in our bosoms. Whom shall a man believe, if not his own conscience? Who knoweth us better than ourselves? 1 Cor. ii. 11, 'For what man knoweth the things of a man, save the spirit of man which is in him?' This judge cannot be suspected of rigour, or partiality, or ill-will; what is nearer, what is dearer to us than ourselves? And partly because of its relation to God; it is called 'the candle of the Lord' Prov. xx. 27. It is in the place of God to us, and therefore, if it condemn us may not God much more? its checks and reproaches are a warning from God; it acteth in his name, and citeth us before his tribunal; and therefore we must not smother and put off troubles of conscience till God put them away. Partly because of the rule it goeth by, which is the law of God, evident, either by the light of nature: Rom. ii. 15, 'Which show the work of the law written in their hearts; their consciences also bearing them witness, and their thoughts in the meanwhile either accusing, or else excusing one another'; or by the light of scripture: Prov. vi. 22, 'Bind my commandment on thy heart; when thou goest, it shall lead thee; when thou sleepest, it shall keep thee; when thou walkest, it shall walk with thee'; it doth but repeat over the law of God to you. It will be heard once; better hear it now, while you have opportunity to correct your error.

[B.] The matter must be discussed, that you may resolve to do as the case shall require.

(1.) In some cases there is an appeal from court to court. In what court doth conscience condemn you? In the court of the law? You ought to subscribe the condemnation is just, to own the desert of sin; and if God should bring it upon you, he is righteous: Nehem. ix. 33, 'Thou art just in all that is brought upon us, for thou hast done right, but we have done wickedly.' But there is a liberty of appeal from court to court: you may take sanctuary at the Lord's grace, and humbly claim the benefit of the new covenant: Ps. cxxx. 3, 4, 'If thou, Lord, shouldest mark iniquity, Lord, who shall stand? but there is forgiveness with thee, that thou shouldest be feared'; and Ps. cxliii. 2, 'And enter not into judgment with thy servant, for in thy sight shall no man living be justified' Deprecate the first court, and beg the favour of the second.

(2.) In other cases there is an appeal from judge to judge. Suppose conscience condemn you in the gospel court, that you are not a sound believer; the case must not be lightly passed over; but you must examine whether there be a sincere bent of heart in you towards God, yea or no. When others question or impeach your sincerity, you appeal to heaven, as Job did, 'My witness is in heaven.' The case is somewhat different when your own hearts question it: but yet you must see whether the judgment of conscience be the judgment of God. Conscience is a judge, but not the supreme judge. It may err both in acquitting and condemning: in acquitting, when from a judge, it becometh an advocate, excusing the partialities of our obedience; so in condemning, when from a judge it becometh an accuser, and exaggerateth incident frailties beyond measure. God may sometimes speak peace in the sentence of his word, when he doth not in the feeling of conscience. Beg of God to interpret your case. Our sincerity is best interpreted by a double testimony. It is well if it be so clear that a single one serveth turn: Rom. ix. 1, 'I say the truth in Christ, I lie not; my conscience also bearing me witness in the Holy Ghost'; and Rom. viii. 16, 'And the Spirit itself bearing witness with our spirits, that we are the children of God.'

(3.) Suppose the worst, that you have no relief by an appeal from court to court, or from judge to judge, yet there is a passing from state to state still allowed us: John v. 24, 'And shall not come into condemnation, but is passed from death to life.' You are in a state of condemnation, but you must get out of it as fast as you can, take the same course that a condemned man would. What is that?

(a.) Acknowledge the justice of it; see you be affected with it. Christ justifieth none but the self-condemned; for he came to seek and to save that which was lost: Luke xviii. 13, 14, 'God be merciful to me a sinner. I tell you, this man went down to his house justified rather than the other: for every one that exalteth himself shall be abased, and he that humbleth himself shall he exalted.' You have no plea but that of a sinner.

(b.) Take heed of resting in this estate, or going on in your sins. There is *sententia lata*, but *dilata*: Eccles. viii. 11, 'Because sentence against an evil doer is not executed speedily, therefore the heart of the sons of men is fully set in them to do evil' There is nothing but the slender thread of a frail life between you and execution; get it repealed quickly, or you are undone forever— 'Their damnation slumbereth not,' 2 Peter iii. 3. God is slow in executing the sentence, as being willing that men should repent; yet it will be executed, it is every day nearer and nearer.

(c.) Embrace the offer of the gospel, and set yourselves in the way of your recovery. Christ hath delivered us from wrath to come, but you must upon warning 'flee from wrath to come' Mat. iii; 7. And then that sentence of death, which you have received in yourselves, will be repealed. The door of grace is always open to those 'who have fled for refuge, to lay hold of the hope set before them,' Heb. vi. 8.

(d.) Make your qualification more explicit, by a holy .and heavenly life: 1 Thes. v. 8, 9, 'But let us who are of the day be sober, putting on the breast-plate of faith and love, and for an helmet, the hope of salvation: for God hath not appointed us to wrath, but to obtain salvation by our Lord Jesus Christ.' The more you live upon the other world, and in a strict obedience to God, the sooner you will make out your qualification: 2 Cor. i. 12, 'For our rejoicing is this, the testimony of our conscience, that in simplicity and godly sincerity we have had our conversation in the world.'

I now proceed to—

Doctrine 2. That our triumph over the fear of condemnation mainly ariseth from the several acts of Christ's mediation.

1st. His death is mentioned 'It is Christ that died'; that is, he hath expiated our sins by his death, and obtained release and pardon for us: and then, 'Who shall condemn? 'This will appear

[1.] By the notions by which it is set forth: a ransom, a mediatorial sacrifice, and a propitiation. A ransom—*lutron anti pollon*, Mat. xx. 28; *antilutron*, 1 Tim. ii. 6. A ransom is a price given to a judge, or one that hath the power of life and death, to save the life of one capitally guilty, and by law bound to suffer death, or some other evil of punishment. This was our case: God was the supreme judge, before whose tribunal man standeth guilty, and liable to death and condemnation; but Christ gave himself as a ransom in our stead, to save us from the condemnation which we had deserved: Job xxxiii. 24, 'Deliver him from going down to the pit; I have found a ransom' From the beginning of the world Christ was known to be a redeemer, who saved the world by a ransom paid; no other way could the effects of the Lord's grace be communicated to us. We receive mercies freely, but they were dearly purchased by Christ. The second notion is that of a mediatorial sacrifice: Isa. liii. 10, 'He shall make his soul an offering for sin'; so Eph. v. 2, 'He gave himself for us, an offering and a sacrifice to God, for a sweet-smelling savour'. Sin is a wrong done to God, and therefore there must be something offered to God in our stead, by way of satisfaction, before he would quit his controversy against us. This Christ hath done. All that was signified by the ancient sacrifices and offerings was accomplished by him: they were slayed, killed, burned, all which are but shadows of what our Lord endured. He is the true and real sacrifice, wherein provoked justice doth rest satisfied, his wrath appeased, and we that were loathsome by reason of sin, made acceptable and well-pleasing unto God. The third notion is that of a propitiation: 1 John ii. 2, 'He gave himself a propitiation for our sins; and not for ours only, but for the sins of the whole world'; and Rom. iii. 25, 'Whom God set forth to be a propitiation through faith in his blood.' This implieth God's being pacified and appeased, so as to become propitious and merciful for ever to sinful man; in which sense he is also said to make reconciliation for the sins of his people, Heb. ii. 17, whereby is meant God's being reconciled to us. This was the great end why Christ died for us, to appease God's wrath and displeasure, and to reduce us into grace and favour with him again, by tendering a full compensation to God for all our sins.

[B.] The effects ascribed to it

(1.) Sin is expiated or purged out: Heb. i. 3, 'When he had by himself purged our sins, he sat down on the right hand of the Majesty on high' As God would not be appeased without a ransom, sacrifice or satisfaction, so could not sin be purged out without bearing the punishment. So the conscience is said to be 'purged from dead works by the blood of Christ' Heb. ix. 4; and Kev. i. 5, 'He hath washed us from our sins in his blood'; that is, done that which will remove the guilt and pollution of it when it is rightly applied to us; and so he is said to 'finish transgression, and make an end of sin' Dan. ix. 24; that is, to destroy the reign of sin, and to seal up the roll and hand writing that was against us, that it may not be imputed and brought into the judgment.

(2.) The sin is pardoned, and the sinner justified: Eph. i. 7, 'In whom we have redemption in his blood, the forgiveness of sins' That is the great benefit which floweth from the death of Christ, which is offered in the New Testament: Acts x. 41, 'To him give all the prophets witness, that through his name, whosoever belie veth in him shall receive remission of sins' And it is sealed and represented in the Lord's supper: Mat. xxvi. 28, 'This is my blood of the new testament, which was shed for the remission of sins'

(3.) The sanctifying the sinner to God: Heb. xiii. 12, 'Jesus, that he might sanctify the people with his own blood, suffered without the gate'; Heb. x. 10, 'By the which will we are sanctified by the offering of Jesus Christ once for all'; so Eph. v. 26, 'That he might sanctify and cleanse it, by the washing of water, through the word'; so John xvii. 1 9, 'That they also might be sanctified through the truth' In these, and many other places, is meant both our dedication to God, and the renovation of our natures, that qualifieth for communion with him.

(4.) The consummation, or the perfecting of the sanctified, as Heb. x. 14, 'By one offering he hath perfected the sanctified forever.' The priests of the law were forced to renew their sacrifices, because they could not completely take away sin; for 'the law made nothing perfect', Heb. vii. 19. Could not yield us sufficient expiation for sin, to justify and sanctify the person, so as to open heaven to him, and a free access to God; but Christ hath fully done this; perfected us forever by one offering. There needeth no other sacrifice, no other satis faction, to remove the guilt and eternal punishment: John xix. 30, TereXeo-To-t, 'All is finished' or perfected; all is undergone that was necessary for the redemption of the elect; there needed no more to satisfy justice or procure salvation for us.

[C.] The sufficiency of it to these ends and effects.

(1.) From the dignity of the person. He had all fulness in him: a fulness of holiness, Col. i. 9; a fulness of the godhead, Col. ii. 9. He was holy and innocent, and also God; and will not the blood of God cleanse us from all our sins?

(2.) The unity of his office and sacrifice. There is but one redeemer, and one sacrifice; and if but one, this is enough: 1 Tim. ii. 5, 'There is one God, and one mediator between God and man, the man Christ Jesus.' One sacrifice: Heb. x. 12, 'But this man, after he had offered one sacrifice for sins for ever, sat down at the right hand of God'; Heb. ix. 26, 'But now once in the end of the world hath he appeared, to put away sin by the sacrifice of himself'; and Rom. v. 18, 'The free gift came upon all, to the justification of life.' The scripture much insists upon this.

(3.) The greatness of his sufferings: Isa. liii. 4-6, 'Surely he hath borne our griefs, and carried our sorrows; yet did we esteem him stricken, smitten of God, and afflicted: but he was wounded for our transgressions, he was bruised for our iniquities; the chastisement of our peace was upon him, and with his stripes we are healed. All we like sheep have gone astray; we have turned everyone to his own way; and the Lord hath laid on him the iniquities of us all'; Phil. ii. 7, 8, 'But made himself of no reputation, and took upon him the form of a servant, and was made in the likeness of men; and being found in fashion as a man, he humbled himself, and became obedient unto death, even the death of the cross'; and Gal. iii. 13, 'Christ hath redeemed us from the curse of the law, being made a curse for us; for it is written, Cursed is every one that hangeth on a tree.' Now, Christians, all this is offered to our faith: the notions, the effects, or ends; the sufficiency of it to these ends and purposes; the price is paid by Christ, and accepted by God. We partake 'of these benefits as soon as we perform the conditions of the gospel; but we triumph when more explicitly we declare ourselves to be true and sound Christians. God doth not look for an expiatory sacrifice at our hands, but a thorough application of what he hath found out for us. This broad foundation laid is not only free for God to build upon, but for us to build upon: if we would enter into his peace, we must take his yoke upon us, and share with him in all conditions.

2. 'Yea rather, that is risen again.' When the apostle saith 'Yea, rather' there is some special thing in Christ's resurrection comparatively above his death, which hath an influence upon our justification. What is it? What is the reason of this connection? Was not Christ's dying every way enough to free us from sin, and from condemnation by sin? Answer, Yes; but yet the visible evidence was by his resurrection; the apostle saith, 1 Cor. xv. 17, 'If Christ be not risen, then are you yet in your sins;' and again, Rom. iv. 25, 'He died for our offences, and rose again for our justification' Christ's death would not have profited us if he had been swallowed up by it, or still detained under the power of it. More particularly

[A.] It is a proof of the truth of his person and office, that he is the Son of God, and the saviour and judge of the world: and therefore usually by this argument the apostles asserted the truth of the gospel, for they were witnesses of his resurrection; and it is said, 1 Peter i. 21, 'God raised him from the dead, that our faith and hope may be in God.' We would not have believed this foundation laid for the great blessings of the gospel had we not so clear a proof. That he is the Son of God is proved: Rom. i. 4, 'Mightily declared to be the Son of God by his resurrection from the dead'; so Acts xiii. 33, 'God hath raised up Jesus from the dead; for it is written, Thou art my Son, this day have I begotten thee' He was the Son of God from all eternity, but then visibly declared to be so. God did, as it were, by that one act own, pronounce, and publicly declare in the audience of all the world, that Christ was his only-begotten Son, one in substance with him eternally. And as the truth of his person, so of his office, that he was the true Messiah that was to restore the lapsed estate of mankind: Acts v. 31, 'Him hath God exalted with his right hand, to be a prince and a saviour, for to give repentance to Israel, and remission of sins.' This was the only sign he would give the Jews, the sign of the prophet Jonah: Mat. xii. 38-40, 'Master, we would see a sign from thee. But he answered and said unto them, An evil and adulterous generation seeketh after a sign, and there shall no sign be given to it but the sign of the prophet Jonas; for as Jonas was three days and three nights in the whale's belly, so shall the Son of man be three days and three nights in. the heart of the earth' So elsewhere he speaketh of destroying the temple of his body, and raising it up after three days, John ii. 19. So for his being the judge of the world: Acts xvii. 31, 'Whereof he hath given assurance to all men, in that he raised him from the dead'; namely, that he is Lord and judge. So that by his resurrection all the clouds about his person vanish. The world have satisfaction enough, if they will take it. There lieth this argument in the case: if Christ had been an impostor or false prophet, neither could he have raised up himself, being a mere man, nor would God have raised him up if he had been a mere deceiver; nor could the devil have raised him to life, no more than make a man out of dead matter. Nor can we reply that Lazarus was raised up from the dead, and so others; and yet not the sons of God, nor saviours and judges of the world.

I answer: Christ died, not a natural death, but in the repute of man as a malefactor, by the hand of the magistrate. Lazarus and others did not give out themselves as the saviours of the world, as Christ did; so the truth of his claim was manifested, and made evident by the resurrection. God would not leave him in the power of death, but raised him up, and assumed him into glory. Therefore it appeared the judgment passed on him was not right, and that he was indeed what he gave out himself to be.

[B.] It is a token of the acceptation of his purchase, or a solemn acquittance, a full discharge of Christ as our mediator and surety; he died to pay our debts. Now the payment is fully made when the surety is let out of prison: Isa. liii. 8, 'He was taken from prison, and from judgment.' His resurrection showeth God hath received the death of Christ as a sufficient ransom for our sins. The continuance of the payment showed the imperfection of it; it is a kind of release; Christ did not break prison, but was brought forth: Heb. xiii. 20, c Now the God of peace, that brought again from the dead our Lord Jesus' As the apostles would not come out of prison till fetched out, Acts xvi. 38, 39, so here.

[C.] He is in a capacity to convey life to others, which, if he had remained in a state of death, he could not do: John xiv. 19, 'Yet a little while, and the world seeth me no more, but ye see me; because I live, ye shall live also.' The life of believers is derived from the life of Christ, without which it cannot subsist. If he had been holden of death, he had never been a fountain of grace or glory to us; we have the merit of his humiliation and the power of his exaltation. Rom. v. 10, 'Much more, being reconciled, we shall be saved by his life'; meaning thereby his life in glory. His death was for the expiation of sin, but the effectual application of it dependeth on his life; so that the faith of sinners may comfortably rest on Christ as one raised and glorified.

[D.] His resurrection was his victory over death, which is the wages of sin. If Christ be risen from the dead, then is sin conquered; for the sting of death is sin. Therefore his resurrection declareth plainly that sin is done away, and so it is a pattern and pledge to assure us of the forgiveness of sins.

3. His exaltation at the right hand of God 'Who is even at the right hand of God.' This confirmeth all the other ends.

[A.] The truth of Christ's dignity and office: John xvi. 10, 'Of righteousness, because I go to my Father'.

[B.] The validity of Christ's satisfaction; for our surety is not only got out of prison, but preferred; not only discharged, but honoured and rewarded, and appeareth in the presence of God. Christ did in effect say to God, as Judah the patriarch did to Jacob concerning Benjamin, Gen. xliii. 9, 'I will be surety for him: thou shalt require him of me: if I bring him not to thee, and set him before thee, let me never see thy face more, but bear the blame for ever' So Christ undertaketh to be responsible for these poor creatures. What they owe put upon my score, as Paul said to Onesimus.

[C.] That he is in a full capacity to convey life to others. All weakness is removed from him; his human nature is glorified and seated in heaven, and his divine majesty and glory is restored to him; so that we may reflect upon him with comfort, as a king on the throne, in his royal palace and place of residence. David was king as soon as anointed b Samuel; but when crowned in Hebron, then did he actually ad minister the kingdom, and reward his servants and followers in the desert. Christ, when lifted up, filleth all things, Eph. iv. 10.

[D.] His victory over his enemies, death and sin; as is fully seen, Ps. ex. 1, 'The Lord said unto my Lord, Sit thou on my right hand, until I make thine enemies thy footstool;' and Heb. x. 13, 'From hence forth expecting, till his enemies be made his footstool.'

But there is somewhat peculiar.

(1.) By entering into heaven he hath opened heaven for us. He hath carried our nature thither, our flesh into heaven, and advanced it at the Father's right hand in glory, and so hath taken possession of heaven for, and in the name of, all believers, that in time they may ascend and be partakers of the same glory: John xiv. 2, 'I go to prepare a place for you.' It was prepared before the world began by the decree of God: Mat. xxv. 34, 'Come, ye blessed of my Father, inherit the kingdom prepared for you from the foundation of the world.' It

was prepared in time by the purchase of Christ: Heb. ix. 15, 'For the redemption of the
trangressions that were under the first testament, that they which are called might receive
the promise of eternal inheritance.' Now he is gone to heaven to pursue and apply that
right; gone thither as our harbinger: Heb. vi. 20, 'Whither the forerunner is for us entered';
opened Paradise again to us, which was formerly shut and closed by our sins.

(2.) By this means we have a friend in heaven, who is always at the right hand of God to
prevent breaches between him and us: 1 John ii. 1, 'And if any man sin, we have an advocate
with the Father, Jesus Christ the righteous'; as David had Jonathan in Saul's court to give
notice of danger, and to interpose, to take off all displeasure conceived against him.' It is a
great privilege, without question, to have a friend in the court of heaven to take up all
differences between God and us, as a merciful and faithful high priest to answer all
accusations of Satan, and hinder wrath from breaking out upon us, as it would do every
moment if we had the desert of our sins.

(3.) His being exalted at the right hand of God noteth that honour and power which is put
upon the Redeemer. He hath received 'all power in heaven and earth,' Mat. xxviii. 18; and
Eph. i. 20, 21, 'God set him at his right hand, far above all principality, and power, and might,
and dominion, and every name that is named, not only in this world, but also in that which is
to come'; so 1 Peter iii. 22, 'He is gone into heaven, angels, authorities, and powers being
made subject to him.' This height of honour to which Christ was exalted shows how much
his friends may trust him, and venture their all in his hands: Ps. ii. 12, 'Blessed are all they
that put their trust in him'; how much his enemies may fear him; every knee must bow to
him; they must either bend or break, Phil. ii. 10. We have not thoughts high enough of the
glory and excellency of Jesus Christ, and therefore the glory and splendour of created things
doth soon dazzle our eyes, and our hearts are hardly held up and fortified against these
discouragements that we must meet with in his service. Surely, since Christ is in the highest
dignity and power with God, and hath all the heavenly hosts and creatures at his command,
we should more encourage ourselves in the Lord; for all this power is managed for the
comfort and defence of the godly, and the terror and punishment of his and their enemies.
This power was given him as God-man, when he entered into heaven, and sat down on the
right hand of Majesty.

(4.) Fulness of grace given him to dispense the Spirit to his redeemed ones: Acts ii. 33,
'Therefore being by the right hand of God exalted, and having received of the Father the
promise of the Holy Ghost, he hath shed forth this which ye now see and hear.' As soon as
he was warm in the throne he poureth out the Spirit, that is the first news that we hear
from him; and presently the virtue of it appeared, three thousand souls were added to the
church that day. Now that is a pledge of what is continually dispensed in the church; there is
still a Spirit sent forth to convince the unbelieving world, and to conquer the opposing
wisdom and power of the flesh; as also to beget and continue life in his people, that they
may actually be put in possession of what he hath purchased for them; for he hath promised
to be with the ministry and dispensation of the word to the end of the world, Mat. xxviii. 20,

meaning by that presence, not only his powerful providence, but his convincing and quickening Spirit.

(5.) The actual administration of his kingdom. He ruleth his church, preserveth his people, and subdueth their enemies. The enemies of Christ are of two sorts, temporal and spiritual. First, His temporal enemies are such as oppose his cause and servants, and seek to suppress his interest in the world. The Jews despitefully used him and his messengers, and they had their doom; wrath came upon them to the uttermost. It is supposed they are intended: Mat. xvi. 28, 'There are some standing here which shall not taste of death till they see the Son of man coming in his kingdom.' In a few years the city, temple, and whole polity of the Jews were destroyed, for the erection of the gospel kingdom. The Romans were the next enemy, who endeavoured the extirpation of Christianity by several persecutions; these were next made the footstool of the King of kings, and after some years that vast empire was destroyed by the inundation of barbarous nations, and the residue marched under the banner of Christ. Within a little time, all these nations which oppose Christ's interest, and per secute his servants, are subdued under him, and either broken in pieces by sundry plagues and judgments, or else brought to submit their necks to Christ's blessed yoke. There is no standing out against the King whom God hath exalted at his right hand. Secondly, The spiritual enemies of Christ's kingdom are sin, Satan, and death, each of which hath a kingdom of its own, opposite to the kingdom of Christ. The apostle telleth us 'that sin reigned unto death,' Rom. v. 21; but he exhorteth, Rom. vi. 12, 'Let not sin reign in your mortal bodies'; and he promiseth, 'that sin shall not have dominion over you' Rom. vi. 14. Satan hath a kingdom opposite to Christ; he is called 'the prince of this world,' by usurpation, John xii. 31. And the devils are called, Eph. vi. 12, 'Rulers of the darkness of this world.' The ignorant, superstitious, carnal part of the world falleth to his share; but Christ hath cast him out, and will still go on to do it. Death hath an empire and kingdom: Rom. v. 14, 'Death reigned from Adam to Moses'; and verse 17, 'By one offence death reigned' Now, for the destruction of these powers was Christ exalted at the right hand of God, and by degrees he doth destroy and subdue them; yet this destruction is not so universal but that sin and Satan and death doth still continue; yet though there be not a total destruction of them, there is an absolute subjection of them to the throne of the mediator. They cannot do any more than Christ permitteth; they cannot hurt those whom God hath given to Christ, in a deadly manner; they cannot hinder the bringing them unto the heavenly kingdom. He doth annihilate the guilt of sin by his death; the dominion, by the power of his Spirit. In the despisers and refusers of his grace sin continueth in its absolute power, but still in a subjection to the throne. The wrath of the mediator is seen in their condemnation and destruction. Satan is destroyed as to his princely power, but so as we must use the means still; at last he shall be judged. Death is 'the last enemy that shall be destroyed' 1 Cor. xv. 26. It will be finally destroyed in the resurrection. For the present it serveth Christ's ends, 1 Cor. iii. 22.

4. His intercession for us. This is a notable prop to faith.

[A.] Christ presents himself, and the merit of his sacrifice, before the face of God, to preserve us in his favour: Heb. ix. 24, 'He appeareth before God for us.' As the high priest did enter with blood into the holy place: Lev. vi. 7, 'The priest shall make an atonement for him.' If he did not interpose before God night and day, how should the accusations of Satan be repelled, breaches prevented, a mutual correspondence preserved between us and God?

[B.] He doth interpose his love, will, and desire for our salvation, and all grace that is necessary thereunto, in all our difficulties, conflicts, and temptations. To intercede is the part of an inferior towards a superior; thus is Christ as mediator to God: John xiv. 16, 'I will pray the Father.' He is to ask his own glory, Ps. ii. 8; therefore what grace is necessary for us. It is a comfort Christ doth not forget us now in heaven, as Pharaoh's butler forgot Joseph, Gen. xl. 23; but it is much more a comfort that he will take notice of our particular case, that he knoweth us by name, and our necessities and wants, and doth particularly intercede for us. Nay, he is mindful of us when we are not mindful of ourselves, for his intercession doth make way for the effectual application of his grace to us when we think not of it. He obtaineth first the convincing, then sanctifying, then comforting Spirit.

[C.] To prevent breaches: 1 John ii, 1, 'We have an advocate with the Father, Jesus Christ the righteous.' An advocate, so he is opposite to our accuser. And Heb. ii. 17, 'He is a merciful and faithful high priest in things appertaining to God, to make reconciliation for the sins of the people.' Merciful to undertake, faithful to accomplish; merciful to us, faithful to God; merciful in dying, faithful in interceding, and so mindful of us at every turn. Surely it is the office of a saviour to be God's instrument in procuring our discharge; if we ourselves should only plead for pardon, having carried ourselves so unworthy of it, it would be uncomfortable to us; but he that hath redeemed us pleadeth for us; we do not go to God alone.

[D.] He presents our prayers, which are made acceptable to God, not as coming from us, but as perfumed with his merits: Heb. viii. 2, and Kev. viii. 3, 'And another angel came and stood at the altar, having a golden censer, and there was given to him much incense, that he should offer it with the prayers of the saints' He hath made tender his own heart by suffering hunger, contempt in the world, exile, weariness, pain of body, heaviness of mind: Heb. iv. 14-16, 'Seeing then, that we have a great high priest, that is passed into the heavens, Jesus the Son of God, let us hold fast our profession; for we have not an high priest which cannot he touched with the feeling of our infirmities, but was in all points tempted like as we are, yet without sin. Let us therefore come boldly unto the throne of grace, that we may obtain mercy, and find grace to help in a time of need.' Therefore come boldly for such mercies as we stand in need of. He knoweth the heart of a tempted man.

Use. You see then, what abundant cause we have to triumph and glory in Christ. You have his humiliation as the ground of your com fort; his exaltation, which qualifieth him to apply it to you, and work it in you; the merit and power. If he had not wrought our deliverance, long might we have borne the wrath we deserved, and had no means to help ourselves. If he should not make continual intercession for you, the remnant of your sin would still bring damnation; if he did not hide your nakedness, and procure your daily pardon, you would every day be your own destroyers; nay, you would not be an hour longer out of hell; if he did not bring you to God, you could have no comfortable access to him in any of your wants and necessities; if he leave you to yourselves to resist one temptation, even to the foulest sins, how quickly would you be borne down, and wallow like a swine in the mire! We can, with Jonah, easily raise the storm, but we know not how to allay it. All, from first to last, must be given and ascribed to God in Christ.

SERMON XLV

Who shall separate us from the love of Christ? Shall tribulation, or distress, or persecution, or famine, or nakedness, or peril, or sword?

Romans viii. 35.

THE triumph over the evil of sin being ended, the apostle beginneth his triumph over afflictions. Here observe

1. The challenge—*Who shall separate us from the love of Christ?*

2. The evils enumerated—*Shall tribulation, or distress, or persecution, or famine, or nakedness, or peril, or sword?*

1. The challenge—who for what. The things mentioned are spoken of as a person; but the chief difficulty is about the meaning of that clause, 'the love of Christ.' Whether it be meant of our love to Christ, or Christ's love to us. Reasons may be given on both sides. (1.) That it is meant of our love to Christ; for tribulation is not like to alienate Christ from us, but us from Christ. This doth rather tend to draw us from loving God, than God from loving us. (2.) That it is meant of Christ's love to us, because it is very unlikely that the apostle would boast of the constancy of his own love; it is more comely to triumph in God's love to us than our love to God. What shall we then determine in the case? I answer, it is meant of both, Christ's love to us, and our love to Christ, but principally of the love of God in Christ to us. First, The object 'us;' it is we are in danger to be separated. Secondly, the word 'separate' also noteth it; to separate us from our own love to Christ is a harsh phrase. Thirdly, It is said, ver. 37, 'Through him that loved us.' And again 'The love of God which is in Christ Jesus our Lord' ver. 34; which is most properly spoken of God's love to us. But this is not exclusive of our love to him, but comprehendeth it rather; therefore it is a mutual love. The apostle speaketh of his love as the cause of ours; for we love, because he loved us first; the comfort is not so great that we love him, as that he loveth us; and the stability of our love dependeth on his.

2. The evils enumerated here are seven kinds of external affliction, under which all the rest are comprehended. (1) Tribulation; whereby is meant common affliction, which doth not amount to death; anything which presseth or pincheth us, disgrace, fines, stripes, imprisonment, banishment, at large. (2.) Distress; when there is no shifting nor way of escape left us, but we are brought into such straits as we know not which way to turn, but are at our wits' ends, and know not how to escape, but must submit to the will of our enemies. (3.) Persecution; when not only cast out, but pursued from place to place; as David by Saul: 1 Sam. xxvi. 20, 'For the king of Israel is come out to seek a flea, as when one doth hunt a partridge in the mountains'; and 2 Sam. xxiv. 14, 'And David said unto God, I am in a great strait'; *Id genus hominum non inquiro, inventos autem, puniri oportere*[73], a law of

---

[73] I do not search for a man of that kind, though if he were found, he ought to be punished

Severus against the Christians. (4.) Famine; when, for fear of persecution, they are forced to shun all cities, towns, villages, and places of resort, and to lurk in deserts and places uninhabited, where many times they suffer great extremity of hunger: Heb. xi. 38, 'They wandered in deserts and mountains, and dens and cares of the earth.' (5.) Nakedness; when their clothes were worn and spent; so it is said of those: Heb. xi. 37, 'They wandered about in sheep-skins and goat skins'; so the apostle Paul, 2 Cor. xi. 27, 'In hunger, cold, and nakedness'; 1 Cor. iv. 11, 'We hunger and thirst and are naked'. (6.) Peril; by which he meaneth imminent dangers; for even in their lurking-places they had no safety. Paul reckoneth up his perils, 2 Cor. xi. 26, 'In perils of water, in perils of robbers, in perils by mine own countrymen, in perils by the heathen, in perils in the city, in perils in the wilderness, in perils in the sea, in perils among false brethren;' and of the Christians of those times he saith 'They stood in jeopardy every hour' 1 Cor. xv. 20. (7.) The last is the sword, whereby he meaneth a violent death. And here the apostle stoppeth; for all enemies can do no more than kill the body, nor can we suffer more by them; a sword may separate body and soul, but it cannot separate us from the love of Christ; and under sword are comprehended axes, gibbets, fires, halters, all sorts of violent deaths. From the whole observe—

Doctrine 1. That it is the usual portion of a Christian in the discharge of his duty to meet with many troubles.

Doctrine 2. That none of these can dissolve the union between them and Christ.

Doctrine 1. That troubles are often the portion of God's people, the primitive Christians here spoken of are a sufficient instance. First, their troubles were for their number many: Ps. xxxiv. 19, 'Many are the troubles of the righteous.' Secondly, for their kinds divers. Christians, by the unthankful world, are exposed to sundry evils and molestations; sometimes they are assaulted by want and shame, by fear and force, by all present and possible evils. Thirdly, for their degree, very grievous; not only vexatious, but destructive. There is a gradation; they molest them, that is tribulation; they follow them close, leave them no way of escape, that is distress; if they remove, still they worry them, and follow them from place to place, then it is persecution; that driveth to great necessities for food, then it is famine; for raiment, then it is nakedness; involveth them in sundry dangers, then it is peril; yea, sometimes they have power to reach life itself, and then it is sword. Now, shall we think that this was proper to that age only, and that the first professors of Christianity were exposed to these sharp and grievous trials, that we might be totally excused from all kind of vexation and trouble? No; we must not indulge such tenderness and delicacy, but must look for our trials also. The bad will ever hate the good; the world is still set upon wickedness, and worse rather than better by long continuance. Certainly the world is the same that ever it was; but considering in whose hands the government of the world is, that raiseth wonder that he should permit it. Therefore let us see the reasons.

1. That we may be conformed to our head, and pledge him in his bitter cup. Jesus Christ was a man of sorrows, and there would be a strange disproportion between head and members if we should live altogether in honour and pleasure: Col. i. 24, 'That I may fill up what is behind of the sufferings of Christ in my flesh.' There is Christ personal and Christ mystical;

the sufferings of Christ personal are complete, and there is nothing behind to be filled up; but the sufferings of Christ mystical are not perfect till every member have their allotted portion. It is an unseemly delicacy to be nice of carrying the cross after Christ. The apostle counted the 'fellowship of his sufferings, and conformity to his death,' an honour and privilege to be bought at the dearest rates, Phil. iii. 10. All things should be dung and dross to gain this experience and honour.

2. God would have his people seen in their proper colours; that they are a sort of people that love him above all that is dear and precious to them in the world, and that they do not own Christ upon extrinsic and foreign motives, that their example may be a help to promote mortification in the world; therefore all his people shall be tried: James i. 12, 'Blessed is the man that endureth temptation; for when he is tried, he shall receive the crown of life which God hath promised to them that love him;' and Rev. ii. 10, 'Behold the devil shall cast some of you into prison, that ye may be tried;' 1 Peter i. 7, 'That the trial of your faith, being much more precious than of gold that perisheth, though it be tried with fire, might be found to praise and honour and glory at the appearing of Jesus Christ.' God will try the foundation that men build upon, and whether his people love him above all, yea or no; and teach the world to subordinate the animal life to the divine and spiritual.

3. God will have the world seen in their proper colours; the far greater part of the world do live an ungodly, sensual life, and they cannot endure those that would disgrace their delights by a contrary course: John xv. 19, 'The world loveth its own; but I have chosen you out of the world, therefore the world hateth you;' 1 Peter iv. 4, 'They think it strange that you run not with them into the same excess of riot.' A contrary course produceth contrary affections and interests; thence cometh their hatred and malignity against the saints, because they upbraid them with their sins. The wicked and the righteous, the spiritual and the carnal, the sensual and the heavenly, the formal and the serious, can no more agree than the wolf and the lamb, the raven and the dove.

4. It is needful that our pride and carnal affections should be broken by the cross: 1 Peter i. 6, 'Ye are in heaviness for a season, if need be' This smart discipline is needful to reclaim us from our wanderings, to cut off the provision for the flesh, which is an enemy; to humble us for sin, which is the greatest evil; to wean us from the world, to make us more mindful of heavenly things, to make us thankful for our deliverance by Christ. How lazy and vain do the best grow when they live in wealth, honour, and power! Graces are eclipsed, duties obstructed, thoughts of heaven few and cold. We often fear the dejection of the godly; we need more fear their exaltation. What lamentable work do they make in the world when they get upper most; so that we have more cause to thank Christ for our afflictions than our prosperity.

Use 1. Is instruction: that we have no reason to doubt of God's favour and presence with us though we be exercised with calamities, and divers calamities. Single calamities are consistent enough with the love of God to his people. God is a Father when he frowneth, as well as when he smileth. Christ was the Son of his love, and yet a man of sorrows. And so for Christians: Rev. iii. 19, 'As many as I love, I rebuke and chasten.' God loveth those most whom he doth not leave to perish with the godless and unbelieving world; and divers calamities, or variety of troubles, tribulation, distress, persecution, famine, nakedness, peril, sword, call it by what name you will, it is all incident to the saints. Some trials, to ordinary sense, seem to speak wrath, utter wrath, rather than love; as when he seemeth to have broken off his ordinary course of kindness to his people, and to cast them out of his protection, leaving them in the hand and will of their enemies, so that they are reproached, troubled, and reduced to great straits and necessities. All this is necessary; for till an utter exigence, carnal supports are not spent, and one trial by continuance is blunted and loseth its edge till God send another; therefore we need not one affliction only, but divers. But how many soever they be, we have no reason to question the love of God: Job v. 19, 20, 'He shall deliver thee in six troubles, yea, in seven there shall no evil touch thee. In famine he shall redeem thee from death, and in war from the power of the sword.' In nakedness he will clothe thee, in persecution preserve thee, in peril protect thee, in distress comfort thee; though it cometh to the greatest trouble, yet we have no cause to despond, as if God had cast us off, or withdrawn his love from us.

2. That if we meet with many troubles, this will be no excuse or plea to exempt us from our duty; for as afflictions should not make us doubt of God's love to us, so they should not make us abate of our love to God: Ps. xliv. 17, 'All this is come upon us, yet we have not forgotten thee, nor have we dealt falsely in thy covenant.' They had suffered hard things, yet all this could not shake their constancy and resolution for God. All our interests were given us that we might have something of value to esteem as nothing for Christ.

3. It showeth us what a good allowance we should make Christ when we enter into covenant with him, and with what thoughts we should take up the stricter profession of Christianity. Many think they may be good Christians, yet their profession shall cost them nothing. This is as if a man should enter himself a soldier, and never expect battle; or a mariner, and promise himself nothing but calms and fair weather, without waves and storms. A life of ease is not to be expected by a Christian here upon earth. If God will suffer us to go to heaven at an easier rate, yet a Christian cannot promise it to himself, but must be a mortified and resolute man, dead to the world, and resolved to hold on his journey to the world to come, whatever weather he meeteth with. Among other of the pieces of the spiritual armour, the apostle biddeth us 'be shod with the preparation of the gospel of peace' Eph. vi. 15. If a man be not thus shod, he will soon founder in hard and rough ground. But what is this preparation of the gospel of peace? Peace noteth our reconciliation and peace with God, and interest in his favour, and love, and peace, arising from the gospel. The law showeth the breach; the gospel the way of reconciliation how it is made up for us. But there is also preparation or readiness of mind; Acts xxi. 13, 'I am ready, not to be bound only, but to die at Jerusalem for the name of the Lord Jesus'; and 1 Peter iii. 15, 'Be ye ready to render a reason of the hope that is in you'; meaning there, not sufficiency of knowledge in the mind, but strength of resolution and will, so that this preparation is a resolution to go through thick and thin, to follow Christ in all conditions. Alas! Else when we have launched out with Christ, we shall be ready to run ashore again upon every storm. Now, that we may

thus resolve, Christ would have us sit down and count the charges, for he would not surprise any. We should be ready to suffer the sharpest afflictions, though it may be the Lord doth not see fit to exercise us with them. God never intended Isaac should be sacrificed; yet, when he would try Abraham, he must put the knife to his throat, and make all things ready to offer him up.

4. How thankful we should be if God call us not to severe trials, such as tribulation, distress, persecution, famine, nakedness, peril, or sword; which the primitive Christians endured, that were purer Christians than we are. If he deal more gently with us, what use shall we make of this indulgence? Manifold (1.) Partly to be more strict and holy; for when we are not called to passive obedience and sufferings, our active obedience should be the more cheerfully per formed: Acts ix. 31, 'Then the churches had rest, and were edified, walking in the fear of the Lord, and in the comfort of the Holy Ghost' Alas! The first Christians suffered more willingly for Christ than we speak of him, and went to the stake more readily than we go to the throne of grace. Oar peace and comfort will cost us more in getting; therefore we should be more eminent in service. (2.) Partly, that we should be more mortified to the world; he that liveth a flesh-pleasing life becometh an enemy to God without temptations: James iv. 4, 'Know ye not, that the friendship of the world is enmity to God? 'Man under trouble is forced; you yield of your own accord; your act is more voluntary; they for a great fear, you for a little pleasure, hazard the hopes of eternal life. (3.) Partly, to be more ready to communicate and distribute to the necessities of others: 1 John iii. 17, 'But whoso hath this world's goods, and seeth his brother hath need, and shutteth up his bowels of compassion from him, how dwelleth the love of God in him? 'He that cannot part with this world's good things freely, will be loth to part with them by constraint. How will you take the spoiling of your goods joyfully, Heb. x. 34, when you part with them as with a drop of blood? Surely he that grudgeth at a commandment will murmur at a providence. (4.) Partly, to bear lighter afflictions patiently: Jer. xii. 5, 'If thou hast run with footmen, and they have wearied thee, how canst thou contend with horses? 'If you cannot bear a disgrace, a frown, a loss of dignity and honour and preferment, how will you bear the loss of life? Heb. xii. 9, 'Ye have not yet resisted unto blood, striving against sin.' (5.) Partly, by diligence in the heavenly life. A man traineth up himself to endure hardness, as a good soldier of Jesus Christ, by degrees; by meekness, and poverty of spirit, and humility, he is fitted to endure tribulation; by resignation and resolute dependence on God, to endure distress; by weanedness from house and home, to endure persecution; by sobriety, to endure famine; by modesty in apparel, to endure nakedness; by close retirements, to endure a prison; by carrying our life in our hand, to endure peril; by heavenliness of mind, to endure death. *Malum est impatientia boni*[74]. If it be irksome to put the body to a little trouble for holy duties, how will you endure tortures and sufferings to such an eminent degree as they did? (6.) That we should not be dismayed when troubles come actually upon us; it is not in the

---

[74] Evil is impatient good.

power of any persecutor on earth to put us out of the favour of God. What do we suffer? Tribulation! And do any enter into the kingdom of God without it? And we have that promise of rest which will sweeten it. Distress! Christ was nonplussed, John xii. 28. You must stick the closer to God who will relieve you in your distresses. Persecution! The Lord Jesus in his cradle was carried into Egypt, Mat. ii. 14. We that know no home in the world should know no banishment; Jesus Christ had not where to lay his head. Famine! Man liveth not by bread only; better our bodies famished than our souls; if we have God to our Father, we have bread to eat the world knoweth not of. Nakedness! Better pass naked out of the world than go to hell with gay apparel; your rags are more honourable than the world's purple. Is it peril? No danger so great as losing Christ and his salvation. Sword! It is the ready way to send you to Christ, who is your bountiful Lord and Master, and to loose you from the body, that you may be ever with the Lord.

Doctrine 2. That none of these things can dissolve the union between Christ and believers.

1. That there is a strict union between Christ and believers, the scripture doth everywhere manifest it; and the word 'separate 'here implieth it, for nothing can be separated, but what was first conjoined. He is the head, and we are the members; we are the spouse, and he is the husband; 1 Cor. xii. 12': He is the head of the church, and the saviour of the body,' Eph. v. 23'; He is the root, and we are the branches' John xv. 5; he is the stock, and we are the graft or scions, Rom. vi. 5.

2. This union is by the Spirit on Christ's part, and faith on ours. By the Spirit: 1 Cor. vi. 17, 'But he that is joined to the Lord is one spirit'; 1 John iii, 24, 'And hereby we know that he abideth in us, by the Spirit which he hath given us'. The bond on our part is faith: Gal. ii. 20, 'And fhe life that I live in the flesh, I live by the faith of the Son of God'; and he is said 'to dwell in our hearts by faith' Eph. iii. 17.

3. Both these bonds imply love, which makes the union more firm and indissoluble. The Spirit is given as the great fruit of Christ's love, so is our faith; and when once it comes so far that Christ in love hath given his Spirit, and we by faith love him again, nothing can unclasp these mutual embraces by which Christ loveth us and we love him. The Holy Ghost, as the bond of union, is given us as the fruit of his love; Christ prayeth, John xvii. 26, 'that the love wherewith thou hast loved me may be in them, and I in them.' What is the love wherewith God loved Christ? The gift of the Spirit: John iii. 34, 35, 'For he whom God hath sent speaketh the words of God; for God giveth not the Spirit by measure to him. The Father loveth the Son, and hath given all things into his hand.' This love is manifested to us, and so is Christ in us. And then faith on our part is a faith work ing by love, Gal. v. 6. Christ hath hold of a believer in the arms of his love; and so a believer hath hold of Christ. A Christian is held by the heart rather than by the head; only some men's religion lieth in their opinions barely, and then they are always wavering and uncertain; bare reason will let Christ go, when love will not permit us to leave him. If men have a faith that never went deeper than their brains and their fancies, this opinion, or bare superficial assent, will let him go; but it is the faith that worketh by love which produceth this stable and close adherence. A Christian is loath to leave Christ, to whom he is married, who hath so loved him, and whom his soul so

loveth. Again, the heart is Christ's strong citadel or castle, where he resideth and maintaineth his interests in us. A sinner will not leave his lusts and worldly profits, because he loveth them; and so a Christian is loath to leave Christ, because of his love to him. Faith resents to the soul what Christ hath done for us: washed us in his blood, and reconciled us to God; espoused us to himself, and spoken peace to our souls.

4. That Christ's love is the cause and reason of ours; and therefore the stability of our love to him dependeth upon his love to us, and it is the reason; Christ loveth us first, best, and most: 1 John iv. 19, 'We love him, because he loved us first'; that is, because of the great things he hath done for us, in a way of satisfaction, to reconcile God to us; and in a way of conversion, to reconcile us to God; and in a way of preparation for our eternal blessedness, in the fruition of God. In a way of satisfaction; it was his love engaged him to die for us: Gal. ii. 20, 'Who loved me, and gave himself for me'; Rev. i. 5, 'Who hath loved us, and washed us in his blood.' This was the internal bosom-cause of all that he did for us. His love in conversion, in that he brought us home to God: Eph. ii. 4, 5, 'For his great love wherewith he loved us, when we were dead in sins, he quickened us.' So his rich preparations for our blessedness: 1 Cor. ii. 9, 'Eye hath not seen, nor ear heard, neither have entered into the heart of man the things which God hath prepared for them that love him;' and 1 John iii. 1, 2, 'Behold what manner of love the Father hath bestowed upon us, that we should be called the sons of God; therefore the world knoweth us not. Behold now are we the sons of God, and it doth not appear what we shall be; but we know that when he shall appear, we shall be like him, for we shall see him as he is.' Now what is of such moment as to cause us to cease loving him who hath loved us at such a high rate? Secondly, it is the effective cause, not an exciting argument only; for his love inclines to improve his power to preserve us in a state of grace. Three things concur to that: his intercession with God, his giving the Spirit to his people, and his government over the world.

[A.] Christ intercedeth for us in all our conflicts and temptations, because he loveth us, and is mindful of us: Heb. ii. 18, 'For that he himself hath suffered, being tempted, he is able to succour them that are tempted;' and Heb. iv. 15, 16, 'For we have not an high priest which cannot be touched with the feeling of our infirmities, but was in all points tempted like as we are. Therefore let us come boldly to the throne of grace, that we may obtain mercy, and find grace to help in a time of need' He knoweth what it is to suffer hunger, and nakedness, and poverty, and exile, and contempt in the world. He knoweth the heart of a tempted man; therefore he will have compassion upon us, and procure seasonable help for us. He knoweth how hard a thing it is to be tempted, and not to sin; he himself was hard put to it, though he had such power to overcome temptations. He sitteth at the right hand of God for this end and purpose.

[B.] His giving the Spirit to help us and relieve us, and preserve his people in temptation: Phil. iv. 13, 'I can do all things through Christ which strengtheneth me'; Phil. i. 19, 'For I know that this shall turn to my salvation, through your prayer, and the supply of the Spirit of Jesus Christ;' 1 John iv. 4, 'Greater is he that is in you than he that is in the world'; 2 Tim. iv. 17,

'Notwithstanding, the Lord stood with me, and strengthened me.' If Christ will stand by us, and keep us in his own hand, what shall separate?

[C.] Christ hath the government of the world, or a power and dominion over all things which may help or hinder his people's happiness; therefore his love inclineth him to order all things so as may be for their good: John v. 22, 'He hath committed all judgment to the Son'; and John iii. 35, 'He hath given all things into his hand'; so Eph. i. 22, 'Head over all things to the church.' Things are not left to the arbitrament[75] or uncertain contingency of second causes, but are under the government of a supreme providence, the administration of which is in the hands of him that loved us; and therefore he will exercise his dominion as shall be for God's glory and our good, and so curb all opposition, and moderate all temptations, as may be consistent with his love and care over us: 1 Cor. x. 13, 'He will not suffer you to be tempted above what you are able'. In short, being so near to God, and having the dispensation of the Spirit and the administration of providence, his great love maketh him pity his people in their necessities; they are his dear purchase, therefore he will not lose them: John xiii. 1, 'Jesus having loved his own, which were in the world, he loved them to the end.' They were in the world when he was to go out of the world left in the midst of waves when he was got ashore. He knew the dangers to which they were exposed; if they miscarry, his own people miscarry; therefore his heart is moved with all their dangers and difficulties; and when we are most in danger, then is love most at work to provide help for us in all our temptations, as the mother keepeth with the sick child.

5. That love which cometh from the impression of this love is of an unconquerable force and efficacy: Cant. viii. 6, 'Love is strong as death, jealousy as cruel as the grave, the coals thereof are as the coals of fire, which hath a most vehement flame. Many waters cannot quench love, neither can the floods drown it; if a man would give all the substance of his house for love, it would utterly be contemned' There the vehemency and unconquerable constancy of love is set forth; it will not be quenched, it will not be bribed. At this rate Christ loved us; his love was as strong, and stronger, than death; he debased himself from the height of all his glory to the depth of all misery for our sakes, suffered death, and overcame all difficulties. His love carried him to us, his love could not be quenched by the waters of affliction, for he 'endured the cross, and despised the shame' Heb. xii. 2. And his love would not be bribed by the offers of preferment: Mat. iv. 9, 'All these things will I give if thou wilt fall down and worship me'. Ease: Mat. xvi. 22, 'Then Peter took him, and began to rebuke him, saying, Be it far from thee, Lord: this shall not be unto thee'. Honour: Mat. xxvii. 40, 42, 'If thou be the Son of God, come down from the cross. Let him come down from the cross, and we will believe him'. None of this could draw him from his work; and in their measure, it is fulfilled in Christians; waters cannot quench it: Acts xxi. 13, 'What mean ye to weep, and break my heart? for I am ready not only to be bound, but to die at Jerusalem'; Kev. xii. 11,

---

[75] arbitration

'And they loved not their lives unto the death'; they have not learned to love at a cheaper rate. It will not be bribed: Mat. xix. 27, 'And Peter said, We have forsaken all, and followed thee'; Luke xiv. 26, 'If any man come to me, and hate not his father, and mother, and wife, and children, and brethren, and sisters, and his own life, he cannot be my disciple' Now this love that is in us, being of such a vehement nature, it can be resisted no more than death or the grave can be resisted. No opposition can quench or extinguish it, no pleasures, or honours, or profits, can bribe it. If men would give all their substance, such a soul will be faithful to Christ; so that by this love Christ maintaineth his interest in our souls. The stony ground could not abide the heat of the sun; the thorny ground was choked with the deceitfulness of riches and voluptuous living. Waters or bribes may carry away some unmortified souls; but sincere love to Christ will not suffer us to be tempted away from him.

Use 1. Is information. How a Christian cometh to be safe in the midst of temptations.

1. It is by Christ's love to us, and ours to him. (1.) His love to us. Once be persuaded that Christ loveth you, then what need you fear? Nothing that he doth will be grievous to you; but how shall I bring my heart to this? His love to sinners is plainly demonstrated in our redemption: Rom. v. 8, 'But God commendeth his love toward us, in that while we were yet sinners Christ died for us.' But his special love to us is shed abroad in our hearts by the Holy Ghost, Rom. v. 5; he giveth the effects and the sense. The general love must be apprehended by faith: 1 John iv. 16, 'We have known and believed the love God hath to us'; and improved by serious consideration: Eph. iii. 18, 19, 'That ye, being rooted and grounded in love, may be able to comprehend with all saints what is the breadth, and length, and depth, and height'; by taking this way to be possessed of this love; Prov. viii. 17, 'I love them that love me, and they that seek me early shall find me'; and the effects of it sought after. What is everyday done more to heal and recover our wounded and self-condemned souls, and to rescue us out of the misery incurred by sin, to appease our griefs and fears? What power against sin? What assistance of grace in your duties and conflicts? 2 Cor. xiii. 5, 'Examine yourselves whether you be in the faith; prove your own selves; know ye not your own selves, how that Jesus Christ is in you, except you be reprobates? 'This is to seek a proof of Christ in you. (2.) For the other, we get it by patience in afflictions, Rom. v. 5; by fruitfulness in obedience: John xiv. 21-23, 'He that hath my commandments, and keepeth them, he it is that loveth me; and he that loveth me shall be loved of my Father, and I will love him, and will manifest myself to him. If a man love me, and keep my commandments, my Father will love him, and we will come unto him, and make our abode with him.' Converse with God in solemn ordinances: Cant. i. 4, 'Draw me, we will run after thee; the king brought me into his chamber; we will be glad, and rejoice in thee; we will remember thy love more than wine.'

2. Our love to Christ. This must be taken in; for it is we are assaulted, not Christ; we are conquerors, not God; nothing shall divorce us. Christ will never forsake a loving soul; nor will a loving soul easily forsake him; they have such an esteem of Christ that all things else are but dung and dross, Phil. iii. 8-10. Let deceived souls desire worldly greatness, they can be satisfied with nothing but Christ; nothing can supply his room in their hearts.

SERMON XLVI

As it is written, For thy sake we are kitted all the day long; we are accounted as sheep for the slaughter. Nay, in all these things we are more than conquerors through him that loved us.

Romans viii. 36, 37.

IN the former of these verses the apostle continueth his challenge, and then in the latter giveth the answer from experience. He continueth the challenge, ver. 36, speaking to the last enumerated 'sword' Lest he should seem to triumph over a feigned enemy, he showeth how the people of God in all ages are not only subject to divers calamities, but even to death itself. He proveth it by a quotation: Ps. xliv. 2, 'For thy sake we are kilted all the daylong.' The words of the psalm seem to relate to the times of Antiochus, when every day they were in danger of death for religion's sake 'As it is written, For thy sake' &c. The answer is written in ver. 37. That in all these things we have had experience, and have found this, that they have no power 'to separate us from the love of Christ'

In the words considered in themselves, observe three things

1. The greatness of the trial—*For thy sake we are killed all the day long.*

2. The absoluteness of their conquest and victory—*In all these things we are more than conquerors.*

3. The author or cause—*Through him that loved us.*

First, The greatness of the trial. The calamity of the people of God in those times is, first, literally expressed; secondly, set forth by a similitude or metaphor.

1. Literally expressed 'For thy sake we are killed all the day long' Where

(1.) The cause—'For thy sake;' out of love to him, and zeal for his glory, and the purity of his worship. This instance showeth, partly, that the true religion is ever-hated in the world: and partly, that for the love of God we ought to endure all manner of extremities. Partly, that it is a blessed thing when our death is not occasioned by our own crimes, but merely for God's sake; when a man doth not 'suffer as an evil doer,' but for righteousness' sake.

2. The grievousness of the trial— 'We are killed'; not spoiled only, but killed. It is further set forth: Heb. xi. 37, 'They were stoned, sawn asunder, tempted, slain with the sword'; that is, put to death several ways. Some think it should not be *epeirasthesan*, but *epurasthesan*, were burnt, or tempted by some cruel kind of death to forsake God. The whole signifieth that the lives of the saints were most cruelly taken away by several kinds of tormenting deaths.

3. The continuance—'All the day long'. Either the church speaketh as a collective body, for a single person can be killed but once now one, then another made away; all hours of the day they were taking or killing some of the brethren; yet the rest were not discouraged; or else 'killed all the day long' must bear this sense, that they were always in fear of death; it did continually hang over their heads, they were no time free, as the apostle saith, 1 Cor. xv. 31, I die daily'. He did daily run the hazard of death.

2. By a similitude—'We are accounted as sheep for the slaughter.' Some take the allusion from sheep appointed for sacrifice. The wicked thought they did God good service in killing the godly, John xvi. 2; and the godly themselves yielded up themselves as a sacrifice to God: 2 Tim. iv. 6, 'I am ready to be offered, and the time of my departure is at hand'; but this is forced. *Probata sphages* rather implieth sheep destined to the shambles. (1.) The similitude importeth, partly, the contempt of the enemies; they made no more reckoning of them than of sheep: Zech. xi. 4, 5, 'Feed the flock of the slaughter, whose possessors slay them, and hold themselves not guilty'; that is, they care no more for their death than they do for the killing of a sheep. (2.) It noteth their own imbecility; they had no power to resist; as Mat. x. 16, 'Behold, I send you forth, as sheep in the midst of wolves' Sheep have no power or means to preserve themselves. (3.) Their meekness; they did no more resist than sheep: Isa. liii. 7, 'He was oppressed, and he was afflicted, yet he opened not his mouth: he is brought as a lamb to the slaughter, and as a sheep before the shearers is dumb, so he opened not his mouth'.

Doctrine Such as resolve upon the profession of Christianity must prepare to give their life for the maintenance of it, when God calls them thereunto.

This seemeth hard; but,

1. Christ requireth it of all: Luke xiv. 26, 'If any man come to me, and hate not his father, and mother, and wife, and children, and brethren, and sisters, yea, and his own life, he cannot be my disciple' It is too late for us to interpose for an abatement when the terms are thus fixed by Christ himself. So our Lord, when he openeth the doctrine of self-denial, he showeth it must extend to life: Mat. xvi. 24, 25, 'He that saveth his life shall lose it' There is nothing so dear to us as life; nothing which nature doth so highly value, and tenderly look to, and so unwillingly let go. Many that can yield in other points cannot yield in this, but then they are not sincere with God; for you must not look upon it as a note of excellency, but the disposition of those who have the lowest measure of saving grace; as appeareth by these clauses, 'If any man will come after me'; and 'He cannot be my disciple.' You will say, What can the strong and eminent Christian do more than part with life? This is not the difference between the strong and the weak Christian, that one can part with a few things for Christ, and the other can part with all; no, all must part with all. Not this, that one can part with his ease, profit, and credit, and the other can part with his life; no, both must part with life. The difference is not in the things to be parted with, but in the degree of the affection; the strongest Christians can die with greater zeal, love, readiness, joy, and so bring more honour to God by their death than weak Christians do, who offer up themselves to God with greater reluctancy and unwillingness.

2. Such have been the trials of God's children in all ages; as the instance is brought from the godly who lived under the law-dispensation. Now, if the saints of old endured such hard things, and tribulation even unto death, then it followeth—

[A.] It is no strange thing: 1 Peter iv. 12, 'Beloved, think it not strange concerning the fiery trial, as if some strange thing had happened unto you'. Our taking the ordinary case of the godly for a strange thing, is that which doth disturb and distemper us. None wondereth at a bitter winter coming after a sweet summer, or a dark night succeeding a bright day, because it is an ordinary thing; so here.

[B.] Then it is no grievous thing, but such as the people of God have endured, when they had not the advantages that we have. A double advantage we have above the saints of the Old Testament.

(1.) They had not such a pattern of self-denial as we have, and that is the death of Christ, which teacheth us to obey God at the dearest rates: Mat. x. 24, 'The disciple is not above his master, nor the servant above his lord.' Christ is a pattern of sufferings; and to look for exemptions from them, is to expect to be better dealt with than he was; we tread upon no step of hard ground but what Christ hath gone there before us, and his steps drop fatness; left a blessing behind him to sweeten the way to us; so Heb. xii. 1-3, 'Look to Jesus, the author and finisher of our faith, who, for the joy that was set before him, endured the cross, despised the shame, and is set down at the right hand of the throne of God. For consider him that endured such contradiction of sinners against himself, lest you be wearied, and faint in your minds.' Jesus is propounded as our example; he endured cruel pains in his body, and bitter sorrows in his soul; deserted by God, contradicted by men, yet he bore all patiently and undauntedly; this is the copy and pattern which is set for our imitation, that we may not sink under our burdens.

(2.) The other advantage. They had not such a clear discovery of eternal life as is now made to us in the promises of the gospel, 2 Tim. i. 10. Since the appearance of our Lord Jesus Christ, life and immortality is brought to light in the gospel. It was but sparingly revealed then, and, to appearance, the covenant ran more in the strain of temporal promises; but now Christ hath struck a thorough light into the other world, and clearly tells us that great is our reward in heaven; and therefore we may rejoice if men persecute us, Mat. v. 11, 12. We will do so, if we believe him. Who would not permit another to take down a shed, if we did believe that he would build a palace for us at his own cost and charges? The reward is so far above the suffering, that certainly now we should more willingly submit to be killed all the day long, and counted as sheep for the slaughter. If the people of God did so heretofore, upon those few glimmerings which they had about eternal life, certainly they had not such a clear prospect into the other world, nor such a visible demonstration of the certainty of it, as we have by the resurrection and ascension of our Lord Jesus Christ.

3. To manifest the truth and reality of our graces, of our faith in Christ, and love to him, and hope of salvation.

[A.] To show our faith; which is such a trusting ourselves in Christ's hands, that we are willing to part with all, even life itself, for his sake. This is called a believing to the saving of our sonls, Heb. x. 39. Sense saith, Save thyself; Faith saith, Save thy soul: Heb. xi. 35, 'They accepted not deliverance, looking for a better resurrection' when stretched out by torture like the head of a drum.

[B.] To show our love. Nothing can or ought to separate us from the love of Christ. God alloweth us to love life, but he will be loved better; for 'his lovingkindness is better than life,'

Ps. lxiii. 3. Now the greatest things must be greatly loved; and then is our love tried, when the blackest dispensations cannot draw us from God. It is the property of love to long to be with Christ, 'which is better for us' Phil. i. 23. Therefore we should be content to have the prison-door opened, that those who have desired and longed to be with Christ may be admitted into his immediate presence, and let out into liberty and joy.

[C.] Hope. We expect within a little while to have our desires accomplished: Jude 21, 'Looking for the mercy of our Lord Jesus Christ unto eternal life.' Will a soul that is at heaven's gate lose all that he hath waited for because the entrance is troublesome? As those that are going to a mask or show, when they come where it is exhibited, must" crowd, and will venture hard for what they hope to see. Now God will have graces tried with difficulties; the crown of victory is not set on our heads if we fight not.

4. Reason. It is necessary to have this preparation of heart, that we may the better deny other things. Life is that which maketh us capable of all the contentments of the flesh and pleasures of the world, and maketh them valuable to us. Now this is a blow at the root, we are prepared for mortification; when we can deny life itself, we can deny all the appendages of life. Therefore so much of Christianity being exercised in self-denial, our Lord would have us once for all bring ourselves to the highest point, that we may do other things the more easily. The apostle's bonds and afflictions did not move him, because he did not 'count his life dear to him' Acts xx. 24. And certainly a man is never dead to the world, and the interests of the animal life, till he be dead to life itself, and is willing to part with it when God pleaseth.

5. This life must be quitted[76]. Now God will have it quitted in obedience; for things of mere necessity have no moral worth in them. Now it is a mighty help to die willingly and comfortably, when we can once lay life at Christ's feet.

Use. To inform us

1. That Christianity wholly draweth us to another world; for life itself is one of the interests that must be hazarded for Christ's sake: 1 Cor. xv. 19, 'If in this life only we had hope, we were of all men most miserable.' Christ would never proselytise us to a religion that should make us miserable. Now it would do so if our only happiness were in this life; for it requireth us not only to deny the conveniences of life, but life itself.

2. Those that take God's word for the other world must expect to have the strength of their faith and love tried. All along this hath been God's way. God would not confirm Adam in innocency before he had let loose a trial upon him; wherein he, failing, brought misery upon himself and. his posterity. After the breach, the father of the faithful is tried: Gen. xxii. 1, with Heb. xi. 17, 'By faith Abraham, when he was tried.' And still God continueth the same course to all believers: James i. 12, 'Blessed is he that endureth temptations; for when he is

---

[76] To behave in a specified way

tried, he shall receive a crown of life.' In the primitive times their baptism was a presage of their slaughter.

3. Those that expect to be tried had need to be well prepared by a due knowledge of the cause, and foresight of, and resolution against, all known dangers.

[A.] By a due knowledge of their cause; that it may be sure it can be said for God's sake. The cause is sometimes more clear and unquestionable, as when it is for a great essential point, and here our courage should be more clear; for then there can be no doubt in the mind whether the cause be good or not, and then all the comforts of Christianity do fall moon the soul directly, and with great power and efficacy; or else more dark, when it is for a particular truth or duty.

First, It may be for the profession of a particular truth, which we are to own in its season, for we must be established in 'the present truth,' 2 Peter i. 12. What is the present truth the godly-wise will soon discern. Whoever compiled the creed, yet the observation is in a great measure good, that the controversies that have happened in the church have succeeded according to the method and order of the articles therein contained. The controversy with the heathen was about the one only and true God; with the Jews, and afterwards with the pseudo-christians, about Christ, his person, natures, offices, states; then about the Holy Ghost, his personality and operations in converting the elect; then about the church. Now, in all such con troverted truths we must show the same zeal the faithful did in former ages. But to return; though it be but for a particular truth, yet we must show our fidelity to Christ. For then we have an occasion to show that our hearts be true to God, and very sincere when we are willing to suffer anything from man rather than renounce the smallest truths of God; for though the matters for which we suffer be not great, yet sincerity is a great point; and though profession thus be forborne, and of exceeding great moment to our peace in some points, yet we 'can do nothing against the truth,' 2 Cor. i. 8. I am not bound always to profess in lesser things; yet, if they will bind me against it, I am to endure all manner of displeasures rather than yield to the lusts and wills of men. Eating of swine's flesh was no great matter, but when they would compel them to it, in affront to God's institution, contempt of God is a great matter, Heb. xi. 25, 36, 37. I say the more of this, because men are apt to translate the scene of their duty to former times or foreign places, if to turn infidels and Turks; as the Jews, if they had lived in the prophets' days: Mat. xxiii. 30, 'If we had been in our fathers' days, we would not have been partakers with them in the blood of the prophets.' How doth God try thee in thine own age?

Secondly, For particular duties, as well as particular truths. In the general, there is less controversy about the commandments than about the creed; the agenda of Christianity are more evident by the light of .nature than the credenda. Yet, because the commandments are general, and human light is imperfect about the application; as the heathens were right in generals, but 'became vain' Rom. i. 20, 21, yet in particular duties we must not be wanting, for that is a sincere heart that will run the greatest hazards rather than commit the smallest sin or omit the smallest duty, when it is a duty, and I am called to perform it. In omission there is a greater latitude than in commission; for *affirmativa non ligant ad semper*[77].

In the general, he that suffereth for a commandment is as acceptable with God as he that suffereth for an article of faith. Though the cause for which we suffer be civil, yet obedience to God is concerned in it; as if a man suffer for being loyal to his prince and the laws, or doing his duty to parents, or because he will not bear false witness, or tell a lie, or subscribe a falsehood, or because he will not disown a brother, 1 John iii. 16. This man is a martyr to God, as well as he is a martyr to Christ, that suffereth for mere Christianity; which I would have you to note, that you may see how much this precept of God, of laying down our lives for his sake, doth conduce, not only to the interest of Christianity, which is a supernatural truth, but to the good of human society, to which even nature will subscribe; and I do it the rather that you may not think Jesus Christ our lawgiver was bloody, or delighted in the destruction of men, when he required that all who would enter into his profession should hate their own lives when just and convenient reasons did call them thereunto. No, by this law he did not only try his servants, but preserved a principle of honesty in the world, and provided for the comfort of them, who being instruments of public good, do often make themselves objects of public hatred. Alas! What comfort could they have in promoting the good of the world, and venturing themselves magnanimously upon all dangers, if God had not provided some better thing for them? All that I shall add as to particular truths and duties is this, partly by way of caution to the persecuting world, that they may consider how much guilt they incur, when for questionable things (so I must speak to them) they run the hazard of opposing the most faithful servants God hath in the world. Usually it is the conscientious that suffer most; others can easily leap out of one sort of profession and practice into another, or else wriggle and distinguish themselves out of their duty by many crafty evasions, whereas the conscientious are held in the noose, meaning to deal with God and the world without equivocation or evasion, in all simplicity and godly sincerity. And shall these be the object of your hatred and severest persecution? It argueth a heart alien from God, and too full of venomous malignity against the better part of the world. Partly, by way of advice to the persecuted, which is double. First, Abate not of your zeal; for 'he that is not faithful in a little will not be faithful in much,' Luke xvi. 10. A good man dareth not allow himself in the least evil; the world counteth him more nice than wise, but God will not count him so; though he should fail in the application of the general rule, yet God will reward him according to his sincerity; it is a love error. Secondly, Not to censure others that see not by his light; in this case, *capiat qui capere potest*—he that can receive it, let him receive it. The general rule is the bound of our charity, but the particular application is the rule of our practice as long as they own the general rule, though they have not insight into these lesser things: Phil. iii. 15, 16, 'Let us therefore, as many as be perfect, be thus minded; and if in anything ye be otherwise minded, God shall even reveal this to you. Nevertheless, where-unto you have attained, let us walk by the same rule, let us mind the same things.' They may sincerely oppose the same things that we assert; and we sincerely assert the same things

---

[77] The affirmative is not always binding.

which they oppose. Now, whether we oppose or assert, let everyone be firmly persuaded in his own mind, and with a modest mind bear the dissensiency[78] of others; nothing will allay the differences in judgment but a mutual submission to this rule, and meekly holding forth light to others.

[B.] By a due foresight of, and resolution against, all known dangers.

(1.) A due sight or forethought of the dangers. Christ will have us sit down and count the charges, and make him a good allowance, as men do in building and warring: Luke xiv. 18, 'For which of you, intending to build a tower, sitteth not down first and counteth the cost, whether he be able to finish it?' and ver. 31, 'Or what king, going to make war against another king, sitteth not down first, and considereth whether he be able with ten thousand to meet him that cometh against him with twenty thousand? 'If we dream of nothing but ease and prosperity, we flatter ourselves; our very baptism implieth a notion of working and fighting; and we must consider what the work and warfare will cost us: Rom. vi. 13, 'Yield your members as instruments of righteousness unto God'; as arms and weapons of righteousness; and the graces of the Spirit are called 'armour of light' Rom. xiii. 12, that is, our warlike attire. Christ himself, when he was baptized, was consecrated as the captain of our salvation; and therefore presently upon his baptism, he was assaulted by the devil. His baptism was an engagement to the same military work to which we are engaged; a war against the devil, the world, and the flesh. He engageth as the general: 1 John iii. 8, 'For this purpose the Son of God was manifested, that he might destroy the works of the devil'; we as common soldiers. His baptism was the taking of the field as general; we undertake to fight in our rank and place. And can we expect that this conflict can be carried on without sore blows? You must know, therefore, what it is to irritate the prince of darkness, and the powers that join with him, and resolve to follow to the conflict even to death, or else we would be excused in a part of our oath of fealty to Christ.

(2.) By a resolution against all known dangers. It will cost us loss of credit: 1 Cor. iv. 13, 'We are made as the filth of the world, and the off-scouring of all things unto this day' Used as the unworthiest creatures in the world, as the sweeping and filth of the city; many were cast forth as unworthy to live in any civil corporation or society of men. It will cost us loss of estate: Heb. x. 34, 'And took joyfully the spoiling of their goods.' There was pretence of law against the Christians, yet much rapine used in the execution of it the word signifieth, it was violently rent and torn from them. Nay, not only so, but they suffered loss of life and limb, and were forced to seal their profession with their blood; and till we come to that resolution, we are not completely faithful with Christ: Heb. xii. 4, 'Ye have not yet resisted unto blood, striving against sin.' As soon as we are regenerate, we renounce the devil and the world, and bid defiance to these things; our life is a continual warfare. Now, if we have a reserve, that as soon as it cometh to danger of death, we will give over, we are not as yet

[78] Dissentient: in opposition to a majority or official opinion

thoroughly resolved to be Christians. The promise runneth, Rev. ii. 10, 'Be thou faithful to death, and I will give thee a crown of life'. The same duty is required of us that was required of Christ. Now Christ was 'obedient to death,' Phil. ii. 7. Many may sustain some reproaches for Christ's sake, make some small losses, sacrifice their weaker lusts, hoping to satisfy God thereby; as Saul destroyed the weaker cattle of Amalek at God's command, but reserved the fattest. No, life and all must be laid at Christ's feet.

4. Thus to be prepared for death should be the great care of a Christian, and many considerations are necessary to press this.

[A.] That God is lord of life, and will dispose of it at his pleasure. He that gave life is the lord of it; for he hath the free disposal of his own gift, to continue it, or take it back, as he shall think fit. It is a mercy that God only and properly hath *potestatem vitae et necis*, the power of life and death; it is not in the power of enemies to take it away at their pleasure; for the sovereign disposal of his creature is in God's hand: Mat. x. 29, 'A sparrow cannot fall upon the ground without our heavenly Father.' It is not in the power of your own hands; for you cannot make one hair black or white; you are not lords of your lives, but guardians. Well then, it is in the power of God alone; and shall not he dispose of his own, and do with it what he pleaseth?

[B.] Many of the lives of birds and beasts go for us daily, and we would be troubled if we should be retrenched of this liberty when our necessities require it; and hath not God a greater right and power over us than we have over the birds and beasts? His right is original, ours by grant and free gift; his power is absolute, ours limited; for the good man is not cruel to his beast; and we sin when we destroy them in wantonness, and sacrifice them to our lusts. We are to give an account of ourselves, and all the creatures which we possess; but God giveth no account of his matters. Now if we count it no cruelty to take the life of the creatures, why should we think of God as cruel, and despising the life of his creatures, because he requireth them to lay down their lives upon just and convenient reasons? There is a greater distance between us and God than between us and the meanest worm.

[C.] If you deny him your life, he can snatch it from you in fury, and take it whether you will or no; if you sin to escape sufferings, you leap into hell to escape a little pain upon earth: Luke xii. 4, 5, 'Arid I say unto you, my friends, be not afraid of them that can kill the body, and after that have no more that they can do. But I will forewarn you whom ye shall fear; fear him, which, after he hath killed, hath power to cast into hell; yea, I say unto you, fear him.' Men may by God's permission kill the body, but God can cast body and soul into hell fire. You think it is a fearful thing to fall into the hands of men; it is indeed *phoberon*, Heb. x. 31, 'a fearful thing to fall into the hands of the living God.' The carriage of your very enemies should awaken your faith; why should you fear them more than they are afraid of God? In persecuting they run the hazard of the wrath of God; in suffering persecution you run the hazard of the wrath of men: your fear justifieth their boldness; if you be afraid of men, they may as well contemn God. They run upon the greater difficulties, and you, by complying with them, incur greater misery than you avoid.

[D.] If the less be countervailed by a greater gain, you have no reason to stick at it. In the general, it is gain to a believer to die: Phil. i. 21, 'For to me to live is Christ, and to die is gain'; and 2 Cor. v. 1, 'For we know, that if our earthly house of this tabernacle were dis solved, we have a building of God, an house not made with hands, eternal in the heavens.' Much more to a martyr God is able to make it up: Mark x. 29, 30, 'Verily I say unto you, There is no man that hath left house, or brethren, or sisters, or father, or mother, or wife, or children, or lands for my sake and the gospel, but he shall receive a hundredfold now in this time, and in the world to come life eternal.' When he calls for you to come home to him by a persecutor's hand, you have death abundantly recompensed. Therefore you may die with the greater confidence and joy; it is not an ordinary place is reserved for you in heaven. The promise is certain, and your dying upon this occasion maketh your claim sure.

Secondly, the absoluteness of their conquest and victory 'We are more than conquerors.'

But there seemeth to be a contradiction between the two branches, the greatness of the trial, and the absoluteness of their conquest: they are killed all the day long, how then are they conquerors, and more than conquerors?

Answer 1. Some refer it to the kind of the conquest; they have a nobler victory than if they conquered them by the sword. The con quest of faith is more than a conquest gotten by a temporal force, and the power of the long sword: 1 John v. 4, 5, 'For whosoever is born of God overcometh the world; and this is the victory that overcometh the world, even our faith. Who is he that overcometh the world, but he that believeth that Jesus is the Son of God?'

2. Others to the degree of victory.

[A.] It is a conquest when we keep what we have: as Job i. 22, 'In all this Job sinned not, nor charged God foolishly'. They are conquerors under trouble who are kept free from sin and provocation; in the hour of trial they stand their ground; however assaulted, their bow abideth in its strength, Gen. xlviii. 24.

[B.] It is more than a conquest when we gain by it. That is, first, when graces are strengthened, that is, a greater spirit of faith cometh upon them: 2 Cor. iv. 13, 'We having the same spirit of faith, according as it is written, I believed, and therefore have I spoken; we also believe, and therefore speak' Their love is more fervent; as fountain water is hottest in coldest weather usually: Mat. xxiv. 12, 'The love of many shall wax cold'; but when their love groweth hotter, and their zeal for God is so great that the minds of persecutors are daunted, then they are more than conquerors. Secondly, When experiences are enlarged, and they have a fresher and more lively sense of God's love to them: Rom. v. 5, c Because the love of God is shed abroad in our hearts, by the Holy Ghost given unto us'; 1 Peter iv. 14, 'If ye be reproached for the name of Christ, happy are ye; for the Spirit of glory and of God resteth upon you; on their part he is evil spoken of, but on your part he is glorified' So one in prison said, *Se divinas martyrum consolationes sensisse*[79]; when they are more secured in the love of God. Thirdly, their reward is increased. Certainly it is above their trouble: 2 Cor. iv. 17, 'For our light afflictions, which are but for a moment, worketh for us a far more exceeding and eternal weight of glory.' It is likely they have more, Mark x. 29, 30. In the Day of Judgment more honour and praise: 1 Peter iv. 6,7,' That the trial of your faith, being much more precious than of gold that perisheth, though it be tried with fire, may be found unto praise and honour and glory at the appearing of Christ Jesus.'

Thirdly, the author or cause of the victory, or the power by which they conquer, through him that loved us. Here observe—

1. That Christ is not estranged from his people by their afflictions, but rather is more tender of them the more they are wronged by others.

2. That loving them, he doth overrule these things, and cause them to become a means to do them good.

3. He doth not only overrule these occurrences of providence, but doth give them the Spirit of grace.

4. That giving them the Spirit of grace, they overcome in his strength, not their own.

5. That Christ's love is more powerful to save us than the world's hatred to destroy us.

Doctrine 2. That a true believer doth not miscarry under his troubles, but overcome them yea, more than overcome them. Here I shall show (1.) The nature of the victory. (2.) How more than conquerors. (3.) Who is this true believer that will be more than a conqueror. (4.) Reasons why more than conquerors. (5.) Application.

First, To explain the nature of this victory; it doth not consist in an exemption from troubles, or suffering temporal loss by them, or utter perishing as to this world, but keeping that which we contend and fight for; we do not vanquish our enemy so as to cause all opposition to cease; yea, or that we shall not temporally perish under it. No, the world needeth not suspect this holy victory of the saints: it is not conquering kingdoms, and becoming masters of other men's possessions, nor seeing our desire upon our enemies. I prove it

1. From Christ's purchase: Gal. i. 4, 'Who died, that he might deliver us from the present evil world' How so? That we should live exempt from all troubles? That the world should never trouble us? No, but that the world should not ensnare and pervert us. His word was to 'save us from our sins,' Mat. i. 21; to 'deliver us from wrath to come,' 2 Thes. i. 10; and to justify and sanctify and glorify us. We have the victory that he hath purchased for us, if the devil and the world do not hinder our fruition and possession of eternal glory.

2. I prove it, partly from the way of dispensation of it; that is intimated in the first promise of the Messiah: Gen. iii. 15, 'I will put enmity between thee and the woman, and between thy seed and her seed; it shall bruise thy head, and thou shalt bruise his heel. Misery being brought into the world by sin, God ordereth it so that some temporal calamities shall remain

---

[79] The witnesses felt divine comfort.

on those that are recovered by grace; indeed it is our Redeemer's work so to moderate these sufferings, that our heel may be only bruised, but our head safe.

3. I prove it from the way of our conflict and combat and con quest. It is not by worldly greatness, visible prosperity, or the strength of outward dominion; but by patience, and contentedness in suffering, even to the Very death. Those that are as sheep appointed to the slaughter, and killed all the day long, are more than conquerors. This is a riddle to carnal sense: we do not call them conquerors in the world who are killed, oppressed, kept under; but yet these are killed all the day long, and yet are more than conquerors, *Scias hominem Christo dicatupi*[80], saith Jerome, *mori posse, vinci non posse*. A Christian may be slain, yet more than a conqueror. The way to conquer here is to be trodden down, and ruined: 2 Cor. iv. 8, 9, 'We are troubled on every side, yet not distressed; we are perplexed, yet not in despair; persecuted, but not forsaken: cast down, but not destroyed.'

4. Our main party and enemy is Satan. You have not only to do with men, who strike at your worldly interests, but with Satan, who hath a spite at your souls: Eph. vi. 12, 'For we wrestle not against flesh and blood, but against principalities, against powers, against the rulers of the darkness of this world, against spiritual wickedness in high places.' God may give men a power over your bodily lives, and all the interests thereof, but he doth not give the devil a power over the graces of the saints, to separate them from God's love. The devil aimeth at the destruction of souls: he can let you enjoy the pleasures of sin for a season, that he may deprive you of your delight in God and celestial pleasures. He can be content you shall have dignities and honours, if they prove a snare to you. The devil seeketh to bring you to troubles, and poverty and nakedness, to draw you from God: 1 Peter v. 8, 9, 'Be sober, be vigilant; because your adversary the devil, as a roaring lion, walketh about seeking whom he may devour: whom resist steadfast in the faith, knowing that the same afflictions are accomplished in your brethren that are in the world.' Satan's temptations are conveyed to the godly by afflictions, by which he seeketh to make them quit the truth, or their duty, or to quit their confidence in God; otherwise he would let such have all the glory in the world, if it were in his power, so you would but hearken to his lure: as he offered it to Christ: Mat. iv. 9, 'And saith unto him, All these things will I give thee, if thou wilt fall down and worship me'. Therefore our victory is not to be measured by our prosperity and adversity, but faithful adherence to God; if he get his will over our bodies, if he get not his will over our souls, you conquer, and not Satan.

5. The ends or things we contend for. The victory must be stated by that; for we overcome if we keep what we fight for. Now our conflict is for the glory of God, the advancement of the kingdom of Christ, our own salvation, and to maintain and keep alive present grace.

[A.] The glory of God. God must he honoured by his people in adversity: 2 Thes. i. 11, 12, 'Wherefore we pray always for you, that God would count you worthy of this calling, and

---

[80] Men learn dedication to Christ.

fulfil all the good pleasure of his goodness, and the work of faith with power, that the name of our Lord Jesus Christ may be glorified in you'; John xxi. 19, 'This he said, signifying by what death he should glorify God'; Phil. i. 20, 'Christ shall be magnified in my body, whether it be by life or by death' When we suffer for his cause, our very sufferings are conquering: 1 Peter iv. 14, 'On your part he is glorified.' When they are reviled, reproached, persecuted: God can bring more honour to himself by the constancy of his people in their troubles and sufferings, than by per mitting them to live in prosperity, and scandalise others by their vanity, sensuality, and pride of conversation. God is usually more honoured by his people at such times when his graces are exercised in the eye of the world, and his people confess him in the midst of persecutions.

[B.] The advancement of Christ's kingdom, in the propagation of the gospel: Kev. xii. 11, 'They overcame by the blood of the Lamb and the word of their testimony, and they loved not their lives to the death.' There is an overcoming, indeed, you will say, to die in the quarrel! Yes, as long as Christ overcometh, a Christian hath that which he looketh for. If their blood may be the seed of the Church, they are content; some convinced, others converted, brethren strengthened and confirmed: Phil. i. 12, 'Those things which happened to me have fallen out rather to the furtherance of the gospel.' His sufferings conduced thereunto as much as his preaching.

[C.] Our own salvation. It is not worldly prosperity and greatness and dominion that we should seek, but that the soul may be saved in the day of the Lord. Indeed, if our aim were at worldly prosperity, and carnal honour and pleasure, then were we clearly overcome when we hazard our worldly interests; but it is heaven that we aim at: and therefore, as Christ 'endured the cross, and despised the shame, for the glory set before him,' Heb. xii. 2, 3; so we must despise the cross for the same ends. 2 Cor. iv. 17, 'These light afflictions, which are but for a moment, shall work in us a far more exceeding and eternal weight of glory;' Rom. viii. 18, 'For I reckon that the sufferings of this present time are not worthy to be compared with the glory that shall be revealed in us'; Heb. x. 34, 'They took joyfully the spoiling of their goods, as knowing in yourselves that you have in heaven a better and an enduring substance,' At length we shall have our promised crown.

[D.] To maintain and keep alive present grace. First, Our faith: 2 Tim. iv. 8, 'I have kept the faith'; when we abide faithful with God, and are not drawn to apostasy by all the flatteries or threatenings of the world. Secondly, Our love to God. Satan's design is to make a breach between God and us: Rom. viii. 38, 39, 'For I am persuaded that neither death, nor life, nor angels, nor principalities, nor powers, nor things present, nor things to come, nor height, nor depth, nor any other creature, shall be able to separate us from the love of God which is in Christ Jesus our Lord' Nothing can separate them from the love of God in Christ; unclasp these mutual embracements whereby Christ and the soul held fast one another: you are in Christ's arms, and Christ in yours. The devil would count it a greater victory to conquer your love than to get a power over your bodies and bodily interests; his design is to keep men from God; if therefore adversity bringeth you the nearer to him, then you conquer. The souls of the faithful are kept closer to God in suffering times than in prosperity, being sensible of the vanity and emptiness of all worldly things, and weaned from them. Whatever befall the body, you keep nearer to God, and have most of his love. Thirdly, Our patience; that is not overcome by the storm and tempests of temptations: Luke xxi. 19, 'In patience possess your souls.' A man keepeth himself as long as he keepeth his patience: James i. 4, 'Let patience have its perfect work.' This is necessary that we may receive our crown: Heb. x. 36, 'For ye have need of patience, that after ye have done the will of God, ye might receive the promise.' Well then, a Christian overcometh, not when he gets the best of opposite interest in the world, but when he keepeth himself in a capacity to enjoy the heavenly inheritance.

Secondly, How more than a conqueror? When he doth not only keep his standing, but gets ground by the temptation: Rom. viii. 28, 'All things shall work together for good to them that love God'; not only bear them, but groweth the better for them. (1.) More holy and more heavenly; as graces, by being exercised, are improved and increased: Heb. xii. 11, 'Wherefore, lift up the hands that hang down, and the feeble knees'; more sensible of the folly of sinning, than at other times. (2.) More joyful; comforts are increased: Rom. v. 3-5, 'And not only so, but we glory in tribulations also, knowing that tribulation works patience, and patience experience, and experience hope, and hope maketh not ashamed, because the love of God is shed abroad in our hearts by the Holy Ghost given unto us;' 2 Cor. xii. 10, 'Therefore I take pleasure in infirmities, in reproaches, in necessities, in persecutions, and distresses, for Christ's sake; for when I am weak, then am I strong;' Acts v. 41, 'They departed from the presence of the council, rejoicing that they were counted worthy to suffer shame for his name;' and so triumpheth most when he seemeth to be most overcome. (3.) More resolute in the profession of godliness: 2 Sam. vi. 22, 'If this be to be vile, I will be more vile and base in mine own eyes.' Courage groweth by sufferings, as trees are more rooted by being shaken: Ps. cxix. 126, 127, 'It is time for thee, Lord, to work; for they have made void thy law. Therefore I love thy commandments above gold, yea, above fine gold.' As a staff is holden the faster, the more another seeketh to wrest it out of our hands.

Thirdly, Who is this true believer that will be more than a conqueror? The victory is sometimes ascribed to faith, 1 John v. 4, 5; sometimes to love: Rom. viii. 35, 'What shall separate us from the love of Christ? 'Love is not only taken passively, for the love where with Christ loveth us, but actively, for the love wherewith we love Christ. I can exclude neither, for the success is here ascribed in the text to Christ's love to us; but there, our love to Christ must be under stood also, for 'what shall separate us from the love of God? 'Shall tribulation, or distress, or persecution, or famine, or nakedness, or peril, or sword? Tribulation is not wont to draw God from loving us, but to draw us from loving of God. And in the text, it is said, 'We are conquerors,' not God is a conqueror. It is we are assaulted, not Christ, and it is our love which the temptation striketh at. Both must be included. Christ hath hold of a believer in the arms of his love, and a believer hath hold of Christ, 1 John iv. 14. Well then, it is faith; but 'faith worketh by love' Gal. v. 6. Christ is rather held by the heart than the hand only. Go to them that make a religion of their opinions, and you will find no such effect. If they have a faith, it is that that never went deeper than their brains and their fancies; but where Christ dwelleth in the heart by faith, there he remaineth constantly, Eph. iii. 17, and flitteth not thence; he resideth as in his strong citadel and castle. A Christian, because be loveth Christ, he will not leave him; as a sinner will not leave his lusts and worldly profits because he loveth them. Faith reports the great love of Christ, what he hath done to pacify God, to bring home the sinner; what in a way of satisfaction, what in a way of conversion; therefore a Christian is loath to leave Christ, who hath so loved his soul, and whom his soul so loveth. A bare belief is only in the head, which is but the entrance into the inwards of the soul; it is the heart is Christ's castle and citadel; a superficial bare assent may let him go, but it is faith working by love that produceth this close adherence.

Fourthly, I come now, in the fourth place, to the reasons why more than conquerors.

1. On God's part.

2. On the believer's part.

1. On God's part. The keeping of the saints is partly a matter of power, and partly a matter of care. Now, if God take the charge of us, surely we must be kept; for God is invincible in his power, and unchangeable in the purposes of his love; or, which is all one, Christ is mighty to save, and ready to save: Isa. lxiii. 1, 'I that speak in righteousness am mighty to save'.

[A.] He is in God's hand, and Christ's hand: John x. 28, 29, 'I give unto them eternal life, and they shall never perish, neither shall any pluck them out of my hand: my Father is greater than all, and none is able to pluck them out of my Father's hand.' They may have many shakings and tossings, as to their spiritual condition, yet their final perseverance, till they come to eternal life, is certain. Surely God and Christ are invincibles; no other creature hath any power but what God gave them at first, and consequently may be taken away at God's pleasure, and is limited by him in the meantime. Therefore, though in themselves they might fail, and be left for ever, yet his power and everlasting arm is able to sustain them; therefore nothing is to be feared if God desert us not; they are in his hand, that is, under his powerful protection. You will say, While they keep close to God, nothing shall ruin them; but God hath undertaken that: Jer. xxxii. 40, 'He will put his fear into their hearts, that they shall never depart from him.' The whole business of our salvation, and all the conditions of it, are in God's hand. God, seeing how man had wasted that stock of grace which he had put into his hands before the fall, resolveth to provide for him in time to come, to keep his heart and will in his own hand, and to guide it by his Spirit, that he might not hazard his estate any more, or be cheated of it by Satan. In man's restitution after the fall, his estate is impaired with respect to the perfection of it in this present life. He is bruised in his heel with diverstemptations and slips into sin; but it is much better in regard of the firmness of it. Man having power in his own hands, lost it quickly, therefore now his whole salvation is in God's hands; both end arid way and means, and all that conduceth thereunto: Col. iii. 3, 'Our life is hid with Christ in God'; not only in point of obscurity, but security; not left any longer to our own keeping; it is in safe hands.

[B.] As God is invincible in his power, so he is unchangeable in the purposes of love; for, according to his unchangeable nature, 'whom he loveth, he loveth to the end' His new-covenant gifts are 'without repentance,' Rom. xi. 29. The matter is made sure between God and Christ: John vi. 39, 'This is my Father's will, that of all that are given me, I should lose nothing, but should raise it up again at the last day.' They are given him by way of recompense, and by way of charge; if he take them into his custody and charge he will be faithful; for he is to give an account for them at the last day by head and poll: Heb. ii. 13, 'Behold land the children which God hath given me.' Christ hath a special charge to keep all those safe -whom God hath given him; and surely he hath sufficient power, and will be careful of his charge to keep them safe.

2. On the believer's part.

[A.] His relation to Christ: he is united to Christ, married to him in the covenant: 1 Cor. vi. 17, 'He that is joined to the Lord is one spirit.' *Impossibile est massam a pasta separari*—leaven kneaded into the dough cannot be got out. Certainly it is a great means of our preservation. Why? First, Partly because from this union of Christ with believers there floweth life, which is not, like the animal life, obnoxious to death and corruption; it is *sperma menon*, 1 John iii. 9'; an incorruptible seed' 1 Peter i. 23'; a fountain of living waters always springing up to eternal life' John iv. 14, Secondly, From this life resulteth a double inclination, which serveth to preserve it and keep it up; which is (1.) A careful avoiding of what is contrary to it; none more tender and timorous of their own infirmities than they who are endowed with it, Prov. xxviii. 14, more watchful against occasions of revolting: 1 Cor, x. 12, 'Therefore, let him that thinketh he standeth, take heed lest he fall.' More diligent in using sanctified means of confirmation: 1 John v. 18, 'He that is begotten of God keepeth himself, and that evil one toucheth him not'. They are chary of that life they have, and those hopes they are called unto: 1 Cor. ix. 27, 'But I keep under my body, and bring it into subjection, lest by any means, when I have preached to others, I myself should be a cast away.' This being their disposition, the Lord by it fulfilleth the purposes of his grace. (2.) A desire to maintain, promote, and increase this life by the use of all gospel means: 1 Peter ii. 2, 'As new-born babes desire the sincere milk of the word, that you may grow thereby'; and James i. 18, 19, 'Of his own will begat he us by the word of truth, that we should be a kind of first-fruits of his creatures. Wherefore, my beloved, let every man be swift to hear.' (3.) The new nature is thus acting as under the care and protection of God, and most especially when we are most in danger to miscarry: Ps. xciv. 18, 'I said, My foot slippeth; then thy right hand held me up'; so Ps. lxxiii. 23, 'Nevertheless, I am continually with thee: thou hast holden me by thy right hand' When was that? See ver. 2, 'But as for rue, my feet were almost gone; my steps had well-nigh slipped.' God supports us by his grace when the temptation is apt to make too great a shock and impression upon us.

[B.] There is something more on the believer's part; there are two graces which have a great influence upon our adherence to God, faith and love.

(1.) Faith hath a great influence upon our victory: 1 John v. 4, 5, 'For whosoever is born of God overcometh the world; and this is the victory that overcometh the world, even our faith. Who is he that overcometh the world, but he that beiieveth that Jesus is the Son of God? 'For though God keepeth us, yet he keepeth us by our faith: 1 Peter i. 5, 'And are kept by the power of God through faith to salvation.' The love and power of the principal cause doth not exclude the means of our preservation. When we consider our great trials, we are apt to apprehend much matter of fear and uncertainty. As heaven is kept for us, so are we kept for heaven, that we may not be lost in the way thither. But how are we kept? By the power of God as the principal agent, through faith, depending upon his promises both for assistance and pardon; for it is a firm, cordial believing that Jesus is the Son of God, and so the great lawgiver of the church, and the fountain of grace to all his people. As a lawgiver, so we make conscience of his precepts, because his threats and promises are greater than all the terrors and allurements of sense. We can set hell against all the terrors of the world, and heaven against all the delightful things of the world, and so are not greatly moved with what befalleth us here. Faith layeth these things before the soul, as if they were before our eyes. Yea more, here is a prison, there is hell, *Domine imperator, tu carcerem, ille Gehennam*[81]; here torments for the body, there God is ready to cast an unfaithful, fearful Christian, both body and soul, into hell fire: here is pomp of living, contentments for the flesh; there are pleasures at God's right hand for evermore: here is worldly glory; there the glory, honour, and immortality of the other world, Rom. ii. 7: here is escape from present torments, there is a better resurrection, Heb. xi. 35. All this belongeth to Christ as a lawgiver. But as he is the fountain of spiritual life and grace, so we receive Christ that he may live in us, and we in him; and so are fortified against inward weakness, and look upon Christ as able to defend us, and to maintain us in the midst of temptations. We have a weak nature; our God is unseen; our great hopes are to come; the flesh is importunate to be pleased, loth to hold out against so many trials. But look to Jesus, the captain of our salvation, and the fountain of our life; we are encouraged, and receive supplies from him: Phil. iv. 13, 'I can do all things through Christ that strengthened me.' The Lord enableth us to abound, or to be abased; to undergo any condition, so we may discharge our duty to Christ. He strengthened our staggering resolution, and helpeth us to be strong in the power of his might for all encounters, Eph. vi. 10. Thus you see how faith helpeth us.

(2.) Love is another grace, and of chief regard in this place. Now I shall show you that love hath an unconquerable force and power in itself, especially where it is accompanied with desire, hope, and delight, as it is in a sincere, gracious heart.

(a.) There is an invincible force in love itself: Cant. viii. 6, 7, 'For love is strong as death, jealousy is cruel as the grave; many waters cannot quench love, nor can the floods drown it. If a man would give all the substance of his house for love, it would be utterly contemned.' Love is of such a vehement nature that we cannot resist it and break the force of it, no more than we can resist death or fire; nothing but the thing loved can quench or satisfy it. Such a

---

[81] Lord emperor, jail for you, hell for him.

vehement love is there kindled in the heart of a believer towards Christ. It maketh such strong and mighty impressions on the heart, that they cannot endure any separation and divorce from Christ. No opposition can extinguish it, no other satisfaction can bribe it, and entice it away from Christ. No opposition can extinguish it; if many waters cannot quench love, nor can floods drown it; waters will quench fire, but nothing can quench love. By waters in scripture are understood afflictions, crosses, and seeming hard dealing from Christ 'All his waves and billows have gone over me,' saith David. Now a sincere love doth so clasp about Christ, that no cross, no rod, nor the blackest dispensations can drive us from him; neither sword, nor famine, nor pestilence. If all the floods of trial and opposition were let out upon it, it cannot quench love; so, also, nothing can satisfy it. Nay, it rejecteth the offers of all enticing objects, which would intrude themselves into Christ's room in the heart. There are two sorts of trials which carry away souls from Christ; left-hand temptations, as crosses and afflictive evils; and right-hand temptations, such as the cares of this world, deceitfulness of riches, and voluptuous living. When the one sort of trials do not prevail, the other may. The thorny ground could endure the heat of the sun, but the good seed choked in it. But true love to Christ will be prevailed over by neither. If a man would give all the substance of his house, that is, all that can be given, to buy away a soul from Christ, it will not do; all this proffer is utterly contemned, with a holy disdain and indignation. No, all things are dung and dross in comparison of the excellency of the knowledge of our Lord, Phil. iii. 8, 9. All essays to cool it, or divert or draw it away, are fruitless. A slight love may be overcome, but a fervent strong love will not. It is a warm love to Christ which maintaineth his interest in the soul; and then neither waters nor bribes, heights nor depths, advantages nor losses, preferments nor persecutions, will cool the believer's affection to Christ. He dare not entertain anything in Christ's room, nor slacken his love to him. No; pleasures and riches and honours will not satisfy him; and troubles and afflictions will not discourage him. Thus a true and sincere love is unconquerable, and will hold out against temptations on all hands.

(b.) This love to Christ is accompanied with desire, hope, and delight. So far as we want the thing which we love, there is desire; and so far as it is likely to be obtained there is hope; and so far as we enjoy the thing which we love, it is accompanied with delight. Now all these are to be found in the love of Christ; and if they be high and strong, the believer overcometh the violence of the temptation.

(i.) It is not easy to draw off a man from his strongest desires. If a man's heart be set upon Christ, he must be with Christ for ever more. What can separate him? Will he be discouraged with tribu lation or distress? Nay, those inflame him. Shall he lose all that he hath longed for because of a little inconvenience to the flesh? No; Paul's groanings for Christ, and desires to be with the Lord, made him labour and strive and endure all the afflictions of the gospel, 2 Cor. v. 8, 9. Death itself may then be borne; for it is but the key to open the prison door, and let out that soul that hath long desired to be with Christ, Phil. i. 23. *Gratias agimus vobis, quod a molestis dominis liberamur*—you do them a favour to send them home to their dear Lord.

(ii.) It is accompanied with hope; they expect within a little while to have their desires accomplished. And will a soul that is at heaven's gates lose all that he hath waited for because the entrance is troublesome? When men have crowded to any mask or show, and have waited long, they will not lose their waiting, though they venture many a knock or broken pate to get in; so when salvation is very near, will a Christian give over his waiting, seeking, and striving for it? Mat. xi. 12, 'Even from the days of John the Baptist the kingdom of heaven suffereth violence, and the violent take it by force.'

(iii.) Delight. We have gotten in part a taste and earnest of our fruition and enjoyment of God and Christ hereafter, and it is very pleasing to the soul; so that the tempter must needs have a hard task to draw off the soul from him in whom he delighteth. Worldly men will not let go their vanities, nor sinful wretches their foulest sins, because they delight in them. Many who never knew what it is to love Christ, and delight in his salvation, do not so earnestly long for, and fixedly hope for the promised blessedness. Now these may be easily taken off, but the other will venture upon the greatest difficulties.

Objection But may not a sound believer be foiled as to his inward man by these afflictive temptations?

Answer Yes, the experience of the saints showeth it too often. But—

1. It is not totally and finally. Their heel is bruised, not only as the outward man is molested by afflictions, but as they may be drawn to some sinful slips and temptations. The heel is the lowest and basest part of the body, far enough from any vital part, the wounds whereof endanger not the life at all. The devil may draw them into some sins, which may cause much unquietness and affliction of spirit; but these wounds are not deadly, and do not quench the life of grace in them; these wounds may be painful, but not mortal 'They shall not be hurt of the second death,' Rev. ii. 11.

2. Upon recovery by repentance. The Lord sanctifieth these falls to them, to make them the more cautious and watchful; so they grow wiser and better, and more resolute, as being warned before by their own bitter cost; as a ball, with the more force it is beaten down, it rebounds the higher; or as a child that hath gotten a knock, or been bitten by a snappish cur, groweth the more wary: Josh. xxii. 17, 'Is the iniquity of Peor too little for us? 'They were not yet whole of the iniquity of Peor, and therefore should be careful not to wound themselves again.

3. All ends in final conquest over Satan: Horn. xvi. 20, 'And the God of peace shall bruise Satan under our feet shortly.' We are now in our combat; it is some conquering to keep up our resistance; but our full triumph is hereafter.

Objection 2. But will it not hurt to press believers to this confidence? Will not this weaken their care and diligence? No.

1. This is pleasing and acceptable to God, to believe that he will perfect and maintain his begun work: Phil. i. 6, 'Being confident of this, that he that hath begun a good work in you will perfect it to the day of Christ.'

2. It is honourable unto God, and doth excite us to praise and thanks giving, when we can trust our interests in his hands with a quiet and well composed mind: 2 Tim. i. 12. 'And I am persuaded that he is able to keep that which I have committed unto him' A Christian, in all respects of time, can bless God for what he hath done: called us when strangers and enemies, 1 Peter ii. 9; what he doth do: 'keepeth the feet of his saints', 1 Sam. ii. 9; for what he will do: 2 Tim. iv.

17, 18, 'Notwithstanding the Lord stood with me, and strengthened me. And the Lord shall deliver me from every evil work, and preserve me to his heavenly kingdom'. To be satisfied in God's conduct is certainly very honourable to him.

3. It is very profitable to the children of God.

[A.] To keep us from falling. God promiseth to keep us, but in his own way; and that engageth us to an entire dependence upon him in the use of means: John xv. 4, 'Abide in me, and I in you'; so 1 John ii. 16, 17, 'Ye shall abide in him'; and then he presently addeth, 'Little children, abide in him' First a promise, and then an exhortation; and then we use the means with the more diligence and encouragement; as Paul had a promise that not one should perish, Acts xxvii. 23, but yet they must all abide in the ship, ver. 31.

[B.] To encourage us to return when fallen. We have some hold-fast on God, when we seek to recover ourselves by repentance: Ps. cxix. 170, 'Let my supplication come before thee; deliver me according to thy word'; and Jer. iii. 4, 'Wilt thou not from this time cry unto me, My father, the guide of my youth?'

4. It is very comfortable, and breedeth that everlasting joy that should be in God's redeemed ones: Isa. xxxv. 10, 'And the ransomed of the Lord shall return, and come to Zion with songs, and everlasting joy upon their heads'. Nay, it begets a heroical spirit when we can bear up on the love of God in the sorest trials.

Use. It cautioneth us not to be dismayed when the people of God seem to be run down by oppositions and reproaches, and the cause of religion to suffer loss, and visibly to go to ruin. No; Christ hath promised that 'the gates of hell shall not prevail against the church', Mat. xvi. 18. All the powers which the devil can muster up cannot destroy Christ's interest in the world; his kingdom is like a rock in the midst of the sea, which, being beaten on every side with waves, standeth unmovable. His people many times may be scattered, oppressed, their profession discountenanced and opposed everywhere, seemingly beaten out of the world; but then the church groweth inwardly, the graces of his people are strengthened and increased, and their hearts bettered, their glory hastened, their profession more honoured and reverenced in the consciences of men; some converted, others confirmed, when the Christians were butchered, and went to wreck everywhere. Oftentimes it falleth out so. When God breaketh that temporal interest to which we lean, he provideth for his own glory and the advancement of the gospel by other and better means; and religion gaineth when it seemeth to lose; as in the primitive times, when the slaughters were frequent, they sought to drive Christians to deny Christ, but they confess him the more; they fumed and chafed, because they could not get their will, and increased their fury, but still the other grew more resolute. Enemies have confessed themselves overcome; so, 'What shall we do to these men? 'Acts iv. 16. When they imprisoned and scourged them, they were at a loss. Sozomen saith of Sapores, that he was tired with destroying the Christians, and at length caused the troubles to cease; so Dioclesian leaves his empire because he could not root out the Christians, but that they still continued.

Use 2. Is to persuade us to get such a degree of faith and love and patience that we may be more than conquerors in all our trials. It is a great degree of heroical fortitude, or a high Christian pitch, which is here described; for mark

1. Here is not one sort of trials, but many: Col. i. 11, 'Strengthened with all patience' It is not enough to overcome one evil, but all; crosses of all kinds 'In all these things.' A little distress a man might bear, but famine and nakedness and sword terrifieth our thoughts; but nothing must be excepted out of our resignation to God.

2. Here is conquest. It ill becometh the godly to faint in affliction: Prov. xxiv. 10, 'If thou faintest in affliction, thy strength is small.' Affliction will try what our strength is. It is one thing to talk of it, another to bear it; there is a great difference between a trial apprehended in our judgment, and felt by sense: Job iv. 3-5, 'Behold, thou hast instructed many, and thou hast strengthened the weak hands; thy words have upholden him that was falling, and thou hast strengthened the feeble knees; but now it is come upon thee, and thou faintest, it toucheth thee, and thou art troubled.' We are other manner of persons in trouble than we seemed to be out of trouble. The well will give good counsel to the sick; it is easy for them that stand on the shore to say to those that conflict with the waves and tempests, Sail thus. When troubles come upon ourselves, we are restless and impatient; the self-confident and presumptuous will find it another thing to bear trouble than to talk of it; but the humble, and those that are sensible of their weakness, will find, that though they are weak, yet the power they are assisted by is mighty; and that God's power is perfected in their weakness; when weak, then strong. That evils, dreadful in the hearing, are not so grievous when God layeth them on us, and giveth us strength to bear them: 2 Cor. xii. 9, 'And he said unto me, My grace is sufficient for thee; for my strength is made perfect in weakness.' They have a quite contrary t experience; when weak, then strong; as the other, who conceited themselves strong, are then weak.

3. We are not only to be conquerors, but more than conquerors. That is

[A.] As to the frame of your hearts; to be not only patient, but cheerful under the cross upon right grounds: Col. i. 11, 'Strengthened 'with all might according to his glorious power, unto all patience and long- suffering with joyfulness'; so Mat. v. 12, 'Rejoice, and be exceeding glad'; and James i. 2, 'Count it all joy when ye fall into divers temptations' If we have no other burden upon us than the affliction itself, let us bless God rather than repine.

[B.] As to the success.

(1) You must not only keep from miscarrying, but get good by the affliction and persecution. It must purge out sin: Isa. xxix. 9, 'By this, therefore, shall the iniquity of Jacob be purged out; and this is all the fruit, to take away his sin'. Make you more pliable to God's will, and

careful to perform your duty: Ps. cxix. 67, 'Before I was afflicted, I went astray, but now have I kept thy word'; ver. 71, 'It is good for me that I have been afflicted, that I might learn thy statutes.' Retrench your carnal liberty and complacency, and bring you to a greater con tempt of the world: Gal. vi. 14, 'But God forbid that I should glory in anything, save in the cross of our Lord Jesus Christ, by whom the world is crucified unto me, and I unto the world.' Quicken you to be more frequent and fervent in prayer: Isa. xxvi. 16, 'Lord, in trouble have they visited thee, they poured out a prayer when thy chastening was upon them'. From what hand soever the evil cometh, these must be the effects of it; this is to be more than a conqueror.

(2.) If you mean to be so, you must get a holy obstinacy; that is to say, an invincible resolution to adhere to God. (1.) A holy obstinacy of faith: Job xiii. 15, 'Though he kill me, I will trust in him'. Satan's great design in all temptations is to crush our confidence. Now, to cast away our confidence is to do ourselves as ill a turn as Satan can wish for: nay, however God deal with you, resolve to cleave to him; let my trouble be what it will, yet I will depend upon God. (2.) A holy obstinacy of love; as he told his master that he should not have a club big enough to drive him from him: Isa. xxvi. 8, 'Yea, in the way of thy judgments, Lord, have we waited for thee: the desire of our soul is to thy name, and to the remembrance of thee' They are resolved to desire and seek after and delight in God. (3.) A holy obstinacy of obedience: Job xvii. 9, 'The righteous shall hold on his way, and he that hath clean hands shall be stronger and stronger' When opposed, vexed by the hypocrite, by disadvantages and pressures, he gathereth strength. (4.) An obstinacy of patience: Luke xxi. 16-18, 'And ye shall be betrayed, both by parents., and brethren, and kinsfolks, and friends, and some of you shall they cause to be put to death: and ye shall be hated of all men for my name's sake; but there shall not an hair of your head perish. In your patience possess ye your souls' Whatever befall you, either by persecution or death itself, it shall not turn to the least disadvantage to you, but greatest gain; for those that suffered death were eternally crowned, and others are under the protection of God; therefore endure with constancy. Lastly, an obstinacy of zeal: Dan. iii. 17, 18, 'Our God is able to deliver us; but if not, we will not serve thy gods, nor worship thy golden image which thou hast set up' Godly resolution is ever requisite in point of religion, and it should not be weakened in us by the greatest sufferings.

Doctrine 3. That it is the love of Christ which secureth believers in their conflicts, and maketh them triumph over temptations. All their victory is, *dia tou agapesantos*.

1. Let me give the emphasis of the expression.

2. Give you the proof of the point.

[1.] It is not power that is here spoken of, but love; it is not 'through him that strengthened us,' but through him that 'loved us'; elsewhere it is *dia tou endunamountos*, Phil. iv. 13, 'I can do all things through Christ that strengthened me.' The effect indeed cometh from the influence of his power, but it is his love which sets his power a-work. The ground and bottom of all his mediatorial dispensations is love, which is more comfortable to us than bare power; for we do not know whether he will exercise that or no.

[B.] It is not our love to Christ, but his love to us which is spoken of; no question but the great manifestations of his love in reconciling God to us by redemption, and us to God by conversion, do leave upon a gracious heart a forcible impression and inclination to love him again, who hath loved us at so dear a rate, and in so tender a manner; and this love is not unserviceable in our preservation. Men are not so easily drawn from him whom they dearly love, and love upon such good and powerful reasons. But the strength of a believer lieth not here, in his love to Christ, but rather in Christ's love to us, which both began, and still continueth our salvation. It began it: John iii. 16, 'God so loved the world, that he sent his only-begotten Son, that whosoever believeth in him, should not perish, but have everlasting life.' And continueth it: 2 Thes. ii. 16, 17, 'Now our Lord Jesus Christ himself, and God, even our Father, which hath loved us, and given us everlasting consolation, and good hope through grace, comfort your hearts, and establish you in every good word and work.' Christ's love continueth to his people till they enjoy the full effects of it: and therefore carrieth them through all temptations till they come to their eternal rest. There lieth our stability, in the unchangeableness of his love.

[C.] It is not barely, Who loveth us now, but Who hath loved us. He speaketh of the past time; it is true, he retaineth still his loving and kind affections to us, but the foundation was long since laid in our redemption and conversion to God. In our redemption c He hath loved us, and washed us in his blood', Rev. i. 5; in our conversion: Eph. ii. 4, 5, 'But God, who is rich in mercy, for his great love where with he loved us, even when we were dead in sins, hath quickened us together with Christ.' In these two acts the foundation was laid of our victory and triumph. By his redemption he purchased all that grace which is necessary for us till we are fully brought home to God; by conversion we are actually instated in it. By the one, jus ad rem, our right to this grace was acquired; by the other we have *jus in re*, we are actually possessed of it. By the one he doth pacify the wrath of God, by the other he doth take us into a near relation to himself, that we may become his own, and so actually under his care and protection. Therefore in these two acts lieth our safety, in that of redemption and conversion. In short, these two acts do both endear us to Christ, and Christ to us. They endear us to Christ; by redemption his people are his dear purchase; if they miscarry, his purchased people miscarry, therefore he will not lose them; they are his own, being bought with the price of his blood, and everyone will provide for his own, 1 Tim. v. 8. The world will love its own, John xiii. 19. Besides, by conversion we are his own by covenant and near relation. We are his spouse; the kindness of espousals is above other kindness: Jer. ii. 2, 'I remember the kindness of thy youth, the love of thine espousals.' The day of conversion is the day of espousals, Cant. iii. 11. Then we are married to the Lord, that we may bring forth fruit unto God. And both these acts doth endear Christ to us; for the glory of his grace and love to sinners doth eminently appear in our redemption; then he commanded his love to us in the great things he purchased and suffered for us. Besides, in conversion, then his love is applied to us, and he taketh us with all our faults; he spake comfortably to us in our ears, and sanctified our souls, and brought us back again to God, and so to our duty and happiness. We can never forget this kindness of his espousals.

[D.] He hath loved us; it not only compriseth the foundation laid, but implieth also some experience on the saint's part. When we consider what he hath done for us already, we may be the more confident of what he is now, and will be to us hereafter. Christ's love is not only seen in our first entrance into covenant, and the eminent passages of our redemption and conversion, but there is an uninterrupted course thereof, from the time of our first closing with him till our final perfection in glory. His whole dealing with them is love; it is to be read in every dispensation of his and condition of ours; it is to be read in the continual supports, gracious helps, daily pardons, which he constantly vouchsafeth to us. Now the saints promise themselves more, because God hath done such great things for their sakes already: 1 Cor. i. 9, 'God is faithful, by whom ye were called unto the fellow ship of his Son, Jesus Christ our Lord'; and 2 Tim. iv. 17, 18, 'Not withstanding, the Lord stood with me, and strengthened me; and the Lord shall deliver me from every evil work, and preserve me to his heavenly kingdom.' When you have tried Christ so often, cannot you yet trust in him? How often hath he performed promises to thee, heard thy cries, helped and saved thee in thy distresses, confuted thy unbelief, and shamed thy disgraceful tears and cares? Shall all these experiences of his love be forgotten? Nay, one mercy is the pledge of another: 2 Cor. i. 10, 'Who hath delivered us from so great a death, and doth deliver; in whom we trust that he will yet deliver us.' Therefore whatever troubles come upon us, we are more than conquerors from him that loved us.

[E.] This triumph is put into the mouths of a people deeply afflicted, or exposed to tribulation, distress, persecution, famine, nakedness, peril, sword; it is these say, 'We are more than conquerors through him that loved us.' Partly, to show that Christ is not estranged from his people by their afflictions and troubles; these do not vacate their interest nor cause his affection to cease 'Whom the Lord loveth, he rebuketh and chasteneth,' Rev. iii. 19. He doth not cease to love them, but rather is more tender of them, more willing to let out more of his love to them, the more they are wronged by others. And partly, also, to beget confidence. Christ's love is more powerful to save us than the world's hatred to destroy us; for here, to the most direful effects of the world's hatred is opposed nothing but the love of Christ as a ground of triumph. We make too much of the world's hatred, if we think we are not safe enough in Christ's love: John xvi. 33, 'In the world ye shall have tribulation, but in me ye shall have peace'; and surely Christ's peace should counterbalance all the world's troubles. Judge you where we are best provided for, by the world's friendship and Christ's hatred, or by the world's hatred and Christ's friendship.

2. The proof of the point—

[A.] By scripture. And there I shall produce two metaphors; the first where Christ's love is compared to a banner: Cant. ii. 4, 'His banner over me is love.' A banner is a military ensign. The church is elsewhere described to be terrible as an army with banners, because of its order and strength. Now what is the banner under which the church fighteth with joy and victory, against sin, Satan, and the world? Christ's ensign is his love to her, that love by which he redeemed us, and converted us, giveth us everlasting consolation, and good hope through grace; this is the love that giveth us victory over all temptations. The other metaphor, where Christ's love is compared to the lining of a chariot: Cant. iii. 10, 'His chariot is paved with love'; meaning that chariot wherein the saints ride in triumph to heaven. Love doth all for us; all the promises run like pipes with streams of love; all providences, or Christ's dispensations towards his people, are nothing else but love.

[B.] By reasons taken from the properties of Christ's love.

(1.) It is a transcendent love. All love, where it is real, is earnest and vehement. Much more the love of Christ, for that is not to be measured by an ordinary standard, for the apostle saith, Eph. iii. 19, 'That you may know the love of Christ, which passeth knowledge.' The love of Christ to lost sinners is so vast, boundless, and infinite, that there is no parallel whereby we may come to the knowledge of it, Rom. v. 17, 13. We may know it as to admiration, but we cannot know it as to comprehension to the full. Somewhat we may know by what is spoken of it in the scripture, somewhat by what we feel in ourselves of the effects of it; yea, we not only may know it, but we ought to know it so far as may inflame our hearts with a love to God, and enable us to be faithful to him, whatever troubles we endure for his sake. Now what may we not promise ourselves from such a love, as is not only above our expression, but above our comprehension? He that died for sinners, will he not be kind to his people?

(2.) It is a tender love, and such as maketh him solicitous for our welfare. We use to say, Res est solicita, plena timoris amor—Love is a solicitous thing, feareth not the danger or trouble of what is beloved. As Jacob was solicitous about Benjamin, lest mischief should befall him in the way; as Epaphroditus had a solicitous care of the Philippians, and of any trouble or sorrow that might happen to them, Phil. ii. 26; such is the care of Christ over his people, especially when they are most in danger; then his love is most at work for them, to provide help and cordials against all temptations. He knoweth our weakness and infirmities; for his people are 'engraven on the palms of his hands,' Isa. xlix. 16; yea, carried in his heart, as the names of the tribes on the breast of the high priest. So Christ 'calleth his own sheep by name, and leadeth them', John x. 3. Now, knowing the danger to which they are exposed, his love doth incline him to pity them, and give them renewed proof of his affection and care over them in their extremities, and doth strangely preserve them in manifold dangers.

(3.) It is a constant and an immutable love: Jer. xxxi. 3, 'With an everlasting love have I loved thee'—God's love is a love of perpetuity, or eternity; his love and affection continueth still the same to us, and shall do so for ever. God reserveth a liberty in the covenant, for correction: Ps. lxxxix. 32, 33, 'Then will I visit their transgressions with the rod and their iniquity with stripes. Nevertheless my loving-kindness will I not utterly take from him, nor suffer my faithfulness to fail'. The sharpest rods and sorest stripes do stand with loving-kindness to them; yea, are rather effects of his love than hatred. But this new covenant-love is immutable.

(4.) It is an operative and effective, not an idle and hidden love. Christ's love were only an affection in the heart, a well-wishing love, there were less comfort in it; but it is a love that breaketh forth in action and real performance. He will readily do good to his people whom he loveth; not only hereafter, when he will accomplish our glorious hopes, but now his love is not without effects. Two I shall mention.

(a.) His ordering all dispensations of providence for our good; this God doth for them that love him, Rom. viii. 28. And surely it is a great testimony of his love to us. They know nothing in religion that know not that Christ's external government is necessary to the preservation of the saints, as well as his internal grace. See Ps. xxv. 3, 'Let none that wait on thee be ashamed; let them be ashamed that transgress without cause'; 1 Cor. x. 13, 'There hath no temptation taken you, but such as is common to man; but God is faithful, who will not suffer you to be tempted above what you are able, but will with the temptation also make a way to escape, that ye may be able to bear it' He withdraweth temptations, that they may not be too strong for feeble souls, and cause despondency in them, and moderateth our afflictions, that they may not trouble or discourage us, but only correct, and keep us from security, vanity, and contempt of holy things. These temptations by troubles and afflictions are let loose to check other temptations to ambition, worldliness, and sensuality; but when they are like to prove temptations themselves, the love of Christ is much seen in his wise and gracious mitigation and removal of them.

(b.) The assistances of his grace, or the operations of his Spirit. Surely the property of love is, *velle amato bonum*. And God giveth the true good to his children; the good we are capable of in this life is the gift of his sanctifying Spirit. Tempted souls find it a needful benefit; and when they seek it, will Christ deny it to them? No, he hath assured them of the contrary: Mat. vii. 9-11, 'Or what man is there of you, whom, if his son ask bread, will he give him a stone? Or if he ask fish, will he give him a serpent? If ye then, being evil, know how to give good gifts to your children, how much more shall your Father which is in heaven give good things to them that ask him?' God will not deal worse with his children than men do with theirs; and that good thing is the Spirit, Luke xi. 13. Use 1. Information.

1. That we cannot secure ourselves by ourselves. The devil is too strong an enemy for sinful, lapsed men to deal withal. He conquered us in innocency; and what may he not do now, when we are divided in ourselves, and have something in us on both sides? Much earthliness, carnality, averseness from God, as well as love to him? Therefore we subsist every moment by the love of Christ, who became the captain of our salvation, Heb. ii. 10, and in whose cause we are engaged, and who giveth us the Holy Spirit, to move us to good, and to restrain us from evil.

2. What confidence we have, or may have, in Christ. The saints overcome by his love; and if you will adhere to him in the greatest hazards, will he fail you? Surely he is kind to his people, and hath given not only such assurance of it in his promises, but such experience of it in the course of his dispensations, that we are still encouraged to wait upon him. He is willing to help his people, for he loveth them; he is able and sufficient, for infinite power is at the beck of his love. And you have tried him, and he never forsook you; will he fail at last? Was all this to trepan[82] men into a deceitful hope?

3. How little we should suspect his love, when to appearance all things go against us. There are two dispensations Christ useth: either disappointing the temptation, or strengthening his people under it. For the first we have cause to bless him, and many times more cause than we are well aware of. *Plures sunt gratice privativae quam positivae*[83], say divines in general; in our case, that of the prophet is verified—'I led Ephraim, but he knew it not.' In preventing our temptations we know not what the love of Christ hath done for us. But for the second, in what he will try us, take heed of misconstruing any act of Christ's love towards us. You think there is some want of love when he permitteth you to furious and boisterous temptations; no, then he meaneth to give you some supereminent grace of the Spirit: 1 Peter iv. 14, 'If ye be reproached for the name of Christ, happy are ye; for the Spirit of glory and of God resteth upon you; on their part he is evil spoken of, but on your part he is glorified.' He loveth you still, but will not manifest his love this way or that way which the flesh pleaseth.

4. It showeth us how much we should love Christ, and adhere to him in the greatest difficulties. Love doth attract and draw love. Ordinary love should be mutual and reciprocal: 2 Kings x. 15, 'Is thine heart right, as mine is with thee?' That is, dost thou affect me, as I do thee? Paul pleadeth it, 2 Cor. vi. 11-13, 'O ye Corinthians, our mouth is open to you, our heart is enlarged. Ye are not straitened in us, but ye are straitened in your own bowels; now for a recompense in the same, be ye also enlarged.' This showeth the justice of it, that we should retaliate; be as kind and affectionate as Christ is to us. But alas! Usually Christ may complain, 2 Cor. xii. 15, 'The more abundantly I love you, the less I am beloved.' Shall we lessen our respects to him?

Use 2. Is to persuade us to give all diligence to this, that we be assured that Christ loveth us. This is known, partly by an external partly by an internal demonstration.

1. The external demonstration is in redemption; surely there is no doubt of that, that Christ came to show the loveliness and goodness of God to the forlorn world. This only needeth consideration and improvement. He that loved us at so costly a rate, will he desert us if we choose his ways, and resolve to adhere to him?

2. The internal demonstration is in conversion, or our receiving the atonement; entering into peace with God, and adopted as children of the family. Sure if you get this one evidence, you shall be brought to glory. When he hath pardoned thy follies and the frailties of thy youth, and called thee when he passed by others, and left them in their sins, what will he not do for thee?

---

[82] perforate (a person's skull) with a trepan.
[83] There is more grace in a negative than a positive.

SERMON XLVII

For I am persuaded, that neither death, nor life, nor angels, nor principalities, nor powers, nor things present, nor things to come, nor height, nor depth, nor any other creature, shall be able to separate us from the love of God, which is in Christ Jesus our Lord.

Romans viii. 38, 39.

THESE words render a reason why believers are more than conquerors in their sorest trials, and do further carry on the apostle's triumph to a fit conclusion of such an excellent discourse. In the text observe

1. The assailants—*Death, life, angels.*

2. The attempt and design—*To separate us from the love of God.*

3. The fruitlessness of it—No creature shall be able to do this.

4. His confidence—*For I am persuaded.*

1. The aggressors and assailants are set forth, either by a particular distribution, or wrapt up in a general expression.

[A.] The particular distribution is made by four pairs or couples.

(1.) Neither death nor life; that is, neither the fears of death nor the hopes of life; this pair is mentioned because death is the 'king of terrors' Job xviii. 14. And among all desirable good things life is the chiefest, and that which maketh a man capable of enjoying all other good things; expressed Job ii. 4, 'Skin for skin, yea, all that a man hath, will he give for his life' Now all assaults from this first pair are in vain, as they tend to separate us from the love of God in Christ. Will you hope to do it by threats of death? A believer will tell you that Christ threateneth eternal death; and this temporal one, be it natural or violent, is but a passage into life eternal. Will you entice him by the baits of life? They have learned to prefer everlasting life before it: Heb. xi. 35, 'Not accepting deliverance, that they might obtain a better resurrection.'

(2.) Second pair—'Nor angels, nor principalities and powers'; that is, the powers of the visible and invisible world; so these two powers are elsewhere coupled: Eph. i. 21, 'Far above all principalities, and powers, and might, and dominion, and every name that is named, not only in this world, but also that which is to come.' So that by principalities and powers worldly powers are intended. Angels is a common word, that implieth good and evil spirits. If you apply it to the good angels, then it is spoken only by way of supposition, if it were possible they could concur in such a design. Such a supposition there is: Gal. i. 8, 'Though an angel from heaven preach any other doctrine to you, let him be accursed.' It is a supposition of an impossible case; but such as conduceth much to heighten the sense of the truth represented. As for evil angels, they make it their work and business to steal away souls from Christ; and if they could, would wrest them out of Christ's own arms. Well then, the good angels seek not to separate us from Christ; the good will not, and the bad cannot. Were it possible for a good angel to dissuade me from my Lord Jesus Christ, I would hold him accursed. Evil angels assault us, but we are preserved by a stronger than they. By the other branch, 'principalities and powers,' he understandeth the potentates of the world, by what title soever distinguished. No powers can overtop the divine and sovereign Lord of the redeemed. The glory of kings and emperors, compared to his glory, is less than the light of a candle compared with the sun in his brightness.

(3.) Third couple—'Nor things present, nor things to come'. Thereby he meaneth all things that had happened, or might hereafter happen to them before their departure out of the world. As we bear up under present pressures, so we need not fear those which are to come. We often forecast what shall become of us if the Lord permit great troubles, trials, and calamities to befall us. A Christian is as sure of things to come as things present. The present hopes, fears, and enjoyments are transitory and contemptible; and future evils will sooner be passed over, for our salvation will be much nearer than when we first believed, Rom. xiii. 11.

(4.) 'Neither neight nor depth.' The creatures above us or below us; neither sublimitary of honours, nor depth of ignominy; dignities do not entice, nor disgraces discourage us. No power, from the highest to the lowest of the creatures; no estate or condition of life, from the highest honour to the lowest beggary, can prevail with us to quit Christ.

[B.] The general expression—'Nor any other creature,' comprising thereby all things on this side God, how amiable or terrible soever they seem. What can creatures do when they are in the hands, and under the care of the creator? Well then, the sense is, that no force or fraud shall untwist the bands and cords of this love; no temptation shall blast, or persecution cause that faith to wither which hath taken root in a good and honest heart.

2. Their attempt or design 'To separate us from the love of God in Christ Jesus our Lord;' that is, from the love wherewith we through Christ love God, and the love wherewith God loved us through Christ; this as the cause, that as the effect, for the embraces are mutual—'We apprehend that for which we are apprehended of Christ', Phil. iii. 10. Only he first layeth hold upon us by his effectual grace, and we lay hold upon him; and our standing dependeth upon our love as a means, and his love as the principal conserving cause.

3. The fruitlessness of the attempt 'Nothing shall be able to separate us from the love of God.' Mark, the apostle doth not only say that nothing shall, but nothing can separate us, which is more emphatical.

4. His confidence—'I am persuaded.' The apostle doth not go by thinking and guessing, but undoubted knowledge. Elsewhere we have two words: 2 Tim. i. 12, 'I know whom I have believed, and I am persuaded that he is able to keep what I have committed to him.' There are two acts of the understanding, apprehension and judication. We must know the grounds, and assent to them: Heb. xi. 13, 'being persuaded of these things, they embraced them' The mind acquiesceth in the evidence of truth, the will in the worth of truth evidenced. Once more: Paul doth not speak of his resolution, what he would do, but his persuasion, what God would do; the first included, but the latter more clearly asserted.

Question The only question which remaineth for explication is, Whether Paul spake this of himself, and in his own person only, or in the name of all believers?

Answer My answer is the same with that which Paul giveth in some what a like case of Abraham: Rom. iv. 23, 24, 'Now it was not writ for his sake alone, but for us also who believe in Jesus.' For he doth not speak this out of any special and personal revelation made to himself, and concerning himself, but that common spirit of faith which falleth upon all believers; and so we may say, as Paul of David: 2 Cor. iv. 13, 'We, having the same spirit of faith, according as it is written, I believed, and therefore have I spoken; we also believe, and therefore speak' My reasons are, first, because he afterwards changeth the number, 'I am persuaded;' but it is *emas*, separate us. Secondly, the grounds are the same to all, the promise the same, and it is the common interest of all the faithful to be preserved in Jesus Christ. If any be weak, and grow not up to this full persuasion and triumph over all doubts and fears, it is their own fault; for this is not so peculiar to Paul; but they also, if they be not wanting to themselves, may be carried to heaven in Christ's triumphant chariot with confidence and rejoicing, notwithstanding all impediments and difficulties in the way. All may; and if they do not, it is because they do not improve the common grounds.

Doctrine 1. This is matter of triumph to believers, to be persuaded that nothing, be it never so great and powerful, can separate them from the love of God in Christ.

1. I shall inquire what is this love of God in Christ.

2. That as long as God loveth us, the people of God apprehend themselves in good condition.

3. That from this love nothing can separate us

4. We ought firmly to be persuaded of this.

1. What is this love of God in Christ? Here I take it actively for the love wherewith he loveth us. Love may be considered—

[A.] As an attribute or a perfection in God; so it is said, 1 John iv. 8, 'God is love.' Which noteth his readiness, self-propension, or inclination to do good.

[B.] As it relateth and passeth out to the creature; so there is a common love and a special love. His common love is set forth: Ps. cxlv. 4, 'The Lord is good to all, and his tender mercies are over all his works.' This love floweth in the channel of common providence. But then there is a special love, which is called his love in Christ: Eph. i. 3, 'Who hath blessed us with spiritual blessing in heavenly places in Christ'. This love may be considered as purposed or ex pressed. As purposed: 2 Tim. i. 9, 'According to his purpose and grace, which was given us in Christ Jesus before the world began' His gracious purposes were from everlasting; he determined within himself that we should receive these fruits of his love through Jesus Christ. As expressed, and that two ways; as revealed in the gospel, and as applied to our hearts.

(1.) The love and free grace of God is revealed in the gospel. There is the discovery of God's goodwill to sinners, and the rich preparation of grace he hath made for those who are truly willing to receive him, therefore called the unsearchable riches of grace, Eph. iii. 8, or those many blessed advantages that belong to Christians.

(2.) As applied to our hearts. The application may be considered as to the effects, or sense (a.) As to the effects. When the gospel is made successful to our conversion, and his eternal love beginneth to take effect: Jer. xxxi. 3, 'I have loved thee with an everlasting love, therefore in loving-kind ness have I drawn thee'; and again, Eph. i. 6, 'He hath made us accepted in the beloved, to the praise of his glorious grace' The people of God are loved from all eternity by his love of benevolence, whereby he willed good unto them, and decreed to bestow good upon them, even when they were children of wrath in the sentence of the law. But there is besides this, the love of complacency, whereby he accepteth of them as being reconciled to him, and acquiesceth in them as his peculiar people, and will bestow all manner of grace upon them.

(b.) As to sense, or our feeling of this love: Korn. v. 5, 'Because the love of God is shed abroad in our hearts' when it is evidenced to us that God hath thus sanctified us, and adopted us into his family, taken us for his children, Rom. viii. 16, and we are encouraged to look for the eternal inheritance as our right and portion. The effects we have in our conversion, called therefore effectual calling; the sense we have by the Lord's confirming grace, or the witness of the Spirit, which God giveth as a reward to his faithful and obedient servants. Experienced, seasoned Christians usually have it in a large measure.

2. The people of God apprehend it as a very blessed and comfortable condition; for here Paul in their name speaketh, that as long as God loveth them, they are not troubled about other things. Death may separate the soul from the body; depth of poverty may separate them, not only from the preferments of the world, but the enjoyment of their own estates; evil angels may disquiet them with temptations, worldly powers exile them from their country, and separate them from their dearest friends and acquaintance; but as long as they are not separated from the love of God in Christ, they are well apaid and contented; for the apostle's triumph is not that he did escape the troubles, but that he was not separated from the love of God in Christ Jesus. Now this cometh, partly from the real worth of the privilege itself, and partly from their esteem and value of it.

[A.] For the real worth of the privilege itself. Surely God's love can make us more happy than the world can make us miserable. Consider a believer as to his present or future condition; he is a blessed man. For the present, his sins are pardoned: Ps. xxxii. 1, 'Blessed is he whose transgression is forgiven, whose sin is covered.' Their natures are healed: 2 Peter i. 4, 'Whereby are given unto us exceeding great and precious promises, that by these we might be partakers of the divine nature, having escaped the corruption that is in the world through lust.' Their ways are directed and ordered: Ps. cxix. 1, 'Blessed are the undefiled in the way, who walk in the law of the Lord' And for the future they have eternal life: 1 John ii. 25, 'And this is the promise he hath promised us, even eternal life' Now these are blessings the world cannot deprive us of, and they are the fruits of distinguishing love; but worldly things, which are subject to the will and power of our enemies, are not: Eccles. ix. 1, 2, 'Love nor hatred cannot be known by these things: all things come alike to all.' These have escaped the greatest misery, and are entitled to the greatest happiness mankind is capable of.

[B.] Their value and esteem of it above all worldly felicities: Ps. iv. 6, 7, 'Many say, Who will show us any good? Lord, lift thou up the light of thy countenance upon us. Thou hast put gladness into my heart, more than in the time that their corn and wine increased;' yea, above life itself: Ps. lxiii. 3, 'Thy loving-kindness is better than life.' They were willing to renounce all to get it, and therefore they are willing to renounce all to keep it: Phil. iii. 7, 8, 'What things were gain to me I counted loss for Christ; yea, doubtless, and I count all things but loss.' He had counted, and did count, to show that he had not repented of his choice. Man is changeable and fickle, highly conceited, for one thing today, and another tomorrow; but the apostle saw no cause to recede from his choice, he continued still of the same opinion. We often affect novelties; are transported when we first change our profession, and repent at leisure. Now if he were to do it again, he would freely do it, supposing it to be gainful. But now to have the favour of God, and to be like him, how valuable a blessing is it! None are true Christians but those that are like-minded, that value his favour above all things; for otherwise God is loved with the respect of an underling, and so cannot have the affection from us that is due to the chiefest good: Ps. lxxiii. 25, 'Whom have I in heaven but thee? And there is none upon earth that I desire besides thee.'

3. That nothing can separate us from the fruition of his love. This will be best seen from the grounds

[A.] The immutability of God's love to the elect. His elective love maketh not only our vocation effectual, but our justification and glorification also, Rom. viii. 30. He will not cease to love us, nor cast off the care of our salvation, till he hath brought it to its final period.

[B.] The infinite merit of Christ. It is in the text, 'The love of God which is in Christ Jesus our Lord.' His free love is carried on to us in that way, for the fruits of his eternal love we cannot obtain but by Jesus Christ. Now his merit is an everlasting merit: he went not to heaven till he had obtained eternal redemption for us, Heb. ix. 12. A purchase that shall ever stand in force.

[C.] The unchangeable covenant, and the promises of God, which irreversibly make over this right to us: 2 Cor. i. 20, 'For all the promises of God are in him, yea, and amen'; and Heb. vi. 18, 'That by two immutable things, in which it was impossible for God to lie, we might have strong consolation.' Surely this should give us a strong consolation, that we have the word of the eternal God for it; that if we run for refuge, and stick there, nothing shall defeat our right.

[D.] The union of a believer with Christ, as a member of his body, and so belonging to his care and protection. For the Lord Christ is a saviour to all those to whom he is truly a head: Eph. v. 23, 'Christ is the head of the church and the saviour of the body.' Therefore every living member of the mystical body is safe; nothing shall dis solve or break that blessed union that is between Christ and believers.

[F.] The almighty power of God and Christ: 1 Peter i. 5, 'Ye are kept by the power of God through faith to salvation.' Heaven is kept for them, and they are kept for heaven. Christ hath promised his almighty power for the safety of believers. As it was he, and not we, that purchased our salvation; so it is Christ, and not we, that must have the keeping of the purchased benefits; and he saith that none shall pluck them out of his hands, and out of the

Father's hands, John x. 28, 29. This is the great security of the fold, that they are under the power of so careful and so able a shepherd. This almighty power of God and Christ doth mightily fortify us against all temptations we meet with in the way to heaven.-

[G.] This right accrueth to believers by virtue of their interest in Christ: 1 Cor. iii. 22, 23, 'All things are yours, whether Paul, or Apollos, or Cephas, or the world, or life, or death, or things present, or to come; all are yours, and you are Christ's, and Christ is God's.' All things are theirs wherein they are concerned, if not in possession, yet in reduction or final use friends, enemies, ordinances, providences; all conditions life, death. If you resolve firmly to obey Christ and adhere to him, you need not fear anything. Now upon these grounds a Christian may conclude that nothing shall separate him from the love of God which is in Christ Jesus our Lord.

4. That we ought firmly to be persuaded of this. Here I shall show you how this persuasion is bred in us.

[A.] By the word of the gospel, discovering to us the whole mystery of our redemption by Christ, with all the consequent benefits. There all God's merciful designs for the justifying, sanctifying, and glorifying the creature are manifested to us as matter of our faith: Acts xix. 8, 'And persuading the things concerning the kingdom of God.' The doctrine and end of his ministry was to persuade men of the necessity of coming out of their lapsed estate and the power of the devil, and to put themselves under the government of the king, whom God hath set upon his holy hill of Zion, that he may defend them against the devil, the world, and the flesh, and at length bring them to everlasting happiness. Again, Acts xxviii. 23, 'And he expounded and testified the kingdom of God, persuading them concerning Jesus' &c., assuring them of his sufficiency to save them. Now this they did, partly by showing the danger of the contrary: 2 Cor. v. 11, 'Knowing, therefore, the terror of the Lord, we persuade men'; and partly by showing the grace and readiness of God to own them in all troubles: Acts xiii. 43, 'Persuading them to continue in the grace of God'. And if men do quarrel at this dispensation, they will not be edified by any other, be it never so extraordinary: Luke xvi. 31, 'Neither will they be persuaded though one should rise from the dead.' There is more reason to persuade the scriptures are true, than if a message were brought to us by a vision or apparition; which would not induce us to quit our sinful habits and customs. Now this is the means, when we receive it, and are persuaded of it.

[B.] By the Spirit: 1 Cor. ii. 12, 'Now we have not received the spirit of the world, but the Spirit which is of God, that we may know the things that are freely given us of God' The Spirit of God is necessary, that we may believe the doctrine of the gospel, and cure our worldly and sensual inclinations; for who else will be brought to for sake the things which he seeth and loveth, for a God and a glory which he never saw?

[C.] By faith, which is a persuasion of the truth of such things as God hath revealed, because God hath revealed them: 1 John iv. 16, 'And we have known, and believed, the love which God hath to us'. It is matter of faith to believe the love and care of God over his people.

[D.] Experience. The persuasion, with application, increaseth our confidence. His love to us in particular is known by what he hath wrought in us and for us; and this increaseth our persuasion, and breedeth in us a holy confidence: 2 Cor. i. 10, 'Who hath delivered us from so great a death, and doth deliver; in whom we trust that he will yet deliver us;' 2 Tim. iv. 17, 18, 'Notwithstanding, the Lord stood with me and strengthened me, and I was delivered out of the mouth of the lion, and the Lord shall deliver me from every evil work' In this persuasion, confirmed, seasoned, experienced Christians do continue, who have not only a true faith in Christ, and a settled love to him, but such as maketh up an evidence in their conscience of their sincerity, and giveth an undoubted persuasion of his love to them.

(1.) They are such as are rooted and grounded in faith. The full comfort of Christianity is reserved for such as are described by the apostle: Col. i. 23, 'If ye continue in the faith, grounded and settled, and be not moved away from the hope of the gospel.' There is an initial faith which may wither, as the grace of the second and third ground; and there is a rooted faith, which will be supported and maintained in the good and honest heart. Therefore it is not sufficient once to assent to the truth of the gospel in our understandings, or embrace the good things offered to us by our will and affections; but we must be rooted and grounded in the faith. Fluctuating opinion, without a well-grounded persuasion, will not serve the turn. Some slight desires and affections to blessedness to come will not maintain us against the several blasts of so many temptations as we meet with; but we must get a faith that will make us indifferent to all worldly things, 'height or depth, life or death.' The sound, world-conquering faith, will only give us safety, and, I am sure, will only give us com fort: 1 John v. 4, 'For whosoever is born of God overcometh the world: and this is the victory that overcometh the world, even our faith.' Such a sound belief of blessedness to come maketh us dead to the present world.

(2.) Such as are rooted and grounded in love. A taste may fail, Heb. vi. 3, 4. A slender, insufficient touch of the love of God upon the soul will not break the force of opposite inclinations and temptations: Eph. iii. 17, 18, 19, 'That ye, being rooted and grounded in love, may be able with all saints to comprehend what is the breadth, and length, and depth, and height, and know the love of Christ, which passeth knowledge.' A sincere love doth so fasten us to Christ, that no temptation is able to shake us or unloose us, for they are acquainted more and more with Christ's love, and admire it, are ravished by it, feel the effects of it. The 'breadth' noteth the great blessings we have by it, or the ample privileges of the new covenant; the 'length,' the duration of it, from one eternity to another; the 'depth 'of it, his profound condescension, fetching us out of hell itself by a painful, cursed, and ignominious death; the 'height,' as it raised us up to the glory of heaven, and that everlasting blessedness. Now none are said to comprehend this but those that are rooted and grounded in love; that is, to comprehend them to their comfort and joy, to comprehend it to their conquest and victory over temptations, to comprehend it as their triumph and confidence; none but those whose hearts are filled with the love of God, and deep experience of his grace in Christ, that have not taken up some light thoughts about it, but are deeply overcome and possessed with a sense of his love, whose heart and soul is towards God; and his wonderful love in Christ is the root and foundation of all their religion. Now these thorough Christians, who are rooted and grounded in faith and love, they are not so much believers in conflict as believers in triumph; and whereas others make a hard shift to get to heaven with much labour, both of flesh and spirit, and many doubts and fears, they keep up a continual rejoicing in God, and find little or no trouble or disturbance in the spiritual life. Lusts are more mortified, and Satan is discouraged, and they are assisted with a larger ex perience of grace than others receive.

Use 1. Is information.

1. To show what cause they have to be ashamed, that are discouraged by smaller temptations; that cannot 'run with the footmen' Jer. xii. 5. The smallest things separate them from the love of God in Christ, or darken the comfort of it in their souls.

2. The great privileges of a Christian. Turn him to what condition you will, raise him or cast him down, kill him or spare his life, you cannot harm him; enrich him, or beggar him, his happiness is not at your command; he is not at the disposal of any creature in the world, devils or men. Crosses and contrary winds blow him to heaven, Cant. iv. 16; and here, death, life, height, depth. If God hath good to do by his life, he will preserve him; if his work is ended, he will take him away by death. All doth better his heart, or hasten his glory.

3. What an advantage those Christians have above others, who make it their business to love God, and count it their happiness to be beloved by him. Take either; first, that make it their business to love God. Love God once, and all that he doth will be acceptable to you, and all that you do will be acceptable to him: for if we love him, nothing will be grievous; not commands grievous, nor trials grievous: 1 John v. 3; Heb. xii. 6, 'Whom the Lord loveth, he chasteneth'. It is from a father; and all that you do is acceptable to God. The lover's mite is better taken, than the vast treasures of enforced service. If you love him, you may be sure he loveth you, John xiv. 21. Secondly, they count it their happiness to be beloved by him; and then under the sorest temptations, it is enough that God loveth them. If he will not take away his loving-kindness from them, it is enough, though he visit them with scourges. Other things will not satisfy them without this, but this satisfieth them in the want of all other things, Ps. cvi. 7.

Use 2. Is to exhort us to several duties.

1. To the great duties of Christianity, which give us an interest in this unchangeable love. I shall instance in faith and love.

[A.] By faith to put our souls in Christ's hands, for there alone we are safe against temptations: 2 Tim. i. 12, 'For I know whom I have believed, and am persuaded, that he is able to keep that which I have committed unto him'; and 1 Peter iv. 19, 'Commit the keeping of your souls to him'; so Ps. xxxvii. 3, 4, 'Trust in the Lord, and do good, so shalt thou dwell in the land; verily thou shalt be fed. Delight thyself in the Lord, and he shall give thee thy heart's desire' It is not a devout sloth or careless negligence, but a resolution to take his way, and adhere to it, trusting him with all events. We may do it upon the confidence of his willing ness, fidelity, and sufficiency. His office showeth his willingness; it is his office to save souls, which he cannot possibly neglect: Luke xix. 10, 'The Son of man came to seek and save that which was lost.' His covenant showeth his fidelity: 1 Cor. x. 13, 'But God is faithful, who will not suffer you to be tempted above what you are able' His nature or his divine power showeth his sufficiency. He is God, Phil. iii. 21, and he is with God, Heb. vii. 25.

[B.] The next great duty is love; for love is the mutual bond between us and Christ, as Christ is the bond of union between God and us. We must not intermit our own love; the love of God keepeth us, and we are bidden to 'keep ourselves in the love of God,' Jude 21; 1 John ii. 27, 28, 'Ye shall abide in him' and then presently, 'Abide in him'; and John xv. 5, 'Abide in me, and I in you'. The greatest danger of breaking is on our part; there is no fear on Christ s part. Now we must use the means, possess the heart with the love of God in Christ. We must believe the love of God, think of it often, not by light thoughts, but let it be radicated in our hearts, and let us rouse up ourselves to love God again, who hath showed so much love to us.

2. Let us forecast all visible dangers, and not fix too peremptorily on temporal happiness. There are a world of vicissitudes in our pilgrimage, but all are ordered for good to a Christian. Let us not too peremptorily fix on life or death, height or depth, but beg of God to sanctify every condition: Phil. iv. 12 'I know how to be abased, and how to abound; to be full, and to be hungry; to abound, and to suffer need.' We are subject to changes; sometimes in credit and sometimes in dis grace, sometimes in sickness and sometimes in health, sometimes rich and sometimes poor; there needeth wisdom to carry ourselves in prosperity, as well as adversity.

3. Let us get our hearts confirmed against these temptations that may assault our confidence life, death. If God prolong life, there is occasion for service; if death cometh, that is our comfort: Rev. xiv. 8, 'Blessed are the dead that die in the Lord'; Phil. i. 20, 'I desire to be dissolved, and to be with Christ, which is much better.' Death is a passage to glory; it shall not separate us from Christ, but join us to him, Phil. i. 23. Lay up this comfort against the hour of death. It is a separation that causeth a nearer conjunction. Then angels. The evil angels are under Christ, Col. i. 16. You are never in Satan's hand, but Satan is in God's hands. Then for principalities and powers. No potentates have any power but what is given them from above: John xix. 11, 'Thou couldest have no power at all against me, were it not given thee from above'; and Christ promiseth, Mat. xvi. 18, 'Upon this rock I will build my church, and the gates of hell shall not prevail against it!' Things present, and things to come. Whatsoever is present is either good or evil; the good things are for our comfort in our pilgrimage, the evil fit us for a happier estate; but we have no assurance of things to come: Mat. vi. 34, 'Sufficient to the day is the evil thereof.' And then height and depth. We are acquainted with the heighth and depth of the love of God; we know a more glorious height, which is heaven; and there is a dismal depth, which is hell. God can provide a harbour for his people; turneth the devil's design quite contrary to his intention.

Made in the USA
Middletown, DE
23 September 2023

39154256R00321